PJ-CJW-185

D0037552

R

California

Fodor's Travel Publications, Inc.
New York and London

F
859.3
F 63
1991

ISBN 0-679-01887-5

"Along the High Sierra," by Colin Fletcher. Copyright © 1964 by Colin Fletcher. Published by Vintage Books and reprinted by permission of Brandt and Brandt Literary Agents, Inc.

Fodor's California

Editors: Kathleen McHugh, Larry Peterson
Editorial Contributors: Bob Blake, Kevin Brass, Toni Chapman, Bruce David Colen, Laura Del Rosso, Vicky Elliott, Pamela Faust, Marie Felde, Sheila Gadsden, Sharon K. Gillenwater, Pamela Hegarty, Mary Jane Horton, Dan Janeck, Marael Johnson, Jacqueline Killeen, Jane Lasky, Maria Lenhart, Jillian Magalaner, Ellen Melinkoff, Maribeth Mellin, David Nelson, Denise Nolty, Carolyn Price, Peter Segal, Dan Spitzer, Aaron Sugarman, Robert Taylor, Casey Tefertiller
Art Director: Fabrizio La Rocca
Cartographer: David Lindroth
Illustrator: Karl Tanner
Cover Photograph: Dale Baker/Photobank

Design: Vignelli Associates

Special Sales

Fodor's Travel Publications are available at special discounts for bulk purchases (100 copies or more) for sales promotions or premiums. Special editions, including personalized covers, excerpts of existing guides, and corporate imprints, can be created in large quantities for special needs. For more information write to Special Marketing, Fodor's Travel Publications, 201 East 50th Street, New York, NY 10022. Inquiries from the United Kingdom should be sent to Fodor's Travel Publications, 20 Vauxhall Bridge Rd., London, England SW1V 2SA.

MANUFACTURED IN THE UNITED STATES OF AMERICA

10 9 8 7 6 5 4 3 2 1

Contents

Foreword

From sea lions barking off Monterey Peninsula and John Muir's "Range of Light," to the temperate and foggy North Coast and the extremes of snow and heat found in the southern deserts, California is diverse enough and vast enough to satisfy nearly any visitor.

This edition of *Fodor's California* covers more California sights than ever before. There are separate chapters on the Wine Country, Lake Tahoe, and the Far North and much expanded treatment of Santa Barbara and Sacramento. There are extended chapters on San Francisco, Los Angeles, and San Diego, with plenty of information for a week's stay, but this book has been written primarily for those travelers who plan to visit several regions of the state. All the writers are local, and they share their best advice on what to see and do up and down the state.

While every care has been taken to ensure the accuracy of the information in this guide, the passage of time will always bring change, and consequently, the publisher cannot accept responsibility for errors that may occur.

All prices and opening times quoted here are based on information supplied to us at press time. Hours and admission fees may change, however, and the prudent traveler will avoid inconvenience by calling ahead.

Fodor's wants to hear about your travel experiences, both pleasant and unpleasant. When a hotel or restaurant fails to live up to its billing, let us know and we will investigate the complaint and revise our entries where the facts warrant it.

Send your letters to the editors of Fodor's Travel Publications, 201 E. 50th Street, New York, NY 10022.

Highlights'91 and Fodor's Choice

Highlights '91

The forces of nature dominated the headlines from California in 1990. Drought conditions for the past four years have made the already dry landscape all the more vulnerable to **brushfires,** and in the summer of 1990 hundreds-of-thousands of acres throughout the state were ablaze. Santa Barbara experienced its worst fires in 30 years; nearly 500 homes were lost, and 49,000 acres were burned, prompting President Bush to declare it a disaster area. Major brushfires also raged in Coronado, near San Diego, and in Riverside; and forest fires in the Sierra Nevada, near Yosemite Valley forced the precautionary evacuation of that National Park.

San Francisco has bounced back from the **1989 earthquake** with characteristic speed and style, and numerous building projects are underway throughout the city. Expansion of the **Moscone Center** convention facility continues, with a new ballroom now complete, and the Moscone Center North set to open in 1993.

The **Ansel Adams Center** is one of the newest additions to the city's cultural scene. Opened in late 1989, the center is run by the Friends of Photography, a non-profit group begun by Adams and other west coast artists in the late 1960s. One of its five galleries is devoted entirely to Adams' work, and the others showcase the history and development of photography.

The army is closing shop at the **Presidio,** 1,500 wooded acres in San Francisco's unspoiled northwest corner, and the property is to be turned over to the city—a transaction which has city planners and developers drooling. The green and shady retreat's fate is anyone's guess, and visitors shouldn't miss the chance to explore the Presidio before it changes hands.

1991 may also be your last chance to catch the San Francisco Giants playing in much-maligned **Candlestick Park.** The Giants' organization is looking for greener pastures (or at least a field not as plagued by fog and high winds), despite the fact that the old stadium held together admirably during the earthquake that interrupted the '89 World Series.

Some classics are appreciated, though, and one local beauty has received a much-needed facelift. The **Sheraton Palace,** whose guest list reads like a Who's Who of the past century—Enrico Caruso, Sarah Bernhardt, Winston Churchill, Nikita Kruschev, among others—underwent a $135 million renovation that added conference rooms, a health spa, and a swimming pool. Revamping of the glass-domed Garden Court, and the Pied Piper Room (home to Maxfield

Parrish's famous painting of the same name), has also been completed.

The area around the **Civic Center** continues to grow, and visitors who haven't been there for a while will be pleasantly surprised by the new additions in this neighborhood. A center of culture and government, it has, in recent years, become a center of fine dining as well, and opera, symphony, and museum goers will find over fifty restaurants in close proximity. Celebrity chef Jeremiah Tower's Stars still rules this roost, but other standouts include the new Monsoon, the Hayes Street Grill, and Zola's.

There's also plenty going on just beyond San Francisco's city limits: **Marine World Africa USA** has opened its new attraction, "Elephant Encounter," in which visitors can meet and feed lumbering behemoths, and spend time talking to their trainers. South of San Jose, **"Hecker Pass: A Family Adventure,"** a $30 million theme park is under construction. It will include a petting zoo, an amphitheater, a pool, boating, and a variety of rides. The **Jack London Square** redevelopment project in Oakland was completed in the summer of 1990. The waterfront has been expanded to bring in more retail and business offices, and a large casual dining area is being added. **Old Oakland,** an historical neighborhood full of shops and restaurants in downtown Oakland has also had extensive renovation.

Drivers in the bay area will still find a few inconveniences resulting from **damage to roadways** during the '89 earthquake. Some sections of freeway ramp remain closed indefinitely, including the heavily trafficked Embarcadero freeway running along Chinatown, the downtown area, and Fisherman's Wharf. Detours can also be expected along routes between the city and Oakland. Those traveling by car should consult the AAA or the San Francisco Convention and Visitors Bureau for an update on road conditions in and around the city.

Long known for its sights—palm trees, movie stars, the Pacific—Los Angeles is increasingly recognizable by certain sounds: the roar of bulldozers, the pounding of steel girders, and all the other auditory trademarks of rampant real estate development. Much of the hammering and concrete-pouring comes courtesy of the travel industry, with a slew of new hotels and tourist attractions in the works.

The redevelopment of **Hollywood** is probably causing the most—and most varied—noise. Despite the protests of some community groups, several buildings are on their way up or down. The area surrounding Mann's (formerly Graumann's) Chinese Theater on Hollywood Boulevard will resemble a war zone, as the Hollywood Promenade rises phoenix-like from the rubble in 1993. The Promenade will house a hotel, shops and restaurants, a 19-story office tower, a theater complex dubbed the American Cinemateque, and a film and broadcast museum.

At water's edge, **Santa Monica** is in the midst of a hotel boom. The beachfront 195-room **Park Hyatt Santa Monica** opened in 1990, as did the 253-room **Guest Quarters Suite Hotel.** The 148-room **Santa Monica Beach Hotel** on the Pacific Coast Highway is set to open in 1992.

West L.A. has not one, but two major art institutions under construction. The dueling museums are the **Armand Hammer Museum of Art and Cultural Center,** the future home of Hammer's $250-million collection is opening in 1991; and the **J. Paul Getty Center,** which will occupy a 110-acre site with views of the Pacific and the Los Angeles basin, scheduled to take its bow sometime in the mid-1990s.

Downtown L.A. isn't exactly quiet, either. Construction should soon be underway on the **Walt Disney Concert Hall,** future home of the Los Angeles Philharmonic. The hall is being designed by local hero Frank Gehry, although the word is that the structure will be simpler and more conservative than typical Gehry creations.

Fans of the **Farmers Market** will appreciate the ongoing make-over of this L.A. landmark, to be completed in the mid-1990s. A movie theater, restaurants, and a 600-room hotel will be added to the existing marketplace, which itself will be enhanced with landscaping, fountains, plazas, and walkways, making this a much more attractive place to spend time.

The first completed link in the 150-mile, $877 million **Los Angeles Metro Rail System** was opened in July, with service between Long Beach and Los Angeles. The **Metro Rail Blue Line** takes 40 minutes to get passengers the 22 miles from Long Beach to Downtown L.A. This line is only the first in the extensive rebuilding of the rail transport system that served the greater Los Angeles area until the advent of freeways. That its portion of the train system went into operation first is a boost for the resurging city of Long Beach. The home of the Queen Mary and the Spruce Goose, Long Beach is undergoing a remarkable transformation. **The Walt Disney Company** has plans for a major development in the area around the two sites, and three new hotels are in the works, and another in neighboring San Pedro; the expansion of the Convention and Entertainment Center continues, and Long Beach Airport is more and more becoming an alternative to LAX.

The wave of redevelopment has even hit downtown **Huntington Beach** in Orange County. Best known as a surfing center, this classic Southern California beach town has added a multiplex movie theater, restaurant, and retail center at the intersection of the Pacific Coast Highway and Main Street. The complex is called Pier Colony. Across the street from the project, the **Huntington Beach pier** is toward the end of a year-long overhaul, that had the landmark shut down for 1990. The second phase of all this bustling will include two or three waterside restaurants.

Inland, at the other end of Orange County, in the little town of Yorba Linda, is one of Southern California's newest attractions, **The Richard Nixon Library and Birthplace.** Built exclusively with private funds, the Library and Birthplace is set on a nine-acre complex that features the house where Nixon was born, and lived with his family until moving to nearby Whittier in 1922. The musuem and library displays include documents, photographs, memorabilia, interactive exhibits, and film and video presentations of the 37th president's life before, during and after his time in office. President Bush, and former presidents Reagan, and Ford, were on hand for the dedication ceremonies, as was, of course, Richard M. Nixon himself.

Fodor's Choice

No two people will agree on what makes a perfect vacation, but it's fun—and it can be helpful—to know what others think. Here, then, is a very personal list of Fodor's Choices. We hope you'll have a chance to experience some of them yourself while visiting California. We have tried to offer something for everyone and from every price category. For detailed information about each entry, refer to the appropriate chapters within this guidebook.

Lodging

Bel Air Hotel, Los Angeles *(Very Expensive)*

Four Seasons Biltmore Hotel, Santa Barbara *(Very Expensive)*

Claremont Hotel, Oakland *(Very Expensive)*

Four Seasons Cleft Hotel, San Francisco *(Very Expensive)*

St. James Club, Los Angeles *(Very Expensive)*

Ventana Inn, Big Sur *(Very Expensive)*

Casa Del Zorro, Anza Borrego *(Moderate)*

Scenic Drives

17-mile Drive, Carmel

Highway 49, the Gold Country

I-80, San Francisco to Truckee (for a cross section of the State)

Kings Canyon Highway (Highway 180)

Mulholland Drive, Los Angeles

Historic Buildings

Coit Tower, San Francisco

General Vallejo's House, Sonoma

Hotel del Coronado, San Diego

Larkin House, Monterey

Mann's Chinese Theater, Hollywood

Mission San Carlos Borromeo, Carmel

State Capitol, Sacramento

Romantic Sites

Buena Vista Winery, Sonoma

Carnelian Room, Bank of America, San Francisco

Emerald Bay, Lake Tahoe

Griffith Observatory, Los Angeles

Highlands Inn, Carmel

Taste Treats

California wines, tasted at the wineries

Chorrizo burrito, burrito stands, Los Angeles

French-fried artichoke hearts, roadside stands, Monterey Peninsula

Fresh salmon steaks, restaurants along the North Coast

Garlic ice cream, Garlic Festival, Gilroy

Orange freeze, Merlino's, Fulton Ave., Sacramento

Ripe peaches, especially in the Central Valley

Sourdough bread and sweet butter, San Francisco

State Parks

Anza-Borrego Desert State Park, Borrego Springs

California State Railroad Museum, Sacramento

Columbia State Historic Park, Columbia

Del Norte Coast Redwoods State Park, Crescent City

Empire Mine State Historic Park, Grass Valley

Marshall Gold Discovery State Historic Park, Coloma

Point Lobos State Reserve, Carmel

San Juan Bautista State Historic Park, San Juan Bautista

Restaurants with Fabulous Atmosphere

Chateau Souverain Restaurant at the Winery, Geyserville

George's at the Cove, LaJolla

Green's, San Francisco

Spago, Los Angeles

St. Orres, Gualala

Ventana Inn, Big Sur

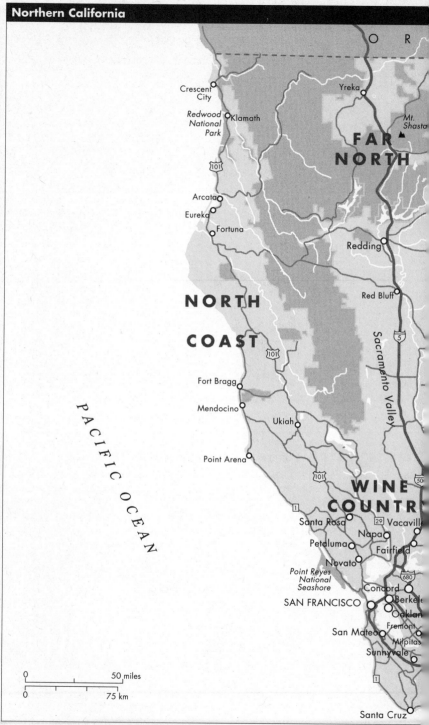

Northern California

Crescent City

Redwood National Park ○Klamath

101

Arcata
Eureka
Fortuna

Yreka

Mt. Shasta

FAR NORTH

Redding

Red Bluff

NORTH

COAST

101

Fort Bragg

Mendocino

Ukiah

Point Arena

101

Sacramento Valley

I-5

50

WINE COUNTR

PACIFIC OCEAN

1

Santa Rosa
Petaluma
Novato

29 Vacaville
Napa
Fairfield

680

Point Reyes National Seashore

Concord
Berkele
Oaklan
Fremont
Milpitas

SAN FRANCISCO

San Mateo

Sunnyvale

| 0 | | 50 miles |
| 0 | | 75 km |

1

Santa Cruz

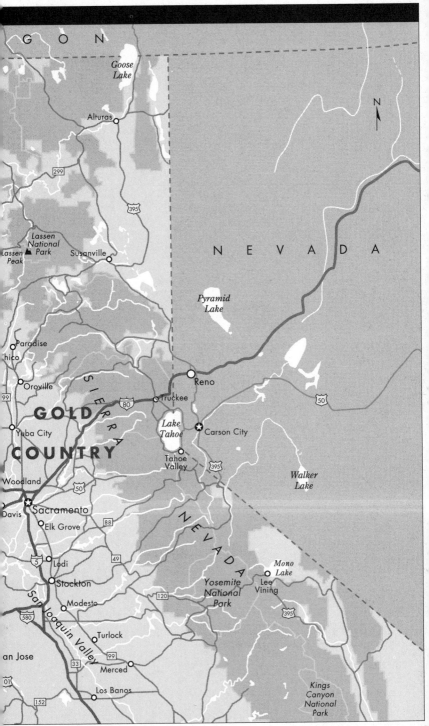

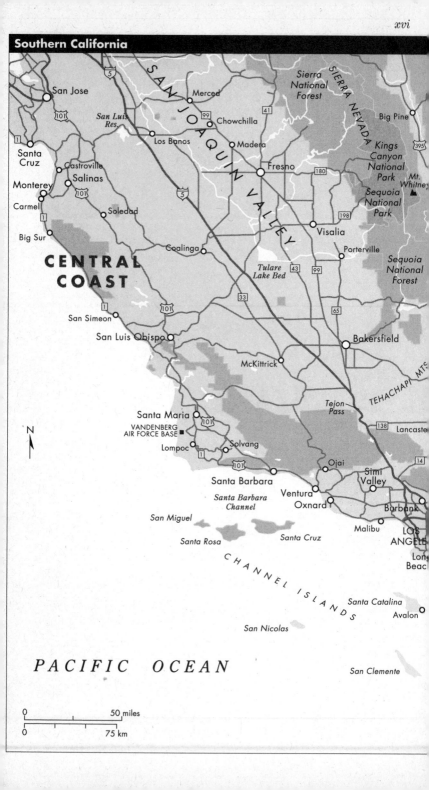

Southern California

PACIFIC OCEAN

CENTRAL COAST

SAN JOAQUIN VALLEY

SIERRA NEVADA

CHANNEL ISLANDS

TEHACHAPI MTS.

Sierra National Forest

Kings Canyon National Park

Sequoia National Park

Sequoia National Forest

Mt. Whitney

San Jose
Merced
Big Pine
San Luis Res.
Chowchilla
Santa Cruz
Los Banos
Madera
Castroville
Fresno
Salinas
Monterey
Carmel
Soledad
Visalia
Big Sur
Porterville
Coalinga
Tulare Lake Bed
San Simeon
San Luis Obispo
Bakersfield
McKittrick
Tejon Pass
Lancaster
Santa Maria
VANDENBERG AIR FORCE BASE
Lompoc
Solvang
Ojai
Simi Valley
Santa Barbara
Ventura
Oxnard
Burbank
Santa Barbara Channel
Malibu
LOS ANGELES
San Miguel
Santa Rosa
Santa Cruz
Long Beach
Santa Catalina
Avalon
San Nicolas
San Clemente

N

0   50 miles
0   75 km

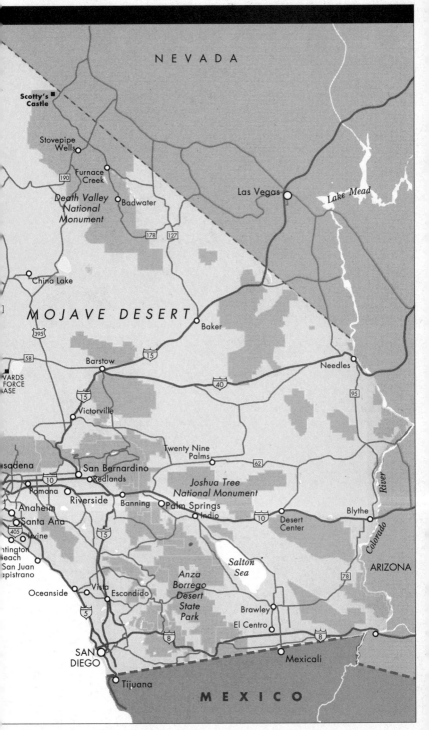

World Time Zones

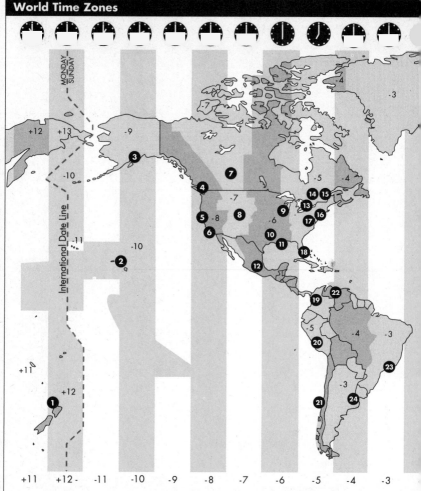

Numbers below vertical bands relate each zone to Greenwich Mean Time (0 hrs.).
Local times frequently differ from these general indications,
as indicated by light-face numbers on map.

Algiers, **29**
Anchorage, **3**
Athens, **41**
Baghdad, **46**
Bangkok, **50**
Beijing, **54**

Berlin, **34**
Bogotá, **19**
Budapest, **37**
Buenos Aires, **24**
Caracas, **22**
Chicago, **9**
Copenhagen, **33**
Dallas, **10**

Delhi, **48**
Denver, **8**
Djakarta, **53**
Dublin, **26**
Edmonton, **7**
Hong Kong, **56**
Honolulu, **2**

Istanbul, **40**
Jerusalem, **42**
Johannesburg, **44**
Lima, **20**
Lisbon, **28**
London (Greenwich), **27**
Los Angeles, **6**
Madrid, **38**
Manila, **57**

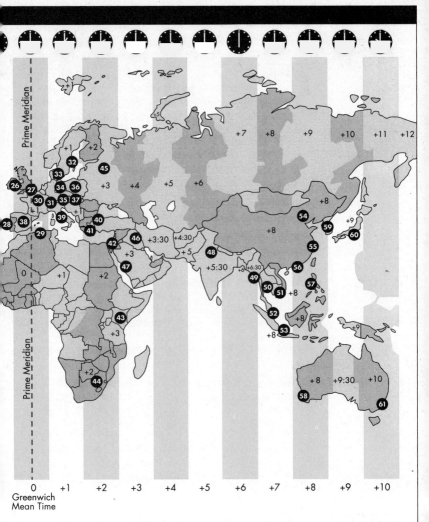

Mecca, **47**
Mexico City, **12**
Miami, **18**
Montreal, **15**
Moscow, **45**
Nairobi, **43**
New Orleans, **11**
New York City, **16**

Ottawa, **14**
Paris, **30**
Perth, **58**
Reykjavík, **25**
Rio de Janeiro, **23**
Rome, **39**
Saigon, **51**

San Francisco, **5**
Santiago, **21**
Seoul, **59**
Shanghai, **55**
Singapore, **52**
Stockholm, **32**
Sydney, **61**
Tokyo, **60**

Toronto, **13**
Vancouver, **4**
Vienna, **35**
Warsaw, **36**
Washington, DC, **17**
Yangon, **49**
Zürich, **31**

Introduction

Coastal California began its migration from somewhere far to the south millions of years ago. It's still moving north along the San Andreas fault, but you've plenty of time to plan your vacation before Santa Monica beach is in the Arctic circle. If you've heard predictions that some of the state may fall into the Pacific, take the long-term view and consider that much of the state has been in and out of the ocean all through its history. The forces that raised the mountains and formed the Central Valley are still at work.

If you want to get a good introduction to the natural history and geology of the state, there is no better place to start than at the Oakland Museum. An impressive light and audio show over a large model of the state explains the geography. Exhibits illustrate the different ecosystems of the state; walking through the exhibit hall is like walking across the state, from the ocean across the Coast Ranges, the Central Valley, and the Sierra Nevada. On another floor, there is a fine collection of artifacts and remains of the state's human history; especially interesting are the Native American baskets, tools, and ceremonial clothing (some are covered with hummingbird feathers!).

Those of you who can't start at the museum but who do travel through at least a few of California's tourist regions will see a wide variety of geography and nature. The state's history often is not as evident as its physical reality. None of the cities is much more than 200 years old (Junípero Serra didn't come to San Diego until 1769), and the most immediate impression is of a 20th-century culture. Still, you will find relics of early days in San Diego, San Francisco, and Los Angeles.

The chapters here are arranged in a generally north-to-south order, but that isn't the way most visitors confront the state. When planning your trip, please keep in mind the very long distances. If you decide to drive between San Francisco and Los Angeles on Highway 1, remember that it is not only more than 400 miles but is a difficult road to drive. Scenic routes, such as Highway 1 along the coast, Highway 49 in the Gold Country, and highways 50 and 120 across the Sierra Nevada, require attention to driving and enough time to allow for frequent stops.

California's North Coast is a dramatically beautiful region, whose main industries are tourism, fishing, and logging. There are no large cities, no large amusement parks, no very luxurious resorts. There isn't even any swimming, because of a cold current that runs down the coast for most of the state (turning out to sea before it reaches Southern California beaches). The ocean keeps the weather temperate, but that doesn't mean that there aren't winter storms. August is often the coldest month of the year here (as it can be in San Francisco, too). What you will find along the North Coast are a wonderful scenic drive (Highway 1 and U.S. 101), many small inns (some of them quite luxurious), interesting restaurants serving locally produced fare, some good galleries, and an increasing number of wineries. This is primarily a region for leisurely exploring. It shouldn't be on the itinerary of anyone not interested in the beauties of nature, because the main attractions are tide pools under coastal cliffs, redwood trees, rhododendron, and banana slugs (a large yellow and black local oddity) in the lush coastal mountains. The Russians settled this region briefly in the 19th century, and there are reminders of their presence.

The two main attractions in the Far North are Mount Shasta, a large volcano that dominates the scenery of the northern part of the state, and Lassen Volcanic National Park. The park is at the southern end of the Cascade Range, and is particularly interesting because of the record of past volcanic activity and evidence of current geothermal activity (such as the Sulphur Works). Even more than the North Coast, this region is for those interested in nature, because lodging and dining opportunities are much more limited. Keep in mind also that much of this region can be very hot in the summer.

The Wine Country is one of California's most popular tourist regions. There are narrow crowded highways and many wineries among the vineyards and valleys of the Coast Ranges north of San Francisco. Many of the wineries are beautiful sites for meals, picnics, or tastings. There are fine bed-and-breakfasts and restaurants specializing in local meat and produce. This is as far north as the Spanish got, and you will see some record of their presence—also of the history of viticulture in the state.

San Francisco is very much a sophisticated, urban environment. There are fine hotels and a greater concentration of excellent restaurants than anywhere else in the state. Because it is so compact, a visitor can do very well without a car, but this is also a fine base for tours up the coast and to the Wine Country. If you want to drive down to Los Angeles from here, you can do it in a day (7–8 hours) if you take I-5 down the Central Valley, but you should budget at least two days if you want to take the coastal route. A long day's drive down U.S. 101 will get you to Santa Barbara, but you'll bypass Monterey and Big Sur.

The Gold Country, also known as the Mother Lode, is the gold-mining region of the Sierra Nevada foothills. There are many historic sites and small towns to explore, many of them of interest to children. Most impressive are the Empire Mine in Grass Valley, the gold discovery site at Coloma, and Columbia State Historic Park, which is a town restored to its Gold Rush condition. As in the Wine Country, there are many B&Bs and small inns, but this is a less expensive, if also less sophisticated, region to visit. In the spring there are wildflowers, and in the fall the hills are colored by bright red berries as well as changing leaves. In the summer, the hills are golden—and hot. Visitors in that season should probably check the weather reports: There are many fine days, but exploring in 90-degree or hotter weather is not much fun. We've included Sacramento in the Gold Country chapter because it is adjacent and because its history was so influenced by the Gold Rush.

Lake Tahoe is famous for its deep blue water and as the largest alpine lake on the continent. It stands up very well to its reputation, despite crowded areas around the Nevada casinos. Lake Tahoe is a four-hour drive from San Francisco along Interstate 80; the traffic to the lake on Friday afternoons and to San Francisco on Sundays is horrendous. If you plan a visit in the winter, remember to carry chains in your car; they are sometimes required even on big I-80. In the summer, it's generally cooler than in the foothills, but still sometimes pretty hot. Luckily, there are lots of beaches where you can swim.

The highlight for many travelers to California is a visit to one of the Sierra Nevada's national parks. Yosemite is the state's most famous park and every bit as sublime as promised. Its Yosemite-type or U-shaped valleys were formed by the action of glaciers on the Sierra Nevada during recent ice ages. Other examples are found in Kings Canyon and Sequoia National Parks (which are adjacent to each other and usually visited together). At all three parks, but especially at the latter two, there are fine groves of Big Trees *(Sequoiadendron gigantea)*, the largest living things in the world. The parks are open year round, with large portions of the higher backcountry closed in winter. Yosemite Valley is only 4,000 feet high, so winter weather is mild, and the waterfalls are beautiful when hung with ice.

The Monterey Peninsula, a two- or three-hour drive south of San Francisco, offers some of the state's most luxurious resorts and golf courses, most interesting historic sites (Monterey was the capital during Spanish and Mexican rule and the state constitution was written here; Junípero Serra is buried at the Carmel Mission), most beautiful coastal scenery (Point Lobos would receive many votes for most treasured state park), and perhaps the most famous scenic drive (the 17-Mile Drive). There are also very good restaurants in Monterey and Carmel and, for those interested, plenty of places to shop, particularly in Carmel. The weather is usually mild year round, but any visitor should be prepared for fog and cool temperatures.

Between Carmel and Santa Barbara is another spectacular stretch of Highway 1, requiring concentration and nerve to drive. This is where you'll find those bridges spanning the cliffs along the Pacific—and Big Sur. Don't expect much in the way of dining, lodging, shopping, or even history until you get down to Hearst Castle. Santa Barbara flaunts its Spanish/Mexican heritage. There's a well-restored mission, and almost all of downtown (including some pleasant shopping areas) is done in Spanish-style architecture. The centerpiece is the Courthouse, built in the 1920s after a disastrous earthquake and displaying some very beautiful tile work and murals.

In certain lights, Los Angeles displays its own Spanish heritage, but much more evident is its cultural vibrancy as a 20th-century center on the Pacific Rim. Hollywood, the beaches, and Disneyland are all within an hour's drive. Also here are Beverly Hills, noted for its shops and mansions; important examples of domestic architecture from throughout the 20th century—and freeways. Dining options are improving, if still not up to the range of San Francisco's choices. Despite the city's reputation for a laidback lifestyle, a visit here can be fairly overwhelming because of the size and variety of the region. Careful planning will help.

San Diego, at the southwestern edge of the state and the country, is usually the first stop. Junípero Serra founded his first mission in Alta California (as opposed to Baja California, which is still part of Mexico) here in 1769. There are historical sites from Mexican and Victorian times, one of the very best zoos in the country, and fine beaches. The weather is very agreeable, so this is a year-round destination.

The California deserts are extensive and varied, and usually divided into two general areas: The Mojave or High Desert and the Colorado or Low Desert. Palm Springs and the new cities nearby (Rancho Mirage, etc.) are filling up with expansive new resorts sporting elaborate gardens, waterfalls, serpentine sidewalks, and—of course—golf courses. That area doesn't offer much of a desert experience, but it has great weather in the winter, and you can use it as an elegant base for exploration. Joshua Tree National Monument is a good day trip (or two trips) from Palm Springs; the northern part is High Desert and the southern part Low Desert, so you can see the difference. Death Valley (*see* The Mojave Desert and Death Valley) and Anza Borrego Desert Park (*see* Excursions from San Diego) are of interest to people who want to explore the beauties of the desert landscape. Anza Borrego is far less developed than Palm Springs, but has a resort and a fancy golf course.

Running 400 miles down the center of the state from below Mount Shasta to the Tehachapi Mountains, lying between the Coast Ranges and the Sierra Nevada, is the Central Valley. We haven't written much about that region (*see* Sacramento in The Gold Country and Red Bluff and Redding in

The Far North) because this is not much of a tourist region. You may drive across some of it on I-80 or down it on I-5, but there isn't much to stop and see, except in the state capital. This is, however, the most important agricultural region in the state and the fastest growing in terms of population.

California is as varied as any state and larger than most, and could be the subject for many visits. Don't expect to visit everything the first time, but if you can plan to travel through several of the state's regions, you will begin to get a feeling for how the state's different cultures and needs (for water or development or the preservation of natural beauty) work together and pull against each other.

1 Essential Information

Before You Go

Visitor Information

A detailed 208-page book, *Discover the Californias*, is available free through the California Office of Tourism (tel. 800/862–2543). The term "the Californias" refers to a useful division of the Golden State into 12 segments; the book sketches in the attractions and the flavor of each area. It also includes a wideranging calendar of yearly events. In addition, the office of tourism can answer many questions about travel in the state. *California Office of Tourism 1121 L St., Suite 103, Sacramento 95814, tel. 916/322–1397.*

There are visitors bureaus and chambers of commerce throughout the state; see individual chapters for listings.

In the United Kingdom, contact the **U.S. Travel and Tourism Administration** (22 Sackville St., Longon W1X 2EA, tel. 071/439–7433).

Tour Groups

General-Interest Tours Most major airlines have sightseeing tours from San Francisco, Los Angeles, and San Diego. If you are flying into any of these cities, check with airlines about the possibilities.

Amtrak offers tours to major attractions in California. For a brochure and special information, tel. 800/872–7245, tours department, or write to **Amtrak Public Affairs** (1 California St., Suite 1250, San Francisco, CA 94111).

Other major providers of tours in California:

California Parlor Car Tours (1101 Van Ness Ave., San Francisco 94109, tel. 415/474–7500 or 800/227–4250) serves all California with motorcoach trips to popular spots such as Lake Tahoe, Yosemite, the Monterey Peninsula, and Hearst Castle. Multilingual capabilities: French, German.

Domenico Tours (751 Broadway, Bayonne, NJ 07002, tel. 800/554–8687 or 201/823–8687) arranges 7-, 10-, 14-, and 18-day tours of California as well as shorter tours organized around special events, such as the Rose Bowl Parade and game on New Year's Day.

Flair Tours Inc. (6922 Hollywood Blvd., Suite 421, Hollywood 90028, tel. 213/466–9822 or 800/223–5247 nationwide or 800/433–5247 within CA) serves all California. It arranges ground transportation by motorcoach and all ground services, and plans tour itineraries. Guides join tours at points of interest. Multilingual capabilities: French, Italian.

Freedom Holidays. (120 Montgomery St., Suite 1270, San Francisco, CA 94101, tel. 213/337–0742 or 800/782–1600 nationwide or 800/451–4440 within CA) serves all California, arranges ground transportation and all ground service, and plans tour itineraries.

Globus Gateway/Cosmos (150 S. Los Robles Ave., Pasadena, CA 91101, tel. 800/556–5454 or 818/449–0919), serving all California, provides charter buses, arranges ground transportation and all ground services, and plans tour itineraries.

Gray Line Tours (6541 Hollywood Blvd., Hollywood, CA 90028, tel. 213/856–5900 or 800/538–5050) provides charter buses, arranges ground transportation and all ground services, and plans tour itineraries. Multilingual guides are available: French, German, Italian, Cantonese, Greek.

Maupintour (Box 807, Lawrence, KS 66044, tel. 800/255–4266 or 913/843–1211) offers tours of the California coast from San Francisco to San Diego and north from San Francisco to Seattle.

Special-Interest Tours
Gold Prospecting

Gold Prospecting Expeditions (18170 Main St., Box 974, Jamestown 95327, tel. 209/984–4653) guides clients in gold panning, dredging, and prospecting in outings that range from one hour to one to two weeks, some involving river rafting and helicopter drop-ins. Special family discount packages.

Rafting, Canoeing, Kayaking

California Rivers (10070 Old Redwood Hwy., Box 1140, Windsor 95492, tel. 707/838–7787) runs easy-water Kiwi Kayak trips lasting from a single summer evening to five days. In difficulty, they range from introducing new paddlers to the romance of paddling on easy waters to offering thrills for seasoned boaters.

O.A.R.S., Outdoor Adventure River Specialists (Box 67, Angels Camp 95222, tel. 209/736–4677) offers one- to four-day rafting trips at several gradations of difficulty in North California on the Salmon and Klamath rivers; in Central California on the three forks of the American River, the Tuolumne, and the Merced; and in South California on the Kern River. The difficulty of the trips is rated on an international scale in terms of the roughest rapid, from I (easy) to VI (unrunnable); these California trips range from II to V. Some class III trips provide overnight accommodations at bed-and-breakfast inns instead of camping. One action-packed trip combines a day of white-water rafting, an overnight at a B&B, and a morning of hot-air ballooning.

Skiing

USAir Great Escape Vacations (tel. 800/223–2929) include air flight, rental car, lodging, and an interchangeable lift ticket good at six North Tahoe resorts: Squaw Valley, Alpine Meadows, Northstar, Homewood, Ski Incline, and Mount Rose.

Wineries

California Wine Adventures (Box 3273, Yountville 94599, tel. 707/944–8168), the first wine-touring business in California, begun in 1973, provides tours of the Napa and Sonoma valleys, using tour leaders from the Napa Valley Docent Council, many of them vintners themselves. Customized tours for one person or large groups, one day or longer are offered. Transportation, lodging, and meals are included. Advance reservations are essential.

Linda Viviani Touring Company, Inc. (500 Michael Dr., Sonoma 95476, tel. 707/938–2100) offers customized tours for one person to 500 people of the Napa, Sonoma, and Russian River wineries. Transportation, tour director, and meals are included. Lodging can be arranged at the Silverado Country Club in Napa or the Sonoma Mission Inn near Sonoma (accommodations at both are in the Very Expensive category). This company also arranges one-day shopping tours of San Francisco or Napa and Sonoma and half-day art tours of Napa Valley galleries.

Package Deals for Independent Travelers

There is a wide range of packages for independent travelers. The large casino-hotels at Lake Tahoe *(see* Chapter 8), for example, will often include a show, cocktails, and breakfast with a special lodging rate. An innovative bed-and-breakfast inn (Murphy's Inn, Grass Valley: *see* Gold Country) offers, in winter, a midweek ski package, a picnic lunch, downhill or cross-country tickets for two, and a spa to enjoy when you return; and in summer, a golf special that includes greens fees, an electric cart, and a carafe of wine.

One call to Heavenly Valley Ski Resort (tel. 702/588–4584) can book a complete ski vacation: a four-night, four-day drive-stay-ski package or a two-night, three-day fly-stay-ski package.

Most airlines have packages that include car rentals and lodging along with your flight. Hotels in major cities often have packages for weekends or for off-season. Packages possibilities sometimes cluster around major tourist attractions; hotels and motels near Disneyland in Anaheim or Marine World/Africa in Vallejo, for instance, offer lodging and admission tickets in a package.

America Fly AAway Vacations (tel. 800/433–7300 or 817/355–1234) offers city packages with discounts on hotels and car rental in San Francisco, Los Angeles, and San Diego. The airline's "Vacation Enchantment" package to the Los Angeles area includes admission to Disneyland. Also check with **United Airlines** (tel. 800/328–6877 or 312/952–4000) and **Continental Airlines** (tel. 800/525–0280) for packages. **American Express** (tel. 800/241–1700) has similar city packages with half-day sightseeing tours.

Packages are increasing in popularity as marketing strategies. Always ask about package options as you are making reservations or thinking about making them. Often chambers of commerce or convention and visitors bureaus will have information for you. Travel agents are good sources, too.

Tips for British Travelers

Passports You will need a valid 10-year passport. You do not need a visa if you are staying for less than 90 days, have a return ticket, and are flying with a participating airline. There are some exceptions to this, so check with your travel agent or with the U.S. Embassy (Visa and Immigration Department, 5 Upper Grosvenor St., London W1A 2JB, Tel. 071/499–3443). Note that the U.S. Embassy no longer accepts applications made in person.

No vaccinations are required for entry into the United States.

Customs If you are 21 or over, you can take into the U.S. (1) 200 cigarettes or 50 cigars or 2 kilos of tobacco, (2) one liter of alcohol, and (3) duty-free gifts to a value of $100. Be careful not to try to take in meat or meat products, seeds, plants, fruits, etc., and avoid drugs and narcotics.

Returning to Britain, you may bring home (1) 200 cigarettes or cigarillos or 50 cigars or 250 grams of tobacco; (2) two liters of table wine and, in addition, (a) one liter of alcohol over 22% by volume (most spirits) or (b) two liters of alcohol under 22% by volume (fortified or sparkling wine); (3) 60 milliliters of perfume and 1/4 liter of toilet water; and (4) other goods up to a value of £32.

Insurance We recommend that you insure yourself to cover health and motoring mishaps. **Europ Assistance** (252 High St., Croydon CR0

1NF, tel. 081/680–1234) is one company that offers this service. It is also wise to insure yourself against trip cancellations and loss of luggage. For free general advice on all aspects of holiday insurance contact the **Association of British Insurers** (Aldermarry House, Queen St., London EC4N 1TT, tel. 071/248–4477).

Tour Operators The price battle that has raged over transatlantic fares has led most tour operators to offer excellent budget packages to the United States. Among those you might consider as you plan your trip are:

Thomas Cook Ltd. (Box 36, Thorpe Wood, Peterborough, Cambridgeshire PE3 6SB, tel. 0733–330300).
Cosmosair plc (Tourama House, 17 Homesdale Rd., Bromley, Kent BR2 9LX, tel. 0614/805799).
Jetsave (Sussex House, London Rd., East Grinstead, West Sussex, RH19 1LD, tel. 0342–312033).
Kuoni Travel Ltd. (Kuoni House, Dorking, Surrey RH5 4AZ, tel. 0306/740500).
Premier Holidays (Premier Travel Center, Westbrook, Milton Rd., Cambridge CB4 1YQ, tel. 0223–355977).
Speedbird (Pacific House, Hazelwick Ave., Three Bridges, Crawley, West Sussex RH10 1NP, tel. 0293/572856).

Airfares We suggest that you explore the current scene for budget-flight possibilities, including **Continental** and **Virgin Atlantic Airways.** Some of these fares can be extremely difficult to come by, so be sure to book well in advance. Also, check on APEX and other money-saving fares, since only business travelers who don't have to watch the price of their tickets fly full-price these days—and find themselves sitting right beside APEX passengers!

At press time, an APEX round-trip fare to San Francisco or Los Angeles costs from £476 up and to San Diego from £479. Another good source of low-cost flights is the small ads found in daily and Sunday newspapers.

When to Go

Any time of the year is the right time to go to California, allowing of course for specific needs and inclinations. There won't be skiable snow in the mountains between Easter and Thanksgiving; there will usually be rain in December, January, and February in the lowlands, if that bothers you; it will be much too hot to enjoy Palm Springs or Death Valley in the summer.

San Francisco, Los Angeles, and San Diego are delightful year round; the Wine Country's seasonal variables are enticing; the coastal areas are almost always mild. You can plan an enjoyable and rewarding trip to California at any time of the year.

The climate varies amazingly in California, not only over distances of several hundred miles but occasionally within an hour's drive. A foggy, cool August day in San Francisco makes you grateful for a sweater, tweed jacket, or light wool coat. Head north 50 miles to the Napa Valley to check out the Wine Country, and you'll probably wear shirt-sleeves and thin cottons.

It's not only over distance that temperatures vary. Daytime and nighttime temperatures in some parts of the state swing widely apart, not only in the mountains where warm, sunny afternoons and cool evenings are expected but in other places as well. Take Sacramento, a city that is at sea level, but in California's Central Valley. In the summer, afternoons can be very warm indeed, in the 90s and occasionally over 100 degrees. But the nights cool down, often with a drop of 40 degrees; it makes for pleasant sleeping, and it also makes a sweater that was distasteful at 2 PM seem wonderful at 11 PM.

It's hard to generalize much about the weather in this varied state. Rain comes in the winter, and there is snow at higher elevations. Summers are dry everywhere. As a rule, if you're near the ocean, the climate will be mild year round, though as you move north, there is more fog. Inland is warmer in the summer and cooler in the winter. As you climb into the mountains, there are more distinct variations with the seasons: Winter brings snow, autumn is crisp, spring is variable, and summer is clear and warm.

Climate The following are average daily maximum and minimum temperatures for the major California cities.

Los Angeles	Jan.	64F	18C	May	69F	21C	Sept.	75F	24C
		44	7		53	12		60	16
	Feb.	64F	18C	June	71F	22C	Oct.	73F	23C
		46	8		57	14		55	13
	Mar.	66F	19C	July	75C	24C	Nov.	71F	22C
		48	9		60	16		48	9
	Apr.	66F	19C	Aug.	75C	24C	Dec.	66F	19C
		51	11		62	17		46	8

San Francisco	Jan.	55F	13C	May	66F	19C	Sept.	73F	23C
		41	5		48	9		51	11
	Feb.	59F	15C	June	69F	21C	Oct.	69F	21C
		42	6		51	11		50	10
	Mar.	60F	16C	July	69F	21C	Nov.	64F	18C
		44	7		51	11		44	7
	Apr.	62F	17C	Aug.	69F	21C	Dec.	57F	14C
		46	8		53	12		42	6

San Diego	Jan.	62F	17C	May	66F	19C	Sept.	73F	23C
		46	8		55	13		62	17
	Feb.	62F	17C	June	69F	21C	Oct.	71F	22C
		48	9		59	15		57	14
	Mar.	64F	18C	July	73F	23C	Nov.	69F	21C
		50	10		62	17		51	11
	Apr.	66F	19C	Aug.	73F	23C	Dec.	64F	18C
		53	12		64	18		48	9

Current weather information on more than 750 cities around the world is only a phone call away. Dialing WeatherTrak at 900/370–8725 will connect you to a computer, with which you can communicate by touch tone—at a cost of 75¢ for the minute and 50¢ a minute thereafter. The number plays a taped message that tells you to dial the three-digit access code for the destination in which you're interested. The code is either the area code (in the United States) or the first three letters of the foreign city. For a list of all access codes, send a stamped, self-addressed envelope to Cities, Box 7000, Dallas, TX 75209. For further information, phone 214/869–3035 or 800/247–3282.

Festivals and Seasonal Events

January **Tournament of Roses Parade and Football Game,** Pasadena. The 102nd annual parade takes place on New Year's Day 1991, with lavish floats, marching bands, and equestrian teams, followed by the Rose Bowl game. (Pasadena Tournament of Roses, 391 S. Orange Grove Blvd., Pasadena 91184, tel. 818/449–4100.)
East-West Shrine All-Star Football Classic, Palo Alto, is America's oldest all-star sports event (1651 19th Ave., San Francisco 94122, tel. 415/661–0291).
Whale Watching. Hundreds of gray whales migrate along the California coast from January through April (California Office of Tourism, 1121 L St., Sacramento 95814, tel. 916/322–1397).

February **AT&T Pebble Beach National Pro-Am,** Carmel. This legendary golf tournament, formerly the Crosby begins in late January and ends in early February (Box 869, Monterey 93942, tel. 408/649–1533).
Bob Hope Chrysler Classic, Indian Wells, PGA West, La Quinta, and Bermuda Dunes (near Palm Springs). This PGA golf tournament is a celebrity-packed pro-am (Box 865, Rancho Mirage 92270, tel. 619/341–2299 or 619/346–8184).
Chinese New Year Celebration. In San Francisco, North America's biggest Chinese community celebrates for a week, ending with the Golden Dragon Parade (Visitor Information Center, Box 6977, San Francisco 94101, tel. 415/391–2000). Los Angeles also has a Chinese New Year Parade (Chinese Chamber of Commerce, 978 N. Broadway, Suite 206, Los Angeles 90012, tel. 213/617–0396).

March **Santa Barbara International Cymbidium Orchid Show.** This is a horticultural spectacular (Box 3006, Santa Barbara 93130, tel. 805/687–0766).
Monterey Wine Festival. Wine tastings, lectures and luncheons are conducted by 200 exhibiting wineries (National Restaurant Association, 150 N. Michigan Ave., Suite 2000, Chicago, IL 60601, tel. 312/853–2525).
Dinah Shore Invitational, Rancho Mirage. The finest female golfers in the world compete for the richest purse on the LPGA circuit (Nabisco Dinah Shore, 1 Raquet Club Dr., Rancho Mirage 92270, tel. 619/324–4546).

April **Ramona Pageant,** Hemet. The poignant love story of Ramona (based on the novel by Helen Hunt Jackson) is presented by a large cast on a mountainside outdoor stage (Ramona Pageant Association, 27400 Ramona Bowl Rd., Hemet 92344, tel. 714/658–3111).
Adobe Tour, Monterey. This tour covers a large number of historic adobe structures and surrounding gardens (Monterey State Historic Park, 525 Polk St., Monterey 93940, tel. 408/649–7118).

May **Jumping Frog Contest,** Angels Camp. Inspired by Mark Twain's story "The Notorious Jumping Frog of Calaveras County," this contest is for frogs and trainers who take their competition seriously (Calaveras County Convention/Visitors Bureau, Angels Camp, 753 S. Main St., Box 111, 95222, tel. 209/736–4444).
Dixieland Jazz Jubilee, Sacramento. The world's largest

Dixieland festival features 100 bands from around the world (Sacramento Traditional Jazz Society, Box 15604, Sacramento 95813, tel. 916/372–5277).

June **International Bicycle Race,** Nevada City. This event is held every year on Father's Day (Nevada City Chamber of Commerce, 132 Main St., Nevada City 95959, tel. 916/265–2692).

Napa Valley Wine Auction, St. Helena. A major wine event, it features open houses, wine tasting, and the auction (Napa Valley Wine Auction, Box 141, St. Helena 94574, tel. 707/963–5246).

July **Lake Tahoe Sail Week,** South Lake Tahoe. Daily races and a lakewide gala are the highlights (Lake Tahoe Visitors Authority, Box 16299, South Lake Tahoe 95706, tel. 916/544–5050).

Carmel Bach Festival. The works of Johann Sebastian Bach are performed for three weeks; events include concerts, recitals, seminars (Box 575, Carmel 93921, tel. 408/624–1521).

August **California State Fair,** Sacramento. The agricultural showcase, with high-tech exhibits, rodeo, horse racing, carnival, big-name entertainment nightly, runs 18 days from August to Labor Day. (Box 15649, Sacramento 95815, tel. 916/924–2000).

Concours D'Elegance, Pebble Beach. At this show you'll see more than 100 of the world's finest automobiles (Box 567, Pebble Beach 93953, tel. 408/649–8500).

September **Renaissance Pleasure Faire,** Novato. Every weekend in August and the first two weekends in September, 3,000 costumed participants stage an Elizabethan harvest festival (Living History Centre, Box B, Novato 94948, tel. 415/892–0937).

Apple Hill Festival, Eldorado County. Fresh apples, baked goods, and family fun are available on farms between South Lake Tahoe and Sacramento. Peak season begins in September and runs throughout October. (Apple Hill Growers, Box 494, Camino 95709, tel. 916/622–9595).

Los Angeles County Fair, Pomona. It's the largest county fair in the world (Box 2250, Pomona 91769, tel. 714/623–3111).

October **Grand National Livestock Exposition, Rodeo, and Horse Show,** San Francisco. A world-class competition, with 3,000 top livestock and horses (Cow Palace, Box 34206, San Francisco 94134, tel. 415/469–6065.).

November **Death Valley '49er Encampment,** Death Valley. Encampment at Furnace Creek commemorates historic crossing of Death Valley in 1849, with fiddlers' contest, art show (Death Valley National Monument, Box 579, Death Valley 92328, tel. 619/786–2331).

Dickens Christmas Fair, Novato. Dickens's London presented by actors and craftspeople. Extends through December weekends (Living History Centre, Box B, Novato 94948, tel. 415/892–0937).

Southern California Grand Prix, Del Mar. Vintage grand prix races, auto expo, and national sports car championship events are included (100 W. Broadway, Suite 760, Long Beach 90802, tel. 213/437–0341).

December **Miners' Christmas Celebration,** Columbia. The fun includes a Victorian Christmas feast, lamplight tours, Christmas theater, children's piñata, costumed carolers, and Los Posadas (Columbia Chamber of Commerce, Box 1824, Columbia 95310, tel. 209/532–4301).

The Shepherd's Play, San Juan Bautista. The annual production by the internationally acclaimed El Teatro Campesino, is performed in the Old Mission (El Teatro Campesino, Box 1240, San Juan Bautista 95045, tel. 408/623–2444).

Christmas Boat Parade of Lights, Newport Beach. For six nights before Christmas, 200 decorated boats parade through the harbor (1470 Jamboree Rd., Newport Beach 92660, tel. 714/ 644–8211).

What to Pack

Clothing   The most important single rule to bear in mind in packing for a California vacation is to prepare for changes in temperature. An hour's drive can take you up or down many degrees, and the variation from daytime to nighttime in a single location is often marked. Take along sweaters, jackets, and clothes for layering as your best insurance for coping with variations in temperature. Include shorts and/or cool cottons unless you are packing for a mid-winter ski trip. Always tuck in a bathing suit. You may not be a beach lover, but the majority of overnight lodgings include a pool, a spa, and a sauna; you'll want the option of using these facilities.

While casual dressing is a hallmark of the California lifestyle, in the evening men will need a jacket and tie for many good restaurants, and women will be more comfortable in something dressier than regulation sightseeing garb.

Considerations of formality aside, bear in mind that San Francisco can be chilly at any time of the year, especially in summer, when the fog is apt to descend and stay. Nothing is more pitiful than the sight of uninformed tourists in shorts, their legs blue with cold. Take along clothes to keep you warm, even if the season doesn't seem to warrant it.

Miscellaneous   Although you can buy supplies of film, sunburn cream, aspirin, and most other necessities almost anywhere in California (unless you're heading for the wilderness), it is a bother, especially if your time is limited, to have to search for staples. Take along a reasonable supply of the things you know you will be using routinely and save your time for sheer enjoyment.

An extra pair of glasses, contact lenses, or prescription sunglasses is always a good idea; the loss of your only pair can damage a vacation.

It is important to pack any prescription medications you need regularly, as well as prescriptions that are occasionally important, such as allergy medications. If you know you are prone to certain medical problems and have good, simple ways of dealing with early manifestations, take along what you might need, even though you may never use it.

Cash Machines

An increasing number of the nation's banks belong to a network of ATMs (automatic teller machines), which gobble up bank cards and spit out cash 24 hours a day in cities throughout the country. There are eight major networks in the United States, the largest of which are Cirrus, owned by MasterCard, and Plus, affiliated with Visa. Some banks belong to more than one network. These cards are not automatically issued; you have to ask for them. If your bank doesn't belong to at least one network, you should consider moving your funds, for ATMs are becoming as essential as check cashing. Cards issued by Visa and MasterCard also may be used in the ATMs, but the fees are usually higher than the fees on bank cards and there is a daily interest charge on the "loan" even if monthly bills are paid on time. Each network has a toll-free number you can call to locate machines in a given city. The Cirrus number is 800/4–CIRRUS; the Plus number is 800/THE–PLUS. Check with your bank for fees and for the amount of cash you can withdraw in a day.

Traveling with Film

If your camera is new, shoot and develop a few rolls of film before leaving home. Pack some lens tissue and an extra battery for your built-in light meter. Invest about $10 in a skylight filter and screw it onto the front of your lens. It will protect the lens and also reduce haze.

Film doesn't like hot weather. If you're driving in summer, don't store the film in the glove compartment or on the shelf under the rear window. Put it behind the front seat on the floor, on the side opposite the exhaust pipe.

On a plane trip, never pack unprocessed film in check-in luggage; if your bags get X-rayed, you can say goodbye to your pictures. Always carry undeveloped film with you through security and ask to have it inspected by hand. (It helps to isolate your film in plastic bag, ready for quick inspection.) Inspectors at American airports are required by law to honor requests for hand inspection; abroad, you'll have to depend on the kindness of strangers.

The old airport scanning machines—still in use in some Third World countries—use heavy doses of radiation that can turn a family portrait into an early morning fog. The newer models—used in all U.S. airports—are safe for anything from five to 500 scans, depending on the speed of your film. The effects are cumulative; you can put the same roll of film through several scans without worry. After five scans, though, you're asking for trouble.

If your film gets fogged and you want an explanation, send it to the **National Association of Photographic Manufacturers,** 550 Mamaroneck Ave., Harrison, NY 10528. They will try to determine what went wrong. The service is free.

Car Rentals

All major car rental agencies serve California, though not all have outlets in every city and airport. Two important suggestions for car rentals: Compare prices, and be sure you understand all the provisions of an agreement before you sign it. Often you will have to pay extra for the privilege of picking up a car in one location and dropping it at another; know the difference in cost, and know how important it is to you. Differing requirements for filling gas tanks can change the cost of the rental. Ask questions.

It's always best to know a few essentials *before* you arrive at the car rental counter. Find out what the collision damage waiver (usually an $8 to $12 daily surcharge) covers and whether your corporate or personal insurance already covers damage to a rental car (if so, bring along a photocopy of the benefits section). More and more companies are holding renters responsible for theft and vandalism damages if they don't buy the CDW; in response, some credit card and insurance companies are extending *their* coverage to rental cars.

Here are toll-free numbers for some of the car rental agencies in California:

Agency Rent-A-Car, tel. 800/843–1143.
American International Rent a Car (AI), tel. 800/527–0202.
Avis, tel. 800/331–1212.
Budget Car and Truck Rental, tel. 800/527–0700.
Dollar Rent a Car, tel. 800/421–6868.
Hertz, tel. 800/654–3131.
National Car Rental, tel. 800/328–4567.
Thrifty Car Rental, tel. 800/367–2277.

Traveling with Children

The watchword for traveling with chidlren is to plan ahead as much as possible. That way, the trip will be a lot more fun for all of you.

In many parts of California, bed-and-breakfast inns are growing in popularity. Small, charming, and usually old, they have a strong appeal for many people. However, if you are traveling with children, you'll have to look carefully to find one that will give you a room at the inn. It's not too surprising; most of these places are furnished with antiques and decorative accessories that are definitely not childproof. Our research shows that you can travel with children in California and occasionally stay at a B&B, but you'll have to plan ahead; look at our listings.

Motels and hotels, with few exceptions, do welcome children. Often they can stay free in the same room with their parents, with nominal charges for cribs and $5–$10 charges for an extra bed. In addition, major hotels usually have lists of baby-sitters so that parents can leave for non-child-related activities.

If you have children, you won't need anyone to tell you to have a good supply of things to keep them busy in the car, on the airplane, on the train, or however you are traveling. If you're traveling by car, you'll have the option of stopping frequently. Just getting the children out of the confines of the car for a little while has an advantage; an even bigger advantage comes when you can stop at a park and the children can run or use a playground.

When you are sightseeing, try to plan some things that will be of special interest to your children. They may tolerate a museum and even show interest in a historic building or two, but put a zoo into the itinerary when you can.

In many ways California is made to order for traveling with children: Disneyland, the San Diego Zoo, the Monterey Aquarium, the San Francisco cable cars, the city-owned gold mine in Placerville, the caverns at Lake Shasta. . . . The list could go on and on.

Publications *Family Travel Times,* an 8- to 12-page newsletter published 10 times a year by TWYCH (Travel with Your Children, 80 Eighth Ave., New York, NY 10011, tel. 212/206–0688). Subscription

($35) includes access to back issues and twice-weekly oppor-
tunities to call in for specific advice.

*Great Vacations with Your Kids: The Complete Guide to Family
Vacations in the U.S.,* by Dorothy Ann Jordon and Marjorie
Adoff Cohen (E.P. Dutton, 2 Park Ave., New York, NY 10016;
$12.95) details everything from city vacations to adventure va-
cations to child-care resources.

Places to Go with Children in Southern California, by Stephan-
ie Kegan (Chronicle Books, 275 Fifth St., San Francisco, CA
94103, tel. 800/722–6657 or 800/445–7577 in CA; $9.95 plus $2
for shipping).

Places to Go with Children in Northern California, by
Elizabeth Pomada (Chronicle Books, same as above).

Eating Out with Kids in San Francisco, by Carole Terwilliger
Meyers (Carousel Press, $7.95). For Carousel Press' catalog of
100–150 family-oriented travel guides and activity books for
kids, send $1 for shipping or a business-size SASE with 45¢
postage to Carousel Press, Box 6061, Albany, CA 94706.

"Kidding around in San Francisco," a free brochure available
from the San Francisco Convention & Visitors Bureau (Box
6977, San Francisco 94101, tel. 415/974–6900.

Hints for Disabled Travelers

California is a national leader in providing access for handicapped people to attractions and facilities. Since 1982 the state
building code has required that all construction for public use
include access for the disabled. State laws more than a decade
old provide special privileges, such as license plates allowing
special parking spaces, unlimited parking in time-limited
spaces, and free parking in metered spaces. Initia from states
other than California are honored.

People with disabilities should plan ahead for travel; check
with providers when you make arrangements for transportation, lodging, and special sightseeing and events. Allow plenty
of time to meet bus, train, and plane schedules. Be sure your
wheelchair is clearly marked if it is carried with other luggage.

Greyhound-Trailways will carry a disabled person and companion for the price of a single fare.

Amtrak (tel. 800/USA–RAIL) advises that you request redcap
service, special seats, or wheelchair assistance when you
make reservations. Also note that not all stations are equipped
to provide these services. All handicapped passengers are entitled to a 25% discount on regular discounted coach fares. A
special children's handicapped fare is also available, offering
qualified kids ages 2–12 a 50% discount on already-discounted
children's fares. Check with Amtrak to be sure discounts are
not exempt when you plan to travel. For a free copy of Amtrak's
Travel Planner, which outlines all its services for elderly and
handicapped, write to Amtrak (National Railroad Corp., 400
N. Capitol St. NW, Washington, DC 20001, tel. 800/872–7245).

The **National Park Service** provides a Golden Access Passport
free of charge to those who are medically blind or have a permanent disability; the passport covers the entry fee for the holder
and anyone accompanying the holder in the same private vehicle and a 50% discount on camping and some other user fees.
Apply for the passport in person at a national recreation facility that charges an entrance fee; proof of disability is required.

For additional information, write to the National Park Service (U.S. Dept. of Interior, 18th and C Sts. NW, Washington, DC 20240).

Society for the Advancement of Travel for the Handicapped (26 Court St., Brooklyn, NY 11242, tel. 718/858–5483 in New York; tel. 213/986–4246 in Los Angeles) is a good source for access information for the disabled. Annual membership is $40; for senior travelers and students, $25.

The Information Center for Individuals with Disabilities (Fort Point Pl., 1st fl., 27–43 Wormwood St., Boston, MA 02210, tel. 617/727–5540) offers useful problem-solving assistance, including lists of travel agencies that specialize in tours for the disabled.

Travel Industry and Disabled Exchange (TIDE, 5435 Donna Ave., Tarzana, CA 91356, tel. 818/368–5648) is an industry-based organization with a $15-per-person annual membership fee. Members receive a quarterly newsletter and information on travel agencies and tours.

Moss Rehabilitation Hospital Travel Information Service (12th St. and Tabor Rd., Philadelphia, PA 19141, tel. 215/329–5715) provides information on tourist sights, transportation, and accommodations for destinations around the world, for a small fee.

Mobility International (Box 3551, Eugene, OR 97403, tel. 503/343–1284) has information on accommodations, organized study, etc., around the world.

Hints for Older Travelers

Many discounts are available to older travelers: Meals, lodging, entry to various attractions, car rentals, tickets for buses and trains, and campsites are among the prime examples.

The age that qualifies you for these senior discounts varies considerably. The American Association of Retired Persons will accept you for membership at age 50, and your membership card will qualify you for many discounts. The state of California will reduce the cost of your campsite if you are at least 62.

If you are 50, our advice is to ask about senior discounts even if there is no posted notice. Ask at the time you are making reservations, buying tickets, or being seated in a restaurant. Carry proof of your age, such as a driver's license, and of course any membership cards in organizations that provide discounts for seniors. Many discounts are given solely on the basis of age, without membership requirement. A 10% cut on a bus ticket and $2 off a pizza may not seem like major savings, but they add up, and you can cut the cost of a trip appreciably if you remember to take advantage of these options.

The American Association of Retired Persons (AARP) (1909 K St. NW, Washington, DC 20049, tel. 202/872–4700). The Purchase Privilege Program offfers discounts on car rentals, sightseeing hotels, motels, and resorts. AARP also arranges group tours through **American Express Vacations** (Box 5014, Atlanta, GA 30302, tel. 800/241–1700 or 800/637–6200 in GA). These and other services are included in the annual dues of $5 per person or per couple. The AARP Motoring Plan offers emergency aid and trip routing information for an annual fee of $33.95 per couple.

Elderhostel (80 Boylston St., Suite 400, Boston, MA 02116, tel. 617/426–7788) is an innovative program for people 60 or over (only one member of a traveling couple needs to be 60 to qualify). Participants live in dorms on 1,200 campuses in the United States and around the world. Mornings are devoted to lectures and seminars, afternoons to sightseeing and field trips. The fee includes room, board, tuition, and round-trip transportation.

National Council of Senior Citizens (925 15th St. NW, Washington, DC 20005, tel. 202/347–8800) is a nonprofit advocacy group with 5,000 local clubs across the country. Annual membership is $12 per person or per couple. Members receive a monthly newspaper with travel information and an ID card for reduced-rate hotels and car rentals.

Mature Outlook (6001 N. Clark St., Chicago, IL 60660, tel. 800/336–6330), a subsidiary of Sears, Roebuck & Co., is a travel club for people over 50, with hotel and motel discounts and a bimonthly newsletter. Annual membership is $9.95 per couple. Instant membership is available at participating Holiday Inns.

September Days Club is run by the moderately priced Days Inns of America (tel. 800/241–5050). The $12 annual membership fee for individuals or couples over 50 entitles them to reduced car rental rates and reductions of 15–50% at 95% of the chain's more than 350 motels.

Greyhound-Trailways (tel. 800/531–5332) and **Amtrak** (tel. 800/USA–RAIL) offer special fares for senior citizens.

Golden Age Passport is a free lifetime pass to all parks, monuments, and recreation areas run by the federal government. Permanent U.S. residents over 62 may pick them up in person at any national park that charges admission. The passport covers the entrance fee for the holder and anyone accompanying the holder in the same private vehicle. It also provides a 50% discount on camping and various other user fees.

The California state park system includes more than 200 locations and provides a $2 discount on campsites (ask for this discount when you make advance reservations) for anyone 62 or over and others in the same private-vehicle.

Publications *The Senior Citizen's Guide to Budget Travel in the United States and Canada* is available for $4.95, including postage, from Pilot Books (103 Cooper St., Babylon, NY 11702, tel. 516/422–2225).
The Discount Guide for Travelers Over 55 by Caroline and Walter Weintz (Dutton, $7.95) lists helpful addresses, package tours, reduced-rate car rentals, etc., in the United States and abroad.

Staying in California

Shopping

In California's big cities, opportunities abound to shop for internationally famed clothing, jewelry, leather goods, and perfumes, often in shops or boutiques set up by French, Ital-

ian, British, or American designers. There are enough specialty shops and fine department stores to keep anyone "born to
shop" busy and happy. *(Note:* San Francisco and Los Angeles
are centers of clothing manufacture; if you're a bargain hunter,
you'll want to explore the factory outlets in both cities.)

If you are shopping for something unique to California, look at
the output of its artists. California is home to a great number of
artists and craftspeople, and you can find their creations from
one end of the state to the other in fine city galleries, in small
neighborhood shops, in out-of-the-way mountain studios, at
roadside stands, and at county fairs. Paintings, drawings,
sculpture, wood carvings, pottery, jewelry, hand-woven fabrics, handmade baskets—the creativity and the output of
California's artists and artisans seems endless. Whatever your
taste and budget, you will probably have no trouble locating
tempting shopping opportunities.

Another California specialty is wine. You can visit wineries in
many parts of the state, not only in the Wine Country north of
San Francisco. Wineries and good wine stores will package
your purchases for safe travel or shipping.

Other possibilities range from antiques to souvenir T-shirts. If
you're flying home from San Francisco, you can make one last
purchase of the city's unique sourdough French bread at the
airport.

Beaches

With almost 1,000 miles of coastline, California is well supplied
with beaches. They are endlessly fascinating: You can walk on
them, lie and sun on them, watch seabirds and hunt for shells,
dig clams, or spot seals and sea otters at play. From December
through April you can watch the migrations of the gray whales.

What you can't always do at these beaches is swim. From San
Francisco north, the water is simply too cold for any but extremely hardy souls. Some beaches, even along the southern
half of the coast, are too dangerous for swimming because of
undertows. Look for signs and postings and take them seriously. Park rangers patrol beaches and enforce regulations, such
as those on pets (dogs must be on leash at all times), alcohol,
dune buggies, and fires.

Access to beaches in California is generally excellent. The state
park system includes many fine beaches, and oceanside communities have their own public beaches. In addition, through
the work of the California Coastal Commission, many stretches
of private property that would otherwise seal off the beach
from outsiders have public access paths and trails. Again, the
best advice is to look for signs and obey them.

Participant Sports

Almost any participant sport you can think of is available somewhere in California at some time of the year. A great many
sports know no time limits and go on year round. Skiing, of
course, depends on the snow and is limited for the most part to
the time between Thanksgiving and April, but golf courses and
tennis courts do a thriving business all year.

Swimming and surfing, scuba diving, and skin diving in the Pacific Ocean are favorite year-round California pleasures in the southern part of the state. On the coast from San Francisco north, the seasons play a limiting role.

California has abundant fishing options: deep-sea fishing expeditions, ocean fishing from the shore, and freshwater fishing in stream, rivers, lakes, and reservoirs. There are many hunting options as well. For information on fishing and hunting licenses and regulations, check with the **California Department of Fish and Game** (1416 9th St., Sacramento 95814, tel. 916/445–3531).

Hiking, backpacking, bicycling, and sailing are popular throughout the state, and you can readily arrange for rental of equipment. River rafting, white-water and otherwise, canoeing, and kayaking are popular, especially in the northern part of the state, where there are many rivers; see individual chapters for detailed information.

Hot-air ballooning is gaining in popularity, although it is not cheap: A ride costs in excess of $100. More and more of the large, colorful balloons drift across the valleys of the Wine Country, where the air drafts are particularly friendly to this sport, and in other parts of California as well.

State and National Parks

State Parks California's state park system includes more than 200 sites; many are recreational and scenic, and some are historic or scientific. A sampling of the variety of state parks: Angel Island in San Francisco Bay, reached by ferry from San Francisco or Tiburon; Anza Borrego Desert, 600,000 acres of the Colorado Desert northeast of San Diego; Big Basin Redwoods, California's first state redwood park, with 300-foot trees, near Santa Cruz; Empire Mines, one of the richest mines in the Mother Lode in Grass Valley; Kings Beach on the shores of Lake Tahoe; Leo Carillo Beach north of Santa Monica; Pismo Beach, with surfing, clamming, and nature trails.

Reservations Most state parks are open year round. Parks near major urban areas and on beaches and lakes are often crowded, and campsite reservations are essential. MISTIX (tel. 800/444–7275) handles all state-park reservations, which may be made up to eight weeks in advance.

For information on California's state parks, contact the **California State Park System** (Dept. of Parks and Recreation, Box 942896, Sacramento 94296, tel. 916/445–6477).

National Parks National parks are administered by the Department of the Interior, and the lands within their boundaries are preserved.

There are five national parks in California: Lassen, Redwood, Sequoia and Kings Canyon, Yosemite, and the Channel Islands. National monuments include Cabrillo, in San Diego; Death Valley; Devil's Postpile, 7,600 feet up in the eastern Sierra Nevada; Lava Beds, in northeastern California; Muir Woods, north of San Francisco; and Pinnacles, in western central California.

There are three national recreation areas: Golden Gate, with 73,000 acres both north and south of the Golden Gate Bridge in San Francisco; Santa Monica Mountains, with 150,000 acres from Griffith Park in Los Angeles to the Ventura County line;

and Whiskeytown-Shasta-Trinity, with 240,000 acres including four major lakes.

For information on specific parks, see the individual chapters or contact the **National Park Service** (450 Golden Gate Ave., San Francisco 94102, tel. 415/556–7230).

Dining

Restaurants are placed in one of four categories—Inexpensive, Moderate, Expensive, and Very Expensive—according to the price of a full dinner for one person. The full dinner includes soup or salad, an entrée, vegetables, dessert, and coffee or tea. The prices does not include drinks, tax, or tip.

Dining is more expensive in major cities than in rural areas. Since price levels vary from one part of California to another, check each chapter for the dollar amount denoted by the category.

Lodging

Overnight accommodations are placed in one of four categories —Inexpensive, Moderate, Expensive, and Very Expensive— according to the amount charged for two people in one room. Since lodging costs vary from one part of the state to another, check each chapter for the dollar amount denoted by the category.

Motel, hotel, and bed-and-breakfast accommodations are listed together in each chapter. Hotels are found primarily in cities and may or may not provide parking facilities. There is usually a charge for parking. Motels have parking space but may not have some of the amenities that hotels typically have: elevators, on-site restaurants, lounges, and room service.

Except for the parking, none of these generalizations is hard and fast. Many motels have restaurants, room service, and other services. Nor is size a distinction. Some hotels are small and have few rooms; some motels have more than 200 rooms.

Bed-and-breakfast inns have become more popular in California in recent years. Most typically, an inn is a large older home, renovated and charmingly decorated with antiques, with a half-dozen guest rooms. Full breakfasts are served at a set time, at a common dining table. Baths may be private or shared. However, these are not hard and fast rules. Sometimes the breakfast is a Continental one. Sometimes the inn is a renovated hotel from the last century with a dozen rooms; occasionally it is a Victorian farmhouse with only three guest rooms.

Few B&Bs allow smoking; virtually none take pets. Antique furniture, delicate fabrics, and the elaborate decorative accessories that are typical of these inns make these restrictions understandable.

On the matter of cost, there is no reliable way of distinguishing among hotels, motels, and B&Bs. A motel may be as lavish and luxurious as a hotel, and you don't necessarily economize by staying in a B&B.

Guest ranches and dude ranches are included in lodging listings, as are resorts. Their range of recreation options is greater than the usual, and this is noted.

Credit Cards

The following credit card abbreviations are used: AE, American Express; CB, Carte Blanche; D, Discover; DC, Diners Club; MC, MasterCard; V, Visa.

Camping

Camping facilities in the state parks are extensive, though you will need reservations. *(See* State Parks, above.) Many popular parks have all spaces reserved several weeks ahead. *California RV Park and Campground Guide* gives information about nearly 300 private parks and campgrounds throughout the state. Send $2 to **California Travel Parks Association** (Box 5648, Auburn, CA 95604).

Smoking

Limitations on smoking are more and more common; if you smoke, be sensitive to restrictions. If you do not smoke, ask for and expect accommodations for nonsmokers on airplanes, in hotels, in restaurants, and in many other public places.

Smoking is banned on all airline routes within the 48 contiguous states, within the states of Hawaii and Alaska, on flights of under six hours to and from Hawaii and Alaska, and to and from the U.S. Virgin Islands and Puerto Rico. The rule applies to both domestic and foreign carriers.

Most hotels and motels have nonsmoking rooms; in larger establishments whole floors are reserved for nonsmokers. Most B&B inns do not allow smoking on the premises.

Most eating places of any size have nonsmoking sections. Many cities and towns in California have ordinances requiring areas for nonsmokers in restaurants and many other public places.

The trend in California, a health-conscious state, is toward more "No Smoking" signs. Expect to see them in many places.

2 Portraits of California

Along the High Sierra

by Colin Fletcher

In 1958 Welch adventurer Colin Fletcher walked the length of California, a six-month trip to "take a look at America." This essay is excerpted from his account of that traverse, The Thousand-Mile Summer. *Other works by Fletcher include* The Man Who Walked Through Time *and the* Complete Walker.

The rest of the world quite rightly sees America as a cockpit of rapacity and exploitation. But it tends to forget that America is also a land of altruistic idealism—an idealism that can give birth to magnificently generous concepts, hammer them into tangibilities, and then throw the whole thing open for the rest of humanity to enjoy.

The world is inclined to remember, for example, that early American settlers slashed and gutted the virgin forests of their new continent; that they slaughtered prodigious herds of buffalo almost into extinction; that they did, in other words, what new settlers had always done, everywhere—wage total war against a Nature that to them was the natural enemy. But the world usually ignores the reverse of this coin.

On the night of September 19, 1870, five men sat around a campfire in what was then the territory of Montana. The men were primarily speculators. To confirm rumors of rich mineral and real-estate potential, they had penetrated deep into the almost unexplored Yellowstone River wilderness. A month's journeying had shown them commercial potential beyond their wildest dreams; but it had also revealed geysers and canyons, lakes and waterfalls, forests and mountain peaks, and a teeming wildlife. Around the last campfire before they returned to civilization, these five hard-headed businessmen discussed the natural impulse to convert their discoveries into personal profit. But remembering the superb beauty they had seen, they spurned the certainty of wealth. They agreed unanimously that private ownership of the Yellowstone region should never be countenanced, and that "it ought to be set aside by the government and forever held to the unrestricted use of the people."

Back in civilization, they registered no land or minerals claims. Instead, they wrote and lectured on the wonders of Yellowstone's natural beauty. Their words swept across the country. Two years later, President Grant signed into law an act creating the world's first National Park. The revolutionary concept of conserving wilderness for its own sake has now spread to every continent. And in enlightened practice America still leads the way. James Fisher, a visiting English naturalist, recently wrote in his *Wild America*, "Never have I seen such wonders or met landlords so worthy of their land. They had, and still have, the power to ravage it; and instead they have made it a garden."

In Death Valley I had seen an attempt to preserve a part of America essentially as it was when the white man came; but

Death Valley has been opened up by roads and amenities, as have most National Parks. In Primitive or Wilderness Areas, all man's travel tools are banned: no roads, no vehicles, no boats. Only hikers and horsemen may use the narrow trails. Compared with some such reservations, the Wild Area in the summit country of the Sierra Nevada above Lake Tahoe is small and almost tame. Its highest peak reaches barely 10,000 feet above sea level. But it is beautiful country. And it is very heavily used.

Lake Tahoe itself—only a four-hour drive for the 3 million people who live around San Francisco Bay—has become northern California's most popular playground. It has something for everybody. People with money to burn flock like moths to the neon lights of the Nevada shore. There they flutter in ecstasy around the one-armed bandits that have moved in from Reno. People with simpler tastes, shorter pockets, and a yearning for suntans congregate along the California shoreline. They fish, swim, water-ski, and finally barbecue without having to move more than two drinks off the highway. People who prefer the outdoors climb up west of the lake into the Wild Area. And there they find wilderness "set aside by the government and forever held to the unrestricted use of the people."

When I climbed up into the Wild Area I found a new sample of America.

At first, it was lake country. Some of the lakes lay open and crisp and sparkling. Others brooded in retirement, like philosophers. Between the lakes, rough stepping-stones led across creeks that vanished into snowdrifts through blue-gray doorways. Sometimes, bare gray rock was the whole scenery—menacing in shadow, bright and inviting in sunlight. But usually, mile after mile, I walked through forest. And always, high above, towered snowcapped peaks.

After two days I came to the infant Rubicon River and began to follow it northward. And now, sometimes, I found myself on the edge of a meadow with a familiar look—a sunlight-and-shadow, almost-too-good-to-be-true, Silver King kind of a look.

In the week I spent wandering through the 50 miles of Wild Area, I met about half a dozen people a day. And I knew that everyone I met shared one thing with me.

All the way from Mexico, well-intentioned inquirers had been saying, "Oh, but there's an easier way than that! Why don't you take the road to So-and-So?" For them, naturally, country was something that had to be passed through on the way from one place to the next. For me, places were refueling points at the end of a stretch of country. Sometimes I had said, "Don't forget, you're interested in *getting* somewhere; I'm interested in *going*." But the idea did not always get over. Now, up in the Wild Area, I knew that everyone looked at the country with the same eyes as I did.

They had little else in common.

I met men, women, and children. Some rode horses. A few led burros—or tried to. The majority labored along under backpacks: packs that perched high on shoulders and packs that wallowed around buttocks; neat packs like bundles back from the laundry and hippopotamic packs like bundles ready to go there; little pouches as convenient as a kangaroo's and murderous millstones that buckled their bearers' knees. And the people I met were as varied as their burdens—as mixed a bunch as any cross-section of people who happen at a given time to find some common interest attracting them to Union Square, Bond Street, or Fifth Avenue.

To be accurate, I did not always quite "meet" them.

There was the evening that there floated across the Rubicon River the authentic nesting sounds of a troop of Girl Scouts.

There was the early morning, ships-that-pass-in-the-night scene beside a small lake. It was a shady, enclosed place that made me think of Walden Pond. The trail skirted one bank, and I walked slowly, trying to see down into the sunlit water. Suddenly I almost trod on a little blue tackle box. It lay open beside the trail, every compartment overflowing with spinners—red, silver, gold. Set there between two moss-covered tree boles, the box was incongruous yet friendly. I looked around. Except for the box and the narrow trail, there was no sign of man's existence. Then I glimpsed movement. A hundred yards away on the far side of the lake a fisherman stood in deep shadow, a mere silhouette against greenery. I leaned on my staff beside the tackle box, watching him. After a while he looked up. I waved. He waved back. Then I went on down the trail, and within twenty paces the lake was hidden and I was back in thick forest.

Often, though, I stopped and talked to those I met.

There was the elderly man who might have been a judge and whose voice and thoughts were quiet and contemplative but who sat astride his horse like Thor taking a weekend off from making thunder.

There were the father and 11-year-old son, engrossed in a private world, their two fly-decked caps close together as they debated which streamer was most likely to tempt the trout of Lake Aloha. We discussed this problem, and even weightier ones. Afterward, as I climbed up beyond the lake, father and son were fishing side by side at the foot of a snow-terraced rock face. They looked very much alone, very much together. Not many youngsters are so lucky, I thought. Not many fathers either.

Then there was the day I climbed a peak on the edge of the Wild Area, overlooking Lake Tahoe. For three hours the panorama had opened out below me with that slow, unfolding growth—inevitable, but full of surprises—that is one of the rewards of climbing a mountain. About noon, almost at the peak, I crossed a rocky spur. And there, 4,000 feet below, I saw the whole huge basin of Lake Tahoe.

I heard myself gasp and say out loud, "My God, what a color!"

I walked up to the peak, sat down beside the metal summit marker, and gave myself up to the blue-and-greenness of forest and lake and sky. The air was all light and space and silence. I leaned back against warm rock. The sun beat down, timelessly.

After a while a scraping sound, as of a fair-sized animal, came from just beyond the summit marker. I fixed my eyes on a ledge, less than 6 feet away. I had noticed that beyond it the rock sloped away quite gently. I waited, every muscle still. And then, up over the ledge, outlined against blue sky, looking straight into my eyes, appeared a boy's head. It stopped dead. It was cheerful, out of breath, and as surprised as I was. It looked very young to be at almost 10,000 feet on its own, even attached to a body.

I felt I ought to say something. "Did you come all the way up by yourself?" I asked.

"Oh no, Mommy's just behind." The boy climbed up onto the ledge. "Yes, there she is." And a little way below us appeared a tall, slim woman in shorts and a red windbreaker. She waved at her son, then stopped. "Ah, the Old Man of the Mountains!" she called out cheerfully.

She walked on up toward us. Her walk was the rare kind that goes equally well with shorts on a mountain and with an evening dress in a ballroom. As she came up close she said, "Oh no, the *Young* Man of the Mountains!" and I felt better.

She had thick, dark hair, and it was difficult to believe that the 11- or 12-year-old boy was her son.

"Isn't it a fantastic view?" she said. "Peter and I often come up. Nowadays, as you see, he gets here first." She sat down, and we discussed climbing mountains and walking from Mexico to Oregon. Her name was Jinny. I found some snow on a sheltered terrace, lit my pressure stove, and brewed tea for the three of us. Jinny provided sandwiches. Afterward I apologized for having no cigarettes to offer.

Jinny smiled. "Oh, I never seem to want to smoke out of doors anyway. I guess . . . I guess I don't really enjoy smoking much. In itself, I mean. At a party now, it's different. A cigarette takes away the taste of the liquor—and without one I'd never know what to do with my hands." She smiled again. "It's wonderful how honest a mountain makes you, isn't it?"

She got up and walked forward and stood looking out over the blueness of Lake Tahoe. Suddenly she stretched her whole body ecstatically. "Oh what a wonderful world it is!" she said. "Three weeks ago my husband and I were in Hawaii, skin-diving and climbing mountains. And now dear old Tahoe again. You know, I feel sorry for people who never discover this kind of thing. The day we left Hawaii, some friends of ours flew in. The moment they got inside the hotel they rushed for a bridge table, and we knew they'd spend their whole vacation playing bridge and drinking. What a waste! I'm afraid we Americans sometimes forget how lucky we are."

I met "Twig" just outside the Wild Area; but he was essentially a part of it. When he bounced up in his jeep, I was changing film beside an old stagecoach road that is one of the Area's boundaries. We sat and talked, looking back up the rock-bound Rubicon Valley.

"Yes, I backpack in whenever I can," said Twig. "But somehow there's not often time these days. That's why I bought this jeep. But walking's the way to travel all right. Ever since Henry Ford, we Americans have been getting soft. I can still remember my great-grandmother, and she'd crossed the United States seven times. And every time except one, when there happened to be an empty wagon, she walked."

Twig nodded up the valley, carrying the gesture far beyond the horizon. "All the way from Mexico, huh?" He sighed. "When I left school, my mother talked me into taking a degree and going into engineering. But I often wish I'd stayed a backwoods cowpuncher and taken pack trains in, like I did when I was a kid. Still, it's good to know that when the pressures build up you can get away from it all and come out to places like this."

It was then, I think, that I realized what was obvious enough really: that the Wild Area was not only a new sample of America; it was a microcosm of The Walk. It was a place where people could do for a few snatched hours or days what I was lucky enough to be doing for six months.

The realization made me more aware of all the small events that sometimes passed unnoticed because they had become part of the fabric of my life: the first clouds of the day forming over distant peaks; a scarlet snow plant sticking up through the carpet of dead leaves and looking at once succulent as strawberries and deadly as a toadstool; a very small trout following an enormous low-flying bumblebee to the river's edge and turning back at the last moment with a flounce of its tail; a turquoise-breasted hummingbird hovering ten inches from my nose and inspecting my red shirt for pollen; a lizard sunbathing on rough granite and looking me over with the critical eye of a mother-in-law elect.

There was one such moment when everything the Wild Area offered—everything The Walk stood for—came together. For three days I had been following the Rubicon River as it grew by slow degrees from brawling infancy into staid maturity. I had just waded across it and was sitting on a grassy bank, putting my boots back on. The cold river had been refreshing, and now the sun was warm. A copper-red dragonfly landed deftly on a blade of grass at the water's edge, so close I could have touched it.

And suddenly thankfulness surged through me. Thankfulness for the moment, for the day, for the freedom of The Walk, for life itself.

I sat quite still, one boot half on, holding my breath and willing memory to imprison that instant of time—to capture and hold every particle of it. I wanted the copper-red dragonfly on its blade of green grass, curving out over the blue Rubicon. I wanted the warm sunshine and the rough grassy bank. I wanted the scent of lupines and the sound of running water. I wanted the deep forest shadow on the far bank. I wanted the snowbanks that hung high above it. I even wanted the mosquitoes on my bare arms. I knew that later I would find it difficult to believe I had really wanted the mosquitoes; but at that moment I was glad for their sakes that they were alive, and I wanted them too.

The moment did not last long. The dragonfly's wings trembled; it flew away. The blade of grass straightened. I finished putting on my boots, heaved the pack onto my back, and started once more down the trail.

Before long the sun dropped behind a line of stark peaks. Down on the valley floor it was suddenly very gray. But I knew that the copper-red dragonfly beside the Rubicon had given me something I would never altogether lose. And I knew that it was for moments like these that people came to the Wild Area.

Wilderness would be worth conserving if it did nothing but make such moments possible. And as I walked I found myself wishing I could thank the five men who had sat around their Yellowstone campfire in the fall of 1870. It would have been satisfying for them to know that their altruism that night—their altruism in a cockpit of rapacity and exploitation—had done so much not only for me but for the nesting Girl Scouts and for Thor astride his horse and for the father and son fishing in Lake Aloha and for Jinny stretching ecstatically on the mountaintop and for Twig in his jeep and for millions of other Americans and for millions more, born and yet to be born, all over the world.

One evening I came down into a steep-sided little valley and found an abandoned ranch house, tucked away and forgotten. As I walked into the homestead, a herd of cattle stampeded away in panic, kicking up clouds of fine dust. The dust hung long afterward among the trees, making the place look as if it had been bombed. I lit my stove on the steps of a crumbling stone hayloft. Dusk fell. Three deer wandered past—vague brown shadows against a background of dying bracken and hanging brown dust. I walked across the farmyard and found a rusty faucet. Close by, a coyote yowled. The sound echoed up the valley.

As I filled my canteen at the faucet, I kept looking at a sage-covered bank. It was some minutes before I understood why I was doing so. Sagebrush is a sign of heat and dryness, of desert or semi-desert; and this sage was the first I had seen since I climbed up into the High Sierra. And all at once I realized that the ridges above me were lower than those I had become used to. The soil was dustier, the trees so much thinner that you almost had to call them spindly.

The mountains were tapering off.

I went back to the old hayloft, sat down beside my stove, and studied the map. The confused highland mass that lay ahead could be called a side branch of the Sierra Nevada, but its elevation was much less than I had realized. It would almost certainly be drier than what I had come to think of as Sierra country. And the foothills soon sank away. Within two days I would be out in semidesert.

Next day I found once more, as I had done when I came near to the end of the desert, that the surest way of savoring something to the full is to become aware that it is almost over.

I climbed an escarpment on the far side of the valley and came back into thick forest. And now I kept noticing, as if they were something new, little things that had become so much a part of my life since I climbed up out of the desert that I had come to take them for granted. The ground sloped gently downward, and soon there were little clearings, thick with skunk cabbage. A rivulet threaded through tall grass. Every ripple and every blade formed a part of the pattern of texture, part of the pattern of light and shade. A crimson columbine curtsied to a turquoise dragonfly. A thin brown snake, basking away its afternoon on a stone, slid off at my approach and swam down into the darkness of a pool. And always, consciously now, I was walking among trees.

All day, as I walked, I found myself listening. In the desert, the cicadas rasp and there is no doubt about it; but in the forest there is sometimes, you think, a buzzing, almost a rasping among the trees. It is a soothing and yet intriguing sound that comes from nowhere and everywhere. Sometimes it is the distorted echo of running water. Sometimes it is the wind in the treetops. And sometimes it is nothing you can name. That day I could not name it, but I heard it more clearly than ever.

All day the ground sloped away. The forest thinned. The trees grew thinner too, became undeniably spindly. The rivulet joined Sagehen Creek, and there was sagebrush again. At first it grew in isolated clumps. Then in large patches. By afternoon it stretched away, acre after acre, as far as I could see down the valley.

Late in the evening, I was almost ready to camp when I saw a man coming toward me on a parallel trail, a few feet to one side. The semi-darkness failed to hide a certain oddness about him, but I could not decide if it lay in his clothes or in his walk or in something else.

I half checked my stride, wanting to talk but not knowing quite how to begin. "Evening," I said.

"Evening," the man answered. He hesitated too, and the black-and-white collie at his heels almost ran into him. Then he resumed his slow, easy stride and vanished into the dusk.

I was still wondering about him when I camped on a dusty sagebrush flat.

While dinner cooked, I did some calculating. I knew that now the mountains were almost over, The Walk would move into a new stage. It was still two hundred miles to the Oregon border, even in a straight line. Walking, it would probably be half as far again. For various reasons—some of them quite sensible—I wanted to be at the boundary by the end of the first week in September. That left me just over three weeks. To make the border on schedule, I would on most traveling days have to walk a good twenty miles.

Before I went to sleep I made up my mind that, no matter what distractions tempted me, the next day would be the first of the 20-milers. And the most important thing was to get moving as early as possible.

I woke at dawn to the sound of bells. A large flock of sheep was browsing slowly toward me. In the center of the dust storm they created, rising up out of it like an iceberg from fog, moved a brown burro with a bell around its neck. By the time I had finished a hurried breakfast, sheep and dust surrounded me.

I had just strapped the sleeping bag onto my pack when a man appeared on the edge of the flock. I recognized him at once. The black-and-white collie still followed at his heels.

"Morning," said the man.

"Morning," I answered.

The man pushed slowly toward me through the sheep. There was indeed something old-fashioned and quaint about his much-worn tweed suit. And something old-fashioned and dignified about the way he moved and about the way he smiled, taking his time over it, as he reached me.

"I hope my sheep have not caused you inconvenience," he said. He spoke with a European accent.

"Not in the least," I said. "I was glad they woke me up."

"Good," said the man. "Very glad." He took tobacco and cigarette papers from a side pocket of his coat.

And suddenly I realized that he must be one of the Basque sheepherders I had been hoping to meet ever since I saw the blackened names on the aspens beside Silver King Creek.

We chatted about the country ahead. The Basque had herded in the Warner Mountains, up near the Oregon border, during World War I. As he talked about it, he rolled a cigarette, coaxing the tobacco into shape with the care of a potter working clay. Once or twice he smiled his slow-emerging smile. It gave him an unexpected kind of Maurice Chevalier charm.

I was settling down for a long discussion when I brought myself up short. As soon as I could do it without rudeness, I tried to explain why I had to push on. Somehow it didn't sound very convincing.

But the Basque smiled understandingly. "You are right," he said, giving his cigarette a final pat. "To start early is the only way."

I pushed through to the edge of the flock. The Basque still stood where I had left him, knee-deep in sheep and the pall of dust. I waved my staff. He waved back.

Then I turned and went down the valley. As I walked, sagebrush scratched at my legs.

Living with the Certainty of a Shaky Future

by John Burks

John Burks is a professor of journalism and humanities at San Francisco State University. He has served as editor-in-chief of two of the city's leading magazines, City *and* San Francisco Focus, *was a* Newsweek *correspondent and managing editor of* Rolling Stone, *and currently edits the quarterly* American Kite.

There's never been any question *whether* there will be another earthquake in San Francisco. The question is how soon. Even the kids here grow up understanding that it's just a matter of time, and from grade school on, earthquake safety drills become routine. *At the first rumble, duck under your desk or table or stand in a doorway,* they are instructed. *Get away from windows to avoid broken glass. When the shaking stops, walk—don't run—outdoors, as far away from buildings as possible.*

Sure as there are hurricanes along the Gulf of Mexico and blizzards in Maine, San Francisco's earthquakes are inevitable. Nobody here is surprised when the rolling and tumbling begins—it happens all the time. Just in the six months following the jarring 1989 earthquake, for instance, seismologists reported hundreds of aftershocks, ranging from the scarcely perceptible to those strong enough to bring down buildings weakened by October's jolt.

The Bay Area itself was created in upheaval such as this. Eons ago, a restless geology of shifting plates deep in the earth gave birth to the Sierra Mountains and the Pacific Coast Range. Every spring when the snows melted, the runoff rushed down from the mile-high Sierra peaks westward across what would eventually be known as California. Here, the runoff ran up against the coastal range, and a vast inland lake was formed.

The rampaging waters from the yearly thaw eventually crashed through the quake-shattered Coast Range to meet the Pacific Ocean, creating the gap now spanned by the Golden Gate Bridge. This breakthrough created San Francisco Bay, one of the world's great natural harbors, its fertile delta larger than that of the Mississippi River. What a fabulous setting for the city-to-be—surrounded on three sides by water, set off by dramatic mountainscapes to the north and south, and blessed by cool ocean breezes.

All this and gold, too. The twisting and rolling of so-called terra firma exposed rich veins of gold at and near ground level that otherwise would have remained hidden deep underground. The great upheaval pushed the Mother Lode to the surface and set the scene for the Gold Rush.

The 1906 earthquake and fire has come to define San Francisco both for itself and the outside world. In the immediate aftermath of the catastrophe, San Franciscans wondered whether they ought to believe the preachers and reformers who declared that this terrible devastation had been wrought upon their wicked city by the avenging hand of God. San Franciscans asked themselves whether, somehow, they had earned it.

But the city was quick to prove its character. Fifty years earlier, six separate fires had destroyed most of San Francisco—yet each time it was rebuilt by a citizenry not ready to give up on either the gold or the city that gold had built. Now, in 1906, heroic firefighters dynamited one of the city's main thoroughfares to prevent the inferno from spreading all the way to the Pacific. The mood of San Franciscans was almost eerily calm, their neighborliness both heartwarming and jaunty. "Eat, drink, and be merry," proclaimed signs about town, "for tomorrow we may have to go to Oakland." No sooner had the flames died than rebuilding began—true to San Francisco tradition. Forty thousand construction workers poured into town to assist the proud, amazingly resilient residents.

The 1906 earthquake provided a chance to rethink the hodge-podge, get-rich-quick cityscape that had risen in the heat of Gold Rush frenzy. City fathers imported the revered urban planner Daniel Burnham, architect of the magnificent 1893 Chicago World's Fair, to re-invent San Francisco. "Make no little plans," Burnham intoned. "They have no power to stir men's souls."

The city's new Civic Center, built under Burnham's direction, was raised to celebrate the city's comeback and is regarded as one of America's most stately works of civic architecture. It's city hall stands as a monument to the city's will to prevail—from its colonnaded granite exterior to its exuberant interior, once described by Tom Wolfe as resembling "some Central American opera house. Marble arches, domes, acanthus leaves . . . quirks and galleries and gilt filigrees . . . a veritable angels' choir of gold." The inscription found over the major's office seems to sum it all up: "San Francisco, O glorious city of our hearts that has been tried and not found wanting, go thou with like spirit to make the future thine."

In 1915, San Francisco dazzled the world with its Panama-Pacific Exposition, designed to prove not only that it was back, but that it was back bigger and better and badder than ever before. An architectural wonderland, the Expo was built on 70 acres of marshy landfill, which later became the residential neighborhood called the Marina District. When the October 1989 earthquake struck, this neighborhood was badly damaged, and became a focus as the entire nation tuned in to see how San Francisco and her people would fare this time around.

Like the gold that surfaced in the Mother Lode, the 1989 quake once again brought out the best in this region's people. Out at Candlestick Park, 62,000 fans were waiting for the start of the World Series between the San Francisco

Giants and the Oakland A's when everything started shaking. They cut loose with big cheer after the temblor subsided. One San Francisco fan quickly hand-lettered a sign and held it aloft: "That was Nothing—Wait Til the Giants Bat." When it became apparent that there would be no ball played that night, the fans departed from the ballpark, just like in a grade school earthquake safety drill, quietly and in good order.

This was what millions of TV viewers across the nation first saw of the local response to this major (7.1) earthquake and, by and large, the combination of good humor and relative calm they observed was an accurate reflection of the prevailing mood around the city. San Franciscans were not about to panic. Minutes after the quake struck, a San Francisco couple spread a lace tablecloth over the hood of their BMW and, sitting in the driveway of their splintered home, toasted passersby with champagne. Simultaneously, across San Francisco Bay, courageous volunteers and rescue workers set to work digging through the pancaked rubble of an Oakland freeway in the search for survivors, heedless that they, too, could easily be crushed in an aftershock. Throughout the Bay Area, hundreds volunteered to fight the fires, clear away the mess, assist survivors, and donate food, money, and clothing.

San Francisco's city seal features the image of a phoenix rising from the flames of catastrophe, celebrating the city's fiery past and promising courage in the face of certain future calamity. The 1989 shake possessed only about one-fortieth the force of the legendary 1906 quake, and all projections point to the inevitability of another Big One, someday, on at least the scale of '06. Often people from other, more stable, parts of the world have trouble understanding how it is possible to live with such a certainty.

The *San Francisco Bay Guardian*, shortly after the 1989 quake, spoke for many Bay Area residents: "We live in earthquake country. Everybody knows that. It's a choice we've all made, a risk we're all more or less willing to accept as part of our lives. We're gambling against fate, and last week our luck ran out. It was inevitable—as the infamous bumper sticker says, Mother Nature bats last."

Former San Francisco Mayor Diane Feinstein explained it this way: "Californians seem undaunted. We [know] we'll never be a match for Mother Nature. But the principal thing that seems to arise from the ash and rubble of a quake is the strong resolve to rebuild and get on with life."

The North Coast

by Dan Spitzer

*A history Ph.D.
and resident of
Northern
California, Dan
Spitzer is the
author of four
travel books based
on five years' work
as a journalist in
Asia, Africa, and
Latin America.*

Within the nearly 400 miles of California coast that lie between the San Francisco Bay and the Oregon border, travelers will encounter some of the most beautiful and rugged landscapes in America. Here in the well-named Redwood Empire are primeval forests of the world's tallest trees, while just off the spectacular shoreline are secluded coves and beaches. Along this coast, you may well see gray whales migrating, seals sunning, and hawks soaring. The region is also rich in history, the domain of Native-American Miwoks and Pomos, Russian trading posts, Hispanic settlements, and more contemporary fishing folk and lumberjacks. All these diverse cultures have left a legacy that still may be experienced. For those in search of untamed natural beauty, great fishing, abundant wildlife, and elegant country inns, the vast panorama of the North Coast is a bit of heaven.

The North Coast is sparsely populated, with only 10 towns housing a population of more than 700 inhabitants. Traditionally, residents of this region made their living from fishing and timber. Today, these industries are depressed. Tourism, however, is doing well. Victorian mansions have been restored to lodge, and fine restaurants founded to feed, the increasing number of visitors.

Getting Around

By Plane **American Eagle,** linked with American Airlines (tel. 415/398–4434 or 800/433–7300), has excellent regular daily service to Eureka-Arcata from San Francisco. This is by far the fastest and most convenient way to reach the redwood country. **Hertz** (tel. 800/654–3131) rents cars at the Eureka-Arcata airport.

By Car If Mendocino is your northernmost destination, the most scenic drive from San Francisco is via Highway 1. With its twists and turns, Highway 1 is slow going. You should allow a full day to drive to Mendocino. Those who wish to explore Point Reyes National Seashore en route might consider an overnight stay at Inverness or in a town along the way. You can return directly to San Francisco in about 3½ hours from Mendocino by taking Highway 1 south to Highway 128, which passes through picturesque farm and forest lands. At Cloverdale, Highway 128 intersects with U.S. 101, which continues south to San Francisco.

If Eureka or a point near the Oregon border is your destination, the quickest way to drive from San Francisco is via U.S. 101. This takes a good six to seven hours if you go straight through. Those with the time and inclination should take the scenic but slow Highway 1, which ultimately intersects with U.S. 101 at Legett. It would be backbreaking to cover the latter route in less than two days.

Although there are excellent services along Highway 1 and U.S. 101, gas stations and mechanics are few and far between on the smaller roads.

By Bicycle For the hardy rider who wishes to take in the full beauty of the North Coast by mountain bike, there are a number of rental services in San Francisco and the major North Coast towns. Two rental shops on the coast are **Point Reyes Bikes** (Hwy. 1, Point Reyes Station, tel. 415/663–1768), and **Mendocino Cyclery** (45040 Main St., Mendocino, tel. 707/937–4744). If you wish to go with a group, call **Backroads Bicycle Touring** (tel. 415/895–1783 or 800/533-2573 outside CA). There are plenty of campsites for long-distance bikers to stay at along the coast.

Important Addresses and Numbers

An excellent source of information on the North Coast is the **Redwood Empire Association.** Its San Francisco office is filled with brochures, and the staff is very knowledgeable. For $2, the association will send you its visitor's guide to the region. Write, or stop at the office (785 Market, 15th floor, San Francisco, CA 94103, tel. 415/543–8334. Open weekdays 9–4:30.).

For **emergency services** on the North Coast, dial 911.

Exploring

Exploring the northern California coast is easiest in a car. Highway 1 is a beautiful, if sometimes slow and nerve-racking, drive. You'll want to stop frequently to appreciate the views, and there are many portions of the highway along which you won't drive faster than 30–40 mph. Even if you don't have much time, you can plan a fine trip, but be realistic and don't plan to drive too far in a day *(see* Getting Around, above).

We've arranged the exploring section for a trip from San Francisco north. The first section follows Highway 1 north past Fort Bragg to its intersection with U.S. 101. The second section follows U.S. 101 through the Redwood Empire.

The North Coast via Highway 1

Numbers in the margin correspond with points of interest on the North Coast maps.

To reach Highway 1, heading north from San Francisco, cross the Golden Gate Bridge and proceed north on U.S. 101 to the Stinson Beach/Route 1 exit. Follow Highway 1 north, and as it ❶ winds uphill, you will see a turnoff for **Muir Woods.**

Muir Woods National Monument and the adjoining Mount Tamalpais State Park are described (as day trips) in the chapter Excursions from San Francisco. Past this turnoff, the town ❷ of **Stinson Beach** has the most expansive sands (4,500 feet) in ❸ Marin County. Along Bolinas Lagoon, you will find the **Audubon Canyon Ranch,** a 1,000-acre bird sanctuary. In the spring, the public is invited to take trails to see great blue heron and great egret tree nestings. There is a small museum with displays on the geology and natural history of the region, a natural history bookstore, and a picnic area. *Tel. 415/868–9244. Donation requested. Open weekends and holidays mid–March– mid–July.*

At the northern edge of Bolinas Lagoon, a couple of miles beyond the Audubon Canyon Ranch, take the unmarked road running west from Highway 1. This leads to the sleepy town of **Bolinas.** Some residents of Bolinas are so wary of tourism that whenever the state tries to post signs, they tear them down. ❹ Birders should take Mesa Road to the **Point Reyes Bird Observatory,** a sanctuary harboring nearly 225 species of bird life. *Tel. 415/868–0655. Admission free. Banding daily Apr. 1–*

Sept. 1; weekends and Wed. Sept. 2–Mar. 31. Visitor center open daily year round.

⑤ As you drive back to Bolinas, go right on Overlook Drive and right again on Elm Avenue until you come to **Duxberry Reef,** known for its fine tide pools.

⑥ Returning to Highway 1, you will pass a pastoral scene of horse farms. About ⅓-mile past Olema, look for a sign marking the turnoff for **Point Reyes National Seashore's Bear Valley Visitors Center.** The center has fine exhibits of park wildlife, and helpful rangers will advise you on beaches, visits to the lighthouse for whale watching (the season for gray whale migration is mid-December through March), and hiking trails and camping. (Camping, for backpackers only, is free; reservations should be made through the visitors center.) No matter what your interests, the beauty of this wilderness is worth your time. A reconstructed **Miwok Indian Village** is a short walk from the visitors center. It provides insight into the daily lives of the first human inhabitants of this region. The lighthouse is a very pretty, 30-to 40-minute drive from the visitors center, across rolling hills that resemble Scottish heath. On busy weekends during the season, parking at the lighthouse may be difficult. If you don't care to walk down—and up—hundreds of steps, you may want to skip the descent to the lighthouse itself. You *can* see whales from the cliffs above the lighthouse, but many people will find the lighthouse view worth the effort. *Tel. 415/663–1092. Admission free. Open weekdays 9–5, weekends 8–5.*

If you choose to stay overnight in this area, there are good country inns and decent restaurants in and around the towns of **Inverness** and **Point Reyes Station.** The architecture and cuisine of Inverness reflect the substantial Czech population here.

The Russian River empties into the Pacific at the fishing town of **Jenner.** If you are lucky, you may see seals sunning themselves off the banks of the estuary. Travelers who wish to move on to the wine-growing region from here can take Highway 116 east from Jenner.

What is perhaps the most dramatic stretch of North Coast shoreline may be seen off Highway 1 between Jenner and Gualala. The road is one series of steep switchbacks after another, so take your time, relax, and make frequent stops to enjoy the unparalleled beauty of this wild coast.

⑦ About 12 miles north of Jenner sits the very well-reconstructed **Fort Ross,** encompassed by a state park. For history buffs, this stop is a *must*, as the state park service has painstakingly recreated the ambience of Russia's major fur-trading outpost in California, built originally in 1812. The Russians brought Aleut sea otter hunters all the way from their Alaskan bailiwicks to hunt pelts for the czar. In 1841, with the coast depleted of seal and otter, the Russians sold their post to John Sutter, later of goldrush fame. After a local Anglo rebellion against the Mexicans, the land fell under U.S. domain, becoming part of the state of California in 1850. At Fort Ross, you will find a restored Russian Orthodox chapel, a redwood stockade, officers' barracks, a blockhouse, and an excellent museum. *Fort Ross State Historical Park, tel. 707/847–3286. Day use: $3. Open daily 10–4:30. Closed Dec. 25 and Jan. 1.*

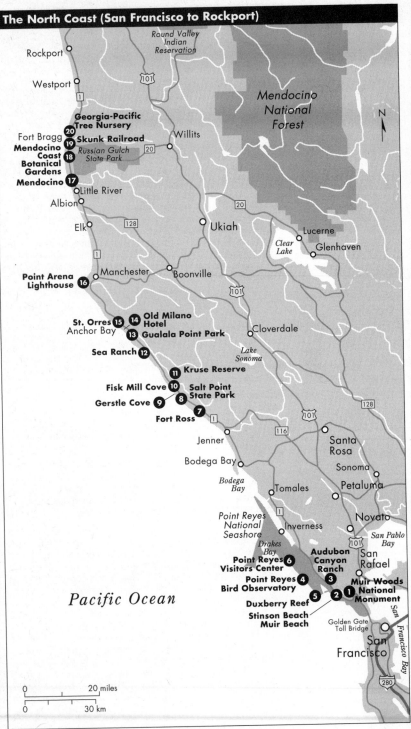

The North Coast (San Francisco to Rockport)

Rockport

Westport

Round Valley
Indian
Reservation

101

1

Mendocino
National
Forest

N

**Georgia-Pacific
Tree Nursery** **20**

Fort Bragg

Skunk Railroad **19**

Willits

**Mendocino
Coast
Botanical
Gardens** **18**

*Russian Gulch
State Park*

20

Mendocino **17**

Little River

Albion

Elk

128

Ukiah

Lucerne

*Clear
Lake*

Glenhaven

20

1

**Point Arena
Lighthouse** **16**

Manchester

Boonville

101

Cloverdale

St. Orres **15** **14** **Old Milano
Hotel**

Anchor Bay

13 **Gualala Point Park**

Sea Ranch **12**

*Lake
Sonoma*

11 **Kruse Reserve**

Fisk Mill Cove **10**

8 **Salt Point
State Park**

Gerstle Cove **9**

7

128

Fort Ross

1

Jenner

116

101

Santa
Rosa

Bodega Bay

Sonoma

Petaluma

*Bodega
Bay*

Tomales

1

Novato

*Point Reyes
National
Seashore*

Inverness

*San Pablo
Bay*

101

*Drakes
Bay*

**Point Reyes
Visitors Center** **6**

**Audubon
Canyon
Ranch**

San
Rafael

**Point Reyes
Bird Observatory** **4**

3

**Muir Woods
National
Monument**

5

2 **1**

Duxberry Reef

Pacific Ocean

**Stinson Beach
Muir Beach**

Golden Gate
Toll Bridge

San Francisco Bay

San
Francisco

280

0   20 miles

0   30 km

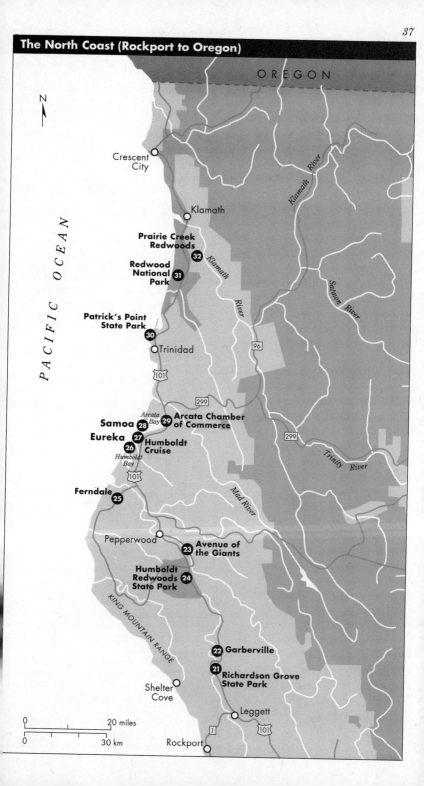

The North Coast (Rockport to Oregon)

OREGON

N

Crescent
City

Klamath

**Prairie Creek
Redwoods**
32

Klamath River

**Redwood
National
Park** **31**

Klamath River

PACIFIC OCEAN

**Patrick's Point
State Park**
30

OTrinidad

[101]

[299]

[96]

Salmon River

[299]

Arcata Bay **29** **Arcata Chamber
of Commerce**

Samoa **28**

Eureka **27**
26 **Humboldt
Cruise**

Humboldt Bay

[101]

Trinity River

Ferndale
25

Pepperwood

Mad River

23 **Avenue of
the Giants**

**Humboldt
Redwoods
State Park** **24**

KING MOUNTAIN RANGE

22 **Garberville**

21 **Richardson Grove
State Park**

Shelter
Cove

Leggett

0   20 miles

0   30 km

[1]   [101]

Rockport

8 About 19 miles north of Jenner, **Salt Point State Park** offers an untamed environment well worth exploring. Visit first the
9 park's **Gerstle Cove,** where you probably will see seals sunning themselves off coastal rocks, and deer in the meadowlands. Note the unusual formations in the sandstone. Called "tafoni," they are the product of hundreds of years of erosion. Also,
10 make the *very* short drive to Salt Point's **Fisk Mill Cove,** where a five-minute walk following the trail uphill will bring you to a bench for a dramatic overview of Sentinel Rock and the pounding surf below. It's all less than a mile off Highway 1. *Tel. 707/ 847–3221. Day use: $3; camping: $10, discount for senior citizens. Open daily.*

11 Not far beyond Fisk Mill Cove, look for the sign to **Kruse Rhododendron Reserve.** Between April and June, be certain to take this turnoff to see the towering pink flowers in this 317-acre reserve. *Admission free. Open daily.*

12 **Sea Ranch** is a controversial development of second homes for the affluent, consisting of 5,000 acres overlooking the Pacific about 10 miles south of Gualala. There was a great outcry by conservationists when this development was announced. To appease the critics, Sea Ranch built trails down to the beaches, which are accessible to the public. Even in the eyes of some environmentalists, the housing here is reasonably congruent with the surroundings; others find the weathered-wood buildings beautiful.

13 For an excellent place to watch whales, check out **Gualala Point Regional Park** (tel. 707/785–2377), where there is picnicking and camping ($10 in summer, $7 in winter). The park is off Highway 1 and is well marked. Just north of the town of Gualala
14 on Highway 1 are two inns worth a visit or a stay. The **Old Milano Hotel,** listed in the National Registry of Historic Places, is an elegant 1905 country inn overlooking Castle Rock.
15 **St. Orres,** with its Russian-style turrets, is also a premiere bed-and-breakfast inn and has one of the best restaurants on the North Coast.

16 For a dramatic view of the surf, take the turnoff north of the fishing village of Point Arena to the **Point Arena Lighthouse** (tel. 707/882–2777). First constructed in 1870, the lighthouse was destroyed by the earthquake that devastated San Francisco in 1906. Rebuilt, it towers 115 feet over the sea. For a small admission fee you can take a tour.

As you head north to Mendocino, you will pass other fine places to stay, perched in and around the coastal cliffs of tiny former lumber ports such as Elk, Albion, and Little River.

17 **Mendocino** is the tourist heartbeat on the North Coast. With its stately Victorian and 19th-century flavor, coupled with its ocean views, the town has become a mecca for artists and visitors alike. See in particular the gingerbread-like **MacCallum House** (45020 Albion St.) and the **Mendocino Hotel** (45080 Main St.), overlooking the sea. There are a number of art galleries to peruse in this eminently walkable town. The **Mendocino Art Center** (45200 Little Lake St., tel. 707/937–5818) has galleries, art classes, concerts, and a theater. A site meriting a stop is the **Kelley House Museum** (45007 Albion St., tel. 707/937–5791), a refurbished 1861 structure. The museum displays historical photographs of Mendocino's logging days, antique cameras, Victorian-era clothing, furniture, and artifacts. Open Friday–

Monday 1–4. On Albion Street you will also see the **Chinese Joss Temple,** dating back to 1871. Another restored structure, the **Ford House,** built in 1854, is on Main Street and serves as the visitors center for **Mendocino Headlands State Park** (tel. 707/ 937–5397, open Fri.–Mon., 1-4 or by appt.). The park itself consists of the cliffs that border the town; access is free.

⑱ Off Highway 1, between Mendocino and Fort Bragg, you will see the **Mendocino Coast Botanical Gardens.** It started as a private preserve in 1962, and the Mendocino Coast Park District acquired 17 acres of the gardens in 1982. Along 2 miles of coastal trails affording views of the sea and observation points for whale watching, you will find a splendid array of flowers, with the rhododendron season peaking from April to June and perennials in bloom from May to September. Fuchsias, heather, and azaleas are resplendent here. This is a fine place to stop for a picnic. *Tel. 707/964–4352. Admission: $5 adults, $4 senior citizens, $3 children 13–17, under 12 free. Open daily Apr.–Oct. 9–5, Nov.–Mar. 10–4.*

Fort Bragg is the commercial heart of Mendocino County. However, unless you are here on business, there is little reason to stay in this nondescript town. It is the headquarters for the **Skunk Train,** on which you may take scenic half- or full-day tours through redwood forests. A remnant of the old logging **⑲** days, the popular **Skunk Railroad,** dating back to 1885, travels 40 miles from Fort Bragg on the coast to the town of Willits, inland on U.S. 101. En route you pass through redwood forests that are not accessible by private car. In summer you have a choice of going partway to the Skunk's Northspur, a 3-hour round trip, or making the 7½-hour journey to Willits and back. *California Western Railroad, Fort Bragg, tel. 707/964–6371. Fort Bragg-Willits: Departs daily 9:20 AM. Admission: $20 adults, $10 children. Fort Bragg-Northspur: third Sat. in June-second Sat. in Sept., departs daily 9:20 AM and 1:35 PM; Apr. 18–June 13 and Sept. 19–Oct. 31, departs Sat. 10 AM and 2 PM. Admission: $16 adults, $8 children.*

⑳ The **Georgia-Pacific Tree Nursery** (Main St. at Walnut St., tel. 707/964–5651) has a visitors center, picnic grounds, and a self-guiding nature trail (open daily 8–4). Those who like fishing can charter boats out of Noyo Harbor, at the southern end of town *(see* Sports, below).

Heading north on Highway 1 from Fort Bragg past the coastal mill town of **Westport,** you will find the venerable highway cut inland around the **King Range,** a stretch of mountain so rugged that road builders found it impossible to construct a major highway through it. Highway 1 joins the larger U.S. 101 at the town of Legett and continues north into the redwood country of Humboldt and Del Norte counties.

The Redwood Empire

㉑ **Richardson Grove State Park,** north of Leggett, along U.S. 101, marks your first encounter with the truly giant redwoods, but you will encounter even more magnificent stands as you head **㉒** north. A few miles below **Garberville,** perched along a lake, is an elegant Tudor resort, the **Benbow Inn.** Even if you are not staying here, stop for a drink or meal to enjoy the architecture and gardens.

㉓ For a treat, be certain to take the turnoff for the **Avenue of the Giants** just north of Garberville. Along this stretch of two-lane blacktop you will find yourself enveloped by some of the tallest trees on the planet, the coastal redwoods. The Avenue of the **㉔** Giants cuts through part of the **Humboldt Redwoods State Park,** 51,222 acres of redwoods and waterways, as the road follows the south fork of the turquoise Eel River. In spring or summer, stop at the park visitors center near Weott (tel. 707/946–2311) for information on the region, its recreational opportunities, and its flora and fauna. The park's **Founders Grove** harbors the tallest tree in the park; at 362 feet, it is less than six feet shorter than the world's tallest tree, found in Redwood National Park.

㉕ Detour 5 miles west of U.S. 101 from Fortuna to **Ferndale.** This stately town maintains some of the most sumptuous Victorian homes in California, many of them originally built by 19th-century Scandinavian dairy farmers and timber barons. The queen of them all is the **Gingerbread Mansion,** 400 Berding Street, formerly a hospital and now a refurbished bed-and-breakfast inn. Numerous shops carry a local map for self-guided tours of this brilliantly preserved town.

The **Ferndale Museum** has a storehouse of antiques from the turn of the century. *515 Shaw Ave., tel. 707/786–4466. Admission: $1 adults, 50¢ children 6–16. Open June–Sept., Tues.–Sat. 11–4, Sun. 1–4; October–May, Wed.–Sat. 11–4, Sun. 1–4; closed January.*

㉖ With 25,000 inhabitants, **Eureka** is the North Coast's largest town. It has gone through cycles of boom and bust, first with mining and later with timber and fishing. There are nearly 100 elegant Victorian buildings in Eureka, many of them well-refurbished. The most splendid is the **Carson Mansion** (at M and 2nd sts.), built in 1885 by the Newsom brothers for timber baron William Carson. Across the street is another Newsom extravaganza popularly known as **The Pink Lady.** For a sense that contemporary architects still have the skills to design lovely Victoriana, see the **Carter House** B&B inn (3rd and L sts.). The **Chamber of Commerce** can provide maps of town and information on how to join organized tours. *2112 Broadway, tel. 707/442–3738. Open June–mid-Sept., weekdays 8:30–7, Sat. 9–5, Sun. 10–3; Sept.–May, closed weekends.*

Old Town Eureka is one of the most outstanding existing Victorian commercial districts in California, with buildings dating from the 1860s to 1915. The **Clarke Museum** has an extraordinary collection of Native American basketry and contains artifacts from Eureka's Victorian, logging, and maritime heritage. *240 E. St., tel. 707/443–1947. Admission free. Open Tues.–Sat. noon–4 and Labor Day, July 4, and Memorial Day. Closed other major holidays.*

On the south end of Eureka stands **Fort Humboldt,** which served as an outpost to guard settlers against the Indians; now it is a state historic park. Ulysses S. Grant was once posted here. On the fort's grounds are re-creations of the logging industry's early days, with a lumber museum, some ancient steam engines, and a logger's cabin. *3431 Fort Ave., tel. 707/445–6567. Open daily 9–5.*

Those who wish to explore the waters around Eureka can take **㉗** a **Humboldt Bay Harbor Cruise.** You can observe some of the region's bird life and sail past fishing boats, oyster beds, and decaying timber mills. *The pier at C St., tel. 707/444–9440. Fare: $4.50 adults, $3.50 children. Departs daily May–Sept., 1, 2:30, and 4 PM.*

28 Across the bridge in Samoa is the **Samoa Cookhouse** (tel. 707/442–1659), a unique example (dating back to about the 1860s) of the lumber town cookhouses that once existed in every mill town. There is a museum displaying antique culinary artifacts, and breakfast, lunch, and dinner are served family style at long wooden tables. *(See* Dining, below.)

Just north of Eureka lies the pleasant college town of **Arcata,** home of Humboldt State University. Arcata is one of the few California burgs that retain a town square. It also has some restored Victorian structures. If you would like to take a self-
29 guided tour, pick up a map from the **Chamber of Commerce.** *1062 G St., tel. 707/822–3619. Open year round, Mon.–Fri., 9–5.*

Take the turnoff to the town of **Trinidad** and follow the road a mile to one of the most splendid harbors on the West Coast. First visited by a Portuguese expedition in 1595, the waters here are now sailed by fishing boats trolling for salmon. The harbor's cove and rock formations lend a sense of untamed yet tranquil beauty to this picturesque bay.

30 Twenty-five miles north of Eureka sits **Patrick's Point State Park.** Set on a forested plateau almost 200 feet above the surf, the park affords good whale and sea lion watching. There are also good tide pools and a small museum with natural history exhibits. *Tel. 707/677–3570. Day use: $3; camping: $10.*

Those continuing north will pass through the 106,000 acres of
31 **Redwood National Park.** After 115 years of intensive logging, this vast region of the tallest trees in the world came under government protection when Lyndon Johnson signed the park into law in 1968. Without question, this was the greatest victory won by California's environmentalists over the timber industry. The park encompasses three state parks (Prairie Creek Redwoods, Del Norte Coast Redwoods, and Jedediah Smith Redwoods) and is more than 40 miles long. *Redwood National Park Headquarters, 1111 2nd St., Crescent City, CA 95531, tel. 707/464–6101.*

Campground reservations for all state parks are usually necessary in summer. Call MISTIX 800/444–7275 (CA only) or 619/452–1950 (out of state) for reservations.

To gain a full sense of what Redwood National Park encompasses, stop at the **Redwood Information Center** in Orick (tel. 707/488–3461). You can drive up the short, steep trail to the world's tallest trees. Whale watchers will find the deck of the visitors center an excellent observation point, and birders will enjoy the nearby **Freshwater Lagoon,** a mecca for migrating waterfowl.

Drive to **Lady Bird Johnson Grove,** just off Bald Hill Road, for the short circular trail to resplendent redwoods dedicated as part of the park by the former first lady. For equally spectacular scenery, take Davison Road (often closed in winter) along a stunning seascape to **Fern Canyon.**

Wildlife lovers will see something truly special just opposite
32 the entrance to Redwood's **Prairie Creek Redwoods State Park.**
Extra space has been paved alongside the parklands, providing
visitors with fine vantage points to observe an imposing herd of
Roosevelt elk grazing in the adjoining meadow. Prairie Creek
also has a beautiful trail fully accessible for the disabled, called
Revelation Trail.

The route of redwoods and sea views will ultimately lead you
past the Klamath River, home of the famous king salmon, to
Del Norte County's largest town, **Crescent City.** Here you can
get any further information you require about the national
park at the headquarters (see above for address).

Travelers continuing north to the Smith River near the Oregon
border will find fine trout and salmon fishing as well as a profu-
sion of flowers. Ninety percent of America's lily bulbs are
grown in this area.

Shopping

Most shops and galleries are open Monday–Saturday, 10–6.
Some are open on Sunday during the summer.

In the charming town of Inverness, **Shaker Shops West** (5 Inverness Way, tel. 415/669–7256) has an exceptional array of
reproduction Shaker furniture and gift items. There is a turn-
of-the-century sensibility to the fine works exhibited here;
open Wednesday through Sunday from 11 to 5. In Point Reyes
Station, **Gallery Route One** (in the Creamery Building, tel. 415/
663–1347) is a nonprofit cooperative of 24 area artists in all media, open Friday through Monday from 11 to 5.

Mendocino has earned its reputation as the artistic heart of the
North Coast. So many fine artists exhibit their wares here that
it is a matter of personal taste as to which galleries will curry
favor with you. The few streets of this compact town are easily
walkable, so look around until you see something you like. One
suggestion is to visit the **Mendocino Art Center** (45200 Little
Lake St., tel. 707/937–5818), where artists teach courses and
display their creations.

In the Redwood Empire, the Victorian village of Ferndale is a
magnet for fine painters, potters, and carpenters. Just walk
down Main Street and stop in to browse at any of the stores
along its three principal blocks.

Eureka has a number of fine art shops and galleries in the district running from C to I streets between 2nd and 3rd streets.
One gallery of note is the **Old Town Art Guild Cooperative** (233 F
St., tel. 707/445–2315). Apart from this district, a recommended gallery is the **Humboldt Cultural Center** (422 1st St.,
tel. 707/442–2611 or 707/442–0278).

Sports

The following sporting attractions and facilities are listed in a
south-to-north order.

Bicycling *See* Getting Around, above.

Canoeing Among the many canoe liveries of the North Coast are **Stanford
Inn by the Sea** (Mendocino, tel. 707/937–5615) and **Benbow Inn**
(Garberville, tel. 707/923–2124).

Golf
Among others, there are courses open to the public at **Bodega Harbour** (Bodega Bay, tel. 707/875–3538), **Little River Inn** (Little River, tel. 707/937–5667), **Benbow Inn** (nine holes, Garberville, tel. 707/923–2124), and **Eureka Golf Course** (tel. 707/443–4808).

Horseback Riding
There are numerous stables and resorts where you may rent horses on the North Coast. Among them are **Five Brooks Stables** (Point Reyes, tel. 415/663–1570), **Sea Horse Guest Ranch** (Bodega Bay, tel. 707/875–2721), **Benbow Inn** (Garberville, tel. 707/923–2124), and **Lazy L Ranch** (Arcata, tel. 707/822–6736).

Fishing
For ocean fishing, there are plenty of outfits from which you can charter a boat with equipment provided. Among them are **Bodega Bay Sportfishing** (tel. 707/875–3344), **Noyo Fishing Center** (Fort Bragg, tel. 707/964–7609) **Lost Coast Landing** (Shelter Cove, tel. 707/986–7624), and **Blue Pacific Charters** (Eureka, tel. 707/442–6682). You can fish for salmon and steelhead in the rivers. There's particularly good *abalone diving* around Jenner, Fort Ross, Point Arena, Westport, Shelter Cove, and Trinidad.

River & Ocean Rafting
For rafting trips on the Salmon and Klamath rivers, contact the **Electric Rafting Company** (Eureka, tel. 707/445–3456) which also runs *Lost Coast Tours* along the coastline in motorized rafts.

Whale Watching
There are a number of excellent observation points along the coast for watching whales during their annual migration season from December through March. Another option is a **whale-watching cruise.** Possibilities include: **Oceanic Society Expeditions** (San Francisco, tel. 415/474–3385), **New Sea Angler and Jaws** (Bodega Bay, tel. 707/875–3495), **Lost Coast Landing** (Shelter Cove, tel. 707/986–7624).

Beaches

Although the waters of the Pacific along the North Coast are fine for seals, most humans find the temperatures downright arctic. Nonetheless, when it comes to spectacular cliffs and seascapes, the settings of North Coast beaches are second to none. So pack a picnic and take in the pastoral beauty of the wild coast. Explore tide pools, watch for seals, or dive for abalone. Don't worry about crowds, for on many of these beaches you will have the sands largely to yourselves. Day use is usually $3 per car.

The following beaches are particularly recommended and are listed in a south-to-north order:

Muir Beach. Located just off Hwy. 1, 3 miles from Muir Woods. Free.
Duxbury Reef. Tide pools. From Bolinas, take Mesa Road off Olema-Bolinas Road; make a left on Overlook Drive and a right on Elm Avenue to the beach parking lot.
Point Reyes National Seashore. Limantour Beach is one of the most beautiful of Point Reyes sands. Free.
Tomales Bay State Park. Take Sir Francis Drake Boulevard off Hwy. 1 toward Point Reyes National Seashore, then follow Pierce Point Road to the park.
Fort Ross State Park. About 9 miles north of Jenner.
Sea Ranch Public Access Trails and Beaches. Off Hwy. 1 south of Gualala.

Manchester State Beach. About 9 miles north of Point Arena.
Agate Beach. Tide pools. Set within Patrick's Point State Park
off U.S. 101 about 25 miles north of Eureka.

Dining

by Bruce Colen

For the past 15 years, Bruce David Colen has been the restaurant and food critic for Los Angeles Magazine. *He has also written on food and travel for* Town & Country, Architectural Digest, Bon Appetit, Connoisseur, Signature, *and* Endless Vacations.

For years, the better dining establishments of the North Coast
specialized in fresh salmon and trout. With the growth of the
tourist industry, a surprising variety of fare ranging from
Mexican to Japanese to Continental haute cuisine is now being
served at good restaurants charging reasonable prices. Unless
otherwise noted, dress is informal. During the winter months,
December to mid–March, tourism slackens on the North
Coast; consequently, restaurant days and/or hours are often
reduced. It is best to call ahead to check the schedule.

Highly recommended restaurants are indicated by a star ★.

Category	Cost*
Very Expensive	over $35
Expensive	$25–$35
Moderate	$15–$25
Inexpensive	under $15

*per person, not including tax, service, or drinks

Albion
Moderate–Expensive
★

The Albion River Inn. Built overlooking the site where the Albion River enters the Pacific, the glassed-in dining room offers spectacular views. The seafood, pasta, and meat dishes are better than average. *Hwy. 1, a few miles south of Mendocino, tel. 707/937–4044. MC, V. Dinner only.*

Arcata
Moderate

Crosswinds. Fine Continental cuisine is served in a comfortable dining room. Classical musicians provide the entertainment. *10th and I sts., tel. 707/826–2133. Reservations advised on weekends. MC, V.*
Ottavio. This comfortable, polished restaurant offers Continental cuisine, from Italian *gnocchi* to Greek *spanakopita*, a spinach and cheese pie. *686 F St., tel. 707/822–4021. MC, V. Closed Mon.*

Bodega Bay
Expensive

The Inn at the Tides. The town's top restaurant is best known for its fish and meat dishes. *Hwy. 1, tel. 707/875–2751. AE, MC, V. Dinner only, Fri. and Sat. Sun. brunch.*

Crescent City
Moderate

Harbor View Grotto. This glassed-in dining hall overlooking the Pacific prides itself on fresh fish. *155 Citizen's Dock Rd., tel. 707/464–3815. No credit cards.*

Elk
Expensive
★

Harbor House. Continental cuisine is served in a dining room overlooking a dramatic seascape. *Rte. 1, 6 mi south of the junction with Hwy. 128, tel. 707/877–3203. Reservations recommended. No credit cards.*

Eureka
Expensive

Carter House. Comfortable, satisfying meals are served in the dining parlor of the contemporary Victorian Carter House. The accent is on California cuisine, featuring the freshest ingredients. *3rd and L sts., tel. 707/444–8062. Reservations recommended. AE, MC, V.*

Moderate–Expensive   **Eureka Inn-Rib Room.** In the dining hall of this Tudor manor, grilled meats are the specialty. *7th and F sts., tel. 707/442-6441. AE, DC, MC, V.*

★   **Lazio's.** Now reopened in its new location, Lazio's has long been a premiere restaurant in Eureka, noted for its seafood. *1st and C sts., tel. 707/443-9717. MC, V.*

Moderate   **Cafe Waterfront.** This restaurant serves decent seafood at reasonable prices. *102 F St., tel. 707/443-9190. MC, V.*

OH's Townhouse. This is a good choice for reasonably priced grilled meats. *206 W. 6th St., tel. 707/443-4652. MC, V.*

Samurai Japanese Cuisine. Decent Japanese fare at a reasonable price is served here. *621 5th St., tel. 707/442-6802. MC, V.*

Inexpensive   **Mazzotti's.** The local favorite for pizza and calzone. *305 F St., tel. 707/445-1912. No credit cards. Closed Sun. lunch.*

Samoa Cookhouse. A local lumberman's watering hole, dating back to the early years of the century, this eatery serves three substantial family-style meals at long wooden tables. Meat dishes dominate the menu. *A short drive from Eureka, across Samoa Bridge, off Rte. 101 on Samoa Rd., tel. 707/442-1659. No credit cards. Closed Sun. lunch.*

Fort Bragg   **The Restaurant.** California cuisine is featured. The dining room
Moderate   doubles as an art gallery. *418 N. Main St., tel. 707/964-9800. Reservations advised. MC, V. Dinner only.*

Garberville   **Benbow Inn.** If you want to dine in style, this is the place. The
Moderate–Expensive   resort's wood-paneled dining room, with fireplace ablaze, of-
★   fers Continental cuisine and fresh salmon and trout. *445 Lake Benbow Dr., off U.S. 101, 2 mi south of Garberville, tel. 707/923-2124. Reservations advised. MC, V. Closed winter.*

Inexpensive–   **Woodrose Cafe.** This unpretentious eatery, a local favorite,
Moderate   serves fresh healthy food, with fish, pasta, and vegetarian specials. *911 Redwood Dr., tel. 707/923-3191. No credit cards.*

Gualala   **Old Milano.** In the dining room of this house, listed in the Na-
Expensive   tional Registry of Historic Places, adequate country meals are served five nights a week. *Hwy. 1, tel. 707/884-3256. Reservations advised. AE, MC, V. Closed Mon.–Tues.*

★   **St. Orres.** From the Russian turrets that top this hotel to the hand-hewed timbers and stained-glass windows, the look and atmosphere here are very special. One of the best restaurants on the North Coast, with equally intriguing cuisine. You have a choice of five entrees (meat or fish), plus soup and salad, at prix fixe. *Hwy. 1, just north of Gualala, tel. 707/884-3335. Reservations recommended. No credit cards. Dinner only. Closed Wed.*

Sea Ranch Lodge Restaurant. Seafood and homemade deserts are served in a dining room overlooking the Pacific. *North of Gualala at 60 Sea Walk Dr., off U.S. 101 at Sea Ranch, tel. 707/785-2371. MC, V.*

Moderate   **Empire Cafe.** The ocean view is a good enough reason in itself to dine here. The focus is on seafood. *Hwy. 1, tel. 707/884-4630. MC, V. Closed lunch Mon.–Fri.*

Inverness   **Manka's.** Excellent Czech cooking is served in a wood-paneled
Moderate–Expensive   dining room warmed by a fireplace. This is the best of
★   Inverness's Eastern European restaurants. *30 Calendar Way, tel. 415/669-1034. Reservations suggested in summer. MC, V. Open Thurs.–Mon. for dinner. Sunday brunch.*

Inexpensive **Grey Whale.** A good stop-off for pizza, salad, pastries, and coffee. Open for lunch and dinner. *On Sir Frances Drake Blvd., in the center of town, tel. 415/669-1244. No credit cards.*

Jenner **River's End.** The Continental/Germanic fare is very good, featuring seafood, venison, and duck dishes. Brunches are exceptional. *Hwy. 1, north end of Jenner, tel. 707/865-2484. MC, V. Closed Mon. and Tues., closed Nov. 30-Mar. 15.*
Moderate-Expensive

Little River **Heritage House.** In a plate-glass dining room overlooking the sea, hearty American meat and fish dishes are featured at a prix fixe for breakfast and dinner. *Hwy. 1, just south of Little River, tel. 707/937-5885. Jacket and tie required. Reservations advised. No dinner. No credit cards.*
Expensive
★

Little River Restaurant. This is a tiny restaurant with the post office and gas station adjoining it, across from the Little River Inn. Appearances aside, this modest eatery serves some of the best dinners in the Mendocino area, featuring steaks and the freshest of seafood. *Hwy. 1, tel. 707/937-4945. Reservations advised. MC, V. Closed Tues.-Thurs. Closed lunch.*

Mendocino **Cafe Beaujolais.** All the rustic charm of peaceful, backwoods Mendocino—with great country cooking to boot. Owner Margaret Fox is a marvelous baker, so be sure to take home several packages of her irresistible *panforte*, made with almonds, hazelnuts, walnuts or macadamia nuts. This is the best place in town for breakfast, and the tree house-like second-story deck is a splendid retreat for a leisurely lunch. If you don't order the delicious chicken-apple sausages, you'll never forgive yourself. *961 Ukiah St., tel. 707/937-5614. Reservations essential. No credit cards. Dinner Thurs.-Sun. Breakfast and lunch, daily. Closed Jan.-Feb.*
Moderate-Expensive
★

MacCallum House Restaurant. Set within a charming, period bed-and-breakfast inn, the redwood-paneled dining room offers a Continental menu and lovely homemade desserts. *45020 Albion St., tel. 707/937-5763. Reservations advised. No credit cards. Closed Jan.-March and Mon. Closed lunch.*

Mendocino Hotel. A 19th-century ambience has been re-created in the wood-paneled dining room, fronted by a glassed-in solarium. Fine fish dishes, and the best wild berry cobblers in California are served. *45080 Main St., tel. 707/937-0511. AE, MC, V.*

Moderate **Sea Gull.** Extremely popular with the local art crowd, this unpretentious spot serves excellent fish, beef, and lamb dishes at reasonable prices. The breakfast omelets and luncheon sandwiches are also good. *On the corner of Lansing and Ukiah sts., tel. 707/937-2100. MC, V.*

Muir Beach **Pelican Inn.** Basic English fare—from fish and chips to prime rib and Yorkshire pudding—is served with imported beers and ales. The atmosphere is wonderful: a wood-paneled dining room warmed by a great stone fireplace and a glass-encompassed solarium, ideal for sunny lunches. *Hwy. 1 at Muir Beach, tel. 415/383-6005. Reservations advised for 6 or more. MC, V. Closed Mon.*
Moderate-Expensive
★

Point Reyes Station **Chez Madeline.** A restaurant featuring above-average French cooking and excellent seafood; its proprietor sometimes entertains by playing classical flute. *Hwy. 1, tel. 415/663-9177. MC, V. Closed Mon. Closed lunch.*
Moderate-Expensive

Station House Cafe. This modest local hangout serves breakfast, lunch, and dinner in a relaxing paneled dining room.

Fresh fish and grilled meats highlight the dinner menu. *Hwy. 1, tel. 415/663–1515. MC, V.*

Stinson Beach
Moderate

Sand Dollar. This pleasant pub serves great hamburgers and other sandwiches for lunch and decent seafood for dinner. An added attraction is the outdoor dining deck. *Hwy. 1, tel. 415/868–0434. No credit cards.*

Trinidad
Moderate–Expensive
★

Larrupin Cafe. Actually located close to Trinidad in the town of Westhaven, Larrupin has earned a widespread reputation for Cajun ribs and fish. Dinner only. *1150 Westhaven Dr., tel. 707/677–0230. Reservations essential. No credit cards. Closed Mon.–Wed.*

Moderate

Merryman's Dinner House. This is a fine oceanfront setting for hungry lovers. Fresh fish is featured. *On Moonstone Beach, tel. 707/677–3111. No credit cards. Closed weekdays in winter.*

Inexpensive–Moderate

Seascape. With a glassed-in dining room and deck for alfresco dining, this is an ideal place to take in the splendor of Trinidad Bay. Great breakfasts, substantial lunches, and good seafood dinners are served. *At the pier, tel. 707/677–3762. MC.*

Lodging

The North Coast offers some of the most attractive lodging in the country, with a range to fit virtually every pocketbook. You will find elaborate Victorian homes, grand old hotels, and modest motels. Many bed-and-breakfasts along the coast are sold out on weekends months in advance, so reserve early. Budget travelers will find youth hostels in Point Reyes National Seashore, Klamath, and Leggett (summer only).

Highly recommended hotels are indicated by a star ★.

Category	Cost*
Very Expensive	over $120
Expensive	$90–$120
Moderate	$50–$90
Inexpensive	under $50

**double room, not including tax*

Albion
Moderate–Very Expensive

Albion River Inn. Overlooking the sea, this attractive inn has sizable rooms, some with fireplaces and Jacuzzis, and provides continental breakfasts. *3790 No. Hwy. 1, Box 100, 95410, tel. 707/937–1919. 20 rooms. Facilities: restaurant (dinner only), horseback riding 15 mi. away. MC, V.*

Arcata
Moderate—Expensive
★

The Plough and the Stars. There's a truly Irish ambience at the Plough. It's hard to imagine a friendlier inn, as the warm hospitality of the hosts makes this former farmhouse a wonderful place to stay. The suite has a wood stove. Breakfast is included. *1800 27th St., 95521, tel. 707/822–8236. 5 rooms, 3 with bath. MC, V.*

Bodega Bay
Expensive–Very Expensive

Inn at the Tides. All the rooms here have a view of the harbor and some have fireplaces. Breakfast is included. *800 Hwy. 1, Box 640, 94923, tel. 707/875–2751. 88 rooms. Facilities: room service, restaurant on weekends, Sunday brunch, cable TV, refrigerator, pool, sauna, Jacuzzi, laundromat. AE, MC, V.*

Crescent City
Inexpensive

Curly Redwood Lodge. True to its namesake, the lodge is built from one huge redwood tree, which produced 57,000 board feet of lumber. The rooms are a decent size, and there is a nice lobby with a fireplace. *701 Redwood Hwy. S, 95531, tel. 707/464–2137. 36 rooms. Facilities: color TV, phone. AE, DC, MC, V.*

Elk
Very Expensive

Harbor House. Constructed in 1916 by a timber company to entertain its guests, this redwood house has a dining room affording a view of the Pacific. Five of the six rooms in the main house have fireplaces. There are also four smallish cottages. Breakfast and dinner are included. *5600 S. Hwy. 1, 95432, tel. 707/877–3203. 10 rooms. No credit cards.*

Expensive–
Very Expensive
★

Elk Cove Inn. Private, romantic cottages perched on a bluff above the pounding surf. One room's shower has a full-length window that shares this magnificient view of the Pacific. Skylights, wood-burning stoves, and hand-embroidered cloths are some of the amenities. A full gourmet breakfast is included. *6300 S. Hwy 1, Box 367, 95432, tel. 707/877–3321. 4 cabin rooms (2 with stoves) plus 3 rooms in 1883 Victorian building, all with bath. No credit cards.*

Eureka
Very Expensive

Eureka Inn. This striking Tudor manor, built in 1922 and now a National Historic Landmark, oozes charm and luxury. The elegant lobby is warmed by a fireplace. *7th and F sts., 95501, tel. 707/442–6441. 105 rooms. Facilities: color TV, phone, pool, sauna, whirlpool. AE, D, DC, MC, V.*

Moderate–
Very Expensive
★

Carter House. For elegance coupled with warmth and hospitality, it is hard to beat Carter House. With a design consonant with the Newsom architecture of the region, Mark Carter has built a truly regal Victorian structure. Most rooms have a view of the Newsom brothers' Carson Mansion as well as of the bay. There is a remarkable sense of airiness, with bay windows accenting two sizable parlors, each with a marble fireplace. On the walls, Carter exhibits fine local artwork, which blends well with the interior. The guest rooms are extraordinary, with Oriental carpets, generous windows, and fine wood furnishings. There is a two-room suite with fireplace and Jacuzzi. Four-course gourmet breakfast, voted the best in the state by *California* magazine, is included. Gourmet dinners are served Thursday–Saturday. *1033 3rd St., 95501, tel. 707/445–1390. 7 rooms. AE, MC, V.*

Moderate–Expensive

Hotel Carter. Situated just across from the Carter House and a block from the Carson Mansion, this tastefully appointed hotel offers a spacious, elegant ambience at reasonable cost. There are Jacuzzis in the deluxe room and suite. Gourmet continental breakfast is included. *Gourmet dinners served Wed.–Sat. 301 L St., 95501, tel. 707/444–8062. 20 rooms. Facilities: color TV. AE, MC, V.*

Ferndale
Expensive–
Very Expensive
★

The Gingerbread Mansion. Many visitors come expressly to stay in this spectacular Victorian home, one of the most romantic of the North Coast's B&B inns. The mansion's carved friezes set off its gables, and turrets dazzle the eye. Inside, the luxury continues with four comfortable parlors warmed by two fireplaces. The rooms seem designed for lovers. Some have fireplaces, some have views of the mansion's elegant English garden, and others have side-by-side bathtubs. Breakfast is included. *400 Berding St. Box 40, 95536, tel. 707/786–4000. 9 rooms with bath. Facilities: bicycles. MC, V.*

Fort Bragg
Moderate–
Very Expensive

Grey Whale Inn. A most comfortable, friendly abode, this inn was once a hospital but doesn't look anything like one today. Two rooms have fireplaces, four have an ocean view, and the deluxe room has a private whirlpool tub and sundeck. Breakfast is included. *615 N. Main St., 95437, tel. 707/964–0640. 14 rooms. AE, MC, V.*

Garberville
Moderate–
Very Expensive
★

Benbow Inn. Set alongside a beautiful lake, this three-story Tudor manor resort is the equal of any in the Redwood Empire. A magnificent fireplace warms the bar/lobby, and all rooms are furnished with antiques. The most luxurious rooms are under the terrace, with fine views of the Eel River; some have fireplaces. *445 Lake Benbow Dr., 95440, tel. 707/923–2124. 55 rooms. Facilities: VCR movies in lounge, restaurant, swimming off private beach, canoeing, tennis, golf, fishing, horseback riding. MC, V. Closed Jan. 3–Apr. 21.*

Sea Ranch
Expensive–
Very Expensive

Sea Ranch Lodge. South of Gualala, the lodge has ocean-view rooms, some with fireplaces and some with hot tubs. Close to beaches, trails, golf. *60 Sea Walk Dr., Box 44, 95497, tel. 707/785–2371. 20 rooms. AE, MC, V.*

Gualala
Moderate–
Very Expensive

Gualala Country Inn. All rooms have both ocean and river views. Some rooms have fireplaces; some have two-person whirlpools; all have color TVs. *Hwy. 1, 95445, tel. 707/884–4343. 20 rooms. MC, V.*

★ **Old Milano Hotel.** Overlooking the sea just north of Gualala, the Old Milano is one of California's premiere B&B inns. Established in 1905, this wonderfully rustic mansion richly deserves its listing in the National Registry of Historic Places. Set amid English gardens, the estate overlooks Castle Rock and a spectacular coast. Tastefully furnished and appointed with exceptional antiques, five of the rooms look out over the ocean, and another looks over the gardens. Those in search of something different will find a caboose with a wood-burning stove. A cottage also comes complete with wood stove and kitchenette. Breakfast is included, and dinners are offered Wednesday–Sunday. Note: no children, no smoking. *38300 Hwy. 1, 95445, tel. 707/884–3256. 9 rooms. Facilities: hot tub. AE, MC, V.*

★ **St. Orres.** Located just north of Gualala, St. Orres is one of the North Coast's most eye-catching inns. Reflecting the Russian influence in the region, St. Orres's main house is crowned by two Kremlinesque towers. The carved wood is accented by balconies and leaded-glass windows. Two of the rooms overlook the sea, while the other six are set over the garden or forest. Ten wonderfully rustic cottages, built behind the main house in a tranquil woods, provide excellent alternative lodging, six with wood stoves or fireplaces. Note: children in cottages only. Breakfast is included; for dinner, the inn's restaurant is considered one of the finest north of San Francisco. *Hwy. 1, 95445, tel. 707/884–3303. 18 rooms. Facilities: private beach, hot tub, sauna. MC, V.*

Inverness
Expensive–
Very Expensive
★

Blackthorne Inn. Rising from the base of a tranquil wooded slope is one of the most stunning North Coast B&Bs. The Blackthorne is architecturally striking, with an octagonal wooden tower sitting above a turreted treehouse. It includes a glass-enclosed solarium and large fireplace as well as a penthouse, the Eagle's Nest, whose skylight provides a view of the stars. Breakfast is included. *266 Vallejo Ave., Box 712, 94937, tel. 415/663–8621. 5 rooms, 2 with private bath. Facilities: hot tub, MC, V.*

Expensive
★
Ten Inverness Way. In a lovely old house, set on a quiet side street, you will find one of the most pleasant B&Bs on the North Coast. The comfortable living room has a classic stone fireplace and piano. The rooms are charming, furnished with comfortable antiques. Breakfast is included. *10 Inverness Way, 94937, tel. 415/669–1648. 4 rooms. Facilities: hot tub. MC, V.*

Jenner
Expensive–
Very Expensive
★
Timber Cove Inn. Set off Highway 1 about 3 miles north of the Russian fort, this attractive resort is one of the more luxurious accommodations of the North Coast. With sweeping views overlooking Timber Cove, more than half the rooms have fireplaces, and the more expensive rooms have hot tubs. The bar and dining hall are festooned with flowers, and there is a Japanese pond at the entrance to the complex. There are also conference and seminar rooms. *2178 N. Hwy. 1, 95450, tel. 707/ 847–3231. 49 rooms. AE, D, DC, MC, V.*

Moderate–
Very Expensive
Fort Ross Lodge. About 1½ miles north of the old Russian fort, the cabins here, most with fireplaces, afford spectacular views of the Sonoma shoreline. *20705 Hwy. 1, 95450, tel. 707/847– 3333. 16 cabins plus 7 hill suites with sauna, in-room hot tub, VCR, and fireplace. Facilities: color TV. AE, MC, V.*

Moderate–Expensive
★
Murphy's Jenner Inn. Several units of this good-value inn have been built along the edge of the Russian River; some have partial ocean views. The large suite has a full kitchen, wood stove, and loft that can accommodate up to eight. Breakfast is included. *10400 Hwy. 1, 95450, tel. 707/865–2377. 10 rooms. Facilities: hot tub available to 3 units. AE, MC, V.*

Inexpensive–
Moderate
Stillwater Cove Ranch. Sixteen miles north of Jenner, overlooking Stillwater Cove, this former boys' school has been transformed into a pleasant, reasonably priced place to lodge. The proprietors have beautified the grounds with peacocks. *22555 Hwy. 1, 95450, tel. 707/847–3227. 7 rooms. No credit cards.*

Klamath
Inexpensive
DeMartin Redwood AYH Hostel. The California coast's northernmost hostel, this turn-of-the-century inn is a stone's throw from the ocean. It is located within Redwood National Park, so hiking begins just beyond its doors. The living room is heated by a wood stove. *U.S. 101 (at Wilson Creek Rd.), 95548, tel. 707/482–8265. No credit cards.*

Little River
Expensive–
Very Expensive
★
Heritage House. This famous resort, where the film *Same Time, Next Year* was shot, has attractive cottages overlooking a stunning seascape. There is a lovely dining room, also with fine Pacific views, serving breakfast and dinner, which are included. *Hwy. 1, 95456, tel. 707/937–5885. 70 rooms. Make reservations well in advance. No credit cards.*

Moderate–
Very Expensive
★
Glendeven. For a tranquil touch of the pastoral, stay at this inn at the north end of Little River. In addition to the attractive New England-style main house, a barn has been transformed into a fine lodging. The owners, both designers, have decorated the guest rooms with antiques, contemporary art, and ceramics, and have instituted an on-site gallery. Many rooms have fireplaces. Breakfast is included. *8221 N. Hwy. 1, 95456, tel. 707/937–0083. 11 rooms. MC, V.*

Mendocino
Very Expensive
★

Stanford Inn by the Sea. For those who wish to experience the quintessence of luxury on the Mendocino coast, this is the place. In sumptuously appointed rooms, each with a deck and fireplace, you can gaze out over the Pacific and the town of Mendocino. The Stanford is adjacent to a llama farm and set along the estuary. Breakfast is included. (This was previously known as the Big River Lodge.) *Just south of Mendocino, east on the Comptche-Ukiah Rd., Box 487, 95460, tel. 707/937–5615. 25 rooms. Facilities: canoes, color TV, stereo, VCRs, coffee makers, telephones, refrigerators, state-of-the-art mountain bikes. AE, DC, MC, V.*

Expensive–
Very Expensive
★

Headlands Inn. A magnificently restored Victorian building dating back to 1868, the inn combines 19th-century charm and contemporary comforts. All rooms have private baths and fireplaces; some overlook a garden and the pounding surf, others offer fine village views. There is also a private cottage on the premises. Gourmet breakfast is served in your room. *44950 Albion St., Box 132, 95460, tel. 707/937–4431. 5 rooms. No credit cards.*

Moderate–
Very Expensive

Mendocino Hotel. The exterior of this fine hotel lends a sense of the Wild West; inside, an elegant atmosphere of Tiffany lamps, polished wood, and Persian carpets prevails. All but 14 of the rooms have a private bath, and the 19th-century decor is appealing. There are also deluxe garden rooms with fireplaces on the property. *45080 Main St., 95460, tel. 707/937–0511. 51 rooms. Facilities: restaurant, bar, telephones. AE, MC, V.*

Mendocino Village Inn. This beautifully refurbished 1882 Queen Anne Victorian inn has a potpourri of motifs, with one room providing an Indian ambience, another a whaling captain's quarters, and a third a homage to Teddy Roosevelt. Many of the rooms have fireplaces, some have ocean views, and others look out on the garden. Breakfast is included. *44860 Main St., Box 626, 95460, tel. 707/937–0246. 12 rooms, 10 with bath. No credit cards.*

Moderate–
Expensive
★

MacCallum House. The most stunning Victorian in Mendocino, this splendid 1882 inn transports you back to another era. Its comfortable period furnishings and antiques provide a turn-of-the-century ambience. In addition to the main house, individual cottages and barn suites are set around a garden with a gazebo. Continental breakfast is included. *45020 Albion St., Box 206, 95460, tel. 707/937–0289. 21 rooms. Facilities: restaurant, bar. MC, V.*

★

Joshua Grindle Inn. This beautiful century-old Victorian inn has a reputation for friendliness. Some rooms have splendid ocean views, and some have fireplaces. Three rooms are in a water tower. There is also a cottage with a Franklin stove. Breakfast is included. *44800 Little Lake Rd., 95460, tel. 707/937–4143. 10 rooms. MC, V.*

Muir Beach
Expensive–
Very Expensive
★

Pelican Inn. A wonderfully atmospheric Tudor-style B&B house reminiscent of 16th-century England, the Pelican is a five-minute walk from splendid Muir Beach. The rooms, filled with antiques, have canopied two- and four-poster beds. On the ground floor, there's an Old English pub complete with dart boards and a selection of British brews. The dining quarter consists of two sections: a romantic rustic wooden and stone hall and a glassed-in solarium, both warmed by fireplaces. *Hwy. 1, 94965, tel. 415/383–6000. 7 rooms. MC, V.*

Point Reyes **National Seashore** *Inexpensive*	**Point Reyes Hostel.** Located within the national seashore and a mere 2 miles from lovely Limantour Beach, this is the best deal for basic budget travelers. Lodging is dorm-style. The family room is limited to families with small children and must be reserved well in advance. *Box 247, Pt. Reyes Station, 94956, tel. 415/663–8811. Send $8 per adult per night with reservation requests; state your gender. Facilities: shared kitchen. No credit cards.*

Shelter Cove
Inexpensive–
Moderate

Beachcomber Inn. There are three good-size rooms, two with kitchenettes and wood-burning stoves, and ocean views. The inn is near the marina and it's an easy walk to the beach. *Write c/o 7272 Shelter Cove Rd., Shelter Cove, 95489, tel. 707/986–7733. 3 rooms. MC, V.*

Trinidad
Moderate–
Expensive
★

Trinidad Bed and Breakfast. Overlooking Trinidad Bay, this delightful inn gets our vote for having the most spectacular sea view on the North Coast. The innkeepers are a treasure trove of information about the nearby wilderness, beach, and fishing habitats. The living room is warmed by a crackling fireplace. Upstairs, three comfortably furnished rooms offer fabulous seascapes. Breakfast is included. *560 Edwards St., Box 849, 95570, tel. 707/677–0840. 4 rooms. Reserve well in advance. No credit cards.*

Tomales Bay
Moderate

Tomales Country Inn. Secluded by trees and bordered by gardens, this Victorian house has a relaxed atmosphere. The owner, Byron Randall, is a painter who has filled the inn with his turn-of-the-century, European-style paintings. Breakfast is included. *25 Valley St., 94971, tel. 707/878–9992. 5 rooms, 2 with bath. No credit cards.*

Westport
Moderate

Howard Creek Ranch. This rustic redwood former ranch, built in 1871, has fine ocean views. It is within 300 yards of the beach. Breakfast included. *40501 Hwy. 1, Box 121, 95488, tel. 707/964–6725. 6 rooms, 3 with bath. Facilities: hot tub, sauna. MC, V.*

Nightlife

If a raucous swinging urban scene is what you are hankering for, the North Coast is not the place for you. Nonetheless, there are some watering holes favored by locals and visitors that should meet the needs of those not quite ready for a good night's sleep after exploring the forest and sea.

The following are listed alphabetically by town.

Bolinas

Smiley's Schooner Saloon. The only nightlife in Bolinas, Smiley's has a pool table and jukebox. *41 Wharf Rd., tel. 415/868–1311.*

Garberville

Benbow Inn. In this elegant Tudor mansion, a pianist can be heard nightly while you are warmed by a romantic fireplace. *445 Lake Benbow Dr., tel. 707/923–2124.*

Mendocino

The Sea Gull. Also an excellent restaurant, the Sea Gull has an upstairs bar that hosts live musical entertainment from jazz to rock Friday and Saturday evenings. *Lansing and Ukiah sts., tel. 707/937–2100.*

Muir Beach

Pelican Inn. Set just outside Muir Beach, this is a wonderful English pub and restaurant, with imported brews on tap, a dart board, and a stone fireplace. *Hwy. 1, tel. 415/383–6005.*

Point Reyes Station **Western Saloon.** If you are in town on the right Friday night, you can dance your jeans off at this favorite local pub. There is dancing on occasional Fridays. Other nights it's a friendly place to meet West Marinites. *Hwy. 1, tel. 415/663–1661.*

4 The Far North

While the rest of California boomed with an influx of high-tech industries, sun-seeking East Coasters, and value-conscious developers, the Far North simply hung up its "gone fishin'" sign. You won't find many hot nightspots or cultural enclaves here, but you will find some of the best hiking, fishing, and hunting the state has to offer. Some Bay area families return to the lakes of the far north year after year. Many enjoy the outdoors from their own piece of paradise—a private houseboat. A good number of retirees have chosen to live out their golden years in the area.

The towering, snow-covered Mount Shasta dominates the land. It can be seen for 100 miles, and qualifies the otherwise flat and fast trip through the valley along I–5 as a scenic drive. The 14,000-foot dormant volcano is surrounded by national and state parks. The natural and artificially created wonders include the bubbling mud pots and sulfur vents of Lassen Volcanic National Park and the immense Shasta Dam.

Almost all of the towns in the Far North are small and friendly, made up of third- and fourth-generation descendants of '49-ers who never cared to leave. Proud of their Gold Rush history, each town, no matter how small, has a museum filled with an impressive collection of artifacts donated by locals. This is the kind of place where people say hello to you as you walk down Main Street.

Getting Around

By Plane Redding Municipal Airport is served by **United Express** and **American Eagle** (which flies daily from San Francisco). Major car rental agencies are located at the airport.

By Train There are **Amtrak** stations in Redding and Dunsmuir.

By Bus **Greyhound-Trailways** buses travel I–5, serving Red Bluff, Redding, Dunsmuir, and Mt. Shasta City. In Redding, a city bus system, "The Ride," serves the local area daily except Sunday (tel. 916/241–2877).

By Car I–5 runs up the center of California through Red Bluff and Redding to the Oregon border. It is an excellent four-lane divided highway. Lassen Park can be reached by Highway 36 from Red Bluff or Highway 44 from Redding; Highway 299 leads from Redding to McArthur-Burney Falls. These are very good two-lane roads that are kept open year round. If you are traveling in winter, however, always carry snow chains in your car.

Important Addresses and Numbers

Tourist Information **Mt. Shasta Chamber of Commerce.** Information pavilion (300 Pine St., Mt. Shasta, 96067, tel. 916/926–4865).

Red Bluff-Tehama County Chamber of Commerce (100 N. Main St., Box 850, Red Bluff 96080, tel. 916/527–6220).

Redding Convention and Visitors Bureau (777 Auditorium Dr., Redding 96001, tel. 916/225–4100).

Shasta Cascade Wonderland Association. Visitor information for the entire region (1250 Parkview Ave., Redding 96001, tel. 916/243–2643).

Emergencies The number for emergency assistance throughout the Far North is 911. This will put you in touch with police, fire, and medical help.

Exploring

Numbers in the margin correspond with points of interest on the Far North map.

The Far North covers a large territory, from the valleys east of the coast range to the Nevada border, and from the almond and olive orchards north of Sacramento to the Oregon border. The entire state of Ohio would fit into this section of the Golden State.

Redding is the urban center of the Far North. It offers the greatest selection of restaurants and the most luxurious accommodations. You'll experience more of the true flavor of this outdoor country at motels in the smaller towns. Many visitors make the outdoors their home for at least part of their stay. Camping, houseboating, and animal pack trips into the wilderness are very popular.

We've arranged the exploring section from south to north, following the mostly flat and fast I-5 with the addition of two day-long side trips. The valley around Redding is hot, even in winter, but cooler temperatures prevail in the higher elevations to the east and north. Be aware that many restaurants and museums have limited hours and sometimes close temporarily during the off-season.

Red Bluff

The turn-off for Red Bluff will take you past a neon-lit motel row, but persevere and explore the roads to the left of the main drag to discover gracefully restored Victorian structures, a fine museum, and a Western-style downtown.

❶ The **Kelly-Griggs House Museum** is a restored 1880's Victorian dwelling with an impressive collection of antique furniture, housewares, and clothing arranged as though a refined Victorian family still resided there. An engraved silver tea server waits on the end table. A "Self Instructor in Penmanship" teaching the art of graceful, flowing handwriting sits on the desk. And eerily life-like mannequins seem frozen in conversation in the upstairs parlor.

The museum's collection includes finely carved china cabinets, Native American basketry, and a turn-of-the-century painting by Thomas Hill, known for his western landscapes. The painting over the fireplace is by Sarah Brown, daughter of abolitionist John Brown, whose family settled in Red Bluff after his execution. Their home is on the self-guided tour map of Red Bluff Victoriana available at the museum. *311 Washington St., tel. 916/527–1129. Admission free. Open Thurs.–Sun. 2–4. Closed holidays.*

❷ North of town on the banks of the Sacramento River is the **William B. Ide Adobe State Historic Park,** which contains the restored homestead of the man who was the first and only president of the California Republic, under the Bear Flag Party proclamation. The republic existed for 25 days in 1846 before it was occupied by the United States. Early furnishings are dis-

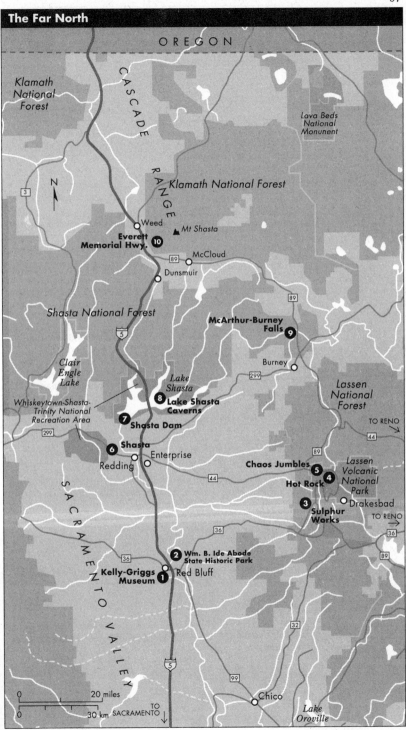

57

The Far North

OREGON

Klamath
National
Forest

CASCADE

3

Weed
▲ Mt Shasta

Everett
Memorial Hwy. 10

McCloud

89

Dunsmuir

Klamath National Forest

Lava Beds
National
Monument

RANGE

Shasta National Forest

5

McArthur-Burney
Falls 9

89

Clair
Engle
Lake

Whiskeytown-Shasta-
Trinity National
Recreation Area

299

Lake
Shasta

Lake Shasta
Caverns 8

Shasta Dam 7

Shasta 6

Enterprise

Redding

Burney

299

Lassen
National
Forest

TO RENO

44

89

Chaos Jumbles 5

Hot Rock 4

Lassen
Volcanic
National
Park

44

3 Sulphur
Works

Drakesbad

TO RENO

36

SACRAMENTO

36

89

2 Wm. B. Ide Abode
State Historic Park

Kelly-Griggs
Museum 1

Red Bluff

VALLEY

36

32

5

99

Chico

Lake
Oroville

0   20 miles
0   30 km   TO
         SACRAMENTO
         ↓

played in the adobe. *21659 Adobe Rd., tel. 916/527–5927. Admission free. Home open 11–4 in summer; park and picnic facilities open year-round from 8 AM–sunset.*

Lassen Volcanic National Park

You'll take Highway 36 east from Red Bluff to this still-active volcano. Except for the ski area, the park is largely inaccessible from late October to early June because of snow. Highway 89 through the park is closed to cars in winter, but open to intrepid cross-country skiers. When free of snow, you can drive Highway 89 north for a meandering 34-mile look at three sides of the world's largest plug volcano.

In 1914 the 10,457-foot Mt. Lassen began a series of 300 eruptions that went on for seven years. Molten rock overflowed the crater; there were clouds of smoke, and hailstorms of rocks and volcanic cinders. Proof of the volcano's volatility becomes evident shortly after you enter the park at the **Sulphur Works Thermal Area.** Boardwalks take you over bubbling mud and hot springs, and through the nauseating sulphur stink of steam vents. Five miles farther along the road you'll find the start of the **Bumpass Hell Trail,** a 3-mile round-trip hike to the park's most interesting thermal-spring area where you'll see hot and boiling springs, steam vents, and mud pots. The trail climbs and descends several hundred feet.

Drive on through forests and past lakes, looking out for deer and wildflowers, to **Hot Rock.** This 400-ton boulder was hurled through the air during the volcano's active period, and was still hot to the touch when locals found it. Although cool now, it's still an impressive sight. Five miles on is **Chaos Jumbles,** created 300 years ago when an avalanche from the Chaos Crags lava domes spread hundreds of thousands of rocks 2 to 3 feet in diameter over 2 square miles.

An important word of warning: Stay on trails and boardwalks near the thermal areas. What may appear to be firm ground can be a thin crust over scalding mud, and serious burns can result. Be especially careful with children!

Lassen is a unique, lovely and relatively uncrowded national park, but services are rather sparse. You'll find a year-round cafe and gift shop at the winter sports area in the southwest corner, open during the busier ski and summer seasons; there's another store (offering fast food and gas) at the Manzanita Lake campground, which is open in the summer only. Admission to the park is $5 per vehicle.

There are seven campgrounds in Lassen Volcanic National Park. Reservations are not accepted; it's first come, first served. For campground and other information, contact Lassen Volcanic National Park (Mineral 96063, tel. 916/595–4444).

The only other lodging in the park is a 100-year-old guest ranch at Drakesbad, which is near its southern border, and isolated from most of the park. Reservations should be made well in advance. *Booking office: 2150 Main St., Suite 7, Red Bluff 96080, tel. 916/529–1512. Open mid-June–late Sept.*

Redding

A few miles west of Redding on Highway 299 are the ruins of
the gold-mining town of **Shasta,** now a **state historic park** with a
few restored buildings. A museum located in the old courthouse has an eclectic array of California paintings as well as
memorabilia including period newspapers advertising "Gold
Dust Bought and Sold," a "Prairie Traveler" guidebook with
advice on encounters with Indians, and the 1860 census of the
once-prosperous town. Continue down to the basement to see
the iron-barred jail cells and step outside to the scaffold where
the murderers were hanged. *Tel. 916/243–8194. Admission: $1
adults; 50¢ children 6–17. Open 10–5. Closed Jan. 1, Thanksgiving, and Dec. 25. Closed Tues. and Wed. Nov.–Feb.*

Lake Shasta

Take the Dam/Project City exit west off I–5 about 12 miles
north of Redding and follow the signs to **Shasta Dam.** You'll be
able to see the mammoth construction from several points; this
is the second-largest and the fourth-tallest concrete dam in the
United States.

Whether you drive across the dam, or park at the landscaped
visitors' area and walk across, you'll see three Shastas: the
dam, the lake spreading before you, and the mountain presid-
ing over it all. At twilight the sight is magical, with Mt. Shasta
gleaming above the not-quite-dark water. The dam is lighted
after dark, but there is no access from 10 PM to 6 AM. In addition
to providing maps and brochures, the **Visitor Information Center**
(tel. 916/275–4463) offers exhibits (June–Aug., weekdays 7–5;
Sept.–May, weekdays 8:30–4). The coffee shop is closed in January and February.

Lake Shasta has 370 miles of shoreline and 21 varieties of fish.
You can rent fishing boats, ski boats, sailboats, canoes,
paddleboats, jet skis, and Windsurfer boards at one of the many
marinas and resorts along the shore. But the houseboat is king
on Lake Shasta, known as the houseboat capital of the world.

Houseboats come in all sizes except small. The ones that sleep
12 to 14 people are 55 feet by 14 feet; the minimum size sleeps
six. As a rule these moving homes come equipped with cooking
utensils, dishes, and most of the equipment you'll need to set up
housekeeping on the water. (You supply the food and linens.)
Renters are given a short course in how to maneuver the boats
before they set out on cruises; it's not difficult.

The houseboats are slow-moving, and life aboard is leisurely.
You can fish, swim, or sunbathe on the flat roof. The shoreline
of Lake Shasta is beautifully ragged, with countless inlets; exploring is fun, and it's not hard to find privacy. Be aware,
however, that the recent drought has considerably diminished
the volume of the lake, making some areas inaccessible.

Expect to spend a minimum of $170 a day for the sleeps-six size
houseboat. Contact the **Shasta Cascade Wonderland Association** (1250 Parkview Ave., Redding, CA 96001, tel. 916/243–
2643) for specifics about the 10 marinas that rent houseboats.

Stalagmites, stalactites, odd flowstone deposits, and crystals
entice visitors of all ages to the **Lake Shasta Caverns.** The two-

hour tour includes a ferry ride across the McCloud arm of the lake and a harrowing bus ride up a steep grade to the cavern entrance. The caverns are a constant 58 degrees year-round, making them a cool retreat on a hot summer day, but you should bring a sweater. All cavern rooms are well lit, and the crowning jewel is the spectacular cathedral room. The guides are friendly, enthusiastic, and informative. *Take the Shasta Caverns Road exit from I–5. Tel. 916/238–2341. Admission: $10 adults, $5 children 4–12. Hourly tours May–Sept., daily 9–4; Oct.–Apr., at 10 AM, noon, and 2 PM. Closed Thanksgiving and Dec. 25.*

Burney Falls

You take the Highway 299 East exit off I–5 just north of Redding, past the town of Burney, and turn north on Highway 89 to get to **McArthur-Burney Falls Memorial State Park.** It's a two-hour round trip drive from I–5, so you may want to plan to spend the day here. Just inside the southern boundary of the park, Burney Creek wells up from the ground and divides into two cascades that fall over a 129-foot cliff into a pool below. The thundering water creates a mist at the base of the falls, often highlighted by a rainbow. Countless ribbonlike falls stream from hidden moss-covered crevices creating an ethereal backdrop to the main cascades. Each day, 100 million gallons of water rush over the falls; Theodore Roosevelt proclaimed them "the eighth wonder of the world." A self-guided nature trail descends to the foot of the falls. There is a lake and beach for swimming. A campground, picnic sites, trails, and other facilities are available. *Rte. 1, Box 1260, Burney 96013, tel. 916/335–2777. Admission: $3 per vehicle for day use.*

Mt. Shasta

If you drive up the valley on I–5, past the 130-million-year-old granite outcroppings of Castle Crags towering over the road, through the quaint old railroad town of Dunsmuir, you'll reach the town of Mt. Shasta, nestled at the base of the huge mountain. If you are interested in hiking on Mt. Shasta, stop at the **Forest Service Ranger Station** (204 West Alma St., tel. 916/926–4511) as you come through town for the latest information on trail conditions or call the **Fifth Season Mountaineering Shop** in Mt. Shasta City (tel. 916/926–3606).

The central Mt. Shasta exit east leads out of town along the **Everett Memorial Highway.** This scenic drive climbs to almost 8,000 feet, and the views of the mountain and the valley below are extraordinary.

If you are wondering where all those eye-catching pictures of Mount Shasta reflected in a lake are shot, take the central Mt. Shasta exit west and follow the signs to **Lake Siskiyou.** This is the only lake in California created solely for recreational purposes. On the way, stop at the oldest **trout hatchery** in California. The pools there literally swarm with over 100,000 trout.

What to See and Do with Children

Almost everything we have described in the Far North of California offers something that children will enjoy: the bubbling mud at Lassen, the houseboats and caverns at Lake Shasta, and the falls at Burney. **Waterworks Park** in Redding has giant water slides, a raging river inner-tube ride, and a children's water playground. *151 N. Boulder Dr., tel. 916/246–9550. Admission: $9.95 adults, $7.95 children 4–11, children under 4 and senior citizens free. Open Memorial Day–Labor Day, daily 10–8.*

Off the Beaten Track

The hand-painted sign along Main Street in **McCloud** reads "Population 1,665, Dogs 462." To reach this time-capsule town, take the Highway 89 exit east from I–5 just south of the town of Mt. Shasta. McCloud began as a lumber company town in the late 1800s, and was one of the longest-lived company towns in the country. In 1965, the U.S. Plywood Corp. acquired the town, its lumber mill, and the surrounding forest land, and allowed residents to purchase their homes. The immense mill has been cut back to a computerized operation, but the spirit of the townsfolk have kept McCloud from becoming a ghost town. Picturesque hotels, churches, a lumber baron's mansion, and simple family dwellings have been renovated, and the 60,000-pound Corliss steam engine that powered the original mill's machinery stands as a monument behind the town's small museum.

Sports

Fishing
You'll need a California fishing license. State residents pay $21, but nonresidents must fork over $55.75 for a one-year license. Both residents and non-residents can purchase a one-day license for $6.75. For information, contact the **Department of Fish and Game** (1416 9th St., Sacramento 95814, tel. 916/445–3531).

For licenses, current fishing conditions, guides, or special fishing packages, contact **The Fly Shop** (4140 Churn Creek Rd., Redding 96002, tel. 916/222–3555), **The Fishin' Hole** (3844 Shasta Dam Blvd., Central Valley, 96019, tel. 916/275–4123), or **Shasta Cascade Wonderland Association** (1250 Parkview Ave., Redding 96001, tel. 916/243–2643).

Golf
Churn Creek Golf Course (8550 Churn Creek Rd., Redding, tel. 916/222–6353). Nine holes, par 36. Carts.

Gold Hills Country Club (1950 Gold Hills Dr., Redding, Oasis Road exit from I–5, tel. 916/246–7867). Eighteen holes, par 72. Carts, club rentals, driving range, pro shop, restaurant.

Lake Redding Golf Course (1795 Benton Dr., Redding, in Lake Redding Park, tel. 916/243–5531). Nine holes, par 62. Pull carts, rentals.

Llama Pack Tours
Shasta Llamas (Box 1137, Mt. Shasta 96067, tel. 916/926–3959) leads three- and five-day trips into the backcountry.

Raft and Canoe Rentals
Park Marina Watersports (2515 Park Marina Dr., Redding, tel. 916/246–8388).

Skiing
Mt. Lassen Ski Park. Inside the southwest entrance of Lassen Volcanic National Park is the only park facility open in winter, with three lifts. The terrain is 40% beginner, 40% intermediate, 20% advanced. Mt. Lassen's summit is 7,200 feet; its base,

6,600 feet; its vertical drop, 600 feet. The longest run is ¾-mile. There is a ski school and a beginner's special: lift, rentals, lessons. The Kids Are People Too program for ages 5–11 includes rentals, lunch, lesson, lifts. Facilities include a cafeteria and rental shop. *Hwy. 36 exit from I–5 at Red Bluff, tel. 916/595–3376. Snow phone: 916/595–4464.*

Mt. Shasta Ski Park. On the southeast flank of Mt. Shasta are three lifts on 300 acres. The terrain is 20% beginner, 60% intermediate, 20% advanced. Mt. Shasta's summit is 6,600 feet; its base, 5,500 feet; its vertical drop 1,100 feet. The longest run is 1.2 miles. Night skiing goes till 10 PM Wednesday–Saturday. There is a ski school with a beginner's special: lifts, rentals, lessons. The Powder Pups program is for ages 4–7. Lodge facilities include food and beverage, ski shop, and rentals. *Hwy. 89 exit east from I–5, just south of Mt. Shasta, tel. 916/926–8610. Snow phone 916/926–8686.*

Snowshoe Tours National Park Service rangers conduct snowshoe tours at Mt. Lassen Ski Park. A variety of natural history topics are covered. Snowshoes and instructions are free. *Weekends at 1:30 PM and daily through the Christmas and Easter holiday periods except Thanksgiving and Dec. 25. Reservations, tel. 916/595–4444.*

Dining

Cafes and simple, informal restaurants are ample in the far north. Most of the fast-food restaurants are clustered in Redding, though they are also found along I–5 in some of the larger communities. The restaurants listed here are of special interest because of their food and/or unique atmosphere. Dress is always casual in the Far North; reservations aren't necessary except where noted.

Highly recommended restaurants are indicated by a star ★.

Category	Cost*
Very Expensive	over $25
Expensive	$20–$25
Moderate	$15–$20
Inexpensive	under $15

per person, not including tax, service, or drinks

Lake Shasta **Tail O' the Whale.** Nautical decor distinguishes this restaurant,
Inexpensive– reminiscent of a ship's prow, overlooking the lake. Seafood,
Moderate beef, poultry, and Cajun pepper shrimp are the specialties. Reservations are recommended for the Sunday brunch served during the summer. *10300 Bridge Bay Rd. (Bridge Bay exit from I–5), tel. 916/275–3021. MC, V.*

Mt. Shasta **Bellissimo.** This bright, Mediterranean-style cafe has an eclec-
Inexpensive tic, creative menu with generous use of fresh herbs and
★ healthful ingredients. Specialties change, but could include curry chicken with apple-raisin chutney, parsley-garlic fettucine with clams, and decadent desserts. There's a special Sunday brunch. *204A West Lake St., tel. 916/926–4461. No credit cards. Limited hours in winter.*

Marilyn's. Everyone greets each other by name at this

Mayberry-esque diner where they serve 10¢ coffee. Even the local deputy orders the regular here. The former stage stop serves hearty breakfasts and sandwiches as well as Italian specialties. Complete dinners including soup and salad cost less than $7. *1136 South Mt Shasta Blvd., tel. 916/926–2720. MC, V.*

Red Bluff
Inexpensive

The Snack Box. This cheerfully renovated Victorian place is decorated in country-French blue and dusty rose. The carved wooden murals, like the omelets, soups and sandwiches, are homemade by the owner. *257 Main St. (1 block from Kelly-Griggs Museum), tel. 916/529–0227. No credit cards. Closed dinner.*

Redding
Moderate
★

Misty's. Two-story windows overlook the Red Lion Inn's pool area at this romantic dinner room with private booths. Specialties include steak Diane and hot rock cuisine, whisky peppercorn steak, and wild mushroom fettucini. The meals are artistically presented, and there's a Sunday brunch. *1830 Hilltop Dr. (at the Red Lion Inn), tel. 916/221–8700. AE, CB, DC, MC, V.*

Inexpensive–
Moderate

J.D. Bennett's. This open, airy garden court restaurant has a turn-of-the-century ambience with etched glass, dark wood, and gaslight fixtures. The diverse menu offers everything from lasagna to Mexican food to filet Mignon. *1800 Churn Creek Rd. (Cypress exit east from I–5), tel. 916/221–6177. AE, MC, V. Closed Dec. 25.*

Inexpensive

Jack's Grill. This steakhouse is usually jam-packed and noisy; it's immensely popular with the natives throughout the territory. It looks like a dive from the outside, but the steaks are famous. *1743 California St., tel. 916/241–9705. MC, V. Closed lunch, closed Sun.*

Lodging

Motel chains, such as Best Western and Motel 6, have accommodations in many of the communities in the Far North, though Redding has the greatest selection by far. Luxury hotels are found only in Redding.

Highly recommended hotels are indicated by a star ★.

Category	Cost*
Very Expensive	over $100
Expensive	$75–$100
Moderate	$50–$75
Inexpensive	under $50

*double room, not including tax

Dunsmuir
Moderate

Railroad Park Resort. At this railroad buff's delight, antique cabooses have been converted to clean, playfully romantic motel rooms in honor of Dunsmuir's railroad legacy. There's also a restaurant in a restored, Orient Express-style dining car, and a full bar in a converted railcar. The nicely landscaped grounds feature a huge logging steam engine and restored water tower. *100 Railroad Park Rd., 96025, tel. 916/235–4440. 19 cabooses with bath. 4 cabins. Facilities: pool, Jacuzzi, organ/piano bar in lounge. AE, MC, V.*

Mt. Shasta **Alpine Lodge.** The clean, standard motel rooms here are deco-
Inexpensive rated in a range of colors. Amenities include in-room coffee. *908
S. Mt. Shasta Blvd., 96067, tel. 916/926–3145. 8 rooms with
bath. 5 family suites. Facilities: pool, spa with Jacuzzi jets.
AE, DC, MC, V.*

Redding **Red Lion Inn.** Nicely landscaped grounds and a large, attract-
Expensive ive patio area with outdoor food service are the highlights here.
★ The rooms are spacious and comfortable. Small pets are
allowed; notify the motel when you make reservations. *1830
Hilltop Dr., 96002. (Hwy. 44 and 299 exit east from I–5), tel.
916/221–8700 or 800/547–8010. 195 rooms with bath. Facilities:
pool, wading pool, whirlpool, putting green, restaurant, coffee
shop, lounge, room service, movies. AE, DC, MC, V.*

Moderate **Vagabond Inn.** The clean, large rooms here feature a cheerful
decor, with flowered drapes and spreads. Continental breakfasts and weekday papers are on the house. Pets are allowed for
a $3 fee. *536 E. Cypress Ave., 96002 (Cypress exit west from
I–5), tel. 916/223–1600 or 800/522–1555. 71 rooms with bath.
Facilities: pool, coffee shop adjacent, movies. AE, CB, DC,
MC, V.*

Camping

There are an infinite number of camping possibilities in the Far
North's national and state parks, forests, and recreation areas.
You'll find every level of rusticity, too, from the well-outfitted
campgrounds in McArthur-Burney State Park, with hot water,
showers, and flush toilets, to isolated campsites on Lake Shasta
that can be reached only by boat. For information about camping in the region, contact the **Shasta Cascade Wonderland
Association** (1250 Parkview Ave., Redding, CA 96001, tel. 916/
243–2643).

Nightlife

Although the larger hotels in Redding usually have weekend
dance bands geared to the younger set, there's not much
nightlife in this outdoors country where the fish bite early. One
wild exception is the **Saddle Horn Saloon** (2655 Bechelli La., behind the bowling alley, Redding, tel. 916/223–3400), the local
ranchers' favorite watering hole. This is a foot-stomping country-western bar where cowboys don their Saturday-best hats
and boots and couples execute a fast-paced Texas two-step.

5 The Wine Country

In 1862, after an extensive tour of the wine-producing areas of Europe, Count Agoston Haraszthy de Mokcsa reported back to his adopted California with a promising prognosis: "Of all the countries through which I passed," wrote the Father of California's viticulture, "not one possessed the same advantages that are to be found in California . . . California can produce as noble and generous a wine as any in Europe; more in quantity to the acre, and without repeated failures through frosts, summer rains, hailstorms, or other causes."

The "dormant resources" that Haraszthy saw in the temperate valleys of Sonoma and Napa, with their balmy days and cool nights, are in full fruition today. While its wines are savored by connoisseurs throughout the world, the area is a fermenting vat of experimentation, a crucible for the latest techniques of grape-growing and wine-making.

In the Napa Valley, it seems that every available inch of soil is combed with neat rows of vines; would-be wine makers with very little acreage can rent the cumbersome, costly machinery needed to stem and press the grapes. Many say that making wine is one way to turn a large fortune into a small one, but that hasn't deterred the doctors, former college professors, publishing tycoons, and airline pilots who come to try their hand at the process.

Twenty years ago the Napa Valley had no more than 20 wineries; today there are almost 10 times that number. In Sonoma County, where the web of vineyards is looser, there are more than 100 wineries, and development is now claiming the cool Carneros region at the head of the San Francisco Bay, deemed ideal for growing the currently favored chardonnay grape.

All this has meant some pretty stiff competition, and the wine makers are constantly honing their skills. They are aided by the scientific know-how of graduates of the nearby University of California at Davis as well as the practical knowledge of the grape growers. They experiment with planting the vine stock closer together and "canopy management" of the grape cluster, as well as with "cold" fermentation in stainless steel vats and new methods of fining, or filtering, the wine.

The emphasis in the past was on creating wines to be cellared, but today "drinkable" wines that can be enjoyed relatively rapidly are in demand. This has led to the celebration of dining as an art in the Wine Country. Many wineries boast first-class restaurants which showcase excellent California cuisine and their own fine wines.

As wine-making gathers momentum, the stretch of highway from Napa to Calistoga recently began to rival Disneyland as the biggest tourist draw in the state. Two-lane Highway 129 slows to a sluggish crawl on weekends throughout the year, and there are acres of vehicles parked at the picnic places, upscale gift shops, and restaurants in the area.

The pace in Sonoma County is less frenetic. While Napa is upscale and elegant, Sonoma is overalls and corduroy, with an air of rustic innocence. But the county's Alexander, Dry Creek, and Russian River Valleys are no less productive of award-winning vintages. The Sonoma countryside also offers excellent opportunities for hiking, biking, camping, and fishing.

In addition to state-of-the-art viticulture, the Wine Country also provides a look at California's history. In the town of Sonoma, you'll find remnants of Mexican California and the solid ivy-covered brick wineries built by Haraszthy and his disciples. The original attraction here was the water. The rush to the spas of Calistoga, promoted by the indefatigable Gold Rush entrepreneur, Samuel Brannan, in the late 19th century, left a legacy of fretwork, clapboard, and Gothic architecture. More recent architectural details can be found at the art nouveau mansion of the Beringer brothers in St. Helena, and the latter-day neoclassical extravaganza of Clos Pegase in Calistoga.

The courting of the tourist trade has produced tensions, and some residents wonder whether projects like the *Wine Train*, now running between Napa and St. Helena, bring the Disneyland atmosphere a little too close to home.

These fears may or may not be realized, but the natural beauty of the landscape will always draw tourists. Whether in the spring, when the vineyards bloom yellow with mustard flowers, or in the fall, when fruit is ripening, this slice of California has a feel not unlike the hills of Tuscany or Provence. Haraszthy was right: This is a chosen place.

Getting Around

By Plane The San Francisco and Oakland airports are closest to the Wine Country. **Greyhound-Trailways** (tel. 415/558–6789) runs buses from the San Francisco Terminal at 7th and Mission streets to Napa (2 each day), Sonoma (1 each weekday), and Santa Rosa (4 each day).

By Bus **Sonoma County Area Transit** (tel. 707/585–7516) and **The Vine** (tel. 707/255–7631), Napa's bus service, provide local transportation within towns in the Wine Country.

By Car Although traffic on the two-lane country roads can be heavy, the best way to get around the Wine Country is by private car. Rentals are available at the airports, and in San Francisco, Oakland, Santa Rosa, and Napa.

The Rider's Guide (484 Lake Park Ave., Box 255, Oakland 94610, tel. 415/653–2553) produces tapes you can play in your car about the history, landmarks, and wineries of the Sonoma and Napa valleys. The tapes are available for $9.95 at Waldenbooks and Books Inc. in San Francisco, Beringer and Sterling Wineries, the Sonoma Mission Inn, and the Calistoga Bookstore.

Guided Tours

Full-day guided tours of the Wine Country usually include lunch, and cost about $50. The guides, many of them winery owners themselves, know the area well, and may bring you to some lesser-known cellars.

Gray Line Inc. (425 Mission St., San Francisco, tel. 415/558–9400) has bright red double-deckers that tour the Wine Country. Reservations are required.
Great Pacific Tour Co. (518 Octavia St., San Francisco, tel. 415/626–4499) offers full-day tours including a picnic lunch to Napa and Sonoma in passenger vans that seat 13.

Maxi Touring Guide Co. (Box 590064, San Francisco, tel. 415/
441–6294) provides air-conditioned van tours of the Wine
Country.

Starlane Tours (416 Francisco, San Francisco, tel. 415/982–
2223) provides full-day tours of Napa and Sonoma wineries;
they offer group and senior rates.

Superior Guide Co. (642 Alvarado St., Suite 100, San Francisco,
tel. 415/550–1352) limits its full-day excursions to 14 passengers. The company offers personalized itineraries on request,
and provides free hotel pickup, and group and senior rates.
Reservations are required.

Wine Train (1275 McKinstry St., Napa 94559, tel. 707/253–2111
or 800/522–4142). Enjoy lunch, dinner, or weekend brunch on
one of several restored 1915 Pullman railroad cars that now run
on the Napa Valley Railroad line between Napa and St. Helena.
Round-trip fare is $25; brunch or luncheon costs $20 and dinner
costs $45 (train fare is reduced to $12.50 for dinner parties of
two or more). During the winter service is limited to Thurs.–
Sun. There is a special car for families with children on the Saturday brunch trip.

Horse-Drawn Vineyard Tours through the Alexander Valley are
offered by Five Oaks Farm (15851 Chalk Hill Rd., Healdsburg
95448, tel. 707/433–2422). The tours run from April through
November, weather permitting, and include lunch or dinner.

Important Addresses and Numbers

Tourist   **Redwood Empire Association** (785 Market St., 15th floor, San
Information   Francisco 94103, tel. 415/543–8334). The *Redwood Empire Visitors' Guide* is available free of charge at the visitors center, or
for $2 by mail.

Napa Chamber of Commerce (1556 1st St., Napa 94559, tel. 707/
226–7455).

Sonoma Valley Visitors Bureau (453 1st St. E, Sonoma 95476,
tel. 707/996–1090).

Sonoma County Convention and Visitors Bureau (10 4th St.,
Ste. 100, Santa Rosa 95401, tel. 707/575–1191).

Calistoga Chamber of Commerce (1458 Lincoln Ave., Calistoga
94515, tel. 707/942–6333).

Healdsburg Chamber of Commerce (217 Healdsburg Ave.,
Healdsburg 95448, tel. 707/433–6935 or 800/648–9922 in CA).

St. Helena Chamber of Commerce (1080 Main St., Box 124, St.
Helena 94574, tel. 707/963–4456).

Emergencies   The emergency number for fire, police, ambulance, and
paramedics is 911, or dial "O" for operator and ask to be connected with the appropriate agency.

Exploring

There are three major paths through the Wine Country: U.S.
101 north from Santa Rosa, Highways 12 and 121 through
Sonoma County, and Highway 29 north from Napa.

From San Francisco, cross the Golden Gate Bridge and follow
Highway 101 to Santa Rosa and points north. Or cross the Gold-
en Gate, go north on Highway 101, east on Highway 37, and
north on Highway 121 into Sonoma. Yet another route runs
over the San Francisco Bay Bridge and along I–80 to Vallejo,
where Highway 29 leads north to Napa.

If you approach the Wine Country from the east you'll travel along I–80, and then turn northwest on Highway 12 for a 10 minute-drive through a hilly pass to Highway 29. From the north, take Highway 101 south to Geyserville, turn southeast on Highway 128, and drive down into the Napa Valley.

Wineries

Choosing which of the 400 or so wineries to visit will be difficult, and the range of opportunities makes it tempting to make multiple stops. Being adventurous will pay off. The wineries along the more frequented arteries of the Napa Valley tend to charge nominal fees for tasting, but in Sonoma County, where there is less tourist traffic, fees are the exception rather than the rule. In Sonoma, you are more likely to run into a wine-grower willing to spend part of an afternoon in convivial conversation than you are along the main drag of Napa Valley, where the waiter serving yards of bar has time to do little more than keep track of the rows of glasses.

Unless otherwise noted, visits to the wineries listed are free.

Highway 29 The town of Napa is the gateway into the famous valley, with its unrivaled climate and neat rows of vineyards. The towns in the area are small, and their Victorian Gothic architecture adds to the self-contained and separate feeling that permeates the valley.

A few miles north of Napa is the small town of Yountville. Turn west off Highway 29 at the Veterans Home exit and then up California Drive to **Domaine Chandon,** owned by the French champagne producer Möet-Hennessy and Louis Vuitton. You can tour the sleek modern facilities of this beautifully maintained property and sample flutes of the *methode champenoise* sparkling wine. Champagne is $3, the hors d'oeuvres are complimentary, and there is an elegant restaurant. *California Dr., Yountville, tel. 707/944–2280. The restaurant is closed Mon. and Tues. Nov.–Apr.; closed dinner Mon. and Tues. May–Oct. Tours daily 11–5, except Mon. and Tues., Nov.–Apr. Closed major holidays.*

Vintage 1870, a 22-acre complex of boutiques, restaurants, and gourmet stores is on the east side of Highway 29. The vine-covered brick buildings were built in 1870, and originally housed a winery, livery stable, and distillery. The adjacent *Vintage Cafe* is housed in the depot Samuel Brannan built in 1868 for his privately owned Napa Valley Railroad; the remodeled railroad cars of the *Napa Valley Railway Inn* accommodate guests (*see* Lodging, below).

Washington Square, at the north end of Yountville, is a new complex of shops and restaurants; **Pioneer Cemetery** where the town founder George Yount is buried, is across the street.

Many premier wine making establishments lie along the route from Yountville to St. Helena.

At **Robert Mondavi,** tasters are required to take the 40- to 60-minute tour before they imbibe. There are concerts on the grounds during the summer. *7801 St. Helena Hwy., Oakville, tel. 707/963–9611. Open daily 11–4. Reservations recommended in summer. Closed major holidays.*

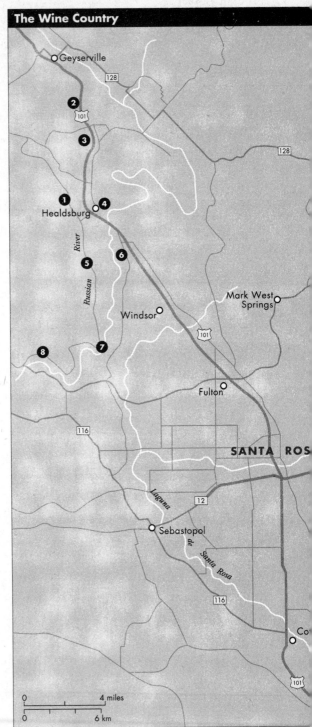

The Wine Country

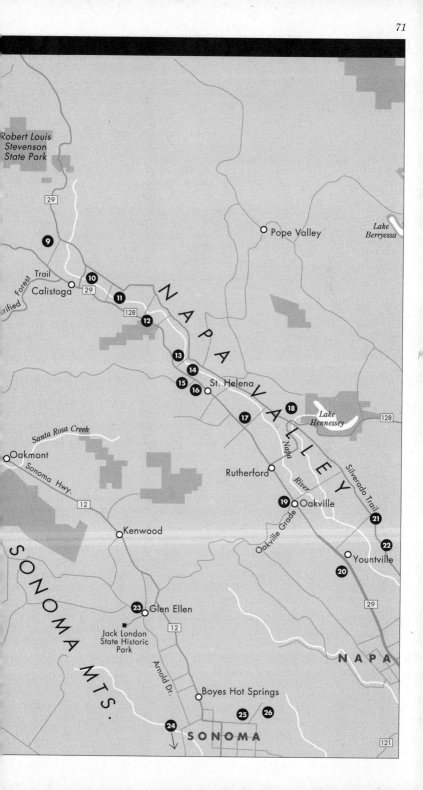

The **Charles Krug Winery** opened in 1861 when Count Haraszthy loaned Krug a small cider press. It is the oldest winery in the Napa Valley. Run by the Peter Mondavi family, it offers vineyard tours, and has a gift shop. *2800 N. Main St., St. Helena, tel. 707/963–5057. Open daily 10–4. Closed major holidays.*

The wine made at **V. Sattui** is sold only on the premises; the tactic draws crowds, as does the huge delicatessen, with its exotic cheeses. Award-winning wines include dry Johannisberg Rieslings, zinfandels, and madeiras. *Main St., at White La., St. Helena, tel. 707/963–7774. Open daily 9–5. Tours by appointment. Closed Christmas.*

The town of St. Helena boasts many Victorian buildings; don't overlook the **Silverado Museum,** two blocks east from Main Street on Adams, with Robert Louis Stevenson memorabilia, including first editions, manuscripts, and photographs. *1490 Library La., tel. 707/963–3757. Admission free. Open Tues.–Sun. noon–4. Closed major holidays.*

Beringer Vineyards has been operating continuously since 1876. Tastings are held in the Rhine House mansion where hand-carved oak and walnut and stained glass show Belgian art nouveau at its most opulent. The Beringer brothers, Frederick and Joseph, built the mansion in 1883 for the princely sum of $30,000. Tours include a visit to the deep limestone tunnels in which the wines mature. *2000 Main St., St. Helena, tel. 707/963–4812. Open daily 9:30–5. Closed major holidays.*

Christian Brothers Greystone Cellars is housed in an imposing stone building, built in 1889 and recently renovated. There are tours every half hour, displays on wine-barrel making, and an unusual collection of corkscrews. *2555 Main St., St. Helena, tel. 707/967–3112. Open daily 10–4:30. Closed major holidays.*

Freemark Abbey Winery was founded in the 1880s by Josephine Tychson, the first woman to establish a winery in California. *3022 St. Helena Highway N, St. Helena, tel. 707/963–9694. Open daily 10–4:30. One tour daily at 2 PM.*

The **Hurd Beeswax Candle Factory** is next door, with a gift shop that specializes in handcrafted candles made on the premises, and two restaurants.

The **Sterling Vineyards** lies on a hilltop to the east as you near Calistoga. The pristine white Mediterranean-style buildings are reached by an enclosed gondola from the valley floor; the view from the tasting room is superb. *1111 Dunaweal La., Calistoga, tel. 707/942–5151. Tram fee: $5 adults, children under 16 free. Open daily 10:30–4:30.*

At **Clos Pegase,** neoclassicism sets the tone. The new winery, commissioned by Jan Schrem, a publisher and art collector, and designed by architect Michael Graves, the exemplar of postmodernism, pays homage to art, wine, and mythology. *1060 Dunaweal La., Calistoga, tel. 707/942–4981. Open 10:30–4:30.*

Calistoga, at the head of the Napa Valley, is noted for its mineral water, hot mineral springs, mud baths, steam baths, and massages. The Calistoga Hot Springs Resort was founded in 1859 by the maverick entrepreneur Sam Brannan, whose ambition was to found "the Saratoga of California." He tripped up over the name at a formal banquet, and it stuck.

One of his cottages, preserved as the **Sharpsteen Museum,** has a magnificent diorama of the resort in its heyday. *1311 Washington St., tel. 707/942–5911. Donations accepted. Open May–Oct., daily 10–4; Nov.–Apr., daily noon–4.*

Chateau Montelena, a vine-covered building built in 1882, is set in Chinese-inspired gardens complete with red pavilions and arched bridges. It's a romantic spot for a picnic if you reserve ahead. *1429 Tubbs La., Calistoga, tel. 707/942–5105. Open daily 10–4. Tours at 11 and 2.*

The **Silverado Trail,** which runs parallel to Highway 29, takes you away from the madding crowd to some distinguished wineries. As you travel north from Napa:

Clos du Val. Bernard Portet, the French owner, produces a celebrated cabernet sauvignon. *5330 Silverado Trail, tel. 707/252–6711. Open daily 10–4.*
Stag's Leap Wine Cellars. The Cabernet Sauvignon was rated higher than many venerable bordeaux wines at a blind tasting in Paris in 1976. *5766 Silverado Trail, tel. 707/944–2020. Open daily 10–4.*
Rutherford Hill Winery. The wine ages in French oak barrels stacked in more than 30,000 square feet of caves. You can tour the nation's largest such facility, and picnic on the grounds. *200 Rutherford Hill Rd., Rutherford, tel. 707/963–7194. Cave tours at 11:30 AM, 1 and 2:30 PM.*
Hanns Kornell Champagne Cellars. Kornell opened his winery in 1952; he is still working here daily. *1091 Larkmead La., just east of Hwy. 29, 4 mi north of St. Helena, tel. 707/963–1237. Open daily 10–4:30.*
The **Calistoga Soaring Center** will give you a bird's-eye view of the whole valley, offering rides in gliders and bi-planes, as well as tandem ski-diving. *1546 Lincoln Ave., tel. 707/942–5592. Fee: $70–$160. Open daily 9 AM–dusk, weather permitting.*

You don't have to be a guest at a spa to experience a mud bath. At **Dr. Wilkinson's Hot Springs,** a $33 fee includes individual mineral-water showers and a mineral-water whirlpool, followed by time in the steam room, and a blanket wrap. For $49, you also get a half-hour massage. Reservations are recommended on weekends. *1507 Lincoln Ave., Calistoga, tel. 707/942–4102. Open daily 8:30–3:30.*

Highway 12 Sonoma is rustic in feeling, anchored by its past. It is the site of the last and the northernmost of the 21 missions established by the Franciscan order of Fr. Junipero Serra, and its central plaza includes the largest group of old adobes north of Monterey. The **Mission San Francisco Solano,** whose chapel and school labored to bring Christianity to the Indians, is now a museum, which contains a collection of 19th-century watercolors by Chris Jorgensen. *114 Spain St. E, tel. 707/938–1519. Admission: $1 adults, 50¢ children 6–17, includes the Sonoma Barracks on the Central Plaza, and General Vallejo's home, Lachryma Montis. Open daily 10–5. Closed Dec. 25, Jan. 1, and Thanksgiving Day.*

Time Out The four-block **Sonoma Plaza** is the largest of its kind in California. An inviting array of shops and food stores looks out onto
the shady park and attract gourmets from miles around. Many
pick up the makings for a first-rate picnic. The **French Bakery**
(466 1st St. E) is famous for its sourdough and cream puffs. The
Sonoma Sausage Co. (453 1st St. W) produces a mind-boggling
selection of bratwurst, bologna, boudin, bangers, and other
Old World sausages. There are good cold cuts, too. The **Sonoma
Cheese Factory** (2 Spain St.), run by the same family for four
generations, makes Sonoma jack cheese and a tangy new creation, Sonoma Teleme. You can peer through the glass windows
at the cheese-making process: great swirling baths of milk and
curds, and the wheels of cheese being pressed flat to dry.

A few blocks west (and quite a hike) is the tree-lined approach
to **Lachryma Montis,** which General Mariano Vallejo, the last
Mexican governor of California, built for his large family in
1851. The Victorian Gothic house is secluded in the midst of
beautiful gardens; opulent Victorian furnishings, including a
white marble fireplace in every room, are particularly noteworthy. The state purchased the home in 1933. *Spain St. W, tel.
707/938–1578. Admission: $1 adults, 50¢ children 6–17. Open
daily 10–5. Closed Dec. 25, Jan. 1, and Thanksgiving Day.*

The **Sebastiani Vineyards,** planted by Franciscans of the
Sonoma Mission in 1825, and later owned by General Vallejo,
were bought by Samuele Sebastiani in 1904. The Sebastianis
recently helped popularize "blush" wines, and Sylvia
Sebastiani has recorded her good Italian home cooking in a family recipe book, "Mangiamo." Tours include an unusual
collection of impressive carved oak casks. *389 4th St. E, tel. 707/
938–5532. Open daily 10–5, closed major holidays.*

The landmark **Buena Vista Winery** (follow signs from the Plaza), set among towering trees and fountains, is a must-see in
Sonoma. This is where, in 1857, Count Agoston Haraszthy de
Mokcsa laid the basis for modern California wine-making,
bucking the conventional wisdom that vines should be planted
on well-watered ground by planting on well-drained hillsides.
Chinese laborers dug the cool aging tunnels 100 feet into the
hillside, and the limestone they extracted was used for the main
house. Although the wines are produced elsewhere today,
there are tours, a gourmet shop, art gallery, wine museum,
and great picnic spots. *18000 Old Winery Rd., tel. 707/938–
1266. Open daily 10–5.*

In the Carneros region of the Sonoma Valley, south of Sonoma,
the wines at **Gloria Ferrer Champagne Caves** are aged in a
"cava," or cellar, where several feet of earth maintain a constant temperature. *23555 Hwy. 121, tel. 707/996–7256. Tasting
$3.50. Open daily 10:30–5:30.*

The well-known **Glen Ellen Winery** uses watercolors painted by
Jan Haraszthy, one of the count's descendants, on its labels; the
originals hang in the tasting room. *1883 London Ranch Rd.,
Glen Ellen, tel. 707/935–3000. Open daily 10–4.*

North of Sonoma, through the Valley of the Moon and in the
hills above Glen Ellen, is **Jack London State Historic Park.** The
House of Happy Walls is a museum of his effects, including his
collection of South Sea artifacts. The ruins of Wolf House,
which London designed, and which mysteriously burned down

just before he was to move into it, lie nearby, and London is buried here. *2400 London Ranch Rd., tel. 707/938–5216. Admission to park, $3 per car; $2 for senior citizens. Park open daily 8 AM–sunset; museum 10–5. Museum closed Jan. 1, Thanksgiving Day, and Dec. 25.*

Highway 101 Santa Rosa is the Wine Country's largest city, and your best bet for a moderately priced hotel room, especially if you haven't reserved in advance.

The **Luther Burbank Memorial Gardens** commemorate the great botanist, who lived and worked on these grounds for 50 years, single-handedly developing modern techniques of hybridization. Arriving as a young man from New England, he wrote: "I firmly believe . . . that this is the chosen spot of all the earth, as far as nature is concerned." The Santa Rosa plum, the Shasta daisy, and the lily of the Nile agapanthus are among the 800 or so plants he developed or improved. In the dining room of his house, a Webster's Dictionary of 1946 lies open to a page in which the verb "burbank" is defined as "to modify and improve plant life." *Santa Rosa and Sonoma aves., tel. 707/576 –5115. Gardens free, open daily 8–5. Home tours: $1, open Apr.–Oct., Wed.–Sun. 10–3:30.*

The wineries of Sonoma County are located along winding roads and are not immediately obvious to the casual visitor; a tour of the vineyards that lie along the Russian River is a leisurely and bucolic experience. *For a map of the area, contact Russian River Wine Rd., Box 127, Geyserville 95441, tel. 707/ 433–6935.*

You could start at the imposing **Korbel Champagne Cellars** for a historical overview, with its photographic documents housed in a former stop of the North West Pacific Railway. *13250 River Rd., Guerneville, tel. 707/887–2294. Open daily 9–4:30.* Traveling down the River Road east of Guerneville, turn left down Westside Road and follow it as it winds past a number of award-winning wineries.

Davis Bynum Winery, an up and coming label, offers a full line of varietal wines that have been doing very well in recent competitions. *8075 Westside Rd., Healdsburg, tel. 707/433–5852. Open daily 10–5.*

The **Hop Kiln Winery** is located in an imposing hop-drying barn, built in the early 1900s, and used as the backdrop for such films as the 1960 *Lassie* with James Stewart. *6050 Westside Rd., Healdsburg, tel. 707/433–6491. Open daily 10–5.*

Lambert Bridge produces some superbly elegant cabernet sauvignons and merlots. *4085 W. Dry Creek Rd., Healdsburg, tel. 707/433–5855. Open daily 10–4:30.*

The **Robert Stemmler Winery** draws on German traditions of wine-making, and specializes in pinot noir. There are picnic facilities on the grounds. *3805 Lambert Bridge Rd., Healdsburg (Dry Creek Rd. exit from Hwy. 101, northwest 3 mi to Lambert Bridge Rd.), tel. 707/433–6334. Open daily 10:30–4:30.*

Lytton Springs Winery produces the archetype of the Sonoma zinfandel, a dark, fruity wine with a high alcohol content. There is still dispute over the origin of this varietal and whether it was transplanted from stock in New England, but the vines themselves are distinctive, gnarled and stocky, many of them more than a century old. *650 Lytton Springs Rd., Healdsburg, tel. 707/433-7721. Open daily 10-4.*

In Healdsburg, back on Highway 101, is **Clos du Bois,** winemaking at its most high-tech. You can tour by appointment, but you'd do better to concentrate on sampling the fine estate wines of the Alexander and Dry Creek valleys that are made here. *5 Fitch St., tel. 707/433-5576. Open daily 10-5.*

South of Healdsburg, off Highway 101, are the **Piper Sonoma Cellars,** a state-of-the art winery that specializes in making champagne. *11447 Old Redwood Hwy., Healdsburg, tel. 707/433-8843. Open daily 10-5.*

Time Out In case you've had enough wine for the day, **Kozlowski's Raspberry Farm** (5566 Gravenstein, Hwy. N. 116) in Forestville makes jams of every berry imaginable. Also in Forestville, **Brother Juniper's** (6544 Front St., Hwy. 116, tel. 707/887-7908) makes a heavenly *Struan* bread of wheat, corn, oats, brown rice, and bran. *Open Mon.-Sat. 9-4:30.*

What to See and Do with Children

In **the Bale Grist Mill State Historic Park** is a flour mill powered by a 36-foot overshot water wheel erected by Dr. Edward Turner Bale in 1846 and since restored. Hiking trails lead from the access road to the mill pond. *3 mi north of St. Helena on Hwy. 29, tel. 707/942-4575. Day use: $1 adults, 50¢ children 7-18. Open daily 10-5.*

Old Faithful Geyser of California is a 60-foot tower of steam and vapor that erupts about every 40 minutes; the pattern is disrupted if there's an earthquake in the offing. One of just three regularly erupting geysers in the world, the spout lasts three minutes. It is fed by an underground river that heats to 350 degrees F. Picnic facilities are available. *1299 Tubbs La., 1 mi north of Calistoga, tel. 707/942-6463. Admission: $3 adults, $2 children 6-11. Open daily 9-6 in summer, 9-5 in winter.*

In the **Petrified Forest,** volcanic eruptions of Mount St. Helena six million years ago uprooted the gigantic redwoods, covered them with volcanic ash, and infiltrated the trees with silicas and minerals, causing petrification. There is a museum, and picnic facilities are available. *4100 Petrified Forest Rd., 5 mi west of Calistoga, tel. 707/942-6667. Admission: $3 adults, $1 children 4-11. Open daily 10-6 in summer, 10-5 in winter.*

A scale steam train at **Train Town** runs for 20 minutes through a forested park with trestles, bridges, and miniature animals. *20264 Broadway, 1 mi south of Sonoma Plaza, tel. 707/938-3912. Admission: $2.40 adults, $1.80 children under 16 and senior citizens. Open mid-June–Labor Day, daily 10:30-5; Sept.–mid-June, weekends and holidays 10:30-5:30. Closed Dec. 25.*

Howarth Memorial Park in Santa Rosa has a lake where canoes, rowboats, paddleboats, and small sailboats can be rented for $3-$4 an hour. The children's area has a playground, pony rides, petting zoo, merry-go-round, and a miniature train. Fishing, tennis, and hiking trails are also available. *Summerfield Rd. off Montgomery Rd., tel. 707/576-5132. Park open* *daily. Children's area open Wed.–Sun. in summer, weekends, spring and fall. Admission to amusements: 25–50¢.*

Off the Beaten Track

You'll see breathtaking views of both the Sonoma and Napa valleys along the hairpin turns of the *Oakville Grade,* which twists along the range dividing the two valleys. The surface of the road is fine, and if you're comfortable with mountain driving, you'll enjoy this half-hour excursion. Trucks are advised not to take this route.

Robert Louis Stevenson State Park, on Highway 53, three miles northeast of Calistoga, encompasses the summit of Mount St. Helena. It was here, in an abandoned bunkhouse of the Silverado Mine, that Stevenson and his bride, Fanny Osbourne, spent their honeymoon in the summer of 1880. The stay inspired Stevenson's "The Silverado Squatters," and Spyglass Hill in *Treasure Island* is thought to be a portrait of Mount St. Helena. The park's 3,000 acres are undeveloped except for a fire trail leading to the site of the cabin, which is marked with a marble tablet, and then on to the summit. Picnicking is permitted, but fires are not.

Shopping

Most wineries will ship purchases. Don't expect bargains at the wineries themselves, where prices are generally as high as at retail outlets. Local residents report that the area's supermarkets stock a wide selection of local wines at lower prices. Gift shops in the larger wineries offer the ultimate in gourmet items—you could easily stock up on early Christmas presents.

Sports

Ballooning This sport has fast become part of the scenery in the Wine Country, and many hotels arrange excursions. Most flights take place soon after sunrise, when the calmest, coolest time of day offers maximum lift and soft landings. Prices depend on the duration of the flight, number of passengers and services (some companies provide pickup at your lodging, champagne brunch after the flight, etc.) You should expect to spend about $150 per person.

Companies providing flights include **Balloons Above the Valley** (Box 3838, Napa 94558, tel. 707/253–2222 or 800/233–7681 in CA); **Napa Valley Balloons** (Box 2860, Yountville 94599, tel. 707/253–2224 or 800/253–2224 in CA); and **Once in a Lifetime** (Box 795, Calistoga 94515, tel. 707/942–6541 or 800/722–6665 in CA).

Bicycling One of the best ways to experience the countryside is on two wheels. Reasonably priced rentals are available in most towns.

Golf Though the weather is mild year-round, in the winter months rain may occasionally prevent your teeing off. Call to check on greens fees at **Fountaingrove Country Club** (1525 Fountaingrove Pkwy., Santa Rosa, tel. 707/579–4653); **Oakmont Inn and Golf Course** (7025 Oakmont Dr., Santa Rosa, tel. 707/539–0415); or **Silverado Country Club** (1600 Atlas Peak Rd., Napa, tel. 707/257–0200).

Dining

by Bruce David Colen

A number of the Wine Country's kitchens are the domains of nationally prominent chefs. The emphasis everywhere on the freshest ingredients goes hand in hand with local bounty: vegetables and fruits, seafood, lamb, and poultry. While some of the restaurants are expensive (dinner at Auberge du Soleil or the Silverado Country Club may run to $50 per person), wonderful local foods are available for picnics.

With few exceptions (which are noted), dress is informal. Where reservations are indicated to be essential, you may need to reserve a week or more ahead during the summer and early fall harvest seasons.

Highly recommended restaurants are indicated by a star ★.

Category	Cost*
Very Expensive	over $35
Expensive	$25–$35
Moderate	$16–$25
Inexpensive	under $16

per person, not including tax, service, or drinks

Calistoga
Expensive
★

Calistoga Inn. With the atmosphere and appeal of a village tavern (but the talents of a big-city chef), the restaurant has nicely prepared California cuisine and excellent fish dishes. First-rate local wines are also featured. *1250 Lincoln Ave., tel. 707/942–4101. Jacket recommended. Reservations suggested. MC, V.*

Moderate

Alex's. This family-style restaurant features roast beef in three different cuts. If you're not in the mood for steak, try one of the several fish entrées or the daily seafood special. Don't pass up the family recipe cheesecake. *1437 Lincoln Ave., tel. 707/942–6868. Dress: informal. Wine and beer. AE, MC, V. Closed Mon.*

Geyserville
Very Expensive
★

Château Souverain Restaurant at the Winery. There is a gorgeous view of the Alexander Valley vineyards from the dining room and terrace. The California/Continental menu is imaginative: Sonoma lamb loin with soy mustard ginger glaze, black peppercorn rosemary lamb essence and Japanese eggplant; grilled marinated quail with smoked pear purée, pancetta, and basil quail essence. *400 Souverain Rd. (take Independence La. exit west from Hwy. 101), tel. 707/433–3141. Jacket and tie at dinner. Reservations advised. Beer, wine. AE, DC, MC, V. Dinner Thurs.–Sat. only; lunch Tues.–Sat., Sun. brunch.*

Healdsburg
Very Expensive
★

Madrona Manor. The chef uses a brick oven, smokehouse, orchard, and herb and vegetable garden to enhance other fresh produce and seafood on his California menus. Dinners and Sunday brunch are served in the dining room and terrace of an 1881 Victorian mansion on a hilltop west of town. À la carte and prix fixe. *1001 Westside Rd., tel. 707/433–4231. Jacket and tie. Reservations advised. Wines. AE, DC, MC, V. Dinner only.*

Moderate

Jacob Horner. The focus here is California cuisine with an emphasis on locally grown vegetables ("no more than two miles

from the restaurant") and fresh seafood, lamb, and duck from
near at hand. An enthusiastic owner-chef has put together a
comfortable, good-looking restaurant on Healdsburg's charming town plaza. There is an extensive, award-winning wine list
with 17 wines served by the glass. _106 Matheson St., tel. 707/
433–3939. Dress: informal. Reservations accepted. Full bar.
AE, MC, V. Closed Sun. No dinner Mon._

Inexpensive-Moderate **Plaza Grill.** Mesquite-grilled meats, fresh fish (orange roughy
en papillote), espresso, and cappucino are served at a small, attractive wine bar on Healdsburg's pretty town plaza. _109–A
Plaza St., tel. 707/431–8305. Dress: informal. Reservations
advised. Beer and wine. MC, V. Closed Mon., Sun. lunch, and
first week in December._

Napa **Silverado Country Club.** There are two dining rooms and a bar
Very Expensive and grill at this large, famous resort. Vintner's Court, with
Continental cuisine, serves dinner only; there is a seafood buffet on Friday night. Royal Oaks offers steak, seafood, and
lobster for dinner; in summer it opens for lunch. The bar and
grill serves breakfast and lunch year-round. _1600 Atlas Peak
Rd., 707/257–0200. Jackets preferred at dinner. Reservations
advised. Full bar. AE, DC, MC, V._

Inexpensive **Jonesy's Famous Steak House.** This longtime institution at the
Napa County Airport is popular with private pilots throughout
the West and with local people. Steaks are prepared on an open
grill, with large hot rocks placed on top of them while cooking.
The building is nothing special: plain and businesslike. _2044
Airport Rd., tel. 707/255–2003. Dress: informal. Reservations
accepted for groups of 6 or more. Full bar. AE, MC, V. Closed
Mon., Jan. 1, Thanksgiving, and a week at Christmas._

Rutherford **Auberge du Soleil.** Sitting on the dining terrace of this hilltop
Very Expensive inn, looking down across groves of olive trees to the Napa Val-
★ ley vineyards, is the closest one can get to the atmosphere and
charm of southern France without needing a passport. The
mood is enhanced by a menu centered around light Provençal
dishes, using the fresh produce of nearby farms. The Auberge
features a fine California, French, and Italian wine list. It is
also a 36-room inn (_see_ Lodging, below). _180 Rutherford Hill
Rd., tel. 707/963–1211. Jacket and tie recommended. Reservations required. Full bar. MC, V._

St. Helena **Starmont at Meadowood.** Three-course prix fixe dinners, an ex-
Very Expensive tensive Napa Valley wine list, and some French wines are
served in this elegantly casual 65-seat restaurant that turns to
the outdoors, maximizing the view over the golf course and
stands of pine trees beyond. There is terrace service in warm
weather. Sunday brunch April–November. _900 Meadowood
La., tel. 707/963–3646. Jacket recommended. Reservations required. Full bar. AE, DC, MC, V._

Moderate-Expensive **Abbey Restaurant.** Greek specialties, seafood, beef, lamb
shanks, and pastitsio are served at lunch and dinner, next door
to Freemark Abbey. _3020 N. St. Helena Hwy. (Hwy. 29), tel.
707/963–2706. Dress: informal. Reservations accepted. Full
bar, wine. AE, MC, V. No dinner Mon. and Tues. Closed Jan. 1,
Easter, Dec. 25._

 Terra. The delightful couple who own this lovely, unpretentious
restaurant in a century-old stone foundry, learned their culinary skills at the side of chef Wolfgang Puck. Hiro Sone was
head chef at L.A.'s Spago and Lissa Doumani was the pastry

chef. The menu has an enticing array of American favorites, prepared with Hiro's Japanese-French-Italian finesse: addictive baked mussels in garlic butter, sauteed Miyagi oysters with jalapeño salsa, home-smoked salmon with golden caviar, grilled quail and polenta, and sweetbreads with asparagus and wild mushrooms. Save room for Lissa's desserts. *1345 Railroad Ave., tel. 707/963–8931. Jacket required. Reservations advised. Wine and beer. MC, V. Dinner only. Closed Tues.*

Tra Vigne. This Napa Valley fieldstone building has been turned into a barn of a trattoria, serving good pizza, pastas, and traditional Italian grilled meats, fish, and fowl. Tra Vigne has terrace dining, weather permitting. The oak-paneled bar is a favorite meeting place for locals and tourists. *1050 Charter Oak Ave., tel. 707/963–4444. Jacket required. Reservations advised. Full bar. AE, MC, V.*

Inexpensive **Fairway Grill and Bar.** California specialties include Meadowood salad (Napa goat cheese with St. Helena olive oil vinaigrette) and grilled marinated chicken breast with cilantro pesto. This is a light, airy, casual restaurant at the Meadowood Resort, where large windows and an outdoor terrace overlook the golf course and croquet lawns. Antique croquet mallets and tennis rackets decorate the walls. *900 Meadowood La., tel. 707/963–3646. Dress: informal. Reservations advised. Full bar. AE, DC, MC, V. No dinner in winter.*

★ **French Laundry.** Long a favorite of surrounding wine makers for its tasty blend of French and California cooking, French Laundry has marvelous fresh-baked breads and croissants. It is also one of the most attractive wine bars in the Wine Country. *Washington and Creek sts., tel. 707/944–2380. Jacket recommended. Reservations advised. Wine and beer. MC, V. Dinner only, Wed.–Sun.*

Santa Rosa **John Ash & Co.** The thoroughly regional cuisine here emphasizes beauty, innovation, and the seasonality of food products grown in Sonoma County. In spring, local lamb is roasted with hazelnuts and honey; in fall, farm pork is roasted with fresh figs and Gravenstein apples. There are wondrous desserts and an extensive wine list. Two dining rooms are in a vineyard setting next to Vintner's Inn. The restaurant also offers Sunday brunch. *4330 Barnes Rd. (River Rd. exit west from Hwy. 101), tel. 707/527–7687. Jacket preferred. Reservations advised. Wine. AE, MC, V. Closed Mon.*

Moderate **Equus.** In this handsome restaurant, the equestrian theme is carried out in redwood carvings, murals, and etched glass. A gallery of Sonoma County wines features nearly 300 bottles hand-picked by their makers. *101 Fountaingrove Pkwy., tel. 707/578–6101. Jacket preferred. Reservations advised. Full bar. AE, DC, MC, V.*

Los Robles Lodge Dining Room. The elegant 150-seat dining room specializes in tableside presentations of chateaubriand, lamb, and flaming desserts. Seafood and sautéed dishes are also featured. This 26-year-old restaurant has a loyal local following. *9255 Edwards Ave. (Steele La. exit west from Hwy. 101), tel. 707/545–6330. Jacket preferred. Reservations advised. Full bar. AE, DC, MC, V. No lunch on major holidays.*

Inexpensive **Omelette Express.** At least 300 omelette possibilities are offered in an old-fashioned restaurant in historic Railroad Square. *112 4th St., tel. 707/525–1690. Dress: informal. No reservations. No alcohol. MC, V. No dinner.*

Sonoma
Expensive

Sonoma Mission Inn. There are two dining rooms as well as a poolside terrace for alfresco meals at this attractive, "contemporary country" resort. The inn is also a spa, so the menu has a wide assortment of light dishes with the accent on fresh salads, fish, and poultry, prepared in nouvelle-California style. The annual Sonoma Wine Auction is held on the inn's grounds, so the extensive wine list should come as no surprise. *18140 Hwy. 12, Boyes Hot Springs, tel. 707/938–9000. Jacket recommended at dinner. Reservations advised. Full bar. AE, DC, MC, V.*

Moderate-Expensive

L'Esperance. The room is small and pretty, with flowered tablecloths to the floor, burgundy overcloths, and burgundy chairs. There is a choice of classic French entrées, such as rack of lamb, plus a "menu gastronomique" that includes hot and cold appetizers, salad, entrée, cheese, dessert, and coffee. Sunday brunch is served. *464 1st St. E (down a walkway off the plaza, behind the French Bakery), tel. 707/996–2757. Dress: informal. Reservations advised. Wine and beer. MC, V. Closed Thurs.*

Piatti. On the ground floor of the recently remodeled El Dorado Hotel, a 19th-century landmark building, this is the Sonoma cousin of the Napa Valley Piatti (*see* below). This very friendly trattoria features a nice selection of grilled northern Italian items. *405 1 St. tel. 707/996–3030. Dress: casual. Full bar. MC, V. No lunch weekends.*

Moderate

Sonoma Hotel Dining Room. Seasonal produce and homemade ingredients are featured in a restaurant with antique oak tables and stained glass. The saloon boasts a magnificent old bar of oak and mahogany. Service on garden patio in summer. *110 W. Spain St., tel. 707/996–2996. Dress: informal. Reservations advised. Full bar. AE, MC, V. No dinner Wed.*

Inexpensive

Gino's Restaurant and Bar. This relaxed, friendly eating and drinking establishment on Sonoma's plaza specializes in fresh seafood and pasta. *420 1st St., tel. 707/996–4466. Dress: informal. No reservations. Full bar. MC, V. Closed Tues.*

La Casa. "Whitewashed stucco, red tile, serapes, and Mexican glass" describes this restaurant just around the corner from Sonoma's plaza. There is an extensive menu of traditional Mexican food: chimichangas, snapper Veracruz, flan for dessert, sangria to drink. *121 E. Spain St., tel. 707/996–3406. Dress: informal. Reservations advised. Full bar. AE, DC, MC, V.*

Yountville
*Expensive-Very
Expensive*
★

Domaine Chandon. Nouvelle seafood, pasta, beef, and lamb are prepared imaginatively and presented beautifully. The architecturally dramatic dining room has views of vineyards and carefully preserved native oaks. There is also outdoor service on a tree-shaded patio. *California Dr. (no number), tel. 707/ 944–2892. Jacket and tie required. Reservations essential. Wine. AE, DC, MC, V. No dinner Mon. and Tues. year round; no lunch Mon. and Tues., Nov.–Apr.*

Moderate-Expensive

Piatti. A small, stylish trattoria with a pizza oven and open kitchen, this cheery place is full of good smells and happy people. Its authentic, light Italian cooking—from the antipasto to the grilled chicken to the *tiramisu*—is the perfect cure for a jaded appetite. The pastas are the best bet. *6480 Washington St., tel. 707/944–2070. Jacket for dinner. Reservations suggested. Full bar. AE, DC, MC, V.*

Moderate

Anesti's Grill and Rotisserie. Rotisserie-roasted lamb, duck, and suckling pig are specialties of this small, cheerful restaurant with a mesquite grill. *6518 Washington St., tel. 707/944–1500. Dress: informal. Reservations advised. Wine and beer. AE, DC, MC, V.*

California Cafe Bar & Grill. Chicken breast with red pepper jam, tapas, warm apple crisp, and an extensive wine list are featured in a large, square room with an open kitchen. There is outdoor service on the terrace. Sunday brunch is also served. *6795 Washington St., tel. 707/944–2330. Dress: informal. Reservations accepted. Full bar. AE, MC, V.*

Mama Nina's. This homey and old-fashioned restaurant serves homemade pasta and fresh grilled fish. There's a children's menu. *6772 Washington St., tel. 707/944–2112. Dress: informal. Reservations advised. Full bar. MC, V. Closed Easter, Thanksgiving, Dec. 24–25. Dinner only.*

★ **Mustard's Grill.** Mesquite-grilled fish, hot smoked meats, fresh local produce, and a good wine list are offered in a simple, unassuming dining room. It's very popular and crowded at prime meal times. *7399 St. Helena Hwy. (Hwy. 29, 2 mi north of Yountville), tel. 707/944–2424. Dress: informal. Reservations essential. Wine and beer. MC, V.*

California Cafe. This is the Wine Country link of a small upscale chain serving bar and grill dishes, plus roast game and a variety of good pastas and salads. The simplest dishes here taste the best. There is a long list of local wines sold by the glass. *6795 Washington St., tel. 707/944–2330. Dress: casual. AE, DC, MC, V.*

Inexpensive **The Diner.** Probably the best known and most appreciated stop-off in the Napa Valley, especially for breakfast. Be sure to have the local sausages and the house potatoes. At night, many of the specials are Mexican. *6476 Washington St., tel. 707/944–2626. No reservations; expect a wait for seating. Wine and beer. AE, MC, V. Closed Mon.*

Lodging

Make no mistake, staying in the Wine Country is expensive. The inns, hotels, and motels are usually exquisitely appointed, and many are fully booked long in advance of the summer season. Since Santa Rosa is the largest population center in the area, it has the largest selection of rooms, many at moderate rates. Try there if you've failed to reserve in advance or have a limited budget.

Highly recommended hotels are indicated by a star ★.

Category	Cost*
Very Expensive	over $100
Expensive	$80–$100
Moderate	$50–$80
Inexpensive	under $50

double room, not including tax

Calistoga **Brannan Cottage Inn.** This exquisite Victorian cottage with
Expensive lacy white fretwork, large windows, and a shady porch is the
★ only one of Sam Brannan's 1860 resort cottages still standing on its original site. The restoration is excellent, and includes elegant stenciled friezes of stylized wildflowers. All rooms

have private entrances. Full breakfast is included. Children under 10 not allowed. *109 Wapoo Ave., 94515, tel. 707/942–4200. 6 rooms. MC, V.*

Moderate-Very Expensive **Mount View Hotel.** This refurbished 1930s art deco hotel provides live music and dancing nightly. Continental breakfast in the lobby is included; the suites also include complimentary wine. *1457 Lincoln Ave., 94515, tel. 707/942–6877. 34 rooms with bath. Facilities: pool, jacuzzi, restaurant, bar. AE, CB, DC, MC, V.*

Moderate **Comfort Inn Napa Valley North.** All the rooms in this motel have one king-size or two queen-size beds, and many have vineyard views. Continental breakfast is included. There are rooms for nonsmokers and handicapped guests, and senior citizen discounts. *1865 Lincoln Ave., 94515, tel. 707/942–9400 or 800/228–5150. 54 rooms with bath. Facilities: movies, natural mineral water pool, spa, sauna, and steam room. AE, DC, MC, V.*

Dr. Wilkinson's Hot Springs. This hot springs spa resort has been in operation for more than 40 years. Reserve ahead for weekends when there are separate fees for mud baths, massages, facials, and steam rooms. Mid-week packages include room and full spa services. *1507 Lincoln Ave., 94515, tel. 707/942–4102. 42 rooms. Facilities: 3 mineral pools. AE, MC, V.*

Mountain Home Ranch. This rustic 75-year-old ranch is on 300 wooded acres, with hiking trails, a creek, and a fishing lake. There are no phones, and just one TV in the dining room. Families are welcome and there are special children's rates. In summer, the modified American plan (full breakfast and dinner) is used; otherwise Continental breakfast is included. Six simple cabins without heat are available from mid-June to Labor Day. They have a separate shower facility, and you must bring your own linens. *3400 Mountain Home Ranch Rd., 94515 (north of town on Hwy. 128, left on Petrified Forest Rd., right on Mountain Home Ranch Rd. to end; 3 mi from Hwy. 128), tel. 707/942–6616. 12 rooms with bath, 6 cabins with half bath. Facilities: pools, tennis. MC, V. Closed Dec.–Jan.*

Healdsburg Very Expensive **Madrona Manor.** A splendid three-story 1881 Gothic mansion, carriage house, and outbuildings sit on eight wooded and landscaped acres. Mansion rooms are recommended: All nine have fireplaces, and five contain the antique furniture of the original owner. The approach to the mansion leads under a stone archway and up a flowered hill; the house looks over the valley and vineyards. Full breakfast is included, and there's a fine restaurant on the premises that serves dinner. Pets are allowed. *1001 Westside Rd., Box 818, 95448, tel. 707/433–4231. 20 rooms with bath. Facilities: pool, restaurant. AE, DC, MC, V.*

Moderate-Very Expensive **Healdsburg Inn on the Plaza.** This renovated 1900 brick building on the attractive town plaza has a bright solarium and a roof garden. The rooms are spacious, with quilts and pillows piled high on antique beds, and clawfoot tubs complete with rubber ducks. Full breakfast, afternoon coffee and cookies, and early evening wine and popcorn are included. *116 Matheson St., Box 1196, 95448, tel. 707/433–6991. 9 rooms. MC, V.*

Moderate **Best Western Dry Creek Inn.** Movies, Continental breakfast, and a complimentary bottle of wine are included at this three-story motel in Spanish Mission style. There is a 24-hour coffee shop next door. Direct bus service from San Francisco Airport is available. *198 Dry Creek Rd., 95448, tel. 707/433–0300; 800/*

528–1234 in CA, 800/222–5784. 102 rooms with bath. Facilities: pool, spa, laundry. AE, DC, MC, V.

Napa
Very Expensive

Silverado Country Club. This luxurious 1,200-acre resort in the hills east of the town of Napa offers cottages, kitchen apartments, and one- to three-bedroom efficiencies, many with fireplaces. There are also two dining rooms, a lounge, a sundries store, seven pools, 20 tennis courts, and two championship golf courses designed by Robert Trent Jones. Fees are charged for golf, tennis, and bike rentals. *1600 Atlas Peak Rd., 94558 (6 mi east of Napa via Hwy. 121), tel. 707/257–0200 or 800/532–0500. 277 condo units. Facilities: golf, restaurant. AE, CB, DC, MC, V.*

Expensive

Chateau. There's a French country inn atmosphere at this modern motel which provides Continental breakfast and a social hour with wine. Movies, in-room refrigerators, handicapped facilities, and senior citizen discounts are available. *4195 Solano Ave., 94558 (west of and adjacent to Hwy. 29; take W. Salvador Ave. exit), tel. 707/253–9300 or 800/253–6272 in CA. 115 rooms. Facilities: pool, spa. AE, CB, DC, MC, V.*

Clarion. This modern, comfortable, and immaculately maintained motel has a restaurant and lounge on the premises, live music in the lounge, movies, and rooms for the handicapped. Pets allowed with $10 fee. *3425 Solano Ave., 94558 (1 block west off Hwy. 29; take Redwood-Trancas exit), tel. 707/253–7433 or 800/333–7533. 191 rooms. Facilities: pool, spa, lighted tennis courts. AE, DC, MC, V.*

Moderate

Best Western Inn Napa. This immaculate, modern, redwood motel with spacious rooms has a restaurant on the premises and same-day laundry and valet service. There are suites as well as rooms for nonsmokers and the handicapped. Small pets are allowed. *100 Soscol Ave., 94558 (Imola Ave. Hwy. 121 exit east from Hwy. 29 to junction of Hwy. 121 and Soscol), tel. 707/257–1930 or 800/528–1234. 68 rooms. Facilities: pool, spa. AE, DC, MC, V.*

John Muir Inn. Continental breakfast and in-room coffee are included at this new, well-equipped three-story motel which has kitchenettes, refrigerators, movies, valet service, and some whirlpool tubs. Rooms for nonsmokers and handicapped guests, and senior citizen discounts are available. *1998 Trower Ave., 94558 (adjacent to Hwy. 29, east at Trower exit), tel. 707/257–7220 or 800/522–8999 in CA. 59 rooms. Facilities: pool, spa. AE, CB, DC, MC, V.*

Rutherford
Very Expensive

Auberge du Soleil. This luxurious French country-style inn has a spectacular view over vineyards and hills, and an excellent restaurant. *180 Rutherford Hill Rd., 94573, tel. 707/963–1211. 48 rooms. Facilities: pool, spa, tennis. AE, MC, V.*

Rancho Caymus Inn. Early California-Spanish in style, this inn has well-maintained gardens and large suites with kitchens and whirlpool baths. There is an emphasis on decorative handcrafts and home-baked breads, and there are unusual beehive fireplaces, tile murals, stoneware basins, and llama blankets. *1140 Rutherford Rd., 94573 (junction of hwys. 29 and 128), tel. 707/963–1777. 26 rooms. Facilities: restaurant. MC, V.*

St. Helena
Very Expensive

Meadowood Resort Hotel. The resort is on 256 wooded acres, with a golf course, croquet lawns, and hiking trails. The hotel is a rambling country lodge reminiscent of turn-of-the-century Rhode Island, and separate bungalow suites are clustered on the hillside. Half of the suites and some rooms have fireplaces. *900 Meadowood La., 94574, tel. 707/963–3646 or 800/458–8080. 70 rooms. Facilities: 2 restaurants, lounge, room service, pool, nine-hole golf course, croquet, par course, tennis, masseuse, wine school. AE, DC, MC, V.*

Expensive-Very Expensive **Harvest Inn.** This English Tudor inn with many fireplaces overlooks a 14-acre producing vineyard and award-winning landscaping. The furnishings are antique, but there are also wet bars, refrigerators, and a wine bar and dance floor in the lobby "Great Room." Dogs are allowed for a $5 fee. *1 Main St., 94574, tel. 707/963–9463 or 800/950–8466. 55 rooms. Facilities: 2 pools, 2 Jacuzzis. AE, MC, V.*

Expensive **Cinnamon Bear Bed and Breakfast.** Built in 1904 as a wedding gift, this house is decorated with a period flavor, including antique quilts and toys and clawfoot tubs. Full breakfast is included. Rooms for nonsmokers are available. *1407 Kearney St., 94574 (from Main St., Hwy. 29, turn west on Adams St., then 2 blocks to Kearney), tel. 707/963–4653. 4 rooms with shared baths. MC, V.*

Hotel St. Helena. This restored 1881 stone hostelry, furnished with antiques and decorated in rich tones of burgundy, aims at Old World comfort. Continental breakfast is included. Smoking not encouraged. *1309 Main St., 94574, tel. 707/963–4388. 14 rooms with bath, 4 rooms with shared baths. AE, DC, MC, V.*

Moderate **El Bonita Motel.** This old-fashioned roadside motel was remodeled with an art deco feeling. The decor is white and gray with streaks of flamingo and blue; a neon calla lily graces the north side. Small rooms have soft, smart furnishings. The 16 rooms in the main motel and six garden rooms with kitchenettes are stylishly furnished. *195 Main St., 94574, tel. 707/963–3216 or 800/541–3284. 22 rooms. Facilities: pool. AE, MC, V.*

Santa Rosa *Very Expensive* **Vintner's Inn.** Set in 50 acres of vineyards, this recently built inn has large rooms, French Provincial furnishings, and woodburning fireplaces. Movies and breakfast are included, and there is an excellent restaurant on the premises. Rooms for the handicapped are available and pets are allowed. *4350 Barnes Rd., 95403 (River Rd. exit west from Hwy. 101), tel. 707/575–7350 or 800/421–2584 in CA. 44 rooms. Facilities: spa. AE, CB, DC, MC, V.*

Moderate-Very Expensive **Doubletree Round Barn Inn.** Many rooms in this large, modern, multistory hotel on a hilltop have views of the valley and vineyards; the Burgundy, Cabernet, Chardonnay, Chablis, and Riesling buildings have especially fine views. Spacious rooms have work-size desks and functional and comfortable furnishings. There are rooms for nonsmokers and the handicapped, and patio rooms overlooking the pool. Golf and tennis are available at the adjacent Fountaingrove Country Club for additional fees; there's a courtesy shuttle to Santa Rosa and a jogging path. *3555 Round Barn Blvd., 95401 (Old Redwood Hwy., exit east from Hwy. 101), tel. 707/523–7555 or 800/833–9595. 252 rooms with bath. Facilities: restaurant, bar, lounge, pool, spa, room service, valet service. AE, DC, MC, V.*

Moderate-Expensive ★ **Fountaingrove Inn.** This new, elegant, and comfortable inn boasts a redwood sculpture, *Equus III*, and a wall of cascading water in the lobby. Rooms have work spaces with modem jacks. Buffet breakfast is included, and there's an exceptional restaurant. Senior citizen discounts and rooms for nonsmokers and the handicapped are available. *101 Fountaingrove Pkwy., 95403, tel. 707/578–6101 or 800/222–6101 in CA. 85 rooms. Facilities: lap pool, spa, room service, movies. AE, CB, DC, MC, V.*

Moderate **Los Robles Lodge.** This pleasant, relaxed motel has comfort-
★ able rooms overlooking a grassy, landscaped pool. Rooms for the handicapped and nonsmokers are available. Pets are allowed except in executive rooms, which have jacuzzis. A DJ provides nightly entertainment. *925 Edwards Ave., 95401 (Steele La. exit west from Hwy. 101), tel. 707/545–6330 or 800/ 552–1001. 105 rooms. Facilities: restaurant, coffee shop, lounge, pool, outdoor Jacuzzi, laundry. AE, DC, MC, V.*

Inexpensive **Best Western Hillside Inn.** Some rooms at this cozy, nicely land-scaped small motel have balconies or patios. Kitchenettes and suites are available. Pets are allowed. *2901 4th St., 95409 (at Farmers La., 2 mi east off Hwy. 101 on Hwy. 12), tel. 707/546–9353 or 800/528–1234. 35 rooms. Facilities: pool, restaurant, sauna, shuffleboard. AE, DC, MC, V.*

Sonoma **Sonoma Mission Inn.** This elegantly restored 1920s resort
Very Expensive blends Mediterranean and early California architecture. It's early Hollywood—you half expect Gloria Swanson to sweep through the lobby. The location is unexpected, off the main street of tiny, and anything but posh, Boyes Hot Springs. The grounds are nicely landscaped, and the accommodations include suites. This is the home of the *The Spa Cookbook*, and there are extensive spa facilities (fee for health club). *18140 Sonoma Hwy. (Hwy. 12 north of Sonoma), Box 1447, 95476, tel. 707/938–9000; 800/358–9022 or in CA, 800/862–4945. 170 rooms. Facilities: restaurant, coffee shop, 2 bars, lounge, 2 pools, weight room, steam room, Jacuzzis, sauna, tennis. AE, CB, DC, MC, V.*

Moderate-Expensive **Best Western Sonoma Valley Inn.** Just one block from the town plaza, this new motel features balconies, handcrafted furni-ture, wood-burning fireplaces, and whirlpool baths. Conti-nental breakfast and a complimentary split of wine are in-cluded. Senior discounts, kitchenettes, and rooms for nonsmokers and the handicapped are available. *550 2nd St. W, 95476, tel. 707/938–9200 or 800/334–5784 in CA. 72 rooms. Fa-cilities: pool, whirlpool, laundry. AE, CB, DC, MC, V.*

Sonoma Hotel. At the edge of Sonoma's plaza, this hotel, built in 1870, has been carefully restored, and each of its rooms fur-nished with antiques in an attempt to re-create a Victorian country inn. There's no television, but Continental breakfast and a complimentary split of wine are included. The restaurant specializes in California country cuisine. *110 W. Spain St., 95476, tel. 707/996–2996. 5 rooms with bath, 12 with shared bath. Facilities: bar. AE, MC, V.*

Windsor **Redwood Royale Hometel.** This clean, no-frills motel is a bar-
Inexpensive gain for an economy-minded family. Each unit has a bedroom, bath, kitchen, and living/dining area, and the rate is the same for one to four persons. Kitchen items are available for rent. The motel is on 2½ acres, and there is secured parking for RVs. *8900 Bell Rd., 95492, tel. 707/838–9771. 80 units. Facilities: pool, laundry. AE, MC, V.*

Yountville **Vintage Inn.** All rooms in this luxurious new inn have fire-
Very Expensive places, whirlpool baths, refrigerators, private verandas or patios, handpainted fabrics, window seats, and shuttered win-

dows. Continental breakfast with champagne and afternoon tea are provided. Bike rental and hot-air ballooning are available in season. *6541 Washington St., 94599, tel. 707/944–1112; 800/982–5539; in CA, 800/351–1133. 80 rooms with bath. Facilities: lap pool, spa, tennis. AE, DC, MC, V.*

Napa Valley Lodge. Spacious rooms overlook vineyards and valley in this California hacienda-style lodge with tile roofs, covered walkways, balconies, patios, and colorful gardens. Freshly brewed coffee is provided in rooms, as well as Continental breakfast and the morning paper. Some rooms have fireplaces and pets are allowed. Kitchenettes and rooms for nonsmokers and the handicapped are available. *Madison St. and Hwy. 29, Box L, 94599, tel. 707/944–2468 or 800/368–2468. 55 rooms. Facilities: exercise room, pool, spa, sauna, valet service, refrigerators. AE, DC, MC, V.*

Moderate-Expensive **Napa Valley Railway Inn.** This unusual establishment is made up of nine vintage railcars on the original track of the Napa Valley Railroad. Each car is now an air-conditioned suite, with sitting area, queen-size brass beds, skylights and bay windows, and full tiled baths. Wine and coffee are provided. *6503 Washington St., 94599, tel. 707/944–2000. 9 rooms with bath. MC, V.*

The Arts and Nightlife

Galleries throughout the Wine Country display the work of local artists: painters, sculptors, potters, and jewelry makers. The **Luther Burbank Performing Arts Center** in Santa Rosa (tel. 707/546–3600, box office open Mon.–Sat. noon–6) has a full calendar of concerts, plays, and other performances with both locally and internationally known performers. Wineries often schedule concerts and music festivals during the summer.

Nightlife in the Wine Country is best savored in a leisurely, elegant dinner at one of the restaurants for which the area is justly famous. Many of the larger hotels and motels often feature live music on weekends.

6 San Francisco

The Golden Gate, sailboats on the bay, the hills and the cable cars, the restored Victorian "Painted Ladies," and the whiteness of the fog—if these are your dreams, they will come to life in San Francisco. As it enters the last decade of the 20th century, however, the city is facing some hard realities: the shift of economic power to Southern California, the AIDS epidemic, and, most recently, the devastating earthquake of October 1989, which caused large-scale destruction and loss of life in the city and the surrounding area. San Francisco may be your dream vacation, but it is also a real city dealing with real problems.

The Bay Area's 1989 earthquake destroyed a number of homes in San Francisco's Marina District and several older industrial buildings south of Market Street, and damaged several major stretches of freeway. Extensions of Interstate 280 and U.S. 101 remained closed into 1990 for repairs, and at press time, the fate of the elevated Embarcadero Freeway remains undecided. In Oakland, the collapsed section of Interstate 880 was demolished, and a permanent replacement may not be completed until the mid-1990s. Visitors who plan to drive to and around San Francisco should consult the AAA or the San Francisco Convention and Visitors Bureau for an update on road conditions.

Arriving and Departing

By Plane
Airports and Airlines
San Francisco International Airport is just south of the city, off U.S. 101. Among the airlines serving San Francisco are Alaska Air, American, Continental, Delta, Republic, Southwest, TWA, United and USAir. International carriers include Air Canada, Canadian Pacific, Japan Air Lines, British Airways, China Airlines, Qantas, Air New Zealand, Mexicana, and Pan American. Many of these same airlines serve the Oakland Airport, which is not much farther away from downtown.

Between the Airport and Downtown
The Airporter (tel. 415/495–8404) provides bus service between downtown and the airport, making the round of downtown hotels. Buses run every 20 minutes, 5 AM–midnight. The fare is $5 one way.

For $9, **Supershuttle** will take you from the airport to anywhere within the city limits of San Francisco. At the airport, after picking up your luggage, call 415/871–7800 and a van will pick you up within five minutes. To go to the airport, make reservations (tel. 415/558–8500) 24 hours in advance.

Taxis to or from downtown take 30 minutes and average $30.

By Train
Amtrak (tel. 800/USA–RAIL) trains (the *Zephyr*, from Chicago via Denver, and the *Coast Starlight*, traveling between San Diego and Seattle) stop at the Oakland Depot, from which buses will take you across the Bay Bridge to the Transbay Terminal at 1st and Mission streets in San Francisco.

By Bus
Greyhound serves San Francisco from a depot at 50 7th Street (tel. 415/558–6789). **Trailways** uses the Transbay terminal at First and Mission streets (tel. 415/982–6400).

By Car
I-80 finishes its westward journey from New York's George Washington Bridge at the Bay Bridge, linking Oakland and San Francisco. U.S. 101, running north–south through the whole

90

Exploring San Francisco *(Boxes Refer to Detail Maps)*

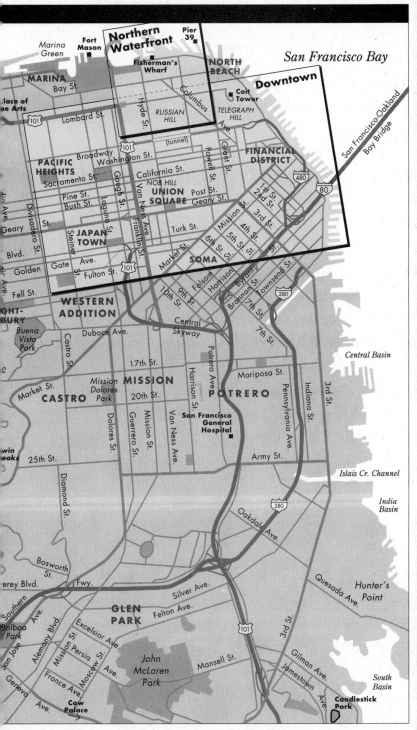

state, enters the city across the Golden Gate Bridge and continues on south down the peninsula, along the west side of the bay.

Getting Around

By BART **Bay Area Rapid Transit** (tel. 415/788–BART) sends air-conditioned aluminum trains at speeds of up to 80 miles an hour across the bay between San Francisco and Oakland, Berkeley, Concord, Richmond, and Fremont in the East Bay. Trains also travel south from the city as far as Daly City. Wall maps in the stations list destinations and fares (85¢–$3). Trains run Monday–Saturday 6 AM–midnight, Sunday 9 AM–midnight.

A $2.60 excursion ticket buys a three-county tour. You can visit any of the 34 stations for up to four hours as long as you exit and enter at the same station.

By Bus The **San Francisco Municipal Railway System,** or **Muni** (tel. 415/673–MUNI), includes buses and trolleys, surface street cars, and the new below-surface street cars as well as cable cars. There is 24-hour service, and the fare is 85¢ (exact change required), with free transfers available.

A $6 pass good for unlimited travel all day on all routes can be purchased from conductors on cable cars.

By Cable Car "They turn corners almost at right angles; cross other lines, and for all I know, may run up the sides of houses," wrote Rudyard Kipling in 1889. In June 1984, the 109-year-old system returned to service after a $58.2-million overhaul. Because the cable cars were declared a National Historic Landmark in 1964, renovation methods and materials had to preserve the historical and traditional qualities of Andrew Hallidie's system. The rehabilitated moving landmark has been designed to withstand another century of use.

The Powell-Mason line (No. 59) and the Powell-Hyde line (No. 60) begin at Powell and Market streets near Union Square and terminate at Fisherman's Wharf. The California Street line (No. 61) runs east–west from Market Street near the Embarcadero to Van Ness Avenue. Adult fare is $2; $1 children 5–17.

By Taxi Rates are high in the city, though most rides are relatively short, and it is almost impossible to hail a passing cab. Weekends are especially difficult. Either phone or use the nearest hotel taxi stand to grab a cab. See the Yellow Pages for numbers of taxi companies.

By Car Driving can be a challenge in San Francisco, what with the hills, the one-way streets, and the traffic. Take it easy, remember to curb your wheels when parking on hills, and use public transportation whenever possible. It's a great city for walking and a terrible city for parking. Finding a spot in North Beach at night, for instance, may be impossible.

Important Addresses and Numbers

Tourist Information The **San Francisco Convention and Visitors Bureau** maintains a visitors information center on the lower level at Hallidie Plaza (Powell and Market streets). The location is very convenient (three blocks from Union Square, near the cable car turnaround and the Powell Street entrance to BART), so it's well worth stopping in. *Weekdays 9–5:30, Sat. 9–3, Sun. 10–2. 24-hour information: tel. 415/974–6900.*

Emergencies **Police and Ambulance.** Telephone 911 for emergency assistance.

Doctor Two hospitals with 24-hour emergency rooms are:

San Francisco General Hospital (1001 Potrero Ave., tel. 415/821–8200).

Medical Center at the University of California, San Francisco (500 Parnassus Ave., at 3rd Ave., near Golden Gate Park, tel. 415/476–1000).

Access Health Care (1604 Union St. at Franklin, tel. 415/775–7766; 26 California at Drumm, tel. 415/397–2881) provides drop-in medical care at two San Francisco locations, daily 8–8. No membership is necessary.

Pharmacies There are no 24-hour pharmacies in San Francisco, though some have extended hours and some deliver.

Walgreen Drugstore. *135 Powell St., near Union Sq., tel. 415/391–4433. Open Mon.–Sat. 8 AM–midnight, Sun. 9 AM–8 PM. AE, MC, V.*

The Mandarin Pharmacy. *895 Washington St., in Chinatown, tel. 415/989–9292. Free deliveries. Open Mon.–Fri. 10–6:30, Sat. 10–6. MC, V.*

Guided Tours

Orientation Tours **Gray Line** offers a variety of tours of the city, the Bay Area, and Northern California. The city tour, on buses or double-decker buses, lasts 3½ hours and departs from the Transbay Terminal at 1st and Mission five to six times daily. Gray Line also picks up at centrally located hotels. *Tel. 415/558–9400. Tours daily. Make reservations the day before. Cost: $21.50 adults, $10.75 children.*

The Great Pacific Tour uses 13-passenger vans for its daily 3½-hour city tour. Bilingual guides may be requested. Pickups at major hotels. Tours are available to Monterey, the Wine Country, and Muir Woods. *Tel. 415/626–4499. Tours daily. Make reservations the day before or, possibly, the same day. Cost: $25 adults, $22 senior citizens, $18 children 5–11, under 5 free.*

San Francisco Scenic Route. Near Escapes (Box 193005, San Francisco 94119, tel. 415/921–1392) has produced an audio cassette with music and sound effects that will take you in your own car "where the tour buses can't go." It will guide you past Fisherman's Wharf, Chinatown, Golden Gate Park, Twin Peaks, Ghirardelli Square, Mission Dolores, the Civic Center, etc. The cassette comes with a route map. It's available in a few local outlets, or you can get it mail-order for $12 (or $14 with Visa or MasterCard).

Special-Interest Tours **Near Escapes** (Box 193005, San Francisco 94119, tel. 415/921–1392) plans unusual activities in the city and around the Bay Area. Recent tours and activities include tours of a Hindu temple in the East Bay, the Lawrence Berkeley Laboratory, the aircraft maintenance facility at the San Francisco Airport, and the quicksilver mines south of San Jose. The Julia Morgan Architectural Tour focuses on the work of one of the most prominent California architects of the early 20th century. Send

$1 and a SASE for a schedule for the month you plan to visit San Francisco.

Walking Tours **Chinese Cultural Heritage Foundation** (tel. 415/986–1822) offers two walking tours of Chinatown. The Heritage Walk leaves Saturday at 2 PM and lasts about 2 hours. *Cost: $9 adults, $2 children under 12.* The Culinary Walk, a 3-hour stroll through the markets and food shops, plus a dim sum lunch, is on Wednesdays at 10:30 AM. *Cost: $18 adults, $9 children.*

City Guides. The Friends of the Library run free walking tours all over the city, lasting 1–1½ hours, slightly longer on weekends. Tours include the Gold Rush City, Historic Market Street, City Hall, North Beach, Coit Tower, Golden Gate Bridge, and the Presidio. *For a monthly schedule, write (and send SASE to) Friends of the Library—City Guides, San Francisco Public Library, Main Branch, Civic Center, San Francisco 94102, tel. 415/558–3981. No reservations. Admission free.*

Dashiell Hammett Tour. Don Herron gives 4-hour, 3-mile literary walking tours designed around the life of Hammett and his character Sam Spade. Tours depart Saturday at noon between May and August from the main library at 200 Larkin Street. *Tel. 415/564–7021. Cost: $5.*

Castro District. Trevor Hailey leads 3½-hour tours focusing on the history and development of the city's gay and lesbian community, beginning at 10 AM most days from Castro and Market streets. *Tel. 415/550–8110. Cost: $25, including breakfast or lunch.*

Exploring

Few cities in the world cram so much diversity into so little space. San Francisco is a relatively small city, with fewer than 750,000 residents nested on a 46.6-square-mile tip of land between the bay and the Pacific Ocean.

San Franciscans cherish the city's colorful past, and many older buildings have been spared from demolition and converted into modern offices and shops. Today the city is again establishing strong commercial relations with the nations of the Pacific Rim. For more than a century, the port city has been trafficking with the peoples of the world. The unusually large number of people with ties to other cultures flavors the cuisine, commerce, and charisma of the city. It also encourages a tolerance for a variety of customs and beliefs.

San Francisco is a maze of one-way streets and restricted parking zones. Public parking garages and lots tend to be expensive, as are the hotel parking spaces. The city's famed 40-plus hills can be a problem for drivers new to the terrain. People who know the city agree that one of the best ways to see and experience its many moods and distinctive neighborhoods is on foot. Those museums on wheels—the cable cars—and the numerous buses or trolleys can take you to or near many of the area's attractions. In the exploring tours that follow, we have often included information on public transportation.

Hills are a daily challenge to visitor and resident alike; good walking shoes are essential. Climate, too, is a consideration in deciding what to wear. There are dramatic temperature changes, especially in summer, when the afternoon fog rolls in. Winds are often a problem, both on the bay and cityside. Year-round, layered clothing will be most adaptable to changing conditions; a cap or scarf and sunglasses will be useful. Casual city togs are appropriate; shorts and tank tops are for Southern California's climate.

Union Square Area

Numbers in the margin correspond with points of interest on the Downtown San Francisco map.

Since 1850, Union Square has been the heart of San Francisco's downtown. Its name derives from a series of violent pro-Union demonstrations staged in the hilly area just prior to the Civil War. This is the center of the city's finest department stores as well as elegant boutiques. There are 40 hotels within a 3-block walk, and the downtown theater district is nearby.

The square is a 2.6-acre oasis of palms, boxwood, and seasonal flowers, peopled with a kaleidoscope of characters: office workers sunning and brown-bagging, street musicians, always at least one mime, several vocal and determined preachers, and the ever-increasing parade of panhandlers. Smartly dressed women and camera-laden tourists usually hurry past the denizens. Throughout the year, the square hosts numerous public events: fashion shows, free noontime concerts, ethnic celebrations, and noisy demonstrations.

Auto and bus traffic is often gridlocked on the four streets bordering the square. Post, Stockton, and Geary are one-way, while Powell runs in both directions along the cable car line. Union Square covers a convenient but costly 4-story underground garage. Close to 3,000 cars use it on busy holiday shopping and strolling days.

❶ Any visitor's first stop should be the **San Francisco Visitors Information Center** (tel. 415/391–2001) in Hallidie Plaza at Powell and Market streets. It is open daily, and the multilingual staff will answer specific questions as well as provide maps, brochures, and information on daily events. The office provides 24-hour recorded information.

The **cable car terminus,** also at Powell and Market, is the starting point for two of the three operating lines. Before 1900, there were 600 cable cars spanning a network of 100 miles. Today, there are 39 cars in the three lines, and the network covers just 12 miles. Most of the cars date from the last century, though the cars and lines had a complete $58.2-million overhaul in the early 1980s. There are seats for about 30 passengers, with usually that number standing or strap-hanging. If possible, plan your cable-car ride for mid-morning or mid-afternoon during the week to avoid crowds. Summertime, there are often long lines to board any of the three systems. (*See* Getting Around, above.)

❷ A 3-block stroll along bustling Powell Street leads to **Union Square,** with its fashionable stores, fine hotels, and photogenic flower stalls, making the square an improvisational stage for local life. Center stage, the Victory Monument, by Robert Ingersoll Aitken, commemorates Commodore George Dewey's victory over the Spanish fleet at Manila in 1898. The 97-foot Corinthian column, topped by a bronze figure symbolizing naval

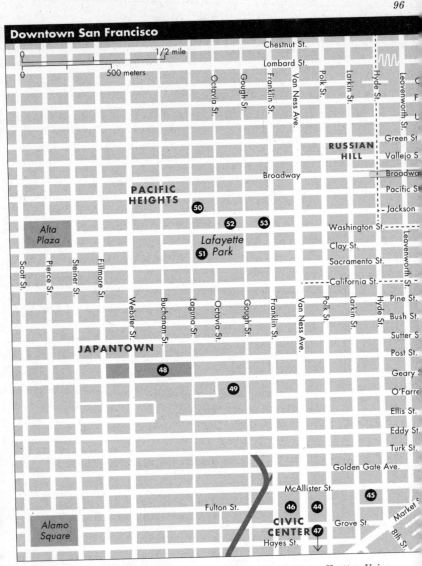

Downtown San Francisco

Chestnut St.
Lombard St.
Octavia St.
Gough St.
Franklin St.
Van Ness Ave.
Polk St.
Larkin St.
Hyde St.
Leavenworth St.

Green St
Vallejo S
RUSSIAN HILL
Broadwa
Pacific St
Jackson

Broadway

PACIFIC HEIGHTS
Washington St.
Clay St.
Sacramento St.
California St.
Leavenworth St.

Alta Plaza

Scott St.
Pierce St.
Steiner St.
Fillmore St.

Lafayette Park

Pine St.
Bush St.
Sutter S
Post St.

Webster St.
Buchanan St.
Laguna St.
Octavia St.
Gough St.
Franklin St.
Van Ness Ave.
Polk St.
Larkin St.
Hyde St.

JAPANTOWN

Geary S
O'Farre
Ellis St.
Eddy St.
Turk St.

Golden Gate Ave.

McAllister St.

Alamo Square

Fulton St.

CIVIC CENTER

Grove St.

Market
8th St.

Hayes St.

Ansel Adams Center, **20**
Bank of America, **11**
Cable Car Museum, **43**
California Historical Society, **50**
Chinatown Gate, **21**
Chinese Culture Center, **25**
Chinese Historical Society, **29**

Chinese Six Companies, **30**
Church of St. Francis of Assisi, **34**
City Hall, **44**
City Lights Bookstore, **35**
Coit Tower, **36**
Crocker Galleria, **8**
Curran Theater, **5**
Embarcadero Center, **18**

Fairmont Hotel, **39**
Ferry Building, **17**
450 Sutter, **9**
Geary Theater, **4**
Grace Cathedral, **38**
Haas-Lilienthal House, **53**
Hallidie Building, **16**
Huntington Hotel, **42**

Hyatt on Union Square, **6**
Japan Center, **48**
Lafayette Park, **51**
Maiden Lane, **7**
Mark Hopkins Hotel, **40**
Mills Building and Tower, **14**
Mission Dolores, **47**
Old Chinese Telephone Exchange, **27**

San Francisco Bay

Chestnut St.
Lombard St.

TELEGRAPH HILL

NORTH BEACH

Columbus Ave.
Grant Ave.
Mason St.
Powell St.
Stockton St.

Embarcadero
Front St.
Davis St.
Drumm St.
Davis St.
Front St.
Spear St.
Steuart St.

CHINATOWN

Montgomery St.
Sansome St.
Battery St.
Kearny St.
Halleck St.

N

UNION SQUARE

Main St.
Beale St.
Fremont St.
1st St.

Maiden Ln.

SOMA

Market St.
Mission St.
New Montgomery St.
2nd St.
3rd St.
Hawthorne St.

4th St.
5th St.
Howard St.

conquest, was dedicated by President Theodore Roosevelt in 1903 and withstood the 1906 quake.

After the earthquake and fire in 1906, the square was dubbed "Little St. Francis" because of the temporary shelter erected for residents of the St. Francis Hotel. The actor John Barrymore was among the guests pressed into volunteering to stack bricks in the square. His uncle, the thespian John Drew, remarked, "It took an act of God to get John out of bed and the United States government to get him to work."

❸ The St. Francis Hotel, on the southwest corner of Post and Powell, was built here in 1904 and gutted by the 1906 disaster. The second-oldest hotel in the city was conceived by Charles Crocker and his associates as an elegant hostelry for their bonanza millionaire friends. Swift service and sumptuous surroundings were hallmarks of the property. A sybarite's dream, the separate Turkish baths had ocean water piped in. A new, larger, more luxurious hotel opened in 1907 to attract loyal clients among the world's rich and powerful. Today, you can relax over a traditional teatime or opt for champagne and caviar in the dramatic art deco Compass Rose lounge in the lobby. Elaborate Chinese screens, secluded seating alcoves, and soothing background music make it an ideal time-out after frantic shopping or sightseeing. For dining before or after the theater (within walking distance), visit the award-winning Victor's. After a breathtaking ride up 30-plus stories in an outside glass-walled elevator, guests enter a warm, wood-paneled lobby area with recessed bookshelves housing leather-bound classics. Floor-to-ceiling windows offer spectacular views of the bay and the city.

Both the Geary and Curran theaters are a few blocks west on
❹ Geary. The **Geary** (415 Geary), home of the renowned American Conservatory Theatre, was damaged during the 1989 earthquake and will remain closed for repairs through late
❺ 1991. The **Curran** (445 Geary) is noted for showcasing traveling companies of the "Best of Broadway." The San Francisco Ticket Box Office Service (STBS) (tel. 415/433-STBS) is in a booth on the Stockton Street side of Union Square, opposite Maiden Lane. Open from noon till 7:30 PM, Tuesday through Saturday, it provides day-of-performance tickets (cash only) to all types of performing arts events at half price.

❻ Just a dash up from STBS, the striking **Grand Hyatt Hotel** offers exciting city views. Stop and examine local sculptor Ruth Asawa's fantasy fountain honoring the city's hills, bridges, and unusual architecture plus a wonder world of real and mythical creatures. Children and friends helped Ms. Asawa shape the hundreds of tiny figures created from baker's clay and then assembled on 41 large panels from which molds were made for the bronze casting. The artist's distinctive designs decorate many public areas in the city. You may see her famous mermaid fountain at Ghirardelli Square.

❼ Pop around the corner into **Maiden Lane,** which runs from Stockton to Kearny streets. Known as Morton Street in the raffish Barbary Coast era, this red-light district reported at least one murder a week. But the 1906 fire destroyed the brothels, and the street emerged as Maiden Lane. It has since become a chic and costly wayfare. The 2 blocks are closed to vehicles from 11 AM until 4 PM. Daytimes, take-out snacks can be enjoyed resting under the gay, umbrella-shaped tables. Masses of daffodils and bright blossoms and balloons bedeck the lane during the annual spring festival. A carnival mood prevails, with zany street musicians, artsy-craftsy people, and throngs of spectators.

Note **140 Maiden Lane:** This handsome brick structure is the only Frank Lloyd Wright building in San Francisco. With its circular, interior ramp and skylights, it is said to have been a model for his designs for the Guggenheim Museum in New York. It now houses the Circle Gallery, a showcase of contemporary art. Be sure to study the unique limited-edition art jewelry designed by internationally acclaimed Erté. *Open Mon.–Wed. and Fri.–Sat. 10–6, Thurs. 10–7, Sun. 11–4.*

❽ Still to be seen is the **Crocker Galleria** at Post and Kearny streets, an imaginatively designed 3-level complex of fine dining and shopping capped by a dazzling glass dome. Sutter Street hosts prestigious art galleries, antiques dealers, smart hotels, and noted designer boutiques. Art deco aficionados will want to linger at the striking medical/dental office building at **❾ 450 Sutter.** Handsome Mayan-inspired designs are used in both the exterior and interior surfaces of the 1930 terra-cotta-colored skyscraper.

Time Out Most stores and shops here open about 9:30–10 AM. Breakfasting beforehand is a way to see the area before the day's traffic and shoppers are out in force. **Mama's** (398 Geary St.) is a long-time favorite for either light or full breakfast selections. Or blow the day's meal budget at **Campton Place Hotel.** Wonderful breads and muffins, delicious hash, and out-of-season fruits are lavishly served. *340 Stockton, tel. 415/781–5155. Reservations suggested for brunch. Open weekdays 7–11 AM, Sat. 8–11:30 AM, Sun. brunch, 8 AM–2:30 PM.*

The Financial District

The heart of San Francisco's commerce is Montgomery Street. It was here in 1848 that Sam Brannan proclaimed the historic gold discovery on the American River. At that time all the streets below Montgomery between California and Broadway were wharves. At least 100 ships were abandoned by frantic crews and passengers caught up in the '49 gold fever. Many of the wrecks served as warehouses or were used as foundations for new constructions.

The financial district is roughly bounded by Kearny Street on the west, Washington Street on the north, and Market Street on the southeast. Workdays it is a congested canyon of soaring skyscrapers, gridlock traffic, and bustling pedestrians. Weekends the quiet streets allow walkers to admire the distinctive architecture. Unfortunately, the museums in corporate headquarters are closed then.

❿ The city's most-photographed high rise is the 853-foot **Transamerica Pyramid** at 600 Montgomery, between Clay and Washington. Designed by William Pereira & Associates in 1972, the $34-million controversial symbol has become more acceptable to local purists as it has gained San Francisco instant recognition worldwide. There is a public viewing area on the 27th floor (open weekdays 9–4). You can relax in the city's only redwood grove along the east side of the building.

⑪ The granite and marble **Bank of America** building dominates the territory bounded by California, Pine, Montgomery, and Kearny streets. The 52-story carnelian marble-covered complex is crowned by a chic cocktail and dining restaurant. As in almost all corporate headquarters, the interiors display impressive original art, while outdoor plazas include avant-garde sculptures. A massive abstract black granite sculpture designed by the Japanese artist Masayuki in the mall has been dubbed the "Banker's Heart" by local wags.

⑫ Diagonally across Montgomery is the **Wells Fargo History Museum** (420 Montgomery St.). There were no formal banks in San Francisco in the early years of the gold rush, and miners often entrusted their gold dust to saloonkeepers. In 1852, Wells Fargo opened its first bank in the city. The History Room displays samples of nuggets and gold dust from major mines, a mural-size map of the Mother Lode, original art by Western artists Charlie Russell and Maynard Dixon, mementos of the poet bandit Black Bart, and letters of credit and old bank drafts. The showpiece is the red century-old Concord stagecoach, which in the mid-1850s carried 15 passengers from St. Louis to San Francisco in three weeks. *Admission free. Open banking days 9–5.*

⑬ The **Russ Building** (235 Montgomery St.) was called "the skyscraper" when it was built in 1927. The Gothic design was modeled after the Chicago Tribune Tower, and until the 1960s it was San Francisco's tallest—at just 31 stories. Prior to the 1906 earthquake and fire, the site was occupied by the Russ House, considered one of the finest hostelries in the city.

⑭ The **Mills Building and Tower** (220 Montgomery St.) was the outstanding pre-fire building in the financial district. The 10-story all-steel construction had its own electric plant in the basement. The original Burnham and Root design of white marble and brick was erected in 1891–92. The 1906 fire damage was slight; its walls were somewhat scorched but were easily refurbished. Two compatible additions east on Bush Street were added in 1914 and 1918 by Willis Polk, and in 1931 a 22-story tower completed the design.

Ralph Stackpole's monumental 1930 granite sculptural groups *Earth's Fruitfulness* and *Man's Inventive Genius*, flank anoth-
⑮ er imposing structure, the **Pacific Stock Exchange** (which dates from 1915), on the south side of Pine at Sansome. The Stock Tower around the corner at 15 Sansome is a 1930 modern classic by architects Miller and Pfleuger, featuring an art-deco gold ceiling and black marble-walled entry. *Pacific Stock Exchange, 301 Pine St., 94104, tel. 415/393–7969. Tours by 2-week advance reservation; minimum 5 persons.*

⑯ Stroll down Sansome Street to Sutter Street. The **Hallidie Building** (130 Sutter St.) was built as an investment by the University of California Board of Regents in 1918 and was named for cable car inventor Andrew S. Hallidie, also a university regent. It is believed to be the world's first all-glass-curtain-wall structure. Architect Willis Polk's revolutionary design hangs a foot beyond the reinforced concrete of the frame. It dominates the block with its reflecting glass and decorative exterior fire escapes that appear to be metal balconies. On the sixth floor is the American Institute of Architects' gallery, open to the public.

From here, it's a short walk back to Union Square.

The Embarcadero and Lower Market Street

⑰ The trademark of the port is the quaint **Ferry Building,** where Market Street meets the Embarcadero. The clock tower is 230 feet high and was modeled by Arthur Page Brown after the campanile of Seville's cathedral. The four great clock faces on the tower, powered by the swinging action of a 14-foot pendulum, stopped at 5:17 AM the morning of April 18, 1906, and stayed that way for the 12 months that followed. The 1896 building survived the quake and is the headquarters of the Port Authority and the World Trade Center. A waterfront promenade extends from this point to the Oakland Bay Bridge. It's great for jogging, enjoying the sailboats on the bay (if the day is not too windy), or enjoying a picnic. Ferries from here operate to Sausalito, Larkspur, and Tiburon.

⑱ Strolling back up Market, one's attention is drawn to the huge **Embarcadero Center** complex, frequently dubbed "Rockefeller Center West." A three-tiered pedestrian mall links the buildings, which include a variety of shops, restaurants, and offices as well as nearby high-rise residential towers and town-house condos. Much attention has been given to attractive landscaping throughout the development. The Hyatt Regency Hotel, Embarcadero Five, designed by John Portman, is noted for the spectacular lobby and 20-story hanging garden. Just in front of the hotel is the Justin Herman Plaza. There are art and crafts shows, street musicians, and mimes on weekends year round. Kite-flying is popular here. A huge concrete sculpture, the Vaillancourt Fountain, has had legions of critics since its installation in 1971. Most of the time the fountain does not work, and many feel it is an awkward eyesore.

⑲ The **Old San Francisco Mint,** at Fifth and Mission streets, reopened as a museum in 1973. The century-old brick and stone building exhibits a priceless collection of gold coins. Visitors tour the vaults and can strike a souvenir medal on an 1869 press. *Admission free. Open weekdays, 10–4.*

South of Market has in recent years been dubbed "SoMa," and it is frequently compared to the highly successful renaissance of New York's SoHo. This is the happening place after dark. The machine shops, printers, and warehouses are losing out to restaurants, bars, discos, and clubs.

⑳ The **Ansel Adams Center,** SoMa's first museum, operates five exhibition galleries for photography, including one always devoted to Adams' work. It is operated by the Friends of Photography, a group Adams helped establish. There is also a bookstore and a library. *250 Fourth St., tel. 415/495–7000. Admission, $3 adults, $2 senior citizens and students. Open Tues.–Sun. 11–6.*

Chinatown

A city within a city, this is the largest Chinese community outside Asia. Approximately 100,000 Chinese live in a 24-block downtown area just south of North Beach (and in the Richmond district's "New" Chinatown). Chinatown has been revitalized by the fairly recent immigration of southeast Asians who have added new character and life to the neighborhood. Downtown

Chinatown is officially defined as reaching from "Bay Street
south to California, and from Sansome at the edge of downtown
west to Van Ness," which includes much of Russian and Nob
hills.

Visitors usually enter Chinatown through the green-tiled
㉑ dragon-crowned **Chinatown Gate** at Bush Street and Grant Avenue. To best savor Chinatown, explore it on foot (it's not far
from Union Square), even though you may find the bustling,
noisy, colorful stretches of Grant and Stockton streets north of
Bush difficult to navigate. Parking is rare, and traffic is impossible. As in Hong Kong, most families shop daily for fresh
meats, vegetables, and bakery products. This street world
shines with much good-luck crimson and gold; giant berib-
boned floral wreaths mark openings of new bakeries, bazaars,
and banks. The nighttime is as busy here as the daytime, with
almost 100 restaurants squeezed into a 14-block area.

㉒ The handsome brick **Old St. Mary's Church** at Grant and California served as the city's Catholic cathedral until 1891
Granite quarried in China was used to build the structure
which was dedicated in 1854. Diagonally across the intersec
㉓ tion is **St. Mary's Park,** a tranquil setting for local sculptor
Beniamino (Benny) Bufano's heroic stainless-steel and rose-
colored-granite Sun Yat Sen. The 12-foot statue of the founder
of the Republic of China was installed in 1937. Bufano's
stainless-steel-and-mosaic statue of St. Francis welcomes
guests at San Francisco International Airport.

Shopping surrounds the stroller on **Grant Avenue.** Much o
what is offered in the countless curio shops is worthless, and
discerning visitors may be dismayed by the gaudy and glitter
gimcrackery. In recent years, however, a growing number o
large department-store-type operations have opened. Mos
feature an ever-growing array of products from the People's
Republic. You'll find, too, that visiting the Chinese markets
even just window-gazing, is fascinating. Note the dragon
entwined lampposts, the pagoda roofs, and the street sign
with Chinese calligraphy.

The city's first house was built in 1836 at the corner of Gran
and Clay; it was destroyed in the 1906 earthquake. Turn righ
㉔ here and a short walk brings you to **Portsmouth Square,** the po
tato patch that became the plaza for Yerba Buena. This is where
Montgomery raised the American flag in 1846. Note the bronze
galleon atop a 9-foot granite shaft. Designed by Bruce Porter
the sculpture was erected in 1919 in memory of Robert Loui
Stevenson, who often visited the site during his 1879–80 resi
dence. Early in the morning, the park is crowded with peopl
performing solemn tai chi rituals.

㉕ From here you can walk to the **Chinese Culture Center,** which
displays frequent exhibits of Chinese-American art as well a
traveling exhibits of Chinese culture. The center also offer
Saturday-afternoon walking tours of historic points in China
town. *In the Holiday Inn, 750 Kearny St., tel. 415/986–1822
Admission free. Open Tues.–Sat. 10–4.*

㉖ A short block south of the Culture Center is the **Pacific Heri
tage Museum,** in the Bank of Canton building. Display
illustrate the artistic, cultural, and economic history of the Pa
cific Basin peoples. *608 Commercial St. near Montgomery, tel
415/362–4100. Admission free. Open daily 10–4.*

You're on the edge of North Beach now and could easily walk over to City Lights bookstore and other North Beach sites.

The original Chinatown burned down after the 1906 earthquake, and the first building to set the style for the new Chinatown is 3 blocks north, at 743 Washington Street. The (27) three-tiered pagoda called the **Old Chinese Telephone** Exchange was built in 1909.

Waverly Place is noted for ornate painted balconies and Chi-(28) nese temples. **Tien Hou Temple** (125 Waverly Pl.) was dedicated to the Queen of the Heavens and Goddess of the Seven Seas by Day Ju, one of the first three Chinese to arrive in San Francisco in 1852.

(29) The **Chinese Historical Society,** off Grant Avenue, traces the history of Chinese immigrants and their contributions to the state's rail, mining, and fishing industries. *17 Adler Pl., tel. 415/391–1188. Admission free. Open Wed.–Sun. noon–4.*

The other main Chinatown shopping street for everyday needs is **Stockton Street,** which parallels Grant. This is the real heart of Chinatown. Shoppers jostle each other as they pick apart the sidewalk displays of Chinese vegetables. Double-parked trucks unloading crates of chickens or ducks add to the all-day traffic jams. You'll see excellent examples of Chinese architecture along this street. Most noteworthy is the elaborate (30) **Chinese Six Companies** (843 Stockton St.) with its curved roof tiles and elaborate cornices. Folk-art murals grace the walls of an apartment building at Stockton and Pacific. Displays of jade and gold glitter from jewelry windows, for the Chinese value these items above all other ornaments.

Time Out Skip a Big Mac; opt instead for dim sum, a variety of pastries filled with meat, fish, and vegetables, the Chinese version of smorgasbord. More than a dozen Chinese restaurants feature this unusual lunch/brunch adventure from about 11 AM to 3 PM. Usually, stacked food-service carts patrol the premises; customers select from the varied offerings, and the final bill is tabulated by the number of different saucers on the table. Dim-sum restaurants tend to be big, crowded, noisy, cheap, and friendly. Suggestions are often offered by nearby strangers as to what is inside the tempting morsels. Two favorites on Pacific Avenue, two blocks north of Washington Street, between Stockton and Powell, are **Hong Kong Tea House** (835 Pacific Ave.) and **Tung Fong** (808 Pacific Ave.). Many of the smaller, inexpensive Chinese restaurants and cafes do not accept credit cards; some serve beer and wine.

It's an easy half-hour walk back downtown to Union Square via (31) the **Stockton Street Tunnel,** running from Sacramento to Sutter. Completed in 1914, This was the city's first tunnel to accommodate vehicular and pedestrian traffic.

North Beach and Telegraph Hill

Like neighboring Chinatown, North Beach, centered on Columbus Avenue north of Broadway, is best explored on foot. In the early days there truly was a beach. At the time of the gold rush, the bay extended into the hollow between Telegraph and Russian hills, forming a beach. North Beach, less than a square mile, is the most densely populated district in the city and is truly cosmopolitan, but much of the old-world ambience still lingers in this easygoing and polyglot bohemia.

Among the first immigrants to Yerba Buena in the early 1840s were young men from the northern provinces of Italy. By 1848, the village, renamed San Francisco, became an overnight boom town with the discovery of gold. Thousands more poured into the burgeoning area, seeking the golden dream. For many, the trail ended in San Francisco. The Genoese started the still-active fishing industry as well as much-needed produce businesses. Later, the Sicilians emerged as leaders of the fishing fleets; eventually they became proprietors of the seafood restaurants lining Fisherman's Wharf. Meanwhile, their Genoese cousins established banking and manufacturing empires.

32 **Washington Square** may well be the daytime social heart of what was once considered "Little Italy." By mid-morning, groups of conservatively dressed elderly Italian men are sunning and sighing on the state of their immediate world—North Beach. Nearby, laughing Asian and Caucasian playmates race through the grass with Frisbees or colorful kites. Multinational denim-clad mothers exchange shopping tips and ethnic recipes. Ancient Chinese matrons stare impassively at the passing parade. Camera-toting tourists focus their lenses on **33** the adjacent Romanesque splendor of **Saints Peter and Paul,** often called "the Italian Cathedral." Built in 1924, it has twin-turreted terra-cotta towers that are local landmarks. On the first Sunday of October, the annual Blessing of the Fleet is celebrated with a mass, followed by a parade to Fisherman's Wharf. Another popular annual event is the Columbus Day pageant.

The 1906 earthquake and fire devastated this area, and the park provided shelter for hundreds of the homeless. **Fior d'Italia,** facing the cathedral, is San Francisco's oldest Italian restaurant. The original opened in 1886 and continued operating in a tent after the 1906 quake until new quarters were ready. Surrounding streets are brimming with savory Italian delicatessens, bakeries, Chinese markets, coffee houses, and ethnic restaurants. Wonderful aromas fill the air. (Coffee beans roasted at **Graffeo** at 733 Columbus, are shipped to customers all over the United States.) You can pick up a good sandwich to go at numerous local delis.

South of Washington Square and just off Columbus is the **34** **Church of Saint Francis of Assisi** (610 Vallejo St.). This 1860 Victorian Gothic building stands on the site of the frame parish church that served the gold-rush Catholic community.

Over the years, North Beach has attracted creative individualists. The "Beat" movement of the 1950s was born, grew up, flourished, and then faltered in this then-predominately Italian enclave. Beat gathering places are gone, and few of the original leaders remain. Poet Lawrence Ferlinghetti still holds **35** court at his **City Lights Bookstore** (261 Columbus St.), but the face of North Beach is changing. The bohemian community has migrated up Grant Avenue, above Columbus. **Grant Avenue** originally called "Calle de la Fundacion," is the oldest street in the city. Each June, a street fair is held on the upper part of Grant, where a cluster of cafes, boutiques, and galleries attracts crowds.

Time Out The richness of North Beach lifestyle is reflected in the numerous cafes. Breakfast at **Caffe Roma** (414 Columbus) and create your own omelet from a list of 11 ingredients. Skip the main room with its pastel murals of cherubs and settle at one of the umbrella-shaded tables on the patio. Moviemaker Francis Ford Coppola is a regular, and the adjoining Millefiori Inn, a charming B&B, frequently hosts film celebrities. Across the street is the **Caffe Puccini** (411 Columbus). It could be Italy: Few of the staff speak English; their cafe latte (coffee, chocolate, cinnamon, and steamed milk) and strains of Italian operas recall *Roman Holiday*. A Saturday morning must is around the corner at **Caffe Trieste** (601 Vallejo). Get there about noon. At 1 PM, the Giotta family's weekly musical begins. The program ranges from Italian pop and folk music to favorite family operas. The Trieste opened in 1956 and became headquarters for the area's beatnik poets, artists, and writers. **Caffe Malvina** (1600 Stockton) started in the 1950s and was among the first U.S. importers of Italian-made espresso machines.

Telegraph Hill residents command some of the best views in the city as well as the most difficult ascent to their aeries. The Greenwich stairs lead up to Coit Tower from Filbert Street, and there are steps down to Filbert on the opposite side of Telegraph Hill. Views are superb en route, but most visitors should either taxi up to the tower or take the Muni bus No. 39 Coit at Washington Square. To catch the bus from Union Square, walk to Stockton and Sutter streets, board the Muni No. 30, and ask for a transfer to use at Washington Square (Columbus and Union streets) to board the No. 39 Coit. Public parking is very limited at the tower, and there are long lines of cars and buses on holidays and weekends winding up the narrow road.

Telegraph Hill rises from the east end of Lombard Street to about 300 feet and is capped with the landmark Coit Tower, dedicated as a monument to the city's volunteer firefighters. Early in the gold rush, an eight-year-old arrived who would become one of the city's most memorable eccentrics: Lillie Hitchcock Coit. Legend relates that at age 17 "Miss Lil" deserted a wedding party and chased down the street after her favorite engine, Knickerbocker No. 5, clad in her bridesmaid finery. She was soon made an honorary member of the Knickerbocker Company, and ever after she signed herself "Lillie Coit 5," in honor of her favorite fire engine. Lillie died in 1929 at the age of 86, leaving the city about $100,000 of her million-dollar-plus estate to "expend in an appropriate manner . . . to the beauty of San Francisco."

36 **Coit Tower** stands as a monument not only to Lillie Coit and the city's firefighters, but also to the influence of the Mexican muralist Diego Rivera. Fresco was Rivera's medium, and it was his style that unified the work of most of the 25 artists who painted the murals in the tower. The murals were commissioned by the U.S. government, a Public Works of Art project. The artists were paid $38 per week. Some were fresh from art schools; others found no market for art in the dark depression days of the early 1930s. An illustrated brochure for sale in the tiny gift shop explains the various murals dedicated to the workers of California. There is a lift to the top providing a panoramic view of both the Bay Bridge and the Golden Gate Bridge; directly offshore is the infamous Alcatraz and just behind it, Angel Island, a hikers' and campers' paradise. Be sure to carry a camera and binoculars.

There are often artists at work in **Pioneer Park** at the foot of the tower. Frequently, small paintings of the scene are offered for sale at modest prices. The impressive bronze statue of Christopher Columbus, "Discoverer of America," was a gift of the local Italian community.

New life and vitality are coming to the hill. Expensive pierfront condominiums, handsome commercial structures, including the impressive Levi Strauss headquarters, attractive restaurants, and young affluent residents are making Telegraph a very desirable habitat.

Nob Hill

Once called the "Hill of Golden Promise," this area became Nob Hill in the 1870s when "the Big Four"—Charles Crocker, Leland Stanford, Mark Hopkins, and Collis Huntington—built their hilltop estates. It is still home to many of the city's "elite" as well as to four of San Francisco's finest hotels.

By 1882, Robert Louis Stevenson called it "the hill of palaces." But the 1906 earthquake and fire destroyed all the palatial mansions. The shell of one survived. The Flood brownstone (1000 California) was built by the Comstock silver baron in 1886 at a reputed cost of $1,500,000. In 1909, the property was purchased by the prestigious **Pacific Union Club.** The 45-room exclusive club remains the bastion of wealthy and powerful men.

Adjacent is a charming small park noted for its festive Christmas decorations and frequent art shows. It was the site of the Collis Huntington home.

Neighbor **Grace Cathedral** (1051 Taylor) is the seat of the Episcopal Church in San Francisco. The soaring Gothic structure took 53 years to build. The gilded bronze doors at the east entrance were taken from casts of Ghiberti's "Gates of Paradise" at the Baptistry in Florence. The superb rose window is illuminated at night. There are often organ recitals on Sundays at 5 PM as well as special programs during the holiday seasons.

What sets the **Fairmont Hotel,** at California and Mason, apart from other luxury hostelries is its legendary history. Since its dazzling 1907 opening, the opulent marble palace has hosted presidents, royalty, and local nabobs. Its eight-room $5,000-per-day penthouse suite was used frequently in the TV series *Hotel.* The lobby sports much red-velvet upholstery, and the stunning Nob Hill spa and fitness club is on the premises. From a terrace at the rear of the building, beyond the shops, you'll have a fine view of the Powell Street cable cars.

The stately **Mark Hopkins Hotel,** across California, is remembered fondly by thousands of World War II veterans who jammed the "Top of the Mark" lounge prior to overseas duty. At California and Powell, the posh **Stanford Court** debuted in 1972, in a remodeled 1909 apartment house. This world-class hotel excels in service and personal attention. The **Huntington** (1075 California) is impeccably British in protecting the privacy of its celebrated guests.

43 The **Cable Car Museum,** at Washington and Mason streets, exhibits photographs, scale models, and other memorabilia of the
cable-car system during its 115 years of service. A 16-minute
film is shown continuously. *Tel. 415/474–1887. Admission free.
Open daily Oct.–Apr. 10–5, May–Sept. 10–6.*

The Civic Center

San Francisco's Civic Center stands as one of the country's
great city, state, and federal building complexes with handsome adjoining cultural institutions. It's the realization of the
theories of turn-of-the-century proponents of the "City Beautiful."

Facing Polk Street, between Grove and McAllister streets, the
44 **City Hall** is a baroque masterpiece of granite and marble, modeled after the Capitol in Washington. Its dome is even higher
than the Washington version, and it dominates the area. Before
the building are formal gardens with fountains, walkways, and
seasonal flower beds. Brooks Exhibit Hall was constructed under this plaza in 1958 to add space for the frequent trade shows
and other events based in the Civic Auditorium on Grove
Street.

San Francisco's increasing numbers of homeless people are often evident in all the city's green spaces. Visitors and residents
should exercise caution while strolling in park areas and deserted business sectors after dark.

45 Across the plaza from the city hall is the main branch of the **San
Francisco Public Library.** History buffs should visit the San
Francisco History Room and Archives on the third floor. Historic photographs, maps, and other memorabilia are carefully
documented for the lay person or research scholar. *Tel. 415/558
–3949. Open Tues. and Fri. noon–6, Thurs. and Sat. 10–6,
Wed. 1–6.*

46 The **Performing Arts Center** encompasses the Veterans Building, the Opera House, and Davies Hall.

On the other (west) side of City Hall, across Van Ness Avenue,
are the Museum of Modern Art, the Opera House, and Davies
Symphony Hall. The northernmost of the three is the Veterans'
Building, whose third and fourth floors house the **Museum of
Modern Art.** The permanent collection includes contemporary
masters Paul Klee, Jackson Pollock, Robert Motherwell, Alexander Calder, Henri Matisse, and Clyfford Still. Traveling
exhibitions bring important national and international paintings, photographs, graphics, and sculpture to the Bay Area.
The Museum Store has a select offering of books, posters,
cards, and crafts. The Museum Cafe serves light snacks as well
as wine and beer. *At McAllister and Van Ness, tel. 415/863-
8800. Admission: $4 adults, $1.50 senior citizens and children
5–16. Open Tues. and Wed. 10–5, Thurs. 10–9, Fri. 10–5, Sat.
and Sun. 11–5. Closed major holidays.*

South of the Veterans Building is the opulent **War Memorial Opera House,** which opened in 1932. There are two seasons: the
13-week international season beginning in mid-September and
the summer season beginning in June. This is the largest opera
company west of New York. Wagner's entire Ring cycle is performed during the summer season every five years (next in
1995).

South of Grove Street, still on Van Ness Avenue, is the $27.5-million home of the San Francisco Symphony, the modern 3,000-plus-seat **Louise M. Davies Symphony Hall,** made of glass and granite. *Grove St. and Van Ness Ave., tel. 415/552–8338. Cost: $3 adults, $2 senior citizens and students. Tours Wed. 1:30 and 2:30, Sat. 12:30 and 1:30. Tours of Davies Hall and the adjacent venues that constitute the Performing Arts Center Mon., every half hour, 10–2:30.*

The San Francisco Opera Shop, across from Davies Hall, carries books, T-shirts, posters, and gift items associated with the performing arts. *199 Grove St., tel. 415/565–6414. Open Mon.–Fri. 11–8, Sat. noon–8, Sun. noon–6.*

47 San Francisco's original civic center is **Mission Dolores,** founded in 1776 at what is now 16th and Dolores streets, about a mile south of city hall. The sixth of 21 missions founded by the Franciscans and the oldest building in the city, it combines Moorish, Mission, and Corinthian styles. Until the gold rush, it was surrounded by farms, and a nearby creek flowed to the bay. It retains the appearance of a small-scale outpost, dwarfed by the towers of the adjacent basilica built in 1916. There is a small museum and cemetery garden. *Tel. 415/621–8203. Donation: $1. Open daily 9–4. Public transportation: Muni Metro J-Church train to 16th St.*

Japantown

Japanese-Americans began gravitating to the neighborhood known as the Western Addition prior to the 1906 quake. Early immigrants arrived about 1860, and they named San Francisco Soko. After the 1906 fire had destroyed wooden homes in other parts of the stricken city, many survivors settled in the Western Addition. By the 1930s the pioneers had opened shops, markets, meeting halls, and restaurants and established Shinto and Buddhist temples. Japantown was virtually disbanded during World War II when many of its residents, including second- and third-generation Americans, were "relocated" into camps. Today, Japantown, or "Nihonmachi," is centered on the slopes of Pacific Heights, north of Geary Boulevard, between Fillmore and Laguna. Annually, the Nihonmachi Cherry Blossom Festival is celebrated for two weekends in April, with a calendar of ethnic events. Walking around Nihonmachi is more than just a shopping and culinary treat; it is a cultural, sensory experience.

From Union Square, take the Muni bus No. 38-Geary or a No. 2, 3, or 4 on Sutter, westbound to Laguna. Remember to have exact change—fares are 85¢, with free transfers good for two changes of vehicle.

Buchanan Street between Bush and Sutter is a good place to start discovering the area. A little less ethnic in appearance, Buchanan leads into the traffic-free **Japan Center Mall** between Sutter and Post, where the buildings are of the shoji screen school of architecture and Ruth Asawa's origami fountain site is in the middle. (*See* Exploring Union Square, above, for more information on Ms. Asawa.)

48 The mall faces the 3-block-long, 5-acre **Japan Center.** In 1968, the multimillion-dollar development created by noted American architect Minoru Yamasaki opened with a three-day folk festival. The 3-block cluster includes an 800-car public garage and shops and showrooms selling Japanese products: electronic products, cameras, tapes and records, porcelains, pearls, and paintings.

The center is dominated by its Peace Plaza and Pagoda located between the East and Kintetsu buildings. Designed by Professor Yoshiro Taniguchi of Tokyo, an authority on ancient Japanese buildings, the plaza is landscaped with traditional Japanese-style gardens and reflecting pools. A graceful *yagura* (wooden drum tower) spans the entrance to the plaza, and the copper-roofed *Heiwa Dori* (Peace Walkway) at the north end connects the East and Kintetsu buildings. The five-tiered 100-foot Peace Pagoda overlooks the plaza, where seasonal festivals are held. The pagoda draws on the tradition of miniature round pagodas dedicated to eternal peace by Empress Koken in Nara more than 1,200 years ago. It was designed by the Japanese architect Yoshiro Taniguchi "to convey the friendship and goodwill of the Japanese to the people of the United States." A cultural bridge modeled after Florence's Ponte Vecchio spans Webster Street.

Time Out At a sushi bar, sample the bite-size portions of lightly seasoned rice and seaweed topped with various kinds of seafood, usually raw. Try to manage the chopsticks, dip (don't drench) your portion in the soy sauce, and experience this typical Japanese favorite. Tea, sake, or excellent Japanese beer accompanies these morsels. One warning—the final bill is counted piece by piece, and it is not unusual to run up a $20 tab per person. **Isobune,** in the Kintetsu Mall in Japan Center (tel. 415/563–1030), is unusual. The sushi chef prepares a variety of sushi, placing each small portion on a small wooden boat that floats on a "river" of water that circles the counter. The customer then fishes out a sampling.

Walk back on Geary to Gough Street. This enclave of expensive high-rise residential towers is known as Cathedral Hill. The dramatic **St. Mary's Cathedral** was dedicated in 1971 and cost $7 million. The impressive Catholic cathedral seats 2,500 people around the central altar. Above the altar is a spectacular cascade made of 7,000 aluminum ribs. Four magnificent stained-glass windows in the dome represent the four elements: the blue north window, water; the palecolored south window, the sun; the red west window, fire; and the green east window, earth. Designed by a team of local architects as well as Pier Nervi of Rome, the Italian travertine church is approached through spacious plazas.

We recommend Japantown and the Western Addition area as daytime diversions for most visitors. Though the hotels and restaurant areas are relatively safe in the evening, it is often difficult to avoid long waits at isolated bus stops and to find a cruising cab. The proximity of the often hostile street gangs living in areas of the Western Addition could cause unpleasant incidents.

Pacific Heights

Although Japantown may be centered on the slopes of Pacific Heights, it is light-years, if not mega-yen, away from the many-splendored mansions and town houses that still dominate some of the city's most expensive ($1 million up) and viewable real estate. Its boundaries are an east-west ridge along the city's northern flank from Van Ness to the Presidio and from California Street to the bay. The area features grand old Victorian homes and, expensively face-lifted, grace tree-lined streets, although here and there glossy, glass-walled condo high rises cut out the view.

Old money and some new, trade and diplomatic personnel, personalities in the limelight, and those who prefer absolute media anonymity occupy the city's most prestigious residential enclave. Receptions at the Gordon Getty mansion can block Broadway traffic while irate demonstrators picket the Soviet Consulate on Green Street. Rolls-Royces, Mercedes, and security systems are commonplace.

Visitors will see the pleasing facades of Queen Anne charmers, English Tudor imports, and Baroque bastions, and strolling can be a jackpot. Many of the structures extend upward for two or more stories, and a distinguishing feature of some of the grand residences is an ornate gate.

Begin your stroll at Webster and Pacific, deep in the heart of the heights. You can get here from Union Square by taking Muni bus no. 3 at Sutter and Stockton streets to Jackson and Fillmore. Turn right and walk one block to Webster.

North on Webster, at 2550, is the massive Georgian brick mansion built in 1896 for William B. Bourn, who had inherited a Mother Lode gold mine. Its architect Willis Polk was responsible for many of the most traditional and impressive commercial and private buildings from the prequake days until the early 1920s. (Be sure to see his 1917 Hallidie Building, 130 Sutter Street; *see* Exploring the Financial District, above.)

Neighbors include a consulate and, on the northwest corner, two classic showplaces. 2222 Broadway is the 3-story Italian Renaissance palace built by Comstock mine heir James Flood. The former Flood residence was given to a religious order. Ten years later, the Convent of the Sacred Heart purchased the Baroque brick Grant house at 2220, and both serve as school quarters today. A second top-drawer school, the Hamlin (2120 Broadway), occupies another Flood property.

Go east on Broadway, and, at the next corner, go right on Buchanan and on to 2090 Jackson Street. One of the most elegant 19th-century houses in the state, the massive red sandstone ❺⓿ Whittier Mansion is headquarters for the **California Historical Society** (tel. 415/567–1848). Period furnishings enhance this fine 1894 beauty, built so solidly that only a chimney toppled over during the 1906 quake. *Open Tues.–Sun. 1–4:30; guided tours Tues.–Fri. 1:30, weekends 1:30 and 3; admission: $3 adults, $1 senior citizens and students.* The adjoining library, **Schubert Hall,** occupies a 1905 baroque wood and stucco gem of a building at 2099 Pacific.

Proceed east another block to Laguna. The Italianate Victorian buildings on the east side of the 1800 block of Laguna Street cost only $2,000–$2,600 when they were built in the 1870s. This block is one of the most photographed in the city.

51 A block south, at Washington Street, is **Lafayette Park,** a 4-block-square oasis for sunbathers and dog-and-Frisbee teams. In the 1860s, a tenacious squatter, Sam Holladay, built himself a big house from wood shipped round the Horn, in the center of the park. Holladay even instructed city gardeners as if the land were his own and defied all attempts to remove him. The house was finally torn down in 1936.

52 The most imposing residence is the formal French **Spreckels Palace** (2080 Washington). Sugar heir Adolph Spreckels' wife was so pleased with architect George Applegarth's work that she commissioned him to design the city's French-inspired museum, the California Palace of the Legion of Honor in Lincoln Park.

Continue south on Gough Street (pronounced "Goff"), which runs along the east side of the park. A number of Queen Anne-style buildings here have been lovingly restored. Three blocks south and one east, at the corner of California and Franklin, is the impressive twin-turreted home built for a gold-rush mining and lumber baron. North on Franklin, at 1735, a stately brick Georgian house was built in the early 1900s for a coffee merchant.

53 At 2007 Franklin is the handsome **Haas-Lilienthal,** built in 1886 at an original cost of $20,000. This grand Queen Anne-style residence survived the 1906 earthquake and fire, and is the only fully furnished Victorian home open to the public. It is operated by the Foundation for San Francisco's Architectural Heritage, and tours are given by volunteer docents. *Tel. 415/441-3004. Admission: $4 adults, $2 senior citizens and students. Open Wed. noon-4, Sun. 11-4:30.*

By the mid-1970s, dozens of San Francisco's shabby gingerbreads were sporting psychedelic-colored facades, and the trend continues. Renovated treasures are found not only in the Haight Ashbury district but increasingly in the Western Addition as well as the Mission Area.

The Northern Waterfront

Numbers in the margin correspond with points of interest on the Northern Waterfront map.

For the sight, sound, and smell of the sea, hop the Powell-Hyde cable car from Union Square to the end of the line. First stop is the National Maritime Museum. After visiting Aquatic Park, start exploring the rest of the waterfront. We recommend casual clothes, good walking shoes, and a jacket or sweater for mid-afternoon breezes or foggy mists.

Or you could begin your day with one of the early morning boat tours that depart from the Northern Waterfront piers. On a clear day (almost always) the morning light casts a warm glow on the different-hued homes on Russian Hill, the weather-aged fishing boats cluttered at Fisherman's Wharf, rosy Ghirardelli Square and its fairy-tale clock tower, and the swelling seas beyond the entrance of the Golden Gate.

San Francisco is famous for the arts and crafts that flourish on the streets. Each day more than 200 of the city's most innovative jewelers, painters, potters, photographers, and leather workers offer their wares for sale. You'll find them at Fisherman's Wharf, Union Square, Embarcadero Plaza, and Cliff House. Be wary; some of the items are foreign factory wares, and some may be overpriced. If you can't live or leave without the item, try to bargain.

1 The **National Maritime Museum** (Aquatic Park, at the foot of Polk Street) exhibits ship models, photographs, maps, and other artifacts chronicling the development of San Francisco and the West Coast through maritime history. *Tel. 415/556–2904. Admission free. Open Wed.–Sun. 10–5; extended hours during the summer.*

2 The museum also includes the **Hyde Street Pier** (2 blocks east), where historic vessels are moored. The *Eureka*, a side-wheel ferry, the *Balclutha*, a steel-hulled, square-rigged vessel built in 1886, and the *C.A. Thayer*, a three-masted schooner, can be boarded. The *Alma*, a scow schooner, and the *Hercules*, a steam tug, can be viewed. The *Wapama*, a wooden steam schooner, is undergoing restoration. *Tel. 415/556–6435. Small admission price. Open daily 10–5; 10–6 in summer.*

The *Pampanito* is a World War II submarine at **Pier 45.** An audio tour has been installed. *Tel. 415/929–0202. Admission: $4 adults; $2 students 12–18, $1 children 6–11, senior citizens, and active military. Open Sun.–Thurs. 9–6, Fri.–Sat. 9–9. There are extended summer hours.*

3 Stroll through **Ghirardelli Square,** across Beach Street from the museum. This charming complex of 19th-century brick factory buildings has been transformed into specialty shops, cafes, restaurants, a cinema, and galleries. Until the early 1960s, the Ghirardelli Chocolate Company's aromatic production perfumed the northern waterfront. Two unusual shops deserve mention. Light Opera specializes in exquisite Russian lacquer boxes. (Gump's on Post Street also shows these sophisticated treasures, priced from about $50 to $20,000). Xanadu Gallery displays museum-quality tribal art from Asia, Africa, Oceania, and the Americas. The array of antique and ethnic jewelry is peerless.

4 Just east of the Hyde Street Pier, the **Cannery** is a 3-story structure built in 1894 to house the Del Monte Fruit and Vegetable Cannery. Now shops, art galleries, and unusual restaurants ring the courtyard. Nearby, additional shopping and **5** snacking choices are offered at the flag-festooned **Anchorage** mall.

A bit farther down at Taylor and Jefferson streets is main-**6** stream **Fisherman's Wharf.** Numerous seafood restaurants are located here, as well as the sidewalk crab pots and counters that offer take-away shrimp and crab cocktails. Ships creak at their moorings; seagulls cry out for a handout. By mid-afternoon, the fishing fleet is back to port. T-shirts and sweats, gold chains galore, redwood furniture, and acres of art—some original—beckon visitors. Wax museums, fast-food favorites, amusing street artists, and the animated robots at Lazer Maze provide diversions for all ages.

Today's tourists have the daily opportunity of enjoying exhilarating cruising on the bay. Among the cruises of the **Red and White Fleet,** berthed at Pier 41, are frequent 45-minute swings under the Golden Gate Bridge and the northern waterfront; fares are $5–$12. Advance reservations are necessary for the

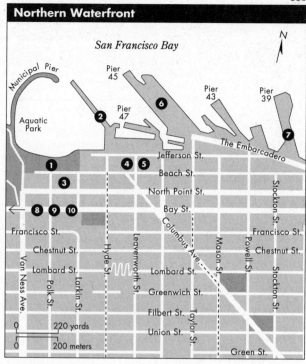

very popular Alcatraz Island tour, allowing a self-guided tour through the prison and grounds. *Advance reservations for individuals from Ticketron, Box 26430, San Francisco, CA 94126; tel. 415/546–2896. Cost: $7.50 adults, $7 senior citizens, $4 children 5–11.*

The **Blue and Gold Fleet,** berthed at Pier 39, provides its passengers with validated parking across the street. The hour-and-a-quarter tour sails under both the Bay and Golden Gate bridges. Barbecue dinner-dance cruises run April to October. *Tel. 415/781–7877. Reservations not necessary. Bay cruise: $12 adults, $6 senior citizens and children 5–18. Dinner-dance cruise: $32 per person (group rates available). Daily departures.*

7 **Pier 39** is the newest of San Francisco's waterfront malls. Dozens of shops with fascinating but often useless merchandise will prove tempting. A myriad of eateries confuses some parents seeking only a traditional soda-and-burger stop. Ongoing free entertainment, accessible validated parking, and nearby public transportation assure crowds most days.

Time Out A great family spot on the Wharf is **Bobby Rubino's** (245 Jefferson). Barbecued ribs, shrimp, chicken, and burgers—there is something tasty for all hands. A favorite with couples is crowded, noisy **Houlihan's** at the Anchorage. It is noted for fancy drinks, fantastic bay views, tasty pizza and pastas, plus nightly music and dancing.

The mellow **Buena Vista Cafe** (2765 Hyde) claims to be the birthplace of Irish coffee stateside; local columnist Stan Delaplane is credited with importing the Gaelic concoction. The BV opens at 9 AM, serving a great breakfast. It is always crowded; try for a view table overlooking nostalgic Victorian Park, with its cable-car turntable.

The Marina and the Presidio

❽ San Francisco's rosy and rococo **Palace of Fine Arts,** at Baker and Beach streets, is at the very end of the Marina, a picture-pretty residential district fronting the bay. The palace is the sole survivor of the 32 tinted plaster structures built for the 1915 Panama-Pacific Exposition. Bernard Maybeck designed the Roman Classic beauty, and legions of sentimental citizens and a huge private donation saved the palace. It was reconstructed in concrete at a cost of $7 million and reopened in 1967. The massive columns, great rotunda, and swan-filled lagoon are familiar in fashion layouts as well as in many recent films. Currently, package tours from Japan are using it as a backdrop for wedding photos with the brides wearing Western-style finery.

The interior houses a fascinating hands-on museum, the **Exploratorium.** It has been called the best science museum in the world. The curious of all ages flock here to try to use and understand some of the 600 exhibits. Be sure to include the pitch-black, crawl-through Tactile Dome in your visit. *Tel. 415/563–7337. Prices and hours subject to change, so call ahead. Admission. $5 adults, $1.50 children 6–17, under 6 free. For the Tactile Dome, reservations required, and a $5 charge includes museum admission. Open Wed.–Sun.*

If you have a car, this is the time to drive through the Presidio. If not, Mini bus No. 38 from Union Square will take you to Park Presidio; from there use a free transfer to bus No. 28 into the Presidio. Headquarters of the U.S. Sixth Army, it was a military post for over 200 years. De Anza and a band of Spanish settlers claimed the area in 1776. It became a Mexican garrison in 1822 when Mexico gained its independence from Spain. In 1846, U.S. troops forcibly occupied it. Now that the army is closing down its operations there, the Presidio's future is uncertain, but the grounds are expected to remain open to the public.

The more than 1,500 acres of rolling hills, majestic woods, and attractive red-brick army barracks present an air of serenity in the middle of the city. There are two beaches, a golf course, and picnic sites. The **Officers' Club,** a long, low adobe, was the Spanish commandante's headquarters, built about 1776, and is the oldest standing building in the city. The **Presidio Army Museum** is housed in the former hospital and focuses on the role played by the military in San Francisco's development. *Tel. 415/561–4115. Admission free. Open Tues.–Sun. 10–4.*

❾ Muni bus No. 28 will take you to the **Golden Gate Bridge** toll plaza. San Francisco celebrated the 50th birthday of the orange suspension bridge in 1987. Nearly 2 miles long, connecting San Francisco with Marin County, the bridge was designed to be able to withstand winds of more than 100 miles an hour. Walkers should wear warm clothing and be prepared for a windy and often misty crossing. The view of San Francisco from the vista point on the Marin side is smashing.

⑩ Fort Point was constructed during 1853–1861 to protect San Francisco from sea attack during the Civil War. It was designed to mount 126 cannons with a range of up to 2 miles. Standing under the shadow of the Golden Gate Bridge, the national historic site is now a museum filled with military memorabilia. Guided group tours are offered by National Park Rangers and there are cannon demonstrations. There is a superb view of the bay from the top floor. *Stairs and a trail lead from the bridge toll plaza to the fort, or it can be reached by driving via Lincoln Blvd. to Long Ave. Tel. 415/556–1693. Admission free. Open daily 10–5.*

From here, hardy walkers may elect to stroll about 3½ miles (with bay views) along the **Golden Gate Promenade** to Aquatic Park and the Hyde Street cable-car terminus.

Golden Gate Park

Numbers in the margin correspond with points of interest on the Golden Gate Park map.

It was a Scotsman, John McLaren, who became manager of the Golden Gate Park in 1887 and transformed the brush and sand into the green civilized wilderness we enjoy today. Here you can attend a polo game or a Sunday band concert and rent a bike, boat, or roller skates. On Sundays, some park roads are closed to cars and come alive with joggers, bicyclists, skaters, museumgoers, and picnickers. There are tennis courts, baseball diamonds, soccer fields, and a buffalo paddock. There are miles of trails for horseback riding in this 1,000-acre urban park.

Because it is so large, the best way for most visitors to see it is by car. Muni buses provide service, though on weekends there may be long waits for transportation. On Market Street, board a westbound No. 5-Fulton or No. 21-Hayes bus and continue to Arguello and Fulton. Walk south about 500 feet to John F. Kennedy Drive.

❶ The oldest building in the park and perhaps San Francisco's most elaborate Victorian one is the **Conservatory,** a copy of London's famous Kew Gardens. The ornate greenhouse was originally brought around the Horn for the estate of James Lick in San Jose. The Conservatory was purchased from the Lick estate with public subscription funds and erected in the park. As well as a tropical garden, there are seasonal displays of many varieties of flowers and plants.

The eastern section of the park has three museums.

❷ The M.H. de Young Memorial Museum has 44 galleries surrounding the spacious Hearst Court, illustrating the cultures of the Western world from the time of ancient Egypt to the 20th century. The major focus is on American art, including the highly acclaimed Rockefeller Collection and the works of Sargent, Copley, and Church. There are prime examples of period furniture and decorative arts as well. The display of traditional arts of Africa, Oceania, and the Americas includes pottery, basketry, sculpture, and ritual clothing and accessories. The collection of classical objects from Egypt, Greece, and Rome includes tapestries, sculptures, and religious art. In addition to its extensive permanent collections, the de Young hosts selec-

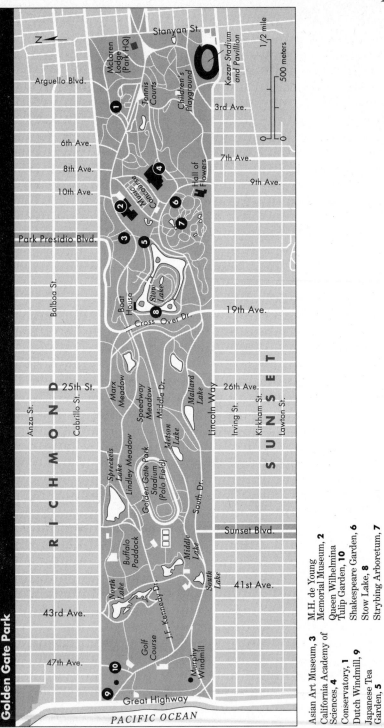

Golden Gate Park

tive traveling shows—often blockbuster events for which there are long lines and an additional charge to enter.

The museum has an outstanding shop with a wide selection of art books, magazines, cards, selected jewelry, and small art objects. The Cafe de Young, which has outdoor seating in the Oakes Garden, serves a complete menu of light refreshments until 4 PM. *Tel. 415/750–3600 or 750–3659 for 24-hour information. Open Wed.–Sun. 10–4:45. Admission: $4 adults, $2 senior citizens and children 12–17, under 12 free. 1st Wed. of the month and 1st Sat. 10–noon, all are free. Note: One admission charge admits you to the de Young, Asian Art, and Legion of Honor museums on the same day.*

❸ The **Asian Art Museum** is located in galleries that adjoin the de Young. This world-famous Avery Brundage Collection consists of more than 10,000 sculptures, paintings, and ceramics that illustrate major periods of Asian art. Very special are the Magnin Jade Room and the Leventritt collection of blue and white porcelains. On the second floor are treasures from Iran, Turkey, Syria, India, Tibet, Nepal, Pakistan, Korea, Japan, Afghanistan, and Southeast Asia. Both the de Young and Asian Art museums have daily docent tours. *Tel. 415/668–8921. Admission collected when entering the de Young. Open Wed.–Sun. 10–4:45.*

❹ The **California Academy of Sciences** is directly opposite the de Young Museum. It is one of the five top natural history museums in the country and has both an aquarium and a planetarium. Throngs of visitors enjoy its Steinhart Aquarium and dramatic 100,000-gallon Fish Roundabout, home to 14,000 creatures. A new addition is a living coral reef with colorful fish, giant clams, tropical sharks, and a rainbow of hard and soft corals. There is an additional charge for Morrison Planetarium shows ($2.50 adults, $1.25 children 17 and under. Tel. 415/750–7141 for daily schedule). The Space and Earth Hall has an "earthquake floor" enabling one to ride a simulated California quake. The Wattis Hall of Man presents lifelike habitat scenes that range from the icy terrain of the Arctic to the lush highlands of New Guinea. Newly renovated is the Wild California Hall, with a 10,000-gallon aquarium tank showing underwater life at the Farallones (islands off the Northern California coast), life-size elephant seal models, and video information on the wildlife of the state. The innovative Life through Time Hall tells the story of evolution from the beginnings of the universe through the age of dinosaurs to the age of mammals. A cafeteria is open daily until one hour before the museum closes. The Academy Store offers a wide selection of books, posters, toys, and cultural artifacts. *Tel. 415/221–5100 or 415/750–7145 (recorded message). Admission: $4 adults, $2 senior citizens and children 12–17, $1 children 6–11. Free 1st Wed. of each month. Open daily July 4–Labor Day 10–7, Wed. to 8:45; open Wed. to 8:45; open daily after Labor Day–July 3, 10–5, Wed. to 8:45. Extended Sun. hours in summer.*

Time Out The **Japanese Tea Garden**, next to the Asian Art Museum, is
❺ ideal for resting after museum touring. This charming 4-acre village was created for the 1894 Mid-Winter Exposition. Small ponds, streams, and flowering shrubs create a serene landscape. The cherry blossoms in spring are exquisite. The Tea

House (tea, of course, and cookies) is popular and busy. *Tel. 415/752–1171. Admission: $2 adults, $1 senior citizens and children 6–12. Free 1st Wed. of each month.*

6 A short stroll from the tea garden is the free **Shakespeare Garden.** Two hundred flowers mentioned by the bard, as well as bronze-engraved panels with floral quotations of his, are set throughout the garden.

7 **Strybing Arboretum** specializes in plants from areas with climates similar to that of the Bay Area, such as the west coast of Australia, South Africa, and the Mediterranean. There are many gardens inside the grounds, with 6,000 plants and tree varieties blooming seasonally. *9th Ave. at Lincoln, tel. 415/661 –1316. Admission free. Open weekdays 8–4:30, weekends and holidays 10–5. Tours leave the book store daily at 1:30 PM.*

The western half of Golden Gate Park offers miles of wooded greenery and open spaces for all types of spectator and partici-
8 *pant sports.* Rent a paddleboat or stroll around **Stow Lake.** The **Chinese Pavilion,** a gift from the city of Taipei, was shipped in 6,000 pieces and assembled on the shore of Strawberry Hill Island in Stow Lake in 1981. At the very western end of the park, where Kennedy Drive meets the Great Highway, is the beauti-
9 **10** fully restored 1902 **Dutch Windmill** and the photogenic **Queen Wilhelmina Tulip Garden.**

Lincoln Park and the Western Shoreline

No other American city provides such close-up viewing of the power and fury of the surf attacking the shore. From Land's End in Lincoln Park you can look across the Golden Gate (the name was originally given to the opening of the San Francisco Bay, long before the bridge was built) to the Marin Headlands. From Cliff House south to the San Francisco Zoo, the Great Highway and Ocean Beach run along the western edge of the city and the Pacific Ocean.

The wind is often strong along the shoreline, summer fog can blanket the ocean beaches, and the water is cold and usually too rough for swimming. Carry a sweater or jacket and bring binoculars.

At the northwest corner of the San Francisco peninsula is **Lincoln Park.** At one time, all the city's cemeteries were here, segregated by nationality. Today, there is an 18-hole golf course with large and well-formed Monterey cypresses lining the fairways. There are scenic walks throughout the 275-acre park, with particularly good views from **Land's End** (the parking lot is at the end of El Camino del Mar). The trails out to Land's End, however, are for skilled hikers only: There are frequent landslides, and danger lurks along the steep cliffs.

Also in Lincoln Park is the **California Palace of the Legion of Honor.** The building itself—modeled after the 18th-century Parisian original—is architecturally exciting and is surrounded by four massive sculptures: Rodin's *Thinker* and *Three Shades* and Anna Huntington's *Joan of Arc* and *El Cid.* The French-based collection is expanding to display a wider range of European artwork. The museum's collection of the sculpture of Auguste Rodin is one of the most famous in the United States. Exhibits include furniture, porcelain, paintings, tapes-

tries, and decorative arts. Rembrandt, El Greco, Titian, Fra
gonard, Corot, Manet, Monet, Degas, and Cezanne ar
represented. The Achenbach print collection contains mor
than 100,000 items and is considered the most important prin
collection in the West. *Legion of Honor Dr., tel. 415/750–3600
24-hour information, tel. 415/750–3659. Daily docent tours
Admission: $4 adults, $2 senior citizens, children under 1
free. Free 1st Wed. of each month and Sat. 10–noon. Open Wed
–Sun. 10–5.*

Cliff House (1066 Point Lobos Ave.), where the road turn
south along the western shore, has existed in several incarna
tions. The original, built in 1863, and several later structure
were destroyed by fire. The present building has restaurants, a
pub, and a gift shop. The lower dining room overlooks **Sea
Rocks** (the barking marine mammals sunning themselves are
actually sea lions).

An adjacent (free) attraction is the **Musée Mécanique,** a collec
tion of antique mechanical contrivances, including peep shows
and nickelodeons. The museum carries on the tradition of ar
cade amusement at the Cliff House. *Tel. 415/386–1170; oper
daily in summer 10–8, winter 11–7.*

Two flights below Cliff House is a fine observation deck and the
Golden Gate National Recreation Area **Visitors Center** (tel. 415,
556–8642; open daily 10–4:30). There are interesting and historic photographs of Cliff House and the glass-roofed **Sutro
Baths.** The baths covered 3 acres just south of Cliff House and
housed six enormous baths, 500 dressing rooms, and several
restaurants. The baths were closed in 1952 and burned in 1966.
You can explore the ruins on your own (the Visitors Center offers information on these and other trails) or take ranger-led
walks on weekends.

Because traffic is often heavy in summer and on weekends, you
might want to take the Muni system from the Union Square
area out to Cliff House. Take the Muni No. 38-Geary Limited
weekdays to 48th and Point Lobos and walk down the hill.
(Weekends and evenings, the Muni No. 38 is marked 48th Avenue.)

Time Out   Cliff House has several restaurants and a busy bar. The **Upstairs Room** (tel. 415/387–5847) features a light menu with a
number of omelet suggestions. The lower dining room, the **Terrace Room** (tel. 415/386–3330), has a fabulous view of Seal
Rocks. Reservations are recommended, and there still may be
a wait for a table, especially at midday on Sunday.

Below the Cliff House are the **Great Highway** and **Ocean Beach.**
Stretching for 3 miles along the western (Pacific) side of the
city, this is a beautiful beach for walking, running, or lying in
the sun—but not for swimming.

At the Great Highway and Sloat Boulevard is the **San Francisco Zoo.** The zoo was begun in 1889 in Golden Gate Park. At its
present home there are 1,000 species of birds and animals, at
least 130 of which have been designated as endangered species.
Among the protected are the snow leopard, Bengal tiger, red
panda, jaguar, and Asian elephant. One of the newest attractions is the greater one-horned rhino exhibit, next to the
African elephants. Gorilla World, a $2-million exhibit, is the

largest and most natural gorilla habitat in a zoo. The circular outer area is carpeted with natural African kikiyu grass, while trees, shrubs, and waterfalls create communal play areas. The $5-million Primate Discovery Center houses 16 endangered species in atriumlike enclosures. One of the most popular zoo residents is Prince Charles, a rare white tiger, the first of its kind to be exhibited in the West. Other popular animals are penguins, wolves, and koalas.

There are 33 "storyboxes" throughout the zoo that when turned on with the blue plastic elephant keys ($1.50) recite animal facts and basic zoological concepts in four languages (English, Spanish, Cantonese, and Tagalog). Many of the recordings have been made by local celebrities: Herb Caen points out the similarities between elephants and politicians; ex-mayor Dianne Feinstein bares all about bears.

The children's zoo has a minipopulation of about 300 mammals, birds, and reptiles plus an insect zoo, a baby animal nursery, and a beautifully restored 1921 Dentzel carousel. A ride astride one of the 52 hand-carved menagerie animals costs 75¢.

Zoo information, tel. 415/661–4844. Admission: $5 adults, $2 children 12–15 and senior citizens, children under 12 free when accompanied by an adult, senior citizens $1 for a quarterly pass. Open daily 10–5. Children's zoo admission: $1, under 3 free. Open daily 11–4.

San Francisco for Free

This is not a cheap town to live in or visit. Lodging and dining are expensive; museums, shopping, the opera, or a nightclub may set you back a bit. It is possible, however, to do much of your sightseeing very cheaply. Walking is often the best way to get around, and it's not very expensive to use the cable cars and buses. Exploring most of Golden Gate Park is absolutely free, and so is walking across the Golden Gate Bridge.

There are several venues for free concerts in San Francisco. The nation's oldest continuous free summer music festival, offering 10 Sunday afternoons of symphony, opera, jazz, pop music, and dance, takes place at **Stern Grove** (Sloat Blvd. at 19th Ave., tel. 415/398–6551) in the Sunset District. Keep in mind that summer in this area near the ocean can be cool. Bring a picnic and enjoy this lovely sunken park surrounded by eucalyptus and redwoods.

There are also free organ concerts Saturdays at 4 PM in the **Palace of the Legion of Honor** (tel. 415/750–3600) in Lincoln Park and free band concerts Sunday and holiday afternoons in the **Golden Gate Park band shell** (tel. 415/558–3706), opposite the de Young Museum.

What to See and Do with Children

The attractions described in the above exploring sections offer a great deal of entertainment for children as well as their families. We suggest, for example, visiting the ships at the **Hyde Street Pier** and spending some time at **Pier 39,** where there is a double-decker Venetian carousel. (*See* Exploring the Northern Waterfront, above.)

Children will find much to amuse them at **Golden Gate Park**, from the old-fashioned conservatory to the expansive lawns and trails. There is another vintage carousel (1912) at the children's playground. The **Steinhart Aquarium** at the California Academy of Sciences has a "Touching Tide Pool," from which docents will pull starfish and hermit crabs for children or adults to feel. The **Japanese Tea Garden,** although crowded, is well worth exploring; climbing over the high, humpbacked bridges is like moving the neighborhood playground toys into an exotic new (or old) world.

It is also possible to walk across the **Golden Gate Bridge.** The view is thrilling and the wind invigorating if the children (and adults) are not overwhelmed by the height of the bridge and the nearby automobile traffic (*see* Exploring the Marina and the Presidio, above).

Many children enjoy walking along crowded **Grant Avenue** and browsing in the many souvenir shops. Unfortunately, nothing —not even straw finger wrestlers, wooden contraptions to make coins "disappear," shells that open in water to release tissue paper flowers, and other true junk—is as cheap as it once was (*see* Exploring Chinatown, above).

The **San Francisco Zoo,** with a children's zoo, playground, and carousel, is not far from **Ocean Beach.** The weather and the currents do not allow swimming, but it's a good place for walking and playing in the surf (*see* Exploring Lincoln Park and the Western Shoreline, above).

The Exploratorium at the Palace of Fine Arts is a preeminent children's museum and is very highly recommended (*see* Exploring the Marina and the Presidio, above).

Finally, we remind you of the **cable cars.** Try to find time for a ride when the crowds are not too thick (mid-morning or afternoon). It's usually easier to get on at one of the turnarounds at the ends of the lines (*see* Getting Around, above).

If you're ready to spend a day outside of the city, consider a trip to Vallejo's Marine World Africa USA (*see* Excursions, below).

Shopping

San Francisco is a shopper's dream—major department stores, fine fashion, discount outlets, art galleries, and crafts stores among the offerings. Most accept at least Visa and MasterCard charge cards, and many also accept American Express, Diner's Club, and Carte Blanche. A very few accept cash only. Ask about traveler's checks; policies vary. The San Francisco *Chronicle* and *Examiner* will have sales advertisements; for smaller innovative shops, check the San Francisco *Bay Guardian*. Store hours are slightly different everywhere, but a generally trusted rule is to shop between 10 AM and 5 or 6 PM Monday–Saturday (until 8 or 9 PM on Thursdays) and noon–5 PM on Sundays. Stores on and around Fisherman's Wharf often have longer summer hours.

If you want to cover most of the city, the best shopping route might be to start at Fisherman's Wharf, then continue in order to Union Square, San Francisco Centre, Crocker Galleria, the

Embarcadero Center, Jackson Square, Chinatown, North Beach, Union Street, and Japan Center.

Shopping Districts
Fisherman's Wharf
San Francisco's Fisherman's Wharf is host to a number of shopping and sightseeing attractions: **Pier 39, the Anchorage, Ghirardelli Square,** and **the Cannery.** Each offers shops, restaurants, and a festive atmosphere as well as outdoor entertainment, such as musicians, mimes, and magicians. Pier 39 includes an amusement area and a double-deck Venetian carousel. One shared attraction in all the centers is the view of the bay and the proximity to the cable-car lines, which can take shoppers directly to Union Square.

Union Square
San Francisco visitors usually head for shopping at Union Square first. It's centrally located in the downtown area and surrounded by major hotels, from the large luxury properties to smaller bed-and-breakfasts. The square itself is a city park under which is built a garage. It is flanked by large stores such as **Macy's, Saks Fifth Avenue, I. Magnin,** and **Neiman Marcus. North Beach Leather** and **Gucci** are two smaller upscale stores. Across from the cable-car turntable at Powell and Market streets is the $140-million **San Francisco Centre** high rise, with the fashionable **Nordstrom** store on the top five floors. Nearby is **Crocker Galleria,** underneath a glass dome at Post and Kearny streets; 50 shops, restaurants, and services make up the financial district shopping center, which is topped by two rooftop parks.

Embarcadero Center
Four modern towers of shops, restaurants, and offices plus the Hyatt Regency Hotel make up the downtown Embarcadero Center at the end of Market Street. Like most malls, the center is a little sterile and falls short in the character department. What it lacks in charm, however, it makes up for in sheer quantity. The center's 175 stores and services include a number of nationally known stores such as **The Limited, B. Dalton Bookseller,** and **Ann Taylor,** as well as more local or West Coast-based businesses such as the **Nature Company, Filian's European Clothing,** and **Lotus Designer Earrings.** Each tower occupies 1 block, and parking garages are available.

Jackson Square
Jackson Square is where a dozen or so of San Francisco's finest retail antiques dealers are located. If your passion is 19th-century English furniture, for example, there's a good chance that something here will suit. Knowledgeable store owners and staffs also can direct you to other places in the city for your special interests. The shops are along Jackson Street in the financial district, so a visit there will put you very close to the Embarcadero Center and Chinatown.

Chinatown
Grant and Bush marks "the Gateway" to Chinatown; here, shoppers and tourists are introduced to 24 blocks of shops, restaurants, markets, and temples. There are daily "sales" on gems of all sorts—especially jade and pearls—alongside stalls of bok choy and ginger root. Chinese silks and toy trinkets are also commonplace in the shops, as are colorful pottery, baskets, and large figures of soapstone and jade.

North Beach
The once largely Italian enclave of North Beach gets smaller each year as Chinatown spreads northward. It has been called the city's answer to New York City's Greenwich Village, although it's much smaller. Many businesses here tend to be small clothing stores, antiques shops, or eccentric specialty shops like **Postermat,** with psychedelic mementos, and **Quanti-**

ty Postcards, with an inventory of thousands of postcards. If you get tired of poking around in the bookstores, a number of small cafes dot the streets and there are lots of Italian restaurants.

Union Street Out-of-towners sometimes confuse Union Square with the popular Union Street, whose main shopping area is actually in another part of town. Nestled at the foot of a hill between the neighborhoods of Pacific Heights and Cow Hollow, this street shines with contemporary fashion and jewelry. Union Street's feel is largely new and upscale, although there are a few antiques shops and some oldtime storekeepers. Shopping here is not limited to apparel, and the options include a good bookstore —**Solar Light Books**—**Union Street Graphics** for posters, and several galleries for crafts, photographs, sculpture, and serigraphs.

Japantown Unlike Chinatown, North Beach, or the Mission, the 5-acre **Japan Center** is contained under one roof. It is actually a mall of stores that are filled with antique kimonos, beautiful tansu chests, and both new and old porcelains. The center always feels a little empty, but the good shops here are well worth a visit. Japan Center occupies the 3-block area between Laguna and Fillmore streets, and between Geary and Post streets.

Participant Sports

One great attraction of the Bay Area is the abundance of activities. Joggers, bicyclists, and aficionados of virtually all sports can find their favorite pastimes within driving distance, and often within walking distance, from downtown hotels. Golden Gate Park has numerous paths for runners and cyclists. Lake Merced in San Francisco and Lake Merritt in Oakland are among the most popular areas for joggers.

For information on running races, tennis tournaments, bicycle races, and other participant sports, check the monthly issues of *City Sports* magazine, available free at sporting goods stores, tennis centers, and other recreational sites.

Bicycling Two bike routes are maintained by the San Francisco Recreation and Parks Department (tel. 415/558–3706). One route goes through Golden Gate Park to Lake Merced; the other goes from the south end of the city to the Golden Gate Bridge and beyond. Many shops along Stanyan Street rent bikes.

Boating and Sailing **Stow Lake** in Golden Gate Park has rowboat, pedalboat, and electric boat rentals. The lake is open for boating from 8:30 AM to 4 PM each spring and summer day. San Francisco Bay offers year-round sailing, but tricky currents make the bay hazardous for inexperienced navigators. Boat rentals and charters are available throughout the Bay Area and are listed under "boat rentals" in the Yellow Pages. A selected charter is **A Day on the Bay** (tel. 415/922–0227). Local sailing information can be obtained at **The Eagle Cafe** on Pier 39.

Fishing Numerous fishing boats leave from San Francisco, Sausalito, Berkeley, Emeryville, and Point San Pablo. They go for salmon outside the bay or striped bass and giant sturgeon within the bay. Temporary licenses are available on the charters. In San Francisco, lines can be cast from San Francisco Municipal Pier, Fisherman's Wharf, or Aquatic Park. Trout fishing is available at Lake Merced. Licenses can be bought at sporting-goods stores. The cost of fishing licenses ranges from $4.50 for one day to $22.50 for a complete state license. For charters, advance reservations are suggested. Some selected sport-fishing charters are listed. Mailing addresses are given, but you're more likely to get a response if you call.

Capt. Ron's Pacific Charters. Fisherman's Wharf. Write to 561 Prentiss St., San Francisco, CA 94110, tel. 415/285–2000.

Capt. Fred Morini. Fisherman's Wharf. Write to 138 Harvard Dr., Larkspur, CA 94939, tel. 415/924–5575.

Muny Bait & Sport Shop. 3098 Polk St., San Francisco, CA 94109, across from Ghirardelli Sq., tel. 415/673–9815. Leaves daily from Fisherman's Wharf.

Wacky Jacky. Fisherman's Wharf. Write Ms. Jacky Douglas at 473 Bella Vista Way, San Francisco, CA 94127, tel. 415/586–9800.

Fitness   **Physical fitness** activities continue to be popular, but most clubs are private and visitors can have trouble finding a workout location. **Sheraton Hotels** have arrangements with neighboring clubs, and the **Burlingame Hyatt,** near the airport, has a workout facility. **24-hour Nautilus** (1335 Sutter, tel. 415/776–2200) is open to the public for a $10 drop-in fee. **Sante West Fitness** (3727 Buchanan, tel. 415/563–6222) offers aerobics, low impact, stretching, and other classes for a $7 drop-in fee.

Golf   San Francisco has four public golf courses, and visitors should call for tee times: **Harding Park,** an 18-hole, par-72 course (at Lake Merced Blvd. and Skyline Blvd., tel. 415/664–4690); **Lincoln Park,** 18 holes, par 69 (34th and Clement, tel. 415/221–9911); **Golden Gate Park,** a "pitch and putt" 9-holer (47th and Fulton, tel. 415/751–8987); **McLaren Park,** a full-size 9-holer, on Sunnydale, between Brookdale and Persia (tel. 415/587–2425). Another municipal course, **Sharp Park,** is south of the city in Pacifica (tel. 415/359–3380).

Tennis   The San Francisco Recreation Department maintains 130 free tennis courts throughout the city. The largest set of free courts is at **Mission Dolores Park,** 18th and Dolores streets, with six courts on a first-come basis. There are 21 public courts in **Golden Gate Park;** reservations and fee information can be obtained by calling tel. 415/566–4800.

Spectator Sports

For the sports fan, the Bay Area offers a vast selection of events, from yacht races to rodeo and baseball. The 49er football games are sold out far in advance, so this isn't a likely activity for visitors.

Baseball   The *San Francisco Giants* play ball at Candlestick Park (tel. 415/467–8000), and the *Oakland A's* play at the Oakland Coliseum (tel. 415/638–0500). These games rarely sell out, and gameday tickets are usually available at the stadiums. Premium seats, however, often do sell out in advance. Remember that Candlestick Park is often windy and cold, so bring along extra layers of clothing to deal with changing weather.

Basketball   The *Golden State Warriors* play NBA basketball at the Oakland Coliseum Arena, October–April. Tickets are available through Ticketron (tel. 415/392–7469).

Rodeo and Horse Shows San Francisco relives its Western heritage each October with the *Grand National Rodeo and Livestock Show* at the Cow Palace (tel. 415/469–6000), just south of the city limits in Daly City. In August, the Cow Palace hosts the *San Francisco Equestrian Festival*, featuring such events as dressage and vaulting.

Tennis The Cow Palace (tel. 415/469–6000) is the site of the *Transamerica Men's Tennis Championships* in September. The *Virginia Slims Women's Tennis Tour* visits the Oakland Coliseum Arena in February.

Yacht Racing There are frequent yacht races on the bay. The local papers will give you details, or you can be an uninformed but appreciative spectator from the Golden Gate Bridge or other vantage points around town.

Beaches

San Francisco's beaches are perfect for romantic sunset strolls, but don't make the mistake of expecting to find Waikiki-by-the-sea. The water is cold, and the beach areas are often foggy and usually jammed on sunny days. They can be satisfactory for afternoon sunning, but treacherous currents make most areas dangerous for swimming. During stormy months, beachcombers can stroll along the sand and discover a variety of ocean treasures: glossy agates and jade pebbles, sea-sculptured roots and branches, and—rarely—glass floats.

Baker Beach Baker Beach is not recommended for swimming; watch for larger-than-usual waves. In recent years, the north end of the beach has become popular with nude sunbathers. This is not legal, but such laws are seldom enforced. The beach is in the southwest corner of the Presidio and begins at the end of Gibson Road, which turns off Bowley. Weather is typical for the bay shoreline: summer fog, usually breezy, and occasionally warm. Picnic tables, grills, day-camp areas, and trails are available.

China Beach From April to October, China Beach, south of Baker at Seacliff and 28th avenues, offers a lifeguard, gentler water, changing rooms, and showers. It is also listed on maps as Phelan Beach.

Ocean Beach South of Cliff House, Ocean Beach stretches along the western (ocean) side of San Francisco. It has a wide beach with scenic views and is perfect for walking, running, or lying in the sun— but not for swimming.

Dining

San Francisco probably has more restaurants per capita than any city in the United States, including New York. Practically every ethnic cuisine is represented. Thus, to select a few restaurants to list here from the vast number available is a very difficult task, indeed. We have chosen one or two restaurants to represent each popular style of dining in various price ranges, in most cases because of the superiority of the food, but in some instances because of a spectacular view or exceptionally beautiful ambience.

We also have endeavored to create a geographical balance in the areas of town most frequented by visitors. This meant leaving out some great places in outlying districts such as Sunset and Richmond. The Richmond district restaurants we have recommended were chosen because they offer a type of experience not available elsewhere.

All listed restaurants serve dinner; they are open for lunch unless specified closed; restaurants are not open for breakfast unless the morning meal is specifically mentioned.

Parking accommodations are mentioned only when a restaurant has made special arrangements; otherwise, you're on your own. There is usually a charge for valet parking. Validated parking is not necessarily free and unlimited; often there is a nominal charge and a restriction on the length of time.

Restaurants do change their policies about hours, credit cards, and the like. It is always best to inquire first.

Highly recommended and unusual restaurants are indicated by a star ★.

Category	Cost*
Very Expensive	over $40
Expensive	$25–$40
Moderate	$15–$25
Inexpensive	under $15

per person, not including tax, service, or drinks

American   A decade ago it was hard to find a decent "American" restaurant in the Bay Area. However, the list keeps growing and becoming more diversified, with categories for Creole-Cajun, California cuisine, Southwestern, barbecue, and the all-American diner.

Very Expensive   **Campton Place.** Famed chef Bradley Ogden left to open his own place, Lark Creek Inn, in Marin County. Now his former sous chef, New Orleans-bred Jan Birnbaum, wears the top toque in carrying on Ogden's innovative approach to American regional cooking with a slight Southern accent, in dishes such as squab with wild rice and pecan gravy. Breakfasts are a big event here, too. The atmosphere is elegant and understated, though the tables are too close for privacy. *340 Stockton St., downtown, tel. 415/781–5555. Jacket required at dinner, tie requested. Reservations required, 2 weeks in advance on weekends. AE, DC, MC, V. Valet parking.*

Expensive   **Fournou's Ovens.** There are two lovely dining areas in the elegant Stanford Court Hotel. This is a multilevel room with tiers of tables, focused on the giant open hearth where many specialties—notably the rack of lamb—are roasted. Some people opt for the flower-filled greenhouses that flank the hotel and offer views of the cable cars clanking up and down the hill. Wherever you sit, you'll find excellent food and attentive service. *905 California St., Nob Hill, tel. 415/989–1910. Jacket required. Reservations advised. AE, MC, V. No lunch weekends. Valet parking.*

★   **Postrio.** Chef Wolfgang Puck's San Francisco restaurant debut in 1989 caused the biggest culinary commotion locally since Alice Waters reinvented the pizza, but Puck claims to have done that in Los Angeles. Postrio has an open kitchen (another trend started by Puck) and a stunning 3-level bar-dining area, high-lighted by palm trees and museum-quality contemporary paintings. The food is Puckish Californian with Mediterranean and Asian overtones, emphasizing pastas, grilled seafood, and house-baked breads. A substantial breakfast is served here, too. *545 Post St., Union Sq. area, tel. 415/776–7825. Dress: informal. Reservations advised. AE, DC, MC, V. Valet parking.*

★ **Stars.** This is the culinary temple of Jeremiah Tower, the superchef who claims to have invented California cuisine. Stars is a must stop on the traveling gourmet's itinerary, but it's also where many local movers and shakers hang out as well as a popular place for post-theater dining—open till the wee hours. The dining room has a clublike ambience, and the food ranges from grills to ragouts to sautées—some daringly creative and some classical. *150 Redwood Alley, Civic Center area, tel. 415/861–7827. Dress: informal. Reservations accepted up to 2 weeks in advance, some tables reserved for walk-ins. AE, DC, MC, V. Closed Memorial Day. No lunch weekends. Valet parking.*

Moderate
★ **Fog City Diner.** This is where the diner and grazing crazes began in San Francisco, and the popularity of this spot knows no end. The long, narrow dining room emulates a luxurious railroad car with dark wood paneling, huge windows, and comfortable booths. The cooking is innovative, drawing its inspiration from regional cooking throughout America. The sharable "small plates" are a fun way to go. *1300 Battery St., Embarcadero area, tel. 415/982–2000. Dress: informal. Reservations advised a week in advance for peak hours. MC, V. Closed Christmas and Thanksgiving.*

MacArthur Park. Year after year San Franciscans acclaim this their favorite spot for ribs, but the oakwood smoker and mesquite grill also turn out a wide variety of all-American fare, from steaks to seafood, in this renovated pre-earthquake warehouse. Breakfast is served weekdays, too. *607 Front St., Embarcadero area, tel. 415/398–5700. Dress: informal. Reservations advised. AE, DC, MC, V. Closed weekend lunch and Christmas. Valet parking in evenings.*

Washington Square Bar & Grill. You're apt to rub elbows with the city's top columnists and writers in this no-frills saloon. The restaurant recently broke with North Beach Italian tradition to offer lighter cooking, though pastas and seafood still lead the menu alongside basic bar fare such as burgers and steaks. Pianist at night; open late. *1707 Powell St., North Beach, tel. 415/982–8123. Dress: informal. Reservations advised. AE, DC, MC, V. Closed most major holidays. Validated parking at garage around the corner on Filbert.*

Caribbean
Moderate
Miss Pearl's Jam House. Since its opening in 1989, this Caribbean hot spot in a Tenderloin motel has been jammed with a younger-than-yuppie crowd at night. But by day it's quiet and lovely with lunch served out by the pool. The chef draws his inspiration from many West Indian islands and the intense flavor of the food more than compensates for its lack of authenticity. *601 Eddy St., tel. 415/775–5267. Reservations accepted only for 10 or more. Dress: informal. MC, V. No lunch Sat. Closed Sun.*

Chinese
For nearly a century, Chinese restaurants in San Francisco were confined to Chinatown and the cooking was largely an Americanized version of peasant-style Cantonese. However, the last few decades have seen an influx of restaurants repre-

Acquarello, **9**
Act IV, Inn at the Opera, **47**
Amelio's, **12**
Angkor Palace, **6**
Bistro Roti, **28**
Blue Fox, **22**
Buce Giovanni, **10**
California Culinary Academy, **44**
Campton Place, **34**
Capp's Corner, **13**
Chevys, **36**
Corona Bar & Grill, **37**
Donatello, **39**
Ernie's, **21**
Fleur de Lys, **42**
Fog City Diner, **16**
Fournou's Ovens, **29**
Gaylord, **4**, **27**
Golden Turtle, **7**
Greens, **1**
Harbor Village, **26**
Harris, **8**
Hayes Street Grill, **48**
Hunan, **17**
Il Fornaio, **15**
Izzy's Steak & Chop House, **2**
Jack's, **23**
Julius Castle, **14**
Khan Toke Thai House, **50**
Kulleto's, **38**
Lascaux, **33**
Le Castel, **53**
Le Central, **32**
MacArthur Park, **19**
Mandarin, **3**
Masa's, **31**
Miss Pearl's Jam House, **43**
North India, **5**
Pacific Heights Bar & Grill, **52**
Pierre, **35**
Postrio, **40**
Sanppo, **51**
690, **45**
Square One, **20**
Stars, **46**
Tadich Grill, **25**
Trader Vic's, **41**
Washington Square Bar & Grill, **11**
Waterfront, **18**
Yamato, **30**
Yank Sing, **24**
Zuni Cafe Grill, **49**

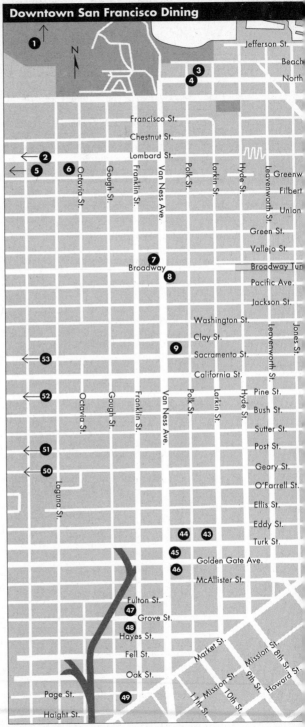

Downtown San Francisco Dining

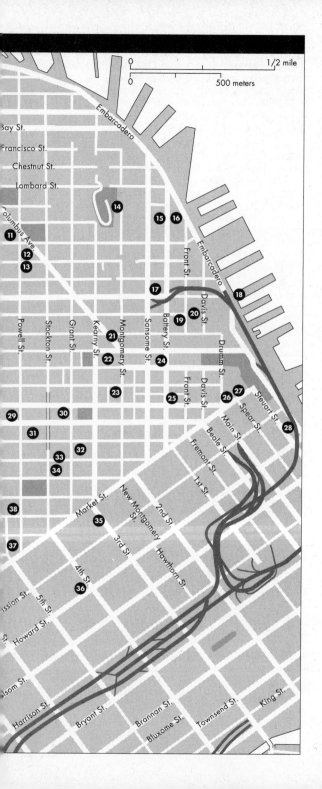

0   1/2 mile

0   500 meters

senting the wide spectrum of Chinese cuisine: the subtly seasoned fare of Canton, the hot and spicy cooking of Hunan and
Szechuan, the northern style of Peking where meat and dumplings replace seafood and rice as staples, and, most recently,
more esoteric cooking, such as Hakka and Chao Chow. These
restaurants are now scattered throughout the city, leaving
Chinatown for the most part to the tourists.

Moderate–Expensive **The Mandarin.** Owner Cecilia Chiang introduced San Francis-
★ cans to the full spectrum of Chinese cooking in 1961, when she
opened the original Mandarin in a tiny Post Street locale. Now
she holds court in a magnificent setting fit for imperial fare,
decorated with paintings and embroideries from her family's
palatial homes in Peking. This is one of the world's great restaurants, and its finest offerings, such as Mandarin duck,
beggar's chicken cooked in clay, and the Mongolian fire pot,
must be ordered a day in advance. Bay view from some tables.
*Ghirardelli Sq., tel. 415/673–8812. Dress: informal. Reserva-
tions advised. AE, DC, MC, V. Closed Christmas and
Thanksgiving. Validated parking in Ghirardelli Sq. Garage.*

Moderate **Harbor Village.** Classic Cantonese cooking, dim sum lunches,
★ and fresh seafood from the restaurant's own tanks are the hallmarks of this 400-seat branch of a Hong Kong establishment,
which sent five of its master chefs to San Francisco to supervise
the kitchen. The setting is opulent, with Chinese antiques and
teak furnishings. *4 Embarcadero Center, tel. 415/781–8833.
Dress: informal. Reservations not accepted noon–1 PM. AE,
MC, V. Free validated parking in Embarcadero Center Garage
evenings and weekends.*

Inexpensive **Hunan.** Henry Chung's first cafe on Kearny had only six tables,
but his Hunan cooking merited six stars from critics nation-
wide. Now he has opened a larger place on Sansome, equally
plain but with 250 seats. Smoked dishes are a specialty, and
Henry guarantees no MSG. *924 Sansome, North Beach, tel.
415/956–7722. Dress: informal. Reservations advised. AE,
DC, MC, V.*

Yank Sing. This teahouse has grown by leaps and branches
with the popularity of dim sum. The Battery Street locale seats
300, and the older, smaller Stevenson site has just been rebuilt
in high-tech fashion. *427 Battery, Embarcadero area and financial district, tel. 415/362–1640. 49 Stevenson, tel. 415/495–
4510. Dress: informal. Reservations advised. AE, DC, MC, V.
No dinner.*

Continental These restaurants strive to combine French, Italian, and other
European cuisines, and dishes are usually served in a formal
setting.

Expensive **Julius Castle.** This turreted landmark building clings to the
cliffs of Telegraph Hill and commands sweeping vistas of the
bay. The food is traditional French and Italian, with an emphasis on pastas, seafood, and veal. The view and the site
compensate for the lack of imagination in the cuisine. *1541
Montgomery St., Telegraph Hill, tel. 415/362–3042. Jacket required. Reservations required. AE, DC, MC, V. No lunch
weekends. Closed Christmas and Thanksgiving. Valet parking.*

Moderate **Jack's.** Little has changed in more than 100 years at this bank-
ers' and brokers' favorite. The menu is extensive, but regulars

opt for the simple fare—steaks, chops, seafood, and stews. The dining room has an old-fashioned, no-nonsense aura, and private upstairs rooms are available for top-secret meetings. *615 Sacramento St., financial district, tel. 415/986-9854. Jacket and tie required. Reservations advised. AE. No lunch weekends. Closed major holidays.*

French French cooking has gone in and out of vogue in San Francisco since the extravagant days of the bonanza kings. A renaissance of the classic haute cuisine occurred in the 1960s, but recently a number of these restaurants closed. Meanwhile, nouvelle cuisine went in and out of fashion, and the pundits say the pendulum is swinging back to the classics. Nevertheless, the city offers a variety of dining choices from bistro to classic to nouvelle.

Very Expensive **Amelio's.** This historic restaurant, a former speakeasy, evokes
★ turn-of-the-century San Francisco. Once known for its Italian food, it was revitalized when the young French chef Jacky Robert became a partner. Robert's food looks as beautiful as it tastes. *1630 Powell St., North Beach, tel. 415/397-4339. Jacket required, tie requested. Reservations advised. AE, DC, MC, V. Closed Christmas and New Year's Day.*

★ **Ernie's.** This famous old-timer recently had a facelift. The dining rooms have been redecorated and a distinguished chef, Marcell Cathala, took charge of the kitchen, preparing innovative and lighter versions of classics from the south of France. Even so, the restaurant is still steeped with the aura of Gay Nineties San Francisco. *847 Montgomery St., North Beach, tel. 415/397-5969. Jacket and tie required. Reservations advised. AE, DC, MC, V. No lunch. Closed major holidays. Valet parking.*

★ **Masa's.** Chef Julian Serrano carries on the tradition of the late Masa Kobayashi. In fact, some Masa regulars say the cooking is even better. The artistry of the presentation is as important as the food itself in this pretty, flower-filled dining spot in the Vintage Court Hotel. *648 Bush St., downtown, tel. 415/989-7154. Jacket required. Reservations should be made precisely 21 days in advance. AE, DC, MC, V. No lunch. Closed Sun. and Mon., first week in July, last week in Dec., and first week in Jan. Valet parking.*

Pierre. French visitors feel right at home at the Meridien Hotel, where the exquisitely appointed Pierre carries on three-star traditions. The menu encompasses both classic and innovative cooking, and the service is some of the smoothest and most unobtrusive in town. From time to time visiting French chefs do special dinners. *50 Third St., Moscone Center area, tel. 415/974-6400. Jacket required. Reservations advised. AE, DC, MC, V. No lunch. Valet parking.*

Expensive–Very **Fleur de Lys.** The creative cooking of chef/partner Hubert Kel-
Expensive ler is earning rave reviews for this romantic spot that some
★ consider the best French restaurant in town. The menu changes constantly, but dishes such as lobster soup with lemongrass are a signature. The intimate dining room, like a sheik's tent, is swathed in hundreds of yards of paisley. *777 Sutter St., downtown, tel. 415/673-7779. Jacket and tie required. Reservations on weekends advised 2 weeks in advance. AE, DC, MC, V. No lunch. Closed Sun., Christmas, New Year's Day, and Thanksgiving. Valet parking.*

★ **Le Castel.** Trends come and go, but Le Castel has adhered to classic French cooking—with a light touch. You'll even find such rarities as calf's brains and bone marrow. The restaurant is housed in a former Victorian residence that was remodeled with a Moorish touch to the interior. *3235 Sacramento St., Presidio Heights, tel. 415/921–7115. Jacket required. Reservations advised. AE, DC, MC, V. No lunch. Closed Sun., Mon., and most major holidays. Valet parking.*

Moderate **Bistro Roti.** Tables in the rear of this new waterfront cafe look out over the bay and bridge, while those at the front surround a boisterous bar. A giant rotisserie and grill turn out succulent chops and roasts, but don't overlook that bistro classic— French onion soup. *155 Steuart St., tel. 415/495–6500. Reservations advised. Dress: informal. AE, MC, V. No lunch weekends.*

California Culinary Academy. This historic theater houses one of America's most highly regarded professional cooking schools. Watch the student chefs at work on the two-tier stage while you dine on classic French cooking. Prix fixe meals and bountiful buffets are served in the main dining room, healthy à la carte lunches are served at Cyril's on the balcony level, and there's a first-floor grill. *625 Polk St., Civic Center area, tel. 415/771–3500. Jacket required. Reservations required in dining room, accepted at Cyril's and the grill for parties of more than 5 or 7, respectively; not accepted for balcony. AE, DC, MC, V. Closed weekends and major holidays.*

Le Central. The quintessential bistro: noisy and crowded, with nothing subtle about the cooking, but the garlicky pâtés, leeks vinaigrette, cassoulet, and grilled blood sausage with crisp french fries keep the crowds coming. *453 Bush St., financial district, tel. 415/391–2233. Dress: informal. Reservations advised. AE, MC, V. Closed Sun. and major holidays.*

Indian The following restaurants serve the cuisine of northern India, which is more subtly seasoned and not as hot as its southern counterparts. They also specialize in succulent meats and crispy breads from the clay-lined tandoor oven.

Moderate **Gaylord.** A vast selection of mildly spiced northern Indian food is offered, along with meats and breads from the tandoor oven and a wide range of vegetarian dishes. The dining rooms at both branches are elegantly appointed with Indian paintings and gleaming silver service. Ghirardelli also offers bay views and an elaborate buffet brunch on Sunday. *Ghirardelli Sq., tel. 415/771–8822; 1 Embarcadero, tel. 415/397–7775. Dress: informal. Reservations advised. AE, DC, MC, V. No lunch Sun. at Embarcadero. Ghirardelli closed Christmas and Thanksgiving; Embarcadero closed Christmas, Labor Day, and New Year's Day. Validated parking at Ghirardelli Sq. Garage and Embarcadero Center Garage.*

North India. Small and cozy, this restaurant has a more limited menu and hotter seasoning than Gaylord. Both tandoori dishes and curries are served, plus a range of breads and appetizers. Everything is cooked to order. *3131 Webster St., Cow Hollow, tel. 415/931–1556. Dress: informal. Reservations advised. AE, DC, MC, V. No lunch weekends. Parking behind restaurant.*

International The following restaurants are truly international in that they draw their inspiration from both Eastern and Western cuisines.

Dining 133

Expensive ★ **Square One.** Chef Joyce Goldstein introduces an ambitious new menu daily with dishes based on the classic cooking of the Mediterranean countries as well as that of Asia and Latin America. The dining room, with its views of the open kitchen and the Golden Gateway commons, is an understated setting for some of the finest food in town. *190 Pacific Ave., Embarcadero area, tel. 415/788–1110. Dress: informal. Reservations advised. AE, MC, V. No lunch weekends. Closed major holidays. Valet parking in evenings.*

Moderate–Expensive **Trader Vic's.** This is the headquarters of Vic's empire. You'll find the usual tikis, the vast array of Cantonese and Polynesian dishes, and the exotic drinks. Concentrate instead on simpler fare such as fresh seafood and Indonesian rack of lamb. The Captain's Cabin is where the local celebs hang out, but you're not likely to get a seat there unless you're known. *20 Cosmo Pl., Downtown, tel. 415/776–2232. Jacket and tie required. Reservations advised. AE, DC, MC, V. No lunch weekends. Closed Christmas and Thanksgiving. Valet parking.*

Moderate **690.** East meets West on a tropical beach at Jeremiah Tower's latest spot. The decor, with its Club Med-style murals, is pure funk. And the food is pure fun—a medley of subtropical flavors and culinary styles from Thai to Moroccan. *690 Van Ness Ave., tel. 415/255–6900. Reservations advised. Dress: informal. AE, MC, V. No lunch Sat.*

Italian Italian food in San Francisco spans the "boot" from the mild cooking of northern Italy to the spicy cuisine of the south. Then there is the style indigenous to San Francisco, known as North Beach Italian—dishes like *cioppino* (a fisherman's stew) and Joe's special (a mélange of eggs, spinach, and ground beef).

Expensive– Very Expensive **Blue Fox.** This landmark restaurant was revitalized in 1988 by John Fassio, son of a former owner, who redecorated the place in a light, subtly formal style. The classic cooking, with a seasonally changing menu, is from the Piedmont region of northern Italy. Pasta and gnocchi are made on the premises, as are the luscious desserts. *659 Merchant, financial district, tel. 415/981–1177. Jacket and tie required. Reservations required. AE, DC, MC, V. No lunch. Closed Sun. and major holidays. Valet parking.*

Donatello. Much of the menu in this elegant restaurant in the Donatello Hotel is drawn from the Emilia-Romagna region of Italy, which is famous for its food, especially the Bolognese pastas. The intimate dining rooms are exquisitely appointed with silk-paneled walls, paintings, and tapestries. Service is superb and low-key. Donatello also serves breakfasts that combine typical American fare with Italian-accented dishes. *Post and Mason sts., downtown, tel. 415/441–7182. Jacket and tie required. Reservations advised. AE, DC, MC, V. No lunch. Validated parking in hotel garage.*

Expensive **Acquarello.** This exquisite little restaurant is a new venture of the former chef/maître d' at Donatello. The service and food are exemplary, and the menu covers the full range of Italian cuisine, from northern to southern styles. Desserts are exceptional. *1722 Sacramento St., tel. 415/567–5432. Reservations advised. Dress: informal. MC, V. No lunch. Closed Sun., Mon. Validated parking across the street.*

Act IV, Inn at the Opera. This intimate, wood paneled dining room—possibly the most romantic in the city—is now the setting for the sophisticated "country Italian" cooking of Michael Hart, the man who put Donatello on the culinary map. Though it's located just behind the Performing Arts Center, Act IV is so special that you'll want to skip the show and spend the entire evening there. Hart turns out an Italian-accented breakfast, too. *333 Fulton St., tel. 415/863–8400. Reservations advised. Jacket required. AE, MC, V. Valet parking.*

Moderate **Buca Giovanni.** Giovanni Leoni showcases the dishes of his
★ birthplace: the Serchio Valley in Tuscany. Pastas made on the premises are a specialty, and the calamari salad is one of the best around. The subterranean dining room is cozy and romantic. *800 Greenwich St., North Beach, tel. 415/776–7766. Dress: informal. Reservations advised. AE, MC, V. No lunch. Closed Sun. and most major holidays.*

Capp's Corner. One of the last of the family-style trattorias, diners sit elbow to elbow at long Formica tables to feast on bountiful six-course dinners. For the budget-minded or calorie-counters, a shorter dinner includes a tureen of soup, salad, and pasta. *1600 Powell St., North Beach, tel. 415/989–2589. Dress: informal. Reservations advised. AE, DC, MC, V. No lunch weekends. Closed Christmas and Thanksgiving. Credit off meal check for parking in garage across the street.*

Il Fornaio. An offshoot of the Il Fornaio bakeries, this handsome tile-floored, wood-paneled complex combines a cafe, bakery, and an upscale trattoria with outdoor seating. The cooking is Tuscan, featuring pizzas from a wood-burning oven, superb house-made pastas and gnocchi, and grilled poultry and seafood. Anticipate a wait for a table, but once seated you won't be disappointed—only surprised by the moderate prices. Breakfast is served in the cafe. *Levi's Plaza, 1265 Battery, Embarcadero area, tel. 415/986–0100. Dress: informal. Reservations advised. MC, V. Closed Christmas and Thanksgiving. Valet parking.*

Kuleto's. The contemporary cooking of northern Italy, the atmosphere of old San Francisco, and an antipasti bar have made this spot off Union Square a hit since it opened in the 1980s. Grilled seafood dishes are among the specialties. Breakfast is served, too. Publike booths and a long, open kitchen fill one side of the restaurant; a gardenlike setting with light splashed from skylights lies beyond. *221 Powell St., downtown, tel. 415/397–7720. Dress: informal. Reservations advised. AE, DC, MC, V. Closed Christmas and Thanksgiving.*

Lascaux. Despite its Gallic name (after the primitive caves in France), the cuisine at this smart new restaurant is primarily Mediterranean with a contemporary Italian accent. Changing menus offer such delights as a fluffy polenta topped with steamed mussels, a torta of sun-dried tomatoes and mascarpone, and grilled seafood with imaginative sauces. Desserts are fabulous. A huge fireplace cheers the romantically lit subterranean dining room. *248 Sutter St., Union Sq. area, tel. 415/391–1555. Dress: informal. Reservations advised. AE, MC, V. No lunch Sat. Closed Sun., Christmas, and Thanksgiving.*

★ **Zuni Cafe Grill.** The Italian-Mediterranean menu and unpretentious atmosphere pack in the crowds from early morning to late evening. A balcony dining area overlooks the large bar area, where both shellfish and drinks are dispensed. A second dining room houses the giant pizza oven and grill. Even the hamburgers have an Italian accent; they're served on herbed focaccio buns. *1658 Market St., Civic Center area, tel. 415/552–2522. Dress: informal. Reservations advised. AE, MC, V. Closed Mon., Christmas, and Thanksgiving.*

Japanese To understand a Japanese menu, you should be familiar with the basic types of cooking: *yaki*, marinated and grilled foods; *tempura*, fish and vegetables deep-fried in a light batter; *udon* and *soba*, noodle dishes; *domburi*, meats and vegetables served over rice; *ramen*, foods served in broth; and *nabemono*, meals cooked in one pot, often at the table. Of course sushi bars are extremely popular in San Francisco; most offer a selection of *sushi* (vinegared rice with raw fish or vegetables) and *sashimi* (raw fish). Western seating refers to conventional tables and chairs; *tatami* seating is on mats at low tables.

Moderate **Yamato.** The city's oldest Japanese restaurant is by far its most beautiful, with inlaid wood, painted panels, a meditation garden, and a pool. Both Western and tatami seating, in private shoji-screened rooms, are offered, along with a fine sushi bar. Come for the atmosphere primarily; the menu is somewhat limited, and more adventurous dining is found elsewhere. *717 California St., Chinatown, tel. 415/397–3456. Reservations advised. AE, DC, MC, V. No lunch weekends. Closed Mon., Christmas, New Year's Day, and Thanksgiving.*

Inexpensive **Sanppo.** This small place has an enormous selection of almost every type of Japanese food: yakis, nabemono dishes, domburi, udon, and soba, plus feather-light tempura and interesting side dishes. Western seating only. *1702 Post St., Japantown, tel. 415/346–3486. Dress: informal. Reservations not accepted. No credit cards. No lunch. Closed Mon. and major holidays. Validated parking in Japan Center Garage.*

Mexican In spite of San Francisco's Mexican heritage, until recently most south-of-the-border eateries were locked into the Cal-Mex taco-enchilada-mashed-beans syndrome. But now some newer places offer a broader spectrum of Mexican cooking.

Moderate **Corona Bar & Grill.** Reed Hearon, a new superstar among local
★ chefs, fills the ever-changing menu with light versions of regional Mexican dishes. His Corona paella, laden with shellfish and calamari, is sensational, as is the chocolate-coated flan. The atmosphere is a mix of old San Francisco (pressed tin ceilings and an antique bar) and old Mexico (handpainted masks and Aztec motifs). *88 Cyril Magnin, downtown, tel. 415/392–5500. Dress: informal. Reservations advised. AE, DC, MC, V. Closed Sun. lunch, Christmas, and Thanksgiving.*

Inexpensive **Chevys.** This first San Francisco branch of a popular Mexican minichain is decked out with funky neon signs and "El Machino" turning out flour tortillas. "Stop gringo food" is the motto here, and the emphasis is on the freshest ingredients and sauces. Of note are the grilled quail and seafood and the fabulous fajitas. *4th and Howard sts., Moscone Center area, tel. 415/543–8060. Dress: informal. Reservations accepted only for parties of 8 or more. MC, V. Closed Christmas and Thanksgiving. Validated parking evenings after 5 and weekends at garage under building (enter from Minna St.).*

Seafood Like all port cities, San Francisco takes pride in its seafood even though less than half the fish served here is from local waters. In winter and spring look for the fresh Dungeness crab best served cracked with mayonnaise. In summer, feast upon Pacific salmon, even though imported varieties are available year-round. A recent development is the abundance of unusual oysters from West Coast beds and the resulting proliferation of oyster bars.

Moderate **Hayes Street Grill.** ★ Eight to 15 different kinds of seafood are chalked on the blackboard each night at this extremely popular restaurant. The fish is served simply grilled, with a choice of sauces ranging from tartar to a spicy Szechuan peanut concoction. Appetizers are unusual, and desserts are lavish. *32 Hayes St., Civic Center area, tel. 415/863-5545. Dress: informal. Reservations should be made precisely 1 week in advance. MC, V. No lunch Sat. Closed Sun. and major holidays.*

Pacific Heights Bar & Grill. Unquestionably the best oyster bar in town, with at least a dozen varieties available each day and knowledgeable shuckers to explain the mollusks' origins. In the small dining rooms, grilled seafood and shellfish stews head the bill of fare. Paella is a house specialty. *2001 Fillmore St, lower Pacific Heights, tel. 415/567-3337. Dress: informal. Reservations advised. AE, MC, V. No lunch Sat. Closed Christmas and Thanksgiving. Valet parking in the evening.*

Tadich Grill. Owners and locations have changed many times since this old-timer opened in the gold-rush era, but the 19th century atmosphere remains, as does the kitchen's special way with seafood. Seating at the counter or in private booths; long lines for a table at lunchtime. *240 California St., financial district, tel. 415/391-2373. Dress: informal. Reservations not accepted. No credit cards. Closed Sat. and holidays.*

The Waterfront. The dramatic, multilevel glass-walled dining room guarantees a bay view from every table. The food doesn't always match the fabulous view, but the fresh fish and pasta are usually above average. Very popular for weekend brunch. *Pier 7, Embarcadero, tel. 415/391-2696. Dress: informal. Reservations required. AE, DC, MC, V. Closed Christmas. Valet parking.*

Southeast Asia In recent years San Franciscans have seen a tremendous influx of restaurants specializing in the foods of Thailand, Vietnam and most recently, Cambodia. The cuisines of these countries share many similarities, and one characteristic in particular: the cooking is always spicy and often very hot.

Inexpensive–Moderate **Khan Toke Thai House.** ★ The city's first Thai restaurant has a lovely dining room, furnished with low tables and cushions, and a garden view. The six-course dinners, with two entrées from an extensive choice, provide a delicious introduction to Thai cooking. (The seasoning will be mild unless you request it hot.) There's classical Thai dancing on Sunday. *5937 Geary Blvd, Richmond district, tel. 415/668-6654. Dress: informal. Reservations advised. AE, MC, V. No lunch. Closed Christmas, Labor Day, and Thanksgiving.*

Inexpensive **Angkor Palace.** One of the loveliest Cambodian restaurants in town, and also the most conveniently located for visitors. The extensive family-style menu offers such exotic fare as fish and coconut mousse baked in banana leaves. You'll have que tions, of course, but you'll find the staff eager to explain the contents of the menu. *1769 Lombard St., tel. 415/931–2830. Reservations advised. Dress: informal. AE, MC, V. No lunch.*

Golden Turtle. This popular Vietnamese cafe is more accessible than its original branch on Fifth Avenue. The menu is also more extensive, with about 50 items, and the decor is more elaborate. There's even a carp pond. *2211 Van Ness Ave., midtown, tel. 415/441–4419. Dress: informal. Reservations accepted only for parties of 3 or more. AE, MC, V. Closed Mon. and last week in Dec.*

Steak Houses Although San Francisco traditionally has not been a meat-and-potatoes town, a few very fine steak houses have opened in recent years. You can also get a good piece of beef at some of the better French, Italian, and American restaurants.

Expensive **Harris.** Ann Harris knows her beef. She grew up on a Texas cat-
★ tle ranch and was married to the late Jack Harris of Harris Ranch fame. In her own elegant restaurant she serves some of the best dry-aged steaks in town, accompanied by Texas red potatoes. But don't overlook the grilled seafood or poultry. *2100 Van Ness Ave., midtown, tel. 415/673–1888. Jacket required at dinner. Reservations recommended. AE, DC, MC, V. No lunch on weekends. Closed Christmas and New Year's Day. Valet parking.*

Moderate **Izzy's Steak & Chop House.** Izzy Gomez was a legendary San Francisco saloonkeeper, and his namesake eatery carries on the tradition with terrific steaks, chops, and seafood, plus all the trimmings like cheesy scalloped potatoes and creamed spinach. A collection of Izzy memorabilia and antique advertising art covers almost every inch of wall space. *3345 Steiner, Marina, tel. 415/563–0487. Dress: informal. Reservations accepted. AE, DC, MC, V. No lunch. Closed Thanksgiving and Christmas. Validated parking at Lombard Garage.*

Vegetarian Vegetarians should also consider Gaylord (*see* above), which offers a wide variety of meatless dishes from the Hindu cuisine.

Moderate **Greens at Fort Mason.** This beautiful restaurant with its bay
★ views is a favorite with carnivores as well as vegetarians. Owned and operated by the Tassajara Zen Center of Carmel Valley, the restaurant offers a wide, eclectic, and creative spectrum of meatless cooking, and the bread promises nirvana. Dinners are à la carte on weeknights, but only a five-course prix fixe dinner is served Friday and Saturday. *Bldg. A, Ft. Mason Marina, tel. 415/771–6222. Dress: informal. Reservations advised. MC, V. Brunch only on Sun. Closed Mon., Christmas, New Year's Day, and Thanksgiving. Public parking at Ft. Mason Center.*

Lodging

Few cities in the United States can equal San Francisco's variety in lodging. There are plush hotels ranked among the finest in the world, renovated older buildings that have the charm of Europe, bed-and-breakfast inns in the city's Victorian "Painted Ladies," and the popular chain hotels and low-rise motels that are found in most cities in the United States.

One of the brightest spots in the lodging picture is the transformation of handsome early-20th-century downtown high rises into small, distinctive hotels that offer personal service and European-style ambience. Another is the addition of ultradeluxe modern hotels, such as the Nikko, Portman, and Mandarin Oriental, that offer attentive Asian-style hospitality. On top of those offerings are the dozens of popular chain hotels, such as Holiday Inn, Sheraton, Hyatt, and Hilton, that continually undergo face-lifts and additions to keep up with the competition.

Because San Francisco is one of the top destinations in the United States for tourists as well as business travelers and convention-goers, reservations are always advised, especially in the May-September peak season.

San Francisco's geography makes it conveniently compact. No matter their location, the hotels listed here are on or close to public transportation lines. Some properties on Lombard and in the Civic Center area have free parking, but a car is more a hindrance than an asset in San Francisco.

Although not as high as those in New York, San Francisco hotel prices may come as a surprise to travelers from less urban areas. Average double room rates downtown and at the wharf are in the $125 range. Motel and hotel rooms can be found for less throughout the city, especially in the Civic Center and Lombard areas. Adding to the expense is the city's 11% transient occupancy tax, which can significantly boost the cost of a lengthy stay.

An alternative to hotels, inns, and motels is staying in private homes and apartments, available through two companies: **American Family Inn/Bed & Breakfast San Francisco** (Box 349, San Francisco, CA 94101, tel. 415/931–3083) and **Bed & Breakfast International-San Francisco** (1181-B Solano Ave., Albany, CA 94706, tel. 415/525–4569).

The **San Francisco Convention and Visitors Bureau** (201 3rd St., San Francisco 94103) each year publishes a free lodging guide with a map and listings of all hotels. There are two telephone reservation services: **Golden Gate Lodging Reservations** (tel. 415/771–6915 or 800/423–7846) and **San Francisco Reservations** (tel. 415/227–1500 or 800/333–8996).

If you are looking for truly budget accommodations (under $40), consider the Adelaide, Grant Plaza (*see* below), or the:

YMCA Central Branch. *220 Golden Gate Ave., San Francisco 94102, tel. 415/885–0460. 102 rooms, 8 with private bath. Facilities: health club, pool, sauna. MC, V.*

Highly recommended hotels are indicated by a star ★.

Lodgings are listed by geographical area and price range.

Category	Cost*
Very Expensive	over $175
Expensive	$100–$175

Moderate	$65–$100
Inexpensive	under $65

double room, not including tax

Civic Center/Van Ness The governmental heart of San Francisco has been undergoing a renaissance that has made it come alive with fine restaurants, trendy night spots, and renovated small hotels.

Expensive **Cathedral Hill Hotel.** Guest rooms were renovated in 1988 at this popular convention hotel. *1101 Van Ness Ave., 94109, tel. 415/776–8200, 800/622–0855 in CA, or 800/227–4730 nationwide. 400 rooms. Facilities: free parking, pool, 2 restaurants, lounge. AE, DC, MC, V.*

Inn at the Opera. A music or ballet lover's heart may quiver at this lovely small hotel, where Mikhail Baryshnikov and Leontyne Price stay when they appear at San Francisco's performing arts centers a block away. Billowing pillows, terrycloth robes, microwave ovens, and servibars in each room. *333 Fulton, 94102, tel. 415/863–8400, 800/423–9610 in CA, or 800/325–2708 nationwide. 48 rooms. Facilities: restaurant, lounge. AE, MC, V.*

Majestic Hotel. One of San Francisco's original grand hotels was meticulously restored and reopened in 1985 with even more stately elegance. Romantic rooms have French and English antiques and four-poster canopy beds. Many also have fireplaces and original clawfoot bathtubs. *1500 Sutter, 94109, tel. 415/441–1100 or 800/869–8966. 60 rooms. Facilities: gourmet restaurant, lounge. AE, DC, MC, V.*

Miyako. In the heart of Japantown is this elegant, recently renovated hotel. The Japanese ambience starts with a greeting by a kimono-clad hostess. Traditional Japanese rooms with tatami mats are available. *1625 Post at Laguna, 94115, tel. 415/922–3200 or 800/533–4567. Facilities: restaurant, 2 lounges, AE, DC, MC, V.*

Moderate **Abigail Hotel.** ★ A former bed-and-breakfast inn, this hotel retains its homey atmosphere with an eclectic mix of English antiques and mounted hunting trophies in the lobby. Hissing steam radiators and sleigh beds set the mood in the antique-filled rooms. Room 211—the hotel's only suite—is the most elegant and spacious. *246 McAllister St., 94102, tel. 415/861–9728, 800/553–5575 in CA, or 800/243–6510 nationwide. 62 rooms. Facilities: European-style restaurant. AE, DC, MC, V.*

Best Western Americania. This hotel stands out for its pink and turquoise Moorish facade. Rooms overlook inner courtyards with fountain or swimming pool. *171 7th St., 94103, tel. 415/626–0200 or 800/444–5816. 142 rooms. Facilities: outdoor pool, sauna, coffee shop, free parking, nonsmoking rooms available. AE, DC, MC, V.*

Holiday Inn-Civic Center. The renovated restaurant and marble-floored lobby have added a touch of elegance. Good location 3 blocks from Civic Center and 2 blocks from Brooks Hall/Civic Auditorium. *50 8th St., 94103, tel. 415/626–6103 or 800/HOLIDAY. 390 rooms. Facilities: restaurant, lounge, outdoor pool. AE, DC, MC, V.*

★ **Lombard Hotel.** This is a European-style hotel with a handsome marble-floored lobby flanked on one side by the Gray Derby restaurant. Rooms were refurbished in 1988 with blondwood furniture and new servibars. Quiet rooms are in the back. Complimentary evening cocktails and chauffeured limousine to

Downtown San Francisco Lodging

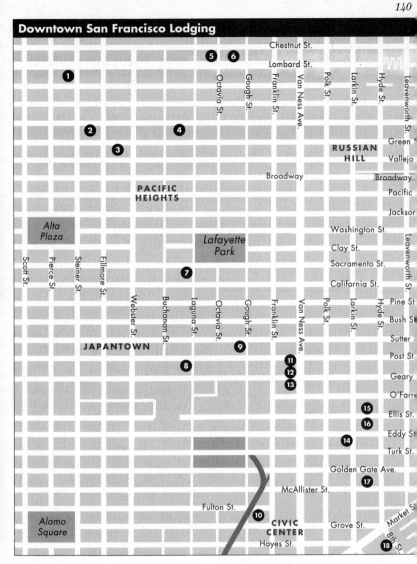

Abigail Hotel, **17**
Atherton Hotel, **16**
Aston Regis Hotel, **33**
Bed and Breakfast
Inn, **4**
Bel Aire Travel
Lodge, **1**
Campton Place, **37**

Cathedral Hill
Hotel, **11**
Cartwright, **25**
Chancellor Hotel, **26**
Essex Hotel, **15**
Fairmont Hotel and
Tower, **22**
Four Season Clift, **32**
Galleria Park, **41**

Grand Hyatt, **36**
Holiday Inn--Civic
Center, **18**
Holiday Inn--Financial
District, **38**
Hotel Diva, **34**
Hotel Nikko--San
Francisco, **29**

Huntington Hotel, **21**
Hyatt Regency--San
Francisco, **40**
Inn at the Opera, **10**
Inn at Union
Square, **27**
King George, **28**
Lombard Hotel, **12**
Majestic Hotel, **9**
Mandarin Oriental, **39**

San Francisco Bay

TELEGRAPH HILL

NORTH BEACH

CHINATOWN

Halleck St.

UNION SQUARE

0   440 yards
0   400 meters

Mansion, **7**
Marina Inn, **5**
Mark Hopkins Inter-Continental, **23**
Miyako, **8**
New Richelieu, **13**
Petite Auberge, **20**
Phoenix Inn, **14**
San Francisco Hilton, **31**
Sheraton Palace, **42**

Sherman House, **3**
Sir Francis Drake, **35**
Stanford Court, **24**
Town House Motel, **6**
Union Street Inn, **2**
Westin St. Francis, **30**

downtown. *1015 Geary St., 94109, tel. 415/673–5232 or 800/227 –3608. 100 rooms. Facilities: restaurant. AE, DC, MC, V.*

The Mansion. This twin-turreted Queen Anne Victorian house was built in 1887 and today is one of the most unusual hotels in the city. Rooms contain an oddball collection of furnishings, and vary from the tiny "Tom Thumb" room to the opulent "Josephine" suite, the favorite of celebrities such as Barbra Streisand. Owner Bob Pritikin's pig paintings and other "porkabilia" are everywhere. *2220 Sacramento St., 94115, tel. 415/929–9444. 19 rooms. Facilities: guests-only restaurant, live nightly entertainment in concert rooms, Bufano sculpture, and flower garden. AE, DC, MC, V.*

New Richelieu Hotel. The Richelieu's rooms have new beds, furniture, and carpeting. Rooms in the back building are larger and have new bathrooms. The lobby has been spruced up with an elegant gray and blue color scheme. *1050 Van Ness Ave., 94109, tel. 415/673–4711 or 800/227–3608. 150 rooms. Facilities: nonsmoking rooms available, gift shop and tour desk in lobby. 24-hour restaurant adjacent. AE, DC, MC, V.*

The Phoenix Inn. Resembling more a '50s-style beachside resort than a hotel in San Francisco's government center, the Phoenix bills itself aptly as an "urban retreat." Bungalow-style rooms, decorated in casual bamboo and original art by San Francisco artists, all face a pool courtyard and sculpture garden. *601 Eddy, 94109, tel. 415/776–1380 or 800/CITY–INN. 44 rooms. Facilities: free parking, lounge, heated swimming pool; Italian restaurant offers room service. AE, DC, MC, V.*

Inexpensive **The Atherton Hotel.** A clean, low-priced hotel with two-level Mediterranean-style lobby. *685 Ellis St., 94109, tel. 415/474– 5720 or 800/227–3608. 80 rooms. Facilities: restaurant, bar. AE, DC, MC, V.*

The Essex Hotel. Italian marble floors in the lobby give this otherwise simple tourist hotel a touch of class. The friendliness of the Australian couple who own it also is a big plus. Popular with German and English tourists. *684 Ellis St., 94109, tel. 415/474– 4664, 800/44–ESSEX in CA, or 800/45–ESSEX nationwide. 100 rooms, 52 with private bath. AE, MC, V.*

★ **Hotel Britton.** Clean and comfortable, with good rates and close to Civic Center. Rooms are attractively furnished, and color TVs offer in-room movies. *112 7th St., at Mission, 94103, tel. 415/621–7001 or 800/444–5819. 80 rooms. Facilities: coffee shop. AE, DC, MC, V.*

Financial District High-rise growth in San Francisco's financial district has turned it into mini-Manhattan, a spectacular sight by night.

Very Expensive **Mandarin Oriental.** The third-highest building in San Francisco's skyline is topped by a luxurious 11-story hotel on the 38th–48th floors. It's the best for spectacular views, especially from the bathrooms in the Mandarin rooms, with their floor-to-ceiling windows flanking the tubs. *222 Sansome, 94104, tel. 415/885–0999 or 800/526–6566. 160 rooms. Facilities: gourmet restaurant, lounge. AE, DC, MC, V.*

Sheraton Palace. One of San Francisco's grand old hotels, the Palace was still undergoing an extensive restoration at press time and was due to reopen at the end of 1990. The fabled Garden Court restaurant, with its leaded glass ceiling, and the clubby Pied Piper lounge, with its namesake Maxfield Parrish painting, have both been renovated; a health club, pool, and air conditioning are a few of the new additions. *2 New Montgom-*

*ery, 94105, tel. 415/392–8600 or 800/325–3535. 528 rooms. Fa-
cilities: 24-hour room service, 2 restaurants, 2 lounges, pool,
health club. AE, DC, MC, V.*

Expensive
★
Galleria Park. Very attractive renovated hotel convenient to
Union Square shopping district. *191 Sutter, 94104, tel. 415/781
–3060, 800/792–9855 in CA, or 800/792–9639 nationwide. 177
rooms. Facilities: rooftop park and jogging track, 2 restaurants, lounge. AE, DC, MC, V.*

Holiday Inn-Financial District. Excellent location in China-
town and five minutes to Union Square and North Beach.
Rooms on 12th floor and above have city and bay views. *750
Kearny, 94108, tel. 415/433–6600 or 800/HOLIDAY. 556 rooms.
Facilities: pool, free parking, restaurant, lounge. AE, DC,
MC, V.*

Hyatt Regency-Embarcadero. The stunning atrium-lobby architecture is the highlight. *5 Embarcadero Center, 94111, tel.
415/788–1234 or 800/233–1234. 803 rooms. Facilities: 2 restaurants, coffee shop, lounge, 24-hour room service, shopping
arcade. AE, DC, MC, V.*

**Fisherman's
Wharf/North
Beach**
Fisherman's Wharf, San Francisco's top tourist attraction, is
also the most popular area for accommodations. All are within a
couple of blocks of restaurants, shops, and cable car lines. Owing to city ordinances, none of the hotels here are more than 4
stories; thus, this is not the area for fantastic views of the city
or bay. Reservations are always necessary, sometimes weeks
in advance during the peak summer months. Some street-side
rooms can be noisy.

Very Expensive
San Francisco Marriott-Fisherman's Wharf. An elegant lobby
and guest rooms set the mood in one of the wharf's newest and
finest hotels. *1250 Columbus Ave., 94133, tel. 415/775–7555 or
800/228–9290. 256 rooms. Facilities: restaurant, 2 lounges, gift
shop. AE, DC, MC, V.*

Expensive
Holiday Inn-Fisherman's Wharf. This large brick-faced hotel
covers nearly 2 square blocks, including the 1984 addition,
which has its own lobby and restaurant. Ongoing renovations
keep the rooms throughout the hotel upgraded. Charley's restaurant in the main building serves three excellent buffets;
lunch features fresh seafood. *1300 Columbus Ave., 94133, tel.
415/771–9000 or 800/HOLIDAY. 580 rooms. Facilities: outdoor
swimming pool, laundry rooms, free parking. AE, DC, MC,
V.*

Ramada Hotel-Fisherman's Wharf. The well-appointed public
areas and guest rooms have all been renovated within the last
few years. *590 Bay, 94133, tel. 415/885–4700 or 800/228–2828.
231 rooms. Facilities: free parking, running track, par golf
course. AE, DC, MC, V.*

Sheraton at Fisherman's Wharf. Rooms and corridors were
handsomely refurnished in 1987 at this sprawling full-service
hotel. Street-side rooms can be noisy; interior courtyard rooms
are the quietest. *2500 Mason St., 94133, tel. 415/362–5500 or
800/325–3535. 525 rooms. Facilities: outdoor pool, 3 restaurants, cocktail lounge. AE, DC, MC, V.*

TraveLodge at the Wharf. This is an attractive hotel whose
rooms were tastefully redecorated in the last few years.
Higher-priced interior rooms (third and fourth floors) have balconies overlooking a landscaped deck/swimming pool and
unobstructed views of Alcatraz. *250 Beach St., 94133, tel. 415/*

392–6700 or 800/255–3050. 250 rooms. Facilities: outdoor pool, restaurant, lounge, free parking. AE, DC, MC, V.

Moderate **Columbus Motor Inn.** This is an attractive motel between the wharf and North Beach with suites ideal for families. *1075 Columbus Ave., 94133, tel. 415/885–1492. 45 rooms. Facilities: free parking. AE, DC, MC, V.*

Inexpensive **San Remo Hotel.** This cozy hotel is reminiscent of a European-
★ style pensione. Renovated during recent years, its smallish rooms and narrow corridors are freshly painted and decorated with plants and antiques. A good location on the border of Fisherman's Wharf and North Beach. *2237 Mason St., 94133, tel. 415/776–8688. 62 rooms; all share baths. Daily rates May–Oct.; weekly rates remainder of year. Facilities: Italian restaurant. MC, V.*

Lombard Street/ Lombard Street, a major traffic corridor leading to the Golden
Cow Hollow Gate Bridge, is sandwiched between two of San Francisco's poshest neighborhoods, Cow Hollow and the Marina district, locations of the fashionable Union Street shopping area and the lovely Marina Green and yacht harbor.

Very Expensive **The Sherman House.** In the middle of an elegant residential dis-
★ trict is this magnificent landmark mansion, the most luxurious small hotel in San Francisco. Each room is individually decorated in Biedermeier, English Jacobean, or French Second-Empire antiques, with tapestrylike canopies covering four-poster beds. Marble-topped wood-burning fireplaces and black granite bathrooms with whirlpool baths complete the picture. There is an in-house restaurant for guests only. *2160 Green St., 94123, tel. 415/563–3600. 15 rooms. Facilities: restaurant, sitting rooms, valet/laundry service, concierge. AE, DC, MC, V.*

Moderate **The Bed and Breakfast Inn.** The first of San Francisco's B&Bs, this is an ivy-covered renovated Victorian home on an alleyway off Union Street. Romantic, cheery rooms with flowery wallpaper include "The Mayfair," a flat with a spiral staircase leading to a sleeping loft. Some rooms are more modest and share baths. *4 Charlton Court, 94123, tel. 415/921–9784. 9 rooms; 5 with private bath. Facilities: breakfast room. No credit cards.*

Bel Aire TraveLodge. This attractive, well-kept motel is in a quiet location ½-block from Lombard. *3201 Steiner, 94123, tel. 415/921–5162 or 800/255–3050. 32 rooms. Facilities: free parking. AE, DC, MC, V.*

Cow Hollow Motor Inn. This is a large, modern motel with lovely rooms that were all renovated in 1988 with thick new burgundy carpeting and rose-colored bedspreads. *2190 Lombard, 94123, tel. 415/921–5800. 117 rooms. Facilities: free parking. AE, DC, MC, V.*

★ **Marina Inn.** Cute B&B-style accommodations are offered at motel prices. Dainty flowered wallpaper, poster beds, country pine furniture, and fresh flowers give the rooms an English country air. Continental breakfast is served in the cozy central sitting room. Turned-down beds and chocolates greet guests at the end of the day. No parking. *3110 Octavia at Lombard, 94123, tel. 415/928–1000. 40 rooms. Facilities: lounge. AE, MC, V.*

Rancho Lombard Motel. This motel has handsome, newly renovated rooms with colonial-style furniture. Some rooms have kitchens and/or bay views. *1501 Lombard, 94123, tel. 415/474–3030. 37 rooms. Facilities: free parking. AE, DC, MC, V.*

Union Street Inn. A retired schoolteacher has transformed this 1902 Edwardian home into a cozy inn. Antiques and fresh flowers are found throughout. *2229 Union St., 94123, tel. 415/346–0424. 6 rooms; 3 with private bath. Facilities: English garden, breakfast room. AE, MC, V.*

Vagabond Inn. This is a beautifully maintained motor inn that overlooks a central courtyard swimming pool. Some fourth- and fifth-floor rooms have views of Golden Gate Bridge. *2550 Van Ness, near Lombard, 94109, tel. 415/776–7500 or 800/522–1555 in CA. 132 rooms. Facilities: outdoor pool, 24-hour restaurant, lounge. AE, DC, MC, V.*

Inexpensive **Edward II Bed and Breakfast.** Standard rooms are smallish and parking is not available, but reasonable prices and a quaint pensione atmosphere offset the drawbacks. *3155 Scott St., at Lombard, 94123, tel. 415/922–3000. 29 rooms; 19 with private bath. Facilities: restaurant, Italian bakery off the lobby. AE, MC, V.*

Marina Motel. This quaint Spanish-style stucco complex is one of oldest motels on Lombard, but it is well kept. All rooms have their own garages. *2576 Lombard, 94123, tel. 415/921–9406. 45 rooms; some with kitchens. Facilities: free parking. AE, MC, V.*

Star Motel. This is a well-maintained motel with basic rooms. Free HBO. *1727 Lombard, 94123, tel. 415/346–8250. 52 rooms. Facilities: free parking. AE, MC, V.*

★ **Town House Motel.** This is a very attractive motel with recently redecorated rooms, one of the best values on Lombard. *1650 Lombard, 94123, tel. 415/885–5163, 800/334–1516 in CA, or 800/255–1516 nationwide. 24 rooms. Facilities: free parking. AE, DC, MC, V.*

Nob Hill Synonymous with San Francisco high society, Nob Hill contains some of the city's best-known luxury hotels. All offer spectacular city and bay views and noted gourmet restaurants. Cable-car lines that cross Nob Hill make transportation a cinch.

Very Expensive **Fairmont Hotel and Tower.** The regal "grande dame" of Nob Hill, the Fairmont has one of the most spectacular lobbies and public rooms in the city. All guest rooms are spacious and finely decorated. Those in the modern tower have the best views; those in the old building have the stately ambience of another era. *950 Mason, 94108, tel. 415/772–5000 or 800/527–4727. 596 rooms. Facilities: health club and spa, gift shops, 7 restaurants, 10 lounges, 24-hour room service. AE, DC, MC, V.*

Huntington Hotel. Understated class is found in this little jewel atop Nob Hill. Sumptuous rooms and suites are individually decorated. The only elevator operators in the city push buttons for guests 24 hours a day. *1075 California, 94108, tel. 415/474–5400, 800/652–1539 in CA, or 800/227–4683 nationwide. 140 rooms. Facilities: 2 restaurants including L'Etoile, lounge. AE, DC, MC, V.*

Mark Hopkins Inter-Continental. Another Nob Hill landmark, "The Mark" is lovingly maintained. Rooms were redone in late 1987 in dramatic neoclassical furnishings of gray, silver, and khaki and with bold leaf-print bedspreads. Bathrooms are lined with Italian marble. Even-numbered rooms have views of the Golden Gate Bridge. *999 California, 94108, tel. 415/392–3434 or 800/327–0200. 392 rooms. Facilities: gift shops, 2 res-*

taurants, lobby lounge, Top of the Mark cocktail lounge with panoramic views. AE, DC, MC, V.

The Stanford Court. This is one of the most highly acclaimed hotels in the United States. The service is so thoughtful that the general manager recently put dictionaries in each room for guests' convenience. One of the city's finest restaurants, Fournou's Ovens, is located here. *905 California, 94108, tel. 415/989-3500 or 800/227-4736. 402 rooms. Facilities: gift shops, 2 restaurants, 2 lounges. AE, DC, MC, V.*

Union Square/Downtown The largest variety and greatest concentration of hotels are near the city's lovely downtown hub, Union Square, where hotel guests find the best shopping, the theater district, and transportation to everywhere in San Francisco.

Very Expensive **Campton Place.** Steps away from Union Square is one of the most highly rated and elegant hotels in San Francisco. Attentive, personal service begins the moment uniformed doormen greet guests outside the marble-floored lobby. *340 Stockton, 94108, tel. 415/781-5555, 800/235-4300 in CA, or 800/647-4007 nationwide. 126 rooms. Facilities: Campton Place restaurant, bar. AE, DC, MC, V.*

Four Seasons Clift. Probably San Francisco's most acclaimed hotel, this stately landmark is the first choice of many celebrities and discriminating travelers for its attentive personal service. Special attention is given to children, with fresh cookies and milk at bedtime. *495 Geary, 94102, tel. 415/775-4700 or 800/332-3442. 329 rooms. Facilities: French Room restaurant, Redwood Room lounge. AE, DC, MC, V.*

Grand Hyatt. Rooms were renovated in 1989 in this hotel that overlooks the square. *345 Stockton, 94108, tel. 415/398-1234 or 800/228-9000. 693 rooms. Facilities: 2 restaurants, 2 lounges, shopping arcade. AE, DC, MC, V.*

Hotel Nikko-San Francisco. Trickling waterfalls and walls of white marble set a quiet, subtle mood at this fine Japanese Air Lines–owned hotel. *222 Mason St., 94102, tel. 415/394-1111 or 800/NIKKO-US. 525 rooms. Facilities: heated indoor pool, health club and spa, 2 restaurants, lounge. AE, DC, MC, V.*

Westin St. Francis. This is one of the grand hotels of San Francisco and a Union Square landmark. Rooms in the original building and modern tower are all recently renovated. *335 Powell, 94102, tel. 415/397-7000 or 800/228-3000. 1,200 rooms. Facilities: 5 restaurants, 5 lounges, shopping arcade. AE, DC, MC, V.*

Expensive **Aston Regis Hotel.** This is one of the finest examples of the new generation of small, renovated hotels. Rooms are large and elegant. *490 Geary, 94102, tel. 415/928-7900 or 800/82-REGIS. 86 rooms. Facilities: restaurant, lounge. AE, DC, MC, V.*

Holiday Inn–Union Square. Good location on cable-car line 1 block from Union Square. *480 Sutter, 94108, tel. 415/398-8900 or 800/HOLIDAY. 400 rooms. Facilities: 30th-floor lounge, restaurant. AE, DC, MC, V.*

Hotel Diva. This hotel attracts the avant-garde set with a high-tech look that sets it apart from every other hotel in San Francisco. *440 Geary, 94102, tel. 415/885-0200 or 800/553-1900. 125 rooms. Facilities: art gallery, breakfast room, restaurant. AE, DC, MC, V.*

Inn at Union Square. Individually decorated rooms with

goosedown pillows and four-poster beds are sumptuous. Continental breakfast and afternoon tea are served before a fireplace in the cozy sitting areas on each floor. *440 Post St., 94102, tel. 415/397–3510 or 800/288–4346. 30 rooms. AE, MC, V.*

Kensington Park. A handsome, high-ceilinged lobby sets the mood of this fine hotel, where afternoon tea and sherry are served. *450 Post, 94102, tel. 415/788–6400 or 800/553–1900. 90 rooms. AE, DC, MC, V.*

★ **Petite Auberge.** The French countryside was imported to downtown San Francisco to create this charming B&B inn. Calico-printed wallpaper, fluffy down comforters, and French reproduction antiques decorate each room. Most have wood-burning fireplaces. Next door is the sister hotel, the 27-room White Swan, similar in style but with an English country flavor. *863 Bush St., 94108, tel. 415/928–6000. 26 rooms. Facilities: breakfast rooms, parlors. AE, MC, V.*

San Francisco Hilton on Hilton Square. A huge expansion and renovation in 1988 made this by far the largest hotel in San Francisco. Popular with convention and tour groups. *1 Hilton Sq. at O'Farrell and Mason sts., 94102, tel. 415/771–1400 or 800/445–8667. 1,907 rooms. Facilities: pool, shopping arcade, 5 restaurants, 2 lounges. AE, DC, MC, V.*

Sir Francis Drake. A multimillion-dollar renovation in 1986 retained the stately elegance. It is famous for its Beefeater-costumed doormen. *450 Powell, 94102, tel. 415/392–7755, 800/652–1668 in CA, or 800/227–5480 nationwide. 415 rooms. Facilities: restaurant, rooftop lounge. AE, DC, MC, V.*

Moderate **The Cartwright.** This is a family-owned hotel in an ideal location
★ with a friendly, personal touch. Rooms have brass or wood-carved beds, small refrigerators, and newly tiled bathrooms. *524 Sutter, 94102, tel. 415/421–2865, or 800/227–3844. 114 rooms. Facilities: coffee shop. AE, DC, MC, V.*

★ **Chancellor Hotel.** This family-owned and -operated hotel has been attracting a loyal clientele since it opened in 1924. The rooms have a new, elegant appearance with polished cherrywood furniture. It is one of the best buys on Union Square. *433 Powell, 94102, tel. 415/362–2004. 140 rooms. Facilities: Italian restaurant, lounge. AE, DC, MC, V.*

Handlery Union Square Hotel. The former Handlery Motor Inn and Stewart Hotel were combined and refurbished at a cost of $5 million in early 1988. The suitelike Handlery Club rooms are larger and more expensive. *351 Geary St., 94102, tel. 415/781–7800 or 800/223–0888. 378 rooms. Facilities: restaurant, outdoor heated pool, nonsmoking rooms. AE, DC, MC, V.*

Hotel Bedford. Big, cheery floral prints dominate the recently renovated guest rooms in this hotel, 4 blocks from Union Square. *761 Post, 94109, tel. 415/673–6040, 800/652–1889 in CA, or 800/227–5642 nationwide. 144 rooms. Facilities: restaurant, English-style pub, in-room movies available to rent. AE, DC, MC, V.*

★ **King George.** Rooms at this charming midsize hotel were renovated in 1988 to give them a more uptown look. The hotel's quaint Bread and Honey Tearoom serves traditional afternoon high tea to the accompaniment of live piano music. *334 Mason, 94102, tel. 415/781–5050 or 800/288–6005. 144 rooms. Facilities: tearoom, lounge. AE, DC, MC, V.*

Monticello Inn. This hotel could boast that "George Washington slept here" and most people would believe it. Recreating a little bit of the American Colonial period in the middle of downtown, the Inn opened in 1987 after a complete renovation. The popular Corona Bar and Grill is off the lobby. *80 Cyril Magnin, 94102, tel. 415/392–8800 or 800/669–7777. 91 rooms. Facilities: restaurant. AE, DC, MC, V.*

The Raphael. A favorite among repeat visitors to San Francisco, the Raphael was one of the first moderately priced European-style hotels in the city. Rooms were redecorated in 1988. The location is excellent. *386 Geary St., 94102, tel. 415/986–2000 or 800/821–5343. 151 rooms. Facilities: restaurant, lounge, in-room HBO. AE, DC, MC, V.*

Vintage Court. Beautifully furnished, elegant rooms with Wine Country theme are featured. Complimentary wine is served before a crackling fire in the lobby in afternoons. *650 Bush, 94108, tel. 415/392–4666, 800/654–7266 in CA, or 800/654–1100 nationwide. 106 rooms. Facilities: Masa's restaurant, lounge. AE, DC, MC, V.*

York Hotel. This very attractive, renovated old hotel is known for its Plush Room cabaret and as the site of a scene in Alfred Hitchcock's *Vertigo, 940 Sutter St., 94109, tel. 415/885–6800 or 800/227–3608. 96 rooms. Facilities: nightclub, fitness center, complimentary chauffeured limousine. AE, DC, MC, V.*

Inexpensive **Adelaide Inn.** The bedspreads may not match the drapes or carpets and the floors may creak, but the rooms are clean and cheap (about $40 for a double room) at this friendly small hotel that is popular with Europeans. Continental breakfast is complimentary. *5 Isadora Duncan Court, off Taylor between Geary and Post, 94102, tel. 415/441–2661, 16 rooms, all share bath. Facilities: sitting room, refrigerator for guest use. MC, V.*

Amsterdam. This European-style pensione is in a Victorian building 2 blocks from Nob Hill. Rooms were renovated in 1988. *749 Taylor, 94108, tel. 415/673–3277 or 800/637–3444. 30 rooms; 10 with shared bath. Facilities: cable TV in rooms, reading room, breakfast room for complimentary breakfast. AE, MC, V.*

Beresford Arms. Complimentary pastries and coffee are served in the hotel's grand old lobby. The suites with full kitchens are a good bargain for families. Standard rooms come queen-size beds and small refrigerators. *701 Post St., 94109, tel. 415/673–2600 or 800/533–6533. 90 rooms. Facilities: some rooms have whirlpool baths. AE, DC, MC, V.*

★ **Grant Plaza.** This bargain-priced hotel at the entrance of Chinatown has small but clean and attractively furnished rooms. No restaurant, but plenty of dining is available nearby. *465 Grant Ave., 94102, tel. 415/434–3883, 800/472–6805 in CA, or 800/472–6899 nationwide. 72 rooms. AE, MC, V.*

Oxford–Cambridge Inn. Clean, comfortable rooms with color TVs and in-room movies are a good value. Complimentary Continental breakfast is served. *25 Mason St., 94102, tel. 415/775–4600 or 800/553–1900. 103 rooms. Facilities: Hofbrau restaurant, rooftop patio. AE, DC, MC, V.*

U.N. Plaza Hotel. This is a well-kept hotel for budget-conscious travelers who don't mind a less-than-desirable location. Large corner suites are ideal for families. Color TVs have in-room movies. *1112 Market St., 94102, tel. 415/626–5200 or 800/553–1900. 136 rooms. Facilities: tour desk in lobby. AE, DC, MC, V.*

The Arts and Nightlife

The best guide to arts and entertainment events in San Francisco is the "Datebook" section, printed on pink paper, in the Sunday *Examiner and Chronicle. The Bay Guardian,* a free weekly newspaper available in racks around the city, lists more neighborhood, avant-garde, and budget-priced events as well as what's current in music and comedy clubs. Another handy reference for San Francisco nightlife is *Key* magazine, offered free in most major hotel lobbies. For up-to-date cultural, sports, and musical events, call the Convention and Visitors Bureau's *Cultural Events Calendar* (tel. 415/391–2001). Those seeking weekly jazz headliners should dial the *KJAZ Jazz Line* (tel. 415/769–4818).

Half-price tickets to many local and touring stage shows go on sale at noon Tuesday–Saturday at the **STBS** booth on the Stockton Street side of Union Square, between Geary and Post streets. **STBS** is also a full-service ticket agency, open until 7:30 PM, for theater and music events around the Bay Area. While the city's major commercial theaters are concentrated downtown, the opera, symphony, and ballet perform at the Civic Center. For recorded information about **STBS** tickets, call 415/433–7827.

The city's two charge-by-phone ticket services are **BASS** (tel. 415/762–2277), with one of its centers in the **STBS** booth, and **Ticketron** (tel. 415/392–7469), with a center in the Emporium-Capwell store, 835 Market Street. Other agencies downtown are the **City Box Office,** 141 Kearny Street in the Sherman-Clay store (tel. 415/392–4400) and **Downtown Center Box Office** in the parking garage at 320 Mason Street (tel. 415/775–2021). The opera, symphony, the ballet's *Nutcracker,* and touring hit musicals are often sold out in advance; tickets are usually available within a day of performance for other shows.

The Arts
Theater

San Francisco's "theater row" is a single block of Geary Street west of Union Square, but a number of commercial theaters are within walking distance, along with resident companies that suggest the city's theatrical diversity. The three major commercial theaters are operated by the Shorenstein-Nederlander organization, which books touring plays and musicals, sometimes before they open on Broadway. The most venerable is the **Curran** (445 Geary St., tel. 415/673–4400), which is used for plays and smaller musicals. The **Golden Gate** is a stylishly refurbished movie theater (Golden Gate Ave. at Taylor St., tel. 415/474–3800), primarily a musicals house. The 2,500-seat **Orpheum** (1192 Market St. near the Civic Center, tel. 415/474–3800) is used for the biggest touring shows.

The smaller commercial theaters, offering touring shows and a few that are locally produced, are the **Marines Memorial Theater** (Sutter and Mason sts., tel. 415/441–7444) and **Theatre on the Square** (450 Post St., tel. 415/433–9500). For commercial and popular success, nothing beats *Beach Blanket Babylon,* the zany revue that has been running for years at **Club Fugazi** (678 Green St. in North Beach, tel. 415/421–4222). Conceived by imaginative San Francisco director Steve Silver, it is a lively, colorful musical mix of cabaret, showbiz parodies, and tributes to local landmarks.

The city's major theater company is the **American Conservatory Theatre (ACT),** which quickly became one of the nation's leading regional theaters when it was founded in the mid-1960s. The company has had its artistic and financial ups and downs, but it remains the standard by which other Northern California resident theaters are judged. It presents a season of approximately eight plays in rotating repertory from October through late spring. The repertory includes Shakespeare, European classics from the 19th and 20th centuries, recent New York successes, and rediscovered American plays from the 1930s and 1940s. The ticket office is at the Geary Theatre (415 Geary St.), but the theater itself was damaged in the 1989 earthquake and will remain closed until late 1991. Meanwhile, ACT performances are being held at several other theaters around the city. *Tickets and information, tel. 415/749–2228. Performances are usually Mon.–Sat. nights with additional matinees.*

At the next level are several established theaters in smaller houses and with lower ticket prices that specialize in contemporary plays. The most reliable are: **Eureka Theatre** (2730 16th St. in the Mission District, tel. 415/558–9898) and the **Magic Theatre** (Bldg. D at Ft. Mason Center, Laguna St. at Marina Blvd., tel. 415/441–8822).

The city boasts a wide variety of specialized and ethnic theaters that work with dedicated local actors and some professionals. Among the most interesting: **The Lamplighters,** the delightful Gilbert and Sullivan troupe that often gets better reviews than touring productions of musicals, performing at the Presentation Theater (2350 Turk St., tel. 415/752–7755); the **Lorraine Hansberry Theatre,** which specializes in plays by black writers (620 Sutter St., tel. 415/474–8800); the **Asian American Theatre** (403 Arguello Blvd., tel. 415/346–8922); and the gay and lesbian **Theatre Rhinoceros** (2926 16th St., tel. 415/861–5079). The **San Francisco Shakespeare Festival** offers free performances on summer weekends in Golden Gate Park (tel. 415/221–0642).

Concerts The completion of Davies Symphony Hall at Van Ness Avenue and Grove Street finally gave the San Francisco Symphony a home of its own. It solidified the base of the city's three major performing arts organizations—symphony, opera, and ballet —in the Civic Center. The symphony and other music groups also perform in the smaller, 928-seat Herbst Theatre in the opera's "twin" building at Van Ness and McAllister Street, the War Memorial Building. Otherwise, the city's musical ensembles can be found all over the map: in churches and museums, in restaurants and outdoors in parks, and in outreach series in Berkeley and on the peninsula. San Francisco Symphony is the city's most stable performing arts organization, playing September–May, with music director Herbert Blomstedt conducting for about two-thirds of the season. Guest conductors often include Michael Tilson Thomas, Edo de Waart, and Erich Leinsdorf. Guest soloists include artists of the caliber of Andre Watts, Leontyne Price, and Jean-Pierre Rampal. The symphony has concentrated on the standard repertoire in recent years as Blomstedt has developed the ensemble's stability and focus. *Davies Symphony Hall, Van Ness Ave. at Grove St., tel. 415/431–5400. Tickets at the Davies Hall box office and BASS agency, tel. 415/762–2277.*

Philharmonia Baroque, a stylish ensemble, has been called the local Baroque orchestra with the national reputation. Its season of concerts, fall through spring, celebrates composers of the 17th and 18th centuries, including Handel, Vivaldi, and Mozart. *Most performances at Herbst Theatre, Van Ness Ave. at McAllister St., tel. 415/552-3656. Tickets also at the STBS booth in Union Sq.*

Dance **San Francisco Ballet.** The ballet has restored much of its luster under artistic director Helgi Tomasson, and both classical and contemporary works have won admiring reviews. The company's primary season runs February–May, with a repertoire including such full-length ballets as *La Fille mal gardée* and a new production of *Swan Lake.* The company is also intent on reaching new audiences with bold new dances, what it likes to call "cutting edge works that will make you take a second look." Like many dance companies in the nation, the ballet presents *The Nutcracker Suite* in December, and its recent production is one of the most spectacular. *War Memorial Opera House, Van Ness Ave. at Grove St., tel. 415/621-3838. Tickets also available at BASS outlets.*

Film The Bay Area, including Berkeley and San Jose, is considered one of the nation's most important movie markets. If there is a film floating around the country or around the world in search of an audience, it is likely that it will eventually turn up on a screen in San Francisco. The Bay Area is also a filmmaking center: Documentaries and experimental works are produced on modest budgets, feature films and television programs are shot on location, and some of Hollywood's biggest directors prefer to live here, particularly in Marin County. In San Francisco, about a third of the theaters regularly show foreign and independent films. The city is also one of the last strongholds of "repertory cinema," with several theaters showing older American and foreign films on bills that change daily.

San Francisco's traditional movie theater center, downtown on Market Street, is pretty much given over to sex and action movies nowadays. First-run commercial movie theaters are scattered throughout the city, although they are concentrated along Van Ness Avenue, near Japantown and in the Marina District. All are accessible on major Muni bus routes, as are the art-revival houses. Several of the most respected and popular independent theaters have been taken over by chains recently, and their policies could change. The San Francisco International Film Festival (tel. 415/931-3456), the oldest in the country, continues to provide an extensive selection of foreign films each spring.

Opera **San Francisco Opera** (Van Ness Ave. at Grove St., tel. 415/864-3330). Founded in 1923 and the resident company at the War Memorial Opera House in the Civic Center since it was built in 1932, the Opera has expanded to a fall season of 13 weeks. Approximately 70 performances of 10 operas are given, beginning on the first Friday following Labor Day. For many years the Opera was considered a major international company and the most artistically successful operatic organization in the United States. International competition and management changes have made recent seasons uneven; in 1988, the governing board appointed a new general director, Lofti Mansouri, formerly head of Toronto's Canadian Opera Company. International opera stars frequently sing major roles here, but the Opera is also well known for presenting the American debuts of singers who have made their name in Europe. In the same way, the company's standard operatic repertoire is interspersed with revivals of rarely heard works.

The Opera was one of the first to present "supertitles," projecting English translations above the stage during performances. The system is used for almost all operas not sung in English. In addition to the fall season, the Opera performs Wagner's *Ring* cycle every five summers, next in 1995. Ticket prices range to a high of about $65, and many performances are sold out in advance. Standing-room tickets are always sold, however, and patrons often sell extra tickets on the opera house steps just before curtain time.

Pocket Opera (tel. 415/346-2780). This lively, modestly priced alternative to "grand" opera gives concert performances, mostly in English, of rarely heard works. Offenbach's operettas are frequently on the bill during the winter-spring season. Concerts are held at various locations.

Another operatic alternative is the **Lamplighters** (*see* Theater, above), which specializes in Gilbert and Sullivan but presents other light operas as well.

Nightlife
Comedy

Cobb's Comedy Club. Bobby Slayton, Paula Poundstone, and Dr. Gonzo are among the super stand-up comics who perform here. *In the Cannery, 2801 Leavenworth at the corner of Beach St., tel. 415/928-4320. Shows Mon. 8 PM, Tues.–Thurs. and Sun. 9 PM, Fri. and Sat. 9 and 11 PM. Cover: $7 weeknights, $9 Fri.–Sat. Minimum: 2 drinks. MC, V.*

Holy City Zoo. Robin Williams ascended like a meteor from an improv group that gained fame here. Terrific stand-up comics, such as local favorite Michael Prichard, headline now. The "Zoo" features comedy nightly, with an open mike for pros and would-be comedians Sunday through Thursday. *408 Clement St., in the Richmond district, tel. 415/386-4242..Shows Sun.–Thurs. 9 PM; Fri.–Sat. 9 and 11 PM. Cover: $4 Sun.–Thurs., $8 Fri.–Sat. Minimum: weekends, 2 drinks, MC, V.*

The Improv. This distinctively San Franciscan outlet for the franchised night club chain is the only comedy club in the heart of downtown, 1 block from Union Square. It books local and nationally known comics and requires them to avoid profanity and material that might be offensive to ethnic groups or either sex. *401 Mason St. at Geary, tel. 415/441-7787. Shows Sun.–Thurs. at 9 PM, Fri. at 9 and 11 PM, Sat. at 8, 10, and 11:45 PM. Cover $6–$8. Minimum: 2 drinks. AE, MC, V.*

The Punch Line. A launching pad for Jay Leno, Robin Williams, and Whoopi Goldberg, the Punch Line features some of the top talents around—several of whom are certain to make a national impact. Note that weekend shows often sell out, and it is best to buy tickets in advance at BASS outlet (tel. 415/762–BASS). *444-A Battery St., between Clay and Washington sts., tel. 415/ 397-7573. Shows Sun. and Tues.–Thurs. 9 PM, Fri. and Sat. 9 and 11 PM, closed Mon. Cover: Sun. and Tues.–Thurs. $5, Fri. and Sat. $9. Minimum: 2 drinks. AE, MC, V.*

Dancing
Emporiums

Bahia Tropical. This spinoff from a nearby Bahia Brazilian restaurant features live samba and other Latin dance music nightly, with combos early in the week and full bands on weekends. *1600 Market St., tel. 415/861–8657. Live music Mon.–Thurs. 9 PM–1 AM, Fri.–Sat. 9:30–1, Sun. 7–11. Cover: $3–$10.*

New Orleans Room. Since the Fairmont's Venetian Room closed, this former Dixieland stronghold has become the hotel's main dance lounge, with a live band recreating the music of the swing era. *950 Mason St., tel. 415/772–5259. Performances Mon. 9 PM–1 AM, Tues.–Sat. 9:30 PM–1:30 AM. Cover: $4.*

Oz. The most popular upscale disco in San Francisco, the land of Oz is reached via a glass elevator. Then, surrounded by a splendid panorama of the city, you can dance on marble floors and recharge on cushy sofas and bamboo chairs. The fine sound system belts out oldies, disco, Motown, and new wave. *335 Powell St., between Geary and Post, in the top floor of the Westin St. Francis Hotel, tel. 415/397–7000. Open nightly 9:30 PM–2 AM. Cover: Sun.–Thurs. $8, Fri. and Sat. $15.*

Pop, Rock, and Blues **Great American Music Hall.** This is one of the great eclectic nightclubs, not only in San Francisco but in the entire country. Here you will find truly top-drawer entertainment running the gamut from the best in blues, folk, and jazz to rock with a sprinkling of outstanding comedians. This colorful marble-pillared emporium will also accommodate dancing to popular bands. Past headliners here include Carmen McRae, B.B. King, Tom Paxton, and Doc Watson. *859 O'Farrell St., between Polk and Larkin, tel. 415/885–0750. Shows: usually 8 PM on weeknights and 8:30 or 9 PM on weekends, but this may vary, so call. Cover: $8–$12. No credit cards.*

I-Beam. One of the most popular of San Francisco's rock dance clubs, the I-Beam features new-wave bands and high-energy rock 'n' roll in a spacious setting. Spectacular lights and lasers enhance your dancing pleasure here. *1748 Haight St., tel. 415/668–6006. Open nightly 9 PM. Cover $3–$12. No credit cards.*

Last Day Saloon. In an attractive setting of wooden tables and potted plants, this club offers some major entertainers and a varied schedule of blues, Cajun, rock, and jazz. Some of the illustrious performers who have appeared here are Taj Mahal, the Zazu Pitts Memorial Orchestra, Maria Muldaur, and Pride and Joy. *406 Clement St., between 5th and 6th aves. in the Richmond district, tel. 415/387–6343. Shows 9 PM nightly. Cover: $5–$7. No credit cards.*

Plush Room. The popularity of this elegant club rises and falls with the cabaret market. *In the Hotel York, 940 Sutter St., tel. 415/885–6800 for information.*

The Saloon. Some locals consider the Saloon the best spot in San Francisco for the blues. Among the headliners here are Charles Musselwhite and Roy Rogers. *1232 Grant St., near Columbus in North Beach, tel. 415/989–7666. Shows 9:30 PM nightly. Cover: $5. Fri.–Sat.; other nights free, but always a 2-drink minimum. No credit cards.*

Slim's. The most popular night club in the South of Market neighborhood features "American roots" music including blues, soul, country, and rockabilly. *333 11th St. near Folsom, tel. 415/621–3330. Shows most nights, 8 and 11 PM. Cover $6–$15. Dinner served, minors admitted. AE, MC, V.*

That's Rich. This rhythm-and-blues club attracts a slightly older crowd and is known for its after-hours jams and weekend "blues and breakfast" sessions. *330 Ritch St. near Brannan, South of Market, tel. 415/896–1988. Open daily at 9 PM. Shows*

Mon.–Wed. 9 PM–2 AM, Fri.–Sat. 1:30 AM–5 AM. Cover $2–$6. AE, MC, V.

The Warfield. This one-time movie palace has been turned into a nightclub, restaurant, and bar, with dancing on the main floor. It features modern rock and headliners such as Alice Cooper and Jerry Garcia. *982 Market St., tel. 415/775–7722. Shows most nights at 8. Admission: $16–$20, 2 drink minimum on main floor. AE, MC, V.*

Jazz **Kimball's.** Jazz greats Stan Getz and Freddie Hubbard have played at this club, which is also a restaurant. *300 Grove St., at Franklin in the Civic Center, tel. 415/861–5555. Shows 8 PM Wed.; 9 and 11 PM Thurs., Fri. and Sat. Cover $8–$12. The additional $5 minimum for food and drink is generally not enforced. AE, MC, V.*

Pasand Lounge. Features Brazilian jazz on Monday and Thursday, with jazz combos playing Wednesday and Friday–Sunday *1875 Union St., in Pacific Heights, tel. 415/922–4498. Shows 9 PM nightly. No cover. Minimum: 2 drinks. AE, MC, V.*

Pier 23. Pier 23 offers the best in bebop jazz, ranging from the Brian Melvin Trio to Kitty Margolis. *At Embarcadero and Pier 23, across from the Fog City Diner, tel. 415/362–5125. Shows Wed.–Sat. 10 PM, Sun. 4–8 PM. No cover. Minimum: 2 drinks. V, MC.*

Skyline Bars **Carnelian Room.** At 781 feet above the ground, enjoy dinner or cocktails here on the 52nd floor, where you may drink in the loftiest view of San Francisco's magnificent skyline. Reservations are a must for dinner here. *Top of the Bank of America Building, 555 California St., tel. 415/433–7500. Open nightly 3 PM–11:30 PM, weekends to 1:30 AM.*

Crown Room. Just ascending to the well-named Crown Room is a drama in itself as you take the Fairmont's glass-enclosed Skylift elevator to the top. Some San Franciscans maintain that this lounge is the most luxurious of the city's skyline bars. Lunch, dinner, and Sunday brunch are served as well as drinks. *24th floor of the Fairmont Hotel, California and Mason sts., tel. 415/772–5131. Open daily 11 AM–1 AM, weekends to 2 AM.*

Equinox. What's unique about the Hyatt's skyline-view bar is its capacity to revolve. *Open daily 11 AM–1:30 AM. The Hyatt also is home to the* **Other Trellis Lounge.** There is no cover charge here for music ranging from classical to jazz. *Both in the Hyatt Regency, Embarcadero Center 5, tel. 415/788–1234.*

Starlite Roof. In this 21st-story glassed-in lounge, you may dance to a band playing primarily '50s and '60s hits. *In the Sir Francis Drake Hotel, Powell and Sutter sts., tel. 415/392–7755. Open nightly 4:30 PM–1 AM. No cover.*

Top of the Mark. This fabled landmark affords fabulous views in an elegant 19th-floor setting. *In the Mark Hopkins Hotel, California and Mason sts., tel. 415/392–3434. Open nightly 4 PM–1:30 AM. Dress formal.*

Excursion to Sausalito

by Robert Taylor

A staff writer for the Oakland Tribune, Robert Taylor lives in San Francisco.

The San Francisco Convention and Visitors Bureau describes Sausalito's location as "the Mediterranean side of the Golden Gate." With its relatively sheltered site on the bay in Marin County, just 8 miles from San Francisco, it appeals to bay area residents and visitors for the same reason: It is so near and yet so far. As a hillside town with superb views, an expansive yacht harbor, the aura of an artists's colony, and ferry service, Sausalito might be a resort within commuting distance of the city. It is certainly the primary excursion for visitors to San Francisco, especially those with limited time to explore the bay area. Mild weather encourages strolling and outdoor dining, although afternoon winds and fog can roll over the hills from the ocean, funneling through the central part of town once known as Hurricane Gulch.

There are substantial homes, including Victorian mansions, in Sausalito's heights, but the town has long had a more colorful and raffish reputation. Discovered in 1775 by Spanish explorers and named Saucelito (Little Willow) for the trees growing around its springs, Sausalito was a port for whaling ships in the 19th century. In 1875, the railroad from the north connected with ferryboats to San Francisco and the town became an attraction for the fun-loving. Even the chamber of commerce recalls the time when Sausalito sported 25 saloons, gambling dens, and bordellos. Bootleggers flourished during Prohibition in the 1920s, and shipyard workers swelled the town's population in the 1940s, when tour guides divided the residents into "wharf rats" and "hill snobs." Ensuing decades brought a bohemian element with the development of an artists' colony and a houseboat community. Sausalito has also become a major yachting center, and restaurants attract visitors for the fresh seafood as well as the spectacular views. Sausalito remains a friendly and casual small town, although summer traffic jams can fray nerves. If possible, visit Sausalito on a weekday—and take the ferry.

Arriving and Departing

By Car Cross Golden Gate Bridge and go north on Highway 101 to the Sausalito exit, then go south on Bridgeway to municipal parking near the center of town. The trip takes ½-hour–45 minutes one way.

By Bus **Golden Gate Transit** (tel. 415/332–6600) travels to Sausalito from First and Mission streets and other points in the city.

By Ferry **Golden Gate Ferry** (tel. 415/332–6600) crosses the bay from the Ferry Building at Market Street and the Embarcadero; **Red and White Fleet** (tel. 415/546–2896) leaves from Pier 41 at Fisherman's Wharf. The trip takes 15–30 minutes.

Guided Tours

Most tour companies include Sausalito on excursions north to Muir Woods and the Napa Valley Wine Country. Among them are **Gray Line** (tel. 415/558–9400), **Great Pacific Tour Co.** (tel. 415/626–4499), and **Dolphin Tours** (tel. 415/441–6810).

Exploring

Numbers in the margin correspond with points of interest on the Sausalito map.

Bridgeway is Sausalito's main throughfare and prime destination, with the bay, yacht harbor, and waterfront restaurants on one side, and more restaurants, shops, hillside homes, and hotels on the other. It is only a few steps from the ferry termi-

1 nal to the tiny landmark park in the center of town: the **Plaza Vina del Mar,** named for Sausalito's sister city in Chile. The park features a fountain and two 14-foot-tall statues of elephants, created for the 1915 Panama-Pacific International Exposition in San Francisco.

2 Across the street to the south is the Spanish-style **Sausalito Hotel,** which has been refurbished and filled with Victorian an-
3 tiques. Between the hotel and the **Sausalito Yacht Club** is another unusual historic landmark, a drinking fountain with the invitation Have a Drink on Sally. It's in remembrance of Sally Stanford, the former San Francisco madam who later ran Sausalito's Valhalla restaurant and became the town's mayor. Actually, the monument is also in remembrance of her dog. There is a sidewalk-level bowl that suggests Have a Drink on Leland.

South on Bridgeway, toward San Francisco, there is an esplanade along the water with picture-perfect views. Farther south are a number of restaurants on piers, including—near the end of Bridgeway at Richardson Street—what was the
4 **Valhalla** and is the oldest restaurant in Sausalito. Built in 1893 as "Walhalla," it was one of the settings for the film *The Lady from Shanghai* in the 1940s, Sally Stanford's place in the 1950s, and most recently a Chart House restaurant.

North on Bridgeway from the ferry terminal are yacht harbors and, parallel to Bridgeway a block to the west, the quieter Caledonia Avenue, with its own share of cafes and shops. There is a pleasant, grassy park with a children's playground at Caledonia and Litho streets, with a food shop nearby for picnic provisions.

Here and there along the west side of Bridgeway are flights of steps that climb the hill to Sausalito's wooded, sometimes rustic and sometimes lavish residential neighborhoods. The stairway just across the street from Vina del Mar Park is
5 named Excelsior, and it leads to the **Alta Mira,** a popular Spanish-style hotel and restaurant with a spectacular view. However, there are vistas of the bay from all these streets.

Where there isn't a hillside house or a restaurant or yacht in Sausalito, there is a shop. Most are along Bridgeway and Princess Street, and they offer a wide assortment of casual and sophisticated clothing, posters and paintings, imported and handcrafted gifts, and the expected variety of T-shirts, ice
6 cream, cookies, and pastries. **The Village Fair** (777 Bridgeway) is a 4-story former warehouse that has been converted into a warren of clothing, craft, and gift boutiques. Craft workers often demonstrate their talents in the shops, and a winding brick path—Little Lombard Street—connects various levels. The shopping complex is a haven during wet weather.

Sausalito's reputation as an art colony is enhanced by the **Art Festival** held during the three-day Labor Day weekend in September. It attracts more than 35,000 visitors to the waterfront area, and there are plans to expand the site and offer direct ferry service from San Francisco. Details are available from the Sausalito Chamber of Commerce (333 Caledonia St., 94965, tel. 415/332–0505).

7 North on Bridgeway, within a few minutes' drive, is the **Bay Model,** a re-creation in miniature of the entire San Francisco

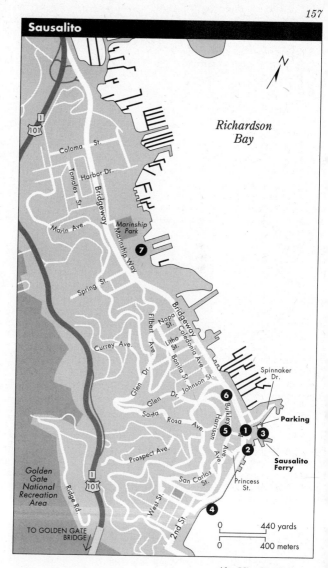

Alta Mira Hotel, **5**
Bay Model, **7**
Plaza Vina del Mar, **1**
Sausalito Hotel, **2**
Sausalito Yacht
Club, **3**
Valhalla, **4**
Village Fair, **6**

Bay and the San Joaquin-Sacramento River delta. It is actually nearly 400 feet square and is used by the U.S. Army Corps of Engineers to reproduce the rise and fall of tides, the flow of currents, and the other physical forces at work on the bay. It is housed in a former World War II shipyard building, where there is a display of shipbuilding history. At the same site is the Wapama, a World War I—era steam freighter being restored by volunteers. *2100 Bridgeway, tel. 415/332–3871. Open Tues. –Fri. 9–4; weekends 10–6; closed Sun. in winter.*

Along the shore of Richardson Bay, north of the Bay Model, are some of the 400 houseboats that make up Sausalito's "floating homes community." In the shallow tidelands, most of them are floating only about half the time, but they are always a fanciful collection of the rustic, the eccentric, the flamboyant, and the elegant.

Dining

Restaurants and cafes line Bridgeway, Sausalito's main street, and specialize in seafood. A variety of sandwiches, salads, and snack foods are also available. The favored restaurants are directly on the bay or on Sausalito's hillside.

Restaurants are listed according to price category.

Category	Cost*
Very Expensive	$30 and up
Expensive	$20–$30
Moderate	$10–$20
Inexpensive	under $10

per person, not including tax, service, or drinks

Moderate–Expensive **Alta Mira.** This is a smart restaurant, with a more formal atmosphere than the downtown cafes, in a Spanish-style hotel a block above Bridgeway. The Alta Mira serves three meals a day, and the specialties are fresh scallops and Pacific salmon, grilled meats, and large crab and shrimp salads. The terrace offers one of Sausalito's best views and is popular for lunch and Sunday brunch. *125 Bulkley Ave., tel. 415/332–1350. Reservations recommended. AE, DC, MC, V.*

Casa Madrona. Another restaurant in a charming hotel, this is a Victorian building surrounded by a landscaped walk and newer rooms stepping down the hill to Bridgeway. Casa Madrona serves American cuisine, with an appealing selection of breakfast and brunch dishes. There is no lunch on Saturday, and only brunch is served on Sunday. Dinner is served nightly. *801 Bridgeway, tel. 415/331–5888. MC, V.*

Moderate **The Spinnaker.** Seafood specialties and homemade pastas are offered in a quietly contemporary building in a spectacular setting on a point beyond the harbor, near the yacht club. You may see a pelican perched on one of the pilings just outside. Lunch and dinner are served daily, brunch on Saturday and Sunday. *100 Spinnaker Dr., tel. 415/332–1500. AE, MC, V.*

Inexpensive–Moderate **Winship Restaurant.** Seafood, pasta, steaks, burgers, and salads are served in a casual nautical setting directly on the

Bridgeway shopping strip. Breakfast and lunch are served every day, dinners Wednesday–Sunday. *607 Bridgeway, tel. 415/ 332–1454. AE, DC, MC, V.*

Excursion to Muir Woods

One hundred fifty million years ago, the ancestors of redwood and sequoia trees grew throughout America. Today the *Sequoia sempervirens* can be found only in a narrow, cool coastal belt from Monterey to Oregon. (*Sequoiadendron gigantea* grows in the Sierra Nevada.) **Muir Woods National Monument,** 17 miles northwest of San Francisco, is a 550-acre park that contains one of the most majestic redwood groves. Some redwoods in the park are nearly 250 feet tall and 1,000 years old. This grove was saved from destruction in 1908 and named for naturalist John Muir, whose campaigns helped establish the National Park system. His response: "This is the best tree-lover's monument that could be found in all of the forests of the world. Saving these woods from the axe and saw is in many ways the most notable service to God and man I have heard of since my forest wandering began."

Arriving and Departing

By Car Take U.S. 101 north to the Mill Valley-Muir Woods exit. The trip takes 45 minutes one-way when the roads are open, but traffic can be heavy on summer weekends, so allow more time.

By Bus **Golden Gate Transit** (tel. 415/332–6600) sends buses from First and Mission streets and other points in San Francisco to Muir Woods.

Guided Tours

Most tour companies include Muir Woods on excursions to the Wine Country, among them **Gray Line** (tel. 415/558–9400) and **Great Pacific** (tel. 415/626–4499).

Exploring

Muir Woods is a park for walking; no cars are allowed in the redwood grove itself. There are 6 miles of easy trails from the park headquarters, crossing streams and passing through ferns and azaleas as well as magnificent stands of redwoods such as Bohemian Grove and the circular formation called Cathedral Grove. No picnicking or camping is allowed, but snacks are available at the visitors center. (There are picnic sites at Mt. Tamalpais; *see* below). The weather is usually cool and often wet, so dress warmly and wear shoes appropriate for damp trails. *Tel. 415/ 388–2595. Open daily 8 AM–sunset.*

Excursion to Berkeley

Berkeley and the University of California are not synonymous, although the founding campus of the state university system dominates the city's heritage and contemporary life. The city of 100,000 facing San Francisco across the bay has other interesting features for visitors. Berkeley is culturally diverse and politically adventurous, a breeding ground for social trends, a

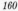

continuing bastion of the counterculture, and an important center for Bay Area writers, artists, and musicians. The city's liberal reputation and determined spirit has led detractors to describe it in recent years as the People's Republic of Berkeley. Wooded groves on the university campus, neighborhoods of shingled bungalows, and landscaped hillside homes temper the environment.

The city was named for George Berkeley, the Irish philosopher and clergyman who crossed the Atlantic to convert the Indians and wrote "Westward, the course of empire takes its way." The city grew with the university, which was created by the state legislature in 1868 and established five years later on a rising plain of oak trees split by Strawberry Canyon. The central campus occupies 178 acres of the scenic 1,282-acre property, with most buildings located from Bancroft Way north to Hearst Street and from Oxford Street east into the Berkeley Hills. The university has more than 30,000 students and a full-time faculty of 1,600. It is considered one of the nation's leading intellectual centers and a major site for scientific research.

Arriving and Departing

By Car Take I–80 east across the Bay Bridge, then the University Avenue exit through downtown Berkeley to the campus, or take the Ashby Avenue exit and turn left on Telegraph Avenue to the traditional campus entrance. The trip takes ½-hour one way (except in rush hour).

By Public Transportation **BART** (tel. 415/788–2278) trains run under the bay to the downtown Berkeley exit; transfer to the Humphrey GoBart shuttle bus to campus. The trip takes from 45 minutes to one hour one way.

Exploring

Numbers in the margin correspond with points of interest on the Berkeley map.

❶ The throbbing heart of the University of California is **Sproul Plaza,** just inside the campus at Telegraph Avenue and Bancroft Way. It's a lively panorama of political and social activists, musicians, food vendors, children, dogs, and students on their way to and from classes at this "university within a park." In **❷** the main lobby of the **Student Union Building** on the plaza is the Visitors Center (tel. 415/642–5215; open 8–5 Monday to Friday). There are maps and brochures for convenient self-guided walks and student-guided tours Monday, Wednesday, and Friday at 10 AM.

The university's suggested tour circles the upper portion of the central campus, past buildings that were sited to take advantage of vistas to the Golden Gate across the bay. The first campus plan was proposed by Frederick Law Olmsted, who designed New York's Central Park, and the university's architects over the years have included Bernard Maybeck and Julia Morgan (who designed Hearst Castle at San Simeon). Be- **❸** yond Sproul Plaza is the bronze **Sather Gate,** built in 1909 and the south entrance to the campus until expansion in the 1960s. **❹** Up a walkway to the right is vine-covered **South Hall,** one of two remaining buildings that greeted the first students in 1873.

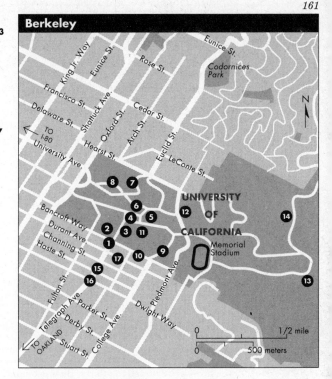

⑤ Just ahead is **Sather Tower,** popularly known as the Campanile, the campus landmark that can be seen for miles. The 307-foot tower was modeled on St. Mark's tower in Venice and was completed in 1914. The carillon, which was cast in England, is played three times a day. In the lobby of the tower is a photographic display of campus history. An elevator takes visitors 175 feet up to the observation deck. *Open daily except university holidays, 10–4:30.*

⑥ Opposite the Campanile is **Bancroft Library,** with a rare book collection and a changing series of exhibits that may include a Shakespeare first folio or a gold-rush diary. On permanent display is a gold nugget purporting to be the one that started the rush to California when it was discovered on January 24, 1848.

⑦ Across University Drive to the north is the **Earth Sciences Building,** with a seismograph for measuring earthquakes. The

⑧ building also contains the **Paleontology Museum,** which has displays of dinosaur bones and the huge skeleton of a plesiosaur. *Open when the university is in session, weekdays 8–5, weekends 1–5 PM.*

⑨ The university's two major museums are on the south side of campus near Bancroft Way. **The Lowie Museum of Anthropology,** in Kroeber Hall, has a collection of more than 4,000 artifacts. Items on display may cover the archaeology of ancient America or the crafts of Pacific Islanders. The museum also houses the collection of artifacts made by Ishi, the lone survivor of a California Indian tribe, who was brought to the Bay

Area in 1911. *Tel. 415/642–3681. Open Tues.–Fri. 10–4:30, weekends noon–4:30.*

⑩ The University Art Museum is a fan-shaped building with a spiral of ramps and balcony galleries. It houses a collection of Asian and Western art, including a major group of Hans Hofmann's abstract paintings, and also displays touring exhibits. On the ground floor is the Pacific Film Archive, which offers daily programs of historic and contemporary films. *2626 Bancroft Way, tel. 415/642–0808. Museum open Wed.–Sun. 11–5. Free museum admission. Film-program information, tel. 415/642–1124.*

Many of the university's notable attractions are outdoors. Just **⑪** south of the Campanile near the rustic Faculty Club is **Faculty Glade** on the south fork of Strawberry Creek, one of the best examples of the university's attempt to preserve a parklike atmosphere. East of the central campus, across Gayley Road, is **⑫** the **Hearst Greek Theatre,** built in 1903 and seating 7,000. Sarah Bernhardt once performed here; now it is used for major musical events.

Above the Greek Theatre in Strawberry Canyon is the 30-acre **⑬ Botanical Garden,** with a collection of 25,000 species. It's a relaxing gathering spot with benches and picnic tables. *Open daily except Christmas, 9–5.*

Perched on a hill above the campus on Centennial Drive is the **⑭** fortresslike **Lawrence Hall of Science,** which is a laboratory, a science education center, and—most important to visitors—a dazzling display of scientific knowledge and experiments. Displays are updated regularly. On weekends there are additional films, lectures, and demonstrations, especially for children. *Tel. 415/642–5132. Nominal admission charge. Open Mon.–Sat. 10–4:30, Sun. noon–5.*

Berkeley is a rewarding city to explore beyond the university. Just south of the campus on **Telegraph Avenue** is the busy, student-oriented district, full of cafes, bookstores, poster shops, and street vendors with traditional and trendy craft items. Shops come and go with the times, but among the neigh-**⑮** borhood landmarks are **Cody's Books** (2454 Telegraph Ave.), **⑯** with its adjacent cafe; **Moe's** (2476 Telegraph Ave.), with a **⑰** huge selection of used books; and **Leopold Records** (2518 Durant Ave.). This district was the center of student protests in the 1960s, and on the street it sometimes looks as if that era still lives. People's Park, one of the centers of protest, is just east of Telegraph between Haste Street and Dwight Way. It's best to avoid this section of Telegraph Avenue at night.

Downtown Berkeley around University and Shattuck avenues is nondescript. However, there are shops for browsing along College Avenue near Ashby Avenue south of campus and in the Walnut Square development at Shattuck and Vine streets northwest of campus. Berkeley's shingled houses can be seen on tree-shaded streets near College and Ashby avenues. Hillside houses with spectacular views can be seen on the winding roads near the intersection of Ashby and Claremont avenues, around the Claremont Hotel (*see* Excursion to Oakland, below). At the opposite side of the city, there are views across the bay from the Berkeley Marina at the foot of University Avenue, west of I–80.

Dining

Berkeley's major restaurants, including those on Shattuck Avenue north of the university, are known for innovative use of fresh local produce. There is an eclectic variety of low-cost international cafes and snack stands in the student area along Telegraph Avenue and more cafes downtown on Shattuck Avenue near the central Berkeley BART station.

Restaurants are listed according to price category.

Category	Cost*
Very Expensive	over $30
Expensive	$20–$30
Moderate	$10–$20
Inexpensive	under $10

per person, not including tax, service, or drinks.

Moderate–Expensive **Cafe at Chez Panisse.** Fresh and innovative light meals (lunch and dinner) are served, including pasta, pizza, salads, and light grilled dishes, upstairs from the mecca for California cuisine. *1517 Shattuck Ave., north of University Ave., tel. 415/548-5525. Same-day reservations accepted. AE, DC, MC, V.*

Moderate **Spenger's Fish Grotto.** This is a rambling, boisterous seafood restaurant, with daily specials and hearty portions. *1919 4th St., near University Ave. and I-80, tel. 415/845-7771. Reservations for 5 or more. AE, DC, MC, V.*

Inexpensive **Kip's.** This is a student hangout, but it is open to everyone. Located upstairs near Telegraph Avenue, with big wooden tables and burgers, pizza, and—of course—beer on tap. *2439 Durant Ave., tel. 415/848-4340. No reservations. No credit cards.*
The Swallow. This is a pleasant cafe at the University Art Museum with fresh sandwiches, salads, soups, and desserts served for lunch and throughout the afternoon. *2626 Durant Ave., tel. 415/841-2409. No reservations. No credit cards. Closed Mon.*

Excursion to Oakland

Originally the site of ranches, farms, a grove of redwood trees, and, of course, clusters of oaks, Oakland has long been a warmer and more spacious alternative to San Francisco. By the end of the 19th century, Mediterranean-style homes and gardens had been developed as summer estates. With swifter transportation, Oakland became a bedroom community for San Francisco; then it progressed to California's fastest-growing industrial city. In recent decades, Oakland has struggled to redefine its identity. However, the major attractions remain: the parks and civic buildings around Lake Merritt, which was created from a tidal basin in 1898; the port area, now named Jack London Square, where the author spent much of his time at the turn of the century; and the scenic roads and parks along the crest of the Oakland-Berkeley hills. Also in the hills is the castlelike Claremont Resort Hotel, a landmark since 1915, as well as more sprawling parks with lakes and miles of hiking trails.

Arriving and Departing

By Car From the Bay Bridge, take I–580 to the Grand Avenue exit for Lake Merritt. To reach downtown and the waterfront, use the I–980 exit from I–580. The trip takes 45 minutes.

By Public Transportation Take BART to Oakland City Center station or Lake Merritt station for the lake and Oakland Museum. The trip takes 45 minutes one way.

Exploring

Numbers in the margin correspond with points of interest on the Oakland map.

If there is one reason to visit Oakland, it is to explore the ❶ **Oakland Museum,** an inviting series of landscaped buildings that displays the state's art, history, and natural science. It is the best possible introduction to a tour of California, and its dramatic and detailed exhibits can help fill the gaps on a brief visit. The natural science department displays a typical stretch of California from the Pacific Ocean to the Nevada border, including plants and wildlife. There is a breathtaking film, *Fast Flight,* that condenses the trip into five minutes. The museum's sprawling history section includes everything from Spanish-era artifacts and a gleaming fire engine that battled the flames in San Francisco in 1906, to 1960s souvenirs of the "summer of love." The California Dream exhibit recalls a century of inspirations. The museum's art department includes mystical landscapes painted by the state's pioneers as well as contemporary visions. There is a pleasant museum cafe for lunch and outdoor areas for relaxing. *1000 Oak St. at 10th St., tel. 415/834 –2413. Admission free. Open Wed.–Sat. 10–5; Sun. noon–7.*

❷ Near the museum, **Lake Merritt** is a 155-acre oasis surrounded by parks and paths, with several outdoor attractions on the ❸ north side. The **Natural Science Center and Waterfowl Refuge** attracts birds by the hundreds during winter months. *At the foot of Perkins St., tel. 415/273–3739. Open Mon. noon–5, Tues.–Sun. 10–5.*

❹ **Children's Fairyland** is a low-key amusement park with a puppet theater, small merry-go-round, and settings based on nursery rhymes. *Grand Ave. at Park View Terrace, tel. 415/452 –2259. Open daily in summer, 10–4:30; closed weekdays in* ❺ *winter.* The **Lakeside Park Garden Center** includes a Japanese garden and many native flowers and plants. *666 Bellevue Ave. tel. 415/273–3208, open daily 10–3 or later in summer; closed Thanksgiving, Christmas, and New Year's Day.*

Jack London, although born in San Francisco, spent his early years in Oakland before shipping out for adventures that inspired *The Call of the Wild, The Sea Wolf, Martin Eden,* and ❻ *The Cruise of the Snark.* He is commemorated by **Jack London Square** at the foot of Broadway with a bronze bust. A livelier ❼ landmark is **Heinhold's First and Last Chance Saloon,** one of his hangouts. Next door is the reassembled Klondike cabin in which he spent a winter. The square is mainly for drinking and dining. Next door, Jack London Village has specialty shops and

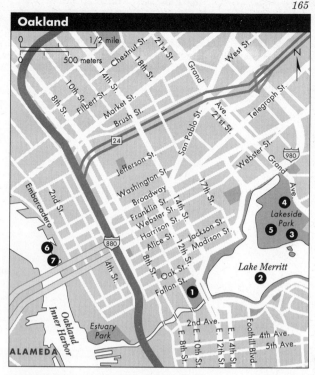

restaurants. The best local collection of the author's letters,
manuscripts, and photographs is in the Jack London Room at
the Oakland Main Library (125 14th St., tel. 415/273–3134).

Oakland's downtown has been undergoing redevelopment for
many years. More stable and pleasant areas for shopping and
browsing, with a selection of cafes, can be found on Lake Shore
Avenue northeast of Lake Merritt, Piedmont Avenue near the
Broadway exit from I–580, and College Avenue west of Broadway in North Oakland. College Avenue is lined with antiques
stores, boutiques, and cafes. The neighborhood surrounds
BART's Rockridge station. Transferring there to the local No.
51 bus will take visitors to the University of California campus,
about 1½ miles away in Berkeley.

Time Out   A drive through the Oakland Hills is spectacular, with open-
space parks and bay views, and a stop on the way at the **Claremont Hotel** (Ashby and Domingo aves., tel. 415/843–3000)
offers fine views, a spot in which to relax, and good food. Drive
north on Claremont to Ashby and on up the hill to the hotel.
From a distance, this sprawling white building with towers and
gables looks like a castle. Surrounded by 22 acres of lush
grounds tucked into the south Berkeley hills, the Claremont is
on the Oakland-Berkeley border, and for years both cities have
claimed it. When a new entrance was built on a different side of
the building, the address changed from Berkeley to Oakland.
The 1915 hotel has been restored and refurbished and turned
into a resort spa facility. The dining room is large and elegant,
with pressed linen, large contemporary paintings, and views

across the bay to San Francisco and the peninsula and north to Mt. Tamalpais. Meals, which fall into the Moderate–Expensive category, feature California cuisine, with seasonal fresh seafood for Sunday brunch and creative sandwiches for lunch.

The East Bay Regional Park District (tel. 415/531–9300) offers 46 parks in an area covering 60,000 acres to residents and visitors. In the Oakland hills is **Redwood Regional Park,** accessible from Joaquin Miller Road off Highway 13, to which Ashby Avenue will lead you. In the Berkeley hills is the 2,000-acre **Tilden Park,** which includes a lake and children's playground and is accessible from Grizzly Peak Boulevard off Claremont Avenue. There are scenic views of the Bay Area from roads that link the hilltop parks: Redwood Road, Skyline Boulevard, and Grizzly Peak Boulevard. Parks are open daily during daylight hours.

Dining

Oakland's ethnic diversity is reflected in its restaurants and cafes. There is a thriving Chinatown a few blocks northwest of the Oakland Museum, a number of seafood restaurants at Jack London Square, and a variety of international fare on Piedmont and College avenues.

Restaurants are listed according to price category.

Category	Cost*
Very Expensive	over $30
Expensive	$20–$30
Moderate	$10–$20
Inexpensive	under $10

per person, not including tax, service, or drinks

Moderate–Expensive **The Bay Wolf.** French inspiration and fresh, regional specialties mark one of the city's best restaurants, in a converted home. *3853 Piedmont Ave., tel. 415/655–6004. Reservations recommended. No lunch weekends. MC, V.*

Inexpensive **Oakland Grill.** Hamburgers, sandwiches, and omelets are among the wide selection in this popular restaurant in the city's produce district. *301 Franklin St., tel. 415/835–1176. No credit cards.*

Ratto's. Salads, sandwiches, soups, and pasta are served in a big, cheerful room adjacent to one of the Bay Area's best international grocery stores, in the Old Oakland Victorian Row restoration. *821 Washington St., tel. 415/832–6503. Lunch, weekdays; take-out orders are prepared in the deli, Mon.–Sat. No credit cards.*

Excursion to Marine World Africa USA

This wildlife theme park is one of Northern California's most popular attractions. It has been a phenomenal success since moving in 1986 from a crowded site south of San Francisco to Vallejo, about an hour's drive northeast. The 160-acre park features animals of the land, sea, and air performing in shows, roaming in natural habitats, and accompanying their trainers to stroll among park visitors. Among the "stars" are killer whales, dolphins, a dozen Bengal tigers, elephants, sea lions, chimpanzees, and a troupe of human water-skiers. There are cockatoos, macaws, flamingos, cranes, and ostriches. There are a whale and dolphin show, a sea lion show, a tiger and lion show, and an elephant and chimpanzee show.

The park is owned by the Marine World Foundation, a nonprofit organization devoted to educating the public about the world's wildlife. The shows and close-up looks at exotic animals serve that purpose without neglecting entertainment. Although the park is a family attraction, it's not just for youngsters. For additional sightseeing, visitors can reach the park on a highspeed ferry from San Francisco, a trip that offers unusual vistas through San Francisco Bay and San Pablo Bay. *Marine World Pkwy., Vallejo, tel. 707/643–6722. Admission: $14–$19; tickets at Ticketron outlets. Open 9:30–5 or later daily in summer; Wed.–Sun. the rest of the year and some school holidays.*

Arriving and Departing

By Car   Take I–80 east to Marine World Parkway in Vallejo. The trip takes one hour one way.

By Bus   **Greyhound-Trailways** (tel. 415/558–6789) from Seventh and Market streets, San Francisco, to Vallejo or **BART** train (tel. 415/781–BART) to El Cerrito Del Norte station; transfer to **Vallejo Transit** line (tel. 707/643–7663) to the park.

By Ferry   **Red and White Fleet's** (tel. 415/546–2896) high-speed ferry departs mornings each day that the park is open from Pier 41 at Fisherman's Wharf. It arrives in Vallejo an hour later. Roundtrip service allows five hours to visit the park. Excursion tickets are $19–$32 and include park admission.

7

The Gold Country

by Vicky Elliott

Before the Gold Rush, California looked toward the coast: The Spanish, despite their hunger for precious metal, had neglected the Sierras. When gold was discovered at Coloma in 1848, everybody headed for the hills, starting the greatest mass migration since the Crusades. It lured people from everywhere in the world, from Austria and Ireland, from England, France, and China; and when it was all over, California was a different place.

Today, the Gold Country lies waiting to be discovered again, once more off the beaten track and ripe with hidden treasure. You can still join a prospecting expedition and try your hand at panning for the flakes deposited by millennia of trickling streams, but the chief reward here is the chance to walk back a little into the past.

At one point in the 1850s, Nevada City was as big a place as Sacramento and San Francisco. Today, it stands out for its sophistication among its neighbors, but, like almost all the towns along Highway 49, which winds the 200-mile length of the historic mining area, its population is in the five-digit range. Time has washed over the Mother Lode; economic opportunities are limited, and consequently there is a homey, unspoiled feel to it that attracts those who are content to live modestly amidst the natural beauty of these rolling hills.

Travelers can experience that lifestyle at bed-and-breakfast inns, many in exquisite Victorian buildings that have been taken down to the studs and lovingly restored. Their sumptuous breakfasts and period atmosphere offer a comfortable and romantic base from which to explore the tumbledown villages and historic sites that speak of the 19th century.

In the frenzy of the Gold Rush, as tents and flimsy wooden buildings sprang up around promising "diggings," comfort was in short supply. During the early years, this was a man's world. After the hard journey around the Horn by ship, or the wearying trek across the continent, everyday life in the claims, under blazing sun or in freezing streams, was tough.

The saloon keepers and canny merchants realized where the real gold was to be made. Nothing came cheap. This was a market where potatoes and onions could command $1 apiece. Entrepreneurs like the storekeeper Samuel Brannan became millionaires.

The labor of panning made way for the crude wooden stamp mill and the arrastre, which were used to break up the gold-bearing rock, as well as for a host of mining techniques imported from all over the world. Hydraulic mining washed whole hillsides away, and as the industry matured, the exploitation of quartz-bearing hard-rock lodes demanded organization and capital that superseded the rough-and-tumble self-government of the first arrivals.

The story of this extraordinary episode in American history, vividly described by Mark Twain and Bret Harte, comes alive in mining towns in various stages of decay, as well as in careful reconstructions including Columbia State Historic Park. The Gold Country may be a backwater, but it repays leisurely exploration.

Getting Around

By Plane Sacramento Metropolitan Airport is the major airport closest to the Gold Country (it's an hour's drive from Placerville, and a little closer to Auburn). San Francisco International Airport is about two hours from Sacramento. Car rentals are available at both airports.

By Bus **Greyhound-Trailways** serves Sacramento, Auburn, Grass Valley, and Placerville from San Francisco. The **Sacramento Transit Authority** buses service points of major interest in downtown Sacramento.

By Car This is the most convenient way to see the Gold Country, since most of its towns are too small to provide a base for public transportation. I–80 intersects with Highway 49 at Auburn; U.S. 50 intersects with Highway 49 at Placerville.

Guided Tours

Gold Prospecting Expeditions (18172 Main St., Box 974, Jamestown 95327, tel. 209/984–4653). Specialists in the field, this outfit offers one-hour gold-panning excursions, two-week prospecting trips, and a good deal in between.

Outdoor Adventure River Specialists (O.A.R.S.) (Box 67, Angels Camp 95222, tel. 209/736–4677). A wide range of white-water rafting trips on the American, Merced, and Tuolumne Rivers are offered from late March through early October.

River City Queen (1401 Garden Hwy., Suite 125, Sacramento 95833, tel. 916/921–1111) runs 1½-hour narrated cruises on the Sacramento River year round. Board at 1207 Front Street.

Matthew McKinley. (Channel Star Excursions, 1207 Front St., No. 18, Sacramento 95814, tel. 916/441–6481 or 800/433–0263). This paddlewheel riverboat offers a variety of excursions, including a happy hour, dinner cruises, and a champagne brunch.

Important Addresses and Numbers

Tourist Information **Amador County Chamber of Commerce** (30 S. Hwy 49–88, Box 596, Jackson 95642, tel. 209/223–0350).

Auburn Area Visitors and Convention Bureau (601 Lincoln Way, Auburn 95603, tel. 916/885–5616 or 800/433–7575 in CA).

Columbia State Historic Park (Box 1824, Columbia 95310, tel. 209/532–4301 or 209/532–0150).

El Dorado County Chamber of Commerce (542 Main St., Placerville 95667, tel. 916/621–5885).

Golden Chain Council of the Mother Lode (Box 7046, Auburn 95604).

Nevada City Chamber of Commerce (132 Main St., Nevada City 95959, tel. 916/265–2692).

Nevada County Chamber of Commerce (248 Mill St., Grass Valley 95945, tel. 916/273–4667 or 800/752–6222 in CA). The Nevada County Chamber is housed in a reproduction of the home owned on this site by the notorious dancer Lola Montez when she moved to Grass Valley in the early 1850s; her bathtub is still there.)

Sacramento Convention and Visitors Bureau (1421 K St., Sacramento 95814, tel. 916/442–5542).

Old Sacramento Visitor Information Center (1104 Front St., Old Sacramento, tel. 916/442–7644).

Tuolumne County Visitors Bureau (Box 4020, 55 W. Stockton St., Sonora 95370, tel. 209/533–4420 or 800/446–1333 in CA).

Emergencies Dial 911 for emergencies throughout the Gold Country to reach police, fire, and medical personnel.

There are several hospitals with 24-hour emergency room service in Sacramento: **Mercy Hospital of Sacramento Promptcare** (4001 J St., tel. 916/453–4424), **Sutter General Hospital** (2801 L St., tel. 916/733–3003), and **Sutter Memorial Hospital** (52nd and F sts., tel. 916/733–1000).

Exploring

From San Francisco, I–80 runs toward the Gold Country via Sacramento; at Auburn, it intersects with Highway 49, which links many of the old Gold Rush communities. Alternatively, you can pick up U.S. 50 at Sacramento; it intersects Highway 49 at Placerville.

Today, unlike Gold Rush times, it's possible to travel the length of Highway 49 in a single day. The winding road is almost entirely two-lane, but it is excellent; there is no roughness or hardship now. It would be a spectacular outing, but on such a tight timetable, you'd miss the fun of wandering through ghost towns and exquisitely restored villages, stopping by the roadside to read historical markers, poking through antiques shops and craft stores, and visiting the foothill vineyards to sample the wines. This is an area where it pays to slow down and take your time.

Highway 49

Numbers in the margin correspond with points of interest on the Gold Country map.

● A two-hour drive from Sacramento to the northern end of Highway 49 is **Downieville,** one of the prettiest of the Gold Rush towns. Stone, brick, and frame buildings seem to cling to the mountainsides, or hug the banks of the fast-moving Yuba River. Along the quiet streets, lovely old houses have been well-maintained or restored. The spare and elegant Methodist church, which dates from 1865, is the oldest Protestant church in continuous use in the state. Drive out Main Street past the last bridge and take a short walk past the PG&E Station to the crystal-clear Yuba River. The river forms pools as it rushes over boulders, and it's a favorite swimming spot. *An information booth in the center of town is open from May to Sept.*

● Wind back down Highway 49 50 miles to **Nevada City,** a Gold Rush town reminiscent of New England with its white houses and picket fences. The **Nevada Theatre** on Broad Street, built in 1865, is California's oldest theatre in continuous use, and a community center for the town.

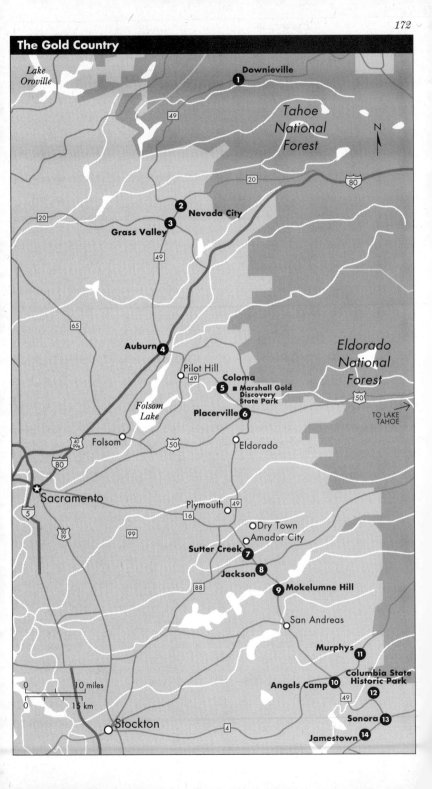

The Gold Country

Lake Oroville

Downieville ❶

Tahoe National Forest

49

20

80

❷ Nevada City

❸
Grass Valley

20

49

65

Auburn ❹

Pilot Hill
49

Coloma
❺ ■ Marshall Gold
Discovery
State Park

Eldorado National Forest

50

TO LAKE TAHOE

Placerville ❻

Folsom Lake

40
99 Folsom

50

Eldorado

80
5

Sacramento

Plymouth 49

16

ODry Town
Amador City

Sutter Creek ❼

Jackson ❽

❾ Mokelumne Hill

88

50
99

99

San Andreas

Murphys
❶❶

4

Columbia State
Historic Park
❶❷

0   10 miles
0   15 km

Angels Camp ❶⓪

49

Sonora ❶❸

Stockton

4

Jamestown ❶❹

Behind the theater, the **Miners Foundry,** also built in 1865, now serves as a cultural center, home to plays, concerts, and such events as the annual Teddy Bear Convention. The cavernous building, housing many Victorian artifacts, holds a Sunday brunch from 9:30 to 11:30, enlivened by musicians. *325 Spring St., tel. 916/265–5040. Open daily 10–5.*

Shopping is a draw in Nevada City. You'll find an enticing selection of antiques, brass, crystal, books, and toys. The town also has a number of good restaurants, not always the case in Gold Country communities.

Time Out | **Sierra Mountain Coffee Roasters** is a cozy and appealing refreshment stop. Excellent coffee, coffee drinks, and homemade pastries are served until late afternoon. It's an informal place —there's a pile of daily papers to read in a booth or outdoors on the quiet patio. *316 Commercial St., corner of York, tel. 916/265–5282. Closed Sun. Open until 11 PM Fri. and Sat.*

❸ South along Highway 49, **Grass Valley** is worth a full day's browsing. More than half of California's total gold production was extracted from the mines of Nevada County, and some of the area's most interesting exhibits on gold mining are to be found here.

The **Empire Mine,** which was worked from 1850 right up to 1956, was one of California's richest quartz mines, and an estimated 5.8 million ounces of gold were brought up from its 367 miles of underground passages. The mine is now a State Historic Park, and its buildings and grounds are open year round. Tours allow you to peer into the deep recesses of the mine, and to view the owner's "cottage," with its exquisite woodwork. The visitors' center has films and exhibits on mining, and you can picnic. *10791 Empire St. (Empire St. exit south from Hwy 49), tel. 916/273–8522. Admission: $1 adults, 50¢ children 6–17. Open daily in winter, 10–5; daily in summer 9–6. Tours and lectures: winter, weekends at 1 and 2; summer, on the hour from 11–4.*

The **North Star Power House and Pelton Wheel Exhibit** boasts a 32-foot-high Pelton wheel, the largest ever built. It was used to power mining operations, and is a forerunner of the modern water turbines that generate hydroelectricity. Period mining equipment and a stamp mill are also on display, as well as one of the few operable Cornish pumps in the country, part of the legacy of the tin miners who migrated here from Cornwall in England. There are hands-on displays for children and a picnic area. *Allison Ranch Rd. and Mill St. (Empire St. exit north from Hwy 49), tel. 916/273–4255. Donation requested. Open May–Oct. 10–5.*

Time Out | A more palpable reminder of the mining past can be had at **Marshall's Pasties,** which still purveys handmade beef and potato pies like those taken down into the shafts in lunch buckets by the Cornish miners who came to work in the hard-rock mines. The apple pasties are good, too. *203 Mill St., tel. 916/272–2844. Open Mon.–Sat. 9:30–6.*

❹ **Auburn,** at the intersection of Highway 49 and I–80 (after 49 crosses under I–80, turn right on Lincoln and follow the signs), is a small old town with narrow climbing streets, cobblestones, wooden sidewalks, and many original buildings. The **Bernhard Museum,** built in 1851 as the Traveler's Hotel, now offers a glimpse of family life in the late Victorian era. *291 Auburn-Folsom Rd., tel. 916/889–4156. Admission: $1 adults, 50¢ for children 6–16 and senior citizens over 65. Open Tues.–Fri. 11–3, weekends noon–4.*

❺ Twenty-five miles farther on is **Coloma,** where gold fever originally broke out. John Sutter erected a sawmill here on the banks of the American River, and it was in the millrace that one of his employees, James Marshall, discovered gold in January 1848. "My eye was caught with the glimpse of something shining in the bottom of the ditch," he recalled later. Unfortunately, the wagon-builder himself never found any more "color," as it came to be called.

Most of Coloma lies within **Marshall Gold Discovery State Historic Park.** Within six months of Marshall's discovery, 2,000 prospectors arrived, and Coloma became the first Gold Rush town. Its population swelled rapidly to 10,000, but as supplies of the precious metal were exhausted, the miners evaporated as quickly as they had come. A replica of Sutter's mill, based on Marshall's drawings, now stands here, with Marshall's cabin and museum; there are areas to picnic and fish. *Tel. 916/622–3470. Day use: $3 per car. Park open daily 8 AM to sunset. Museum open daily 10–5 in summer; 11–4:30 Labor Day–Memorial Day. Closed Dec. 25, Jan. 1, and Thanksgiving.*

❻ Follow Highway 49 south 10 miles into **Placerville,** which has shed its former name of Hangtown, a graphic allusion to the summary nature of frontier justice. Placerville today has the distinction of being one of the only cities in the world to own a gold mine. The **Gold Bug Mine** has two fully lighted shafts, one of which dead-ends at a gold-flecked vein, while the other follows an uphill trail. A shaded stream runs through the park, and there are picnic facilities. *Bedford exit north from Hwy. 49 to Gold Bug Park, tel. 916/622–0832. Admission free, 50¢ for self-guided tour of mine. Park open daily 8 AM–sunset; mine open April–Oct.*

Placerville is the largest town on Highway 49. Driving south through rolling countryside, you'll pass villages that amount to little more than a few antiques stores and perhaps a cafe, with crumbling brick buildings and the ubiquitous historical markers: Plymouth, Drytown, Amador City.

❼ **Sutter Creek** is another matter, well-kept and totally unspoiled, its white homes carefully restored, with green shutters and picket fences. The stores clustered along Highway 49 are worth a closer look, and the wooden sidewalks evoke the feeling of the muddy roads of the 19th century.

A detour here along Shake Ridge Road to **Volcano** will take you past Daffodil Hill, which, from March to mid-April, comes alive with color. Dutch colonists planted the bulbs here, and the daffodils have propagated themselves riotously since. The village of Volcano, once a town of 5,000 people, with 17 hotels and 35 saloons, is a faithful reflection of a vanished age: Nothing has been tampered with, and its general store and theater are still in use, as they have been for 140 years or more.

Driving south from Sutter Creek, Highway 49 climbs sharply, twists and turns, and then rewards you with a wonderful view

8 over the mining town of **Jackson.** An old white church sits on a knoll, its small cemetery spread out around it, and from this vantage point, the brick buildings below cluster tightly. Seen up close, however, the town is a motley assortment of modern businesses and buildings in various states of repair; it has the dubious distinction of closing its bordellos only as recently as 1956.

9 Seven miles south along Highway 49 is the town of **Mokelumne Hill,** Moke Hill for short. Unlike busy Jackson, the county seat, this little village is frozen in an earlier time. Many of the buildings are constructed in light-brown rhyolite tuff, a stone common in much of the Gold Country. Where there are sidewalks, they are wooden, like the small, frail-looking houses on the hilly side streets.

10 Another 20 miles along the highway is **Angels Camp,** famed chiefly for its jumping-frog contest in May, based on Mark Twain's "The Jumping Frog of Calaveras County," one of his first stories to attract public notice. Twain was not impressed by the hospitality he experienced during his stay here in 1865; he described the coffee as "day-before-yesterday dishwater." At the north end of town is a museum with an interesting collection of minerals and early artifacts. *Tel. 209/736–4444. Open daily 10–3.*

11 East on Highway 4, and less than 10 miles up the road, is **Murphys,** with its white picket fences and Victorian houses. In **Murphys Hotel,** opened in 1856 as the Sperry & Perry and still operating, is a guest register recording the visits of Horatio Alger and Ulysses S. Grant, who joined the 19th-century swarms who came to visit the giant sequoias in **Calaveras Big Trees State Park,** about 15 miles farther east on Highway 4. *Tel. 209/ 795–2334. Day use: $3 per car. Open daily.*

Another spectacle of nature 4 miles out of Murphys, on the Vallecito-Columbia highway, is **Moaning Cavern,** a vast underground chamber with ancient crystalline rock formations. *Tel. 209/736–2708. Admission: $5.75 adults, $2.50 children, $2 senior citizens. Open 9–6 in summer, 10–5 in winter.*

Back on Highway 49 driving south, there is a breathtaking ride across the bridge over the Melones Reservoir and an indication of the rugged terrain in a part of California where the rivers have dug deep canyons. Horse-drawn wagons must have found it rough going.

12 A well-marked turnoff leads to **Columbia State Historic Park,** a pleasingly executed mix of preservation and restoration. The "Gem of the Southern Mines" comes as close to a Gold Rush town in its heyday as you can get, although there are more ice-cream parlors than saloons today. You can still ride a stagecoach and pan for gold; street musicians give lively performances on the banjo, the fiddle, and the stump; and there is a blacksmith working at his anvil. Elegant lodging can be found at the City Hotel or Fallon House, both dating from the 1850s, and the Fallon Theater presents plays year round. Columbia's candy store makes its own old-fashioned confectionery: licorice sticks, horehound drops, and fudge. *Exhibits and demonstrations daily 10–6.*

13 Highway 49 is the main street in **Sonora.** Don't miss the beautiful **St. James Episcopal Church,** built in 1860, the second-oldest frame church in California. In winter, the ski traffic passes through Sonora on the way along Highway 108 to Lake Tahoe 30 miles east.

The road turns west for a few miles out of Sonora, and heads to ⓮ **Jamestown** whose **Railtown 1897 State Historic Park** includes 26 acres of trains, a station, a roundhouse, and facilities for maintaining trains. There are slide presentations, guided tours, and train excursions on the weekends. The park is open daily from spring through fall. *Tel. 209/984–3953. Admission: $2 adults, $1.25 children; train excursions: $8 adults, $4 children.*

Sacramento

Numbers in the margin correspond with points of interest on the Sacramento map.

A major gateway to the Gold Country, Sacramento has its own slice of Gold Rush history, as the point from which gold prospectors fanned out to seek their fortunes. Sacramento predates the Gold Rush, but came into its own as a center for financial transactions and the shipping of provisions to the prospecting fields, ultimately becoming the western terminus of the Pony Express, the transcontinental railroad, and the telegraph. One of the largest restoration projects in the United States has spruced up the old city, an airy island marooned on its plot to one side of the state capital's extravagant high rises. Today, its cobbled streets are paced by horse-drawn carts laden with visitors, and covered walkways frame magnificent commercial premises whose tall windows and high ceilings offer a revealing glimpse into 19th-century shopping.

❶ The **visitor's center** (1104 Front St., tel. 916/442–7644) is housed in a former depot for passengers and freight bound down the river to San Francisco by steamship. *Open daily 9–5.*

❷ The **Eagle Theater** (925 Front St.) was California's first, built in 1849. A reconstruction done in 1976 is in regular use now. The ❸ **Sacramento History Center** was once the nerve center of the town: mayor's offices, council chambers, jail, and policemen's quarters, among other things. It now offers a streamlined, well-presented introduction to the history of Sacramento and its surroundings, complete with gold pans that you can sift yourself, a thatched Indian hut, memorabilia from the world wars, and a colorful stack of turn-of-the-century cans of local produce. *101 I St., tel. 916/449–2057. Admission: $2.50 adults, $1 children 6–17, $1.50 senior citizens. Open Tue.–Sun. 10–5. Closed Dec. 25, Jan. 1, and Thanksgiving.*

❹ Old Sacramento's biggest draw is the **California State Railroad Museum,** 100,000 square feet exhibiting 21 restored locomotives and railroad cars in perfect working order, including the Governor Stanford, the Central Pacific locomotive that steamed from Sacramento to Promontory Point to mark the completion of the transcontinental railroad. You can walk through a post-office car and peer into the cubbyholes and canvas bags of mail, or go through a sleeping car that simulates the swaying on the roadbed and the flashing lights of a passing town at night. On weekends from May through Labor Day, a steam-powered excursion train runs several miles down the river to Miller Park every hour on the hour from 10 to 5 from the depot on Front Street. *125 I St., at 2nd and I sts., tel. 916/448–4466. Admis-*

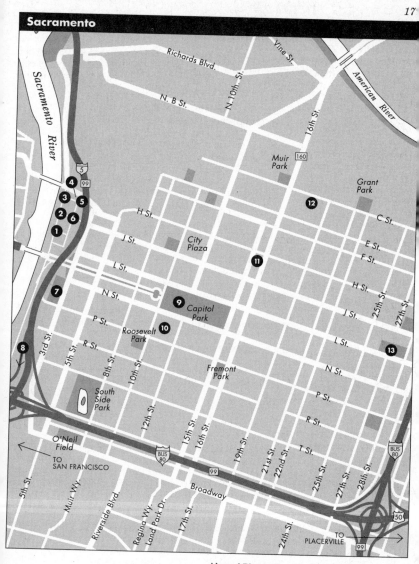

Sacramento

Almond Plaza, **12**

B.F. Hastings
Building, **6**

California State
Archives, **10**

California State
Railroad Museum, **4**

Crocker Art
Museum, **7**

Eagle Theater, **2**

Governor's
Mansion, **11**

Huntington, Hawkins
& Co. Store, **5**

Sacramento History
Center, **3**

State Capitol, **9**

Sutter's Fort, **13**

Towe Ford
Museum, **8**

Visitor's Center, **1**

sion: $3 adults, $1 children 6–17. Open daily 10–5. Closed Dec. 25, Jan. 1, and Thanksgiving.

⑤
⑥ The **Huntington, Hawkins & Co. Store** hardware exhibit at 111 I Street is open daily 11–5. The **B.F. Hastings Building** (2nd and J sts.) includes the first Sacramento chambers of the California State Supreme Court, built in 1854.

⑦ The **Crocker Art Museum,** a few blocks from old Sacramento, is the oldest art museum in the West, with a collection of European, Asian, and California art, including "Sunday Morning in the Mines," a large canvas depicting the mining industry of the 1850s. The museum's lobby and magnificent ballroom retain the original 1870s woodwork, plaster moldings, and imported tiles. *216 O St., tel. 916/449–5423. Admission: $2.50 adults, $1.50 senior citizens, and $1 children 7–17. Open Tues. 1–9, Wed.–Sun. 10–5. Closed Dec. 25, Jan. 1, Thanksgiving, and July 4.*

⑧ A recent attraction is the **Towe Ford Museum,** a collection of more than 150 vintage cars, embracing every year and model manufactured by the Ford company for 50 years, starting in 1903. *2200 Front St., tel. 916/442–6802. Admission: $5 adults, $4.50 senior citizens, $2.50 young adults 14–18; $1 children 5–13. Open daily 10–6. Closed Dec. 25, Jan. 1, and Thanksgiving.*

⑨ The **state capitol** was built in 1869 and was extensively restored recently. The lacy plasterwork of the rotunda, 120 feet high, has the complexity and color of a Fabergé Easter egg. There are free guided tours daily every hour from 9 to 4, and there are also tours of the well-kept grounds, 2 blocks wide and 5 blocks long, whose plants and shrubs from all over the world are clearly identified. *Capitol Ave. and 10th St., tel. 916/324–0333. Admission free. Open daily 9–5 spring and summer; weekdays 9–5, 10–5 fall and winter. Closed Dec. 25, Jan. 1, and Thanksgiving.*

⑩ The **California State Archives** has a wealth of documents on the history of the state, including the oldest collection of Western newspapers, and a catalog of all those eligible to vote at the turn of the century. *1020 O St., tel. 916/445–4293. Open weekdays 8–5. Closed major holidays.*

⑪ The historic **Governor's Mansion** was originally the palatial residence of Albert Gallatin, one of the partners in the Central Pacific Railroad, and subsequently home to 13 California governors—until Ronald Reagan turned it down in 1967. *16th and H sts., tel. 916/323–3047. Admission: $1 adults, 50¢ children 6–17. Closed Mon. Tours on the hour 10–4.*

⑫ Well worth visiting also is the Blue Diamond cooperative's **Almond Plaza,** the world's largest almond-processing factory, with tours that fill you in on the myriad uses of the almond—as butter, powder, paste and oil. The variety of almond delicacies on sale in the gift shop is amazing. *1701 C St., tel. 916/446–8587 or 800/225–NUTS. Open weekdays 9–5:30, gift shop also Sat. 10–4. Tours at 9 AM, 10 AM, 1 PM, and 2 PM.*

⑬ **Sutter's Fort** is the settlement from which Sacramento grew, founded in 1839 by the Swiss immigrant John Augustus Sutter. Its thick walls now surround an adobe house and workshops for gunsmiths, blacksmiths, and candlemakers. Behind the fort is a museum displaying local Indian artifacts. *27th and L sts., tel.*

916/445–4422. Admission: $1 adults, 50¢ children 6–17. Open daily 10–5. Closed Dec. 25, Jan. 1, and Thanksgiving.

Dining

Given the small population of the Gold Country (only two towns, Auburn and Placerville, approach a population of 10,000), there are a disproportionately large number of good restaurants. Many of the menus are ambitious: In addition to standard American, Italian, and Mexican fare, there is Continental, French, and California cuisine, with an emphasis on innovation and the freshest ingredients. The national fast-food chains are few and far between—the population isn't large enough to support them. It's not difficult, though, to find the makings for a good picnic in most Gold Country towns.

Sacramento is enjoying a period of prosperity and expansion, and it offers a wide range of eating places for its growing population; restaurants listed are all located in Old Sacramento or downtown. Unless otherwise noted, dress is informal.

Highly recommended restaurants are indicated by a star ★.

Category	Cost*
Very Expensive	over $30
Expensive	$20–$30
Moderate	$10–$20
Inexpensive	under $10

per person, not including tax, service, or drinks

Amador City
Expensive

Au Relais. Candlelight, crystal, fresh flowers, and rose-hued table linens glow against an unusual apothecary's counter in this French country dinner house. A rock fireplace is filled with flowers in warm weather. The menu features French adaptations of California cuisine, with many fresh fish entrées and an emphasis on fresh produce elegantly presented. The wine list includes French and Californian vintages. *14220 Hwy 49, tel. 209/267–5636. Reservations advised. MC, V. Closed Mon.–Tues.*

Auburn
Moderate

Butterworth's. Housed in a handsome Victorian mansion on a hillside overlooking Old Auburn, this restaurant features American regional cuisine with copious servings and a Sunday brunch. *1522 Lincoln Way, tel. 916/885–0249. Reservations accepted. Jacket and tie advised. AE, MC, V. Closed Mon. Closed lunch Sat.*

★ **Headquarter House.** This restaurant is set on a hilltop within the Dunipace Angus Ranch, with a lounge on the top floor overlooking pine trees. Part of the view includes a nine-hole golf course, open to the public and inexpensive. The varied menu emphasizes California cuisine, with a good choice of fresh seafood. *14500 Musso Rd., tel. 916/878–1906. Reservations advised. AE, CB, DC, MC, V.*

Lou La Bonte. This is a homey, long-established restaurant serving hearty American food for breakfast, lunch, and dinner; some Italian dishes are included on the dinner menu. There is entertainment and dancing in the bar on weekends. *13460 Lin-*

coln Way, tel. 916/885-9193. Reservations accepted. AE, CB,
DC, MC, V.

Inexpensive **Auburn Joe's.** This is an informal but nicely appointed restaurant with a pleasant atmosphere, offering an American menu for lunch, dinner, and breakfast on weekends. Beef, lamb, and seafood are emphasized, with some Italian specialties. *13480 Lincoln Way, tel. 916/885-3090. Reservations advised. AE, CB, DC, MC, V.*

Cafe Delicias. Located in a picturesque building in Old Auburn, this Mexican restaurant has an extensive menu, and the helpings are generous. One dinner choice is *carne asada a la Tampiquena*—steak grilled with spices, onions, and bell peppers, served with a cheese enchilada, rice, and beans. *1591 Lincoln Way, tel. 916/885-2050. No reservations. MC, V. Closed Tues.*

Mary Belle's. This cozy, friendly coffee shop in an Old Auburn brick building serves simple American breakfasts and lunches; the hot oatmeal is perfect. There are salads, sandwiches, desserts, a soda fountain, and an extensive breakfast menu. *1590 Lincoln Way, tel. 916/885-3598. No reservations. MC, V.*

Coloma **Vineyard House.** In this Victorian country inn, dating from
Expensive 1878, the small dining rooms have fireplaces or wood-burning stoves, flower-painted chandeliers, and early California memorabilia. The menu is American, with chicken, beef, seafood, and pasta. Chicken and dumplings are a house specialty. Sunday brunch is served. *Cold Springs Rd., off Hwy. 49; tel. 916/ 622-2217. Reservations advised. MC, V. Closed Mon. No lunch.*

Columbia **City Hotel.** This authentically restored 1850s hotel and dining
Expensive room serves regional American cuisine, using fresh local produce stylishly prepared and served with flair. The California wine list is comprehensive. An adjoining bar, also restored, is called the What Cheer Saloon, after the liquor store of that name that once operated here. *Main St. (in Columbia State Park), tel. 209/532-1479. Reservations advised. AE, MC, V.*

Cool **The Nugget.** In this unassuming setting, not far from Auburn,
Inexpensive Jens Hoppe, who was born in Germany, draws on the cooking he learned at home, producing some delectable goulash and tender Wiener schnitzels. *Hwy 49, tel. 916/823-1294. Reservations advised. No credit cards. Closed Mon. dinner.*

Downieville **The Forks.** This small, cheerful restaurant on the Downie River
Inexpensive– provides outdoor service on a flagstone patio at the water's
Moderate edge in summer. The American menu offers beef, chicken, homemade soup, salads, sandwiches, and 12 varieties of tea. There is a short, very reasonably priced California wine list. *Main St., tel. 916/289-3479. Summer reservations advised. MC, V. Closed weekend lunch and Mon. dinner.*

Grass Valley **Owl Tavern.** This cozy and comfortable brick tavern, built in
Moderate– 1852, specializes in magnificent steaks, which guests select
Expensive from a display case, prepared by the chef at an open grill. There's also trout, lobster, and pork chops. Cornish pasties, sandwiches, and salads are available at lunch. Desserts are homemade. *134 Mill St., tel. 916/273-0526. Reservations advised. AE, DC, MC, V. No lunch Sun.*

Jackson **Teresa's.** This long-established Italian restaurant has a local cli-
Moderate entele. The menu features daily specials, and includes home-

made ravioli, fresh minestrone daily, and a fine selection of veal, scampi, and other Italian classics. *1235 Jackson Gate Rd., tel. 209/223-1786. Reservations advised. MC, V. Closed Wed.–Thurs; closed lunch Sun., dinner from 2 PM.*

Inexpensive **The Balcony.** This popular, unpretentious restaurant offers Continental cuisine with daily specials such as chicken marsala and veal piccata. The lunch menu includes quiches and crepes. Senior citizens receive discounts. *164 Main St., tel. 209/223-2855. Reservations advised. AE, MC, V. Closed dinner, Mon. and Tues., closed lunch Sun.*

Jamestown
Moderate–
Expensive
Jamestown Hotel. Old oak sideboards, cut-glass lamps, and rocking chairs in the lobby set the tone in this restored Gold Rush hotel. Continental dishes and steaks are served at dinner; salads, sandwiches, and omelets are offered at lunch. Service is in the dining room or the garden patio. Sunday brunch is served. *18153 Main St., tel. 209/984-3902. Reservations advised. AE, MC, V.*

Nevada City
Very Expensive
York Street Blues. Flowered wallpaper, tablecloths, gaslight, and candlelight create an intimate atmosphere at this dinner theater where the price of the dinner includes an evening's entertainment. The menu isn't long; it features prime rib, chicken, and vegetarian dishes. *203 York St., tel. 916/265-6363. Reservations advised. No credit cards. May–Nov., open for lunch weekdays, dinner theater Fri.–Sun., with Sun. matinee; dinner theater only, Fri.–Sun., Dec.–April.*

Moderate–
Expensive
Country Rose. The exterior of this old brick and stone building, complete with the original iron shutters from Gold Rush days, blends well with the antiques in this French country restaurant. A lengthy menu features seafood, beef, lamb, chicken, and ratatouille. In the summer, there is outdoor service on a leafy patio. *300 Commercial St., tel. 916/265-6248. Reservations advised. AE, MC, V. Closed Sun. lunch.*

Friar Tuck. Lots of dark wood and secluded booths give an old-English ambience to this restaurant. The specialty of the house is fondue. A pot of bubbling hot peanut oil is brought to your table; you cook your own scallops, shrimp, chicken, or steak, and then dip the morsels into a variety of sauces. Seafood, beef, chicken, and pasta dishes are also offered. A children's menu is available. *111 N. Pine St., tel. 916/265-2262. Reservations advised. AE, MC, V. Closed lunch and Mon., Tues.*

Peter Selaya's California Restaurant. Stained glass, lace curtains, antique sideboards, and old-fashioned high-back oak dining chairs set the mood in this long-established dinner house. The menu is international, with an emphasis on seafood. Desserts and espresso are a specialty. *320 Broad St., tel. 916/265-5697. Reservations advised. AE, MC, V. Closed Mon.*

Moderate **National Hotel.** This is the oldest continuously operating hotel west of the Rockies (and perhaps the Mississippi), founded in 1856. The menu includes steaks, seafood, and oriental and Continental specialties. *211 Broad St., tel. 916/265-4551. Reservations advised. AE, MC, V.*

Posh Nosh. They bake their own bread every day at this restaurant, which offers deli fare and California cuisine. Everything on the lunch menu is available for takeout: sandwiches, salads, and bagel baskets. There's a good wine list, as well as 20 varieties of imported beer, and a dozen domestic brands. Dinner features fresh seafood, including lobster, and there are vegetarian selections, as well as cream puffs with fresh straw-berries. You can dine on the garden patio in nice weather. *318 Broad St., tel. 916/265–6064. Reservations advised for dinner. AE, MC, V.*

Trolley Junction Cafe. The expansive windows of this sparkling new restaurant take advantage of the setting beside a creek, waterfall, and waterwheel. The American menu features hearty breakfast choices and salads and sandwiches for lunch. *400 Railroad Ave., tel. 916/265–5259. Reservations advised. MC, V.*

Placerville **Smokehouse 1898.** An airy two-level restaurant with garden de-
Moderate   cor offers traditional American food, including barbecued chicken, steak, and ribs, as well as Continental selections. *311 Main St., tel. 916/622–1898. Reservations advised. AE, MC, V. Closed Mon.*

Inexpensive **Apple Cafe.** This light, spacious coffee shop has a superb setting, looking out over valleys and mountains. It features homemade dishes including biscuits and gravy, and soup. Breakfast is served all day. *2740 U.S. 50, tel. 916/626–8144. No reservations. No credit cards. No dinner.*

★   **Powell Bros. Steamer Co.** The decor is nautical in this seafood restaurant with old brick walls and dark wood. The menu is primarily shellfish, served in stews, pastas, chowders, cocktails, and sandwiches, and cooked in big steamers—nothing is fried. *425 Main St., tel. 916/626–1091. No reservations. MC, V.*

Sacramento **The Firehouse.** A restored firehouse, dating from 1853, this
Very Expensive luxuriously opulent restaurant offers fine cuisine, with elaborate Continental entrées. Less formal, but highly agreeable, are the outdoor lunches served in the leafy cobbled courtyard to the tinkle of fountains, weather permitting, from April through September. *1112 2nd St., tel. 916/442–4772. Jacket and tie advised at dinner. Reservations advised. AE, MC, V. Closed Sun. and major holidays.*

Moderate– **California Fat's.** The ultimate in postmodern decor, this restau-
Expensive rant is built on three levels with a splashy, two-story waterfall and a California Pacific menu featuring dishes from the Pacific Rim. Its banana cream pie is famous. *1015 Front St., tel. 916/441–7966. Reservations recommended. AE, MC, V. Closed Dec. 25, Jan. 1, and Thanksgiving.*

Moderate **Fat City.** Once Sam Brannan's general merchandise store, it's now a study in art deco, incorporating the Leadville, Colorado bar behind which the unsinkable Molly Brown served before she made off on the Titanic. *1001 Front St., tel. 916/446–6768. No reservations. AE, MC, V. Closed Dec. 25, Thanksgiving.*

Los Padres. At this spacious Mexican establishment in Old Sacramento with lofty ceilings and handsome Mexican furnishings, traditional dishes from Baja California are featured. *106 J St., tel. 916/443–6376. Reservations required for groups of 10 or more. AE, MC, DC, CB, V. Closed Dec. 25 and Thanksgiving.*

The Virgin Sturgeon. This restaurant is rustic and casual, and plumb on the Sacramento River; you can dine on the deck and watch the water rush by. The simple American menu offers seafood, steaks, chicken, and salads, but no desserts. *1577 Garden Hwy, tel. 916/921–2694. Reservations required for groups of 10 or more. MC, V. Closed Dec. 25.*

Inexpensive
★
The Old Spaghetti Factory. An old Western Pacific Railroad station has been transformed into an Italian family restaurant, complete with fringed lampshades and velvet settees. Menu highlights are the pasta specialties, crusty bread, and spumoni. *1910 J. St., tel. 916/443–2862. No reservations. No credit cards. Closed for lunch weekends and Dec. 25.*

Sonora
Moderate
★
Hemingway's Cafe Restaurant. The owner of this charming restaurant feels a kinship with Ernest Hemingway, whose love of fishing and hunting is reflected in the menu. Italian, French, and Spanish touches in the entrées commemorate the great man's European travels. The California/Continental cuisine emphasizes fresh foods; the chalkboard menu changes daily and follows the seasons. The wine list features award-winning selections, and many unusual imported beers are stocked. *362 S. Stewart, tel. 209/532–4900. Reservations advised. AE, MC, V. Closed Mon., weekend lunch, Tues. dinner.*

Sutter Creek
Expensive
Pelargonium. An old California bungalow has been reworked into a restaurant; the walls of the small rooms are crowded with art. The California cuisine features seafood and new specials weekly, such as trout stuffed with crab, or roast lamb served with three-cheese polenta and tomato-basil topping. *Hwy. 49 at Hanford St., tel. 209/267–5008. Reservations advised. Closed Wed. and Thurs. Closed lunch.*

Lodging

Among the treasures of the Gold Country today are its inns, many of them in beautifully restored buildings dating back to the 1850s and 1860s and furnished with period pieces. If you came here for the history, there's no better way to get a taste of the past. In Sacramento, the lodgings listed are all in the downtown area, close to Old Sacramento, the capitol, and Sutter's Fort. Highly recommended hotels are indicated with a star ★.

Category	Cost*
Very Expensive	over $80
Expensive	$60–$80
Moderate	$45–$60
Inexpensive	under $45

double room, not including tax

Amador City
Moderate
Mine House Inn. On a steep hillside overlooking tiny Amador City, the headquarters of the Keystone Consolidated Mining Co., more than a century old, have been transformed into an inn furnished with original Victorian antiques. Continental breakfast is included. No pets. *Box 266, Hwy 49, 95601, tel. 209/ 267–5900. 7 rooms. Facilities: pool, open from Memorial Day until the end of Sept. No credit cards.*

Angels Camp
Moderate
Gold Country Inn. This modern, air-conditioned two-story motel provides queen-size beds and a coffeemaker in each room. There is a coffee shop next door. *Box 188, 720 S. Main, Hwy 49, 95222, tel. 209/736–4611. 40 rooms. Facilities: cable TV. AE, MC, V.*

Auburn
Moderate–Expensive

Auburn Inn. This beige and brown multistory inn, built in 1984, is exceptionally well-maintained. The decor is country-style, with chintz draperies and earth tones. There are king- and queen-size beds, suites, nonsmoking rooms, and rooms with facilities for the handicapped. *1875 Auburn Ravine Rd., 95603 (Foresthill exit north from I–80), tel. 916/885–1800 or 800/272–1444 in CA. 81 rooms. Facilities: pool, spa, laundry, cable TV. AE, CB, DC, MC, V.*

Inexpensive

Country Squire Inn. This three-story motel is built around a spacious central area, and has modern rooms decorated in browns and blues. Suites are available. Pets are allowed. There is a restaurant next door. *13480 Lincoln Way, 95603 (Foresthill exit south off I–80), tel. 916/885–7025. 80 rooms. Facilities: pool, spa, cable TV. AE, CB, DC, MC, V.*

Coloma
Expensive

Coloma Country Inn. A restored Victorian bed and breakfast that was built in 1852, this inn is set on 5 acres and offers fishing and canoeing on its own pond. The rooms have antique double beds, and private sitting areas; the decor features quilts, stenciled friezes, and fresh flowers. Country breakfasts are served. No children, pets, or smoking are allowed. Hot-air ballooning and white-water rafting can be arranged. Reservations recommended. *Box 502, 2 High St., 95613, tel. 916/622–6919. 5 rooms, 2 with shared bath. No credit cards.*

Moderate
★

Vineyard House. This 1878 country inn, outfitted with handsome antiques and thick carpets, is built on the site of a prize-winning winery, whose owner turned to wine-making when the Gold Rush petered out. The setting is romantic; the ruins of the wine cellars lie behind flower gardens. Continental breakfast is included. The restaurant and lounge are open every evening from May through September and closed Mondays in winter. No pets. *Box 176, Cold Springs Rd., 95613 (off Hwy 49), tel. 916/622–2217. 7 rooms with shared baths. MC, V.*

Columbia
Expensive

City Hotel. The rooms in this restored 1856 hostelry are elaborately furnished with period antiques. Two balcony rooms overlook Main Street, and the three parlor rooms open onto a second-floor sitting room. Rooms have private half-baths with showers nearby; robes and slippers are provided. Continental breakfast is served in the upstairs parlor, and a dining room is open for lunch and dinner. No pets. *Main St. (inside Columbia State Park), Box 1870, 95310, tel. 209/532–1479. 9 rooms with half-bath. Facilities: saloon. AE, MC, V.*

*Moderate–
Very Expensive*

Fallon Hotel. The state of California recently restored this 1857 hotel to Victorian grandeur. The lobby and rooms are furnished with 1890s antiques. Each accommodation has a private half-bath; there are also men's and women's showers. Continental breakfast is served; if you occupy one of the five balcony rooms, you can sit outside with your coffee and watch the town wake up. Smoking is not allowed; one room is equipped for the handicapped. *Washington St. (inside Columbia State Park, next to the Fallon House Theater), Box 1870, 95310, tel. 209/532–1470. 14 rooms with half bath. AE, MC, V.*

Inexpensive

Columbia Gem Motel. Rustic cottages and six simple air-conditioned motel rooms are set among pine trees. Senior citizens receive discounts. *Columbia Hwy (1 mi from Columbia State Park), Box 874, 22131 Parrot's Ferry Rd., 95310, tel: 209/532–4508. 12 rooms. Facilities: cable TV. MC, V.*

Downieville
Inexpensive

Dyer's Resort-Motel. This small, cheerful, spotlessly clean motel on the Yuba River has a coffee percolator and color TV in each room; some kitchenettes are available. *9 Water St. (first right from Hwy 49), Box 406, 95936, tel. 916/289-3308. 13 rooms. Facilities: pool. MC, V.*

Grass Valley
Expensive–
Very Expensive
★

Murphy's Inn. An immaculate white house in a leafy setting (there is a giant sequoia in the back yard), this outstanding B&B, built in 1866, used to be the mansion of a gold mine owner. Some guest rooms have the original wallpaper, three have fireplaces, and all have antique beds and gas chandeliers. The spacious veranda is festooned with ivy. There are award-winning full breakfasts; Belgian waffles and eggs Benedict are specialties. Smoking and pets are not allowed; there are kennel facilities nearby. *318 Neal St., 95945, (Colfax Hwy 174 exit from Hwy 49, left on S. Auburn), tel. 916/273-6873. 8 rooms. Facilities: swimming spa. AE, MC, V.*

Moderate

Best Western Gold Country Inn. This well-kept two-story motel has contemporary rooms decorated in warm colors; 58 rooms have small refrigerators, and 16 have kitchens. Some rooms adjoin each other. Small pets are allowed. *11972 Sutton Way, 95945 (Brunswick Rd. exit east from Hwy 49), tel. 916/273-1393 or 800/528-1234. 84 rooms. Facilities: pool, spa. AE, DC, MC, V.*

Jackson
Moderate

Best Western Amador Inn. An up-to-date motel with rooms decorated in blue, rose, and light brown. Some rooms have fireplaces, and a few kitchenettes are available. No pets. *200 S. Hwy 49, Box 758, 95642, tel. 209/223-0211 or 800/528-1234. 119 rooms. Facilities: restaurant, lounge, pool, cable TV. AE, DC, MC, V.*

Jamestown
Moderate–
Very Expensive

Jamestown Hotel. Each room in this old brick building with Gold Rush-era furnishings is individually decorated with quilts, rocking chairs, flags, and other 19th-century artifacts, as well as a private Victorian bath. Continental breakfast is included. No pets. October through May is the value season with 20% discounts. *Main St., Box 539, 95327, tel. 209/984-3902. 8 rooms with bath. AE, MC, V.*

Moderate

Sonora Country Inn. This new three-story motel is decorated in subdued pastels. Continental breakfast is included. Small pets are welcome. Half the rooms are for nonsmokers; there are facilities for the handicapped. *Hwy 108 between Jamestown and Sonora, Box 1040, 95327, tel. 209/984-0315 or 800/847-2211 in CA. 59 rooms. Facilities: pool. AE, CB, DC, MC, V.*

Murphys
Expensive

Dunbar House. This restored 1880 home in a pleasant setting is filled with antiques and quilts, and offers refreshments, complimentary wine, and a full country breakfast. No pets; smoking is not allowed. *271 Jones St., 95247, tel. 209/728-2897. 4 rooms. MC, V.*

Inexpensive–
Moderate

Murphys Hotel. The rooms are rustic in this restored 1855 hotel, which was visited by Mark Twain and Ulysses S. Grant. It has retained its period charm, but the modern rooms in the adjoining motel are more comfortable. Children are welcome; pets are allowed in the motel only. *457 Main St., 95247, tel. 209/728-3454. 21 rooms. Facilities: restaurant, lounge. AE, MC, V.*

Nevada City
Very Expensive

Grandmere's Bed and Breakfast Inn. This large white wedding cake of a house was built in 1856 and restored in 1985 in a country French style. The antiques, fabrics, and flower arrangements are superb, and the gardens beautifully landscaped. Full breakfast is included. Smoking is not allowed. *449 Broad St., 95959, tel. 916/265–4660. 6 rooms. MC, V.*

Expensive– Very Expensive **The Red Castle.** A town landmark, this 1860 Gothic Revival mansion stands on a hillside overlooking Nevada City. Its brick with white icicle trim, porches, and gardens add to the charm. The rooms, some of which look over the town, have antique furnishings and are elaborately decorated. A full buffet breakfast is served. No pets. *109 Prospect St., 95959, tel. 916/265–5135. 6 rooms with bath, 2 with shared bath. MC, V.*

Moderate–Expensive **Northern Queen.** This bright, pleasant, two-story motel has a lovely creekside setting. Accommodations include new or remodeled motel units; eight two-story chalets and eight rustic cottages with efficiency kitchens are located by a trout pond in a secluded, wooded area. Rooms have small refrigerators. Facilities for the handicapped are available. Pets are not allowed. *400 Railroad Ave., 95959 (Sacramento St. exit off Hwy 49), tel. 916/265–5824. 75 rooms. Facilities: heated pool (year round), spa, restaurant, cable TV. MC, V.*

Placerville *Expensive* **Fleming Jones Homestead Bed and Breakfast.** This 1883 farmhouse on 11 acres is only a few miles out of Placerville, but the atmosphere is distinctly rural. Exotic poultry and ducks wander through the rose gardens and vegetable beds; burros and ponies graze in the adjoining fields. Rooms are furnished with antiques, Victorian memorabilia, and teddy bears. A full breakfast is served. No pets; smoking is not allowed. *3170 Newtown Rd., 95667 (Hwy 50 east from Hwy 49, then Newtown Rd./Pt. View exit south), tel. 916/626–5840. 6 rooms with bath. No credit cards.*

Moderate **Days Inn.** The clean and comfortable rooms here have bright flowered bedspreads and curtains. There is a coffee shop next door. *1332 Broadway, 95667 (Hwy 50 east from Hwy 49, then Schnell School exit south), tel. 916/622–3124. 45 rooms. AE, DC, MC, V.*

Sacramento *Very Expensive* **Holiday Inn Capitol Plaza.** This high-rise hotel offers fine views of the Sacramento River and the capitol building from its upper-floor rooms and top-floor restaurant and lounge. Old Sacramento is just across the road, and the capitol is 8 blocks away. The modern rooms and suites are furnished in pastels and accented with brass. Pets are allowed. *300 J St., 95814, tel. 916/446–0100 or 800/HOLIDAY. 368 rooms, 5 suites. Facilities: 3 restaurants, 2 lounges, pool, sauna, health club, garage. AE, CB, DC, MC, V.*

Expensive– Very Expensive **Briggs House Bed and Breakfast Inn.** The large, well-decorated rooms are true to the period in this stately, spacious 1901 Victorian building. The breakfasts, included in the rates, are worthy of a gourmet. Smoking is not allowed. Bicycles are available for loan. *2209 Capitol Ave., 95816, tel. 916/441–3214. 7 rooms. Facilities: sauna. AE, MC, V.*

Expensive **Vagabond Inn.** Pastel print bedspreads brighten the neutral colors in this comfortable motel close to Old Sacramento. Continental breakfast, coffee, tea, and newspapers are complimentary. There are rooms for nonsmokers, facilities for the disabled, and senior citizens discounts. Pets are allowed with a $3 deposit. A restaurant and lounge are adjacent. *909 3rd St.,*

95814 (J St. exit off I–5), tel. 916/446–1481 or 800/522–1555. 107 rooms. Facilities: pool. AE, CB, DC, MC, V.

Moderate–Expensive
★
Hotel El Rancho Resort. This 17-acre resort offers outstanding recreational facilities; the rooms and suites are decorated in contemporary pastels with wicker accents. There is an excellent restaurant and lounge. *1029 W. Capitol Ave., West Sacramento, 95691 (Jefferson St. exit north off Business Loop 80), tel. 916/371–6731 or 800/952–5566 in CA. 245 rooms. Facilities: kitchenettes, pool, sauna, lighted tennis courts, racquetball, fitness center with aerobics, Nautilus, and free weights, 1.2–mi par course, massage. AE, CB, DC, MC, V.*

Moderate
Best Western Sandman. The contemporary rooms are decorated in beige and brown at this two-story motel on the banks of the Sacramento River. The location is convenient, at a freeway exit out of Old Sacramento. Small pets are allowed. Senior citizens receive a discount. *236 Jibboom St., 95814 (Richards Blvd. exit west from I–5), tel. 916/443–6515 or 800/528–1234. 115 rooms. Facilities: restaurant, pool, whirlpool. AE, CB, DC, MC, V.*

Inexpensive
Motel Orleans. This is a bright, well-maintained two-story economy hotel with simple contemporary rooms, just one freeway exit from Old Sacramento. Pets are allowed with a $5 deposit. A coffee shop is adjacent. *228 Jibboom St., 95814 (Richards Blvd. exit west from I–5), tel. 916/443–4811. 70 rooms. Facilities: pool. AE, MC, V.*

Sonora
Moderate–Expensive
Ryan House Bed and Breakfast Inn. Rose gardens and a hammock add to the pleasure of this 1855 farm homestead, furnished with country antiques. A full breakfast is served. *153 S. Shepherd St., 95730, tel. 209/533–3445. 4 rooms with shared bath. AE, V.*

Sonora Inn. This inn stands on the site of the first hotel established by a woman in the Gold Country; its original Victorian facade was plastered over in the 1920s during the vogue of Spanish Mission architecture. The roomy lobby, restaurant, and lounge have tiled floors. There is a newer motel attached, where small pets are permitted. *160 S. Washington St., 95370, tel. 209/532–7468 or 800/321–5261 in CA. 61 rooms. Facilities: pool (unheated). AE, MC, V.*

Moderate
Best Western Sonora Oaks Motor Hotel. This 1984 motel is located away from Sonora's crowded central area. The style is modern, with print bedspreads accenting the blue, green, or burgundy colors of the rooms and suites. A 24-hour restaurant and lounge is adjacent. *19551 Hess Ave., 95730 (3 mi east from Hwy 49 on Hwy 108), tel. 209/533–4400, 800/528–1234. 70 rooms. Facilities: pool, spa, cable TV, movies. AE, DC, MC, V.*

Inexpensive
Gunn House Bed & Breakfast. The original adobe house here was built in 1850. It was the first two-story building in town, the home of a newspaperman from Philadelphia who championed the rights of Chinese laborers. It has since been enlarged, restored, and furnished with antiques and air-conditioning. Continental breakfast is served in the old-fashioned lounge on the premises. Pets are not allowed. *286 S. Washington St., 95370, tel. 209/532–3421. 18 rooms. Facilities: pool. AE, MC, V.*

Sutter Creek
Very Expensive
★

The Foxes Bed & Breakfast. The rooms in this house, built in 1857, are handsome, with high ceilings, antique beds, and lofty armoires topped with floral arrangements. All rooms have queen-size beds; three have wood-burning fireplaces. A menu allows guests to select a full breakfast, brought to each room on a silver service. No pets; no smoking allowed. *Box 159, 77 Main St., 95685, tel. 209/267–5882. 6 rooms. MC, V.*

Expensive–
Very Expensive

Hanford House Bed & Breakfast. A modern brick building that evokes an earlier period with its California antiques and spacious rooms. The beds are queen-size, and a hearty Continental breakfast is served. Pets are not allowed. One room offers wheelchair access, and there is a rooftop deck. *61 Hanford St., Box 1450, 95685 (Hwy 49), tel. 209/267–0747. 9 rooms with bath. MC, V.*

★ **Sutter Creek Inn Bed & Breakfast.** This white and green New England-style house, dating from the 1850s, is something of a legend in the bed and breakfast business. The rooms are comfortable and highly individual, furnished with a homey melange of antiques, wood-burning fireplaces, and unique hanging beds, suspended on chains from the ceiling. The gardens are spacious, with a variety of tables, chairs, and chaises, and the parlor is stocked with books and games. Breakfast, a communal affair, is lavish. No pets. *Box 385, 75 Main St., 95685, tel. 209/267–5606. 19 rooms. No credit cards.*

8 Lake Tahoe

With a shoreline more than 6,000 feet above sea level in the Sierra Nevada, Lake Tahoe is one of California's most spectacular natural attractions—even if a third of the lake is in Nevada. Visitors to the 482-square-mile Lake Tahoe Basin are also divided. About half of them arrive intent on sightseeing, hiking, fishing, camping, and boating, while the rest head directly for the casinos on the Nevada side of the lake where gambling is legal. During some summer weekends it seems that absolutely every tourist—100,000 at peak periods—is in a car on the 72-mile shoreline, looking for historic sites and uncrowded beaches, or parking places, restaurants, motels. But the crowds and congestion don't exist at a vantage point overlooking Emerald Bay early in the morning, or on a trail in the national forests that ring the basin, or on a sunset cruise on the lake itself, which is 22 miles long and 12 miles wide.

Placid vistas contrast with the lake's violent formation and dramatic history. About 25 million years ago the Tahoe Basin sank between the uplifting Sierra Nevada and an eastern offshoot of the Carson Range. Lava flowing from Mt. Pluto on the north blocked the basin's outlet. During the Ice Age, glaciers scoured the landscape. Now mountains rise 4,000 feet above the lake, and as much as 500 inches of snow falls in the winter at upper elevations. Sixty-three streams flow into the lake, but only the Truckee River flows out, and it never reaches the ocean. The lake's deepest point is 1,645 feet, and the brilliant blue and blue-green color can be breathtaking, but protecting its clarity is a continuing and often controversial campaign.

For centuries, before the lake was sighted by explorers Kit Carson and John C. Fremont in 1844, it was a summer gathering place and sacred site for Washoe Indians. The California gold rush lured emigrants over the treacherous Sierra north and south of the lake, and Nevada's silver bonanza enticed prospectors east from California a few years later. Hotels and resorts sprang up in the 1850s and 1860s, but the Tahoe Basin's forests were nearly stripped of trees for silver mining operations. By the turn of the century wealthy Californians were building lakeshore estates, some of which survive. Improved roads brought the less affluent in the 1920s and 1930s, when modest, rustic bungalows began to fill the wooded shoreline. The first casinos opened in the 1940s, and ski resorts also brought a development boom as the lake became a year-round attraction. Road construction and other building projects, however, washed soil and minerals into the lake, leading to a growth of algae that threatened its fabled clarity. (Objects can still be seen to a depth of 75 feet.) The environmental movement gained strength in the 1970s, resulting in a moratorium on new construction on the lakeshore and development of a master plan for future growth.

The lake has long been a summer refuge from California's hot Central Valley and the Nevada desert. July and August daytime temperatures are in the 70s, with nighttime lows in the 40s. In the winter, the average daytime high is 36 degrees, the nighttime low 18. Ski resorts open at the end of November, sometimes with machine-made snow, and operate as late as May. Organized summer activities begin at the end of May, when the U.S. Forest Service Visitors Center opens on the south shore. Most accommodations, restaurants and some parks are open year round, although September and October, when crowds have thinned but the weather is still pleasant, may be the most satisfying time to visit Lake Tahoe.

Getting Around

By Plane Two airports provide good access to Lake Tahoe. **Reno Cannon International,** 58 miles northeast of the lake, is served by a number of national and regional airlines. Rental cars are available from the major agencies. There is shuttle bus service to the lake during peak travel periods, and the largest hotel/casinos offer their own transportation, for a fee. **Lake Tahoe Airport** on Hwy. 50, 3 miles south of the lake's shore, is served by American Airlines and American Eagle with smaller jet planes from San Francisco, San Jose and Los Angeles. Rental cars are also available.

By Train There is an **Amtrak** station in Truckee; tel. 800/USA–RAIL, 800/872–7245 in CA.

By Bus **South Tahoe Area Ground Express (STAGE)** (tel. 916/573–2080) runs 24 hours along U.S. 50 and through the neighborhoods of South Lake Tahoe. On the lake's west and north shores, **Tahoe Area Regional Transit (TART)** (tel. 916/581–6365 or 800/325–8278 in NV) runs between Tahoma and Incline Village Monday–Saturday from 6:30 AM to 6:30 PM. **Greyhound Bus** (tel. 916/587–3822) runs among Sacramento, Truckee, and Reno and between Sacramento and South Lake Tahoe. Free shuttle buses run among the casinos, major ski resorts, and motels of South Lake Tahoe.

By Car Lake Tahoe is 198 miles northeast of San Francisco, a four- to five-hour drive, depending on weather and traffic. The major route is I–80, which cuts through the Sierra Nevada about 14 miles north of the lake; from there state highways 89 and 267 reach the north shore. U.S. 50, which begins at I–80 in Sacramento, is the more direct highway to the south shore. U.S. 395 runs south toward the lake from Reno. These are all-weather highways, although there may be delays as snow is cleared during major storms. Tire chains should be carried, and are provided by rental car agencies, from October to May. Avoid the heavy traffic leaving the San Francisco area for Tahoe on Friday afternoons and returning on Sunday afternoons.

By Taxi There is some taxi service available at Tahoe: **North Shore Taxi** (tel. 916/546–3181) and **Taxi Service** (Truckee, tel. 916/587–6336).

Guided Tours

Gray Line (2570 Pacchino, Reno 89512, tel. 702/329–1147) runs daily tours to Emerald Bay, South Lake Tahoe, Carson City, and Virginia City. Other tour providers are **Showboat Lines** (Box 12119, Zephyr Cove, NV 89448, tel. 702/588–6688) and **Tahoe Limousine Service** (Box 10211, South Lake Tahoe 95731, tel. 916/577–2727).

Important Addresses and Numbers

Tourist Information **Lake Tahoe Visitors Authority** (Box 16299, South Lake Tahoe 95706, tel. 916/544–5050 or 800/822–5922).
North Lake Tahoe Chamber of Commerce (950 N. Lake Blvd., Box 884, Tahoe City 95730, tel. 916/583–2371).

Tahoe North Visitors and Convention Bureau (950 N. Lake Blvd., Suite 3, Box 5578, Tahoe City 95730, tel. 916/583–3494 or 800/824–6348).

Ski Phone (tel. 415/864–6440) for 24-hour skiing and weather conditions.

Road Conditions (tel. 916/577–3550).

Emergencies The emergency number throughout the Tahoe area is 911. This will put you in touch with police, fire, and medical help. Make a point of knowing your location.

Exploring

Numbers in the margin correspond with points of interest on the Lake Tahoe map.

The most common way to explore the Lake Tahoe area is to drive the 72-mile road that follows the shore, through wooded flatlands, past beaches, climbing to vistas on the rugged west side of the lake, descending to the busiest commercial developments and casinos. It takes about three hours, but it can be frustrating during peak visiting periods, such as summer holiday weekends when the population swells to 100,000. Obviously, it's best to stop at parks, picnic areas, and scenic lookouts rather than sightseeing entirely from a car. There are many hiking trails, some of them easy, paved paths; with access from the shoreline highway, they offer a quick escape from the traffic. Free maps and information are available at the U.S. Forest Service's Visitors Center (*see* below). The scenic highway around the lake is marked as Highway 28 on the north and northeast shore, U.S. 50 on the south, and Highway 89 on the southwest and west. Highway 89 may be closed at D.L. Bliss State Park when there is a heavy snowfall.

❶ We'll begin a tour around the lake at **Stateline,** actually two towns called Stateline, one on either side of the California–Nevada border. Traveling west along U.S. 50, turn left at Ski ❷ Run Boulevard and drive up to the **Heavenly Valley Ski Resort.** Whether you're a skier or not, you'll want to ride 2,000 feet up on the 50-passenger Heavenly Valley Tram partway up the mountain to 8,000 feet. There you'll find a memorable view of Lake Tahoe and the Nevada desert. The Top of the Tram restaurant, open daily during tram hours, offers basic American food and cafeteria service. It serves lunch, dinner, and Sunday brunch in summer, lunch only in winter. *Tram information, tel. 916/541–1330. Dinner reservations, tel. 916/544–6263. Tram hours, June–Sept., daily 10–10; Nov.–May 9–4. Adult round trip, $9.50, children 3–12, $5.*

Return to U.S. 50 and turn left, heading west toward South Lake Tahoe, the largest community on the lake. As the lakeshore route becomes Highway 89 in Tahoe Valley, commercial development gives way to more wooded national forest lands. You'll notice pleasant bike trails, well off the road. At ❸ **Pope-Baldwin Recreation Area,** take in the Historic Estates Tour (tel. 916/541–5227). Three grand mansions built more than 100 years ago have been restored, and are open for viewing in the summer.

❹ The **Lake Tahoe Visitors Center** on Taylor Creek is operated by the U.S. Forest Service, and offers far more than answers to visitors' questions. This stretch of lakefront is a microcosm of

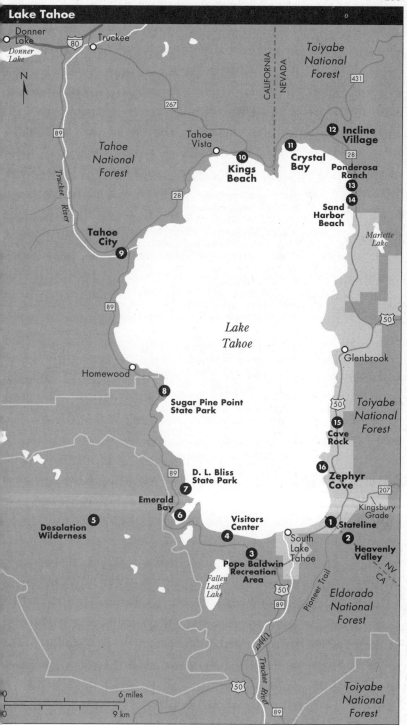

Lake Tahoe

Donner
Lake
*Donner
Lake*

Truckee

*Toiyabe
National
Forest*

431

N

89

267

*Tahoe
National
Forest*

Tahoe Vista

28

10
**Kings
Beach**

11
**Crystal
Bay**

12 **Incline
Village**

28

**Ponderosa
Ranch**

13

14

**Sand
Harbor
Beach**

*Truckee
River*

89

**Tahoe
City**

9

*Marlette
Lake*

89

*Lake
Tahoe*

50

Glenbrook

Homewood

8

**Sugar Pine Point
State Park**

50

*Toiyabe
National
Forest*

15
**Cave
Rock**

89

**D. L. Bliss
State Park**

16

**Zephyr
Cove**

207

7

**Emerald
Bay**

6

Kingsbury
Grade

**Desolation
Wilderness**

5

**Visitors
Center**

4

1 **Stateline**

South
Lake
Tahoe

2

**Heavenly
Valley**

3

**Pope Baldwin
Recreation
Area**

*Fallen
Leaf
Lake*

50

Pioneer Trail

NV

CA

*Eldorado
National
Forest*

89

Upper Truckee River

0   6 miles

0   9 km

50

89

*Toiyabe
National
Forest*

CALIFORNIA NEVADA

the area's natural history, with the site of a Washoe Indian settlement; self-guided trails through meadow, marsh, and forest; and an underground display with windows on Taylor Creek (in the fall, you may see spawning salmon digging their nests.) *Open daily June–Sept., weekends in Oct. Tel. 916/573–2674 in season; at other times of the year, 916/573–2600.*

❺ To the west is the vast **Desolation Wilderness,** a 63,473-acre preserve of granite peaks, glacial valleys, subalpine forests, and more than 80 lakes. Access for hiking, fishing, and camping is by trail from outside the wilderness preserve; Meeks Bay and Echo Lake are two starting points. Permits (free) are required for access at any time of the year from the Forest Service Visitors Center or headquarters (870 Emerald Bay Rd., Box 731002, South Lake Tahoe, CA 95731, tel. 916/573–2600).

❻ The winding road next takes you to **Emerald Bay,** famed for its jewel-like shape and color of its waters. The road is high above the lake at this point; from Emerald Bay Lookout you can survey the whole scene, which includes Tahoe's only island. From the lookout a 1-mile trail leads down to **Vikingsholm,** a 38-room estate built in the 1920s by Lora Knight, inspired by Norwegian and Swedish castles of the 11th century. It's a rugged stone building with a partial sod roof, furnished with Scandinavian antiques and reproductions. Be forewarned that the trail leads down and that the hike back up is steep. *Tel. 916/525–7277. Admission: $1 adults, 50¢ children under 18. Open July–Sept. daily 10–4.*

Another way to see Emerald Bay close up is to take one of the daily cruises across its waters. *The Tahoe Queen,* a glass-bottom sternwheeler, travels year round on 2½-hour cruises from Ski Run Marina off U.S. 50 in South Lake Tahoe. (Tel. 916/541–3364. Daytime and sunset dinner/dance cruises. Fare: $12.50 adults, $4.50 children under 12. From April 21 through November 4 the MS *Dixie* sails from Zephyr Cove Marina to Emerald Bay. (Tel. 702/588–3508. Daytime, dinner and cocktail cruises. Fare: $10 adults, $4 children 4–12). **Tahoe Cruises** (tel. 916/541–3364) travels from the south shore to Tahoe City. Fare: $16.50.

❼ Beyond Emerald Bay is **D.L. Bliss State Park,** which shares with the bay 6 miles of shoreline and 268 family campsites. At the north end of the park is Rubicon Point, which overlooks one of the lake's deepest spots. *Tel. 916/525–7277; day use; $3 per vehicle; closed in winter.*

❽ The main attraction at **Sugar Pine Point State Park** is the **Ehrman Mansion,** a stately, stone-and-shingle 1903 summer home that displays the "rustic" aspirations of the era's wealthy residents. It is furnished in period style. *Tel. 916/525–7232. Open July–Sept., daily 11–4. Admission free. State Park day use fee: $3.*

❾ At **Tahoe City,** Highway 89 turns north from the lake to Squaw Valley; Highway 28 continues around the lake. You'll cross the Truckee River, the lake's only outlet. Fanny Bridge is the best observation point to see the river's giant trout and the rows of visitors leaning over the railing, which gave the bridge its name. The **Gatekeeper's Log Cabin Museum** in Tahoe City provides one of the best records of the area's past, with Washoe and Paiute Indian artifacts as well as 19th-century settlers' memorabilia. *139 W. Lake Blvd., tel. 916/583–1762. Admission free. Open May 15–Oct. 15 daily 11–5.*

⑩ Traveling east on Highway 28 you will reach the 28-acre **Kings Beach State Recreation Area,** one of the lakeshore parks open
⑪ year-round; **Crystal Bay** just over the Nevada border, with the towering Cal-Neva hotel/casino; and the affluent residential
⑫ community of **Incline Village.**

⑬ The **Ponderosa Ranch** is east of Incline Village on Highway 28. The site of the popular television series *Bonanza* includes the Cartwrights' ranch house, a western town, and a saloon and offers horseback riding and hayrides. *Tel. 702/831–0691. Admission: $6.50 adults, $5.50 children 5–11. Open daily April–Oct. 9:30–6.*

⑭ **Sand Harbor Beach** is one of the lake's finest, and so popular it's sometimes filled to capacity by 11 AM on summer weekends. Evenings are something else: a pop music festival in July, Shakespeare festival in August. *Festival information, tel. 916/583–9048.*

Now you meet U.S. 50 again and travel past scenic vistas. The
⑮ road passes through **Cave Rock,** through 25 yards of solid stone.
⑯ Six miles from Cave Rock, you'll come to **Zephyr Cove,** with a beach and a marina that is home to tour boats. Just ahead you see the towers of the casinos at Stateline, and you've come full circle.

What to See and Do with Children

Except for gambling and the floor shows in Nevada, most attractions and activities around the lake are family-oriented. The Forest Service is the best resource, and the Visitors Center at Taylor Creek the prime site. In the summer, the center gives discovery walks and nighttime campfires with songs and marshmallow roasts. The Stream Profile Chamber provides a peek underwater in Taylor Creek. There are Native American exhibits at the Visitors Center and at the Gatekeeper's Museum in Tahoe City. Other options range from bike rentals to flashy video arcades in many casinos.

In the winter, there is a snow play area that rents saucers at **Granlibakken** (tel. 916/583–6203), just south of Tahoe City on Highway 89. Ski areas have classes for children as young as three. **Borges Carriage and Sleigh Rides** in South Lake Tahoe (tel. 916/541–2953) and some ski resorts have sleigh rides.

Off the Beaten Track

For a closer look at the scenery around the lake, consider a two- to three-hour raft trip down a 4-mile stretch of the Truckee River from Tahoe City to the River Ranch. The self-guided float trip is operated mid-May through September. Contact **Mountain Air Sports** (tel. 916/583–5606, $15 adults, $10 children under 12) or **Truckee River Rafting** (tel. 916/583–9724, $15 adults, $10 children under 12). For another perspective that goes above the mountain trams, **CalVada Seaplanes Inc.** (tel. 916/525–7143) provides rides over the lake for $36–$65 per person, depending on the length of the trip.

The most tragic reminder of the High Sierra's past is **Donner Memorial State Park** just off I–80 2 miles west of Truckee. During the ferocious winter of 1846–47 a westbound party led by George Donner was trapped here. The Pioneer Monument stands on a pedestal 22 feet high, the depth of the snow that winter. Of 89 people in the group, only 47 lived; some survived eating bark, mice, and the flesh of the dead. The Immigrant Museum shows a film hourly about the Donner Party's plight; other displays include the history of other settlers, and railroad development through the Sierra. *Tel. 916/587–3841. Open daily 10–4. Closed Jan. 1, Thanksgiving, Dec. 25.*

Participant Sports

For most of the popular sports at Lake Tahoe, summer or winter, you won't have to bring much equipment with you, an important factor if you're traveling by air or have limited space. Bicycles and boats are readily available for rent at Lake Tahoe. Golf clubs can be rented at several area courses. Most of the ski resorts have rental shops.

Golf These courses in the Lake Tahoe area have food facilities, pro shops, cart rentals, and putting greens.

Edgewood Tahoe. 18 holes, par 72. Driving range. Cart mandatory. *U.S. 50 and Lake Pkwy., behind High Sierra Casino, Stateline, tel. 702/588–3566. Open 7–6.*
Incline Championship. 18 holes, par 72. Driving range. Cart mandatory. *955 Fairway Blvd., Incline Village, tel. 702/832–1144. Open 6 AM–6:30 PM.*
Incline Executive. 18 holes, par 58. Cart mandatory. *690 Wilson Way, Incline Village, tel.702/832–1150. Open 7:30–5:30.*
Lake Tahoe Golf Course. 18 holes, par 71. Driving range. *U.S. 50 between South Lake Tahoe Airport and Meyers, tel. 916/577–0788. Open 6 AM–8 PM.*
Northstar-at-Tahoe. 18 holes, par 72. Driving range. Cart mandatory before noon. *Hwy 267 between Truckee and Kings Beach. Tel. 916/587–0290. Open 7:30 AM–dark.*

Skiing The Tahoe Basin ski resorts boast the largest concentration of skiing in the country and its most breathtaking winter scenery. There are 15 downhill ski resorts and 12 nordic ski centers, with more cross-country skiing available on thousands of acres of public forests and parklands. Among the resorts are Heavenly Valley, the nation's largest, covering 20 square miles, and Squaw Valley, site of the 1960 Winter Olympics. There are many ski packages: lodging and lift tickets; lift tickets, rentals, and lessons; airline tickets, lodging, skiing, and auto rental. Ask questions when you are planning an excursion and you may find some bargains. Many resorts at Tahoe offer free or discounted skiing to beginners.

Free shuttle-bus service is available between most ski resorts and hotels and lodges.

Alpine Meadows Ski Area. The high base elevation and a variety of sun exposures give Alpine the longest season in Tahoe, mid-November to Memorial Day. Of its 2,000 acres, 25% are beginner, 40% intermediate, 35% advanced. Its 13 lifts handle 16,000 skiers per hour. The summit elevation is 8,637 ft.; base, 6,835 ft.; vertical drop, 1,800 ft. The longest run is 2.5 mi. There is a ski school and a children's snow school for three- to six-year-olds. The expansive day lodge has a large sun deck, restaurant, bar, cafeteria. There is an overnight RV area. *North shore, be-*

tween Truckee and Tahoe City on Hwy 89. Box 5279, Tahoe City 95730, tel. 916/583-4232. Snow information, tel. 916/583-6914.

Diamond Peak at Ski Incline. This is a newly expanded and improved north shore resort at Incline Village. The terrain is 18% beginner, 49% intermediate, 33% advanced. Its seven lifts can handle 3,700 skiers per hour. The summit is 8,540 ft.; base, 6,700 ft.; vertical drop, 1,840 ft. The longest run is 2.5 mi. Family ticket rates and special all-inclusive "Learn-to-Ski" packages are available. The Child Ski Development Center is for ages three to seven. The full-facility base lodge has a mountaintop barbecue. *Box AL, Incline Village, NV 89450, tel. 702/ 832-1177 or 800/468-2463.*

Diamond Peak Cross Country. This brand-new, high-elevation cross-country ski area offers spectacular views of Lake Tahoe. Its 2,600 acres of rolling terrain are 15% beginner, 70% intermediate, 15% advanced. There are 30 km. of groomed trails and open wilderness trails. Elevation is 8,200 feet; the longest trail, 6 km. Besides a ski school, there is a beginner special that includes trail pass, rentals, and lesson. *Box AL, Incline Village, NV 89450, tel. 702/832-1177.*

Heavenly Valley Ski Resort. Located in the heart of the South Lake Tahoe area, this is America's largest ski resort, with nine mountain peaks and 20 square miles of ski terrain of which 25% is beginner, 50% intermediate, and 25% advanced. Its 24 lifts carry 31,000 skiers each hour. The summit is 10,100 ft.; base, 6,550 ft. (CA) and 7,200 ft. (NV); vertical drop, 3,600 ft. Its longest run is 3 mi. The resort has a ski school, three base lodges, and four on-mountain lodges. *Ski Run Blvd., Box 2180, Stateline, NV 89449, tel. 916/541-1330 or 800/243-2836.*

Homewood Ski Area. On Tahoe's quiet west side, this family ski area offers spectacular views: 90% of Homewood's trails overlook the lake. Of 1,100 acres, 20% are beginner, 50% intermediate, 30% advanced. There are 10 lifts. Homewood's summit is 7,880 ft.; and its base, 6,230 ft.; vertical drop, 1,650 ft. and its longest run, 2 mi. Ski school, rentals, and sports shops are available. Restaurants and lounges are at two base lodges, food and beverages are at midmountain facilities with a large deck and superb view of the lake. Senior citizens 60 and over can ski for $9 at any time. *6 mi south of Tahoe City on Hwy 89, Box 165, Homewood 95718, tel. 916/525-7256.*

Kirkwood Ski Resort. Thirty five miles south of Lake Tahoe, this large resort has extensive trails and the highest base elevation in northern California. Its 2,000 acres are 15% beginner, 50% intermediate, 35% advanced. There are 11 lifts. Kirkwood's summit is 9,800 ft.; its base, 7,800 ft.; vertical drop, 2,000 ft., and longest run, 2.5 mi. Facilities include a ski school, Mighty Mountain for children 4–12, child care, and two base lodges with restaurants and bars. Also available are a beginner special, free shuttle bus from Lake Tahoe, and hotel packages. *Off Hwy 88, Box 1, Kirkwood, CA 95646, tel. 209/258-6000; for lodging, tel. 209/258-7000; for snow conditions, tel. 209/258-3000.*

Northstar-at-Tahoe. Northstar is a complete resort, with lodging and full amenities. Its 1,700 acres of tree-lined ski runs are 25% beginner, 50% intermediate, 25% advanced, with 9 lifts. The summit is 8,600 ft.; base, 6,400 ft.; vertical drop, 2,200 ft. and longest run, 2.9 mi. Northstar has a ski school; adult beginner package; all-day junior lesson program ("Starkids," for ages 5–12). It has 50 km of groomed and tracked wilderness trails for cross-country; beginner 30%, intermediate 40%, advanced 30%. The base is 6,200 ft.; vertical drop, 600 ft. and longest trail, 12 mi. Lessons, guided tours, and rentals are available. Packages may include lodging, lifts, ski school, ski rental, child care, rental car. *Off Hwy 267 between Truckee and North Shore. Box 129, Truckee 95734, tel. 916/562–1010 or 800/ 533–6787. Snow information, tel. 916/562–1330.*

Sierra Ski Ranch. This is a little farther away, but the slopes are usually uncrowded and it has spectacular views of the lake. Of 2,000 acres, 20% are beginner, 60% intermediate, 20% advanced, and there are 11 lifts. The summit is 8,852 ft.; base, 6,640 ft.; vertical drop, 2,212 ft. The longest run is 3.5 mi. Ski school and children's snow school are available. Base lodge has three cafeterias, rental and retail shops; plus a lodge and cafe on top of mountain. Beginner specials are available. *On U.S. 50, 12 mi west of South Lake Tahoe, Box 3501, Twin Bridges 95735, tel. 916/659–7453. Snow phone, tel. 916/659–7475.*

Squaw Valley USA. There are vast, open slopes here, at the site of the 1960 Winter Olympics on 8,300 acres of skiable terrain, which includes 25% beginner, 45% intermediate, 30% advanced. Its 34 lifts have an uphill lift capacity of 47,370 skiers per hour. (Squaw Valley is the only resort in the world that offers a "no waiting in a lift line or your money back" guarantee.) The summit is 9,050 ft.; base, 6,200 ft.; vertical drop, 2,850 ft. and longest run, 3 mi. A ski school is for skiers of all ages and abilities; 10 Little Indians snow school is for children. Day care is available for infants six months to three years. First-time skiers ski free midweek. Base facilities and both Gold Coast and High Camp Complex on upper mountain have a variety of food and beverages. Ski rentals and a wide range of packages are available. *Between Truckee and Tahoe City on Hwy 89, Squaw Valley 95730, tel. 916/583–6985 or 800/545–4350. Snow information, tel. 916/583–6955.*

Tahoe Nordic Ski Center. This cross-country center, north of Tahoe City offers 2,000 acres, 67 km of trails, 30% beginner, 40% intermediate, 30% advanced. Its summit is 7,880 ft.; base, 6,550 ft.; vertical drop, 1,000 ft. and longest trail, 25 km. Facilities include a ski school and beginners special: trail pass, rentals, lesson. *Off Hwy 28, north of Tahoe City, Box 1632, Tahoe City 95730, tel. 916/583–9858 or 916/583–0484.*

Swimming There are 36 public beaches ringing Lake Tahoe. Swimming is permitted at many of them, but since Tahoe is a high mountain lake with fairly rugged winters, only the hardiest will be interested, except during midsummer. Even then the water warms to only 68°F. Lifeguards are on duty at some of the swimming beaches, and yellow buoys mark safe areas where motorboats are not permitted. Opening and closing dates for beaches vary with the climate and available park service staffing. There may be a parking fee of $1 or $2.

Gambling

You don't need a roadside marker to know when you've crossed from California into Nevada. The lake's water and the pine trees may be identical, but the flashing lights and elaborate marquees of the casinos announce legalized gambling with a bang. Nevada got gambling in 1931, and nearby Reno soon proclaimed itself "the biggest little city in the world." In 1944 Harvey's Wagon Wheel Saloon and Gambling Hall, little more than a rustic cabin, brought gambling to Lake Tahoe, and com petition soon flourished in the Stateline area. Now, in addition to the big casinos, visitors will find slot machines in every conceivable location, from gas stations to supermarkets.

The major casinos are also hotels and, more recently, resorts. Four are clustered on a strip of Highway 50 in Stateline, two others on the north shore at Crystal Bay and Incline Village. They are open 24 hours a day, 365 days a year, offering craps, blackjack, roulette, baccarat, poker, keno, pai gow, bingo, and vast arrays of slot machines—1,850, for instance, at Harrah's.

The hotel/casinos compete by offering celebrity entertainers in their showrooms, restaurants and lounges open around the clock, and frequent refurbishing that has transformed many of the Western settings to a more contemporary international style. Some casino restaurants are elegant settings designed to attract upscale visitors; on the other hand, Bill's Casino in Stateline has installed a McDonald's to reach a younger crowd.

Dining

Restaurants at Lake Tahoe range from rustic wood-and-rock decor to elegant French, with a stop along the way for Swiss chalet and spare modern. The food, too, is varied: delicate Continental sauces, mesquite-broiled fish, wild boar in season.

Separate listings are given here for the north and south shores. Casino restaurants are described under lodging. There are also many fast-food restaurants and coffee-shop chains in South Lake Tahoe and some in Tahoe City. Unless otherwise noted, dress is informal for all restaurants. Even the most elegant and expensive Tahoe eating places welcome customers in the casual clothes that are considered appropriate in this year-round mecca for vacationers.

Highly recommended restaurants are indicated by a star ★.

Category	Cost*
Very Expensive	over $30
Expensive	$20–$30
Moderate	$16–$20
Inexpensive	under $16

per person, not including tax, service, or drinks

North Shore
Expensive

Le Petit Pier. The decor in this lakeside dinner restaurant with fine views is French Provincial and romantic. The menu features French classics, such as roast duckling with a blueberry sauce. There is an award-winning wine list. *7250 N. Lake Blvd., Tahoe Vista, tel. 916/546-4464. Reservations advised. Full bar. AE, DC, MC, V.*

Moderate–Expensive

La Playa. This dinner house on the lake features a Continental menu, with outdoor service an option in the summer. Seafood is a specialty. *7046 N. Lake Blvd., Tahoe Vista, tel. 916/546-5903. Reservations advised. Full bar. AE, MC, V.*

Moderate

Captain Jon's. The dining room is small and cozy, with linen cloths and fresh flowers on the tables and a fire burning on a raised brick hearth on chilly evenings. The lengthy dinner menu is country French, with two dozen different daily specials; the emphasis is on fish. The lounge is in a separate building on the water, with a pier where guests can tie up their boats. In summer, lunch is served in the lounge and on the deck. *7220 N. Lake Blvd., Tahoe Vista, tel. 916/546–4819. Reservations advised. Full bar. AE, DC, MC, V. Closed Mon.*

★ **Wolfdale's.** An intimate dinner house on the lake, Wolfdale's offers Japanese/California cuisine. The menu changes weekly; there are a small number of imaginative entrées such as grilled Chinese pheasant with plum sauce and shitake mushrooms and baked Norwegian salmon with saffron scallop sauce. *640 N. Lake Blvd., Tahoe City, tel. 916/583–5700. Reservations advised. Full bar. MC, V. Closed Tues.*

Inexpensive–
Moderate

Gar Woods Grill and Pier. This elegant but casual lakeside restaurant recalls the lake's past, with wood paneling, a river-rock fireplace, and boating photographs. It specializes in grilled foods, along with pasta and pizza. Lunch and dinner are served daily in summer; in winter, dinner nightly and Sunday brunch. *5000 N. Lake Blvd., Carnelian Bay, tel. 916/546–3366. Reservations accepted. MC, V.*

★ **Jake's on the Lake.** Continental food is served in spacious, handsome rooms featuring oak and glass on the water at the Boatworks Mall. There is an extensive seafood bar; the varied menu includes meat and poultry but emphasizes fresh fish. Lunch is served daily in summer. *780 N. Lake Blvd., Tahoe City, tel. 916/583–0188. Dress: collared shirts for men in the evening. Reservations accepted. AE, MC, V.*

★ **River Ranch.** From the terrace of this old-fashioned lodge with a stellar setting beside the Truckee River you can almost get your feet wet. The food is decidedly American, with fresh fish, smoked herb chicken and barbecued ribs from a wood-burning oven, and wild game: pheasant, chukar partridge, rabbit, quail, goose, elk, venison, wild boar, and buffalo. The restaurant is open for dinner all year, with appetizers from 3:30 PM, and service on the terrace in summer. Lunch is served daily in summer. *Hwy 89 between Truckee and Tahoe City, at Alpine Meadows turn, tel. 916/583–4264. Reservations accepted. Full bar. AE, MC, V.*

★ **Sunnyside Restaurant and Lodge.** An expansive lakefront deck with steps down to the beach and the water fronts this handsome wooden lodge. The large lounge features rock fireplaces, comfortable sofas, a seafood bar, and snacks. The Chris Craft dining room, decorated in mahogany with carpets and upholstery in maroon and blue, is trim and sleek. Seafood is a specialty of the Continental menu. *1850 W. Lake Blvd., Tahoe City, tel. 916/583–7200. Reservations accepted. Full bar. MC, V. No lunch in winter.*

Tahoe House. Combining Swiss and California cuisine, this casual and somewhat rustic dinner house features an elegant menu: veal, lamb, beef, fresh pasta and seafood, fresh-baked breads, and a large selection of homemade desserts. In season, try the strawberry torte with white chocolate mousse. A children's menu is available. *625 W. Lake Blvd., Tahoe City, tel. 916/ 583–1377. Reservations advised. Full bar. AE, MC, V.*

Inexpensive

Cafe Cobblestone. A basically American menu is served for breakfast and lunch (and dinner on winter weekends and during the summer high season) in a casual Tyrolean decor. Salads are a specialty; there is also a good variety of quiches, omelets and sandwiches. *475 N. Lake Blvd., Tahoe City, tel. 916/583–2111. No reservations. Gourmet beers and wine. AE, MC, V.*

South Shore
Moderate–Expensive

The Chart House. An American menu featuring steak and seafood is presented in a dinner house with a panoramic lake view. There is a children's menu. *Kingsbury Grade, tel. 702/588–6276. Reservations accepted. Full bar. AE, MC, V.*

Christiania Inn. Located at the base of Heavenly Valley's tram, this inn offers fireside dining among antiques in a Swiss country decor. The American/Continental menu emphasizes fresh seafood, prime beef, and veal. There is an extensive wine list. Midday buffets are served on holidays, and brunch is featured on Sundays. Appetizers, soups, and salads are available in the lounge daily after 2 PM. *3819 Saddle Rd., South Lake Tahoe, tel. 916/544–7337. Reservations advised. Full bar. AE, MC, V.*

Moderate

Zackary's Restaurant. The ambience here is casual and intimate. The menu is Continental, offering fresh fish and traditional dishes. *Round Hill Mall, Zephyr Cove, tel. 702/588–2108. Full bar. AE, MC, V.*

Swiss Chalet. The Swiss decor is carried out with great consistency, making this one of the town's more attractive restaurants. The Continental menu features Swiss specialties, veal dishes, fresh seafood, and home-baked pastries. There is a children's menu. *2540 Tahoe Blvd., South Lake Tahoe, tel. 916/544–3304. Reservations advised. Full bar. AE, MC, V. Closed Mon., Easter, Nov. 23–Dec. 5, Dec. 25.*

Inexpensive–Moderate

The Greenhouse. Hanging plants, white linen cloths, a brick fireplace, and a coppertop bar create the ambience here. The Continental menu includes veal Marsala, tournedos of lamb, and prawns à la cognac. *4140 Cedar Avenue, Box RRR, South Lake Tahoe 95729, tel. 916/541–5800. Reservations advised. AE, DC, MC, V.*

Tahoe Seasons Restaurant. Located at the Tahoe Seasons Resort in Heavenly Valley, this comfortable restaurant has eight fireplaces. Breakfast is served, and at dinner the menu is Continental, with some American fare. *3901 Saddle Rd., South Lake Tahoe, tel. 916/541–6700. Reservations advised. Full bar. AE, MC, V.*

Lodging

Accommodations at Lake Tahoe are as varied as everything else at this prime vacation spot. Quiet inns on the water, motel rooms in the heart of the casino area, rooms at the casinos themselves, lodges close to the ski runs—the most deluxe of lodgings and inexpensive bases for your vacation are all here. Just remember that during the summer months and the ski season, the lake is crowded; plan in advance for a place to stay. Spring and fall give you a little more leeway and lower rates. Lake Tahoe has two telephone reservation services: Tahoe North Visitors and Convention Bureau, 800/824–6348; for the south shore, Lake Tahoe Visitors Authority, 800/822–5922.

The listing of lodgings is divided between the north and south shores. The large hotel/casinos are listed at the end of each geographical section.

Highly recommended hotels are indicated with a ★.

Category	Cost*
Very Expensive	over $100
Expensive	$75–$100
Moderate	$50–$75
Inexpensive	under $50

double room, not including tax

North Shore Hotels
Very Expensive

Tahoe Vista Inn & Marina. Located at the northern tip of Lake Tahoe, this small, luxurious inn has suites only. Each has a living room, fireplace, kitchen, jetted bath tub, separate bedroom, and private lanai overlooking the lake. The decor is opulently modern, with white sofas, glass coffee tables, blond wood, and fieldstone gas-jetted fireplaces. *7220 N. Lake Blvd., Tahoe Vista 95732, tel. 916/546–4819 or 800/662–3433. 7 suites. Facilities: boat slip, restaurant, lounge. AE, DC, MC, V.*

Expensive–Very Expensive ★

Sunnyside Lodge. This modern mountain lodge is in a location that soaks up the sun. The setting features large lakefront decks and a marina. Rooms are decorated in an elegant country style with plaid bedspreads, pottery lamps, and caned chairs. Each room has its own deck and lake and mountain views. Continental breakfast is provided. *1850 W. Lake Blvd., Tahoe City 95730, tel. 916/583–7200 or 800/822–2754 in CA. 23 rooms. MC, V.*

Moderate–Expensive

Tahoe City TraveLodge. Overlooking Lake Tahoe and the Tahoe City Golf Course, the newly refurbished motel rooms here offer king- and queen-size beds with flowered spreads, desks, and high-nap carpets; there is fresh-ground coffee in each room. A restaurant and lounge are adjacent. Senior citizens receive discount. *455 N. Lake Blvd., Box 84, Tahoe City 95730, tel. 916/ 583–3766. 47 rooms with bath and shower/massage. Facilities: heated pool, whirlpool on deck with lake view. AE, DC, MC, V.*

Tahoe Sands Resort. This is a pleasant older motel at a quiet spot on the lakeshore. The spacious grounds and ample play facilities make it attractive to family groups. Some rooms have fireplaces and kitchenettes. *6610 N. Lake Blvd., Tahoe Vista 95732, tel. 916/546–2592. 67 rooms. Facilities: beach, pool, putting green, playground for children, laundry facilities. AE, DC, MC, V.*

Inexpensive–Expensive ★

River Ranch. This is a small, cozy old lodge with an exceptional setting immediately on the Truckee River, close to Alpine Meadows and Squaw Valley skiing. The rooms feature antiques and balconies overlooking the river. There is a good restaurant and lounge on the first floor. *Box 197, Tahoe City 95730, tel. 916/583–4264 or 800/535–9900 in CA. 22 rooms. Facilities: tennis. AE, MC, V.*

North Shore Hotel/Casinos
Expensive–Very Expensive

Cal Neva Lodge Resort Hotel/Casino. Most rooms in this remodeled hotel on Highway 28 at Crystal Bay have views of Lake Tahoe and the mountains. There is an arcade with video games for children, cabaret entertainment, and 22 cabins with living rooms. The restaurants are Lake View (coffee shop) and Sir Charles Fine Dining. *Box 368, Crystal Bay 89402, tel. 702/832–*

4000 or 800/225–6382. 220 rooms. Facilities: cable tv, pool, sauna, whirlpool, wedding chapel. AE, DC, MC, V.

Hyatt Lake Tahoe Resort Hotel/Casino. This luxurious hotel on the lake was entirely renovated in 1989; some rooms have fireplaces. A children's program and rental bicycles are available. The restaurants are Hugo's Rotisserie, Ciao Mein Trattoria (Oriental/Italian), and Sierra Cafe (open 24 hours). *Lakeshore and Country Club Dr., Box 3239, Incline Village 89450. Tel. 702/831–1111. 460 rooms. Facilities: beach, pool, spa, sauna, tennis, movies (fee), health club, laundry, valet parking lot, entertainment. AE, DC, MC, V.*

South Shore Hotels
Expensive–
Very Expensive
★

Inn by the Lake. This luxury motel across the road from the beach is far from the flashy casinos, but convenient to them by free shuttle bus. The rooms and bathrooms are spacious and comfortable, furnished in contemporary style (blond oak, pale peach, light teal blue). All rooms have balconies; some have lake views, wet bars, and kitchenettes. Continental breakfast is served in the lobby each morning. Children under 12 stay free in room with parents. A senior-citizen discount is available. *3300 Lake Tahoe Blvd., Box 849, South Lake Tahoe 95705, tel. 916/542–0330 or 800/877–1466. 100 rooms. Facilities: heated pool, 2-level spa, sauna, movies, laundry. AE, DC, MC, V.*

Tahoe Seasons Resort. Built among pine trees on the side of a mountain across from the Heavenly Valley ski area, this resort has outfitted each room with a fireplace, spa, and minikitchen (sink, refrigerator, and microwave). Dark orange and green are the dominant colors in the contemporary decor; all beds are queen-size. *3901 Saddle Rd., South Lake Tahoe 95729, tel. 916/ 541–6700 or 541–6010. 160 rooms. Facilities: restaurant, lounge, room service, pool, whirlpool, tennis, paddleball, indoor parking, valet garage, free Lake Tahoe Airport and casino shuttle. AE, MC, V.*

Expensive
★

Best Western Station House Inn. This pleasant inn was completely renovated in 1983, and has won design awards for its exterior and interior. The rooms are subtly decorated in mauve and are nicely appointed, with king- and queen-size beds and double vanity baths. The location is good, near a private beach and yet close to the casinos. American breakfast is complimentary October 1–May 31. A senior-citizen discount is available. *901 Park Ave., South Lake Tahoe 95729, tel. 916/542–1101 or 800/822–5953 in CA. 101 rooms. Facilities: restaurant, lounge, pool, hot tub. Shuttle service to casinos. AE, DC, MC, V.*

Moderate–Very
Expensive

Lakeland Village Beach and Ski Resort. A townhouse-condominium complex located along 1,000 feet of private beach, Lakeland Village has a wide range of accommodations: studios, suites, and town houses, all with kitchens and fireplaces. *3535 Lake Tahoe Blvd., South Lake Tahoe 95705, tel. 916/541–7711 or 800/825–8246. 214 units with bath. Facilities: beach, boating and fishing pier, 2 pools, wading pool, spa, saunas, movies, laundry. AE, DC, MC, V.*

Moderate–Expensive

Flamingo Lodge. This motel has completely refurbished rooms decorated in contemporary blues and tans, many with refrigerators or wet bars and all with in-room fresh ground coffee. The lodge's grounds are spacious. There is an adjacent coffee shop. *3961 Lake Tahoe Blvd., South Lake Tahoe 95729, tel. 916/544–5288. 90 rooms. Facilities: pool, sauna, hot tub, laundry. AE, DC, MC, V.*

Moderate **Best Western Lake Tahoe Inn.** Located next to Harrah's Casino on U.S. 50, this large motel is nicely situated on 6 acres of grounds, with gardens and the Heavenly Valley Ski Resort directly behind. Rooms are modern, decorated in pastel pinks, purple, and mauve. *Box II, South Lake Tahoe 95729, tel. 916/ 541–2010. 400 rooms. Facilities: restaurants, lounge, 2 heated pools, hot tub, 1-day valet service. AE, DC, MC, V.*

Inexpensive– **Royal Valhalla Motor Lodge.** On the lake at Lakeshore Boule-
Moderate vard and Stateline Avenue, this motel has simple modern rooms decorated in earth tones with queen-size beds. There is some covered parking. A senior-citizen discount is available. *Drawer GG, South Lake Tahoe 95729, tel. 916/544–2233. 80 rooms, 20 with kitchenettes. Facilities: pool, laundry. AE, DC, MC, V.*

Inexpensive **Tahoe West Motor Lodge.** A long-established motel that is
★ proud of its repeat business, Tahoe West is 2 blocks from the beach and the downtown casinos. The exterior is rustic in appearance. The rooms are newly furnished, and the beds are queen-size. Coffee and doughnuts are served in the lobby. *4082 Pine Blvd., South Lake Tahoe 95729, tel. 916/544–6455 or 800/ 522–1021. 59 rooms, 12 with kitchenettes. Facilities: pool, sauna, spa, private beach privileges. Shuttle service to casinos and ski areas. AE, DC, MC, V.*

South Shore **Caesars Tahoe Resort.** This luxurious 16-story hotel/casino,
Hotel/Casinos built in 1980, is on U.S. 50 in the casino area. Each room has a
Expensive– view of Lake Tahoe or the encircling mountains and a massive
Very Expensive bathtub "reminiscent of ancient Rome." There is top-name entertainment in the 1,600-seat Circus Maximus and the Cabaret. Games include dice, 21, roulette, big six, French roulette, baccarat, poker, sic bo, pai gow, and hundreds of slot machines. Race and sports book is also available. Restaurants include Empress Court (Chinese), Evergreen Buffet (international), Cafe Roma (24-hour meals), Le Posh (Continental, with tableside service), Primavera (Italian), Broiler Room, and Yogurt Palace. *Box 5800, South Lake Tahoe, CA 95729, tel. 702/ 588–3515 or 800/648–3353 for reservations and show information. 440 rooms. Facilities: heated indoor pool, saunas, whirlpool, tennis (fee), health club (fee), movies, valet garage, parking lot. AE, DC, MC, V.*

Harrah's Tahoe Hotel/Casino. Harrah's is a luxurious 18-story hotel/casino on U.S. 50 in the casino area. Most guest rooms have two full bathrooms, each with a television and telephone; many rooms have views of the lake and the mountains; each has a private bar and refrigerator. There is a supervised children's arcade. Harrah's has a four-star Mobil rating and a five-diamond rating from the American Automobile Association. Top-name entertainment is presented in the South Shore Room and Stateline Cabaret. There are more than 150 table games (blackjack, craps, baccarat, pai gow, keno, roulette, poker, big six, bingo), and 1,850 slot machines. Race and sports book are also available. Restaurants include The Summit (Continental), The Forest (buffet), Corner Deli (New York-style), Holland's Donut Factory, Friday's Station (steaks and seafood), Sierra Restaurant (24-hour breakfast, lunch, and dinner), Swensen's Ice Cream Parlor. *Box 8, Stateline, NV 89449, tel. 702/588– 6606 or 800/648–3773. 535 rooms. Facilities: heated indoor pool, hot tubs, health club, valet garage, parking lot, 24-hour room and valet service, pet kennel. AE, DC, MC, V.*

Harvey's Resort Hotel/Casino. Today it's another luxurious mirrored 18-story hotel/casino on U.S. 50 in the casino area, but in the 1940s Harvey's was the original casino, part of a small service station at Lake Tahoe. Harvey's is the largest Tahoe resort, with well-appointed rooms, six restaurants, 10 cocktail lounges, and a complete health spa. Cabaret revues and contemporary bands perform in the Theatre Lounge. Games include blackjack, craps, roulette, baccarat, and many slot machines. Restaurants include Cafe Metro, Carriage House Restaurant, El Dorado Buffet, Sage Room Steak House, Top of the Wheel (Continental), El Vaquero (Mexican), and Seafood Grotto (seafood and Chinese). *Box 128, Stateline, NV 89449, tel. 702/588–2411 or 800/648–3361. 575 rooms. Facilities: tennis, valet parking, garage. AE, DC, MC, V.*

Expensive **High Sierra Casino/Hotel.** This old-West hotel is currently undergoing a $15-million renovation in an effort to attract upscale patrons. The decor imitates French Beaux Arts design, with elegant molded wood and mirrors. Games include blackjack, craps, roulette, keno, mini baccarat, and many slot machines. The Pine Cone Lounge and Lily's feature entertainment. Four refurbished restaurants range from a 24-hour cafeteria to gourmet dining. *Box C, Stateline, NV 89449, tel. 702/588–6211 or 800/322–7723 outside NV. 537 rooms. Facilities: 4 restaurants, pool, wading pool, hot tubs. AE, DC, MC, V.*

Nightlife

Major nighttime entertainment is found at the casinos. The top venues are the **Circus Maximus** at Caesar's Tahoe and the **South Shore Room** at Harrah's, each theater as large as many Broadway houses. Typical headliners are Jay Leno, Dionne Warwick, Willie Nelson, Kenny Rogers, and Johnny Mathis; their shows are more concerts than the extravaganzas of Las Vegas.

Two performances a night is the norm in the big showrooms, and reservations are almost always required for superstar shows. A dinner show will cost $30–$40 including the meal, plus tip and Nevada's 16% sales and entertainment tax. A cocktail show runs $15–$30 at most places, but can run up to $50 at Caesars. Smaller casino cabarets sometimes have a cover charge or drink minimum. There are also lounges with no admission charge, featuring jazz and pop music soloists and groups. Even these performers don't try to compete all night with gambling; the last set usually ends at 2:30 or 3 AM.

Lounges around the lake may offer pop and country music singers and musicians, and in the winter the ski resorts do the same. Summer alternatives are outdoor music events, from chamber quartets to jazz bands and rock performers, at Sand Harbor and the Lake Tahoe Visitors Center amphitheater.

9 The Sierra National Parks

by Barbara
Elizabeth Shannon

Yosemite, Sequoia, and Kings Canyon National Parks are famous throughout the world for their unique sights and experiences. Yosemite, especially, should be on your "don't miss" list. Unfortunately, it's on everyone else's as well. In summer the park is very crowded—you should have advance reservations and at least several days to spend. We don't recommend any of these parks as day trips; save them for your next trip to California if you don't have time now. We also recommend that you make your plans far enough in advance so you can stay in the parks themselves, not in one of the "gateway cities" in the foothills or Central Valley. You'll probably be adjusting to a higher altitude and exercising a fair amount, so save your energy for exploring the park, not driving to and from it.

Yosemite National Park

Yosemite Valley is one of the most famous sights (or collection of sights) in California. The surrounding granite peaks and domes (El Capitan, Half Dome) rise more than 3,000 feet above the valley floor; two of the waterfalls that cascade over the valley's rim are among the world's 10 highest; and the Merced River, placid here, runs through the valley. Millions of people visit Yosemite every year. There is no arguing with the claim that especially in the summer, it's very crowded. Such extravagant praise has been written of this valley (by John Muir and others) and so many beautiful photographs taken (by Ansel Adams and others), that you may wonder if the reality can possibly measure up. For almost everyone, it does; Yosemite reminds them of what "breathtaking" and "marvelous" mean.

Yosemite Valley comprises only seven of the more than 1,000 square miles of national park here. The western boundary dips as low as 2,000 feet in the chaparral-covered foothills; the eastern boundary rises to 13,000 feet at points along the Sierra crest. Much of this country is accessible primarily to backpackers and horseback riders (and thus beyond the scope of this guide), but there are many sites to be explored by visitors who do not want to range too far from their cars.

The falls are at their most spectacular in May and June. By the end of the summer, some may have dried up, or nearly so. They begin flowing again in late fall with the first storms. During the winter, they may be hung with ice. Yosemite Valley is open year round. The Vintners' Holidays in December and Chefs' Holidays in January entice "off-season" visitors with free seminars by well-known gourmets. Featured chefs present unique, although relatively pricey ($50 per person), banquet dinners at the culmination of each session. Because the valley floor is only 4,000 feet high, snow does not stay long. It is possible to camp even in the winter (January highs are in the mid-40s, lows in the mid-20s). Tioga Pass Road is closed in winter (roughly from late October through May), so you can't see Tuolumne Meadows then. The road to Glacier Point beyond the turnoff for Badger Pass is also not cleared in winter.

Admission to the park is $5 per car for a week's stay; $2 per person if you don't arrive in a car. For $15, you can purchase a one-year pass to Yosemite. A Golden Eagle pass ($25) is good for a year at all national parks and monuments.

Getting Around

Because of the free shuttle bus that runs around Yosemite Valley (8 AM–11 PM in the summer, 9–10 the rest of the year), it is possible to visit the park without your own car. From 8–8 in the summer, another free shuttle runs from Wawona to Big Trees. Campers are not allowed on this road.

By Plane You could fly into one of the large California airports (San Francisco or Los Angeles) or one of the smaller Central Valley airports (Sacramento, Fresno) and then either rent a car or take public transportation to Yosemite.

By Bus **Yosemite Via** (tel. 209/722–0366) and **Cal Yosemite Tours** (tel. 209/383–1563) run buses from Merced (north of Fresno, also on Highway 99) to Yosemite Valley. Both make connections with Greyhound and Amtrak.

By Car Yosemite is a four- to five-hour drive from San Francisco and a six-hour drive from Los Angeles. From the west, three highways come to Yosemite; all intersect with Highway 99, which runs north–south through the Central Valley. Highway 120 is the northernmost route—the one that travels farthest and slowest through the foothills. If you are exploring the Gold Country along Highway 49, you may want to come this way. The more traveled routes are Highway 140 from Merced and Highway 41 from Fresno. Highway 140 is the major route; Highway 41 provides the most dramatic first view of the valley, after you come out of the Wawona Tunnel.

If you are coming from the east, you could cross the Sierra from Lee Vining on Highway 120 (Tioga Pass). This route takes you over the Sierra crest, past Tuolumne Meadows, and down the west slope of the range. It's scenic but the mountain driving may be stressful for some, and it's only open in the summer. Carry chains at any time of the year; the eastern entrance to the park at Tioga Pass is at nearly 10,000 feet. (Road conditions, tel. 619/873–6366).

Guided Tours

California Parlor Car Tours (Cathedral Hill Hotel, 1101 Van Ness Ave., San Francisco 94109, tel. 415/474–7500 or 800/227–4250) offers several tours that include Yosemite (along with Monterey or Hearst Castle) and depart from either San Francisco or Los Angeles. Some tours are one-way. Lodging and some meals are included; you can choose to stay in either Yosemite Lodge or the Ahwahnee (there's a difference in price, of course). We recommend that you not consider any tour that leaves you less than one full day in the valley (and that is cutting it very short!).

Important Addresses and Numbers

General Information **National Park Service, Information Office** (Box 577, Yosemite National Park, CA 95389, tel. 209/372–0265; 209/372–0264 for a 24-hour recording) or **National Park Service, Fort Mason** (Bldg. 201, San Francisco, CA 94123, tel. 415/556–0560).

Reservations **Yosemite Area Road Conditions** (tel. 209/372–4605).

Camping and Recreation Information (tel. 209/372–4845).

Northern California Road Conditions (tel. 619/873–6366).

Yosemite Park and Curry Company (Central Reservations, 5410 E. Home, Fresno, CA 93727, tel. 209/252–4848).

Exploring

Numbers in the margin correspond with points of interest on the Yosemite National Park map.

Although there is certainly more to see in Yosemite National Park than the valley, this is the primary or only destination for many visitors, especially for those who won't be making backpack or pack-animal trips. Your first view of Yosemite Valley will vary, depending on the road you take. Because the valley is only 7 miles long and averages less than 1 mile wide, you can visit sites in whatever order you choose and return to your favorites at different times of the day.

At Yosemite Village, near the east end of the valley, you'll find the park headquarters, a restaurant, store, and gas station, the Ahwahnee Hotel, Yosemite Lodge, a medical clinic, and the

❶ visitors center. The **Visitors Center** is staffed by park rangers and provides information and wilderness permits (necessary for any overnight backpacking). There are exhibits on natural and human history as well as an adjacent Indian Cultural Museum, and a re-created Ahwahneechee village. *Tel. 209/372–2099. Open daily 9–8, with extended hours in summer.*

During the summer, a visitor center at Tuolumne Meadows and a Yosemite Association bookstore at Mariposa Grove are also open.

❷ **Yosemite Falls** is the highest waterfall in North America and the fifth-highest in the world. The upper falls (1,430 feet), the middle cascades (675 feet), and the lower falls (320 feet) combine for a total of 2,425 feet and, when viewed from the valley, appear as one waterfall. From the parking lot there is a ⅓-mile trail to the base of the falls. (The Yosemite Falls Trail starts from Sunnyside Campground and is a strenuous 3½-mile climb that rises 2,700 feet.)

If you arrive in Yosemite via the Wawona Road, your first view of the valley (in John Muir's words "a revelation in landscape

❸ affairs that enriches one's life forever") will include **Bridalveil Fall,** a filmy fall of 620 feet that is often diverted as much as 20 feet one way or the other by the breeze. Indians called it Pohono ("puffing wind"). There is another very short (⅓-mile) trail from a parking lot on the Wawona Road to the base of the fall.

❹ Across the valley, **Ribbon Fall** (1,612 feet) is the valley's highest single fall, but it also dries up first in the summer.

Vernal and Nevada falls are on the Merced River at the east end

❺
❻ of the valley. **Vernal Fall** (317 feet) is bordered by fern-covered black rocks, and rainbows play in the spray at the base. **Nevada Fall** (594 feet) is the first major fall as the river comes out of the high country. Both falls can be viewed from Glacier Point or visited on foot from Happy Isles, east of Yosemite Village. The roads at this end of the valley are now closed to private cars, but a free shuttle bus runs frequently from the village. From May through September, the nature center with ecology exhibits at Happy Isles is open.

210

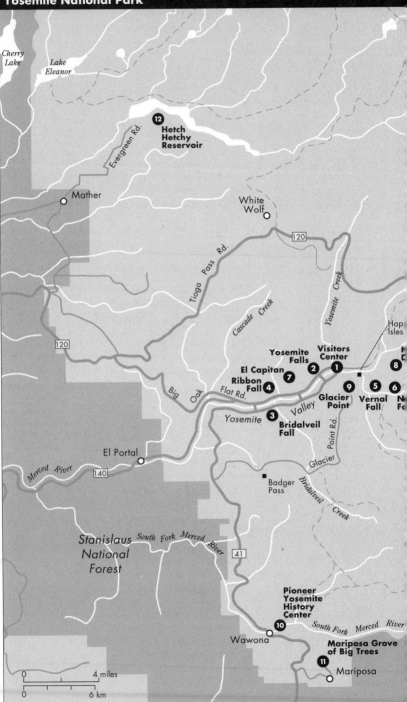

Yosemite National Park

Cherry Lake

Lake Eleanor

12 Hetch Hetchy Reservoir

Evergreen Rd.

○ Mather

White Wolf ○

120

Tioga Pass Rd.

Cascade Creek

Yosemite Creek

120

Big Oak Flat Rd.

Yosemite Falls
El Capitan
Ribbon Fall **4**
7
2
Visitors Center **1**

Hap Isles

8

9 **Glacier Point**
5 **Vernal Fall**
6

3 **Bridalveil Fall**
Yosemite Valley

Glacier Point Rd.

N Fo

Merced River

El Portal ○

140

Glacier

Badger Pass ■

Bridalveil Creek

Stanislaus National Forest

South Fork Merced River

41

Pioneer Yosemite History Center

Wawona ○ **10**

South Fork Merced River

Mariposa Grove of Big Trees

11 Mariposa ○

0 ___ 4 miles
0 ___ 6 km

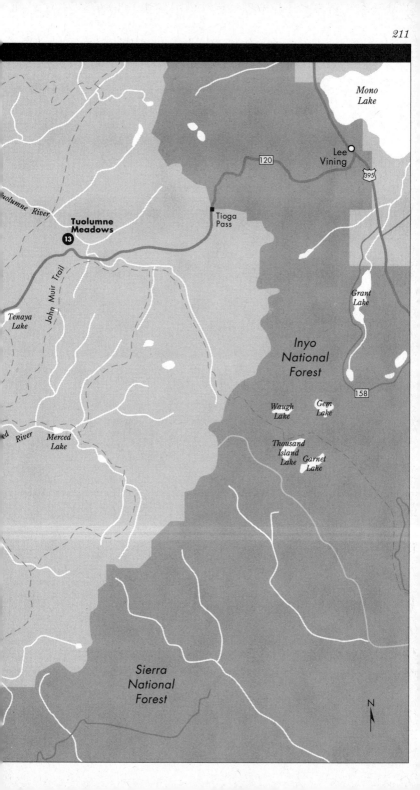

The hike on a paved trail from Happy Isles to the bridge at the base of Vernal Fall is only moderately strenuous and less than 1-mile long. It's another steep ¾-mile along the Mist Trail up to the top of the fall, and then another 2½ miles to the top of Nevada Falls. This is the beginning of the famous John Muir Trail, which leads south over 200 miles through the High Sierra to Mount Whitney.

Most famous among Yosemite's peaks are El Capitan and Half Dome. **El Capitan** is the largest exposed granite monolith in the world, almost twice the height of Gibraltar. It rises 3,593 feet above the valley, with an apparently vertical front thrust out from the valley's rim. **Half Dome** is the most distinctive rock in the region: 8,842 feet altitude, 4,733 feet above the valley floor. The west side of the dome is fractured vertically and cut away to form a 2,000-foot cliff.

Glacier Point offers what may be the most spectacular view of the valley and the High Sierra that you can get without hiking. The Glacier Point Road leaves Highway 41 about 23 miles southwest of the valley; it's then a 16-mile drive, with fine views into higher country. From the parking area, walk just a few hundred yards and you'll be able to see Nevada, Vernal, and Yosemite falls as well as Half Dome and other peaks. This road is closed beyond the turnoff for Badger Pass Ski Area in the winter.

At the **Pioneer Yosemite History Center** in Wawona (on Highway 41) are local historic buildings moved here from their original sites. A living history program in summer re-creates Yosemite's past.

Farther down the Wawona Road (36 miles from the valley) is the **Mariposa Grove of Big Trees.** This fine grove of *Sequoiadendron gigantea* can be visited on foot or on the one-hour tram rides ($5 adults, $2 senior citizens and children 5–11) that run regularly during the summer (May–Oct. 9–6). The Grizzly Giant is the oldest tree here; its age is estimated to be 2,700 years; its base diameter is 30.7 feet, its circumference 96.5 feet, and its height 210 feet. The famous Wawona Tunnel Tree fell during the winter of 1968–69 (did anyone hear it?), but two other tunnel trees remain. A museum presents information on the big trees.

Hetch Hetchy Reservoir is about 40 miles from Yosemite Valley, via Big Oak Flat Road and Highway 120. The reservoir supplies water and power (some of which is sold at a profit) to San Francisco. Some say John Muir died of heartbreak when this beautiful valley was dammed and buried beneath 300 feet of water in 1913. Interior Secretary Donald Hodel made headlines in 1987 when he suggested that the lake might be drained and the valley restored to reduce some of the crowding in Yosemite. Not surprisingly, San Francisco politicians were irate and state environmentalists were intrigued.

The Tioga Pass Road (Highway 120) crosses the Sierra Nevada and meets U.S. 395 at Lee Vining. This scenic route (open only in summer) will take you past **Tuolumne Meadows,** the largest alpine meadow in the Sierra. There are campgrounds, a gas station, store, and visitor center. This is the trailhead for many backpack trips into the High Sierra, but there are also shorter day hikes you can take. Remember, though, to give yourself time (a day or two, at least) to get acclimated to the altitude:

Moderate
($10–$20)

Mountain Room Broiler. The food becomes second̶̶̶ you see the spectacular Yosemite Falls through th̶ room's window-wall. Best bets are steaks, chops, roa̶ and a fresh herb-basted roast chicken. *Yosemite Villa̶ 209/372–1281. Reservations advised. Dress: casual. AĿ̶ MC, V. Dinner only Apr.–Oct. and holiday weeks; closea̶ week in winter.*

Inexpensive
($5–$15)

Four Seasons Restaurant. An upscale, rustic setting with hi̶ finish natural wood tables, lots of greenery and local flora. T̶ breakfast is hearty and all-American; dinner offerings cov̶ the beef, chicken, and fish spectrum, plus vegetarian fare. Yo̶ *semite Lodge, Yosemite Village, tel. 209/372–1269. Reserva-̶ tions advised. Dress: casual. AE, DC, MC, V.*

Lodging

If you aren't into camping, there is still a wide range of accommodation choices in Yosemite, from rustic tent cabins to the rustic luxury of the Ahwahnee Hotel. Most rooms are in the valley, but there are also tent cabins at Tuolumne Meadows and White Wolf (on Tioga Pass Road). White Wolf also has a few cabins with private baths (no electricity). Reservations should be made well in advance, especially for summer travel. At other times, you can always call and try; you might get a room for the next week.

All reservations are made through the **Yosemite Park & Curry Company** (Central Reservations, 5410 E. Home, Fresno, CA 93727, tel. 209/252–4848). Price categories are based on the cost of a room for two people.

ery Expensive
($170–$190)

Ahwahnee Hotel. This grand 1920s-style mountain lodge is constructed of rocks and sugar-pine logs, with exposed timbers and spectacular views. The Grand Lounge and Solarium are decorated in a style that is a tribute to the local Miwok and Paiute Indians. The decor in the rooms continues that motif; modern facilities include TVs. The Ahwahnee was renovated for the 1990 centennial. *123 rooms. Facilities: restaurant, lounge, pool, tennis. AE, DC, MC, V.*

Moderate
($22–$85)

Yosemite Lodge. The lodge has various rooms, from fairly rustic motel-style rooms with two double beds, decorated in rust and green, to very rustic cabins with no baths—all within walking distance of Yosemite Falls. *484 rooms. Facilities: restaurant, lounge, pool. AE, DC, MC, V.*

Inexpensive–
Moderate
($20–$68)

Curry Village. These are plain accommodations: cabins with bath and without, tent cabins with rough wood frames and canvas walls and roofs. It's a step up from camping (linens and blankets are provided), but food or cooking are not allowed because of the animals. If you stay in a cabin without bath, the showers and toilets are centrally located, as they would be in a campground. *180 cabins, 426 tent cabins, 8 hotel rooms. Facilities: cafeteria, pool, rafting (fee), skating (fee), horseback riding (fee). AE, DC, MC, V.*
Housekeeping Cabins. These are also rustic cabins, set along the Merced River, but you can cook here.

8,575 feet. From Yosemite Valley, it's 55 ⫶
Meadows and 74 miles to Lee Vining.

Sports

Bicycling If you want to bicycle around the valley, bike
Yosemite Lodge or **Curry Village.**

Fishing You will have to buy a fishing license if you wa
residents pay $21 for a year's license. Nonres
out $55.75; residents and non-residents may ⫶
license for $6.75.

Hiking Hiking is the primary sport here. If you are hik
steep trails, remember to stay on the trail. C
effect of the altitude on your endurance. If you ⫶
overnight, you'll need a wilderness permit, av⫶
centers or ranger stations. At press time, ther⫶

Rock Climbing **Yosemite Mountaineering** (tel. 209/372–1244 S
372–1335 June–Aug.) conducts beginner throug
rock climbing and backpacking classes. A one-
cludes a hands-on introduction to climbing. Cl
April through September.

Skiing Cross-country and downhill skiing are availa⫶
Pass, off the Glacier Point Road (tel. 209/372–133
outdoor skating rink at Curry Village.

Dining

With precious few exceptions, the best meals av
National Parks are probably those cooked on por⫶
the various campgrounds. But, after all, one doe⫶
derness preserves expecting to find gourmet ⫶
Moreover, there is a snack bar in Yosemite Villag
coffee shops and a cafeteria at the Ahwahnee a⫶
Lodge. Even so, if you are just there for a day, ⫶
want to waste precious time hunting about for fo⫶
stop at a grocery store on the way in and fill up y
and ice chest with the makings of a picnic to enjo
umbrellas of giant fir trees. Price categories are ⫶
cost of a full dinner for one, excluding drinks, tax, ⫶

Expensive **Ahwahnee Hotel.** With the huge sugar-pine log bea⫶
($15–$25) ports, and the big roaring fireplace, you can ima⫶
★ dining in a hunting lodge, built by one of the railro⫶
barons of the last century. Stick with what they ⫶
eaten: steak, trout, prime rib, all competently prepa⫶
rations of Californians make a ritual of spending Chr⫶
New Year's here, so make reservations well in advan⫶
ite Village, tel. 209/372–1489. Reservations advis⫶
and tie required. AE, DC, MC, V.

★ **Erna's Elderberry House.** As a special treat going t⫶
ing, Yosemite, stop at this countryside gem, where t⫶
Vienna-born Erna Kubin, offers bountiful Co⫶
California cuisine, along with dishes from the mo⫶
country she's visited. Prix fixe, six-course dinne⫶
nightly. *48688 Victoria La., Oakhurst, tel. 209/683–6⫶*
et advised. Reservations advised. MC, V. Dinner We⫶
lunch Wed.–Fri., Sunday brunch.

Camping

Reservations for camping are required year-round in Yosemite Valley and from spring through fall outside the valley. They are strongly recommended at any time. Reservations for all campgrounds in Yosemite are made through **Ticketron,** in person or by writing to them (Box 62429, Virginia Beach, VA 23462, tel. 900/454–5454—75¢ for first minute). You can reserve campsites no sooner than eight weeks in advance, and should indicate the name of the park, the campground, and your first, second, and third choice of arrival dates. Fees vary. If space is available, you can also make reservations in person at the Campground Reservations Office in Yosemite Valley, but we strongly recommend making them ahead of time.

Sequoia and Kings Canyon National Parks

The other two Sierra national parks are usually spoken of together. The adjacent parks share their administration and their main highway. Although you may want to concentrate on either Kings Canyon or Sequoia, most people visit both parks in one trip.

Like Yosemite, Sequoia and General Grant national parks were established in 1890. The General Grant National Park, with the addition over the years of the Redwood Canyon area and the drainages of the South and Middle Forks of the Kings River, became Kings Canyon National Park. Both Sequoia and Kings Canyon now extend east to the Sierra crest. The most recent major addition was to Sequoia in 1978, to prevent the development of the Mineral King area for winter sports.

The major attractions of both parks are the big trees (*Sequoiadendron gigantea*—the most extensive groves and the most impressive specimens are found here) and the spectacular alpine scenery. These trees are the largest living things in the world. They are not as tall as the coast redwoods (*Sequoia sempervirens*), but they are much more massive and older. The exhibits at the visitors centers and the interpretive booklets that you can carry on many of the trails will explain the special relationship between these trees and fire (their thick, squishy bark protects them from fire and insects) and how they live so long and grow so big.

The parks encompass land from only 1,200 feet high to more than 14,000 feet. Mount Whitney, on the eastern side of Sequoia, is the highest mountain (14,495 feet) in the contiguous United States. The greatest portion of both parks is accessible only by foot or pack animal. The Generals Highway (46 miles from Highway 180 in Kings Canyon National Park to the Ash Mountain Entrance in Sequoia National Park) links the major groves in the two parks and is open year round.

Summer is the most crowded season, but even then it is much less crowded than at Yosemite. Fall is an especially good time to visit. The rivers will not be as full, but the weather is usually warm and calm and there are no crowds. Snow may remain on the ground in the sequoia groves into June, but is usually gone by mid-month. The flowers in the Giant Forest meadows hit their peak in July.

The entrance fee is $5 per car for a week's stay in both parks. A Golden Eagle pass ($25) will get you into all national parks and monuments for a year.

Getting Around

By Car From the south, enter Sequoia National Park via Highway 198 from Visalia; from the north, enter Kings Canyon National Park via Highway 180 from Fresno. Both highways intersect with Highway 99, which runs north–south through the Central Valley. If you are driving up from Los Angeles, take Highway 65 north from Bakersfield to Highway 198 east of Visalia.

Highways 198 and 180 are connected through the parks by the Generals Highway, a paved two-lane road that is open year round (carry chains in winter). Drivers of RVs and drivers who are not comfortable with mountain driving should probably avoid the southern stretch between the Ash Mountain Entrance and Giant Forest. These 16 miles of narrow road rise almost 5,000 feet and are very twisty, but with care and without undue haste, this is a spectacular drive. Few roads up the west slope of the Sierra rise so quickly through the foothills and offer such spectacular views up into the high country. The rest of the Generals Highway is a well-graded, wide two-lane road and a pleasure to drive.

Highway 180 beyond Grant Grove to Cedar Grove and the road to Mineral King are open only in summer. Both roads, especially the latter, which is unpaved in sections, may present a challenge to inexperienced drivers. Do not expect to drive quickly, especially into Mineral King. Campers more than 30 feet long are not allowed on the Mineral King road.

Guided Tours

For those who must see but not necessarily savor, **KOA Tours** leads one-day trips in vans from Visalia (in the Central Valley) to Giant Forest and Grant Grove. They visit Crescent Meadows, Tharp's Log, and Moro Rock and have lunch at the cafeteria at Giant Forest Village before heading on to the General Sherman Tree and Grant Grove. The tours leave at 8 AM and return at 5:30–6 PM. That's a lot of driving and a lot to see in one day, so we recommend these tours only for those who want to see the largest living things, but can't spend more than a day in the mountains. They also offer tours from Fresno for six or more people. *Tel. 209/651–0100 or 800/322–2336 in CA. Tours daily May–Oct., when weather permits during the rest of the year. Fare: $19.95 adults, $14.95 children.*

Within the park, you can take van tours of Giant Forest ($7.95 adults, $6.95 senior citizens, $4.95 children under 12) or of King's Canyon ($13.95 adults, $11.95 senior citizens, $6.95 children). Sign up for either tour at the Giant Forest Lodge.

Important Addresses and Numbers

General Information: *Sequoia and Kings Canyon National Parks* (Three Rivers, CA 93271, tel. 209/565–3456, Mon.–Fri. 8–4:30 or 209/565–3351, recording) or *National Park Service,*

Fort Mason (Bldg. 201, San Francisco, CA 94123, tel. 415/556–0560).

Reservations: *Sequoia Guest Services* (Box 789, Three Rivers, CA 93271, tel. 209/561–3314 for both parks).

Exploring

Numbers in the margin correspond with points of interest on the Sequoia and Kings Canyon National Parks map.

If you take Highway 180 to the parks, you enter Kings Canyon National Park at the Big Stump Entrance, just southwest of ❶ Wilsonia (a private community with some services) and **Grant Grove.** This was the grove (or what remained of a larger grove decimated by logging) that was protected as General Grant National Park in 1890. It is now the most highly developed area of Kings Canyon National Park. A walk along the 1-mile Big Stump Trail, starting near the park entrance, will demonstrate the effects of heavy logging on these groves.

At Grant Grove Village, you will find a visitor center, gas station, grocery store, campground, coffee shop, and lodging. The visitor center has exhibits on the natural (and human) history of *Sequoiadendron gigantea* and the area. Books and maps describing the region are available. Detailed maps of the trails at this and the other major areas of the two parks are available for $1 each at all the visitor centers.

A spur road leads west less than 1 mile to the General Grant Grove. A short, easy ⅓-mile trail leads through the grove and is accessible to disabled travelers. The most famous tree here is the General Grant, the nation's Christmas tree. In total mass it is not as large as the General Sherman Tree in Sequoia, but it is nearly as tall and just as wide at its base. The Gamlin Cabin is one of several pioneer cabins that can be visited in the parks. A large sequoia was cut for display at the 1876 Philadelphia Exhibition; the Centennial Stump still remains.

❷ Actually in Sequoia National Forest, **Hume Lake** is a reservoir built early this century by loggers; today it is the site of many Christian camps. There is also a public campground. This is a pretty, small lake with distant views of high mountains. If it's hot and you're desperate for a place to swim, you might want to make this side trip. It's accessible by side roads off the Generals Highway east of—or off Highway 180 north of—Grant Grove. There are fine views of Kings Canyon from either road, but the route from the Generals Highway is easier to drive.

Beyond the turnoff for Hume Lake, Highway 180 (Kings River Highway) is closed in winter (usually November–April). In the ❸ summer, you can take this for a spectacular drive to the **Cedar Grove** area, a valley along the South Fork of the Kings River. It's a one-hour drive from Grant Grove to the end of the road where you turn around for the ride back. Although it is steep in places, this is not a difficult road. Built by convict labor in the 1930s, the road clings to some dramatic cliffs along the way, and you should watch out for falling rocks. The highway passes the scars where large groves of big trees were logged at the beginning of the century, and it runs through dry foothills covered with yuccas that bloom in the summer and along the South Fork itself. There are amazing views down into what may

Sequoia and Kings Canyon National Parks

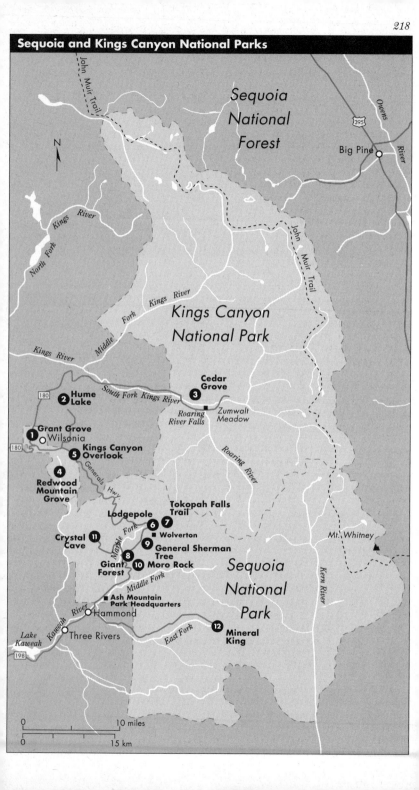

Sequoia National Forest

Big Pine

Owens River

[395]

John Muir Trail

Kings River

North Fork

Middle Fork Kings River

Kings River

Kings Canyon National Park

John Muir Trail

South Fork Kings River

[180]

② **Hume Lake**

③ **Cedar Grove**

Roaring River Falls   Zumwalt Meadow

① **Grant Grove**   Wilsonia

[180]

⑤ **Kings Canyon Overlook**

Roaring River

④ **Redwood Mountain Grove**

Generals Hwy.

Tokopah Falls Trail

Lodgepole

⑥ **⑦**

■ Wolverton

Marble Fork

Crystal Cave **⑪**

⑨ **General Sherman Tree**

⑧

Giant Forest

⑩ **Moro Rock**

Sequoia National Park

▲ *Mt. Whitney*

Middle Fork

■ Ash Mountain Park Headquarters

Kern River

Hammond

Kaweah River

Three Rivers

Lake Kaweah

East Fork

⑫ **Mineral King**

[198]

0 ___ 10 miles

0 ___ 15 km

be the deepest gorge on the continent, at the confluence of the two forks, and up the canyons to the High Sierra.

Cedar Grove, named for the incense cedars that grow there, has campgrounds and lodging, a small ranger station, cafeteria, snack bar, convenience market, and gas station. Horses are available and a good way to explore this country. There are also short trails (one around Zumwalt Meadow, one to the base of Roaring River Falls), and this is the trailhead for many backpackers. This is a lovely day trip if you are staying at Grant Grove or Giant Forest; pack a picnic lunch if you can.

The **Generals Highway** begins south of Grant Grove and runs through this smaller portion of Kings Canyon National Park, through a part of Sequoia National Forest, and then through Sequoia National Park to the Giant Forest and on to the southern entrance to these parks at Ash Mountain.

❹ The **Redwood Mountain Grove** is the largest grove of big trees in the world. There are several paved turnouts (about 4 miles from the beginning of the highway) from which you can look out over the grove (and into the smog of the Central Valley), but the grove is only accessible on foot or horseback. Less than 2 miles **❺** farther, on the north side of the road, a large turnout (**Kings Canyon Overlook**) offers spectacular views into the larger portion of Kings Canyon National Park (the backcountry). You can look into the deep canyons of the South and Middle Forks of the Kings River. If you drive east on Highway 180 to Cedar Grove along the South Fork, you will see these canyons at much closer range.

❻ **Lodgepole,** in a U-shape canyon on the Marble Fork of the Kaweah River, is a developed area with campground, snack bars, grocery store, gas station, and a market complex including a deli, grocery store, gift shop, ice cream parlor, public showers, public laundry, and post office. The visitor center here has the best exhibits in the parks and a small theater for showing films about the park. The Lodgepole Nature Center is geared toward children. The trees here are lodgepole pines, not sequoia, because the canyon conducts cold air down from the high country.

A very short marked nature trail leads from behind the visitor center down to the river. Except when the river is flowing fast (be very cautious), this is a good place to rinse one's feet in cool water, because the trail runs past a "beach" of small rocks along the river.

❼ The **Tokopah Falls Trail** is a more strenuous, 2-mile hike up the river from the campground (pick up a map at the visitor center), but it is also the closest you can get to the high country without taking a long hike. This is a lovely hike, but remember insect repellent during the summer, when mosquitoes can be ferocious.

❽ Four miles beyond Lodgepole you will come to the **Giant Forest**. This is still the most developed area of the parks, with the greatest concentration of accommodations, although plans call for moving these to the Clover Creek area. In the meantime, this is a magical place to stay because of the concentration of varied trails through a series of sequoia groves. There are a grocery store, cafeteria, and two gift shops at Giant Forest Village and a wide range of accommodations at Giant Forest

Lodge. The Lodge also runs a full-service dining room and a gift shop during the summer.

Whether you are staying here or elsewhere in the parks, get the map of the local trails and start exploring. The well-constructed trails range in length from 1–5 miles. They are not paved, crowded, or lined with barricades, so you quickly get the feeling of being on your own in the woods, surrounded by the most impressive trees you are ever likely to see.

Be sure to visit one of the meadows. They are lovely (especially so in July when the flowers are in full bloom), and you can get some of the best views of the big trees across them. Round Meadow, behind Giant Forest Lodge, is the most easily accessible, with a new ¼-mile, wheelchair-accessible "Trail For All People." Crescent and Log meadows are accessible by slightly longer trails. Tharp's Log, at Log Meadow, is a very small and rustic pioneer cabin built in a fallen sequoia. There is also a log cabin at Huckleberry Meadow that children will enjoy exploring.

❾ The most famous tree here is the **General Sherman Tree.** If you aren't up for hiking at all, you can still get to this tree. There is usually a ranger nearby to answer questions, and there are benches so you can sit and contemplate the largest living thing in the world. The tree is 274.9 feet tall and 102.6 feet around at its base, but what makes this the biggest tree is the fact that it is so wide for such a long way up: The first major branch is 130 feet up.

The Congress Trail starts here and travels past a series of large trees and younger sequoias. This is probably the most popular trail in the area, and it also has the most detailed booklet, so it is a good way to learn about the ecology of the groves. You can pick up the booklet from a machine (it takes quarters) near the General Sherman Tree.

A 2½-mile spur road takes off from the Generals Highway near the village and will lead you to other points of interest in the Giant Forest area as well as to the trails to Crescent and Log meadows. The road actually goes through the Tunnel Tree (there is a bypass for RVs that are too tall to fit). Auto Tree is merely a fallen tree onto which you can drive your car for a photograph (if that seems like a reasonable idea to you).

❿ This is also the road to **Moro Rock,** a granite monolith 6,725 feet high, which rises from the edge of the Giant Forest. During the depression, the Conservation Corps built a fabulous trail up to the top. There are 400 steps and, although there is usually a railing, the trail often climbs along narrow ledges over steep drops. If the haul to the top doesn't daunt you, the view is spectacular. Southwest you look down the Kaweah River to Three Rivers, Lake Kaweah, and—on clear days—the Central Valley. Northeast you look up into the High Sierra. Below, you look down thousands of feet to the Middle Fork of the Kaweah River.

⓫ **Crystal Cave** is the only of Sequoia's many caves that is open to the public, and then only on guided tours of the stalagmites and stalactites. You'll have a ½-mile hike from the parking lot down to the cave. Bring a sweater, because the temperature is only 50 degrees. *9 mi southeast of Giant Forest on spur road of Generals Hwy. Admission: $3 adults, $1.50 children 6–11 and* *senior citizens. Open daily June–August; Fri.–Mon. May–September. Tours 10–3.*

⑫ The **Mineral King** area is a recent addition to the parks. In the 1960s the U.S. Forest Service planned to have Walt Disney Productions develop a winter sports resort here, but the opposition of conservation groups led to its incorporation in Senarrow, twisty, and steep road that takes off from Highway 198 at Hammond. The road is only 25 miles long, but budget 90 minutes each way from Highway 198. This is a tough but exciting road to a beautiful high valley. There are campgrounds and a ranger station; facilities are limited but some supplies are available. Many backpackers use this as a trailhead, and there are a number of fine trails for strenuous day hikes.

Sports

Fishing Fishing licenses are required for all anglers. State residents pay $21 for a year's license, nonresidents are charged $55.75. Residents and nonresidents may purchase a 1-day license for $6.75.

Hiking As in Yosemite, hiking is the primary sport. Talk to the rangers at the visitor centers about which trails they recommend when you are there. Keep in mind that you will have to become acclimated to the altitude (over 6,000 feet at Giant Forest) before you can exert yourself fully.

Horseback Riding Horseback riding is available at **Grant Grove, Cedar Grove, Wolverton Pack Station** (between Lodgepole and Giant Forest), and **Mineral King.** Ask at the visitor centers for specifics.

Swimming If you get hot and need a swim, try **Hume Lake** (*see* Exploring, above). Don't try to swim in the fast-running Sierra rivers.

Winter Sports In the winter, you can ski or snowshoe. There is cross-country skiing at Grant Grove and Giant Forest. Rentals and tours are offered by **Sequoia Ski Touring Center** (209/565–3435) at Wolverton and Grant Grove. There are 52 miles of cross-country ski trails at **Montecito-Sequoia** (tel. 800/227–9900), off the Generals Highway between the two parks.

Rangers lead snowshoe walks through Grant Grove and Giant Forest on winter weekends. You can also use the shoes on the cross-country trails at these two areas. Snowshoes can be rented from Sequoia Ski Touring at Wolverton.

Dining

Dining in Sequoia and Kings Canyon national parks is even less of a gourmet experience than in Yosemite, but acceptable food is available. Again, we suggest that you bring food (especially snacks, fresh fruit, and beverages) with you. It will give you more freedom in planning your day. There are casual places to eat at Giant Forest Village, Lodgepole, Grant Grove, and Cedar Grove. The food is not expensive and will satisfy hunger pangs. There is a restaurant at Giant Forest Lodge where you can get a more formal dinner; there is a nice salad bar and good if not inspired American food. Dinner costs $15–$20 per person.

Food should not be left overnight in cars, because bears might be tempted to break in.

Lodging

There is a range of accommodations available in the parks, but you will not find any luxurious rooms. There are hotel/motel-type accommodations at Giant Forest, Stoney Creek (on the Generals Highway), and Cedar Grove. The rooms have one or two double beds and showers but are minimally furnished. They are clean and functional. Rooms cost up to $83 a night for two.

At Giant Forest, there are rustic one- or two-room cabins with baths. At Giant Forest and Grant Grove there are extremely rustic tent-cabins, with rough wood walls, canvas roofs, and wood-burning stoves. Linen, blankets, firewood, and oil lamps are provided. There are centrally located rest rooms and showers. You can cook at these cabins; some have wood-burning cookstoves on their patios. Be sure not to leave any food outside for the animals. Cabin rates are about $35 a night for two.

All reservations should be made through **Sequoia Guest Services** (Box 789, Three Rivers, CA 93271, tel. 209/561–3314). For summer visits, make reservations well in advance. Reservations are recommended for visits at any time of the year because it's a long way out if there's no room at the inn.

Camping

Reservations are accepted only at Lodgepole Campground and only for stays between Memorial Day and Labor Day. Make reservations through **Ticketron,** in person at one of their locations or by writing (Box 62429, Virginia Beach, VA 23462, tel. 900/370–7070—75¢ for first minute). You can reserve campsites up to eight weeks in advance, and should indicate the name of the park, the campground, and your first, second, and third choice of arrival dates. Fees vary. Some campgrounds in Sequoia National Forest (such as Landslide, a very small campground 3 miles from Hume Lake) are just about as convenient as those in the two national parks.

10 The Monterey Peninsula

*by Maria
Lenhart*

*A native of the
Monterey area,
Maria Lenhart
lives in San
Francisco and
writes for
magazines and
newspapers,
including* Travel
Holiday, Travel &
Leisure, *and the*
Christian Science
Monitor.

"The interest is perpetually fresh. On no other coast that I know shall you enjoy, in calm, sunny weather, such a spectacle of ocean's greatness, such beauty of changing color or such degrees of thunder in the sound." What Robert Louis Stevenson wrote of the Monterey Peninsula in 1879 is no less true today— it still provides a spectacle that is as exciting on the first visit as on the twenty-third.

Located almost at the exact center of the California coast, the Monterey Peninsula has been blessed by nature in a number of unique ways. Here are deep green forests of Monterey cypress, oddly gnarled and wind-twisted trees that grow nowhere else. Here also is a vast undersea canyon, larger and deeper than the Grand Canyon, that supports a rich assortment of marine life from fat barking sea lions to tiny plantlike anemones.

The peninsula holds a unique place in California history that is evident in its carefully preserved adobe houses and missions. With the arrival of Father Junípero Serra and Commander Don Gaspar de Portola from Spain in 1770, Monterey became both the military and ecclesiastical capital of Alta California. Portola established the first of California's four Spanish presidios, while Serra founded the second of 21 Franciscan missions, later moving it from Monterey to its current site in Carmel.

When Mexico revolted from Spain in 1822, Monterey remained the capital of California under Mexican rule. The town grew into a lively seaport, drawing Yankee sea traders who added their own cultural and political influence. Then, on July 7, 1846, Commodore John Sloat arrived in Monterey and raised the American flag over the Custom House, claiming California for the United States.

Monterey's political importance in the new territory was shortlived, however. Although the state constitution was framed in Colton Hall, the town was all but forgotten in the excitement caused by the discovery of gold at Sutter's Mill near Sacramento. After the gold rush, the state capital moved from Monterey and the town became a sleepy backwater.

At the turn of the century, however, the Monterey Peninsula began to draw tourists with the opening of the Del Monte Hotel, the most palatial resort the West Coast had ever seen. Writers and artists also discovered the peninsula, adding a rich legacy that remains to this day.

For visitors, the decline of Monterey as California's most important political and population center can be seen as a blessing. The layers of Spanish and Mexican history remain remarkably undisturbed, while the land and sea continue to inspire and delight.

Getting Around

By Plane Monterey Peninsula Airport (tel. 408/373-3731) is 3 miles from downtown Monterey and is served by **American Eagle** (tel. 800/433-7300), **Sky West/Delta** (tel. 800/453-9417), **United Airlines** and **United Express** (tel. 800/241-6522) with daily service from San Francisco and Los Angeles. **USAir** (tel. 800/435-9772) has daily service from Los Angeles.

By Car Heading south from San Francisco, the drive can be made comfortably in three hours or less. The most scenic way is to follow

Highway 1 down the coast, an enjoyable ride past pumpkin and artichoke fields and the beachside communities of Half Moor Bay and Santa Cruz. Unless the drive is made on sunny week-ends when locals are heading for the beach, the two-lane coast highway takes no longer than the freeway routes.

Of the freeway routes available from San Francisco, the most enjoyable is to follow I-280 south and connect with Highway 17 just south of San Jose. Taking Highway 17 south over the redwood-forested Santa Cruz mountains, the route connects with Highway 1 in Santa Cruz. The other standard route is to follow U.S. 101 in San Jose) to Highway 156 near Salinas and head east to Monterey. Traffic in San Jose can be horrendous; avoid rush hours, which start early.

From Los Angeles, the drive to Monterey can be made in less than a day by heading north on U.S. 101 to Salinas and then heading west on Highway 68. The spectacular but slow alterna-tive is to take U.S. 101 to San Luis Obispo and then follow the hairpin turns of Highway 1 up the coast. Allow at least three extra hours if you do.

The Rider's Guide (Box 255, 484 Lake Park Ave., Oakland 94610, tel. 415/653-2553) produces a tape you can play in your car about the history, landmarks, and attractions of the Monte-rey peninsula.

By Train The closest train connection to the Monterey Peninsula is Amtrak's *Coast Starlight*, which makes a stop in Salinas during its run between Los Angeles and Seattle (tel. 800/USA-RAIL).

By Bus From San Francisco, **Greyhound-Trailways** (tel. 415/558-6789) serves Monterey six times daily on a trip that takes up to four hours.

For getting around on the peninsula by bus, **Monterey-Salinas Transit** (tel. 408/424-7695) provides frequent service between towns and many major sightseeing spots and shopping areas for a modest fare.

Scenic Drives

17-Mile Drive Although some sightseers balk at the $5 per car entrance fee to enter this enchanted forest, it is well worth the price to explore this 8,400-acre microcosm of the Monterey coastal landscape. The main entrance gates to the 17-Mile Drive can be found off Lighthouse Avenue in Pacific Grove and off Highway 1 and North San Antonio Avenue in Carmel.

Once inside, the drive presents a primordial nature preserve existing in quiet harmony with palatial estates. Among the nat-ural treasures are many prime examples of the rare Monterey cypresses, trees so gnarled and twisted that Robert Louis Ste-venson once described them as "ghosts fleeing before the wind." The most photographed of them all is the **Lone Cypress,** a weather-sculpted tree growing out of a rocky outcropping above the waves. A turn-out parking area makes it possible to stop for a view of the Lone Cypress, but walking out to it on the precipitous outcropping is no longer allowed. Two other natu-ral landmarks to note are **Seal Rock** and **Bird Rock,** two islands of bird and marine life teeming with harbor seals, sea lions, cor-morants, and pelicans.

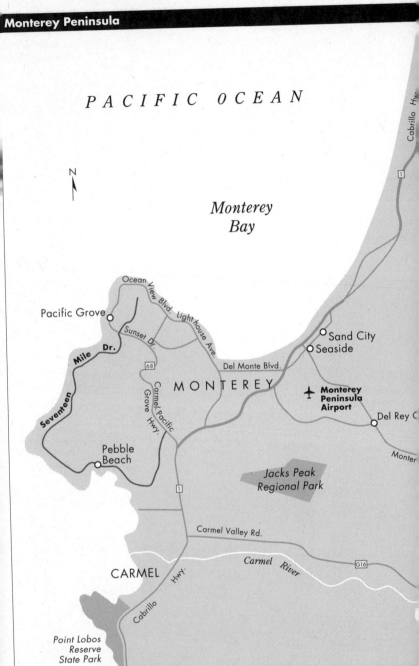

PACIFIC OCEAN

N

Monterey
Bay

Ocean View Blvd.

Pacific Grove

Sunset Dr.

Light house Ave.

Seventeen Mile Dr.

68

Del Monte Blvd.

Sand City

Seaside

Carmel-Pacific Grove Hwy.

MONTEREY

Monterey
Peninsula
Airport

Del Rey C

Monter

Pebble
Beach

1

Jacks Peak
Regional Park

Carmel Valley Rd.

CARMEL

Cabrillo Hwy.

Carmel River

G16

Point Lobos
Reserve
State Park

Cabrillo Hwy.

1

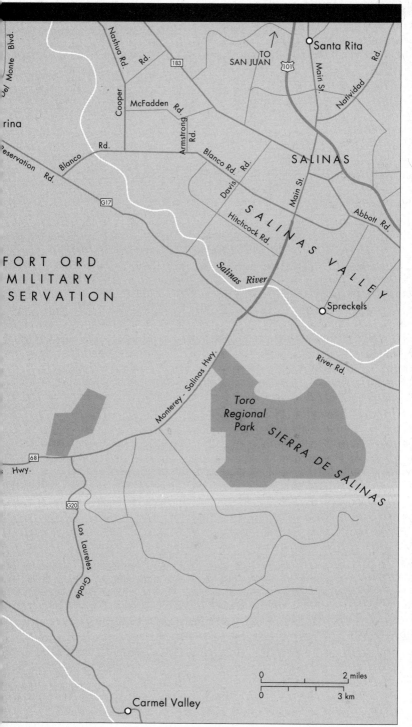

As enticing as the natural scenes are along the drive, those created by man are part of the attraction as well. Perhaps no more famous concentration of celebrated golf courses exists anywhere in the world, particularly the **Pebble Beach Golf Links,** with its famous 18th hole, around which the ocean plays a major role. Even if you're not a golfer, views of impeccable greens can be enjoyed over a drink or lunch at the **Lodge at Pebble Beach** or the **Inn at Spanish Bay,** the two resorts located along the drive.

Among the stately homes, many of which reflect the classic Monterey or Spanish-Mission style that is typical of the region, the most impressive is the **Crocker Marble Palace,** a waterfront estate designed after a Byzantine castle, located not far from the Carmel entrance to the drive. The baroque-style mansion is identifiable by dozens of marble arches, and the grounds even feature a beach area with water heated by underground pipes.

Carmel Valley Road
A world away from the cypress forests and tide pools of the coast are the pastoral ranchlands of Carmel Valley. The rolling meadows studded with oak trees are especially compelling during the spring, when the grass is lush, green, and blooming with bright gold California poppies and blue lupines.

Carmel Valley Road, which turns inland at Highway 1 just south of Carmel, is the main thoroughfare through this secluded enclave of horse ranchers and other well-heeled residents who prefer the valley's perpetually dry, sunny climate to the fog and wind on the coast. A pleasant two hours or so can be spent ambling up the road and back, perhaps in combination with a hike or picnic at **Garland Ranch Regional Park,** or poking around the crafts shops and art galleries in tiny Carmel Valley village.

Another popular stop along the road is the tasting room at the beautiful small **Château Julien** winery, known for its chardonnay and merlot. Personal tours of the winery can be arranged by calling ahead. *Tel. 408/624–2600. Open weekdays 8:30–5, weekends 11–5.*

An enjoyable loop drive can be made by turning off Carmel Valley Road onto **Los Laureles Grade,** a 6-mile winding road that heads over the mountains to Highway 68, ending at a point about halfway between Monterey and Salinas. Located along Highway 68 is the award-winning **Ventana Vineyards,** which has a tasting room. *Tel. 408/372–7415. Open daily noon–5.*

Guided Tours

Seacoast Safaris (tel. 408/372–1288) offers both custom tours and half-day tours of the Monterey Peninsula, which include the 17-Mile Drive, Carmel shopping, Cannery Row, and winetasting. Rates include minivan transportation and sightseeing with guides who are longtime area residents.

Steinbeck Country Tours (tel. 408/625–5107) offers a variety of excursions for individuals and group charters, including Scenic Highlights and Wineries of Monterey County tours. Rates include transportation and guide service.

Motorcoach tours departing from San Francisco that feature the Monterey Peninsula in their Northern California itineraries include **California Parlor Car Tours** (tel. 415/474–7500 or 800/227–4250) and **Gray Line** (tel. 415/558–9400).

Important Addresses and Numbers

Tourist
Information

The Monterey Peninsula Chamber of Commerce (380 Alvarado St., Monterey 93940, tel. 408/649–1770) and The Salinas Chamber of Commerce (119 E. Alisal St., Salinas 93901, tel. 408/424–7611) are both open weekdays 8:30–5.

Emergencies Dial 911 for police and ambulance in an emergency.

Doctor The Monterey County Medical Society (tel. 408/373–4197) will refer doctors on weekdays, 9–5. For referrals at other times, call Community Hospital of Monterey Peninsula (23625 Holman Hwy., Monterey, tel. 408/624–5311). The hospital has a 24-hour emergency room.

Pharmacies There are no all-night pharmacies, but for emergencies there is the Pharmacy Department at the Community Hospital of Monterey Peninsula (*see* above). Sand n' Surf in Carmel at Sixth and Junipero (tel. 408/624–1543) has a pharmacy open weekdays 9–6:30, Sun. and holidays 9–2.

Exploring

Despite its compact size, the Monterey Peninsula is packed with many diversions, and it requires longer than a weekend to do more than skim the surface. Although most communities are situated only a few minutes' drive away from each other, each is remarkably different in flavor and in attractions.

For those with a strong interest in California history and historic preservation, the place on which to concentrate is Monterey, where you need at least two full days to explore the adobe buildings along the Path of History, a state historic park encompassing much of the downtown area. Fans of Victorian architecture will want to allow extra time in Pacific Grove, where many fine examples have been preserved and often house restaurants or bed-and-breakfast inns.

In Carmel you can shop till you drop, although a day fighting the summer and weekend hordes through boutiques, art galleries, houseware outlets, and gift shops is usually enough for most people. After that, the incomparable loveliness of the Carmel coast can restore the spirit if not the pocketbook.

The climate can also vary on the peninsula. A sweater or windbreaker is nearly always necessary along the coast, where a cool breeze is usually blowing and the fog is on the way in or out. The situation a few miles inland can be different, however, particularly during the summer, when temperatures in Salinas or Carmel Valley can be a good 15 or 20 degrees warmer than those in Carmel and Monterey.

Although a car is handy for getting from town to town, most of the Monterey Peninsula is best seen on foot. Parking is especially difficult in Carmel and in the vicinity of the Monterey Bay Aquarium on Cannery Row. Take comfortable shoes for negotiating village streets, ambling along the shoreline, and hiking through nature preserves. A good pair of binoculars is also highly recommended; you never know when a playful otter or even a migrating gray whale may splash into sight.

Carmel

Numbers in the margins correspond with points of interest on the Carmel map.

Although the community has grown quickly over the years and its population quadruples with tourists on weekends and during the summer, Carmel retains its identity as a quaint "village" where buildings have no street numbers and live music is banned in the local watering holes. Indeed, there is still a villagelike ambience for visitors wandering the side streets at their own pace, poking into hidden courtyards and stopping at a Hansel-and-Gretel-like cafe for tea and crumpets.

Carmel has hokey gift emporiums, but most of the wares in its hundreds of shops are distinctive and of high quality. Classic sportswear, gourmet cookware, and original art are among the best buys to be found along the main street, Ocean Avenue, and its cross streets. Just as notable is the architecture of many of the shops, a charming mishmash of ersatz English Tudor, Mediterranean, and other styles.

In recent years, the popularity of shopping in Carmel has led to the creation of several attractive, nicely landscaped shopping malls. **Carmel Plaza,** in the east end of the village proper, consists of more than 50 shops, restaurants, and small branches of major department stores. **The Barnyard** and **the Crossroads** are just southeast of the village off Highway 1.

Time Out   **Patisserie Boissiere,** a Carmel Plaza cafe reminiscent of a country French inn, is the perfect place to take a break from shopping. Light entrées and French pastries are offered. *On Mission Ave. between Ocean and 7th aves. tel. 408/624–5008. MC, V. Open daily except on Christmas Day.*

Before it became an art colony in the early 20th century and long before it became a shopping and browsing mecca, Carmel was an important religious center in the early days of Spanish California. That heritage is preserved in one of the state's loveliest historic sites, the Mission San Carlos Borromeo del Rio Carmelo, more commonly known as the **Carmel Mission.** Founded in 1770 and serving as headquarters for the mission system in California under Father Junípero Serra, the Carmel Mission exists today with its stone church and tower dome beautifully restored. Adjoining the church is a tranquil garden planted with California poppies and a series of museum rooms that depict an early kitchen, Father Serra's Spartan sleeping quarters, and the oldest college library in California. *Rio Rd. and Lausen Dr., tel. 408/624–3600. Open Mon.–Sat. 9:30–4:30. Sun. 10:30–4:30. Donations suggested.*

Scattered throughout the pines in Carmel are the houses and cottages that were built for the steady stream of writers, artists, and photographers who discovered the area decades ago. Among the most impressive dwellings is **Tor House,** a stone cottage built by the poet Robinson Jeffers in 1918 on a craggy knoll overlooking the sea. The low-ceilinged rooms are filled with portraits, books, and unusual art objects, such as a white stone from the Great Pyramid in Egypt. The highlight of the small estate is Hawk Tower, a detached edifice set with stones from the Great Wall of China and a Roman villa, which served as a

Carmel

Bird Rock

Seal Rock

Spyglass Hill

Cyprus Point

PEBBLE BEACH

Stevenson Dr.

Forest Lake Rd.

Seventeen Mile Dr.

Mile Dr.

Seventeen Mile Dr.

Sunset Point

Seventeen Mile Dr.

Pescadero Point

Pebble Beach Golf Course

Arrowhead Point

2nd Ave.

5th Ave.

Ocean Ave. **1**

Lincoln Ave.

Monte Verde St.

San Antonio Ave.

Mountain View Ave.

CARMEL

Scenic Rd.

Carmel Beach

Carmel Bay

Rio Rd. **4**

5

2

3

Cabrillo Hwy.

Carmel River State Beach

6

N

The Pinnacle

Terminal Rock

Granite Point

Monterey Cypress Grove

Sea Lion Rocks

7

Point Lobos State Reserve

0   1 mile

0   1 km

The Barnyard, **2**
Carmel Mission, **4**
Carmel Plaza, **1**
Carmel River State Park, **6**
The Crossroads, **3**
Point Lobos State Reserve, **7**
Tor House, **5**

retreat for the poet's wife, Una, an accomplished musician. The docents who lead tours are very well-informed about the poet's work and life. His home and life present a fascinating story, even if you are not a fan of Jeffers's poetry. *26304 Ocean View Ave., tel. 408/624–1813. Admission: $5 adults, $3.50 college students, $1.50 high school students. Tours by appointment on Fri. and Sat. between 10–4.*

Carmel's greatest beauty, however, is not to be found in its historic and architectural landmarks. Nature has done the most impressive work here, particularly in forming the rugged coastline with its pine and cypress forests and countless inlets. Happily, much of the coastal area has been set aside for public enjoyment.

6 **Carmel River State Park,** stretches for 106 acres along Carmel Bay. On sunny days the waters appear nearly as turquoise as those of the Caribbean. The park features a sugar-white beach with high dunes and a bird sanctuary that is a nesting ground for pelicans, kingfishers, hawks, and sandpipers. *Off Scenic Rd., south of Carmel Beach tel. 408/649–2836.*

7 The park is overshadowed by **Point Lobos State Reserve,** a 1,250-acre headland just south of Carmel. Roads have been kept to a minimum, and the best way to explore is to walk along the extensive network of hiking trails. Especially good choices are the Cypress Grove Trail, which leads through a forest of rare Monterey cypresses clinging to the rocks above an emerald-green cove, and Sea Lion Point Trail, where sea lions, otters, harbor seals, and (during certain times of year) migrating whales can be observed. Part of the reserve is an undersea marine park open to qualified scuba divers. *Hwy 1, tel. 408/624 –4909. Admission: $3 per car, $2 if senior citizen is traveling. Open May–Sept., daily 9–7; Oct.–Apr., 9–5.*

Monterey's Path of History

Numbers in the margin correspond with points of interest on the Monterey map.

A good way to begin exploring Monterey is to start with the beginnings of the town itself—the beautifully preserved collection of adobe buildings contained in the **Monterey State Historic Park** (tel. 408/649–7118). Far from being an isolated period museum, the park facilities are an integral part of the day-to-day business life of the town, with some of the buildings serving as government offices, restaurants, banks, and private residences. Others are museums illustrating life in the raw young seaport as it developed from a colonial Spanish outpost to its brief heyday as California's political center.

The best way to enjoy the park is on a 2-mile self-guided walking tour outlined in a brochure called the "Path of History," available at the Chamber of Commerce or at many of the landmark buildings contained in the park. *Tour package for multiple sites: $3.50 adults, $2 children.*

1 A logical beginning to the walking tour is at the **Custom House** across from Fisherman's Wharf. Built by the Mexican government in 1827 and considered the oldest government building west of the Rockies, this 2-story adobe was the first stop for sea traders whose goods were subject to duty fees. Its grandest day in Monterey's history came in 1846, when Commodore John

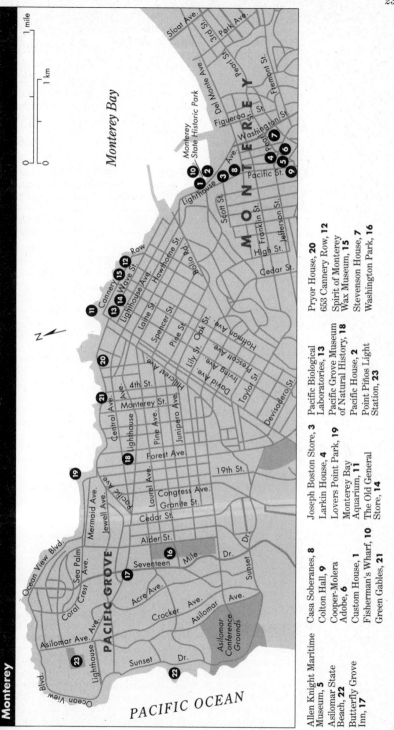

Monterey

Monterey Bay

MONTEREY

PACIFIC GROVE

PACIFIC OCEAN

1 mile
1 km

N

Allen Knight Maritime Museum, **5**
Asilomar State Beach, **22**
Butterfly Grove Inn, **17**

Casa Soberanes, **8**
Colton Hall, **9**
Cooper-Molera Adobe, **6**
Custom House, **1**
Fisherman's Wharf, **10**
Green Gables, **21**

Joseph Boston Store, **3**
Larkin House, **4**
Lovers Point Park, **19**
Monterey Bay Aquarium, **11**
The Old General Store, **14**

Pacific Biological Laboratories, **13**
Pacific Grove Museum of Natural History, **18**
Pacific House, **2**
Point Piños Light Station, **23**

Pryor House, **20**
653 Cannery Row, **12**
Spirit of Monterey Wax Museum, **15**
Stevenson House, **7**
Washington Park, **16**

Sloat raised the American flag over the building and claimed California for the United States. Now the lower floor displays examples of a typical cargo from a 19th-century trading ship. *1 Custom House Plaza, tel. 408/649–7118, Admission: free. Open daily 10–4, Mar.–Oct. 10–5.*

② The next stop along the path should be **Pacific House,** a former hotel and saloon that is now a museum of early California life. There are Gold-Rush relics, historic photographs of old Monterey, and a costume gallery with lacy Mexican shawls and tiny kid slippers from the colonial days. *10 Custom House Plaza, tel. 408/649–2907. Admission: $1, 50¢ for children. Open daily 10–4, Mar.–Oct. 10–5.*

③ Monterey's most historic gift shop is the **Joseph Boston Store,** located in the Casa Del Oro adobe, a tiny store that first opened for business in 1849, with woodwork from a shipwrecked Portuguese whaler. Now staffed with volunteers from the Monterey History and Art Association, the shop is stocked with antiques, tea, and a potpourri of gift items. *Scott and Oliver sts. Open Wed.–Sat. 10–5, Sun. noon–5.*

④ Farther along the Path of History is the **Larkin House,** one of the most architecturally significant homes in California. Built in 1835, the 2-story adobe with a veranda encircling the second floor is a blend of Mexican and New England influences that became known as the Monterey style. The rooms are furnished with period antiques, many of them brought from New Hampshire to Monterey by the Larkin family. *Jefferson St. and Calle Principal. Admission: $1, 50¢ for children. Tours on the hour Mar. 1–Nov. 1, 10–4; Nov. 1–Mar. 1, 10–3. Closed noon–1 PM and Tues.*

⑤ Next door, the **Allen Knight Maritime Museum** is devoted to the private collection of maritime artifacts of former Carmel mayor Allen Knight. The highlight among the exhibits of ship models, scrimshaw items, and nautical prints is the enormous multifaceted Fresnel Light from the Point Sur Lighthouse. *550 Calle Principal, tel. 408/375–2553. Open Sept. 15–June 15, Tues.–Fri. 1–4, Sat.–Sun. 2–4; June 16–Sept. 14, Tues.–Fri. 10–4, Sat.–Sun. 2–4.*

⑥ The largest site along the Path of History is the recently restored **Cooper-Molera Adobe,** a 4-acre complex that includes an early California house dating from the 1820s, a gift shop, a screening room where an introductory slide presentation is shown, and a large garden enclosed by a high adobe wall. The tile-roofed house is filled with antiques and memorabilia, mostly from the Victorian era, that illustrate the life of a prosperous pioneer family. *Polk and Munras sts. Admission: $1, 50¢ for children. Tours on the hour 10–3, Mar.–Oct. 10–4. Closed 1–2 and Wed.*

⑦ For literary and history buffs, one of the path's greatest treasures is the **Stevenson House,** named in honor of Robert Louis Stevenson, author of *Treasure Island* and other classics, who boarded there briefly in a tiny upstairs room. In addition to Stevenson's room, which is furnished with items from his family's estate, there is a gallery of the author's memorabilia and several charming period rooms, including a children's nursery stocked with Victorian toys and games. *530 Houston St. Admission: $1, 50¢ for children. Tours on the hour 10–3, Mar.–Oct. 10–4. Closed noon–1 PM. Closed Wed.*

A historic house with an entirely different feel is the low-ceilinged **Casa Soberanes,** a classic adobe structure that once housed the commander of the Spanish Presidio. *336 Pacific St. Admission: $1. Tours on the hour 10–4, Mar.–Oct. 10–4. Closed 1–2 Tues. and Thurs.*

California's equivalent of Independence Hall is **Colton Hall,** a white edifice where a convention of delegates met in 1849 to draft the first state constitution. Now the historic building, which has served as a school, courthouse, and county seat, is a museum furnished as it was during the constitutional convention. The extensive grounds outside the hall also include a more notorious building, the Old Monterey Jail, where inmates languished behind thick granite walls. *Pacific between Madison and Jefferson sts., tel. 408/375–9944. Open March–Oct., daily 10–5; Nov.–Feb., 10–4. Closed noon–1 weekends.*

Although not on the Path of History, the **Monterey Peninsula Museum of Art** is just across the street from Colton Hall. The museum is especially strong on artists and photographers who have worked in the area, a distinguished lot that includes Ansel Adams and Edward Weston. Another focus of the museum is folk art from around the world; the collection ranges from Kentucky hearth brooms to Tibetan prayer wheels. *559 Pacific St., tel. 408/372–7591. Admission free. Open Tues.–Sat. 10–4, Sun. 1–4.*

Fisherman's Wharf and Cannery Row

Inevitably, visitors are drawn toward the waterfront in Monterey, if only because the mournful barking of sea lions that can be heard throughout the town makes its presence impossible to ignore. The whiskered marine mammals are best enjoyed while walking along **Fisherman's Wharf,** an aging pier crowded with souvenir shops, fish markets, seafood restaurants, and popcorn stands.

Although tacky and touristy to the utmost, the wharf is a good place to visit, especially with children. For years, an organ grinder with a costumed monkey has entertained crowds at the entrance to the wharf. Farther down, you can buy a bag of squid to feed the sea lions that beg from the waters below.

From the wharf, a footpath along the shore leads to **Cannery Row,** a street that has undergone several transformations since it was immortalized in John Steinbeck's 1944 novel of the same name. Steinbeck's street was crowded with sardine canneries processing, during their peak, nearly 200,000 tons of the smelly silver fish a year. During the mid-1940s, however, the sardines mysteriously disappeared from the bay, causing the canneries to close.

Over the years the old tin-roof canneries have been converted to restaurants, art galleries, and minimalls with shops selling T-shirts, fudge, and plastic otters. A recent trend, however, has been toward a more tasteful level of tourist development along the Row, including several attractive inns and hotels. The Monterey Plaza Hotel (400 Cannery Row) is a good place to relax over a drink and watch for otters.

The most important recent development on Cannery Row has been the opening of the spectacular **Monterey Bay Aquarium,** a $50-million window on the sea waters just outside its back

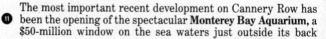

doors. The aquarium has proved so popular that visitors should expect long lines and sizable crowds on weekends, especially during the summer. Braving the crowds is worth it, however, especially to see the 3-story Kelp Forest exhibit, the only one of its kind in the world, and a re-creation of the sea creatures and vegetation found in Monterey Bay. Among other standout exhibits are a bat-ray petting pool, where the flat velvetlike creatures can be touched as they swim by; a 55,000-gallon sea otter tank; and an enormous outdoor artificial tide pool that supports anemones, crabs, sea stars, and other colorful creatures. *886 Cannery Row, tel. 408/649–6466. Admission: $8 adults, $5.75 students and senior citizens, $3.50 children 3–12. Tickets can be purchased ahead from Ticketron, tel. 408/247–7469 or 415/392–7469. Open daily 10–6. Closed Christmas. AE, MC, V.*

Although Steinbeck would have trouble recognizing the street today, there are still some historical and architectural features from its colorful past. One building to take note of is **653 Cannery Row,** with its tiled Chinese dragon roof that dates from 1929. A weathered wooden building at 800 Cannery Row was the **Pacific Biological Laboratories,** where Edward F. Ricketts, the inspiration for Doc in Steinbeck's novel, did much of his marine research. Across the street, the building now called **The Old General Store** is the former Wing Chong Market that Steinbeck called Lee Chong's Heavenly Flower Grocery.

On a more kitschy note, characters from the Steinbeck novel are depicted in wax at the **Spirit of Monterey Wax Museum,** which recently added new lighting and animation and a 25-minute description of the history of the area over the past 400 years, with Steinbeck as narrator. *700 Cannery Row, tel. 408/375–3770. Admission: $4.95 adults, $3.95 students and senior citizens, children under 7 free. Open daily, 9 AM–9 PM.*

Pacific Grove

If not for the dramatic strip of coastline in its backyard, Pacific Grove could easily pass for a typical small town in the heartland. Beginning as a summer retreat for church groups a century ago, the town has retained some of its prim and proper Victorian heritage in the host of tiny board and batten cottages and stately mansions lining its streets.

Even before the church groups migrated here, however, Pacific Grove had been receiving thousands of annual guests in the form of bright orange and black monarch butterflies. Known as "Butterfly Town USA," Pacific Grove is home to the monarchs that migrate south from Canada and the Pacific Northwest and take residence in the pine and eucalyptus groves between October and March. Seeing a mass of butterflies hanging from the branches like a long fluttering veil is unforgettable.

Although many of their original nesting grounds have vanished, two good spots for viewing butterflies remain. The largest is **Washington Park** at the corner of Pine Avenue and Alder Street; the other is a grove adjoining the **Butterfly Grove Inn** at 1073 Lighthouse Avenue.

If you are in Pacific Grove when the butterflies are not, an approximation of this annual miracle is on exhibit at the **Pacific Grove Museum of Natural History.** In addition to a finely crafted butterfly tree exhibit, the museum features a collection of 400 mounted birds native to Monterey County and a film presentation about the monarch butterfly. *165 Forest Ave., tel. 408/372-4212. Admission free. Open Tues.–Sun. 10–5.*

A prime way to enjoy Pacific Grove is to walk or bicycle along its 3 miles of city-owned shoreline, a clifftop area following Ocean View Boulevard that is landscaped with succulents and native plants and has plenty of park benches on which to sit and gaze at the sea. A variety of marine and bird life can be spotted here, including colonies of cormorants that are drawn to the **⑲** massive rocks rising out of the surf. **Lovers Point Park,** located midway along the waterfront, is a pleasant grassy area in which to stop and picnic.

Although it is difficult to turn away from the gorgeous coast, the other side of Ocean View Boulevard has a number of imposing turn-of-the-century mansions that are well worth your **⑳** attention. One of the finest is the **Pryor House** at number 429, a massive shingled structure with a leaded and beveled glass doorway built in 1909 for an early mayor. At the corner of 5th **㉑** Street and Ocean View is **Green Gables,** a romantic Swiss Gothic-style mansion, now a bed-and-breakfast inn, with steeply peaked gables and stained-glass windows.

㉒ Another beautiful coastal area in Pacific Grove is **Asilomar State Beach,** on Sunset Drive between Point Piños and the Del Monte Forest. The 100 acres of dunes, tide pools, and pocketsize beaches from one of the region's richest areas for marine life. The deep tide pools support 210 species of algae and are alive with sea urchins, crabs, and other creatures.

The oldest continuously operating lighthouse on the West **㉓** Coast is also a museum open to the public, the **Point Piños Light Station.** Visitors can learn about the lighting and foghorn operations and wander through a small museum containing historical memorabilia from the U.S. Coast Guard. *Ocean View Blvd. at Point Piños, tel. 408/372-4212. Admission free. Open weekends 1–4 PM.*

Salinas

While Monterey turns its face toward the sea, Salinas, a half-hour inland and a world away in spirit, is deeply rooted as the population center of a rich agricultural valley. This unpretentious town may lack the sophistication and scenic splendors of the coast, but it is of interest to literary and architectural buffs.

The memory and literary legacy of Salinas native John Steinbeck are well-honored here. The author's birthplace, a Victorian frame house, has been converted to a lunch-only restaurant called the **Steinbeck House,** which is run by the volunteer Valley Guild. The restaurant contains some Steinbeck memorabilia and presents a menu featuring locally grown produce. *132 Central Ave., tel. 408/424-2735. Reservations advised. Open weekdays for two sittings at 11:45 AM and 1:15 PM.*

Steinbeck did much of his research for *East of Eden*, a novel partially drawn from his Salinas boyhood, at what is now called the **Steinbeck Library.** The library features tapes of interviews with people who knew Steinbeck and a display of photos, first editions, letters, original manuscripts, and other items pertaining to the novelist. *110 W. San Luis, tel. 408/758-7311.*

Admission free. Open Mon.–Thurs. 10–9, Fri.–Sat. 10–6.

Salinas's turn-of-the-century architecture has been the focus of an ongoing renovation project, much of which is centered on the original downtown area on South Main Street, with its handsome stone storefronts. One of the finest private residences from this era is the **Harvey-Baker House,** a beautifully preserved redwood house built for the city's first mayor in 1881. *238 E. Romie La., tel. 408/757–8085. Open first Sun. of each month 1–4 PM, and weekdays by appointment.*

Of even earlier vintage is the **Jose Eusebio Boronda Adobe,** the last unaltered adobe home from Mexican California open to the public in Monterey County. Located in the meadows above the Alisal Slough, the house, which suffered some damage in the 1989 earthquake, is a treasure trove of early furniture and artifacts from the period. *333 Boronda Rd., tel. 408/757–8085. Admission free. Open weekdays 10–2, Sun. 1–4, Sat. by appointment.*

San Juan Batista

A sleepy little hamlet tucked off U.S. 101 about 20 miles north of Salinas, San Juan Batista is a nearly unaltered example of a classic California mission village. Protected from development since 1933, when much of it became **San Juan Batista State Historic Park,** the village is about as close to early 19th-century California as you can get. *Tel. 408/623–4881. Admission: $1 adults; children 6–17 50¢. Open daily 10–4:30.*

The centerpiece for the village is the wide green plaza ringed by historic buildings that include a restored blacksmith shop, a stable, a pioneer cabin, and jailhouse. Running along one side of the square is **Mission San Batista,** a long, low colonnaded structure founded by Father Lasuen in 1797. A poignant spot adjoining it is **Mission Cemetery,** where more than 4,300 Indian converts are buried in unmarked graves.

After the mission era, San Juan Batista became an important crossroads for stagecoach travel. The principal stop in town was the **Plaza Hotel,** a collection of adobe buildings with furnishings from the 1860s. Next door, the **Castro-Breen Adobe,** once owned by survivors from the Donner party and furnished with Spanish colonial antiques, presents a view of domestic life in the village.

More contemporary pursuits in San Juan Batista include poking through the numerous antiques shops and art galleries lining the side streets of the village. In August the village holds a popular annual flea market.

What to See and Do with Children

Beaches. While local waters are generally too cold and turbulent for children (or adults, for that matter), the Monterey Municipal Beach east of Wharf No. 2 has shallow waters that are warm and calm enough for wading. Another good beach for kids is Lovers Point Park on Ocean View Boulevard in Pacific Grove, a sheltered spot with a children's pool and picnic area. Glass-bottom boat rides, which permit viewing of the plant and sea life below, are available during the summer.

Dennis the Menace Playground (Fremont St. and Camino El Estero, Monterey). Delightful Lake El Estero Park is the setting for this imaginative playground whose name pays tribute to one of its developers, cartoonist and longtime local resident Hank Ketcham. Among the features are a maze made from hedges, free-form play equipment, and a Southern Pacific steam locomotive. Rowboats and paddleboats can be rented on Lake El Estero, a U-shaped lake that is home to a varied assortment of ducks, mud hens, and geese.

Edgewater Packing Co. (640 Wave St., Monterey, tel. 408/649–1899). The centerpiece of this converted sardine cannery and processing plant is an antique carousel with hand-carved animals and mermaids that is as much fun to ride now as it was in 1905. A candy store and game arcade are among the other attractions.

Roller Skating. Roller skates can be rented for the old-fashioned rink at Del Monte Gardens. *2020 Del Monte Ave., Monterey, tel. 408/375–3202. Closed Mon. and Tues.*

Children will enjoy the Monterey Bay Aquarium, the Museum of Natural History, and the Point Piños Lighthouse (*see* Exploring, above). Also popular is whale-watching (*see* Participant Sports, below).

Off the Beaten Track

A few miles north of Monterey near the tiny harbor town of Moss Landing is one of only two federal bird sanctuaries in California, the **Elkhorn Slough** (Hwy. 1, Moss Landing, tel. 408/728–2822). There are 2,500 acres of tidal flats and salt marshes that form a complex environment supporting more than 300 species of birds and fish. A 1-mile walk along the meandering canals and wetlands can reveal swans, pelicans, loons, herons, and egrets. You can wander at leisure or take a guided walk *on weekends at 10 AM and 1 PM and visit the heron rookery. Open Wed.–Sun. 9–5. Admission: $2.25 over 16, free for under 16.*

Shopping

Art Galleries Although few artists can afford the real estate, Carmel's heritage as a thriving art colony lives on in dozens of art galleries scattered throughout the town. A wide and eclectic assortment of art—everything from 19th-century watercolors to abstract metal sculpture—is available for browsing and purchase in galleries in Carmel and elsewhere on the peninsula.

At the **Bennett Sculpture Gallery** in Carmel, brothers Bob and Tom Bennett sell limited-edition bronze sculptures designed and created in their foundry near Sacramento. *Ocean and Juniper aves., tel. 408/625–1085. Open daily 10–6.*
The Coast Gallery Pebble Beach presents the work of contemporary wildlife and marine artists in forms that range from etchings to bronze sculpture. *The Lodge at Pebble Beach, 17-Mile Dr., Pebble Beach, tel. 408/624–2002. Open daily 9–5.*
The Masterpiece Gallery features early California Impressionists and the nostalgic work of James Peter Cost, as well as that of his daughter, Shelley Anne Cost, who specializes in floral

and pastoral California themes. *Dolores St. and 6th Ave., Carmel, tel. 408/624–2163. Open daily 10–6; Sat. 6–10.*

Classic impressionism and traditional realism are the foci of the **Cottage Gallery,** which displays paintings and sculpture. *Mission St. and 6th Ave., Carmel, tel. 408/624–7888. Open daily 10–5.*

The **Bill W. Dodge Gallery** features one of the largest collections of contemporary folk art in the West, including Dodge's own turn-of-the-century-style paintings, posters, and prints. *Dolores St. between 5th and 6th aves., Carmel, tel. 408/625–5636. Open daily 10–5.*

At **GWS Galleries,** which features the work of nationally recognized artists, the primary themes and styles are Western, wildlife, marine, aviation, Americana, and landscape. Museum-quality framing is offered. *26390 Carmel Rancho La., Carmel, tel. 408/625–2288. Open Mon.–Sat. 10–5:30, Sun. 11–4.*

The **Highlands Sculpture Gallery** is devoted to indoor and outdoor sculpture, primarily work done in stone, bronze, wood, and metal by West Coast artists. *Dolores St. between 5th and 6th aves., Carmel, tel. 408/624–0535. Open daily 10:30–4:30.*

Photography West Gallery exhibits a changing spectrum of well-known 20th-century photography and features the work of Ansel Adams, who lived and worked in the region for many years. *Ocean Ave. and Dolores St., Carmel, tel. 408/625–1587. Open weekdays 11–5, Sat. 10–6, Sun. 10–5.*

Gift Ideas   In a region known for superb golf courses, one can find the ultimate in golf equipment and accessories. At **John Riley Golf** customers can get custom-made golf clubs manufactured on the premises. *601 Wave St., Monterey, tel. 408/373–8855. Open Mon.–Sat. 9–5, Sun. noon–5.*

Unusual gifts for golfers can be found at **Golf Arts and Imports,** which features antique golf prints and clubs, rare golf books, and other golfing memorabilia. *Dolores St. and 6th Ave., Carmel, tel. 408/625–4488. Open Mon.–Sat. 10–5, Sun. 10–3.*

The illustrations of Beatrix Potter are in evidence everywhere at **Peter Rabbit and Friends,** which offers toys, nursery bedding, books, music boxes, party supplies, and other items embellished with characters and scenes from Potter's children's tales. *Lincoln Ave. between 7th and Ocean aves., Carmel, tel. 408/624–6854. Open Mon.–Sat. 10–5, Sun. 11–5.*

One of the best places for books on marine life and attractive gifts with a marine life theme is the **Monterey Bay Aquarium Gift Shop,** which offers everything from posters and art prints to silk-screened sweatshirts and lobster-shaped wooden napkin rings. *886 Cannery Row, Monterey, tel. 408/649–6466. Open daily 10–6.*

Participant Sports

Bicycling   The Monterey Peninsula is wonderful biking territory, with bicycle paths following some of the choicest parts of the shoreline, including the 17-Mile Drive and the waterfront of Pacific Grove. Bikes can be rented from **Bay Bikes** (640 Wave St., Monterey, tel. 408/646–9090). Pickup and delivery to hotels is possible in the summer season.

Adventures by the Sea (299 Cannery Row, tel. 408/372–1807) has biking packages that combine rentals with restaurant vouchers or with tickets good for the Monterey Bay Aquarium. Tour packages for groups as well as for walking tours are available.

Mopeds can be rented from **Monterey Moped Adventures** (1250 Del Monte Ave., tel. 408/373–2696). A free practice lesson is included in the rental price; a driver's license is required.

Fishing Rock cod is a relatively easy catch in Monterey Bay, with salmon and albacore tuna also among the possibilities. Most fishing trips are a half day or a full day in duration, leave from Fisherman's Wharf in Monterey, and can include options such as equipment rental, bait, fish cleaning, and a one-day license. Boat charters for groups and trips for individuals are available.

Fishing trips in Monterey are offered by **Monterey Sport Fishing** (96 Fisherman's Wharf, tel. 408/372–2203), **Randy's Fishing Trips** (66 Fisherman's Wharf, tel. 408/372–7440), and **Sam's Fishing Fleet** (84 Fisherman's Wharf, tel. 408/372–0577).

Golf With 19 golf courses, most of them commanding strips of choice real estate, it is not surprising that the Monterey Peninsula is sometimes called the golf capital of the world. Beginning with the opening of the Del Monte Golf course in 1897, golf has long been an integral part of the social and recreational scene in the area.

Many hotels will help with golf reservations or offer golf packages; inquire when you make lodging reservations.

Several of the courses are within the exclusive confines of the 17-Mile Drive, where the Del Monte forest and the surging Pacific help make the game challenging as well as scenic. The most famous of these courses is **Pebble Beach Golf Links** (17-Mile Dr., tel. 408/624–3811), which takes center stage each winter during the AT&T Pro-Am, known for years as the "Crosby," where show business celebrities and pros team up for what is perhaps the world's most glamorous golf tournament. Such is the fame of this course that golfers from around the world make it one of the busiest in the region, despite greens fees that are well over $100. (You do get a refund of the $5 fee for the 17-Mile Drive.) Reservations are essential.

Another famous course in Pebble Beach is **Spyglass Hill** (Spyglass Hill Rd., tel. 408/624–3811), where the holes are long and unforgiving to sloppy players. With the first five holes bordering on the Pacific, the views offer some consolation.

A newer addition to the Pebble Beach scene is **Poppy Hills** (17-Mile Dr., tel. 408/625–2035), a creation of Robert Trent Jones, Jr. that opened in 1986 and has been named by *Golf Digest* as one of the top 20 courses in the world.

The newest course in Pebble Beach is the **Spanish Bay Golf Links** (tel. 408/624–3811), which opened on the north end of the 17-Mile Drive in late 1987. Spanish Bay, which hugs a choice stretch of shoreline when not reaching deep into the Del Monte Forest, is designed in the rugged manner of a traditional Scottish course with sand dunes and coastal marshes interspersed among the greens.

Less experienced golfers and those who want to sharpen their iron shots can try the shortest course in Pebble Beach, the nine-hole **Peter Hay** (17-Mile Dr., tel. 408/624–3811).

Just as challenging as the Pebble Beach courses is the **Old Del Monte Golf Course** (1300 Sylvan Rd., tel. 408/373–2436) in Monterey, the oldest course west of the Mississippi. The greens fees are among the most reasonable in the region.

Another local favorite, with greens fees only a fraction of those in Pebble Beach, is **Pacific Grove Golf Links** (Asilomar Blvd., tel. 408/375–3456). Designed by Jack Neville, who also designed the Pebble Beach Golf Links, the course features a back nine with spectacular ocean views and iceplant-covered sand dunes that make keeping on the fairway a must.

Although lacking in ocean views, golf courses in Carmel Valley offer the company of deer and quail wandering across the greens. One of the choicest is **Rancho Cañada Golf Club** (Carmel Valley Rd., tel. 408/624–0111), with 36 holes, some of them overlooking the Carmel River.

Up the road a few miles is the **Golf Club at Quail Lodge** (8000 Valley Greens Dr., tel. 408/624–2770), which has a course made beautiful and challenging by several lakes incorporated into its design. The course is private but is open to guests at the adjoining Quail Lodge and by reciprocation with other private clubs.

Guests at the nearby Carmel Valley Ranch resort have access to the private Peter Dye-designed **Carmel Valley Ranch Resort** course (1 Old Ranch Rd., tel. 408/626–2510), which has a front nine running along the Carmel River and a back nine reaching well up into the mountains for challenging slopes and spectacular views.

Seven miles inland from Monterey, off Highway 68, is **Laguna Seca Golf Club** (1 York Rd., tel. 408/373–3701), a course with an 18-hole layout designed by Robert Trent Jones, Jr., and open to the public.

Horseback Riding A great way to enjoy the Del Monte Forest, which has more than 34 miles of bridle trails, is by reserving a horse from the **Pebble Beach Equestrian Center** (Portola Rd., tel. 408/624–2756). You can ride on your own or in a group ride scheduled twice daily.

Kayaking Sea kayaking is an increasingly popular sport in Monterey Bay, giving paddlers a chance to come face to face with otters, sea lions, harbor seals, and dolphins. Kayak rentals, basic instruction, and escorted tours are offered by **Monterey Bay Kayaks** (693 Del Monte Ave., Monterey, tel. 408/373–KELP).

Scuba Diving Although the waters are cold, the marine life and kelp beds attract many scuba divers to Monterey Bay. Diving lessons and rental equipment are available at **Aquarius Dive Shops** (2240 Del Monte Ave., Monterey, tel. 408/375–1933 and 32 Cannery Row, Suite #4, tel. 408/375–6605.

Tennis Public courts are available in Monterey and Pacific Grove; information is available through **Monterey Tennis Center** (tel. 408/372–0172) and **Pacific Grove Municipal Courts** (tel. 408/372–5650). Nonmembers are eligible to play on the courts at the **Carmel Valley Inn Swim and Tennis Club** (Carmel Valley Rd. and Los Laureles Grade, Carmel Valley, tel. 408/659–3131).

If tennis is a top vacation priority, you may want to stay at a resort where instruction and facilities are part of the scene. Among the resorts most geared for tennis are the Lodge at Pebble Beach, the Inn at Spanish Bay, Hyatt Regency Monterey, Hilton Resort of Monterey, Quail Lodge, and Carmel Valley Ranch Resort. *See* the Lodging section below for details.

Whale-watching On their annual migration between the Bering Sea and Baja California, 45-foot gray whales can be spotted not far off the Monterey coast. Although they sometimes can be spotted with binoculars from shore, a whale-watching cruise is the best way to see these magnificent mammals up close. The migration south takes place between December and March, while the migration north is from March to June. Late January is considered the prime viewing time, when their numbers in Monterey Bay peak.

Even if no whales are in sight, however, the bay cruises nearly always include some unforgettable marine-life encounter that can range from watching a cluster of sea lions hugging a life buoy to riding the waves alongside a group of 300 leaping porpoises. Whale-watching cruises, which usually last about two hours, are offered by **Monterey Sport Fishing** (96 Fisherman's Wharf, Monterey, tel. 408/372–2203), **Randy's Fishing Trips** (66 Fisherman's Wharf, Monterey, tel. 408/372–7440, and **Sam's Fishing Fleet** (84 Fisherman's Wharf, tel. 408/372–0577).

Spectator Sports

Car Racing Five major races take place each year on the 2.2-mile, 11-turn **Laguna Seca Raceway** (SCRAMP, Box 2078, Monterey 93942, tel. 408/648–5100 or 800/367–9939). They range from Indianapolis 500–style CART races to a historic car race featuring more than 150 restored race cars from earlier eras.

Rodeo One of the oldest and most famous rodeos in the West is the annual **California Rodeo** (Box 1648, Salinas 93902, tel. 408/757–2951) in Salinas, which takes place during a week of festivities starting in mid-July.

Dining

by Bruce David Colen There is no question that the Monterey area is the best and richest place to dine, along the coast, between Los Angeles and San Francisco. The surrounding waters abound with fish, there is wild game in the foothills, and the inland valleys are the vegetable basket of California, while nearby Castroville prides itself on being the Artichoke Capital of the World. The region also takes pride in producing better and better wines. San Francisco's conservative streak extends this far south, when it comes to dress—"casual" means attractive resort wear.

Highly recommended restaurants are indicated by a star ★.

Category	Cost*
Very Expensive	over $50
Expensive	$35–$50

Moderate	$20–$35
Inexpensive	under $20

per person, not including tax, service, or drinks.

Carmel
Expensive

The Covey at Quail Lodge. Continental cuisine is served in an elegant restaurant with a romantic lakeside setting. Specialties include swordfish with avocado in a curried cream sauce, black-currant duck, abalone, and sea scallop mousse. *8205 Valley Greens Dr., tel. 408/624–1581. Jacket and tie required. Reservations advised. AE, DC, MC, V. Dinner only.*

French Poodle. The service is attentive in this intimate dining room with framed maps of French wine regions on the walls. Specialties on the traditional French menu include duck breast in port. *Junipero and 5th Ave., tel. 408/624–8643. Reservations advised. Dress: informal. AE, DC. Dinner only. Closed Sun. and Wed.*

★ **Pacific's Edge.** This restaurant's dramatic views of ancient cypress trees and pounding surf combine with a staff headed by two of the nation's best chefs—Brian Whitmer and chocolatier Bruno Feldeisen—to create the most memorable dining experience along the entire California coast. *Hwy 1, Carmel-by-the-Sea, tel. 408/624–3801. Reservations advised. Jacket required. AE, DC, MC, V.*

Raffaello. A sparkling, elegant rendezvous in one of the loveliest parts of Carmel, the menu offers very good Northern Italian dishes with French overtones. There's excellent pasta, Monterey Bay prawns with garlic butter, local sole poached in champagne, and the specialty of the house, chicken *alla Fiorentina. Mission St., between Ocean and 7th aves., tel. 408/624–1541. Reservations recommended. Jacket and tie required. AE, CB, DC, MC, V. Closed lunch, closed Tues.*

Moderate **Crème Carmel.** This bright and airy small restaurant has a California French menu that changes according to season. Specialties include sea bass stuffed with Dungeness crab and beef tenderloin in cabernet sauce. *San Carlos St., near 7th Ave., tel. 408/624–0444. Reservations advised. MC, V.*

Flaherty's Seafood Grill & Oyster House. This is a bright blue-and-white-tiled fish house that serves bowls of steamed mussels, clams, cioppino, and crab chowder. Seafood pastas and daily fresh fish selections are also available. *6th Ave. and San Carlos St., tel. 408/624–0311. No reservations. MC, V.*

The Gold Fork. Continental cuisine that makes use of fresh local ingredients in such appetizers as calamari puffs and artichoke bisque is served in a charming country-French dining room with a vaulted ceiling. Other specialties include steaks and a weekly game selection. *Ocean Ave. between 3rd Ave. and Dolores St., tel. 408/624–2569. Reservations advised. AE, DC, MC, V. Dinner only. Closed Mon.*

Hog's Breath Inn. Clint Eastwood's place provides a convivial publike atmosphere in which to enjoy no-nonsense meat and seafood entrees with sautéed vegetables. *San Carlos St. and 5th Ave., tel. 408/625–1044. Reservations advised. MC, V.*

Pine Inn. An old favorite with locals, this Victorian-style restaurant with an outdoor gazebo area for lunch offers a traditional American menu, including pork loin, roast duck, and beef Stroganoff. *Ocean Ave. and Monte Verde St., tel. 408/624–3851. Reservations advised. AE, MC, V.*

★ **Rio Grill.** The best bets in this attractive Santa Fe–style setting are meat and seafood (such as fresh tuna) cooked in an oakwood smoker. There's a good California wine list. *Hwy 1 and Rio Rd., tel. 408/625–5436. Reservations advised. MC, V.*

Inexpensive **Friar Tuck's.** This busy wood-paneled coffee shop serves huge omelets and 17 varieties of hamburgers, including one topped with marinated artichoke hearts. *5th Ave. and Dolores St., tel. 408/624–4274. No reservations. No credit cards. No dinners.*

Shabu Shabu. Light meat and seafood dishes, cooked at the table, are the specialties in this country-style Japanese restaurant. *Ocean and 7th aves., tel. 408/625–2828. Reservations advised. AE, MC, V.*

Swedish Restaurant. This quaint cafe with a fireplace and Scandinavian decor features Swedish pancakes, homemade rye bread, and meatballs for breakfast and lunch. *Dolores St. and 7th Ave., tel. 408/624–3723. No reservations. No credit cards.*

Thunderbird Bookstore and Restaurant. The Thunderbird is a very well-stocked bookstore and a good place to enjoy a light lunch or dinner and browse among the books. A hearty beef soup, sandwiches, and cheesecake are the bestsellers. *3600 The Barnyard, Hwy 1 at Carmel Valley Rd., tel. 408/624–1803. MC, V.*

Monterey **Delfino.** The Monterey Plaza Hotel has an elegant dining room
Expensive built over the waterfront on Cannery Row. Fresh seafood, veal medallions, and angel-hair pasta with prawns are among the standouts on the California-Italian menu. *400 Cannery Row, tel. 408/646–1700. Reservations advised. AE, DC, MC, V.*

★ **Fresh Cream.** Ask the area natives where to go for pleasant, light, imaginative California cuisine, and nine out of ten will recommend this charming little restaurant in Heritage Harbor. Be sure to try the squab and quail from nearby farms. *100 Pacific St., tel. 408/375–9798. Reservations recommended. Dress: casual. MC, V. Beer and wine. Closed lunch, closed Mon.*

Neil De Vaughn's. Since 1953 this classic restaurant has occupied a choice waterfront site on Cannery Row. The Continental menu includes mock turtle soup, cheese fondue, sweetbreads, and sole Felipe. *654 Cannery Row, tel. 408/372–2141. Reservations advised. AE, DC, MC, V.*

The Old House. For Old Monterey atmosphere, this location in the historic pink Sanchez adobe is hard to beat. Specialties include duck confit, cassoulet, and game dishes. *500 Hartnell St., tel. 408/373–3737. Reservations advised. AE, MC, V. Dinner only.*

Sardine Factory. The interiors of an old processing plant on Cannery Row have been turned into five separate dining areas, including a glass-enclosed garden room. The decor is from the gaslight era with lots of Gay '90s touches. The menu stresses fresh seafood prepared in an elegant, Italian manner. There's a great wine list. *701 Wave St., tel. 408/373–3775. Reservations recommended. Jacket required. AE, CB, DC, MC, V. Closed lunch.*

★ **Whaling Station Inn.** A pleasing mixture of rough-hewn wood and sparkling white linen makes this both a festive and a comfortable place in which to enjoy some of the best mesquite-grilled fish and meats in town. There are excellent artichoke appetizers and fresh salads. *763 Wave St., tel. 408/373–3778. Reservations advised. AE, DC, MC, V. Dinner only.*

Moderate **Clock Garden.** The wide-ranging eclectic decor includes a collection of antique clocks. There's a Continental menu, with a variety of fresh fish, veal, pork, lamb, and chicken dishes that can be followed by wonderful, rich desserts. *565 Abrego St., tel. 408/375–6100. Reservations advised. AE, MC, V.*

Ferrante's. Gorgeous views of both town and bay are seen from this Northern Italian restaurant at the top of the Sheraton. Pasta and seafood combinations such as spinach fettuccine with clams are especially good. *350 Calle Principal, tel. 408/649–4234. Reservations advised. AE, DC, MC, V.*

★ **The Fishery.** Popular with locals, this restaurant features a mixture of Asian and Continental influences in both food and decor. Specialties include broiled swordfish with saffron butter and fresh Hawaiian tuna with macadamia-nut butter. *21 Soledad Dr., tel. 408/373–6200. MC, V. Dinner only. Closed Sun. and Mon.*

Hammerheads. Located in what was once the town firehouse, the restaurant's main attraction is the Chocoholic Bar laden with all the desserts you can eat. There are five varieties of duck on the dinner menu. *414 Calle Principal, tel. 408/372–3463. Reservations advised. AE, DC, MC, V.*

Mara's Restaurant. Greek and Armenian dishes such as hummos, shish kebab, moussaka, and a chicken and lemon soup called *avgolemono* are featured at this family restaurant. *570 Lighthouse Ave., tel. 408/375–1919. Reservations advised. MC, V. Dinner only.*

Steinbeck Lobster Grotto. Pacific views on three sides highlight this long-established Cannery Row spot known for Maine lobster and local catches. Also good are bouillabaisse, cioppino, and seafood casseroles. *720 Cannery Row, tel. 408/373–1884. Reservations advised. AE, DC, MC, V. Dinner only.*

Surdi's. Meals at this pleasant stucco restaurant start with an impressive antipasto salad bar. Along with traditional pasta dishes, a house specialty is chicken Monterey baked with cream and artichoke hearts. *2030 Fremont St., tel. 408/646–0100. Dress: casual. Reservations advised. AE, DC, MC, V.*

Inexpensive **Abalonetti.** From a squid-lover's point of view, this casual wharfside restaurant is the best place in town. Get it served in a variety of ways: deep-fried, sautéed with wine and garlic, or baked with eggplant. *57 Fisherman's Wharf, tel. 408/375–5941. No reservations. AE.*

Beau Thai. Located across from the Monterey Bay Aquarium, this plant-filled local favorite features such dishes as beef curry with tamarind sauce and spicy noodle dishes. *807 Cannery Row, tel. 408/373–8811. Reservations advised. AE, DC, MC, V.*

Old Monterey Cafe. Breakfast, which can include fresh-baked muffins and eggs Benedict, is served all day here. It's also a good place to relax with a cappuccino or coffee made from freshly ground beans. *489 Alvarado St., tel. 408/646–1021. No reservations. MC, V.*

Sancho Panza. While the basic Mexican dishes may not be extraordinary, the atmospheric setting in this low-ceilinged 1841 Casa Gutierrez adobe along the Path of History definitely is. *590 Calle Principal, tel. 408/375–0095. AE, DC, MC, V.*

Pacific Grove **Gernot's.** The ornate Victorian Hart Mansion is a delightful
Expensive setting in which to dine on seafood and game served with light sauces. California French specialties include pheasant with green peppercorns and roast venison. *649 Lighthouse Ave., tel.*

408/646–1477. Reservations advised. Dress: informal. AE, MC, V. Dinner only. Closed Mon.

★ **Old Bath House.** A romantic, nostalgic mood permeates this dining room in a converted bathhouse overlooking the water at Lovers Point. A seasonal Continental menu stresses local seafood and produce, with salmon and Monterey Bay prawns particularly worth ordering, when available. *620 Ocean View Blvd., tel. 408/375–5195. Reservations advised. Jacket required. AE, DC, MC, V.*

Moderate **Fandango.** With stone walls and country furniture, this restaurant has the earthy feel of a Southern European farmhouse. Complementing it are robust flavors from southern France, Italy, Spain, Greece, and North Africa, with a menu ranging from couscous and paella to canneloni. *223 17th St., tel. 408/373 –0588. Reservations advised. AE, DC, MC, V.*

Inexpensive **Peppers.** This pleasant white-walled cafe offers fresh seafood and traditional dishes from Mexico and Latin America. The red and green salsas are excellent. *170 Forest Ave., tel. 408/373– 6892. Reservations advised. AE, MC, V. Closed Tues.*

The Tinnery. The simple, clean lines of this contemporary dining room are framed by picture-window views of Monterey Bay. The eclectic menu ranges from Japanese teriyaki chicken to Mexican burritos to English fish and chips. *631 Ocean View Blvd., tel. 408/375–5195. Reservations advised. AE, DC, MC, V.*

Pebble Beach **The Bay Club.** This new restaurant decorated in pleasant pas-
Expensive tels overlooks the coastline and golf links at the Inn at Spanish Bay. Continental specialties include truffle ravioli in lobster sauce and veal chop with rosemary butter. *2800 17-Mile Dr., tel. 408/647–7500. Reservations advised. Jacket required. AE, DC, MC, V. Dinner only.*

★ **Club XIX.** Classic French dishes are served in an intimate, cafe-style restaurant at the Lodge at Pebble Beach, with views of Carmel Bay and the 18th green. *17-Mile Dr. and Portola Rd., tel. 408/624–3811. Reservations advised. Jacket required. AE, DC, MC, V.*

Lodging

A recent hotel and resort boom on the Monterey Peninsula has given travelers a far greater choice of accommodations, especially on the most deluxe level, than ever before. The luxury resort scene is particularly flourishing in Carmel Valley and Pebble Beach, where several country clublike spreads have opened recently.

In Monterey, the trend has been toward sophisticated hotels, some with the same range of services and amenities offered by top hotels in San Francisco. Some of the newer hotels are a bit impersonal and clearly designed for conventions, but others pamper the individual traveler in grand style.

While large resorts and hotels have been opening elsewhere on the peninsula, Pacific Grove has quietly turned itself into the bed-and-breakfast capital of the region. Many of the town's landmark Victorian houses, some more than a century old, have been converted to charming inns with brass beds and breakfast buffets laden with cranberry muffins and baked pears.

Rates in the Monterey area are often as high as in a major city, especially during the April–October high season, when even modest motels may charge $100 a night for a double room.

Highly recommended hotels are indicated by a star ★.

Category	Cost*
Very Expensive	over $150
Expensive	$100–$150
Moderate	$60–$100
Inexpensive	under $60

double room, not including tax

Carmel
Very Expensive
★

Highlands Inn. The hotel's unparalleled location on high cliffs above the Pacific just south of Carmel gives it views that stand out even in a region famous for them. Accommodations are in plush condominium-style units with wood-burning fireplaces, ocean view decks, and full kitchens; some have spa tubs. *Hwy 1, Box 1700, 93921, tel. 408/624–3801 or 800/538–9525; 800/682–4811 in CA. 145 rooms. Facilities: pool, whirlpools, restaurant, lounges, entertainment. AE, D, DC, MC, V.*

Tally Ho Inn. This is one of the few inns in Carmel's center that has good views out over the bay. There are suites and penthouse units with fireplaces and a pretty English garden courtyard. Continental breakfast and after-dinner brandy are included. *Monte Verde St. and 6th Ave., tel. 408/624–2232 or 800/624–2290 in CA. 14 rooms. MC, V.*

Tickle Pink Country Inn. Just up the road from the Highlands Inn, this small, secluded inn also features spectacular views. Simple but comfortable accommodations include Continental breakfast. *155 Highland Dr., 93923, tel. 408/624–1244 or 800/635–4774. 34 rooms. AE, MC, V.*

Expensive

Carmel Mission Inn. Located on the edge of Carmel Valley, this attractive modern inn has a lushly landscaped pool and Jacuzzi area and is close to the Barnyard and Crossroads shopping centers. Rooms are large, some with spacious decks. *Hwy 1 and Rio Rd., 3665 Rio Rd., 92923, tel. 408/624–1841 or 800/348–9090. 165 rooms. Facilities: restaurant, bar, pool, Jacuzzi. AE, CB, D, DC, MC, V.*

Carriage House Inn. This attractive small inn with a rustic wood-shingled exterior has rooms with open-beam ceilings, fireplaces, down comforters, and sunken Japanese baths. Continental breakfast, wine and hors d'oeuvres are included. *Junipero Ave. between 7th and 8th aves., Box 1900, 93921, tel. 408/625–2585 or 800/422–4732 in CA. 13 rooms. AE, CB, D, DC, MC, V.*

★ **Cobblestone Inn.** Recent renovations to this former motel have created an English-style inn with stone fireplaces in all the rooms and the sitting room area. Quilts and country antiques, along with a complimentary breakfast buffet and afternoon tea, contribute to the homey touch. *8th and Junipero aves., Box 3185, 93921, tel. 408/625–5222. 24 rooms. AE, MC, V.*

Wayside Inn. Within easy walking distance of shops and restaurants, this attractive brick and wood inn has some units with fireplaces and full kitchens; all come with Continental breakfast and morning paper. *Mission St. and 7th Ave., Box 1900,*

93921, tel. 408/624–5336 or 800/422–4732 in CA. 21 rooms. AE, CB, D, DC, MC, V.

Moderate–Expensive
★
Lobos Lodge. Pleasant pink stucco units in an oak and pine setting on the edge of the business district feature fireplaces and private brick patios. Continental breakfast is included. *Monte Verde St. and Ocean Ave., Box L–1, 93921, tel. 408/624–3874. 30 rooms. AE, MC, V.*

Pine Inn. This traditional favorite with generations of Carmel visitors features Victorian-style decor complete with grandfather clock, flocked wallpaper, and marble-topped furnishings. Located in the heart of the shopping district, the inn has its own brick courtyard of specialty shops. *Ocean Ave. and Lincoln St., Box 250, 93921, tel. 408/624–3851 or 800/228–3851. 49 rooms. Facilities: dining room. AE, CB, DC, MC, V.*

Carmel Valley
Very Expensive
★
Carmel Valley Ranch Resort. This new addition to the resort scene is a stunning mix of contemporary California architecture with such down-home touches as handmade quilts, woodburning fireplaces, and watercolors by local artists. Rooms feature cathedral ceilings, oversize decks, and fully stocked wet bars. *1 Old Ranch Rd., 93923, tel. 408/625–9500 or 800/4CARMEL. 100 rooms. Facilities: restaurant, pool, golf (fee), tennis club and courts, saunas, Jacuzzis. AE, CB, DC, MC, V.*

Quail Lodge. One of the area's most highly regarded resorts is beautifully situated on the grounds of a private country club where guests have access to golf and tennis. There are also 853 acres of wildlife preserve, including 11 lakes, frequented by deer and migratory fowl. The rooms, which are clustered in several low-rise buildings, are spacious and modern, with a mixture of Oriental and European decor. *8205 Valley Greens Dr., Carmel 93923, tel. 408/624–1581 or 800/538–9516; 800/682–9303 in CA. 100 rooms. Facilities: restaurant, 2 pools, 2 lounges, bar, Jacuzzi, putting green, golf (fee), tennis. AE, CB, DC, MC, V.*

Stonepine. The former estate of the Crocker banking family has been converted to an ultradeluxe inn nestled in 330 pastoral acres with riding trails and an equestrian center. The main house, richly paneled and furnished with antiques, offers eight individually decorated suites and a private dining room for guests only. Less formal but still luxurious suites are also available in the ranch-style Paddock House. *150 E. Carmel Valley Rd., Box 1543, 93924, tel. 408/659–2245. 12 rooms. Facilities: dining room, pool, tennis, weight room, archery, mountain bikes, horseback riding. AE, DC, MC, V.*

Moderate–Expensive
Robles Del Rio Lodge. This pine-paneled charmer in a gorgeous setting of rolling meadows and oak forests dates from 1928. Rooms and cottages feature country-style decor with Laura Ashley prints, and the grounds include a large pool and sunbathing area, and hiking trails. *200 Punta Del Monte, 93924, tel. 408/659–3705. 31 rooms. Facilities: restaurant, lounge, pool, tennis, sauna, hot tub. MC, V.*

Valley Lodge. In this small, pleasant inn, there are rooms surrounding a garden patio and separate one- and two-bedroom cottages with fireplaces and full kitchens. Continental breakfast and morning paper are included. *Carmel Valley Rd. at Ford Rd., Box 93, 93924, tel. 408/659–2261 or 800/641–4646 in CA. 31 rooms. Facilities: pool, Jacuzzi, sauna, small fitness center. AE, D, MC, V.*

Monterey
Very Expensive

Doubletree Hotel. Adjacent to the downtown conference center, this hotel is geared more toward convention groups and business travelers than toward vacationers seeking local ambience. Rooms, some with good views of Fisherman's Wharf and the bay, are attractively furnished. Resort amenities include three tennis courts and a round swimming pool with adjoining Jacuzzi. *2 Portola Plaza, 93940, tel. 408/649–4511 or 800/528–0444. 374 rooms. Facilities: 2 restaurants, pool, tennis (fee), garage (fee). AE, CB, D, DC, MC, V.*

Hyatt Regency Monterey. While the rooms and general atmosphere are less glamorous than at some other resorts in the region, the Hyatt does offer excellent golf and tennis facilities, two pools, and a par course jogging track. Continental breakfast is included. *1 Old Golf Course Rd., 93940, tel. 408/372–1234 or 800/824–2196 in CA. 579 rooms. Facilities: restaurant, lounge, entertainment, pools. AE, CB, D, DC, MC, V.*

Monterey Sheraton. This large, convention-oriented hotel sticks out like a pale pink 10-story sore thumb in the middle of Monterey's quaint downtown. Rooms are small, but many have good views of the town and bay. *350 Calle Principal, 93940, tel. 408/649–4234 or 800/325–3535. 338 rooms. Facilities: restaurant, lounge, Jacuzzi, pool, health club, garage. AE, CB, DC, MC, V.*

★ **Spindrift Inn.** This elegant small hotel on Cannery Row boasts the street's only private beach and a rooftop garden overlooking Monterey Bay. Indoor pleasures include spacious rooms with sitting areas, Oriental rugs, fireplaces, canopied beds, down comforters, and other luxuries. Continental breakfast brought to the room on a silver tray and afternoon tea are included. *652 Cannery Row, 93940, tel. 408/646–8900 or 800/225–2901; 800/841–1879 in CA. 41 rooms. AE, CB, DC, MC, V.*

Expensive–Very
Expensive

★ **Hotel Pacific.** Unlike other new hotels in downtown Monterey that clash with the early California architecture and small-town ambience, the Hotel Pacific is an attractive adobe-style addition that fits right in. All rooms are suites, handsomely appointed with four-poster feather beds, hardwood floors, Indian rugs, fireplaces, wet bars, and balconies or patios. Continental breakfast and wine and cheese in the afternoon are included. *300 Pacific St., 93940, tel. 408/373–5700 or 800/225–2903; 800/554–5542 in CA. 104 rooms. AE, CB, D, DC, MC, V.*

Monterey Hotel. Originally opened in 1904, this quaint small downtown hotel reopened in 1987 after an extensive restoration that left its oak paneling and ornate fireplaces gleaming. Standard rooms are small but well-appointed with antiques; master suites offer fireplaces and spa tubs. Complimentary Continental breakfast, afternoon tea, and wine and cheese in the evening are included. *406 Alvarado St., 93940, tel. 408/375–3184 or 800/727–0960. 45 rooms. AE, DC, MC, V.*

★ **Monterey Plaza.** This sophisticated full-service hotel commands a superb waterfront location on Cannery Row, where frolicking otters can be observed from the wide outdoor patio and from many of the room balconies. The architecture and decor, a blend of early California and Oriental styles that retains a little of the old cannery design, harmonizes well with the site. *400 Cannery Row, 93940, tel. 408/646–1700 or 800/631–1339; 800/334–3999 in CA. 290 rooms. Facilities: restaurant, bar, movies, garage (fee). AE, D, DC, MC, V.*

Expensive

Monterey Hotel Resort. The rooms are nondescript but have large private decks, some overlooking the pool area. Resort amenities include tennis courts, saunas, and a large indoor whirlpool. *1000 Aguajito Rd., 93940, tel. 408/373–6141 or 234–5697. 204 rooms. Facilities: restaurant, pool, tennis, sauna, Jacuzzi, putting green. AE, DC, MC, V.*

Victorian Inn. Under the same ownership as the Spindrift Inn, this hotel 2 blocks above Cannery Row has a more casual feel but also offers such in-room comforts as fireplaces, private balconies or patios, and Continental breakfast. Some rooms have ocean views. Wine and cheese are served in the antique-filled lobby during the afternoon. *487 Foam St., 93940, tel. 408/373–8000 or 800/225–2902; 800/232–4141 in CA. 68 rooms. AE, CB, D, DC, MC, V.*

Moderate–Expensive **Best Western Monterey Beach.** This Best Western offers a great waterfront location about 2 miles north of town with panoramic views of the bay and the Monterey skyline. The rooms are nondescript, but the grounds are pleasantly landscaped and feature a large pool with a sunbathing area. *2600 Sand Dunes Dr., 93940, tel. 408/394–3321 or 800/528–1234. 195 rooms. Facilities: restaurant, lounge, pool. AE, CB, D, DC, MC, V.*

Cannery Row Inn. This is a modern small hotel on a street above Cannery Row with bay views from the private balconies of many rooms. Gas fireplaces and complimentary Continental breakfast are among the amenities. *200 Foam St., 93940, tel. 408/649–8580. 32 rooms. Facilities: Jacuzzi, garage. AE, MC, V.*

Otter Inn. This low-rise hotel with a rustic shingle exterior is 2 blocks above Cannery Row and has bay views from most of the rooms. Rooms are spacious, with fireplaces and private hot tubs in some. *571 Wave St., 93940, tel. 408/375–2299. 31 rooms. AE, MC, V.*

Moderate **★ Arbor Inn.** This unusually attractive motel has a friendly, country-inn atmosphere. Continental breakfast is served in a pine-paneled lobby with a tile fireplace. There is an outdoor Jacuzzi, and rooms are light and airy, some with fireplaces and some with accessibility for the handicapped. *1058 Munras Ave., 93940, tel. 408/372–3381 or 800/351–8811 in CA. 56 rooms. Facilities: hot tub. AE, D, DC, MC, V.*

★ Monterey Motor Lodge. A pleasant location on the edge of Monterey's El Estero park gives this motel an edge over its many competitors along Munras Avenue. Indoor plants and a large secluded courtyard with pool are other pluses. Continental breakfast is included. *55 Camino Aguajito, 93940, tel. 408/372–8057 or 800/558–1900. 45 rooms. Facilities: pool, restaurant. AE, CB, D, DC, MC, V.*

Pacific Grove **Centrella Hotel.** A handsome century-old Victorian mansion *Expensive* and garden cottages with clawfoot bathtubs and wicker and brass furnishings house the Centrella Hotel. Depending on the time of day, a sideboard in the large parlor is laden with breakfast treats, cookies and fruit, or hors d'oeuvres. *612 Central Ave., 93950, tel. 408/372–3372; 800/372–3372. 26 rooms, 24 with bath. MC, V.*

★ Gosby House Inn. This lovely yellow Victorian B&B in the town center has 22 individually decorated rooms, almost all with private bath and some with fireplaces. Breakfasts and afternoon hors d'oeuvres are served in a sunny parlor or before the fireplace in the living room. *643 Lighthouse Ave., 93950, tel. 408/375–1287 or 800/527–8828. 22 rooms, 20 with bath. AE, MC, V.*

★ **Green Gables Inn.** Originally built a century ago by a Pasadena judge to house his mistress, this Swiss Gothic B&B retains an air of Victorian romance. Stained-glass windows framing an ornate fireplace and other details compete with the spectacular bay views. The breakfast buffet is tempting, as are afternoon hors d'oeuvres served with wine, sherry, or tea. *104 5th St., 93950, tel. 408/375–2095. 11 rooms, 7 with bath. AE, MC, V.*

Martine Inn. While most B&Bs in Pacific Grove are Victorian houses, this one is a pink stucco Mediterranean-style villa overlooking the water. The rooms, most of which have ocean views, are individually decorated with such unique items as a Chinese wedding bed and a mahogany bedroom set featured at the 1969 World's Fair. Full breakfast, wine, and hors d'oeuvres are included. *255 Oceanview Blvd., 93950, tel. 408/373–3388. 19 rooms. AE, MC, V.*

Moderate– Inexpensive ★ **Asilomar Conference Center.** A pleasant summer camplike atmosphere pervades this assortment of 28 rustic but comfortable lodges in the middle of a 100-acre state park across from the beach. Lodging is on the American plan. Reservations should be made at least a month before arrival. *800 Asilomar Blvd., Box 537, 93950, tel. 408/372–8016. 313 rooms. Facilities: restaurant, pool. No credit cards.*

Pebble Beach *Very Expensive* **The Inn at Spanish Bay.** Under the same management as the Lodge at Pebble Beach, this 270-room resort sprawls on a breathtaking stretch of shoreline along 17-Mile Drive. The resort has a slightly more casual feel, although the 600-square-foot rooms are no less luxurious. The inn is adjacent to its own tennis courts and golf course, but guests also have privileges at all the Lodge facilities. *Box 1418, 2700 17-Mile Dr., 93953, tel. 408/647–7500 or 800/654–9300. 270 rooms. Facilities: 3 restaurants, clubhouse grill, tennis, pool. AE, DC, MC, V.*

★ **The Lodge at Pebble Beach.** A renowned resort since 1916, the Lodge features quietly luxurious rooms with fireplaces and wonderful views. The golf course, tennis club, and equestrian center are also highly regarded. Guests of the lodge have privileges at the Inn at Spanish Bay. *17 Mile Dr., Box 1418, Pebble Beach, 93953, tel. 408/624–3811 or 800/654–9300. 161 rooms. Facilities: 3 restaurants, coffee shop, lounge, pool, sauna, beach, golf (fee), tennis (fee), riding (fee), weights, massage. AE, DC, MC, V.*

The Arts and Nightlife

The area's top venue for the performing arts is the **Sunset Community Cultural Center** (San Carlos, between 8th and 10th aves., tel. 408/624–3996) in Carmel, which presents music and dance concerts, film screenings, and headline performers throughout the year. Facilities include the cathedral-domed Sunset Theater and the Forest Theater, the first open-air amphitheater built in California.

The Arts *Special Events* Performing arts festivals have a long tradition in the Monterey area, with the most famous drawing thousands of spectators. Ordering tickets as far in advance as possible is often essential. The oldest performing arts festival on the peninsula is the **Carmel Bach Festival** (Box 575, Carmel, 93921, tel. 408/624–1521), which has presented the work of Johann Sebastian Bach and his contemporaries in concerts and recitals for more than 50 years. The highlight of the three-week event, starting in mid-July, is a candlelit concert held in the chapel of the Carmel Mission Basilica.

Nearly as venerable is the celebrated **Monterey Jazz Festival** (Box JAZZ, Monterey, 93942, tel. 408/373–3366), which attracts jazz and blues greats from around the world to the Monterey Fairgrounds for a weekend of music each September.

Another popular jazz event is **Dixieland Monterey** (177 Webster St., Suite A-206, Monterey, 93940, tel. 408/443–5260), held on the first weekend of March, which features Dixieland bands performing in cabarets, restaurants, and lounges throughout Monterey, as well as a Saturday morning jazz parade downtown.

For blues fans, there is the **Monterey Bay Blues Festival** (tel. 408/394–2652), which is held in June at the Monterey Fairgrounds, featuring entertainment and soul food.

The Custom House Plaza in downtown Monterey is the setting for free outdoor performances during the **Monterey Bay Theatrefest** (tel. 408/649–6852), which is held on weekend afternoons and evenings during most of the summer.

Concerts One of the nation's most highly regarded metropolitan symphonies, the **Monterey County Symphony** (Box 3965, Carmel, 93921, tel. 408/624–8511), performs a series of concerts throughout the year in Monterey, Salinas, and Carmel. Programs range from classical to pop and often include guest artists.

The **Chamber Music Society of the Monterey Peninsula** (Box 6283, Carmel 93921, tel. 408/625–2212) presents a series of concerts featuring guest artists such as the Juilliard String Quartet and the New York Philomusica. Dance, classical music, and operatic concerts are sponsored by the **Salinas Concert Association** (318 Catharine St., Salinas, tel. 408/758–5027), which presents a series of featured artists between April and October at the Sherwood Hall in Salinas.

Film The **Monterey Institute of Foreign Study** (440 Van Buren St., Monterey, tel. 408/626–1730) sponsors regular screenings of notable foreign films. Classic films are also shown on Thursdays in the community room of the **Monterey Public Library** (625 Pacific St., Monterey, tel. 408/646–3930).

Theater **California's First Theater** (Scott and Pacific sts., tel. 408/375–4916) is home to the Troupers of the Gold Coast, who perform 19th-century melodramas year round in the state's oldest operating little theater, a historic landmark dating from 1846 on Monterey's Path of History.

Specializing in contemporary works, both comedy and drama, is the **GroveMont Theater,** a repertory company performing at the GroveMont Arts Center (320 Hoffman Ave., Monterey, tel. 408/649–6852) that has won considerable acclaim. Also part of the GroveMont Center is the **Poetic Drama Institute,** which often features solo dramatic performances and poetry readings.

American musicals, both old and new, are the focus of the **New Wharf Theater** (Fisherman's Wharf, Monterey, tel. 408/649–2332), where a local cast is often joined by Broadway actors, directors, and choreographers.

Nightlife   **Kalisa's** (851 Cannery Row, Monterey, tel. 408/372–8512). This
Cabaret   long-established, freewheeling cafe in a Cannery Row landmark building offers a potpourri of entertainment that can
include belly dancing, flamenco, jazz, folk dancing, and magic.

Bars and   **Boiler Room** (625 Cannery Row, Monterey, tel. 408/373–1449).
Nightclubs   Most nights feature comedy shows, followed by dancing to live
rock music. There is occasional country and western dancing
and entertainment.

The Club (Alvarado and Del Monte sts., Monterey, tel. 408/646
–9244). This popular night spot has dancing to Top-40 music
nightly, plus changing entertainment that includes rock bands,
comedy, and male striptease.

Doc Ricketts' Lab (95 Prescott, Monterey, tel. 408/649–4241).
Live rock bands perform nightly 1 block above Cannery Row.

Doubletree Hotel (2 Portola Plaza, Monterey, tel. 408/649–
4511). Popular music entertainment is offered nightly except
Sundays in the Brasstree Lounge.

Highlands Inn (Hwy. 1, Carmel, tel. 408/624–3801). There is piano music nightly in the Lobos Lounge; dancing on weekends in
the Fireside Lounge.

Hyatt Regency (1 Old Golf Course Rd., Monterey, tel. 408/372–
1234, ext. 59). Dancing and live music are on tap in the Whis-
pers Lounge from Monday through Saturday.

Lodge at Pebble Beach (17-Mile Dr., Pebble Beach, tel. 408/624
–3811). You'll find easy listening entertainment in the Cypress
Room and Terrace Lounge; there's a jazz band on Friday and
Saturday evenings.

Mark Thomas Outrigger (700 Cannery Row, Monterey, tel. 408/
372–8543). Top-40 dance music is played by live bands on Friday and Saturday night.

Monterey Hotel Resort (1000 Aguajito Rd., Monterey, tel. 408/
373–6141). You can dance to live popular music on weekends in
the Rendez Vous Lounge.

Monterey Plaza Hotel (400 Cannery Row, Monterey, tel. 408/
646–1700). Piano music and a guitarist are to be heard in a romantic setting overlooking the bay in the Delfino Lounge.

Monterey Sheraton (350 Calle Principal, Monterey, tel. 408/649
–4234). Live jazz is offered nightly in the Monterey Bay Club.

Sly McFlys (700 Cannery Row, Monterey, tel. 408/649–8050).
This popular local watering hole has a pub atmosphere.

Discos   **Brick House.** (220 N. Fremont St., Monterey, tel. 408/375–
6116). There is dancing to Top-40 music with a DJ and big-
screen video.

Safari Club (1425 Munras Ave., Monterey, tel. 408/649–1020).
Again, dancing to Top-40 music with local DJ at the Ramada
Inn. Open Friday and Saturday noon to 2 AM.

11 The Central Coast

Introduction

The stretch of coastline between Carmel and Santa Barbara, a distance of about 250 miles, is some of the most breathtaking in California. Around Big Sur, the Santa Lucia Mountains drop down to the Pacific with dizzying grandeur. The area is sparsely populated, dotted with small towns, grazing cattle, and hillsides of wildflowers. Its inhabitants relish their isolation among the redwoods at the sharp edge of land and sea.

Traditionally, Big Sur has attracted individualists—the novelist Henry Miller comes to mind—drawn by the intractability of the terrain. Farther south, the junction of land and sea is less precipitous, there are more sandy beaches and fewer cliffs, and the facilities for tourists are better developed. The main attraction here, Hearst Castle on Enchanted Hill, was built by another famous individualist of a more gregarious bent, William Randolph Hearst.

The rolling hills in the southern part of the region support a number of wineries whose standing is rising steadily. Solvang is a popular stopover for hearty fare on the route north or south, and the artists' colony and resort town of Ojai is half an hour north of Santa Barbara. From Solvang, it is an hour's drive south to Santa Barbara, the first glimpse of the sand, surf and sun of Southern California.

The traditions of Spanish California, of unhurried hospitality and easy living, are kept alive here: Santa Barbara works hard to maintain its relaxed atmosphere and cozy scale, 90 miles from the metropolitan sprawl of Los Angeles. Wedged as it is between the Pacific and the Santa Ynez Mountains, the city never had much room for expansion. The mountains to the north protect its sunny climate, and the emphasis is on the outdoors. The focus of the town is the waterfront, with its Mediterranean feeling, its beaches, pier, and harbor. The downtown area, which retains much of its Spanish architectural heritage, is geared to the city's principal trade: tourism. Up in the hills, in Montecito and Hope Ranch, lie the expensive ranch homes of celebrities.

Highway 1, which runs through most of this region, was the first in the country to be declared a scenic highway, in 1966. Barring fog or rain, the coast is almost always in view from the road. In some sections, the waves break on rocks 11,200 feet below; in others, the highway is just 20 feet above the surf. The two-lane road is good, but it twists, and traffic, especially in the summer months, can be very slow. Allow plenty of time and sit back and enjoy the scenery.

Getting Around

By Plane American and American Eagle (tel. 800/433–7300), Sky West/Delta (tel. 800/453–9417), and United and United Express (tel. 800/241–6522) fly into **Santa Barbara Municipal Airport** (tel. 805/967–5608), 8 miles from downtown on Marxmiller Road.

Santa Barbara Airbus (tel. 805/964–7374) runs to and from the airport and shuttles travelers between Santa Barbara and Los Angeles Airport. **Aero Airport Limousine** (tel. 805/965–2412) serves Los Angeles Airport. **Metropolitan Transit District** (tel.

805/963–3364) bus #11 runs from the airport to the downtown transit center.

By Car The only way to see the most dramatic section of the central coast, the 70 miles between Big Sur and San Simeon, is by car. By heading south on Highway 1, you'll be on the ocean side of the road and get the best views. Don't expect to rush. The road is narrow and twisting with a single lane in each direction, making it difficult to pass slower traffic or the many lumbering RVs that favor the route. In fog or rain, the drive can be nerve-wracking. U.S. 101 from San Francisco to San Luis Obispo is the quicker, easier alternative, but it misses the coast entirely. U.S. 101 and Hwy. 1 join north of Santa Barbara. Both, eventually dividing, continue south through southern California.

By Bus Major bus lines avoid Hwy. 1, preferring the speedier inland routes. There is, however, local service in several towns. From Monterey and Carmel, the public transit service (tel. 408/899–2555) operates daily bus runs to Big Sur April–September. From San Luis Obispo, **North Coastal Transit** (tel. 805/541–BUSS) runs buses around the town and out to the coast on regular schedules. Local service is also provided by the Santa Barbara Metropolitan Transit District (tel. 805/963–3364).

By Train Amtrak (tel. 800/USA-RAIL) runs the *Coast Starlight* train along the coast from Santa Barbara to San Luis Obispo, but there it heads inland for the rest of the route to the San Francisco Bay Area and Seattle. Local numbers are, in Santa Barbara, tel. 805/687–6848; in San Luis Obispo, tel. 805/541–5028.

Guided Tours

California Parlour Car Tours (Cathedral Hill Hotel, 1101 Van Ness Ave., San Francisco 94109, tel. 415/474–7500 or 800/227–4250) offers a number of tours that include the central coast area. Lasting three to eleven days, these are one-way trips from San Francisco to Los Angeles (or vice versa) that travel along the coast in 36-passenger buses, visit Hearst Castle, Santa Barbara, and Monterey and may also include time in Yosemite or Lake Tahoe. There are certainly advantages to such organized touring, especially in a region where driving is so demanding, but there are also disadvantages. (We recommend that you steer clear of any tour that takes you to Yosemite for less than one full day; readers have been disappointed in the past. Save Yosemite for a trip when you have enough time.)

Santa Barbara Trolley Co. (tel. 805/565–1122) has five daily, regularly scheduled runs in Santa Barbara. Motorized San Francisco-style cable cars deliver visitors to major hotels, shopping areas, and attractions. Stop or not as you wish and pick up another trolley when ready to move on. All depart and return to Stearns Wharf. *Fare: $3 adults, $2 children.*

Historic walking tour (tel. 805/967–9869). A longtime Santa Barbara resident takes small groups on walking tours of gardens and historic buildings. Mornings and afternoon tours begin at the courthouse lobby.

Important Addresses and Numbers

Tourist Information An excellent selection of free pamphlets on accommodations, dining, sports, and entertainment is available at the **Visitors**

Information Center (1 Santa Barbara St. at Cabrillo Blvd., tel. 805/965–3021. Open Mon.–Sat. 9–5, Sun. 10–4). Before arriving, contact **Santa Barbara Conference and Visitors Bureau** (222 E. Anapamu St., 93101, tel. 805/966–9222).

Information on other towns along the central coast is available from:

Big Sur Chamber of Commerce (Box 87, 93920, tel. 408/667–2100).
San Luis Obispo Chamber of Commerce (1039 Chorro St., 93401, tel. 805/543–1323).
Cambria Chamber of Commerce (767 Main St., 93428, tel. 805/927–3624).
San Simeon Chamber of Commerce (Box 1, 9190 Hearst, 93452, tel. 805/927–3500).
Solvang Visitors Bureau (1571 Mission Dr., 93463, tel. 805/688–6144).
California Dept. of Parks and Recreation (in Big Sur, tel. 408/667–2315.)

Emergencies Dial 911 for **police** and **ambulance** in an emergency.

Doctor Emergency care is available at **St. Francis Hospital** (601 E. Micheltorena St., Santa Barbara, tel. 805/568–5711 or 962–7661).

Road Conditions Dial 408/757–2006 for information.

Exploring

You can drive up to Santa Barbara from Los Angeles in a few hours. If you fly into town, a car is not absolutely necessary. Exploring all of California's central coast is a rewarding and memorable experience, providing you have a car and plenty of patience. For the 90 miles from Big Sur to Morro Bay, plan for three to four hours on the road. Along this stretch there are 300 turnouts offering ample opportunity to gaze out on the always changing coastline. From mid-December through January, look for migrating gray whales. In the spring, California's vibrant orange native poppy is common along the drive.

Once you start south from Carmel, there is no route off the coast until all the way to Cambria where Highway 46 connects with U.S. 101 inland. Nearly everything you want to see is right along the coastal highway, including the state parks and beaches in the Big Sur region and Hearst Castle in San Simeon. For the attractive shops and restaurants of Cambria, a short loop off of Highway 1 runs through the town's twin villages and connects again back on Highway 1 a few miles later. At Morro Bay, Highway 1 makes its move inland for 13 miles, where it connects with U.S. 101 at San Luis Obispo. From there south, in place of the dramatic coastal scenery, you are rewarded with the driving ease of U.S. 101. This passes the crowded but lively town of Pismo Beach and then travels gently rolling hills for 70 miles to the turnoff for the short drive to Solvang.

The entire 210 miles from Big Sur to Santa Barbara *can* be tackled in a long day, but that won't leave time to enjoy the drive or stop at Hearst Castle or anywhere in between. A better choice is to plan on several days, with time to explore Hearst Castle, Santa Barbara, and (if it's to your taste) Solvang. The time spent along the Big Sur coast will vary wide-

ly depending on your desire to hike or explore rocky beaches;
you'll want to stop and appreciate the view, anyway.

South along Highway 1

*Numbers in the margin correspond with points of interest on
the Central Coast map.*

If you start your coastal trip from the north, you'll be quickly
treated to the quintessential view of California's coast, the elegant concrete arch of **Bixby Creek Bridge.** Just 13 miles south of
Carmel, this view is every photographer's dream. There is a
small parking area on the north side from which to take a photo
or to start a walk across the 550-foot span.

Five miles south and you'll see the **Point Sur Light Station** atop
a sandstone cliff. The century-old beacon is open to the public
on ranger-led tours on Sunday mornings at 9:30. Call the Big
Sur State Park District (tel. 408/667–2315) for tour times.

The small developed area of the Big Sur valley begins a few
miles south. Pfeiffer Big Sur State Park, gas, groceries, hotels,
and restaurants are all clustered along the highway within the
next 7 miles.

One of the few places where you may actually set foot on the
coastline you have been viewing from the road is at **Pfeiffer
Beach.** The road to the beach is immediately past the Big Sur
Ranger Station; follow it for 2 miles. The picturesque beach is
at the foot of the cliffs, and a hole in one of the big sea-washed
rocks lets you watch the waves break first on the sea side and
then again on the beach side. The water is too cold and the surf
too dangerous for swimming much of the year, however.

On the ocean side of Highway 1, a towering 800 feet above the
water, is **Nepenthe,** a favorite hangout with tourists and locals.
The restaurant's deck can be an excellent place to take a break
from a rather stressful if very beautiful drive. Rita Hayworth
and Orson Welles spent their honeymoon here. Downstairs is a
craft and gift shop, displaying among other items the work of
Kaffe Fassett. The famous knitting designer grew up at Nepenthe.

A few miles south is **Julia Pfeiffer Burns State Park** (tel. 408/
667–2315), where a short and popular hike is a nice way to
stretch your legs. The trail leads up a small valley to a waterfall. You can go back the same (easier) way or take a loop that
leads you along the valley wall, with views out into the tops of
the redwood trees you were just walking among. There are picnic and camping areas as well as access to the beach.

For the next dozen miles, it is just you, the road, and the coast.
At Lucia there is a gas station and the beginnings of civilization
again. Among the many picnic areas and campgrounds along
the way from here to San Simeon is **Jade Cove,** one of the best
known areas on the coast in which to hunt for jade. Rock hunting is allowed on the beach, but you may not remove anything
from the walls of the cliffs.

It is 30 miles up to the Enchanted Hill, where the **Hearst San
Simeon State Historical Monument,** one of California's most
popular sites for visitors, perches in solitary splendor. You may
resent being herded into buses at the bottom of the hill, but
that indignity is amply rewarded by the neoclassical extrava-

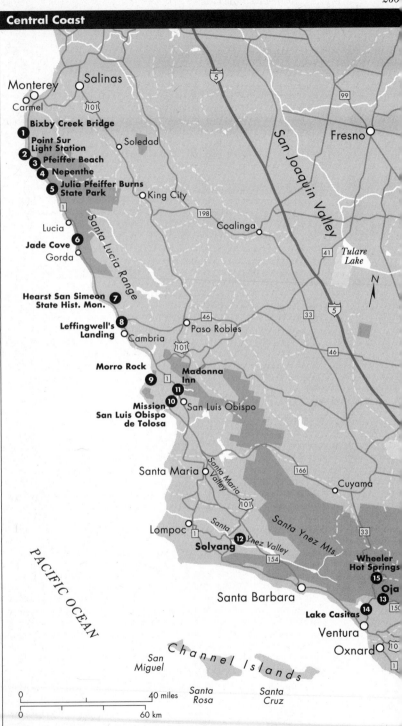

Central Coast

Monterey
Carmel
Salinas

Bixby Creek Bridge ❶

Point Sur
Light Station ❷
Pfeiffer Beach ❸
Nepenthe ❹
Julia Pfeiffer Burns ❺
State Park

Soledad

King City

Lucia
Jade Cove ❻
Gorda

Santa Lucia Range

Coalinga

Fresno

San Joaquin Valley

Tulare
Lake

N

Hearst San Simeon ❼
State Hist. Mon.

Leffingwell's ❽
Landing
Cambria

Paso Robles

Morro Rock
❾
Madonna
Inn
❶❶
❶❿
Mission
San Luis Obispo
de Tolosa

San Luis Obispo

Santa Maria

Santa Maria
Valley

Cuyama

Lompoc

Santa
Ynez Valley
Solvang ❶❷

Santa Ynez Mts.

Wheeler
Hot Springs
❶❺
Ojai
❶❸
Lake Casitas ❶❹

Santa Barbara

Ventura

Oxnard

PACIFIC OCEAN

San
Miguel

Channel Islands

Santa
Rosa

Santa
Cruz

0   40 miles

0   60 km

gance of the millionaire's mansion at the top, with its marble halls and reflecting pools. On the way up, you may catch a glimpse of a zebra, one of the last descendants of William Randolph Hearst's magnificent private zoo.

The newspaper magnate commissioned the celebrated architect Julia Morgan to design his grandiose residence, and work began on it in 1919. Built to house his extensive entourage, not to mention houseguests from Hollywood, it was also intended as a showcase for his impressive collection of art, gathered from around the world. It was completed in 1947.

A new visitors' center offers an introduction to the life of this master of the yellow press and inspiration for Orson Welles's film _Citizen Kane_. Admission is free, but tours of the estate generally require advance reservations (tickets can be bought at the grounds, but tours fill up quickly). There is a choice of four tours, each about two hours long, and covering a considerable distance on foot. _Reservations are usually required: tel. 619/452–1950 or 800/444–7275; sometimes it is possible to gain admission directly. Tours daily 8:20 AM–3 PM (later in summer). Admission: $10 adults, $5 children 6–12. Closed Thanksgiving, Christmas, and New Year's Day. Reservations may be made up to 8 weeks in advance._

Cambria, an artists' colony full of turn-of-the-century homes, is located a few minutes south of San Simeon. Moonstone Beach Drive, which runs along the coast, is lined with motels, and **❽ Leffingwell's Landing,** a state picnic ground at its northern end, is a good place for tide-pooling and watching otters. The woodsy part of town, which boasts several fine restaurants, is divided into the newer West Village and the original East Village, each with its own shops and galleries, and many reminders of the Welsh miners who settled here in the 1890s.

You'll come to the end of the coastal ribbon of Highway 1 at Morro Bay, separated from the ocean by a 4½-mile sandspit and the causeway built in the 1930s out to the huge monolith of **❾ Morro Rock.** You can make the quick drive out to the rock (an extinct volcano), with the sheltered harbor (home of a large fishing fleet) on one side and the crash of waves on the other. Morro Rock is a wildlife preserve to protect nesting areas of endangered peregrine falcons. The town center includes a huge chess board with human-size pieces.

San Luis Obispo, halfway between San Francisco and Los Angeles, is home to two notable institutions: California Polytechnic State University, known as Cal Poly, and the wonderfully garish Madonna Inn. A list of self-guided historic walks through the treelined downtown is available from the **❿** Chamber of Commerce. Among the places to see is the **Mission San Luis Obispo de Tolosa** (805/543–6850) at the heart of the downtown. The Ah Louis Store, 800 Palm Street, was established in 1884 to serve the Chinese laborers building the Pacific Coast and Southern Pacific railroads, and it still operates. If you happen to be in town on Thursday night, don't miss the weekly farmers' market and street fair along Higuera Street.

⓫ Even if you don't stay at the **Madonna Inn,** drop by the cafe and shops for a taste of the gilt cherubs, pink bar stools, pink trash cans, pink lampposts, and all the other assorted froufrou that has made the place famous. You'll notice something is up at the "Flintstone"-like gas station made entirely of big boulders. Begun in 1958 by Alex Madonna, a local highway contractor, and his wife, Phyllis, today each of the more than 100 rooms has its own theme. The cave rooms, complete with waterfalls for showers, are among the most popular. *100 Madonna Rd. (take the Madonna Rd. exit from U.S. 101), tel. 805/543-3000.*

Avila Beach, a usually quiet beach town a short detour off Highway 1/U.S. 101, comes alive on weekends when Cal Poly students take over. A bit farther down the highway, 20 miles of wide sandy beaches begin at the town of Pismo Beach, where U.S. 101 and Highway 1 go their separate ways. The action at this busy community centers on the shops and arcades near the pier.

Leave the beach scene behind and head inland to a taste of Denmark in the town of **Solvang,** about an hour's drive south of U.S. 101 to the turnoff of Highway 246 at Buellton and then less than 5 miles east. There is no question when you've reached Solvang: Suddenly the architecture turns to half-timbered buildings, windmills, and flags galore. Clearly aimed to appeal to tourists, there is nonetheless a genuine Danish heritage here and more than two-thirds of the town is of Danish descent. The more than 200 shops selling Danish goods and an array of knickknacks and gift items are all within walking distance, many along Copenhagen Drive and Alisal Road. Stop by the narrow and jammed coffee shop attached to Birkholm's Bakery, Alisal Road, to try the Danish pastry. It is one of a half dozen aroma-filled bakeries in town.

Everything but the palm trees outside the Bethania Lutheran Church, Atterdag Road at Laurel Avenue, is traditional; the Danish services are open to the public.

From Buellton, U.S. 101 heads back to the coast, where it joins Highway 1 again and runs east to Santa Barbara, about 3 miles away.

A half-hour drive east of Santa Barbara over the narrow and winding Highway 150 will put you in **Ojai,** a surprisingly rural town whose surroundings are reminiscent of earlier days in California. You'll see acres of ripening orange and avocado groves. Moviemaker Frank Capra used the Ojai Valley as backdrop for his 1936 classic, *Lost Horizon.* Be aware that the valley can sizzle in the summer when temperatures reach 90 degrees.

The works of talented local artists can be seen in the Spanish-style shopping arcade along the main street. Each Sunday they display their paintings and crafts at the outdoor exhibition in the Security Bank parking lot (205 W. Ojai Ave.). The Art Center (113 S. Montgomery, tel. 805/646-0117) features art exhibits, theater, and dance.

A stroll around town should include a stop at Bart's Books (30? W. Matilija, tel. 805/646-3755), an outdoor store sheltered by native oaks and overflowing with used books. *Open Tues.–Sun. 10–5:30.*

Nearby **Lake Casitas** on Highway 150 offers boating, fishing, and camping. It was the venue for the 1984 Olympic rowing events.

A special draw for Ojai is a hot spring that makes use of natural mineral water in the hills nearby. The spa at **Wheeler Ho**

Springs emerges like an oasis 7 miles from town on Highway 33. Its tall palms and herb gardens are fed by an adjacent stream, and natural mineral waters fill the four redwood hot tubs and a large pool at the well-kept spa. Massage is also available. A restaurant on site offers dinner Thursday through Sunday and weekend brunch. *16825 Maricopa Hwy, tel. 805/646-8131. Open Mon. and Wed.–Fri. 10–9, Sat. 9 AM–10 PM, Sun 9–9. Reservations advised at least a week in advance, especially for spa.*

Santa Barbara

Numbers in the margin correspond with points of interest on the Santa Barbara map.

Santa Barbara's attractions begin with the ocean, with most everything along Cabrillo Boulevard. In the few miles between the beaches and the hills, you pass the downtown and then reach the old mission and, a little higher up, the botanic gardens. A few miles farther up the coast, but still very much in Santa Barbara, is the exclusive residential district of Hope Ranch. To the east is the district called Montecito, where Charlie Chaplin built the Montecito Inn to house visiting guests during the days he was making movies in Santa Barbara before moving to Hollywood. Montecito is also where the exclusive San Ysidro Ranch is located.

Because the town is on a jog in the coastline, it faces south, making directions confusing. Up the coast is west, and down toward Los Angeles is east. The mountains are north.

Everything is so close, the 8-mile drive to the airport seems like a long trip. A car is handy, but not essential. The beaches and downtown are easily explored by bicycle or on foot. The Santa Barbara Trolley takes visitors to most of the major hotels and sights, which can also be reached on the local buses.

The Visitors Information Center publishes a free guide to a scenic drive that circles the town with a detour into the downtown. It passes the harbor, beaches, Hope Ranch, and the old mission, offers fine views on the way to Montecito, and returns to the beaches. You can pick up the drive, marked with blue "Scenic Drive" signs, anywhere along the loop. A free guide to the downtown, the "Red Tile Walking Tour," is also available free from the tourist office. It hits historical spots in a 12-block area.

The town of Goleta, the home of the University of California at Santa Barbara, is located a few miles up the coast via U.S. 101.

❶ If you decide to start at the Pacific and move inland, then one of the first spots to visit is **Stearns Wharf** on Cabrillo Boulevard at the foot of State Street. You can drive out and park on the pier, then wander through the shops or stop for a meal at the wharf's restaurants or snack bar. First built in 1872, then rebuilt in 1981 after a fire, the wharf extends 3 blocks into the Pacific. It is a fine place to look back on the city for a sense of its size and general layout.

❷ The nearby **Santa Barbara Yacht Harbor** is sheltered by an artificial breakwater at the west end of Cabrillo Boulevard. You can take a ½-mile paved walk along the breakwater, check out the tackle and bait shops, or hire a boat from here.

264

Santa Barbara

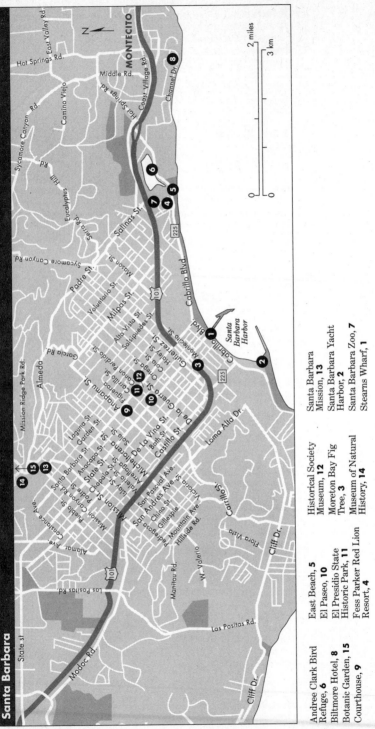

N

MONTECITO

Santa Barbara Harbor

2 miles
3 km

Andree Clark Bird
Refuge, **6**

Biltmore Hotel, **8**

Botanic Garden, **15**

Courthouse, **9**

East Beach, **5**

El Paseo, **10**

El Presidio State
Historic Park, **11**

Fess Parker Red Lion
Resort, **4**

Historical Society
Museum, **12**

Moreton Bay Fig
Tree, **3**

Museum of Natural
History, **14**

Santa Barbara
Mission, **13**

Santa Barbara Yacht
Harbor, **2**

Santa Barbara Zoo, **7**

Stearns Wharf, **1**

3 Planted in 1877, the **Moreton Bay Fig Tree,** at Chapala Street and Highway 101, is so huge it reportedly can provide shade for 10,000 people. In recent years the tree has become a gathering place for an increasing number of homeless people.

Back along Cabrillo, sandy beaches stretch for miles. The sprawling reddish Spanish-style hotel across from the beach is
4 the **Fess Parker Red Lion Resort.** Parker, the actor who played Davy Crockett and Daniel Boone, owned the oceanfront acreage and spent years trying to convince city fathers to allow him to develop a hotel. He finally did, and the hotel opened in 1987 as the largest in Santa Barbara.

5 Just beyond the hotel is the area's most popular beach, **East**
6 **Beach,** at the east end of Cabrillo. Nearby is the **Andree Clark Bird Refuge,** a peaceful lagoon and gardens. *1400 E. Cabrillo Blvd. Admission free.*

7 Adjoining the lagoon is the **Santa Barbara Zoo,** a small lushly landscaped home to big-game cats, elephants and exotic birds. *500 Ninos Dr., tel. 805/962–6310. Admission: $4 adults, $2 senior citizens and children 2–13. Open daily in winter 10–5; daily in summer 9–6.*

Where Cabrillo Boulevard ends at the lagoon, Channel Drive
8 picks up and, a short distance east, passes the **Biltmore Hotel,** now owned by the Four Seasons chain. For more than 60 years, the rich have come here to indulge in quiet elegance.

To reach the downtown area, return to Cabrillo and head inland
9 along State Street. **The Courthouse,** in the center of downtown, has all the grandeur of a Moorish palace. In fact, as you wander the halls, admiring the brilliant hand-painted tiles and spiral staircase, you forget you are in a public courthouse until a handcuffed group of juvenile offenders marches through. This magnificent building was completed in 1929 at the height of the city's cultural reawakening. An elevator to the tower takes visitors to a panoramic view of the city and a fine place to take photos. The second-floor supervisors' ceremonial chambers contains murals painted by the artist who did backdrops for Cecil B. DeMille's silent films. *1100 block of Anacapa St., tel. 805/962–6464. Open weekdays 8–5, weekends 9–5. Free 1-hour guided tours Tues.–Sat. 2 PM.*

10 Walking south you'll pass **El Paseo,** a shopping arcade built around an old adobe home. There are several such arcades in this area and many small art galleries. A few blocks north is the
11 **El Presidio State Historic Park.** Built in 1782, the presidio was one of four military strongholds established by the Spanish along the coast of California. The guardhouse, El Cuartel, is one of the two original adobe buildings that remain of the complex and is the oldest building owned by the state. *123 E. Cañon Perdido St., tel. 805/966–9719. Admission free. Open daily 10:30–4:30.*

12 A block away is the **Historical Society Museum,** with an array of items from the town's past, including a silver-clad riding saddle and a collection of fancy ladies' fans. *136 E. De la Guerra St., tel. 805/966–1601. Admission free. Open Tues.–Sat. 10–5, Sun. noon–5.*

A short distance from downtown (take State St. north and
13 make a right on Los Olivos) at the base of the hills is the **Santa Barbara Mission,** the gem of the chain of 21 missions estab-

lished in California by Spanish missionaries in the late 1700s.
One of the best preserved of the missions, it still functions as a
Catholic church. *Laguna St. Admission: adults $1, children
under 16 free. Open daily 9–5.*

⑭
⑮ Continuing north a block you pass the **Museum of Natural
History,** 2559 Puesta del Sol, and then the **Botanic Garden,** 1 ½
miles north of the mission. The 60 acres of native plants are particularly beautiful in the spring. *1212 Mission Canyon Rd., tel.
805/682–4713. Admission $3 adults. Open daily 8:30 AM–
sunset. Guided tours Thurs., Sat., Sun. 10:30 AM and Sun. 2
PM.*

What to See and Do with Children

Santa Barbara Zoo. Youngsters particularly enjoy the scenic
railroad and barnyard petting zoo (*see* Exploring, above).

Beach playground. For children who tire of the beach quickly,
there is an elaborate jungle gym play area at Santa Barbara's
East Beach, next to the Cabrillo Bath House.

Whale bones. Outside the Museum of Natural History in Santa
Barbara is the skeleton of a blue whale, the world's largest
creature. Kids are dwarfed by the bones and invited to touch
them (they just can't climb on them) (*see* Exploring, above).

Off the Beaten Track

Channel Islands Hearty travelers will be rewarded with a day visit or overnight
camping trip to one of the five Channel Islands that often ap-
pear in a haze off the Santa Barbara horizon. The closest of the
islands and the most often visited is Anacapa Island, 11 miles
off the coast. The islands' remoteness protected them, providing a nature enthusiast's paradise—both underwater and on
land. In 1980 the islands became the nation's 40th national
park, and the water a mile around each is protected as a marine
sanctuary.

On a good day, you'll view seals, sea lions, and an array of bird
life. From December through March, migrating whales can be
seen close up. On land, tide pools alive with sea life are often
accessible. Underwater, divers view fish, giant squid, and coral. Off Anacapa Island, scuba divers can see the remains of a
steamship that sank in 1853. Frenchy's Cove on the west end of
the island has a swimming beach and fine snorkeling.

A visit to the islands can be a rugged trip, often in rough waters. You can charter a boat and head out on your own, if you
wish, but most visitors make the 40-minute drive south to the
Ventura Harbor. There, a park-district concessionaire carries
small groups to the islands for day hikes, barbecues, and primitive overnight camping.

Boat trips. *Island Packers* provide day trips to the islands and
overnight camping to three of them. Boats link up with National Park naturalists for hikes and nature programs. A limited
number of visitors is allowed on each island and unpredictable
weather can limit island landings. *Reservations are essential in
the summer. 1867 Spinnaker Dr., Ventura 93001, tel. 805/642–
7688.*

Wineries Centered around the Solvang area is a California wine-making region with much of the variety but none of the glitz of the famed Napa Valley in Northern California. Most of the region's 22 wineries are located in the rolling hills in either the Santa Maria or Santa Ynez valleys. A leisurely tour of the entire area can easily take all day, but many wineries are no more than a short detour off U.S. 101. These are generally small wineries. Only some offer guided tours, but most have tasting rooms run by helpful staff. You can arrange your tour to assure you are in town for lunch, but why not pack a lunch and take advantage of the picnic areas provided at many of the wineries?

Pamphlets with detailed maps and listings of each winery are readily available at motels and tourist centers all along the coast. A map for a self-guided driving tour is available free from the Santa Barbara County Vintners' Association (Box WINE, Los Olivos 93441, tel. 805/688–0881).

Shopping

Antiques A dozen antiques and gift shops are clustered in restored Victorian buildings on Brinkerhoff Avenue, 2 blocks west of State Street at West Cota Street, in Santa Barbara.

Arcade In all, 32 shops, art galleries, and studios share the courtyard and gardens of El Paseo, a shopping arcade rich in history. Lunch at the outdoor patio is a nice break from a downtown tour. *Between State and Anacapa sts. at Cañon Perdido St. in Santa Barbara.*

Beach Wear If you want to go home with the absolute latest in California beach wear, stop by **Pacific Leisure,** which specializes in volleyball fashions, shorts, tops, and beach towels. *808 State St., Santa Barbara, tel. 805/962–8828. Open Mon.–Sat. 10–6, Sun. noon–5.*

Beaches

Santa Barbara's beaches don't have the big surf of beaches farther south, but neither do they have the crowds. A short walk from the parking lot can usually find you a solitary spot. Be aware that fog often hugs the coast until about noon in May and June.

East Beach. At the east end of Cabrillo Boulevard, this is *the* beach in Santa Barbara. There are lifeguards, volleyball courts, a jogging and bike trail, and the Cabrillo Bath House with a gym, showers, and changing rooms open to the public.

Arroyo Burro Beach. Located a little west of the harbor on Cliff Drive at Las Positas Road, this state beach has a small grassy area with picnic tables and sandy beaches below the cliffs. The Brown Pelican Restaurant on the beach is nice for breakfast.

Goleta Beach Park. To the north in Goleta, this is a favorite with the college kids from the nearby University of California campus. The easy surf makes it perfect for beginning surfers and families with young children.

State Beaches. West of Santa Barbara on Highway 1 are El Capitan, Refugio, and Gaviota state beaches with campsites, picnic tables, and fire pits. East of the city is the state beach at Carpinteria, a sheltered, sunny and often crowded beach.

Participant Sports

Bicycling All through Solvang you'll see people pedaling along in quadricycles, or four-wheel carriages. Those and other bikes are available at **Surrey Cycle Rental** (486 1st St., tel. 805/688–0091). In Cambria, bikes may be rented from **Cambria Bikes** (tel. 805/927–5510).

Camping There are many campsites along Highway 1, but they can fill up early any time but winter. In Big Sur, campsites are at Pfeiffer Big Sur and Julia Pfeiffer Burns state parks. Near Hearst Castle, camping is available at several smaller state parks (San Simeon, Atascadero, Morro Bay, and Montana de Oro). Most of the sites require advance reservations from MISTIX reservation service (tel. 800/444–7275 or 619/452–1950).

Fishing There is access to freshwater- and surf-fishing spots all along the coast. For deep-sea trips, **Virg's Fish'n** (tel. 805/772–1222) offers day trips out of Morro Bay all year. Also in Morro Bay is **Bob's Sportfishing** (tel. 805/772–3340).

Glider Rides Rides of 15–20 minutes are offered weekends, 10–5, at the Santa Ynez Airport near Solvang (tel. 805/688–8390).

Hiking There are miles of hiking trails in the Ventana Wilderness, with trailheads at state parks and picnic areas on Highway 1 from Big Sur to San Simeon. Twelve miles east of Solvang is Cachuma Lake, a jewel of an artificial lake offering hiking as well as fishing and boating.

Santa Barbara Sports

Bicycling Santa Barbara's waterfront boasts the level, two-lane Cabrillo Bike Lane. In just over 3 easy miles, you pass the city zoo, bird refuge, beaches, and harbor. There are restaurants along the way, or you can stop for a picnic along the palm-lined path looking out on the Pacific. Rent bikes from **Beach Rentals** (8 W. Cabrillo Blvd., tel. 805/963–2524; open 8 AM to sunset in winter, and 8 AM–11 PM in summer). It also has roller skates for hire. Bikes can also be rented from the **Cycles 4 Rent** concession near the pool at Fess Parker's Red Lion Resort (633 E. Cabrillo, tel. 805/564–4333, ext. 444).

Boating Charter or rent 14- to 50-foot sailboats and powerboats from **Sailing Center of Santa Barbara,** which also has a sailing school (Breakwater near the harbor, tel. 805/962–2826 or 800/776–0070).

Fishing Surface and deep-sea fishing are possible all year. Fully equipped boats leave the harbor area for full- and half-day trips, dinner cruises, island excursions, and whale-watching from **SEA Landing** (Cabrillo Blvd. at Bath, tel. 805/963–3564).

Golf Play nine or 18 holes at the **Santa Barbara Golf Club** (Las Positas Rd. and McCaw Ave., tel. 805/687–7087). **Sandpiper Golf Course,** 15 miles west in Goleta, offers a challenging course that used to be a stop on the women's professional tour. (7925 Hollister Ave., Goleta, tel. 805/968–1541).

Horseback Riding San Ysidro Ranch hotel offers trail rides for parties of no more than six into the foothills by the hour (900 San Ysidro La., Montecito, tel. 805/969–5046. Reservations advised; hotel guests only on Sat.).

Tennis Many hotels have their own courts, but there are also excellent public courts. Day permits, for $3, are available at the courts. **Las Positas Municipal Courts,** 1002 Las Positas Road, has six lighted courts. Large complexes are also at the **Municipal Courts,** near Salinas Street and Highway 101, and **Pershing Park,** Castillo and Cabrillo.

Volleyball The east end of East Beach has more than a dozen sandlots. There are some casual, pickup games, but be prepared—these folks play serious volleyball.

Spectator Sports

Polo The public is invited to watch the elegant game at the **Santa Barbara Polo Club,** 7 miles east in Carpinteria. *Take the Santa Claus La. exit from Hwy 101, turn left under the freeway and then left again onto Via Real. The polo grounds are ½-mile farther, surrounded by high hedges. Tel. 805/684-6683. April–Oct., Sun. Modest admission.*

Dining

by Bruce David Colen

Although you will find some chain restaurants in the bigger towns, the Central Coast from Big Sur to Solvang is far enough off the interstate rush to assure that each restaurant and cafe has its own personality—from chic to down-home and funky. You'll find a few burger places, but they won't come with golden arches. In almost all cases, the restaurants will be right off Highway 1.

There aren't many restaurants along the coast from Big Sur until you reach Hearst Castle, where there is a large, new snack bar in the visitors center. From there south, however, the commercial fishing industry assures daily fresh fish in many of the restaurants. The stretch of Highway 1 in and around San Simeon is a popular tour-bus route, and restaurants catering to large groups offer solid, if routine, American fare. Generous quantities of prime rib for dinner and bacon and eggs for breakfast can always be found. Cambria, true to its British-Welsh flavor, provides a taste of English cooking complete with peas and Yorkshire pudding, but the offerings range far beyond that. In Solvang, where the tone turns to Danish, count on traditional smorgasbord and sausages.

The variety of good food in Santa Barbara is astonishing for a town its size. Menu selections range from classic French to Cajun to fresh seafood, and the dining style from tie-and-jacket and reservations necessary to shorts-and-T-shirt hip. A leisurely brunch or lunch will take the best advantage of the beach and harbor views afforded by many restaurants and cafes. At the Biltmore's acclaimed and expensive Sunday brunch, however, all attention is on the spread of fresh fruits, seafood, and pastries. Served in the hotel's airy glass-roof courtyard, it is a perfect choice for special occasions.

But a tasty and satisfying meal certainly doesn't have to cost a fortune. If it is good, cheap food with an international flavor you are after, follow the locals to Milpas Avenue on the east edge of downtown. A recent count there found three Thai restaurants, a Hawaiian, a Greek, and a New Mexican food place. Freshly made tortillas are easily found in the markets on

Milpas, particularly at La Super Rica, one of Julia Childs' favorites for a quick, authentic Mexican snack.

Highly recommended restaurants are indicated by a star ★. Casual dress is acceptable, unless otherwise noted.

Category	Cost*
Very Expensive	over $50
Expensive	$40–$50
Moderate	$15–$40
Inexpensive	under $15

per person, without tax, service, or drinks

The following abbreviations for credit cards have been used: AE, American Express; CB, Carte Blanche; DC, Diners Club; MC, MasterCard; V, Visa.

Big Sur
Expensive
★
Ventana Restaurant. The low, wide, modern/rustic stone and wood dining room is attractive; the terrace, with views over golden hills down to the ocean, is spectacular. Even if it's foggy along the highway, it may be sunny and warm up here. Noted for its handling of the light touches of California cuisine, the menu features grilled veal chops, sliced duck, occasional and unexpected game dishes, and some creative sandwiches. Weekend brunches on the patio are a real event. *Off Hwy 1, near the south end of town, tel. 408/667–2331. Reservations advised on weekends. AE, DC, MC, V.*

Moderate
Deetjen's Big Sur Inn. The restaurant is in the main house of the old, funky inn. There are four small dining rooms, none with more than four tables. Classical music enhances the stylish fare that includes roast duckling for dinner and wonderfully light and flavorful whole-wheat pancakes for breakfast (there is no lunch). *Hwy 1, south end of Big Sur, tel. 408/667–2377. No credit cards.*

Glen Oaks Restaurant. Food critics praise the originality of the food served in this small, simply decorated dining room. The restaurant, owned by a husband and wife team, emphasizes fresh ingredients, mesquite grilling, fish, and pasta. *Hwy 1, north end of town, tel. 408/667–2623. MC, V. Closed Mon.*

Inexpensive–
Moderate
★
Nepenthe. You'll not find a more spectacular coastal view between Los Angeles and San Francisco. The 800-foot-high cliff site, overlooking lush meadows to the ocean below, was once owned by Orson Welles and Rita Hayworth. The food is adequately average—from roast chicken with sage to sandwiches and hamburgers—so it is the one-of-a-kind location, in the one and only magnificent Big Sur, that rates the star. An outdoor cafe serves lunch until nightfall. *Hwy 1, south end of town, tel. 408/667–2345. Reservations for large parties only. AE, MC, V. No breakfast. Full bar.*

Cambria
Moderate
Brambles Dinner House. This is the best-known restaurant in Cambria, but it can be hit-or-miss. Specialties include fresh salmon cooked over a seasoned oak fire, blackstrap molasses bread, prime rib, and Yorkshire pudding. *4005 Burton Dr., tel. 805/927–4716. Reservations advised. AE, DC, MC, V. No lunch.*

Sylvia's Rigdon Hall. Delicate pink floral china sets the tone for this dinner house with a British flavor. The Spencer steak marinated in Jack Daniels is a favorite; also featured are a chicken curry mulligatawny soup and prime rib. *4022 Burton Dr., tel. 805/927–5125. MC, V. Dinner only. Closed Christmas Day.*

Inexpensive– Moderate ★ **The Hamlet at Moonstone Gardens.** This is in the middle of a plant nursery. The enchanting patio garden is perfect for lunch. The upstairs dining room—sleek chrome and lavender with fireplace and grand piano—looks over the Pacific or the gardens. Service can be slow, but no one seems to mind. Fish of the day comes poached in white wine; other entrées range from hamburgers to rack of lamb. Downstairs is the Central Coast Wine Center, where you can taste wines from more than 50 wineries. *East side Hwy 1, tel. 805/927–3535. No reservations. MC, V. Closed Dec.*

Mustache Pete's. This lively, upbeat place with overhead fans and baskets of flowers features Italian food, with seafood, pasta, and poultry selections. *4090 Burton Dr., tel. 805/927–8589. AE, MC, V.*

Morro Bay *Moderate– Expensive* **Dutch's Fine Dining.** In a house built of stone quarried from the big Morro Rock, the restaurant features crab *quo vadis* (with artichoke hearts and button mushrooms) and lobster thermidor, as well as steaks and fresh fish. *2738 N. Main St., tel. 805/ 772–8645. AE, DC, MC, V. Lunch weekdays, dinner daily.*

Moderate **Dorn's.** This very pleasant seafood cafe overlooks the harbor and main square. It looks like a Cape Cod cottage, with blue walls, wainscoting, awnings, and bay windows. Breakfast, lunch, and dinner are served; dinner features excellent fish and native abalone. *801 Market St., tel. 805/772–4415. No credit cards.*

Inexpensive ★ **Margie's Diner.** This clean and attractive, Mom-and-Pop type diner-cafe, serves generous portions of All-American favorites: ham or steak and eggs, three-egg omelets, chili, nine versions of hamburger, hot and cold sandwiches, fried chicken steak, and deep dish apple pie. You name it, but don't forget the milkshakes. Top quality produce is used and service is excellent. *1698 N. Main St., tel. 805/772–2510. No credit cards.*

Ojai *Moderate* **Wheeler Hot Springs Restaurant.** The menu changes weekly but always features herbs and vegetables grown in the spa's garden. In Ojai, 6 miles north on Highway 33. *16825 Maricopa Hwy., tel. 805/646–8131. Closed Mon.–Wed.*

San Luis Obispo *Inexpensive– Moderate* **Madonna Inn.** This visual Disneyland has to be seen to be believed. It is the ultimate in kitsch, from rococo bathrooms to pink-on-pink, frou-frou dining areas. You come to ogle, not necessarily to dine, although the latter is perfectly adequate, stopby cooking, with decor-matching desserts. *100 Madonna Rd., tel. 805/543–3000. Dress: informal. No credit cards.*

San Simeon *Moderate* **Europa.** A Hungarian touch brings egg dumplings and paprika to the unexpected menu in an area of traditional fare. Crisp linen tablecloths brighten the small dining room. Steaks are featured as well as specialties from Italy and Vienna. Weekend brunch is served. *9240 Castillo Dr. (Hwy 1), tel. 805/927–3087. AE, MC, V. Closed Sun. Dinner only.*

Inexpensive– Moderate **San Simeon Restaurant.** This restaurant makes the most of its proximity to Hearst Castle, with a mind-boggling decor of imitation Greek columns, statues, and tapestries. There is a standard American menu; prime rib is the big draw. The dark dining room opens to views of the Pacific across the highway. *East side Hwy 1, tel. 805/927–4604. Reservations advised in summer. AE, MC, V.*

Santa Barbara **Downey's.** Chef-owner John Downey was the first to introduce
Expensive Santa Barbara to the assorted pleasures of *nouvelle*-California cooking, and local admirers have kept this charming little restaurant crowded ever since. Try the in-house cured prosciutto, the local mussels with a chile sauce, fresh sea bass and asparagus, or grilled duck or lamb, with local wild mushrooms. *1305 State St., tel. 805/966–5006. Reservations required. Jacket required. Closed lunch. MC, V.*

El Encanto. Sitting on the awninged dining terrace of this hilltop hotel, one has a marvelous view of Santa Barbara's red-tiled roofs stretching down to the harbor below. It is like being on the French or Italian Riviera, and chef James Sly provides the matching cuisines, from bouillabaisse to pasta with lobster sauce. There's also an abundance of fresh, local salads. *1900 Laseun Rd., tel. 805/687–5000. Reservations required. Jacket required. AE, DC, MC, V.*

★ **Michael's Waterside.** Started with the financial help of the Roux brothers, who own London's Waterside Inn and the three-star LeGavroche, this beautiful Victorian house, facing a bird sanctuary, is a romantic gem. And there is nothing about chef Michael Hutchings's *haute*-California cuisine to spoil the mood: "cultured" abalone, mushroom mousse with escargot, gruyère cheese soufflé; baked king salmon, Santa Barbara prawns and ranch-bred squab, and lovely rich desserts. *50 Los Patos Way, tel. 805/969–0307. Reservations required. Jacket and tie required. AE, DC, MC, V. Open for dinner and Sunday brunch.*

Moderate– **The Harbor Restaurant.** This place tops annual surveys on
Expensive where locals like to take out-of-town guests. The lovely seascape makes it particularly pleasant for breakfast or lunch. The restaurant specializes in fresh seafood, local catches, and Maine lobster; and there is an oyster bar on the second floor. *210 Stearns Wharf, tel. 805/963–3311. Dress: casual; jackets required in Santa Barbara Room. AE, CB, DC, MC, V.*

The Stonehouse. This farmhouse restaurant, part of the San Ysidro Ranch, features the best light French-California cuisine in Santa Barbara. For lunch order chef Marc Ehrler's Mediterranean-style pizza while sitting on the deck. At night, the cooking gets more serious, with game, roasts, and fresh fish entrées. *900 San Ysidro La., 805/969–5046. Reservations required. Jacket required. MC, V.*

Moderate **The Palace Cafe.** This stylish and lively restaurant has won acclaim for its Cajun and Creole food. If the dishes aren't spicy enough, each table has its own bottle of hot sauce. Only dinner is served, and be prepared for a wait. It's lots of noisy fun. *8 E. Cota St., tel. 805/966–3133. Dress: informal. Reservations accepted for 5:30 PM seating only. AE, MC, V.*

Pane & Vino. This is a tiny trattoria, with an equally small sidewalk dining terrace, in one of Santa Barbara's tree-shaded, flower-decked shopping centers. The cold antipasto is very good, as are grilled meats and fish, pastas and salads. There's a nearby water trough and hitching post for the visiting horsey set. *1482 E. Valley Rd., tel. 805/969–9274. Reservations advised. Closed Sun. No credit cards.*

Inexpensive **Castagnola Bros. Fish Galley.** Here's an unassuming spot a quick 2 blocks from the beach where wonderfully good, fresh fish comes served on paper plates. Most of the tables are outside on the patio, but a few fast-food style booths share the interior with the fish market, the other half of this enterprise. It closes at 6 PM, 9 PM on weekends. *205 Santa Barbara St., tel. 805/962–8053. No credit cards.*

East Beach Grill. Watch the waves break and the world go by at a surprisingly pleasant outdoor cafe right on the beach. It's a step above the usual beach stand with friendly table service, real plates, and cutlery. Basic breakfast fare is followed by hot dogs and burgers for lunch. *At the Cabrillo Bath House, East Beach, tel. 805/965–8805. No credit cards. Closed 3:30 daily.*

Joe's Cafe. The vinyl checked tablecloths and simple round stools at the hefty wooden counter tell the story: nothing fancy, but solid American cafe fare in generous portions. A popular hangout and drinking spot, particularly for the younger crowd. The martinis are great. *536 State St., tel. 805/966–4638. AE, MC, V. Closed Sun. lunch.*

Solvang
Moderate–Expensive

Danish Inn. The smorgasbord is popular, but there are also steaks and many Continental-style items to choose from. Dining is more formal here than in most Solvang restaurants. Atmosphere: lace curtains and a cozy fireplace. *1547 Mission Dr., tel. 805/688–4813. Reservations advised. AE, MC, V.*

Inexpensive–Moderate

Restaurant Mollenroen. A busy upstairs dining room serves smorgasbord and other Danish specialties. It has a cheerful, light setting, with fresh flowers on the tables and booths. The local folks come here for a good meal at good prices. *435 Alisal Rd., tel. 805/688–4555. AE, DC, MC, V.*

★ **Royal Scandia Restaurant.** Despite the size (there are three dining rooms), this restaurant is decorated like an old Danish cottage, with vaulted ceilings, rafters, and lots of brass and frosted glass. You can dine on the patio protected by glass and brick. The menu caters to traditional American tastes, with a few Danish items. *420 Alisal Rd., tel. 805/688–8000. AE, DC, MC, V.*

Inexpensive

Little Belgium Inn. This cafe with outdoor patio does a booming business at breakfast and lunch. Waffles of all kinds and grilled Danish sausage are among the offerings. Inside, the cafe is sunny and pleasant, though it can get crowded. *475 1st St., tel. 805/688–0095. MC, V.*

Lodging

The lodging choices in Big Sur, though few in number, range from the dramatic Ventana Inn to the rustic and funky Deetjen's Big Sur Inn. Neither cater to children, but the Big Sur Lodge is the perfect place for them. You won't find many hotels or motels between Big Sur and San Simeon. In castle country—from San Simeon to San Luis Obispo—there are many moderately priced hotels and motels, some nicer than others, but mostly just basic lodging. Only the Madonna Inn, the all-pink, one-of-a-kind motel in San Luis Obispo, is worthy of a stay for its own sake. Be sure you make reservations ahead of time, well ahead in the summer. Remember that there may not be another town just down the road with more lodging options.

Bargain lodging is hard to come by in Santa Barbara, where high-end resorts are more the style. Long a favorite getaway for congestion-crazed Los Angeles residents, the resorts promise, and usually deliver, pampering and solitude in romantic settings. The beach area is certainly the most popular locale for lodging. It is also where you will find the largest concentration of moderately priced motels. Many places offer discounts in the winter season. Come summer weekends, when 90% of the town's 46,000 motel and hotel rooms are filled, reservations well in advance are strongly advised.

Highly recommended lodgings are indicated by a star ★.

Category	Cost*
Very Expensive	over $150
Expensive	$100–$150
Moderate	$60–$100
Inexpensive	under $60

*for a double room, not including tax

Big Sur
Very Expensive
★
Ventana Inn. A getaway that is essential California chic—restful and hip. Rooms, scattered in clusters on a hillside above the Pacific, are done in natural woods, and the floors are cool tile. Activities here are purposely limited to sunning at poolside—there is a clothing-optional deck—and walks in the hills nearby. Rates include an elaborate Continental breakfast and afternoon wine and cheese (featuring California wines). *Hwy 1, 93920, tel. 408/667–2331 or 800/628–6500 in CA. 59 rooms. Facilities: 2 pools, spa, restaurant, gift shop. Minimum stay 2 nights on weekends, 3 on holidays. AE, DC, MC, V.*

Moderate
Big Sur Lodge. Located inside Pfeiffer Big Sur State Park, this is the best place in Big Sur for families. Motel-style cottages are set around a meadow surrounded by redwood and oak trees. Some have fireplaces, some kitchens. *Hwy. 1, Box 190, 93920, tel. 408/667–2171. 61 rooms. Facilities: pool, sauna. MC, V.*

Deetjen's Big Sur Inn. Built in bits and pieces in the '20s and '30s, this place is charming, but also rustic and not always comfortable. There are no locks on the doors, the heating is by wood-burning stove in half of the rooms, and your neighbor is often heard through the walls. Still, it's a special place, set among redwood trees with each room individually decorated and given a name like "Château Fiasco." *Hwy 1, south end of town, 93920, tel. 408/667–2377. 20 rooms, 13 with bath. Facilities: restaurant. No credit cards.*

Cambria
Moderate
★
Best Western Fireside Inn. This modern motel has spacious rooms decorated in cream and peach, with sofas and upholstered lounge chairs (plus refrigerators and coffee makers). Some have whirlpools. Ask for a room with a fireplace and an ocean view. Continental breakfast is served in a room adjacent to the pool. The landscaping is very attractive, and the inn is just across from the beach. *6700 Moonstone Beach Dr., 93428, tel. 805/927–8661 or 800/528–1234. 46 rooms. Facilities: heated pool, spa. AE, DC, MC, V.*

Cambria Pines Lodge. The lodge's buildings are set in 25 acres of pine trees above the town, with peacocks wandering the grounds. There is a big stone fireplace in the lounge, and all the furnishings—new and old—fit the decor of the 1920s, when the lodge was built. *2905 Burton Dr., 93428, tel. 805/927–4200. 100 rooms. Facilities: bar, restaurant. AE, MC, V.*

★ **San Simeon Pines Resort Motel.** There is a quiet lodgelike feel here, directly across from Leffingwell's Landing, a state picnic area on the rocky beach. Areas are set aside for adults and families. *7200 Moonstone Beach Dr., Box 117, San Simeon 93452, tel. 805/927–4648. 60 rooms. Facilities: children's playground, nine hole golf, pool, shuffleboard. AE, MC, V.*

Inexpensive **Bluebird Motel.** Located between the east and west villages, this older motel was recently fully redecorated, and includes a homey lounge for hanging out. *1880 Main St., 93428, tel. 805/ 927–4634. 31 rooms. AE, MC, V.*

Morro Bay **The Breakers.** Rooms in this motel, ½-block from the water-
Moderate front, are decorated in pastels—each with a different wallpaper—and traditional furniture. Most have ocean views, some have fireplaces, all have coffee makers and refrigerators. *Morro Bay Blvd. at Market, Box 110, 93443, tel. 805/772–7317. 25 rooms. Facilities: heated pool, spa, cable TV. AE, D, DC, MC, V.*

Ojai **Ojai Valley Inn and Country Club.** Reopened by Hilton Interna-
Very Expensive tional in January 1988 after a $40 million renovation, the hotel
★ is set in landscaped grounds lush with flowers. The enormously peaceful setting comes with hillside views in nearly all directions. Some of the nicer rooms are in the original adobe building, where the best of the old—like huge bathrooms—is enhanced with contemporary touches. The suites in cabanas are more expensive. Interesting works by the famed local artists are featured throughout the resort. *Country Club Rd., 93023, tel. 805/646–5511 or 800/422–OJAI. 218 units. Facilities: championship golf course, lighted tennis courts, 2 pools, men's and women's sauna and steam room, complimentary bicycles, 2 restaurants, bar. AE, CB, D, DC, MC, V.*

Inexpensive **Los Padres Inn.** This is a modern hotel on the main street of town across from the Soule Park Golf Course. *1208 E. Ojai Ave. 93023, tel. 805/646–4365. 31 units. Facilities: pool, whirlpool. AE, CB, D, DC, MC, V.*

San Luis Obispo **Madonna Inn.** A designer's imagination gone berserk, this
Moderate– place is as much a tourist attraction as a place to stay. Each
Expensive room is unique. "Rock Bottom" is all stone, even the bathroom.
★ The "Safari Room" is decked out in animal skins. "Old Mill" features a waterwheel that powers cuckoo clock-like figurines. *100 Madonna Rd., 93401, tel. 805/543–3000 or 800/543–9666. 109 rooms. Facilities: ballroom, 2 restaurants, wine cellar, 2 gift shops, gourmet shop. No credit cards.*

Inexpensive **Motel Inn.** If it is nostalgia rather than comfort you seek, this place bills itself as the world's first motel. Small bungalows with stucco exterior and flat red-tile roofs make you feel like you are on the set of an old B movie. Although they are old, the rooms are kept clean and the grounds are nicely lush. *2223 Monterey St., 93401, tel. 805/543–4000. Facilities: pool, bar. AE, D, MC, V.*

San Simeon **Holiday Inn.** This is a newish 2-story motel with comfortable
Moderate rooms opening on an interior corridor. The rooms are standard Holiday Inn-style, decorated in blue and rust. *9070 Castillo Ave. (Hwy 1), 93452, tel. 805/927–8691 or 800/465–4329. 100*

rooms. *Facilities: heated pool, restaurant, lounge, room service. AE, D, DC, MC, V.*

Inexpensive **San Simeon Lodge.** Built in 1958, the exterior looks its age, but the modernized rooms have nice touches, like matching spreads and curtains. *9520 Castillo Dr. (Hwy 1), 93452, tel. 805/927–4601. 63 rooms. Facilities: pool, restaurant, bar, lounge. AE, CB, DC, MC, V.*

Santa Barbara **Fess Parker's Red Lion Resort.** This is a sprawling resort com-
Very Expensive plex with a slightly Spanish flair. Two- and three-story stucco
★ buildings are located directly across the street from the beach. This is Santa Barbara's newest luxury hotel and, with its huge and lavishly appointed lobby, a showplace for the chain. Spacious rooms, all with either private patio or balcony, and many with ocean views, are furnished with pastels and light wood. *633 E. Cabrillo Blvd., 93103, tel. 805/564–4333 or 800/879–2929. 360 rooms. Facilities: pool, sauna, tennis courts, exercise room, Jacuzzi, gift shop, lounge with dance floor, 2 bars, cafe, 2 restaurants. AE, CB, D, DC, MC, V.*

Four Seasons Biltmore. Santa Barbara's grande dame has been spruced up with a $15 million face-lift by its new owners. A decor featuring muted pastels and bleached woods gives the cabanas a light, airy touch without sacrificing the hotel's reputation for understated elegance. It's a bit more formal than elsewhere in Santa Barbara, with lush gardens and palm trees galore. *1260 Channel Dr., 93108, tel. 805/969–2261 or 800/332–3442. 236 rooms. Facilities: olympic pool, whirlpool, croquet, shuffleboard, racquet ball, health club, casino, putting green, tennis courts, 2 restaurants, bar. AE, CB, DC, MC, V.*

San Ysidro Ranch. At this luxury "ranch" you can feel at home in jeans and cowboy boots, but be prepared to dress for dinner. A hideout for the Hollywood set, this romantic place hosted John and Jackie Kennedy on their honeymoon. Guest cottages, some with antique quilts and all with wood-burning stoves or fireplaces, are scattered among 14 acres of orange trees and flower beds. There are 500 acres more left in open space to roam at will on foot or horseback. The hotel welcomes children and pets. *900 San Ysidro La., Montecito, 93108, tel. 805/969–5046. 43 rooms. Facilities: pool, tennis courts, horseback riding, croquet, badminton, restaurant. AE, MC, V. Minimum stay: 2 days on weekends, 3 days on holidays.*

Moderate–Expensive **Ambassador by the Sea.** Near harbor and Stearns Wharf, this place has a real California beach feel. Sun decks overlook the ocean and bike path. Complimentary breakfast is included. *202 W. Cabrillo Blvd., 93101, tel. 805/965–4577. 32 units. Facilities: pool, 2 units with kitchenettes. AE, D, DC, MC, V.*

Pacific Crest Motel. A block from East Beach on a quiet residential street, this motel has clean and comfortable rooms, avoiding the austerity of some budget operations. Kitchens are available. *433 Corona Del Mar Dr., 93103, tel. 805/966–3103. 26 rooms. Facilities: pool, laundromat. AE, D, DC, MC, V. Minimum stay: 2 nights on weekends, 3 on holidays.*

Santa Barbara Inn. Wicker and floral prints give a Polynesian feel to this 3-story motel, directly across the street from East Beach. Many rooms have ocean views, but the lower-price ones with mountain views also look over the parking lot. *435 S. Milpas, 93103, tel. 805/966–2285 or 800/231–0431. 71 rooms. Facilities: pool, whirlpool, restaurant. AE, DC, MC, V.*

Villa Rosa. The atmosphere is of a private home. Housed in a

50-year-old Mediterranean house a block from the beach, the rooms and intimate lobby are decorated with a southwestern style. Rates include Continental breakfast and wine and cheese in the afternoon. *15 Chapala St., 93101, tel. 805/966–0851. 18 rooms. Facilities: pool, spa. AE, MC, V.*

Inexpensive **Motel 6.** Low price and great location near the beach are the pluses for this no-frills place. Reserve well in advance all year. *443 Corona Del Mar Dr., 93103, tel. 805/564–1392. 52 units. Facilities: heated pool. AE, DC, MC, V.*

Solvang **Chimney Sweep Inn.** All the rooms are pleasant, but it is the
Moderate– cottages in the backyard that are extra special (and expensive).
Very Expensive Built in a half-timbered style, they were inspired by the C. S. Lewis's children's book, The Chronicles of Narnia. The cottages have kitchens. In the garden are a waterfall and fish pond. Complimentary Continental breakfast includes hot apple cider. *1554 Copenhagen Dr., 93463, tel. 805/688–2111 or 800/824–6444. 28 rooms. Facilities: spa, garden. AE, MC, V.*
Sheraton Royal Scandinavian Inn. This member of the chain follows the Danish theme of the town. The rooms—in Danish decor, of course—have nice touches, like handpainted furniture. The large, brick and darkly timbered lobby has a fireplace and overstuffed chairs. *400 Alisal Rd., 93463, tel. 805/688–8000 or 800/624–5572. 133 rooms. Facilities: restaurant, lounge, pool, Jacuzzi. AE, DC, MC, V.*

Inexpensive **Solvang Gaard Lodge.** This was Solvang's first motel and is still as comfortable and friendly as you could want. Some of the old-Danish-style rooms are rented to full-time residents, others to repeat visitors who come to spend a week or more in a quiet place, just beyond the center of things. *293 Alisal Rd., 93463, tel. 805/688–4404. 21 units. AE, MC, V.*

The Arts and Nightlife

The Arts Santa Barbara prides itself on being a top-notch cultural center. It supports its own professional symphony and chamber orchestra and an impressive art museum. The proximity to the University of California at Santa Barbara assures an endless stream of visiting artists and performers.

The performing arts find a home in two theaters that are themselves works of art. The enormous Moorish-style **Arlington Theater** on State Street is home to the Santa Barbara Symphony. You can also catch a first-run movie there. The **Lobero,** a state landmark, at the corner of Anacapa and Cañon Perdido streets, shares its stage with community theater groups and touring professionals.

The works housed in the **Museum of Art** range from Greek and Roman collections to Grandma Moses's vistas. There's also a fine collection of antique dolls. *1130 State St., tel. 805/963–4364. Admission $3 adults, $1.50 children under 16. Open Tues.–Sat. 11–5, Sun. noon–5, Thurs. 11–9. Tours are led Tues.–Sun. at 2 PM.*

For a more casual art experience, catch the beachfront display of wares from local artists and craftspeople each Sunday from 10 AM to dusk along Cabrillo Boulevard.

The **Santa Barbara Arts Council** (1236 Chapala St., tel. 805/966 -7022) provides information on performances and events and also has a gallery space for emerging local artists.

Music   Since 1971, the **San Luis Obispo Mozart Festival** (Box 311, San Luis Obispo, tel. 805/543–4580) has been held early in August. The settings include the Mission San Luis Obispo de Tolosa and the Cal Poly Theater. There are afternoon and evening concerts and recitals—by professionals and well-known visiting artists—as well as seminars and workshops. Not all the music is Mozart; you'll hear Haydn and other composers. The Festival Fringe offers free concerts outdoors.

Theater   Boo and hiss the villains year round at the **Great American Melodrama** (Hwy. 1, tel. 805/489–2499) in the small town of Oceano, south of San Luis Obispo.

From June through September, the **Pacific Conservatory of the Performing Arts** (420 2nd St., tel. 805/688–7688) hosts a repertory of plays in the half-timbered open-air Solvang Festival Theater.

Film   The **Santa Barbara International Film Festival,** (1216 State St. # 201, tel. 805/963–0023) held in March, draws the celebrity crowd, with premieres and screenings of American and international films.

Nightlife   Most of the major hotels offer nightly entertainment during the summer season and live weekend entertainment all year. To see what's scheduled at the hotels and many small clubs and restaurants, pick up a copy of the free weekly *Santa Barbara Independent* newspaper for an extensive rundown.

Dancing   **Zelo.** This is a high-energy restaurant that doubles as a progressive rock and punk dance club featuring offbeat videos and innovative lighting. *630 State St., tel. 805/966–5792. Closed Mon.*

12 Los Angeles

You're preparing for your trip to Los Angeles. You're psyching up with Beach Boys cassettes on your car radio or perhaps some Hollywood epics on the VCR. You've pulled out your tropical Hawaiian shirts and tennis shorts. You've studied the Mexican menu at Taco Bell. Maybe you're even doing a crash regimen at your local tanning salon and aerobics studio so you won't *look* like a tourist when you hit the coast.

Well, relax. *Everybody's* a tourist in LaLa Land. Even the stars are star-struck (as evidenced by the celebrities watching the other celebrities at Spago). Los Angeles is a city of ephemerals, of transience, and above all, of illusion. Nothing there is quite real, and that's the reality of it all. That air of anything-can-happen—and it often does—is what keeps thousands moving to this promised land each year and millions more vacationing in it. Not just from the East or Midwest, mind you, but from the Far East, Down Under, Europe, and South America. It's this influx of cultures that's been the lifeblood of L.A. since its Hispanic beginning.

We cannot predict what *your* Los Angeles will be like. You can laze on a beach or soak up some of the world's greatest art collections. You can tour the movie studios and stars' homes or take the kids to Disneyland, Magic Mountain, or the *Queen Mary/Spruce Goose*. You can shop luxurious Beverly Hills' Rodeo Drive or browse for hipper novelties on boutique-lined Melrose Avenue. The possibilities are endless—rent a boat to Catalina Island, watch the floats in Pasadena's Rose Parade, or dine on tacos, sushi, goat cheese pizza, or just plain hamburgers, hot dogs, and chili.

None of this was imagined when Spanish settlers founded their Pueblo de la Reina de Los Angeles in 1781. In fact, no one predicted a golden future for the desert-dry Southern California until well after San Francisco and Northern California had gotten a good head start with their own gold rush. The dusty outpost of Los Angeles eventually had oil and oranges, but the golden key to its success came on the silver screen: the movies. If the early pioneers of Hollywood—religiously conservative fruit farmers—had gotten their way, their town's name would never have become known for the fruition of cinema and entertainment.

In mid-century, the U.S. automakers and oil companies lobbied against an urban mass transit system in Southern California in order to sell more cars and gasoline. Free-spirited Californians drove blithely on, indulging their independence until one day, late in the 1950s, the smog got thick enough to kill. Mandatory emission controls have helped clear up that problem. Nevertheless, check the papers daily to ascertain the air quality. Because the 700 miles of freeways are so full, a metro subway system is finally being dug to offer another solution to the smog problem. Perhaps not too little, but already too late: The first phase of the system won't be ready until sometime during the 1990s.

No city embraces the romance of the automobile as does Los Angeles. Cars themselves announce the wealth, politics, and taste of their drivers. Vanity license plates, a California innovation, condense the meaning of one's life into seven letters (MUZKBIZ). Sun roofs, ski racks, and cardboard windshield visors sell better here than anywhere else. You are what you drive—a thought worth remembering when you rent a car. Yes, Lamborghinis are available, even by the hour.

The distance between places in Los Angeles explains the ethnic enclaves that do not merge, regardless of the melting-pot appearance of the city. It would be misleading of us to gloss over the tensions between racial and ethnic groups learning to share Los Angeles. More notable for visitors, however, is the rich cultural and culinary diversity this mix of peoples creates.

Arriving and Departing

By Plane
Airports and Airlines

The new, improved **Los Angeles International Airport** (LAX, tel. 213/646–5252) is the largest airport in the area. It was revamped for the 1984 Olympics as a two-level airport with departures on the upper level, arrivals on the lower level. More than 85 major airlines use LAX, the third-largest airport in the world in terms of passenger traffic. There are a multitude of restaurants, shops, and newsstands at LAX, and even the spectacular Host International theme restaurant with its futuristic architecture and 80-foot observation deck.

Among the major carriers that serve LAX are Air Canada (tel. 800/422–6232), America West (tel. 800/228–7862), American (tel. 800/433–7300), Braniff (tel. 800/752–4556), British Airways (tel. 800/247–9297), Continental (tel. 800/525–0280), Delta (tel. 800/221–1212), Japan Airlines (tel. 800/525–3663), Northwest (tel. 800/225–2525), Pan Am (tel. 800/221–1111), Southwest (tel. 800/531–5601), TWA (tel. 800/221–2000), United (tel. 800/241–6522), and USAir (tel. 800/428–4322).

Between the Airport and Center City

A dizzying array of ground transportation is available from LAX to all parts of Los Angeles and its surroundings. A **taxi** ride to downtown Los Angeles can be a 20-minute drive, if there is no traffic. In Los Angeles, however, that is a big if. Visitors should request the flat fee ($24 at press time) to downtown, or choose among the several ground transportation companies that offer set rates.

SuperShuttle (tel. 213/417–8988; advance reservations, tel. 213/338–1111), with door-to-airport service, is one of the most popular. Cost depends on where one goes; LAX to downtown hotels runs $11. Vans hold a maximum of seven passengers, so you will not be treated like a sardine. SuperShuttle operates 24 hours a day from all the Los Angeles-area airports. You can use the SuperShuttle courtesy phone after you get your luggage, and the van will be there within about 15 minutes.

L.A. Top Shuttle (9100 S. Sepulveda Blvd., #128, tel. 213/670–6666) features door-to-door service and low rates; it costs $10 per person to travel from LAX to hotels in the Disneyland/Anaheim area.

For the ultimate in Los Angeles transportation, try a **limousine** from the airport to your hotel and start your L.A. experience right. Most limo companies have a three-hour minimum, but the following companies charge a flat rate for airport service, ranging from $65 to $75: **Jackson Limousine** (tel. 213/734–9955), **West Coast Limousine** (tel. 213/756–5466), and **Dav-El Livery** (tel. 213/550–0070). Many of the cars have a bar, stereo, TV, and cellular phone.

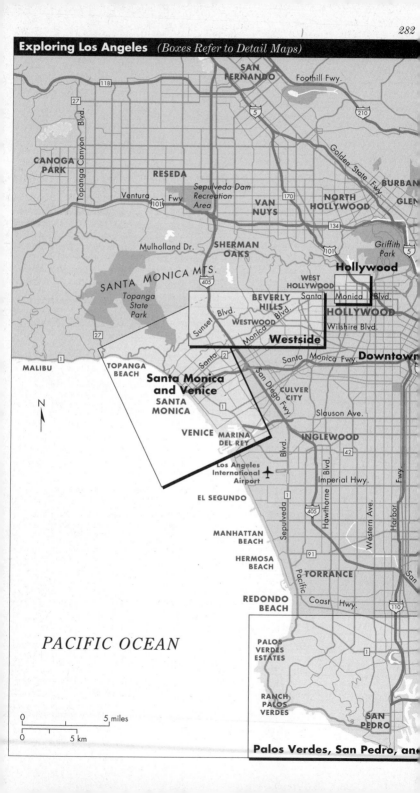

Exploring Los Angeles *(Boxes Refer to Detail Maps)*

SAN FERNANDO

Foothill Fwy.

118

27

210

Golden State Fwy.

CANOGA PARK

RESEDA

Ventura

101

Fwy

Sepulveda Dam Recreation Area

170

VAN NUYS

NORTH HOLLYWOOD

BURBAN

GLEN

Mulholland Dr.

SHERMAN OAKS

134

101

Griffith Park

5

SANTA MONICA MTS.

405

Hollywood

WEST HOLLYWOOD

Santa

Monica Blvd.

Topanga State Park

BEVERLY HILLS

WESTWOOD

Sunset Blvd.

Monica Blvd.

HOLLYWOOD

Wilshire Blvd.

27

Westside

MALIBU

1

TOPANGA BEACH

Santa

2

Santa Monica Fwy.

Downtown

San Diego Fwy.

Santa Monica and Venice

SANTA MONICA

Santa Monica Fwy.

N

1

CULVER CITY

Slauson Ave.

VENICE

MARINA DEL REY

INGLEWOOD

42

Los Angeles International Airport

Blvd.

Blvd.

Hawthorne

Western Ave.

Fwy

Harbor

EL SEGUNDO

Sepulveda

Imperial Hwy.

1

405

MANHATTAN BEACH

HERMOSA BEACH

91

TORRANCE

San

REDONDO BEACH

Pacific

Coast Hwy.

110

PACIFIC OCEAN

PALOS VERDES ESTATES

1

0 ____ 5 miles

0 ____ 5 km

RANCH PALOS VERDES

SAN PEDRO

Palos Verdes, San Pedro, an

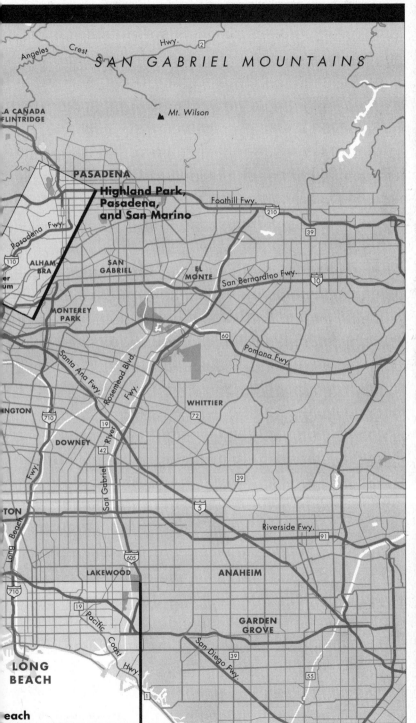

Flyaway Service (7610 Woodley Ave., Van Nuys, tel. 818/994–5554) offers transportation between LAX and the eastern San Fernando Valley for around $5. For the western San Fernando Valley and Ventura area, **The Great American Stage Lines** (tel. 805/656–4190) brown and gold buses go to and from Woodland Hills, Thousand Oaks, Oxnard, and Ventura. **RTD** (tel. 213/626–4455) also offers limited airport service.

The greater Los Angeles area has a collection of smaller, more local airports. **Ontario Airport** (tel. 714/984–1207) serves the San Bernardino-Riverside area, and is located about 35 miles east of Los Angeles. This airport books a variety of domestic flights on: Air LA, Alaska Airlines, American, America West, Continental, Delta, Northwest, SkyWest, Southwest, TWA, United, United Express, and USAir. Ground transportation possibilities include: SuperShuttle as well as Inland Express (tel. 714/626–6599), Empire Airport Transportation (tel. 714/884–0744), and Southern California Coach (tel. 714/978–6415).

Burbank Airport (tel. 818/840–8847) serves the San Fernando Valley with commuter, and some longer flights. Alaska Airlines, Alpha Air, American, America West, Delta, LA Helicopter, SkyWest, States West, TWA, United, United Express, and USAir are represented.

By Car Three main interstate routes take drivers into the Los Angeles area. I-5 runs from Canada to Mexico, through Seattle, Sacramento, and San Diego. It is known as the Golden State or Santa Ana Freeway here. I-10 crosses the country from Florida to Los Angeles and is known locally as the Santa Monica Freeway. I-15 comes into the area from the northeast, from Montana through Las Vegas and San Bernardino.

By Train Los Angeles can be reached by a few different routes on **Amtrak** (tel. 800/USA–RAIL). On overnight trips several sleeping accommodations are available. The *Coast Starlight* is a superliner that travels along the spectacular California coast. It offers service from Seattle-Portland and Oakland-San Francisco down to Los Angeles. Amtrak's *San Joaquin* train travels a route through the Central Valley from Oakland to Bakersfield, where passengers transfer to an Amtrak bus that takes them to Los Angeles. The *Sunset Limited* goes to Los Angeles from New Orleans, the *Eagle* from San Antonio, and the *Southwest Chief* and the *Desert Wind* from Chicago.

The Spanish mission-style Union Station at 800 North Alameda Street is one of the grande dames of railroad stations.

By Bus **Greyhound-Trailways** (tel. 800/237–8211) offers a large variety of scheduled bus routes throughout the country at the lowest prices around. The Los Angeles terminal is at 208 East Sixth Street, on the corner of Los Angeles Street.

Getting Around

By Bus A bus ride on the **Southern California Rapid Transit District (RTD)** (tel. 213/626–4455) costs $1.10 and 25¢ for each transfer, so it's certainly a bargain when you consider the distances that can be covered for that price.

By Taxi You probably won't be able to hail a cab on the street in Los Angeles. Instead, you must phone one of the many taxi companies; the metered rate is $1.60 per mile. Two of the more reputable companies are **Independent Cab Co.** (tel. 213/385–8294 or 385–TAXI) and **United Independent Taxi** (tel. 213/653–5050). United accepts MasterCard and Visa.

By Limousine For total luxury and a real taste of the Los Angeles way of life, try a limousine. It's the most relaxing way to view a city of this caliber and not all that much more expensive than other forms of transportation (if you split the fare among a group of eight or less). Limousines come equipped with everything from a full bar and telephone to a hot tub and a double bed—depending on your needs.

A few limo services are **Dav-El Livery** (tel. 213/550–0070), **First Class** (tel. 213/476–1960), and **Le Monde Limousine** (tel. 213/271–9270, 818/887–7878).

By Car It really is almost necessary to have a car when visiting Los Angeles. *See* Chapter 1 for a list of some of the rental agencies.

The accompanying map of the freeway system should help you place the names and numbers on a generalized map of the area, but we recommend that you not set out without obtaining a more detailed map than this. *Thomas Guides*, books with excellent maps of the entire county, are widely available at bookstores and elsewhere. If you plan to do a lot of exploring, you may find one worthwhile. Ask the advice of people at your hotel or of friends before you start out; take notes, then have a good time. Despite what you've heard, traffic is not always a major problem outside of rush hours, considering you're in the land of valet parking. Parking can be a challenge, though, because this is a crowded and busy city.

Important Addresses and Numbers

Tourist Information **Visitor Information Center,** Arco Plaza, Level B, 6th and Flower sts., tel. 213/689–8822. Open Mon. through Sat. 8–5.
Greater Los Angeles Visitor and Convention Bureau, 515 S. Figueroa, 90071, tel. 213/624–7300.
Beverly Hills Visitors and Convention Bureau, 239 S. Beverly Dr., 90212, tel. 213/271–8174. Open weekdays 8:30–5.
Santa Monica Visitors Center, 1400 Ocean Ave. (in Palisades Park), tel. 213/393–7593. Open daily 10–4. Write to 2219 Main St., 90405.
Hollywood Visitors Center, 6541 Hollywood Blvd., 90028, tel. 213/461–4213. Open weekdays 9–5.
Pasadena Convention and Visitors Bureau, 171 S. Los Robles Ave., 91101, tel. 818/795–9311. Open weekdays 9–5, Sat. 10–4.

Emergencies Dial 911 for **police** and **ambulance** in an emergency.

Doctor **Los Angeles Medical Association Physicians Referral Service,** tel. 213/483–6122. Open weekdays 9–4:45. Most larger hospitals in L.A. have 24-hour emergency rooms. A few are **St. John's Hospital and Health Center** (1328 22nd St., tel. 213/829–5511), **Cedar-Sinai Medical Center** (8700 Beverly Blvd., tel. 213/855–5000), and **Hollywood Presbyterian Medical Center** (1300 N. Vermont Ave., tel. 213/660–3530).

24-Hour Pharmacies **Horton and Converse Pharmacy** (6625 Van Nuys Blvd., Van Nuys, tel. 818/782–6251).
Bellflower Pharmacy (9400 E. Rosecrans Ave., Bellflower, tel. 213/920–4213).

Los Angeles Freeways

SAN FERNANDO

Foothill Fwy.

118

5

Golden State Fwy.

210

Angeles Crest Hwy.

2

LA CAÑADA FLINTRIDGE

170

Hollywood Fwy.

VAN NUYS

NORTH HOLLYWOOD

BURBANK

GLENDALE

PASADENA
Foothill Fwy.

210

101

Ventura Fwy.

134

SHERMAN OAKS

Griffith Park

5

2

Pasadena Fwy.

Huntington Dr.

SAN MARINO

110

101

WEST HOLLYWOOD

BEVERLY HILLS

Santa Monica Blvd.

ALHAMBRA

SAN GABRIEL

405

Sunset Blvd.

WESTWOOD

HOLLYWOOD

Wilshire Blvd.

Dodger Stadium

San Bernardino Fwy.

Santa Monica

Blvd.

Blvd.

DOWNTOWN

110

MONTEREY PARK

10

2

Santa Monica Fwy.

10

60

Pomona Fwy.

SANTA MONICA

San Diego Fwy.

CULVER CITY

La Cienega Blvd.

La Brea

Western Ave.

72

Santa Ana Fwy.

Rosemead Blvd.

VENICE

MARINA DEL REY

Lincoln Blvd.

Slauson Ave.

INGLEWOOD

42

Manchester Ave.

Firestone

HUNTINGTON PARK

Blvd.

Long Beach Blvd.

710

19

River Fwy.

Los Angeles International Airport

Harbor Fwy.

DOWNEY

42

5

EL SEGUNDO

1

Imperial Hwy.

405

Hawthorne Blvd.

Crenshaw Blvd.

Western Ave.

Rosecrans Ave.

MANHATTAN BEACH

Sepulveda

San Gabriel River

605

Alcondra Blvd.

Lakewood Blvd.

HERMOSA BEACH

91

COMPTON

TORRANCE

Pacific Coast Hwy.

San Diego Fwy.

Long Beach Fwy.

LAKEWOOD

REDONDO BEACH

Sepulveda Blvd.

110

PACIFIC OCEAN

Willow St.

710

PALOS VERDES ESTATES

1

19

Pacific Coast Hwy.

Ocean Blvd.

11

RANCH PALOS VERDES

SAN PEDRO

LONG BEACH

N

0 ____ 5 miles

0 ____ 5 km

Horton and Converse (11600 Wilshire Blvd., tel. 213/478–0801, and 3875 Wilshire Blvd., tel. 213/382–2236. Open until 2 AM).

Surf and Weather Call 213/451–8761 for all beach information, pollution alerts.

Guided Tours

Los Angeles is such a hodgepodge of different locales and such a wealth of sightseeing possibilities that it can be mind-boggling. In order to get a feel for the whole city, the traditional tour in a big bus is probably the best way to start. These are priced fairly (about $25) and run frequently. Then, after you see what interests you most about the city, think about taking a smaller tour. Several companies offer more specific ones—shopping, Hollywood landmarks, historical locations.

Orientation Tours **Gray Line** (1207 W. 3rd St., 90017, tel. 213/856–5900). One of the best known tour companies in the country, Gray Line offers several tours of Los Angeles in big tour buses that pick up from more than 140 hotels in Los Angeles. There are more than 24 reasonably priced tours to choose from: tours to attractions such as Disneyland, Universal Studios, *Queen Mary* and *Spruce Goose*, and Catalina Island. "The Premiere Tour" (Hollywood, Beverly Hills, and the City of Los Angeles) will give you the best overview of the city. It lasts most of the day. Reservations must be made in advance; many hotels can book tours for you.

StarLine Sightseeing Tours (6845 Hollywood Blvd., Hollywood 90028, tel. 213/463–3131) has been showing people around Los Angeles in large touring buses since 1935. StarLine picks up at most area hotels. Tours are offered in English, French, German, and Spanish. There are tours to Knott's Berry Farm, Disneyland, and all the usual places; especially popular is the four-hour "Stars' Homes Tour."

Casablanca Tours (Roosevelt Hotel, 7000 Hollywood Blvd, Cabana 4, Hollywood 90028, tel. 213/461–0156) offers a more personalized look at Hollywood and Beverly Hills. The four-hour tour, which can be taken in the morning or afternoon, starts in Hollywood; join it there or be picked up at most centrally located hotels. Tours are in minibuses with a maximum of 12 or 13 people, and prices are equivalent to those of the large-bus tours. Guides are college students with a high-spirited view of the city.

Special-Interest Tours **Grave Line Tours** (Box 931694, Hollywood 90093, tel. 213/876–0920) digs up the dirt on notorious suicides and visits the scenes of various murders, scandals, and other crimes via a luxuriously renovated hearse. It's a clever, off-the-beaten-track tour in the true sensationalist spirit of Hollywood. Two-hour tours daily at noon; $30 per person reserved, $25 standby.

Hollywood on Parade Tour (Graham Hill Enterprises, Box 11414, Burbank 91510, tel. 818/843–3415) has been showing visitors the inner workings of Hollywood for 10 years and takes people to the *real* Hollywood not seen on larger tours. Production minibuses and picture vehicles are used for the tours, which usually book only about six or seven people and last four hours. Vans pick up at Hollywood and Burbank hotels, or meet people at a specified location.

The Next Stage (Box 35269, Los Angeles 90035, tel. 213/939–2688) is for visitors to Los Angeles who want something really different. Such intrepid souls should check with Marlene Gordon, whose innovative tour company offers an ever-changing selection of tours for 4–46 people, ranging from Victorian L.A. and Underground L.A. (in which all the places visited are underground) to the favorite Insomniac Tour that visits the flower market and other places in the wee hours of the morning.

LA Today Custom Tours (Elinor Oswald, 14964 Camarosa Dr., Pacific Palisades 90272, tel. 213/454–5730) also has a wide selection of offbeat tours. With preplanning, individuals can join in with larger (8–50), custom groups for seasonal and cultural events—garden tours, theater events, the Rose Bowl.

Personal Guides **Tour Elegante** (15446 Sherman Way, Van Nuys, tel. 818/786–8466) extends the perks of a personal guide, without the usual expense. Tours with a few people in a Lincoln touring car can come to less than $50 per person.

Elegant Tours for the Discriminating (tel. 213/472–4090) is a personalized sightseeing and shopping service for the Beverly Hills area. Joan Mansfield offers her extensive knowledge of Rodeo Drive to one to three people at a time. For those unfamiliar and intimidated shoppers, this is the perfect way to plunge into the street. Lunch is included and the price depends on the time spent and places covered.

Judith Benjamin Personally Designed Sightseeing (2210 Wilshire Blvd., #754, Santa Monica 90403, tel. 213/826–8810) also matches your interests with sightseeing outings. Judith will design architectural tours, museum tours, shopping tours, or jazz nightclub safaris—anything you might want to see in Los Angeles.

L.A. Nighthawks (Box 10224, Beverly Hills 90213, tel. 213/859–1171). If you have heard about the hot Los Angeles night scene but are afraid to tackle it on your own, this service will do it for a few people at a rather hefty price. In this case, you get what you pay for, and you pay for royal treatment—limousine, guide, gourmet dinner, tips, and tax, as well as immediate entry into L.A.'s hottest night spots. For a group of eight, prices come down considerably because vans or tour buses are used. Nighthawks proprietor, Charles Andrews, a music writer and 20-year entertainment-business veteran, has been featured on *Eye on LA* and other television shows for this innovative approach to nighttime entertainment.

Exploring Los Angeles

In a city where the residents think nothing of a 40-mile commute to work, visitors have their work cut out for them. To see the sites—from the Huntington Library in San Marino to the *Queen Mary* in Long Beach—requires a decidedly organized itinerary. Be prepared to put miles on the car. It's best to view Los Angeles as a collection of destinations, each to be explored separately, rather than to jump willy-nilly from place to place. In this edition, the major sightseeing areas of the Los Angeles area have been divided among seven major tours: Downtown; Hollywood; Wilshire Boulevard; Westside; Santa Monica, Venice, Pacific Palisades, and Malibu; Palos Verdes, San Pedro, and Long Beach; and Highland Park, Pasadena, and San Marino.

These tours are followed by short sections describing an assortment of other attractions, things to do for free, and things to see and do with children.

Downtown Los Angeles

Numbers in the margin correspond with points of interest on the Downtown Los Angeles map.

All those jokes about Los Angeles being a city without a downtown are simply no longer true. They might have had some ring of truth to them a few decades ago when Angelenos ruthlessly turned their back on the city center and hightailed it to the suburbs without a single look back. There *had* been a downtown, once, when Los Angeles was very young, and now the city core is enjoying a resurgence of attention from urban planners, real estate developers, and intrepid downtown office workers who have discovered the advantages of living close to the office. Consequently, a tour cuts through more than a century of history and colorful ethnic neighborhoods. During the day, downtown is relatively safe and quite interesting.

Downtown Los Angeles can be explored on foot or bus. Getting around to the major sites in downtown Los Angeles is actually quite simple, thanks to DASH (Downtown Area Short Hop). This minibus service travels in a loop past most of the attractions listed here. Every ride costs 25¢, so if you hop on and off to see attractions, it'll cost you each time. The cost is worth it, though, because you can travel quickly and be assured of finding your way. Whether you begin your tour at ARCO, as suggested, or decide to start at Olvera Street or Chinatown, DASH will get you around. The bus stops every 2 blocks or so. *DASH (tel. 800/874–8885) runs weekdays 6:30–6:30, Sat. 9–5.*

Begin your walk in the Los Angeles of today. Your walk will take you from the most modern buildings back in time past Art Deco movie palaces to the very oldest adobe in the city.

ARCO Plaza is hidden directly under the twin ARCO towers. This subterranean shopping mall is jam-packed with office workers during the week, nearly deserted on weekends. The ❶ **Greater Los Angeles Visitor and Convention Bureau** is housed on level B. It offers free information about attractions all over Los Angeles as well as advice on public transportation. *695 S. Figueroa St., tel. 213/689–8822. Open weekdays 9–5.*

❷ Just north of ARCO, the **Westin Bonaventure Hotel** (404 S. Figueroa St., tel. 213/624–1000) is unique in the L.A. skyline: five shimmering cylinders in the sky, with not a 90-degree angle in sight. Designed by John Portman in 1974, it remains a science-fiction fantasy. Non-guests can use only one elevator that rises through the roof of the lobby to soar through the air outside to the revolving restaurant and bar on the 35th floor. Food is expensive here. A better bet is to come for a drink (still overpriced) and nurse it for an hour as L.A. makes a full circle around you.

In the 19th century, Bunker Hill was the site of many stately mansions. Thanks to bulldozers, there's not much of a hill left, but this downtown area is being redeveloped, and two major sites here showcase visual arts (painting, sculpture, and environmental work), and media and performing arts.

Downtown Los Angeles

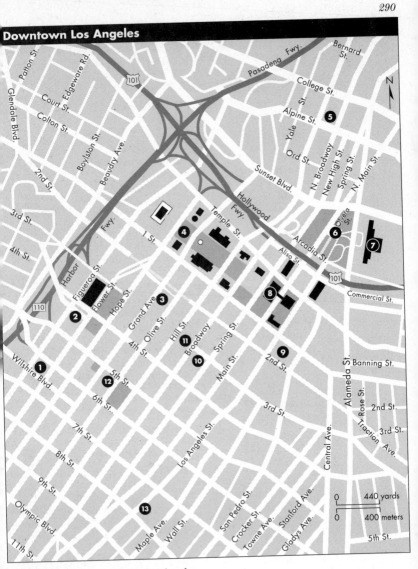

Biltmore Hotel, **12**
Bradbury Building, **10**
Chinatown, **5**
El Pueblo State
Historic Park, **6**
Garment District, **13**
Grand Central
Market, **11**

Greater Los Angeles
Visitor and Convention
Bureau, **1**
Little Tokyo, **9**
Los Angeles City
Hall, **8**
Museum of
Contemporary Art, **3**
Music Center, **4**
Union Station, **7**
Westin Bonaventure
Hotel, **2**

3 The **Museum of Contemporary Art** houses a permanent collection of international scope, representing modern art from 1940 to the present. Included are works by Mark Rothko, Franz Kline, and Susan Rothenberg. The red sandstone building, designed by Japan's renowned architect Arata Isozaki, opened in late 1986. Pyramidal skylights add a striking geometry to the 7-level, 98,000-square-foot building. Don't miss the gift shop or the lively Milanese-style cafe. *250 S. Grand Ave., tel. 213/626–6222. Open Tues.–Wed. and weekends 11–6, Thurs. 11–8. Admission: $4 adults, children under 12 free. Admission free to all Thurs. after 5 PM.*

4 Walk north to **The Music Center,** which has become the cultural center for Los Angeles since it opened in 1969. The Dorothy Chandler Pavilion, the largest and grandest of the three theaters, was named after the widow of the *Los Angeles Times* publisher who was instrumental in fund-raising efforts to build the complex. The round Mark Taper Forum building, in the middle, seats only 750 and seems almost cozy. Most of its offerings are of an experimental nature, many of them on a pre-Broadway run. The Ahmanson, at the north end, is the venue for many musical comedies. The plaza has a fountain and sculpture by Jacques Lipchitz. *1st St. and Grand Ave., tel. 213/972–7211. Free 70-min. tours are offered Tues.–Sat. 10–1:30. Call for reservations.*

5 L.A.'s **Chinatown** runs a pale second to the San Francisco version, but it still offers visitors an authentic slice of life, beyond the tourist hokum. Bordered by Yale, Bernard, Alameda, and Ord, the neighborhood's main street is North Broadway, where, every February, giant dragons snake down the center of the pavement during Chinese New Year celebrations. More than 15,000 Chinese and Southeast Asians (mostly Vietnamese) actually live in the Chinatown area, but many times that number regularly frequent the markets (filled with exotic foods unfamiliar to most Western eyes) and restaurants (dim sum parlors are currently the most popular).

6 **El Pueblo State Historic Park** preserves the "birthplace" of Los Angeles (no one knows exactly where the original 1781 settlement was), the oldest downtown buildings, and some of the only remaining pre-1900 buildings in the city. Comprising 44 acres and including the Plaza and Olvera Street, the state park is bounded by Alameda, Arcadia, Spring, and Macy streets. *The Visitors Center is in Sepulveda House, 622 N. Main St., tel. 213/628–1274. Open weekdays 10–3, Sat. 10–4:30. Most shops and restaurants in the park are open daily 10–9.*

Olvera Street is the heart of the park and one of the most popular tourist sites in Los Angeles.

With its cobblestone walkways, piñatas, mariachis, and authentic Mexican food, Olvera Street should not be dismissed as a mere approximation of Old Mexico, or a gringo version of the real thing. Mexican families come here in droves, especially on weekends and Mexican holidays, because to them it feels like the old country.

Begin your walk of the area at the Plaza, between Main and Los Angeles streets. The wonderful Mexican-style park lulls you with shady trees, a central gazebo and plenty of benches, and walkways for strolling. Frequently on weekends mariachis and folkloric dance groups perform here. In an oversize velvet sombrero, you can have your photo taken astride a stuffed donkey (a takeoff of the zebra-striped donkeys that are a tradition on the streets of Tijuana).

Head north up Olvera Street proper. Mid-block is the Sepulveda House, site of the Visitors Center and a renovation project. The Eastlake Victorian was built in 1887 as a hotel and boardinghouse. Pelanconi House, completed in 1855, was the first brick building in Los Angeles and has been used by La Golondrina restaurant for more than 50 years. During the 1930s, famed Mexican muralist David Alfaro Siqueiros was commissioned to paint a mural on the south wall of the Italian Hall building. The patrons were not prepared for the anti-imperialist mural depicting the oppressed workers of Latin America held in check by a menacing American eagle; it was immediately whitewashed into oblivion. It remains under the paint to this day, as preservationists from the Getty Conservation Trust work on ways to restore the mural. (Ask to see copies of the mural at the visitors' center.)

Walk down the east side of Olvera Street to mid-block and pass the only remaining sign of Zanja Ditch ("mother ditch"), which supplied water to the area in the earliest years. Avila Adobe (open weekdays 10–3), built in 1818, is generally considered the oldest building still standing in Los Angeles. This graceful, simple adobe is designed with traditional interior courtyard. It is furnished in typical 1840 fashion.

On weekends, the restaurants are packed and there is usually music in the plaza and along the street. Two Mexican holidays, Cinco de Mayo (May 5) and Independence Day (September 16) also draw huge crowds—and long lines for the restaurants. To see Olvera Street at its quietest and perhaps loveliest, visit late on a weekday afternoon. The long shadows heighten the romantic feeling of the street and there are only a few strollers and diners milling about.

South of the plaza is an ambitious area that has undergone recent renovation but remains largely underutilized. Except for docent-led tours, these magnificent old buildings remain closed, awaiting some commercial plan (à la Ghirardelli Square in San Francisco) that never seems to come to fruition. Buildings seen on tours include the Merced Theater, Masonic Temple, Pico House, and the Garnier Block—all ornate examples of the late 19th-century style. Under the Merced-Theater and Masonic Temple are the catacombs, secret passageways and old opium dens used by Chinese immigrants. Tours depart Tuesday–Saturday 10–1, on the hour. Meet at the Old Firehouse (south side of plaza), an 1884 building that contains early fire-fighting equipment and old photographs.

Time Out The Olvera Street restaurants run the gamut from fast-food stands to comfortable, sit-down dinner houses. The most authentic food is at **La Luz del Dia,** at the southwest corner of the street. Here are served traditional Mexican favorites like barbecued goat and pickled cactus as well as such standbys as tacos and enchiladas. Best of all are the handmade tortillas. You haven't tasted real tortillas until you've tried handmade ones like these (the only ones on the street), which are patted out in a practiced rhythm by the women behind the counter.

❼ **Union Station** (800 N. Alameda St.) directly east of Olvera Street across Alameda, is one of those quintessentially California buildings that seemed to define Los Angeles to moviegoers all over the country in the 1940s. Built in 1939, its Spanish mission style is a subtle combination of streamlined modern and Moorish. The majestic scale of the waiting room is definitely worth a visit. Imagine it in its heyday, as Carole Lombard or Groucho Marx or Barbara Stanwyck might alight from a train and sashay through.

❽ **Los Angeles City Hall** is another often-photographed building. It's been used in "Dragnet," "Superman," and other TV shows. Opened in 1928, the 27-story City Hall remained the only building to break the 13-story height limit (earthquakes, you know) until 1957. Although other buildings (e.g., the Bonaventure) may afford higher views, City Hall offers a 45-minute tour and ride to the top floor observation deck. *200 N. Spring St., tel. 213/485–4423. Tours are by reservation only, weekdays mornings at 10 and 11.*

❾ **Little Tokyo** is the original ethnic neighborhood for Los Angeles' Japanese community. Though most Japanese now have deserted the downtown center for suburban areas like Gardena and West Los Angeles, Little Tokyo remains a cultural focal point. Nisei (the name for second-generation Japanese) Week is celebrated here every August with traditional drums, obon dancing, a carnival, and a huge parade. Bounded by First, San Pedro, Third, and Los Angeles streets, Little Tokyo has dozens of sushi bars, tempura restaurants, trinket shops, and even an eel-only restaurant. The Japanese American Cultural and Community Center presents events such as kabuki theater straight from Japan.

Broadway between First and Ninth is one of Los Angeles' busiest shopping streets. The shops and sidewalk vendors cater to various clienteles with bridal shops, immigration lawyers, and cheap stereos. First-floor rental space is said to be the most expensive in the city, priced even higher than in Beverly Hills. It can be an exhilarating slice-of-life walk, past the florid old movie theaters like the Mayan and the Million Dollar, and the still-classy-no-matter-what Bradbury Building.

❿ The 5-story **Bradbury Building** (304 S. Broadway, tel. 213/489–1893) remains a marvelous specimen of architecture, serenely anchoring the southeast corner of Third and Broadway and keeping its nose above the hustle and bustle of the street. Once the site of turn-of-the-century sweatshops, it now houses genteel law offices. The interior courtyard with its glass skylight and open balconies and elevator is picture-perfect—and naturally another popular movie locale. The building is only open on weekdays and its owners prefer that you not wander too far past the lobby.

⓫ **Grand Central Market** is the busiest market in the city and a testimony to L.A.'s diversity. The block-through market of colorful and exotic produce, herbs, and meat draws a faithful clientele from the Hispanic community, senior citizens on a budget, and money-is-no-object Westside matrons seeking rare foodstuffs for their recipe adventures. Even if you don't plan to buy even one banana, Grand Central Market is a delightful place to browse. The produce stalls are piled high with the ripest, reddest tomatoes. The herb stalls promise remedies for all your ills. Mixed among them are fast-food stands (one Chinese but most Mexican). *317 S. Broadway. Open Mon.–Sat. 9–6, Sun. 10–4.*

⑫ The **Biltmore Hotel** (515 S. Olive St.) rivals Union Station for sheer majesty in the Spanish Revival tradition. The public areas have recently been restored; the magnificent, hand-painted wood beams brought back to their former glory.

⑬ **The Garment District** (700–800 blocks of Los Angeles St.) is an enclave of jobbers and wholesalers who sell off the leftovers from Los Angeles's considerable garment industry production. The Cooper Building (860 S. Los Angeles St.) is the heart of the district and houses several of what local bargain-hunters consider to be the best pickings.

Hollywood

Numbers in the margin correspond with points of interest on the Hollywood map.

Hollywood. The name once defined movie stars, glamour, the Big Time. The big studios were here; starlets lived in sorority-like buildings in the center of town; the latest movies premiered at the Chinese and the Pantages.

Those days are gone. Paramount is the only major studio left, and some celebrities may live in the Hollywood Hills, but certainly not in the "flats." Hollywood is no longer Hollywood. These days it is, even to its supporters, a seedy town that could use a good dose of urban renewal. Why visit? Because the legends of the Golden Age of the Silver Screen are heavy in the air. Because this is where "they" were: Judy Garland lived here, so did Marilyn Monroe, and Lana Turner. Because visitors are able to look past the junky shops and the lost souls who walk the streets to get a sense of yesterday. Even today, no visit to Los Angeles is truly complete without a walk down Hollywood Boulevard.

❶ Begin your tour of Hollywood simply by looking to the **Hollywood sign** in the Hollywood Hills that line the northern border of the town. Even on the smoggiest of days, the sign is visible for miles. It is north of Beachwood Canyon, approximately 1 mile east of Hollywood and Vine. The sign was erected in 1923 as a promotional scheme for a real estate development called Hollywoodland. (The sign originally read "Hollywoodland"; "land" was taken down in 1949.) Standing high on Mount Lee, the 50-foot-high letters seem to be an ongoing lure for vandals and pranksters. There has been only one known suicide off the letters (in 1932), but every year there are several alterations (dopers turning it into "Hollyweed", right-wingers into "Ollywood" during the Iran-Contra hearings).

❷ **Hollywood and Vine** was once considered the heart of Hollywood. The mere mention of the intersection inspired thoughts of starlets and movie moguls passing by, on foot and in jazzy convertibles. These days, Hollywood and Vine is far from the action. Pedestrian traffic is—well, pedestrian. No stars. No starlets. The big Broadway department store on the southwest corner is closed. The intersection is little more than a place for visitors to get their bearings.

❸ Capitol Records Building. When Capitol decided to build its headquarters building just north of Hollywood at 1756 North Vine, two big Capitol talents of the day (singer Nat King Cole and songwriter Johnny Mercer) suggested that it be done in the shape of a stack of records. It opened in 1956, the very picture of '50s chic. These days, it doesn't seem so odd.

❹ The Palace, just across the street at 1735 North Vine, was opened in 1927 as the Hollywood Playhouse. It has played host to many shows over the years, from Ken Murray's "Blackouts" to Ralph Edwards's "This Is Your Life." It is now the site of popular rock concerts.

❺ The Pantages Theater, at 6233 Hollywood, just east of Vine, opened in 1930, the very height of movie theater opulence. From 1949 to 1959, it was the site of the Academy Awards presentations.

❻ The Hollywood Walk of Fame is at every turn as you make your way through downtown Hollywood on foot. The sidewalks of Hollywood feature dark gray terrazzo circles embedded with pink-colored stars with the name of a Hollywood legend in brass in the center. In 1960, at the northwest corner of Highland Avenue and Hollywood Boulevard, the first eight names were unveiled: Olive Borden, Ronald Colman, Louise Fazenda, Preston Foster, Burt Lancaster, Edward Sedgwick, Ernest Torrence, and Joanne Woodward. In the years since, 1,800 others have been added. Being walked on, day after day, may be a celebrity's dream, but it does not come cheap. The personality in question (or, for instance, the record company) must pay for the honor: $3,500. Walk a few blocks and you'll quickly find that not all the names are familiar. Many are stars from the earliest days of Hollywood. To aid in the identification, celebrities are identified by one of five logos: a motion picture camera, a radio microphone, a television set, a record, or theatrical masks. Here's a guide to a few of the more famous stars on the Walk of Fame: Marlon Brando at 1765 Vine, Charlie Chaplin at 6751 Hollywood, W.C. Fields at 7004 Hollywood, Clark Gable at 1608 Vine, Marilyn Monroe at 6774 Hollywood, Rudolph Valentino at 6164 Hollywood, and John Wayne at 1541 Vine.

❼ Frederick's of Hollywood (6608 Hollywood Blvd., tel. 213/466–8506) is one of Hollywood's more infamous spots. Until recently, a gaudy lavender building, Frederick's was restored in 1989 to its original understated fushia-and-gray art deco look. Inside, it houses the famous name in trashy lingerie and is a popular tourist spot, if only for a good giggle.

❽ Hollywood Wax Museum. It's not the same as seeing them in the flesh, but the museum can offer visitors sights that real life no longer can (Mary Pickford, Elvis Presley, and Clark Gable) and a few that even real life never did (Rambo and Conan). A short film on Academy Award winners is shown daily. *6767 Hollywood Blvd., tel. 213/462–8860. Open Sun.–Thurs. 10 AM–midnight, Fri. and Sat. 10 AM–2 AM. Admission: $7 adults, $5 children.*

❾ It took the residents quite a few years to stop calling **Mann's Chinese Theatre** (6925 Hollywood Blvd., tel. 213/464–8111) "Grauman's Chinese," but now the new owners seem to have a firm hold on the place in the public's eye. The theater opened in 1927 with the premier of Cecil B. de Mille's *King of Kings.* The architecture is a fantasy of Chinese pagodas and temples as

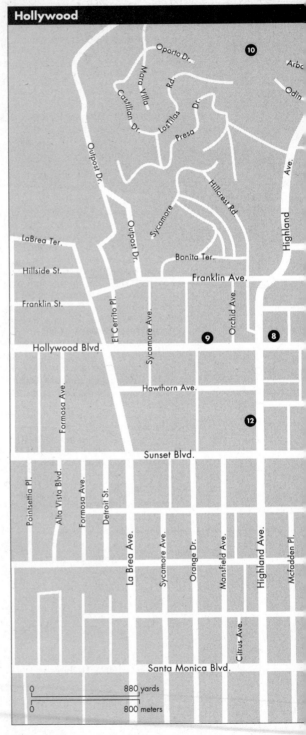

Hollywood

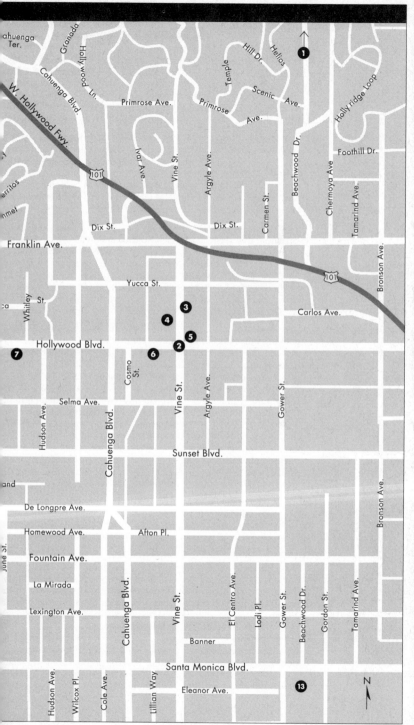

only Hollywood could turn out. Although you'll have to buy a movie ticket to appreciate both the interior trappings and the exterior excess, the courtyard is open for browsing. You'll see the famous cement hand and foot prints. The tradition is said to have begun at the premiere itself, when actress Norma Talmadge accidentally stepped in the wet cement. Now more than 160 celebrities have added their footprints, handprints, and even a few oddball impressions like Jimmy Durante's nose. Space has pretty much run out and, unlike the Walk of Fame on the sidewalks, these cement autographs are by invitation only.

10 Summer evening concerts at the **Hollywood Bowl** have been a tradition since 1922, although the shell has been replaced several times. The 17,000-plus seating capacity ranges from boxes (where local society matrons put on incredibly fancy alfresco preconcert meals for their friends) to cement bleachers in the rear. Some people prefer the back rows of the bleachers for their romantic appeal.

The official concert season begins in early July and runs through mid-September with performances on Tuesday, Thursday, and the weekend. The programs range from jazz to pop to classical. Evenings can be chilly (even after 90-degree days), so bring a sweater and wear comfortable shoes. A night at the Bowl involves considerable walking. *2301 N. Highland Ave., tel. 213/850–2000. Grounds open daily in summer, 9–sunset. Call for program schedule.*

11 The **Hollywood Studio Museum** sits in the Hollywood Bowl parking lot, east of Highland Avenue. The building, recently moved to this site, was once called the Lasky-de Mille Barn and it was where Cecil B. de Mille produced the first feature-length film, *The Squaw Man.* In 1927, the barn became Paramount Pictures, with the original company of Jesse Lasky, Cecil B. de Mille, and Samuel Goldwyn. The museum shows the origin of the motion picture industry. There's a re-creation of Cecil B. de Mille's office, with original artifacts and a screening room offering vintage film footage of Hollywood and its legends. An excellent gift shop sells quality vintage memorabilia like autographs, photographs, and books. *2100 N. Highland Ave., tel. 213/874–2276. Open Tues.–Fri. 11–4, weekends 10–4. Admission: $3.50 adults, $2.50 children.*

12 **Hollywood High School** at 1521 North Highland Avenue, has been attended by such stars as Carol Burnett, Linda Evans, Ricky Nelson, and Lana Turner. Today, the student body is as diverse as Los Angeles itself, with just about every ethnic group represented.

Many of Hollywood's stars, from the silent-screen era on, are
13 buried in **Hollywood Memorial Cemetery,** a few blocks from Paramount Studios. Walk from the entrance to the lake area and you'll find the crypt of Cecil B. de Mille and the graves of Nelson Eddy and Douglas Fairbanks, Sr. Inside the Cathedral Mausoleum is Rudolph Valentino's crypt (where fans, the press, and the famous Lady in Black turn up every August 23, the anniversary of his death). Other stars interred in this section are Peter Lorre and Eleanor Powell. In the Abbey of Palms Mausoleum, Norma Talmadge and Clifton Webb are buried. *6000 Santa Monica Blvd., tel. 213/469–1181. Open daily 8–5.*

Wilshire Boulevard

Wilshire Boulevard begins in the heart of downtown Los Angeles and runs west, through Beverly Hills and Santa Monica, and ends at the cliffs above the Pacific Ocean. In 16 miles it moves through poor immigrant neighborhoods to middle-class ones and on through a corridor of the highest-priced high-rise condos in the city. Along the way (within a few blocks of each other) are many of L.A.'s top architectural sites, museums, and shops.

This linear tour can be started at any point along the way, but to really savor a true cross section of the city, it takes a Bullocks-west approach. It would be better to skip Koreatown, and pare down the museum time than to do only one stretch. All these sites are on Wilshire or within a few blocks north or south of it.

"One" Wilshire is just another anonymous office building in downtown Los Angeles. Begin, instead, a few miles westward. As you move from Wilshire Boulevard's downtown beginning, you pass through neighborhoods now populated by recent immigrants from Central America. In the early years, however, this area was home to many of the city's wealthy citizens, as the faded Victorian houses on the side streets attest.

As the population crept westward, the distance to downtown shops began to seem insurmountable, and the first suburban department store branch, **I. Magnin Wilshire** (3050 Wilshire Blvd., tel. 213/382–6161) was opened in 1929. To appreciate the real splendor of the store, enter from the rear. The behind-the-store parking lot was not only quite an innovation in 1929 but also the first accommodation a large Los Angeles store made to the automobile age. Study the ceiling of the porte cochère, where a mural depicts early-20th-century history. Inside, the store remains a well-preserved monument to the Art Deco age. The walls, the elevators, and the floors are the height of late 1920s style.

Koreatown begins almost at I. Magnin Wilshire's back door. Koreans are one of the newest and largest groups in this melting pot of a city. Arriving from the old country in better shape financially than most immigrant groups and settling in the area south of Wilshire Boulevard, along Olympic Boulevard between Vermont and Western avenues, the Korean community has slowly grown into a full-fledged enclave with active community groups and newspapers. The area is teeming with Asian restaurants (not just Korean but also Japanese and Chinese, because Koreans are fond of those cuisines). Many of the signs in this area are in Korean only.

At the southwest corner of Wilshire Boulevard and Western Avenue is the **Wiltern Theater,** one of the city's best examples of art deco. The 1930 zigzag design has been recently restored to its splendid turquoise hue. Inside, the theater is magnificently opulent, in the grand tradition.

Continuing west on Wilshire, the real estate values start to make a sharp climb. The mayor of Los Angeles has his official residence in **Getty House,** at 605 South Irving Boulevard, 1 block north of Wilshire in the Hancock Park district. This is one of the city's most genteel neighborhoods, remaining in vogue since its development in the 1920s. Many of L.A.'s old monied families live here in English Tudor homes with East Coast landscaping schemes that seem to defy the local climate and history. The white-brick, half-timber house was donated to the city by the Getty family.

Miracle Mile, the strip of Wilshire Boulevard between La Brea and Fairfax avenues, was so dubbed in the 1930s as a promotional gimmick to attract shoppers to the new stores. The buildings went into a decline in the '50s and '60s, but the area is now enjoying a strong comeback. Exceptionally striking art deco buildings like the Darkroom (5370 Wilshire Blvd.) and the El Rey Theater (5519 Wilshire Blvd.) stand out as examples of period design. In Callender's Restaurant (corner of Wilshire and Curson), there are recent murals as well as old photographs that effectively depict life on Miracle Mile during its heyday.

Across Curson Avenue is Hancock Park (not to be confused with the residential neighborhood of the same name). The park is home to two of the city's best museums as well as the city's world-famous fossil source, **La Brea Tar Pits.** Despite the fact that *brea* means tar in Spanish and to say "La Brea Tar Pits" is redundant, the name remains firm in local minds. These tar pits were known to the earliest inhabitants of the area and were long used to seal leaky boats and roofs. In the early 20th century, geologists discovered that the sticky goo contained the largest collection of Pleistocene fossils ever found at one location. Remains of more than 200 varieties of birds, mammals, plants, reptiles, and insects have been discovered here. Statues of the "mammoths" in the big pit near the corner of Wilshire and Curson depict the way in which many of them were entombed: Edging down to a pond of water to drink, the animals were caught in the tar and unable to extricate themselves.

The pits were formed about 35,000 years ago when deposits of oil rose to the earth's surface, collected in shallow pools, and coagulated into sticky asphalt. More than 100 tons of fossil bones have been removed in the 70 years since excavations began here, and there are several pits scattered around Hancock Park as a reminder of nature's superiority over man. Construction in the area has had to accommodate these oozing pits; in nearby streets and along sidewalks, little bits of tar continue to ooze up—unstoppable.

Also in Hancock Park, the **George C. Page Museum of La Brea Discoveries** is a satellite of the Los Angeles County Museum of Natural History. The modern Page Museum is set, bunkerlike, half underground; a bas relief around four sides depicts life in the Pleistocene era. The museum has more than a million Ice-Age fossils. Exhibits include reconstructed, life-size skeletons of mammals and birds whose fossils were recovered from the pits: saber-tooth cats, mammoths, wolves, sloths, eagles, and condors. Several large murals and colorful dioramas review the history of the Pleistocene era. The glass-enclosed Paleontological Laboratory permits observation of the ongoing cleaning, identification, and cataloguing of fossils excavated from the nearby asphalt deposits. *The La Brea Story* and *Dinosaurs, the Terrible Lizards* are short documentary films shown every 15–30 minutes, or so. A hologram magically puts flesh on "La Brea Woman," and a tar contraption shows visitors just how hard it would be to get free from the sticky mess. An excellent gift shop offers nature-oriented books and trinkets. *5801 Wilshire Blvd., tel. 213/936–2230. Open Tues.–Sun. 10–5. Admission: $3 adults, 75¢ children; free the second Tues. of the month.*

The **Los Angeles County Museum of Art,** also in Hancock Park and the largest museum complex in Los Angeles, has grown considerably in the past few years as a result of generous donations from local patrons who are determined to put Los Angeles on the map, art-wise. The original buildings (Ahmanson Gallery, Frances and Armand Hammer Wing, and Leo S. Bing Center) have been joined by the Robert O. Anderson Building and the Pavilion for Japanese Art. The museum's new Wilshire Boulevard facade sports spiffy glass tile.

The Ahmanson Gallery, built around a graceful central atrium, houses a permanent collection of paintings, sculptures, graphic arts, costumes, textiles, and decorative arts from a variety of cultures and periods, prehistoric to present. Included are works by Picasso, Rembrandt, Veronese, Dürer, Hals, La Tour, and Winslow Homer. One of the Western world's largest collections of Indian, Nepalese, and Tibetan art is housed here. Major changing exhibitions are presented in the Frances and Armand Hammer Wing.

The Robert O. Anderson Building was completed in the fall of 1986. This 115,000-square-foot gallery features 20th-century art from the museum's permanent collection and traveling exhibits. The new Pavilion for Japanese Art houses the Sinen-Kan collection of more than 300 Japanese scroll paintings and screens.

The Leo S. Bing Center contains the Art Rental Gallery, the Bing Theater, Art Research Library, and the indoor-outdoor cafeteria-style Plaza Cafe. The museum provides many cultural activities, including film series, concerts, lectures, tours of the collections, and student programs. The Museum Shop carries books, magazines, postcards, posters, antiquities, jewelry, and gifts.

The museum, as well as the adjoining Page Museum and Hancock Park itself, is brimming with visitors on warm weekend days. Although crowded, it can be the most exciting time to visit the area. Mimes and itinerant musicians ply their trades. Street vendors sell fast-food treats and there are impromptu soccer games on the lawns. To really study the art on display though, a quieter weekday visit is recommended. *5905 Wilshire Blvd., tel. 213/857–6111. Open Tues.–Fri. 10–5, weekends 10–6. Admission: $5 adults, $4 children.*

The **Craft and Folk Art Museum,** across Wilshire, is sure to fascinate visitors with its exhibits of contemporary crafts as well as folk crafts from around the world. The museum's collections include Japanese, Mexican, American, and East Indian folk art, textiles, and masks. Six to eight major exhibitions are planned each year. The museum's library and media resources center are open to the public. The museum shop displays merchandise relating to each current exhibition, quality work by expert craftspeople, folk art from around the world, original postcards, and educational materials. *5814 Wilshire Blvd., tel. 213/937–5544. Open Tues.–Sun. 10–5. Admission: free, except for special events.*

Continue west on Wilshire a few blocks to the corner of Fairfax Avenue. On the northeast corner is the May Co. department store, another 1930s landmark with a distinctive curved corner.

Head north on Fairfax a few blocks to the **Farmers Market.** Thanks to tour bus operators and its own easygoing, all-year-outdoor setting, this is a popular stop for L.A. city tours. When it first opened in 1934, the market sold produce straight from the farm at bargain prices. These days, the produce is still tantalizing but definitely high-priced. No longer stocked with farm-fresh produce, the stands offer out-of-season peppers and tiny seedless champagne grapes from Chile at top prices. In mid-winter, the overflowing outdoor produce stands are a delightful sight.

In addition to produce stands, there are dozens of cooked-food stalls selling Cajun gumbos, Mexican enchiladas, fish and chips, frozen yogurt, pizza, and hamburgers. During lunch hours, the outdoor tables are packed, so visitors must scout around and grab one that is just being vacated. Gift shops display souvenir trinkets, and gourmet stands will ship dried fruits, nuts, and other goodies all over the world. *6333 W. 3rd St., tel. 213/933–9211. Open Mon.–Sat. 9–6:30, Sun. 10–5. Open later in summer.*

Time Out   **Kokomo** is not only the best place to eat in the Farmer's Market, it's got some of the best new-wave diner food anywhere in L.A. Lively, entertaining service is almost always included in the reasonable prices. *Located on the 3rd St. side of the market.*

North of the market, Fairfax becomes the center of Los Angeles's Jewish life. The shops and stands stretching north from Beverly Boulevard are enlivened with friendly conversation between shopkeepers and regular customers. Canter's Restaurant, Deli, and Bakery (419 N. Fairfax, tel. 213/651–2030) is the traditional hangout.

Westside

Numbers in the margin correspond with points of interest on the Westside map.

The Westside of Los Angeles, which to residents means from La Brea Avenue westward to the ocean, is where the rents are the most expensive, the real estate values sky high, the restaurants (and the restaurateurs) the most famous, the shops the most chic. It's the good life Southern California-style, and to really savor the Southland, spend a few leisurely days or half days exploring the area. Short on amusement parks, historic sites, museums, and other traditional tourist attractions, it more than compensates with great shopping districts, exciting walking streets, outdoor cafes, and lively nightlife.

The Westside can be best enjoyed in at least three separate outings, allowing plenty of time for browsing and dining. Attractions #1–4 are in the West Hollywood area; #5–8 in Beverly Hills, and #9–10, in Westwood. But the Westside is small enough to allow you to visit four or five of these sites at once, depending on your interests.

West Hollywood is a glitzy section of Los Angeles. Once an almost forgotten parcel of county land surrounded by the city of L.A. and Beverly Hills, it became an official city several years back. The West Hollywood attitude—trendy, stylish, with plenty of disposable income—spills over beyond the formal borders.

① **Melrose Avenue,** which isn't exactly in West Hollywood, nevertheless remains firmly fixed in residents' minds as *very* West Hollywood. If you're entertained by punks, people in spiked hairdos, and just about the most outlandish ensembles imaginable, Melrose is the place for you. Would-be rock stars and weekend punkers hang out and provide quite a show for the ordinary folks. The busiest stretch of Melrose is between Fairfax and La Brea avenues. Here you'll find one-of-a-kind boutiques and small, chic restaurants for more than a dozen blocks. Park on a side street (the parking regulations around here are vigorously enforced—a rich vein for the city's coffers) and begin walking. The quintessential Melrose shops are Soap Plant and Wacko, on the same block near the corner of Martel Avenue. Gaudy both inside and out and offering the most bizarre trinkets and books, these shops are just plain fun. Other busy shops: War Babies (clothes from the armies of the world) and Rene's (offbeat records and a local skateboarders' hangout as well).

Time Out Melrose has no shortage of great eateries. Part of any visit here is trying to pick one from the dozens of choices: Thai, Mexican, sausages, yogurt, Italian, and more. The ultimate Melrose "joint" is **Johnny Rocket's** (7507 Melrose Ave., tel. 213/651–3361), a very hip '50s-style diner near the corner of Gardner Street. It's just stools at a counter, the best of old-time rock and roll on tape, and great hamburgers, shakes, and fries—and almost always crowded, with people lined up behind the stools to slip in the moment they are vacated. Off-hours are best.

② **Beverly Center** (8500 Beverly Blvd. at La Cienega, tel. 213/854–0070) is that hulking monolith dominating the corner of La Cienega and Beverly Boulevard. Designed as an all-in-one stop for shopping, dining, and movies, it has been a boon to Westsiders—except those who suffer the congestion by living too close. Parking is on the second through fifth floors, shops on the sixth and seventh, and movies and restaurants on the eighth. The first floor features Irvine Ranch Market, a state-of-the-art gourmet grocery that is a booby trap for impulse buyers who love to try new foods. At the northwest corner, the Hard Rock Cafe (look for the vintage green Cadillac imbedded in the roof) always has a line of hungry customers (salivating for not only burgers but also a chance to see celebrities, who often come here). Upstairs in the center proper are two major department stores, dozens of upscale clothing boutiques, 14 movie theaters, and a wide variety of restaurants (Mandarin Cove, Siam Orchid, plus cookie shops, and pizza and hamburger stands).

③ West Hollywood is the center of Los Angeles' thriving interior-decorating business. **The Pacific Design Center** (8687 Melrose Ave., tel. 213/657–0800) has been dubbed the "Blue Whale" by residents. The all-blue-glass building was designed by Cesar Pelli in 1975 and houses to-the-trade-only showrooms filled

Westside

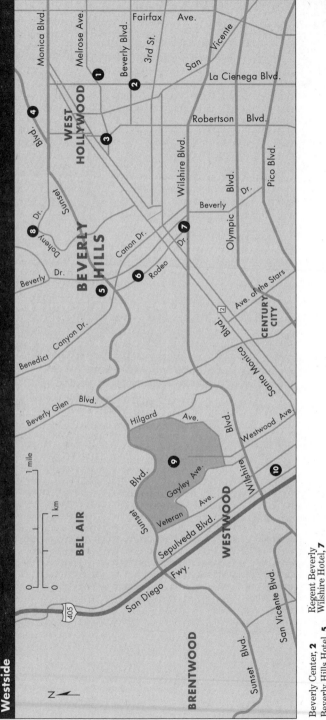

N

Beverly Center, **2**
Beverly Hills Hotel, **5**
Greystone Mansion, **8**
Melrose Avenue, **1**
Pacific Design
Center, **3**

Regent Beverly
Wilshire Hotel, **7**
Rodeo Drive, **6**
Sunset Strip, **4**
UCLA, **9**
Westwood Memorial
Park, **10**

with the most tempting furnishings, wallpapers, and accessories. In 1988, the center added a second eye-catching building by Pelli, this one clad in vivid green glass. Most of the showrooms discourage casual browsers, but the building is open and anyone can stroll the halls and rubberneck in the windows.

The same rules apply for Robertson Boulevard, the name given to the outside-PDC showrooms that surround the Blue Whale. They are not confined to Robertson Boulevard but are well represented on Beverly Boulevard and Melrose Avenue. This section is exceptionally walkable, and residents often walk their dogs here in the evening (even driving them to the area to do their walking) so they can browse the well-lighted windows. A few of the showrooms will accommodate an occasional retail buyer, so if you see something you'd die for, it's worth an inquiry inside.

4 **Sunset Strip** was famous in the '50s and depicted in the '60s in "77 Sunset Strip," but it was popular even in the 1930s when nightclubs like Ciro's and Mocambo were in their heyday. This windy, hilly stretch is a visual delight, enjoyed both by car (a convertible would be divine) or on foot. Drive it once to enjoy the hustle and bustle, the vanity boards (huge billboards touting new movies, new records, new stars), the dazzling shops. Then pick a section and explore a few blocks on foot. The Sunset Plaza section is especially nice, with expensive shops and a few outdoor cafes (Tutto Italia, Chin Chin) that are packed for lunch and on warm evenings. At Horn Street, Tower Records (a behemoth of a record store with two satellite shops across the street), Book Soup (finally, a literary book store in L.A.!), and Spago (tucked a half block up the hill on Horn) make a nice browse, especially in the evening.

At Doheny Drive, where Sunset Boulevard enters the world-famous and glamorous city of Beverly Hills, the glitz of the Strip ends as suddenly as it began. All at once the sidewalk street life gives way to expansive, perfectly manicured lawns and palatial homes, all representative of what the name Beverly Hills has come to mean.

5 West of the Strip a mile or so is the **Beverly Hills Hotel** (9641 Sunset Blvd., tel. 213/276–2251). Dubbed the "Pink Palace," its quiet Spanish Colonial Revival architecture and soft pastel exterior belie the excitement inside, where Hollywood moguls make deals over margaritas in the Polo Lounge and where many stars keep permanent bungalows as second homes.

It is on this stretch of Sunset, especially during the day, that you'll see hawkers peddling maps of stars' homes. Are the maps reliable? Well, that's a matter of debate. Stars do move around, so it's difficult to keep any map up to date. But the fun of looking at some of these magnificent homes, regardless of whether they're owned by a star of the moment, makes many people buy such maps and embark on such tours.

Beverly Hills was incorporated as a city early in the century and has been thriving ever since. As a vibrant, exciting city within the larger city, it has retained its reputation for wealth and luxury, an assessment with which you will agree as you drive along one of its main thoroughfares, Santa Monica Boulevard (which is actually two parallel streets at this point: "Big Santa Monica" is the northern street; "Little Santa Monica," the southern one).

Within a few square blocks in the center of the city are some of the most exotic, not to mention high-priced, stores in Southern California. Here one can find such items as $200 pairs of socks wrapped in gold leaf, and stores that take customers only by appointment. A fun way to spend an afternoon is to stroll famed **❻ Rodeo Drive** between Santa Monica and Wilshire boulevards. Some of the Rodeo (pronounced ro-DAY-o) shops may be familiar to you because they often furnish clothing for major network television shows and get their names to appear among the credits. Others, such as Gucci, have a worldwide reputation. Fortunately, browsing is free (and fun), no matter how expensive the merchandise. Several nearby restaurants have outside patios where you can sit and sip a drink while watching the fashionable shoppers stroll by.

❼ The **Regent Beverly Wilshire Hotel** (9500 Wilshire Blvd., tel. 213/275–4282) anchors the south end of Rodeo, at Wilshire. Opened in 1928, and vigorously expanded and renovated since, the hotel is often home to visiting royalty and celebrities, who arrive amid much fanfare at the porte cochère in the rear of the old structure. The lobby is quite small for a hotel of this size and there is little opportunity to meander; you might stop for a drink or meal in one of the hotel's restaurants.

❽ The **Greystone Mansion** was built by oilman Edward Doheny in 1923. This Tudor-style mansion, now owned by the city of Beverly Hills, sits on 16 landscaped acres and has been used in such films as *The Witches of Eastwick* and *All of Me*. The gardens are open for free self-guided tours, and peeking in the windows (only) is permitted. *905 Loma Vista Dr., Beverly Hills, tel. 213/550–4796. Open daily 10–5.*

One of Beverly Hills's mansions opens its grounds to visitors. The **Virginia Robinson Gardens** are 6.2 terraced acres on the former estate of the heir to the Robinson department store chain. A guide will take you on an hour-long tour of the gardens, the exquisite exteriors of the main house, guest house, servants' quarters, swimming pool, and tennis court. A highlight of the tour is the collection of rare and exotic palms. Because the garden's administrative people are trying to keep a low profile to avoid congestion in the cul-de-sac where this garden is situated, visitors must call for reservations and be told the address and directions. *Tel. 213/276–5367. Two tours daily, Tues.–Thurs. 10 AM and 1 PM, Fri. 10 AM. Admission: $3.*

Westward from Beverly Hills, Sunset continues to wind past **❾** palatial estates and passes by the **University of California at Los Angeles.** Nestled in the Westwood section of the city and bound by LeConte, Sunset, and Hilgard, the parklike UCLA campus is an inviting place for visitors to stroll. The most spectacular buildings are the original ones, Royce Hall and the library, both in Romanesque style. In the heart of the north campus is the Franklin Murphy Sculpture Garden with works by Henry Moore and Lachaise dotting the landscaping. For a gardening buff, UCLA is a treasure of unusual and well-labeled plants. The Mildred Mathias Botanic Garden is located in the southeast section of the campus and is accessible from Tiverton Avenue. Maps and information are available at drive-by kiosks at major entrances, even on weekends. Free, 90-minute, guided walking tours of the campus are offered on weekdays. The campus has several indoor and outdoor cafes plus bookstores that sell the popular UCLA Bruins paraphernalia. *Tours (tel. 213/825–4574) Mon.–Fri. at 10:30 AM and 1:30 PM. Meet at 10945 LeConte St., Rm 1417, on the south edge of the campus, facing Westwood.*

The **Hannah Carter Japanese Garden,** located in Bel Air just north of the campus, is owned by UCLA and may be visited by making phone reservations two weeks in advance (tel. 213/825–4574).

Directly south of the campus is Westwood, once a quiet college town and now one of the busiest places in the city on weekend evenings. It's so busy during the summer, in fact, that many streets are closed to car traffic, and visitors must park at the Federal Building (Wilshire and Veteran) and shuttle over. However you arrive, Westwood remains a delightful village filled with clever boutiques, trendy restaurants, movie theaters, and colorful street life.

The village proper is delineated on the south by Wilshire Boulevard, which is now a corridor of cheek-by-jowl office buildings whose varying architectural styles can be jarring, to say the least. Tucked behind one of these behemoths is **Westwood Memorial Park** (1218 Glendon Ave.). In this most unlikely place for a cemetery is one of the most famous graves in the city: Marilyn Monroe is buried in a simply marked wall crypt. For 25 years after her death, her former husband Joe DiMaggio had six red roses placed on her crypt three times a week. Also buried here is Natalie Wood.

Santa Monica, Venice, Pacific Palisades, and Malibu

Numbers in the margin correspond with points of interest on the Santa Monica and Venice map.

The towns that hug the coastline of Santa Monica Bay reflect the wide diversity of Los Angeles, from the rich-as-can-be Malibu to the neighboring yuppie-seedy mix of Venice. Life is lived outdoors here. While there are several small museums and historical sites on the way, the emphasis here is on being out in the sunshine, always within sight of the Pacific. Visitors might savor the area in two sections: Santa Monica to Venice in one day and Pacific Palisades to Malibu in another.

From Santa Monica to Venice   Santa Monica is a sensible place. A tidy little city, 2 miles square, the ethnic population is largely British (there's an English music hall and several pubs here), attracted perhaps by a cooler and foggier climate than that found in the rest of Southern California. The sense of order is reflected in the economic-geographic stratification: the most northern section has broad streets lined with superb, older homes. Driving south, real estate prices drop about $50,000 every block or so.

Begin exploring at **Santa Monica Pier,** located at the foot of Colorado Avenue and easily accessible for beach-goers as well as drive-around visitors. Cafes, gift shops, a psychic adviser, bumper cars, and arcades line the truncated pier, which was severely damaged in a storm a few years ago. The 46-horse carousel, built in 1922, has seen action in numerous movies and television shows, most notably the Paul Newman-Robert Redford film *The Sting. Tel. 213/394–7554. Carousel rides 50¢*

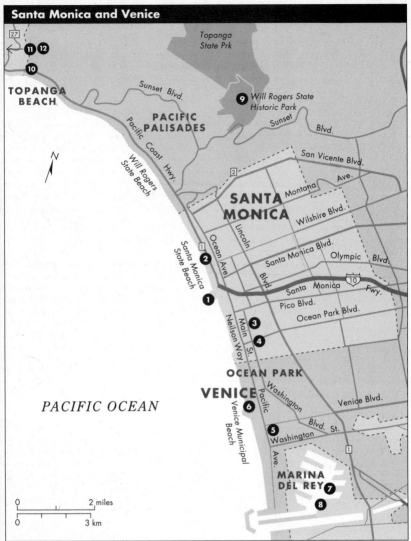

Santa Monica and Venice

Topanga
State Prk

Will Rogers State
Historic Park 9

Sunset Blvd.

TOPANGA
BEACH

PACIFIC
PALISADES

Sunset Blvd.

Pacific Coast Hwy.

Will Rogers State Beach

San Vicente Blvd.

2

SANTA
MONICA

Montana Ave.

Wilshire Blvd.

Lincoln

Ocean Ave.

Santa Monica State Beach

1

Santa Monica Blvd.

Olympic Blvd.

2

Santa Monica Fwy.

10

Pico Blvd.

Ocean Park Blvd.

Blvd.

3

Neilson Way

Main St.

4

OCEAN PARK

VENICE

Washington

Pacific

Venice Blvd.

PACIFIC OCEAN

Venice Municipal Beach

6

5

Blvd. St.

Washington

Ave.

1

MARINA
DEL REY

7

8

0   2 miles
0   3 km

Adamson House , **11**

Burton Chase Park, **7**

Fisherman's Village, **8**

J.Paul Getty
Museum, **10**

Malibu Lagoon State
Park, **12**

Pacific Ave./Venice
Blvd. Canals, **5**

Palisades Park, **2**

Santa Monica Heritage
Museum, **4**

Santa Monica Museum
of Art, **3**

Santa Monica Pier, **1**

Venice Boardwalk, **6**

Will Rogers State
Park, **9**

adults, 25¢ children. Open in summer, Tues.–Sun. 10–9; in winter, weekends 10–5.

② **Palisades Park** is a ribbon of green that runs along the top of the cliffs from Colorado Avenue to just north of San Vicente Boulevard. The flat walkways are usually filled with casual strollers as well as joggers who like to work out with a spectacular view of the Pacific as a backdrop. It is especially enjoyable at sunset.

The Visitor Information Center is located in the park at Santa Monica Boulevard. It offers bus schedules, directions, and information on Santa Monica-area attractions. *Tel. 213/393–7593. Open daily 10–4.*

Santa Monica has grown into a major center for the L.A. art **③** community and the brand new **Santa Monica Museum of Art** promises to boost that reputation. Designed by prominent local architect Frank Gehry, the museum presents the works of performance and video artists and exhibits lesser-known painters and sculptors. *2437 Main St., tel. 213/399–0433. $3 adults, $1 artists, students, and senior citizens. Open Wed., Thurs. 11–8, Fri.–Sun. 11–6.*

④ The **Santa Monica Heritage Museum,** housed in an 1894 vintage, late-Victorian home once owned by the founder of the city, was moved to its present site on trendy Main Street in the mid-1980s. Three rooms have been fully restored: the dining room in the style of 1890–1910; the living room, 1910–1920; and the kitchen, 1920–1930. The second-floor galleries feature photography and historical exhibits as well as shows by contemporary Santa Monica artists. *2612 Main St., tel. 213/392–8537. Open Thurs.–Sat. 11–4, Sun. noon–4.*

The museum faces a companion home: Another Victorian delight that is now the Chronicle restaurant has been moved to the site. These two dowagers anchor the northwest corner of the funky Main Street area of Santa Monica. Several blocks of old brick buildings here have undergone a recent rejuvenation (and considerable rent increases) and now house galleries, bars, cafes, omelet parlors, and boutiques. During warm months, it is an extremely popular place and rivals only Westwood as a stroll-and-dine area. With such proximity to the beach, parking can be tight on summer weekend days. Best bets are the city pay lots behind the Main Street shops, between Main and Neilson Way.

Venice was a turn-of-the-century fantasy that never quite came true. Abbot Kinney, a wealthy Los Angeles businessman, envisioned his little piece of real estate, which then seemed so far from downtown, as a romantic replica of Venice, Italy. He developed an incredible 16 miles of canals, floated gondolas on them, and built scaled-down versions of the Saint Mark's Church and other Venice landmarks. The name remains but the connection with the Old World Venice is flimsy. Kinney's project was bothered by ongoing engineering problems and disasters and soon drifted into disrepair. The arcaded "palaces" at Windward and Pacific streets house fast-food **⑤** restaurants, liquor stores, and boutiques. Three small **canals** and bridges remain and can be viewed from the southeast corner of Pacific Avenue and Venice Boulevard. Gone are the amusement park, swank seaside hotels, and gondoliers.

What's left is a colorful mishmash of street life: the liveliest waterfront walkway in Los Angeles, known as both Ocean Front ❻ Walk and the **Venice Boardwalk.** It begins at Washington Street and runs north. Save this visit for a weekend, any weekend. There is plenty of action year round: Bikini-clad rollerskaters gather a crowd around them as they put on impromptu demonstrations, vying for attention with the unusual breeds of dogs that locals love to prance along the walkway. A local body-building club works out on the adjacent beach, and strollers find it impossible not to stop and ogle the pecs as these strong men lift weights.

At the south end of the boardwalk, along Washington Street near the Venice Pier, roller skates as well as bicycles (some with baby seats) are available for rent.

Time Out   The boardwalk is lined with fast-food stands and food can then be brought a few feet away to be enjoyed as a beachy picnic. But for a somewhat more relaxing meal, stand in line for a table at **Sidewalk Cafe** (1401 Ocean Front Walk, tel. 213/399–5547). Wait for a patio table, where you can watch the wildly dressed free spirits parade by. Despite their flamboyant attire, they seem like Sunday wild ones, and it's amusing to imagine them in their sedate Monday-go-to-work suits. The cafe is open daily for breakfast, lunch, and dinner.

Just south of Venice is a quick shift of the time frame. Forget Italy of the Renaissance, or even of the turn of the century. Marina del Rey is a modern and more successful, if less romantic, dream than Venice. It is the largest man-made boat harbor in the world, with a commercial area catering to the whims of boat owners and boat groupies alike.

For boatless visitors, the best place to savor the marina is from ❼ **Burton Chase Park,** at the end of Mindinao Way. Situated at the tip of a jetty and surrounded on three sides by water and moored boats, this small, 6-acre patch of green offers a cool and breezy place to watch boats move in and out of the channel, and it's great for picnicking.

❽ **Fisherman's Village** is a collection of cute Cape Cod clapboards housing shops and restaurants. It's not much of a draw unless you include a meal or a snack or take one of the 45-minute marina cruises that depart from the village dock, run by Hornblower Dining Outs. *13755 Fiji Way, tel. 213/301–6000. Open in summer daily 11–4; in winter, weekends, 11–4. Cruises leave every hour, weekdays noon–3, weekends 11–5. Tickets: $5 adults, $3.50 senior citizens, $4 children.*

A Tour of Pacific   The drive on Pacific Coast Highway north of Santa Monica to-
Palisades and   ward Malibu is one of the most pleasant in Southern California,
Malibu   day or evening. The narrow-but-expensive beachfront houses were homes of movie stars in the 1930s.

❾ Spend a few hours at **Will Rogers State Historic Park** in Pacific Palisades and you will understand quite easily why all of America fell in love with this cowboy-humorist in the '20s and '30s. The 2-story ranch house on Rogers's 187-acre estate is a folksy blend of Navajo rugs and Mission-style furniture. Rogers's only extravagance was raising the roof several feet (he waited until his wife was in Europe to do it) to accommodate his penchant for practicing his lasso technique indoors. The nearby museum features Rogers memorabilia. The short films of him using the lasso will leave even sophisticated city slickers breathless, and hearing his homey words of wisdom is a real mood lifter.

Rogers was quite a polo fan, and in the '30s, his front yard polo field attracted such friends as Douglas Fairbanks for weekend games. The tradition continues with free games scheduled most summer weekends. The park's broad lawns are excellent for picnicking. For postprandial exercise, there's hiking on miles of eucalyptus-lined trails. Those who make it to the top will be rewarded with a panoramic view of the mountains and ocean. Neighborhood riders keep their horses at the stable up the hill and are usually agreeable to some friendly chatter (no rental horses, alas). *14253 Sunset Blvd., Pacific Palisades, tel. 213/454–8212. Call for polo schedule.*

⑩ The **J. Paul Getty Museum** contains one of the country's finest collections of Greek and Roman antiquities (and a few items of uncertain provenance). The building is a re-creation of a 1st-century Roman villa. The main level houses sculpture, mosaics, and vases. Of particular interest are the 4th-century Attic stelae (funerary monuments) and Greek and Roman portraits. The newly expanded decorative arts collection on the upper level features furniture, carpets, tapestries, clocks, chandeliers, and small decorative items made for the French, German, and Italian nobility, with a wealth of royal French treasures (Louis XIV to Napoleon). Richly colored, brocaded walls set off the paintings and furniture to great advantage.

All major schools of Western art from the late 13th century to the late 19th century are represented in the painting collection, which emphasizes Renaissance and Baroque art and includes works by Rembrandt, Rubens, La Tour, Van Dyck, Gainsborough, and Boucher. Newly added are Old Master drawings, and medieval and Renaissance illuminated manuscripts.

The museum itself has a fascinating history. Getty began collecting art in the '30s, concentrating on the three distinct areas that are represented in the museum today: Greek and Roman antiquities, Baroque and Renaissance paintings, and 18th-century decorative arts. In 1946, he purchased a large Spanish-style home on 65 acres of land in a canyon just north of Santa Monica to house the collection. By the late '60s, the museum could no longer accommodate the rapidly expanding collection and Getty decided to build an entirely new museum, which was completed in 1974. Getty's estimated $1.3-billion bequest upon his death in 1976 appreciated to $2.1 billion with the 1984 takeover of Getty Oil by Texaco.

The bookstore carries art books, reproductions, calendars, and a variety of scholarly and general-interest publications. A self-service lunch is available in the indoor-outdoor Garden Tea Room. There are no tours, but docents give 15-minute orientation talks. Summer evening concerts (reservations required) are given on an irregular basis, with the lower galleries open at intermission. Parking reservations are necessary and there is no way to visit the museum without using the parking lot unless you are dropped off or part of a bus tour. Reserve one week in advance by calling or writing to the museum's Reservations Office. *17985 Pacific Coast Hwy., Malibu, tel. 213/458–2003. Admission free. Open Tues.–Sun. 10–5.*

⑪ **Adamson House** is the former home of the Rindge family, which owned much of the Malibu Rancho in the early 20th century. Malibu was quite isolated then, when all visitors and supplies arrived by boat at the nearby Malibu Pier (and it can still be isolated these days by rock slides that close the highway). The Moorish-Spanish house, built in 1928, has been recently opened to the public and may be the only chance most visitors get to be inside a grand Malibu home. The Rindges had an enviable Malibu lifestyle, decades before it was trendy. The house is right on the beach (high chain-link fences keep out curious beach-goers). The family owned the famous Malibu Tile Company, and their home is encrusted with some of the most magnificent tilework in rich blues, greens, yellows, and oranges. Even an outside dog shower, near the servants' door, is a tiled delight. Docent-led tours help visitors to envision family life here as well as to learn about the history of Malibu and its real estate (you can't have one without the other). *23200 Pacific Coast Hwy., Malibu, 213/456–8432. Admission free. Open Wed.–Sat. 10–1:30.*

⑫ Adjacent to Adamson House is **Malibu Lagoon State Park** (23200 Pacific Coast Hwy., Malibu), a haven for native and migratory birds. Visitors must stay on the boardwalks so that the egrets, blue herons, avocets, and gulls can enjoy the marshy area. The signs that give opening and closing hours refer only to the parking lot; the lagoon itself is open 24 hours and is particularly enjoyable in the early morning and at sunset. Luckily, street-side parking is available then (but not at midday).

Palos Verdes, San Pedro, and Long Beach

Numbers in the margin correspond with points of interest on the Palos Verdes, San Pedro, and Long Beach map.

Few local residents take advantage of Long Beach's attractions; if they should take a day to see the *Queen Mary* when their in-laws visit from Michigan, they are astounded to discover Long Beach's impressive skyline. How could this big city, the fifth-largest in the state, be right here without them really knowing about it? Allow a generous half-day or more to explore the *Queen Mary* complex. Plump up the itinerary with a glorious drive through Palos Verdes and a few short stops at local historic sites and parks.

The drive on Pacific Coast Highway around Palos Verdes Peninsula takes you soaring high about the cliffs. An aerial shot of this area was used in the original opening on television's *Knot's Landing*. Marineland once stood on these cliffs, but it was recently closed and demolished. The real estate in these small peninsula towns, ranging from expensive to very expensive, is zoned for stables, and you'll often see riders along the streets (they have the right of way).

❶ **Wayfarers Chapel** was designed by architect Lloyd Wright, son of Frank, in 1949. He planned his modern glass church to blend in with an encircling redwood forest. The redwoods are gone (they couldn't stand the rigors of urban encroachment), but another forest has taken their place and the breathtaking combination of ocean, trees, and structure remain. This "natural church" is a popular wedding site. *5755 Palos Verdes Dr. S, Rancho Palos Verdes, tel. 213/377–1650. Chapel open on the*

313

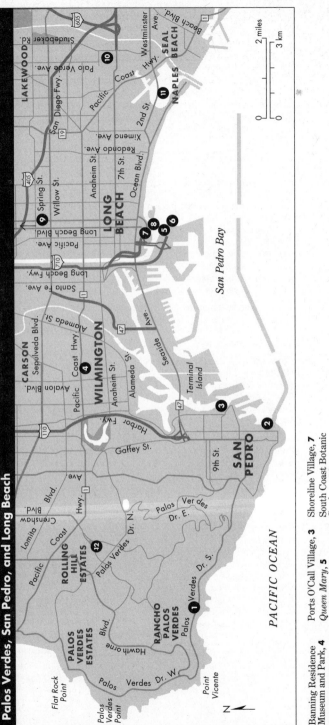

Palos Verdes, San Pedro, and Long Beach

Banning Residence Museum and Park, **4**
Cabrillo Marine Museum, **2**
Naples, **11**

Ports O'Call Village, **3**
Queen Mary, **5**
Rancho Los Alamitos, **10**
Rancho Los Cerritos, **9**
Shoreline Aquatic Park, **8**

Shoreline Village, **7**
South Coast Botanic Gardens, **12**
Spruce Goose, **6**
Wayfarers Chapel, **1**

odd-numbered hours 9–5 (weddings are held on even-num-
bered hours); office open 9–5; grounds open 7 AM–8 PM.

San Pedro shares the peninsula, but little else, with the Palos
Verdes towns. Here, the cliffs give way to a hospitable harbor.
The 1950s-vintage executive homes give way to tidy 1920s-era
white clapboards, and horses give way to boats. San Pedro (the
locals ignore the correct Spanish pronunciation—it's "San Pee-
dro" to them) is an old seafaring community with a strong Mediterranean and Eastern European flavor. There are enticing
Greek and Yugoslavian markets and restaurants throughout
the town.

❷ Cabrillo Marine Museum is a gem of a small museum dedicated
to the marine life flourishing off the Southern California coast.
Recently moved from a nearby boathouse to a modern Frank O.
Gehry-designed building right on the beach, the museum is
popular with school groups because its exhibits are instructive
as well as fun. The 35 saltwater aquariums include a shark tank
and a see-through tidal tank that gives visitors a chance to see
the long view of a wave. On the back patio, docents supervise as
visitors plunge their hands into a shallow tank to touch starfish
and sea anenomes. *3720 Stephen White Dr., San Pedro, tel. 213/*
548–7546. Admission free. Parking: $4. Open Tues.–Fri.
noon–5, weekends 10–5.

If you're lucky enough to visit at low tide, take time to explore
the tide pool on nearby Cabrillo Beach (museum staff can direct
you). The rich and active life is accessible to humans for only a
short time each day.

❸ Ports O'Call Village, a commercial rendition of a New England
shipping village, is an older version of Fisherman's Village in
Marina del Rey, with shops, restaurants and fast-food windows. *Berth 77, San Pedro, tel. 213/831–0996. 1-hr cruises*
depart from village dock. Call for schedule. Fare: $7 adults, $3
children.

❹ Banning Residence Museum and Park, in Wilmington, is a
pleasant, low-key stop before the razzle-dazzle of the *Queen*
Mary. In order to preserve transportation and shipping interests for the city of Los Angeles, Wilmington was annexed in the
late 19th century. Mostly less than ½-mile wide, this narrow
strip of land follows the Harbor Freeway from downtown south
to the port.

General Phineas Banning was an early Los Angeles entrepreneur who is credited with developing the harbor into a viable
economic entity. He built a 24-room Greek Revival-style mansion overlooking the harbor and named the area Wilmington (he
was from Delaware). Part of the estate has been preserved in a
20-acre park that offers excellent picnicking possibilities. A
100-year-old wisteria, near the arbor, blooms in the spring. *401*
E. M St., Wilmington, tel. 213/548–7777. Admission $2. The
interior of the house can be seen only on docent tours, Tues.–
Thurs., weekends 12:30–3:30 on the hour.

Long Beach began as a seaside resort in the 19th century and,
during the early part of the 20th century, was a popular destination for Midwesterners and Dust Bowlers in search of a
better life. They built street after street of modest wood
homes.

❺ The first glimpse of the **Queen Mary**—the largest passenger ship ever built—as she sits so smugly in Long Beach Harbor is disarming. What seemed like sure folly when Long Beach officials bought her in 1964 has turned out to be an attention-getting and money-making bonanza that has put the city on the proverbial map. She stands permanently moored at Pier J.

The 50,000-ton *Queen Mary* was launched in 1934, a floating treasure of art deco splendor. It took a crew of 1,100 to minister to the needs of her 1,900 demanding passengers. This most luxurious of luxury liners is completely intact, from the extensive wood paneling to the gleaming nickel- and silver-plated handrails and the hand-cut glass. Tours are available; guests are invited to browse the 12 decks and witness, close up, the bridge, staterooms, officers' quarters, and engine rooms. There are several restaurants on board, and visitors may even spend the night in the first-class cabins, now the Queen Mary Hotel. *Pier J, Long Beach, tel. 213/435–3511. Admission: $17.50 adults, $9.50 children for all-day combination ticket to both the* Queen Mary *and the* Spruce Goose. *Guided 90-min tours leave every 30 min beginning at 10:30 AM. Open July 4–Labor Day, daily 9–9; rest of year, daily 10–6.*

❻ Just a short walk away from this most amazing ship is a most amazing plane, the **Spruce Goose,** housed in a 12-story aluminum dome. The *Spruce Goose* was Howard Hughes's folly. It is the largest wooden aircraft ever built, with a 320-foot wingspan. Designed by Hughes in 1942, it made its first and only flight on November 2, 1947. Multimedia displays surrounding the plane explain its history. Howard Hughes memorabilia is also on view. New under the *Spruce Goose* dome is *Time Voyager,* "a multisensory entertainment journey." With narration aimed at children, passengers board a 100-seat flight module to experience time periods past and present. It's free with admission. *See* Queen Mary *for times and prices.*

❼ **Shoreline Village** is the most successful of the pseudo-New England harbors here. Its setting, between the Long Beach skyline and the *Queen Mary,* is reason enough to stroll here, day or evening (when visitors can enjoy the lights of the ship twinkling in the distance). In addition to gift shops and restaurants there's a 1906 carousel with bobbing giraffes, camels, and horses. *Corner of Shoreline Dr. and Pine Ave., tel. 213/435–5911. The carousel is open daily 10–10 in summer, 10–9 the rest of the year. Rides are 75¢.*

❽ **Shoreline Aquatic Park** (205 Marina Dr.) is literally set in the middle of Long Beach Harbor (another inspired landfill project) and is a much-sought-after resting place for RVers. And for kite-flyers: The winds are wonderful here. Casual passersby can enjoy a short walk where the modern skyline, the quaint Shoreline Village, the *Queen Mary,* and the ocean all vie for attention. The park's lagoon is off-limits for swimming, but aquacycles and kayaks can be rented during the summer months.

❾ **Rancho Los Cerritos** is a charming Monterey-style adobe built by the Don Juan Temple family in 1844. Monterey-style homes can be easily recognized by two features: They are always 2 stories high, and they have a narrow balcony across the front. Imagine Zorro here, that swashbuckling hero of the rancho era, jumping from the balcony to rescue Don Juan Temple's lovely daughter. The 10 rooms have been furnished in the style of the period and are open for viewing. Don't expect a Southwest fantasy here with primitive Mexican furniture and cacti in the garden. The Temple family shared the prevalent taste of the period. They might have lived in Southern California, but the East Coast and Europe still set the style, emphasizing fancy, dark woods and froufrou Victorian bric-a-brac. The gardens here were designed in the 1930s by well-known landscape architect Ralph Cornell and have been recently restored. *4600 Virginia Rd., Long Beach, tel. 213/424–9423. Open Wed.–Sun. 1–5. Self-guided tours on weekdays. Free 50-min guided tours on weekends hourly 1–4.*

⑩ **Rancho Los Alamitos** was built in 1806 when California still belonged to Spain. There's a blacksmith shop in the barn. *6400 E. Bixby Hill Rd., Long Beach, tel. 213/431–3541. Open Wed.–Sun. 1–5. Hour-long, free tours leave every 30 min.*

⑪ The **Naples** section of Long Beach is known for its pleasant and well-maintained canals. Canals in Naples, you ask? You're right, this is a bit of a misnomer. But better misnamed and successful in Naples than aptly named and a big bust in Venice, a few miles north. Naples, California, is actually three small islands in man-made Alamitos Bay. It is best savored on foot. Park near Bayshore Drive and Second Street, and walk across the bridge, where you can begin meandering the quaint streets bearing Italian names. This well-restored neighborhood boasts eclectic architecture—vintage Victorian, Craftsman bungalow, and Mission Revival. You may spy a real gondola or two on the canals. You can hire them for a ride, but not on the spur of the moment. Gondola Getaway offers one-hour rides, usually touted for romantic couples, although the gondolas can accommodate up to four people. *5437 E. Ocean Blvd., Naples, tel. 213/433–9595. Rides: $45 a couple, $10 each additional person. Reservations essential, at least 1–2 weeks in advance.*

⑫ **South Coast Botanic Gardens** began life ignominiously—as a garbage dump-cum-landfill. It's hard to believe that as recently as 1960, truckloads of waste were being deposited here. With the intensive ministerings of the experts from the L.A. County Arboreta Department, the dump soon boasted lush gardens with plants from every continent except Antarctica. The gardens are undergoing an ambitious five-year reorganization of all the plants into color groups. Self-guided walking tours take visitors past flower and herb gardens, rare cacti, and a lake with ducks. Picnicking is limited to a lawn area outside the gates. *26300 Crenshaw Blvd., Rancho Palos Verdes, tel. 213/377–0468. Admission: $3 adults, $1.50 children. Open daily 9–4:30.*

Highland Park, Pasadena, and San Marino

Numbers in the margin correspond with points of interest on the Highland Park, Pasadena, and San Marino map.

The suburbs north of downtown Los Angeles are endowed with much of the richest architectural heritage in Southern California as well as several fine museums. The Highland Park area can be explored in a leisurely afternoon. Pasadena could take a full day, longer if you want to savor the museums' collections.

A Tour of Highland Park To take advantage of the afternoon-only hours of several sites here, and to enjoy a relaxed Old California patio lunch or dinner, this tour is best scheduled in the afternoon.

Once past Chinatown, the Pasadena Freeway (Highway #110) follows the curves of the arroyo (creek bed) that leads north from downtown. During the early days of Los Angeles this was the main road north, where horse-and-buggy travelers made their way through the chaparral-covered countryside to the small town of Pasadena. In 1942, the road became the Arroyo Seco Parkway, the first freeway in Los Angeles (later renamed the Pasadena Freeway). It remains a pleasant drive in non-rush-hour traffic, with the freeway lined with old sycamores and winding up the arroyo like a New York parkway.

Highland Park, midway between downtown Los Angeles and Pasadena, was a genteel suburb in the late 1800s, where, despite the decidedly Southwest landscape, the Anglo population tried to keep an East coast feeling alive in their architecture. The streets on both sides of the freeway are filled with faded beauties, classic old clapboards that have gone into decline in the past half century.

❶ Heritage Square is the ambitious attempt by the Los Angeles Cultural Heritage Board to save some of the city's architectural gems of the 1865–1914 period from the wrecking ball. During the past 20 years, four residences, a depot, a church, and a carriage barn have been moved to this small park from other parts of the city. The most breathtaking building here is Hale House, built in 1885. The almost-garish colors of both the interior and exterior are not the whim of some aging hippie painter but rather a faithful re-creation of the palette that was actually in fashion in the late 1800s. The whitewashing we associate with Victorian structures was a later vogue. The Palms Depot, built in 1886, was moved to its present site from the Westside of L.A. The actual transport of the building, down city streets and up freeways, is documented in photomurals on the depot's walls. *3800 Homer St., off Ave. 43 exit, tel. 818/449–0193. Admission: $4.50 adults, $3 children 12–17. Open weekends noon–4. Tours begin at 12:15, 1:15, 2:15 and 3:15 on Sun. only.*

❷ El Alisal was the home of eccentric Easterner-turned-Westerner-with-a-vengeance, Charles Lummis. This Harvard graduate was captivated by Native American culture (he founded the Southwest Museum), often living the lifestyle of the natives, much to the shock of the staid Angelenos of the time. His home, built from 1898 to 1910, is constructed of boulders from the arroyo itself, a romantic notion until recent earthquakes have made the safety of such homes questionable. The art nouveau fireplace was designed by Gutzon Borglum, the sculptor of Mount Rushmore. *200 E. Ave. 43, tel. 213/222–0546. Admission free. Open Thurs.–Sun. 1–4.*

❸ The Southwest Museum is the huge Mission Revival building that stands halfway up Mount Washington and can be seen from the freeway. It contains an extensive collection of Native American art and artifacts, with special emphasis on the people of the Plains, Northwest Coast, Southwest United States, and northern Mexico. The basket collection is outstanding. *234 Museum Dr., off the Ave. 43 exit, tel. 213/221–2163. Admission: $3 adults, children free. Open Tues.–Sun. 11–5.*

Casa de Adobe, **4**
El Alisal, **2**
Gamble House, **7**
Heritage Square, **1**
Huntington Library,
Art Gallery, and
Botanical Gardens, **14**
Huntington Sheraton
Hotel, **13**
Kidspace, **12**
Lawry's California
Center, **5**
Norton Simon
Museum, **8**
Old Town Pasadena, **9**
Pacific Asia
Museum, **11**
Pasadena Historical
Society, **10**
Rose Bowl, **6**
Southwest Museum, **3**

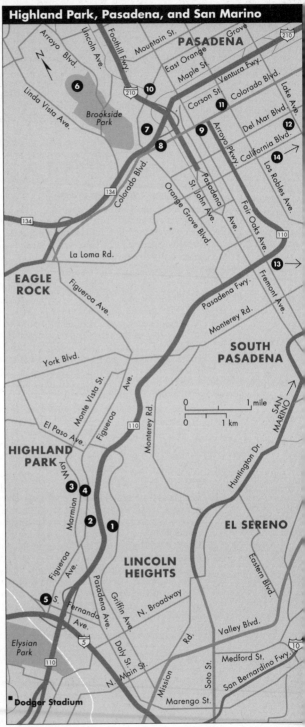

Highland Park, Pasadena, and San Marino

④ Casa de Adobe is a satellite of the Southwest Museum and is located directly below it at the bottom of the hill. What appears to be the well-preserved, authentically furnished hacienda of an Old California don is actually a 1917 re-creation of a 19th-century rancho. The central courtyard plan is typical. *4605 Figueroa St., tel. 213/221–2163. Admission free. Open Tues.–Sat. 11–5, Sun. 1–5.*

Time Out **Lawry's California Center** is a more recent attempt to capture
⑤ the romance of Old Mexico—Zorro and Ramona all rolled up in one—but this one leaves no doubt that it is a recent construction. It is *Sunset* magazine come to life, with bougainvillea-covered patios and flowers in pots at every turn, winter and summer. A spice-blending company, Lawry's offers free tours of its plant on weekdays, but the best reason to come here is to enjoy a patio meal. Lunches, both cafeteria-style and full service, are served year-round 11–3. Fiesta dinners are served (May–Oct.) nightly under the stars to the accompaniment of strolling mariachis. Wine and gourmet shops stay open late for after-dinner browsing. *570 W. Ave. 26, Los Angeles, tel. 213/225–2491. Open daily.*

Pasadena and San Marino

Although now absorbed into the general Los Angeles sprawl, Pasadena was once a distinctly defined, and refined, city. Its varied architecture, augmented by lush landscaping, is the most spectacular in Southern California. If time is short, visitors should consider driving past the Gamble House, through Old Town and then on to the grand old neighborhood of the Huntington Library, spending most of their time there.

⑥ The Rose Bowl (991 Rosemont Ave.) is set at the bottom of a wide area of the arroyo in an older, wealthy neighborhood that must endure the periodic onslaught of thousands of cars and party-minded football fans. The stadium is closed except for games and special events such as the monthly Rose Bowl Swap Meet. Held the second Sunday of the month, this is considered the granddaddy of West Coast swap meets.

⑦ Gamble House, built by Charles and Henry Greene in 1908, is the most spectacular example of Craftsman-style bungalow architecture. The term bungalow can be misleading, because the Gamble House is a huge 2-story affair. To wealthy Easterners such as the Gambles, who commissioned the Greenes to build them a vacation house, this type of home seemed informal compared with the mansions to which they were accustomed. What makes visitors swoon here is the incredible amount of hand craftsmanship: the hand-shaped teak interiors, the Greene-designed furniture, the Louis Tiffany glass door. The dark exterior has broad eaves, with many sleeping porches on the second floor. *4 Westmoreland Pl., tel. 818/793–3334. Admission: $4 adults, children free. Open Thurs.–Sun. noon–3. Tours are given Tues. and Thurs. approximately every hour, Sun. noon–12:45.*

⑧ The Norton Simon Museum will be familiar to television viewers of the Rose Parade. The TV cameras position themselves to take full advantage of the sleek, modern building as a background for the passing floats. Like the more famous Getty

Museum, the Norton Simon is a tribute to the art acumen of an extremely wealthy businessman. In 1974, Simon reorganized the failing Pasadena Museum of Modern Art and assembled one of the world's finest collections, richest in its Rembrandts, Goyas, Degases, and Picassos—and dotted with Rodin sculptures throughout.

Rembrandt's development can be traced in three oils—*The Bearded Man in the Wide Brimmed Hat, Self Portrait,* and *Titus.* The most dramatic Goyas are two oils—*St. Jerome* and the portrait of *Doña Francisca Vicenta Chollet y Caballero.* Down the walnut and steel staircase is the Degas gallery, enriched in 1984 with *Waiting,* a delicate study of two ballerinas that was acquired jointly with the Getty Museum. Picasso's renowned *Woman With Book* highlights a comprehensive collection of his paintings, drawings, and sculptures.

Also strong are the museum's Impressionists (van Gogh, Matisse, Cezanne, Monet, Renoir, et al.) and Cubists (Braque, Gris). Older works range from Southeast Asian artworks from 100 BC, and bronze, stone, and ivory sculptures from India, Cambodia, Thailand, and Nepal.

The museum's wealth of Early Renaissance, Baroque, and Rococo art works could fill an art history book. Church works by Raphael, Guariento, de Paolo, Filippino Lippi, and Lucas Cranach give way to robust Rubens maidens and Dutch landscapes, still lives and portraits by Frans Hals, Jacob van Ruisdal, and Jan Steen. And a magical Tiepolo ceiling highlights the Rococo period. The most recent addition to the collection are seven 19th-century Russian paintings.

The bookstore has posters, prints, and postcards. There are no dining facilities. *411 W. Colorado Blvd., tel. 818/449–6840. Admission: $3 adults, children free. Open Thurs.–Sun. noon–6.*

9 Half a mile east of the museum, **Old Town Pasadena** is an ambitious, ongoing restoration. Having fallen into seedy decay in the past 50 years, the area is being revitalized as a blend of restored brick buildings with a yuppie overlay. Rejuvenated buildings include bistros, elegant restaurants, and boutiques. On Raymond Street, the Hotel Green, now the Castle Apartments, dominates the area. Once a posh resort hotel, the Green is now a faded Moorish fantasy of domes, turrets, and balconies reminiscent of the Alhambra but with, true to its name, a greenish tint. Holly Street, between Fair Oaks and Arroyo, is home to several shops offering an excellent selection of vintage '50s objects, jewelry, and clothes. This area is best explored on foot. Old Town is bisected by Colorado Boulevard, where, on New Year's Day, throngs of people line the street for the Rose Parade.

Time Out If browsing the Holly Street shops leaves you both nostalgic and hungry, walk down Fair Oaks to the **Rose City Diner.** Classic diner fare, from chicken-fried steak and eggs to macaroni and cheese, is served in an *American Graffiti* setting. Bebop singers roam the joint from 11 AM to 3 PM every Sunday, for added '50s flavor. *45 S. Fair Oaks, tel. 818/793–8282. Open daily 6:30 AM–2 AM.*

10 The **Pasadena Historical Society Library and Museum** are housed in Fenyes Mansion. There are also 4 acres of well-landscaped gardens. *170 N. Orange Grove Blvd., tel. 818/577–1660. Admission: $4 adults, children free. Open Tues., Thurs., and Sun. 1–4.*

⓫ The Pacific Asia Museum is the gaudiest Chinese-style building in Los Angeles outside of Chinatown. Designed in the style of a northern Chinese imperial palace with a central courtyard, it is devoted entirely to the arts and crafts of Asia and the Pacific Islands. Most of the objects are on loan from private collections and other museums, and there are usually changing special exhibits that focus on the objects of one country. A bookstore and the Collectors Gallery shop sell fine art items from members' collections. The extensive research library can be used by appointment only. *46 N. Los Robles Dr., tel. 818/449–2742. Admission: $3 adults, children free. Open Wed.–Sun. noon–5.*

⓬ Kidspace is a children's museum housed in the gymnasium of an elementary school. Here kids can talk to a robot, direct a television or radio station, dress up in the real (and very heavy) uniforms of a fire fighter, an astronaut, a football player, and more. A special "Human Habitrail" challenges children by changing architectural environments, and "Illusions" teases one's ability to perceive what is real and what is illusion. *390 S. El Molino Ave., tel. 818/449–9144. Admission: $3. Open during the school year, weekends 12:30–5, Wed. 2–5; longer hours during summer and other school vacation periods.*

⓭ The **Huntington Hotel and Cottages** (1401 S. Oak Knoll Ave., tel. 818/792–0266) is situated in Pasadena's most genteel neighborhood of Oak Knoll, close to San Marino. Although all the original buildings were closed in 1986 because of an inability to conform to earthquake regulations, this hotel, built in 1906, is still worth a visit, if only for its 23 acres of beautifully landscaped grounds, which in selected areas visitors may walk around. Features include the Japanese gardens and the Picture Bridge. You can still make reservations here, but only for the 106 newer rooms.

⓮ The **Huntington Library, Art Gallery, and Botanical Gardens** is the area's most important site. If there's only time for a quick drive through the area and one stop, this should be it. Railroad tycoon Henry E. Huntington built his hilltop home in the early 1900s. It has established a reputation as one of the most extraordinary cultural complexes in the world, annually receiving more than half a million visitors. The library contains 6 million items, including such treasures as a Gutenberg Bible, the earliest known edition of Chaucer's *Canterbury Tales*, George Washington's genealogy in his own handwriting, and first editions by Benjamin Franklin and William Shakespeare. In the library's hallway are five tall hexagonal towers displaying important books and manuscripts.

The art gallery, devoted to British art from the 18th and 19th centuries, contains the original *Blue Boy* by Gainsborough, *Pinkie*, a companion piece by Lawrence, and the monumental *Sarah Siddons as the Tragic Muse* by Reynolds.

The Huntington's awesome 130-acre garden, formerly the grounds of the estate, now includes a 12-acre Desert Garden featuring the largest group of mature cacti and other succulents in the world, all arranged by continent. The Japanese Garden is outstanding, with traditional Japanese plants, stone ornaments, a moon bridge, a Japanese house, a bonsai court, and a Zen rock garden. Besides these gardens, there are collections of azaleas and 1,500 varieties of camellias, the world's largest public collection. The 1,000-variety rose garden displays its collection historically so that the development leading to today's roses can be observed. There are also herb, palm, and jungle gardens plus a Shakespeare garden, where plants mentioned in Shakespeare's plays are grown.

Because of the Huntington's vastness, a variety of orientation options is available for visitors. They include: a 12-minute slide show introducing the Huntington, a 1¼-hour guided tour of the gardens; a 45-minute audio tape about the art gallery (which can be rented for a nominal fee); a 15-minute introductory talk about the library; and inexpensive, self-guided tour leaflets.

In 1980, the first major facility constructed on the Huntington grounds in more than 60 years opened. The $5-million Huntington Pavilion offers visitors unmatched views of the surrounding mountains and valleys, and houses a bookstore, displays, and information kiosks as well. Both the east and west wings of the pavilion display paintings on public exhibition for the first time. The Ralph M. Parsons Botanical Center at the pavilion includes a botanical library, a herbarium, and a laboratory for research on plants. There is no picnicking and pets are not allowed. A refreshment room is open to the public. *Oxford Rd., San Marino, tel. 818/405–2275. Donation requested. Open Tues.–Sun. 1–4:30. Reservations required Sun. (tel. 818/449–3901).*

Other Places of Interest

Burbank Studios. Warner Brothers and Columbia Studios share this lot. A two-hour guided walking tour is available. Because the tours involve a lot of walking, dress comfortably and casually. This tour is somewhat technical, more centered on the actual workings of filmmaking than the one at Universal. It varies from day to day to take advantage of goings-on on the lot. Most tours see the backlot sets, prop construction department, and sound complex. *400 Warner Blvd., Burbank, tel. 818/954–1008. Tours given weekdays at 10 and 2. Admission: $22. No children under 10 permitted. Reservations essential, one week in advance.*

Exposition Park (Figueroa St. at Exposition Blvd., Los Angeles). This beautiful park was the site of the 1932 Olympics, and the impressive architecture still stands. Adjoining the University of Southern California, Exposition Park is the location of two major museums: the California Museum of Science and Industry (tel. 213/744–7400; open daily 10–5) and the Natural History Museum (tel. 213/744–3411; open Tues.–Sun. 10–5), the fourth largest such museum in the country. Also included in the 114-acre park is the Los Angeles Swimming Stadium (home of Los Angeles aquatic competitions), which is open to the public in summer, and the Memorial Coliseum, the site of college football games. There are plenty of picnic areas on the grounds as well as the sunken Rose Garden.

Forest Lawn Memorial Park. This 300-acre formally landscaped area features a major collection of marble statuary and art treasures, including a replica of Leonardo da Vinci's *The Last Supper* done entirely in stained glass. In the Hall of the Crucifixion–Resurrection, is housed one of the world's largest oil paintings incorporating a religious theme, "The Crucifixion" by artist Jan Styka. The picturesque grounds are perfect for a leisurely walk. Forest Lawn was the model for the setting of Evelyn Waugh's novel *The Loved One*.

Many celebrities are buried here, some more flamboyantly than others. Silent screen cowboy star Tom Mix is said to be buried in his good-guy clothes: white coat, white pants, and a belt buckle with his name spelled out in diamonds. Markers for Walt Disney and Errol Flynn are near the Freedom Mausoleum. Inside the mausoleum are the wall crypts of Nat King Cole, Clara Bow, Gracie Allen, and Alan Ladd. Clark Gable, Carole Lombard, Theda Bara, and Jean Harlow are among the luminaries buried in the Great Mausoleum. *1712 S. Glendale Ave., Glendale, tel. 213/254–3131. Open daily 8–5.*

Forest Lawn Memorial Park—Hollywood Hills. Just west of Griffith Park on the north slope of the Hollywood Hills, this 340-acre sister park to Forest Lawn Glendale is dedicated to the ideal of American liberty. Featured are bronze and marble statuary, including Thomas Ball's 60-foot Washington Memorial and a replica of the Liberty Bell. There are also repro--ductions of Boston's Old North Church and Longfellow's Church of the Hills. A film entitled *The Many Voices of Freedom* is shown daily, and Revolutionary War documents are on permanent display. Among the famous people buried here are Buster Keaton, Stan Laurel, Liberace, Charles Laughton, and Freddie Prinze. *6300 Forest Lawn Dr., Hollywood, tel. 213/254–7251. Open daily 8–5.*

Gene Autry Western Heritage Museum. Both movie and real-life versions of the American West are celebrated via memorabilia, artifacts, and art. The collection includes Teddy Roosevelt's Colt revolver, Buffalo Bill Cody's saddle, and Annie Oakley's gold-plated Smith and Wesson guns alongside video screens showing clips from old Westerns. Set on the eastern edge of Griffith Park, the structure draws from Spanish Mission and early Western architecture. *4700 Zoo Dr., Los Angeles, tel. 213/667–2000. Open Tues.–Sun. 10–5. Admission: $4.75 adults, $3.50 senior citizens, $2 children 2–12.*

Griffith Observatory and Planetarium. Located on the south side of Mount Hollywood in the heart of Griffith Park, the Planetarium offers dazzling daily shows that duplicate the starry sky. A guide narrates the show and points out constellations. One of the largest telescopes in the world is open to the public free for viewing every clear night. Exhibits display models of the planets with photographs from satellites and spacecraft. A laserium show is done nightly, and other special astronomy shows are offered frequently. As seen in *Rebel Without a Cause*, the observatory sits high above Los Angeles and from the outside decks and walkways offers a spectacular view of the city; it's very popular on warm evenings. *Griffith Park, tel. 213/664–1191. Enter at Los Feliz and Vermont entrance. Hall of Science and telescope are free. Call for schedule of planetarium shows. Admission: $3 adults, $1.50 children; Laserium show: $6 adults, $5 children. Open Tues.–Fri. 2–10, weekends 12:30–10.*

Hollyhock House. Frank Lloyd Wright designed a number of homes in the Los Angeles area. Hollyhock House was his first, built in 1921, and commissioned by heiress Aline Barnsdall. It was done in the pre-Columbian style Wright was fond of at that time, and used as a unifying theme a stylized hollyhock flower, which appears in a broad band around the exterior of the house and even on the dining room chairs. Now owned by the city (as is Barnsdall Park, where it is located), it has been restored and furnished with originals and reproductions of Wright's furniture. His furniture may not be the comfiest in the world but it sure looks perfect in his houses. *4800 Hollywood Blvd., Hollywood, tel. 213/662–7272. Admission: $1.50 adults, $1 senior citizens, children free. Tours conducted Tues.–Thurs., hourly 10–1, Sat., and the 1st, 2nd, and 3rd Sun. of the month hourly, noon–3.*

Mulholland Drive. One of the most famous streets in Los Angeles, Mulholland makes its very winding way from the Hollywood Hills across the spine of the Santa Monica Mountains west almost to the Pacific Ocean. Driving its length is slow but is rewarded with sensational views of the city, the San Fernando Valley, and the expensive homes along the way. For a quick shot, take Benedict Canyon north from Sunset Boulevard, just west of the Beverly Hills Hotel, all the way to the top and turn right at the crest, which is Mulholland. There's a turn-out within a few feet of the intersection, and at night, the view of the valley side is incredible.

NBC Television Studios. Ninety-minute tours of the largest color television facilities in the United States explain communication satellites and videotape processes. Studio I, where "The Tonight Show" is taped, is part of the tour, as are the huge prop warehouse and makeup and wardrobe departments. Some lucky groups have a chance to see NBC stars like Johnny Carson arrive for their shows. The morning tours are recommended because there is more activity then. Tickets are also available for tapings of NBC shows. *3000 W. Alameda Ave., Burbank, tel. 818/840–3537. Admission: $6.75 adults, $4.50 children. Tours weekdays 8:30–4, Sat. 10–4, Sun. 10–2.*

Universal Studios. This is the best place in Los Angeles to see behind the scenes of the movie industry. The five- to seven-hour Universal tour is an enlightening and amusing (if a bit sensational) day at the world's largest television and movie studio, complete with live shows based on "Miami Vice," *Conan the Barbarian,* and the "Star Trek" series. It stretches across more than 400 acres, many of which are traversed during the course of the tour by trams featuring witty running commentary provided by enthusiastic guides. Visitors experience the parting of the Red Sea, an avalanche, and a flood, and have the opportunity to meet a 30-foot-tall version of the legendary King Kong. They live through an encounter with a runaway train and an attack by the ravenous killer shark of *Jaws* fame. And now, thanks to the magic of Hollywood, visitors can experience the perils of The Big One—an all-too-real simulation of an 8.3 earthquake complete with collapsing earth, deafening train wrecks, floods, and other life-threatening amusements.

Afterward, visitors relax in the snack bar and picnic area, before they go on to the Entertainment Center, the longest and last stop of the day, where they stroll around to enjoy various shows. In one theater animals beguile you with their tricks; in another you can pose for a photo session with the Incredible Hulk. Visit Castle Dracula and confront a variety of terrifying monsters. At the Screen Test Theater, visitors may find themselves being filmed as extras in films already released and recut to include them. *100 Universal Pl., Universal City, tel. 818/508-9600. Admission: $21 adults, $15.50 senior citizens and children 3–11. Box office open daily. 9:30–3:30.*

Watts Towers (1765 E. 107th St.). This is the folk-art legacy of an Italian immigrant tile setter, Simon Rodia, and one of the great folk structures in the world. From 1920 until 1945, without helpers, this eccentric and driven man erected three cement towers, using pipes, bed frames, and anything else he could find, and embellished them with bits of colored glass, broken pottery, seashells, and assorted discards. The tallest of the towers is 107 feet. Plans are underway to stabilize and protect this unique monument, often compared to the 20th-century architectural wonders created by Barcelona's Antonio Gaudi. It's well worth a pilgrimage for art and architecture buffs (or anyone else, for that matter).

Los Angeles for Free

In Los Angeles, every day is a free event in terms of nature; the sun, sand, and ocean can alone fill a vacation. But there are plenty of other free activities, events, and cultural attractions to keep busy even those with limited budgets. Many of the attractions (e.g., the cemeteries and El Pueblo State Historic Park) described in the exploring sections above are free. Consider also the following:

Christmas Boat Parades. During December, many local marinas celebrate Christmas in a special way. Boat owners decorate their boats with strings of lights and holiday displays and then cruise in a line for dockside visitors to see. Call for specific dates: Marina del Rey, tel. 213/822–0119; Port of Los Angeles, tel. 213/519–3508.

Rose Parade. Seen from the streets (rather than the bleachers), the Rose Parade is as free as it is on television. Arrive before dawn and dress warmly. Thousands of residents prefer to watch on television and then go out to east Pasadena a day or two later to view the floats, which are parked there for a few days for observation. *Corner of Sierra Madre Blvd. and Washington St., Pasadena. Call for viewing hours: tel. 818/449–7673.*

Santa Monica Kite Flying. The beach just north of the Santa Monica Pier is filled with dozens of elaborate kites during these monthly celebrations. It's all very low-key with no rules, no judging, no prizes. Just arrive sometime after noon. There are kites for sale if you don't have one. A wonderful way to spend the afternoon on the beach. *Santa Monica Beach, end of Colorado St., at Santa Monica Pier, Santa Monica, tel. 213/822–2561.*

Santa Monica Mountains Nature Walks. The rangers and docents of the many parks in the Santa Monica Mountains (the Hollywood Hills are part of these) offer an ambitious schedule of walks for all interests, ages, and levels of exertion. These include wildflower walks, moonlight hikes, tide pool explorations, and much more. Several outings are held every day. For updated information, call the National Park Service (tel. 818/597–9192).

Westwood Sidewalk Art and Craft Show. One of the best crafts shows in the city for almost two decades, this show is held the first weekend in May. Streets are closed off, and hundreds of vendors set up shop on the sidewalks and streets, offering a stellar display of paintings, pottery, quilts, and more. Call for dates (tel. 818/475–4574).

What to See and Do with Children

Children will enjoy many, if not most, of the attractions described in the preceding exploring sections, particularly Kidspace in Pasadena and the Cabrillo Marine Museum in San Pedro. Here are a few more possibilities, most of them found in Griffith Park, the largest urban park in the country.

Magic Mountain. This is the only real amusement park actually in Los Angeles County. (Depending on where you are staying, it may or may not be closer than Disneyland.) There are 260 acres of rides, shows, and entertainment. The roster of major rides is headlined by Shock Wave, the first stand-up roller coaster in the West. It's a two-minute, ½-mile ride that goes 55 miles per hour once the initial 90-foot drop is made. Condor soars up 112 feet in the air and suspends thrill-seekers in open capsules to give them a taste of what flight is really like. There's also the Roaring Rapids, a simulated white-water wilderness adventure complete with whirlpools, waves, and rapids; the Colossus, the largest dual-track wood roller coaster ever built, offering two "drops" in excess of 100 feet and experiencing speeds up to 62 miles per hour, and the Revolution, a steelcoaster with a 360-degree, 90-foot vertical loop. On the Z-Force ride, passengers ride upside down, and the recently added Ninja is a suspended roller coaster.

At **Children's World,** youngsters can enjoy a playground of bright colors, shapes, and textures, and a rope bridge to the Wizard's Castle. Children's World is a minipark with scaled-down rides, such as the Red Baron's Airplane and the Little Sailor Ride.

Other attractions at the park include a puppet theater, celebrity musical revues, Dixieland jazz, rock concerts, and the Aqua Theater high-diving shows. Spillikin's Handcrafters Junction is a four-acre compound in which wares and skills ranging from blacksmithing to glassblowing are exhibited. *Magic Mountain Pkwy., off I–5, Valencia, tel. 818/992–0884. Admission: $22 adults, $11 children 48" and under. Open daily mid-May–Labor Day 10–10 (later on weekends); rest of the year, open weekends and holidays.*

Griffith Park **Los Angeles Zoo.** The zoo, one of the major zoos in the United States, is noted for its breeding of endangered species. Koala bears and white tigers are the latest additions. The 113-acre compound holds more than 2,000 mammals, birds, amphibians, and reptiles. Animals are grouped according to the geographical areas in which they are naturally found—Africa, Australia, Eurasia, North America, and South America. A tram is available for stops at all areas. Seeing the zoo calls for a lot of walking, seemingly all uphill, so strollers or backpacks are recommended for families with young children. The zoo is beautifully landscaped, and areas for picnicking are available. The animals are in well-kept, spacious areas with imaginative settings for roaming and climbing. Some not-to-be-missed features at the zoo: Adventure Island, a new children's zoo offering interactive exhibits and featuring animals of the American Southwest; a walk-through bird exhibit with more than 50 different species from all over the world; a koala area, where the furry creatures live amid eucalyptus trees in an environment similar to their native Australia. *Junction of the Ventura (134) and Golden State (I–5) freeways, Griffith Park, tel. 213/666–4090. Admission: $5.50 adults, $2.25 children. Open daily 10–5.*

Merry-Go-Round in Griffith Park. Just up the road from the real pony rides, this 1926-vintage carousel offers safe and melodic rides for families. The broad lawn nearby was the scene of some of the most colorful "love-ins" of the 1960s.

Pony Rides. Most kids in L.A. (and their parents before them) had their first pony ride at the track in Griffith Park. Two-year-olds are routinely strapped on and paraded around on the slowest of old nags. These days, the event is dutifully recorded on videotape. The ponies come in three speeds: slow, medium, and fast. The slow ones are the best, for all ages. The faster ones are jarring, and the kids seem disappointed. To round out an eventful morning (the lines are long in late afternoon), there are stagecoach rides and a miniature train ride that makes a figure eight near the pony rides. *Crystal Springs Dr., Griffith Park, tel. 213/664–3266. Use entrance near Golden State Freeway (I–5) and Los Feliz Blvd. Pony rides $1 for two rounds; stagecoach rides $1; miniature train rides $1.50 adults, $1.25 children. Open in summer, weekdays 10–5:30, weekends 10–6:30; rest of year: open Tues.–Fri. 10–4, weekends 10–5.*

Travel Town. This is a collection of airplanes, trains, and other early transportation replicas. Fifteen vintage railroad cars are resting here, all welcoming the onslaught of climbing and screaming children, who love to run from car to car, jump in the cab, scramble through the cars, and jump off the high steps. The collection includes a narrow-gauge sugar train from Hawaii, a steam engine, and an old L.A. trolley. Travel Town goes beyond just trains, with a collection of old planes such as World War II bombers as well as an old fire engine, milk wagon, buggies, and classic cars. A miniature train takes visitors on a ride around the area. *5200 Zoo Dr., Griffith Park, tel. 213/662–5874. Admission free. Open weekdays 10–4, weekends 10–5.*

Off the Beaten Track

The Flower Market. Just east of the downtown high rises, in the 700 block of Wall Street, is a block-long series of stores and stalls that opens up in the middle of the night to sell wholesale flowers and house plants to the city's florists, who rush them to their shops to sell that day. Many of the stalls stay open until late morning to sell leftovers to the general public at the same bargain prices. And what glorious leftovers they are: Hawaiian ginger, Dutch tulips, Chilean freesia. The public is welcome after 9 AM and the stock is quickly depleted by 11 AM. Even if you don't buy, it's a heady experience to be surrounded by so much fragile beauty.

Laurel and Hardy's Piano Stairway. One of the most famous scenes in the history of movies is one in *The Music Box* where Laurel and Hardy try to get a piano up an outdoor stairway. This Sisyphean tale was filmed in 1932 at 923–927 Vendome Street (where the stairway remains today much as it was then), in the Silverlake section of Los Angeles, a few miles northeast of downtown.

Orcutt Ranch Horticultural Center (23600 Roscoe Blvd., Canoga Park, tel. 818/883–6641). Once owned by William Orcutt, a well-known geologist who was one of the excavators of the La Brea Tar Pits, this ranch is a surprisingly lush and varied garden in the west San Fernando Valley. Orcutt is filled with interesting little areas to explore, such as the rose garden, herb garden, a stream banked with shady trees and ferns (a wonderful picnic site). On the last Sunday of the month, the house, in which the Orcutts lived, is open to the public. Two weekends a year (late June or early July) the extensive orange and grapefruit groves are open for public picking. It's a chance to enjoy the valley as it was in the years when groves like these covered the landscape for miles. You'll need an A-frame ladder or a special pole for dislodging the fruit up high. Bring along grocery sacks.

Pig Murals (3049 E. Vernon Ave., Vernon). Vernon Avenue is the heart of Los Angeles' meat-packing industry, and to be stuck in traffic on Vernon Avenue on a hot summer afternoon is an odorific experience not soon forgotten. Nevertheless, for aficionados of offbeat sites and/or street murals, seeing the Pig Murals on the outside walls of the Farmer John Company is great fun. Probably the first public murals in Los Angeles, they were painted originally by Leslie Grimes, who was killed in a fall from the scaffolding while painting. They depict bucolic scenes of farms and contented pigs, rather an odd juxtaposition to what goes on inside the packing plant.

Beaches

The beach scene is very much a part of the Southern California lifestyle. There is no public attraction more popular in L.A. than the white, sandy playgrounds of the deep blue Pacific.

From the L.A. civic center, the easiest way to hit the coast is by taking the Santa Monica Freeway (I–10) due west. Once you reach the end of the freeway, I–10 turns into the famous Highway 1, better known in Southern California as the Pacific Coast Highway (PCH), which continues up to Oregon. Other basic routes from the downtown area include Pico, Olympic, Santa Monica, or Wilshire boulevards, which all run east-west through the city. Sunset Boulevard offers a less direct but more scenic drive to the beaches, starting near Dodger Stadium, passing through Hollywood, Beverly Hills, and Pacific Palisades, and eventually reaching the Pacific Ocean 1 mile south of Malibu. The RTD bus lines, L.A.'s main form of public transportation until the new Metro Rail is completed, runs every 20 minutes to and from the beaches along each of these boulevards.

Los Angeles County beaches (and the state beaches operated by the county) have lifeguards. Public parking (for a fee) is available at most. The following beaches are listed in north-south order. Some are excellent for swimming, some for surfing (check with lifeguards for current conditions for either activity), others better for exploring.

Leo Carillo State Beach. This beach, along a rough and mountainous coastline, is most fun at low tide, when a spectacular array of tide pools blossoms for all to see. Rock formations on the beach create some great secret coves for picnickers looking for solitude. There are hiking trails, sea caves and tunnels, and whales, dolphins, sea lions, and otters are often seen swimming in the kelp beds off shore. The waters here are rocky and best for experienced surfers and scuba divers; fishing is good. Picturesque campgrounds are set back from the beach. *36000 block of PCH, Malibu, tel. 818/706–1310. Facilities: parking, lifeguard, rest rooms, showers, fire pits.*

Zuma Beach County Park. This is Malibu's largest and sandiest beach, and a favorite spot for surfing. It's also a haven for high school students who've discovered Nautilus Plus. *30050 block of PCH, Malibu, tel. 213/457–9891. Facilities: parking, lifeguard, rest rooms, showers, food, playground, volleyball.*

Westward Beach/Point Dume State Beach. Another favorite spot for surfing, this half-mile-long sandy beach has tide pools and sandstone cliffs. *South end of Westward Beach Rd., Malibu, tel. 213/457–9891. Facilities: parking, lifeguard, rest rooms, food.*

Paradise Cove. With its pier and equipment rentals, this sandy beach is a mecca for sport fishing boats. Though swimming is allowed, lifeguards are only there during the summer. *28128 PCH, Malibu, tel. 213/457–2511. Facilities: parking, rest rooms, food.*

Surfrider Beach/Malibu Lagoon State Beach. The steady 3–5 foot waves make this beach, just north of Malibu Pier, a great long-board surfing beach. The International Surfing Contest is held here in September. Water runoff from Malibu Canyon forms a natural lagoon, a sanctuary for many birds. Take a romantic sunset stroll along the nature trails. *23200 block of PCH, Malibu, tel. 818/706–1310. Facilities: parking, lifeguard, rest rooms, picnicking, visitor center.*

Las Tunas State Beach. Las Tunas is small (1,300 feet long, covering a total of only 2 acres), narrow, and sandy, with some rocky areas, and it's set beneath a bluff. Surf fishing is the biggest attraction here. There is no lifeguard, and swimming is not encouraged because of steel groins set offshore to prevent erosion. *19400 block of PCH, Malibu, tel. 213/457–9891. Facilities: parking, rest rooms.*

Topanga Canyon State Beach. The rocky beach stretches from the mouth of the canyon, making it great for surfing, down to Coastline Drive. Catamarans dance in these waves and skid onto the sands of this popular beach, where dolphins sometimes come close enough to shore to startle sunbathers. *15100, Malibu, tel. 213/394–3266. Facilities: parking, lifeguard, rest rooms, food.*

Will Rogers State Beach. This wide, sandy beach is several miles long, with an even surf. Parking is limited to the Castle Rock section, but there is plenty of beach, volleyball, and bodysurfing parallel to the pedestrian bridge. *16000 block of PCH, Pacific Palisades, tel. 213/394–3266. Facilities: parking, lifeguard, rest rooms.*

Santa Monica Beach. This is one of L.A.'s most popular beaches. In addition to a pier and a promenade, a man-made breakwater just offshore has caused the sand to collect and form the widest stretch of beach on the entire Pacific Coast. Wider beaches mean more bodies! If you're up for some sightseeing on land, this is one of the more popular gathering places for L.A.'s young, toned, and bronzed. All in all, the 2-mile-wide beach is well equipped with bike paths, facilities for the disabled, playgrounds, and volleyball. *West of PCH, Santa Monica, tel. 213/394–3266. Facilities: parking, lifeguard, rest rooms, showers.*

Venice Municipal Beach. While the surf and sands of Venice are fine, the main attraction here is the boardwalk. Venice combines the pure beef of some of L.A.'s most serious body builders with the productions of lively crafts merchants and street musicians. There are roller skaters and break dancers to entertain you and cafes to feed you. You can rent bikes at Venice Pier Bike Shop (21 Washington St.) and skates at Roller Skates of America (64 Windward Ave.) or Skatey's (102 Washington St.). *1531 Ocean Front Walk, Venice, tel. 213/394–3266. Facilities: parking, rest rooms, showers, food, picnicking.*

Playa Del Rey. South of Marina Del Rey lies a beach not quite as famous as its neighbors but known to its nearby residents as one of the more underrated beaches in Southern California. Its sprawling white sands stretch from the southern tip of Marina Del Rey almost two miles down to Dockweiler Beach. The majority of the crowds that frequent these sands are young. One of the more attractive features of this beach is an area called Del Rey Lagoon. Located right in the heart of Playa Del Rey, this grassy oasis surrounds a lovely pond inhabited by dozens of ducks, and offers picnickers barbecue pits and tables to help nourish an afternoon outing. *6660 Esplanade, Playa Del Rey. Facilities: Parking, lifeguard, rest rooms, food.*

Dockweiler State Beach. There are consistent waves for surfing at this beach, and it is not crowded, due to an unsightly power plant with towering smokestacks parked right on the beach. While the plant presents no danger to swimmers in the area, its mere presence, combined with the jumbo jets taking off overhead from L.A.'s International Airport, make this beach a better place to work out than to lay out. There is firewood for sale for barbecues on the beach; beach fires are legal in this area as long as they are contained within the special pits that are already set up along the beach. *Harbor Channel to Vista Del Mar and Grand Ave., Playa Del Rey, tel. 213/322–5008. Facilities: parking, lifeguard, rest rooms, showers.*

Manhattan State Beach. Here are 44 acres of sandy beach for swimming, diving, surfing, and fishing. Polliwog Park is a charming, grassy landscape a few yards back from the beach. Ducks waddle around a small pond, picnickers enjoy a full range of facilities including grills and rest rooms, and there is even a series of rock and jazz concerts held here in the summer. *West of Strand, Manhattan Beach, tel. 213/372–2166. Facilities: parking, lifeguard, rest rooms, showers, food.*

Redondo State Beach. The beach is wide, sandy, and usually packed in summer; parking is limited. The Redondo Pier marks the starting point of the beach area, which continues south for more than 2 miles along a heavily developed shoreline community. Storms have damaged some of the restaurants and shops along the pier, but plenty of others are still functioning. Excursion boats, boat launching ramps, and fishing are other attractions. *Foot of Torrance Blvd., Redondo Beach, tel. 213/372–2166. Facilities: parking, lifeguard, rest rooms, showers, food.*

Shopping

Most Los Angeles shops are open from 10 to 6, although many remain open until 9 or later, particularly at the shopping centers, on Melrose Avenue, and in Westwood Village during the summer. Melrose shops, on the whole, don't get moving until 11 AM but are often open on Sundays too. At most stores around town, credit cards are almost universally accepted and traveler's checks are also often allowed with proper identification. If you're looking for sales, check the *Los Angeles Times*.

Shopping Districts When asked where they want to shop, visitors to Los Angeles inevitably answer, "Rodeo Drive." This famous thoroughfare is not only high-high-end—and therefore, somewhat limited—it is also only one of many shopping streets. In our opinion, serious shoppers should not restrict their spending to that area of town. To discover the full scope of what Los Angeles has to offer, consider other parts of this huge metropolitan area for shopping expeditions. Remember, though, that distances between each can be vast, so don't choose too many different stops in one day. If you do, you'll spend more time on the road than you will discovering worthwhile buys.

Downtown Although downtown Los Angeles has many enclaves to explore, we suggest that the bargain hunter head straight for the **Cooper Building** (860 S. Los Angeles St., (tel. 213/622–1139). Eight floors of small clothing and shoe shops (mostly for women) offer some of the most fantastic discounts in the city. Grab a free map in the lobby, and seek out as many of the 82 shops as you can handle. Nearby are a myriad of discount outlets selling everything from shoes to suits to linens.

Near the Hilton Hotel, **Seventh Street Marketplace** (tel. 213/955–7150) is worth a visit. It's an indoor-outdoor multilevel shopping center with an extensive courtyard that boasts many busy cafes and lively music.

Melrose Avenue West Hollywood, especially Melrose Avenue, is where young shoppers should try their luck, as should those who appreciate vintage styles in clothing and furnishings. The 1½-mile stretch of intriguing, one-of-a-kind shops and bistros extends from La Brea to a few blocks west of Crescent Heights; it is definitely one of Los Angeles's hottest shopping areas. Top shops on the avenue include: **Industrial Revolution** (7560 Melrose) for hi-tech furnishings; **Betsey Johnson** (7311 Melrose) for vivid, hip women's fashions; **Ecru** (7428 Melrose) for designer clothing by Ana Salazar, John Galliano, and Uomo for men and women; **Modern Living** (8125 Melrose) for top 20th-century home design from Phillipe Starck, Ettore Sottsass, and Massino Isosaghini. Farther west is the incomparable **Maxfield** (8825 Melrose), where, it seems, all of Hollywood's richest and most fashionable luminaries shop for clothing.

Westwood Westwood Village, near the UCLA campus, is a young and lively area for shopping. The atmosphere is invigorating, especially during summer evenings when there's a movie line around every corner, all kinds of people strolling the streets (an unusual sight in L.A. where few locals ever walk anywhere), and cars cruising along to take in the scene.

Beverly Center and Environs Mall shopping is so important in Los Angeles that it is actually a sociological phenomenon. The **Beverly Center** (tel. 213/854–0070), bounded by Beverly Boulevard, La Cienega Boulevard, San Vicente Boulevard, and Third Street, covers more than 7 acres and contains 200 stores. Since its opening in spring 1982, the mall has continually catered to an upscale market. Many European designers—Laura Ashley, Linea Uomo, Alexio, Melwanis, and others—have opened retail outlets here, as have unusual American shops. The shopping center is anchored by The Broadway department store on one end, Bullocks on the other. Inside, there are also some interesting restaurants (like the Kisho-an, a Japanese restaurant known for its fine sushi, and the Hard Rock Cafe, known for its bargain cuisine and fascinating decor, starting with the 1959 Caddy that looks as if it dove into the roof of the building above the restaurant) and one of L.A.'s finest cineplexes, with 14 individual movie theaters. It's also worthwhile to venture outside the confines of the Beverly Center to discover some real attention-getting shops.

The **Pacific Design Center** (corner of Melrose Ave. and San Vicente Blvd., tel. 213/657–0800) is where leading interior designers find the best in home furnishings and accessories for clients who aim to impress. Set in two startlingly big colored glass buildings—known to locals as the Blue Whale and the Green Giant—with a few exceptions, the PDC's exclusive showrooms sell only to the trade. If you would like to do more than look here, contact LA Design Concepts, an interior design shopping service (8811 Alden Ave., LA 90048, tel. 213/276–2109). A design professional will guide you through the PDC for $15 an hour, offer advice and order items for you at less than half the standard industry markup of 33 percent. More of the same kinds of design stores, many of which *are* open to the public, can be found on Robertson Avenue, between Beverly Boulevard and Third Street, and on Melrose near Robertson.

Century City **Century City Shopping Center & Marketplace** (tel. 213/277–3989) is set among gleaming steel office buildings. Here, in the center of a thriving business atmosphere, is an open-air city kind of mall. Besides The Broadway and Bullocks, both department stores, you'll find Sasha of London for trendy shoes and bags, Ann Taylor for stylish but not outlandish clothing, the Pottery Barn for contemporary furnishings at comfortable prices, and Gelson's, a gourmet food market where you'll find California wines—a great gift to take home. There are five restaurants on the premises, which, incidentally, used to be 20th Century Fox Film Studios' back lot. Among them are Langan's Brasserie, affiliated with a famous London dining spot; and Stage Deli, the kind of New York-style deli that previously was hard to find in L.A. Also at Century City is the AMC Century 14 Theater Complex, which opened in 1987.

West Los Angeles **The Westside Pavilion** (tel. 213/474–6255) is a pastel-colored post-modern mall on Pico and Overland boulevards. The two levels of shops and restaurants run the gamut from high-fashion boutiques for men and women to a store devoted solely to travelers' needs, large and small. The department stores are the May Company and Nordstroms. You'll also find Muppet and Stuff, filled with novelties commemorating the television show; and Mr Gs for Kids, a good place for children's gifts.

Santa Monica Another worthwhile and multifaceted area, farther west and next to the ocean, offers both malls and street shopping. **Santa Monica Place Mall** (315 Broadway, tel. 213/394–5451) is a 3-story enclosed mall that's nothing special. Next-door, **Santa Monica Promenade** (tel. 213/393–8355) is an open-air arena of shops with pedestrian walkways and a landscaped island. A light, airy atrium views all three floors of the mall at once, and from particular points you can see the Pacific in the background. Robinson's and The Broadway are department stores in this complex.

Montana Avenue is home to a dozen blocks that have evolved into an L.A. version of New York City's Columbus Avenue. Boutique after boutique of quality goods can be found along Montana from Seventh to Seventeenth streets. The stretch of **Main Street** leading from Santa Monica to Venice (Pico Blvd. to Rose Ave.) also makes for a pleasant walk, with a collection of good restaurants, unusual shops and galleries, and an ever-present ocean breeze.

Beverly Hills We've saved the most famous section of town for last. **Rodeo Drive** is often compared with such famous streets as Fifth Avenue in New York and the Via Condotti in Rome. Along the several blocks between Wilshire and Santa Monica boulevards, you'll find an abundance of big-name retailers—but don't shop Beverly Hills without shopping the streets that surround illustrious Rodeo Drive. There are plenty of treasures to be purchased on those other thoroughfares as well.

Browse around. Among the many shops and boutiques you'll pass are Fred Hayman (273 N. Rodeo Dr., tel. 213/271–3000) and Bijan. At this illustrious store, (formerly Giorgio), one does not merely shop for the glitzy American and European clothing, accessories, and footwear; one also refreshes oneself at the stunning Oak Bar that separates the women's from the men's clothes. **Bijan** (420 N. Rodeo Dr., tel. 213/273–6544) is a store where you shop by appointment only. Bijan claims that many Arabian sheiks and other royalty shop here along with some of the wealthiest men in the United States. Many designs are created specially by the owner.

Other top shops include: **Polo/Ralph Lauren** (444 N. Rodeo Dr.) and the **Torie Steele** boutiques (414 N. Rodeo Dr.) for designs from Valentino, Fendi, Maud Frizon and Krizia.

Even Beverly Hills has a shopping center, though owners wouldn't dare call their collection of stores and cafes a mall. It's the **Rodeo Collection,** located between Brighton Way and Santa Monica Boulevard (421 N. Rodeo Dr., tel. 213/271–4478), and it's the epitome of opulence and high fashion. Many famous European designers who have never had freestanding stores on the West Coast have opened their doors in this piazzalike area of marble and brass.

Department Stores **The Broadway.** This complete department store offers merchandise in the moderate price range, from cosmetics, to housewares, to linens, to clothing for men and women. There are stores throughout Los Angeles. *The Beverly Center at 8500 Beverly Blvd., tel. 213/854–7200.*
Bullocks. More upscale than The Broadway, Bullocks has an extensive collection of clothing for men and women, housewares and cosmetics. Stores are throughout Southern California. *The Beverly Center, 8500 Beverly Blvd., tel. 213/854–6655.*
I. Magnin. This large store has many designer labels for men and women, and a good handbag and luggage department, with branches throughout Southern California. The flagship store (called I. Magnin Wilshire) is an art deco landmark in the Wilshire district. *3050 Wilshire Blvd., tel. 213/382–6161.*
The May Company. Modestly priced clothing and furniture without glitz or glitter are offered in these stores throughout Southern California. *Downtown at 6067 Wilshire Blvd., tel. 213/938–4211.*

Saks Fifth Avenue. The Los Angeles version of this New York store isn't as impressive as the one you'll find across the street from St. Patrick's Cathedral in Manhattan. Still, the buyers have good taste. There are several locations, but the best is at *9600 Wilshire Blvd. in Beverly Hills, tel. 213/275–4211.*

Nordstrom. This Seattle-based department store infiltrated Southern California within the past decade and has brought with it a wide selection of clothing for men and women as well as a reputation for fine customer service, a huge shoe department, and the entertainment of popular music played on the store's grand piano. There are several locations, but the best is at the *Westside Pavilion at 500 N. Pico Blvd., West Los Angeles, tel. 213/470–6155.*

Robinson's. This high-end department store has many women's selections, few men's selections, a good housewares department, and stores throughout Southern California. *9900 Wilshire Blvd., Beverly Hills, tel. 213/275–5464.*

Buffums. This is a conservative and not very impressive department store carrying moderately priced goods of all description at stores throughout Southern California. *145 S. Central Ave. in the Glendale Galleria, tel. 818/240–8600.*

Specialty Shops	
Antiques	L.A.'s poshest antiquarian niche is Melrose Place. Among the shops are **Rose Tarlow Antiques** (8454 Melrose Pl., tel. 213/653–2122), **Licorne** (8432 Melrose Pl., tel. 213/852–4765) and **Le Lion et La Licorne** (8445 Melrose Ave., tel. 213/653–7470), operated by French emigrés who sell fine 17th- through 19th-century furnishings. **Panache** (8445 Melrose Ave., tel. 213/653–9436) provides an eclectic assortment of furniture and objects at the area's most reasonable prices.

For more intrepid hunters, Western Avenue (between 1st and 2nd sts.) offers some truly valuable finds in some very low key shops, including: **French Kings Antiques** (135 S. Western Ave., tel. 213/383–4430) with furniture, bronzes and clocks; **Used Stuff** (151 S. Western Ave., tel. 213/487–5336) for English imported furniture; and **Antiques Etcetera** (153 S. Western Ave., tel. 213/487–5226), which resembles a jumble of estate and garage sales.

The Antique Guild (8800 Venice Blvd., tel. 213/838–3131). You'll find treasures from all over the world in a gigantic inventory in this warehouse-size space.

Books **Book Soup** (8818 Sunset, West Hollywood, tel. 213/659–3110). This Sunset Strip shop stocks a wide variety of volumes, with particularly strong photography, film, new fiction, and international magazine sections.

The Bodhi Tree (8585 Melrose, West Hollywood, tel. 213/659–1733). If the metaphysical is of interest, this is the place to learn about it.

Artworks (170 S. La Brea, West Hollywood. 213/934–2205). All manner of art and photography books are stocked in this tiny space that shares a building with several art galleries and a terrific little cafe.

Children's Clothing **Splash** (12109 Ventura Blvd., Studio City, tel. 818/762–6123). Shop here if you like to dress your child (newborn to toddlers) in the latest fashions.

Gifts and Crafts **Freehand** (8413 W. 3rd St., West Hollywood, tel. 213/655–2607). The salespeople are extremely helpful at this great shop filled with ceramics, jewelry, pottery, and handmade clothing created by area artists.

Craft and Folk Art Museum Shop (5814 Wilshire Blvd., tel. 213/ 937–5544). Next to a small craft museum, this tiny shop emphasizes ethnic as well as American contemporary items.

Del Mano Gallery (11981 San Vicente Blvd., Brentwood, tel. 213/476–8508). Owners Jan Peters and Ray Leier are known for finding the nation's top contemporary art. For a decade, they have sold everything from hand-crafted sweaters and handbags to glass and ceramic treasures.

Tesoro (319 S. Robertson, tel. 213/273–9890). This large boutique stocks everything from trendy Swid–Powell dishware to Southwestern blankets, ceramics and art furniture. The range of work by area artists is well worth browsing.

Wild Blue (7220 Melrose, West Hollywood, tel. 213/939–8434). At this small boutique of California pottery, ceramics, jewelry, and art furniture, the artists tend toward bright colors.

Jewelry **Kenneth Jay Lane** (441 N. Rodeo Dr., tel. 213/273–9588) sells the work of its owner, a leading designer of faux jewels; you've seen his designs on "Dynasty," "Dallas," and "Falcon Crest."

Pavé (1128 Montana, Santa Monica, tel. 213/458–3492). This store features contemporary gold, silver, and platinum pieces and a great repair department.

Leather **North Beach Leather** (8500 Sunset, West Hollywood. tel. 213/ 652–3224). Here is a great selection of clothing made of leather and suede, for both men and women.

Musical Recordings **Aron's Record** (7725 Melrose, tel. 213/653–8170). There is an extensive selection of old records, perhaps the largest on the West Coast, and low prices on new albums.

CD Bonzai (8250 W. 3rd St., tel. 213/653–0800). This all-CD shop is tiny but full of finds.

Secondhand Clothing **American Rag** (150 S. La Brea Ave., tel. 213/935–3154). Inexpensive, downtown chic clothes for men and women. Much of their stock is "previously owned," though some items are on the racks for the first time.

Charlie's (115 N. LaBrea, tel. 213/931–2486). This West Hollywood shop sells a cornucopia of '50s and '60s clothes, with a few choice furnishings as well. The place is big on evening gowns. The selection is vast and the prices are fair.

Toys **Imaginarium** (Century City Shopping Center, 10250 Santa Monica Blvd., tel. 213/785–0227). Children are encouraged to play in this store, known for toys that are both nonviolent and educational.

Participant Sports

If you're looking for a good workout, you've come to the right city. Los Angeles is one of the major sports capitals in the United States. The near-perfect climate allows sports enthusiasts to play outdoors almost year-round, and during some seasons it's not impossible to be surfing in the morning and snow skiing in the afternoon . . . all in the same city!

Bicycling In the last few years, Los Angeles has made a concerted effort to upgrade existing bike paths and to designate new lanes along many major boulevards for cyclists' use. Perhaps the most famous bike path in the city, and definitely the most beautiful, can be found on the beach. The path starts at Temescal Canyon and works its way down to Redondo Beach. San Vicente Boulevard in Santa Monica has a nice wide lane (5 miles long) next to the sidewalk for cyclists. Balboa Park in the San Fernando Valley is another haven for two-wheelers.

Fishing Shore fishing is excellent on many of the beaches. Pier fishing is another popular method of hooking your dinner. The Malibu, Santa Monica, and Redondo Beach piers each offer nearby bait and tackle shops, and generally pull in a healthy catch. If you want to break away from the piers, however, the **Malibu Pier Sport Fishing Company** (2300 Pacific Coast Hwy., tel. 213/456–8030) and the **Redondo Sport Fishing Company** (233 N. Harbor Dr., tel. 213/372–2111) have half-day and full-day charters. Half-day charters, from 8 AM to 1 PM, run about $16 per person, while full-day charters are about $40. You can rent a pole for $5.50. Sea bass, halibut, bonita, yellowtail, and barracuda are the usual catch.

For something with a little more bite, there are a number of fishing charters out of Marina Del Rey, like **The Widow Maker** (tel. 213/306–9793), that will take you hunting for thresher shark. Threshers are common in the Santa Monica Bay and are almost as big as marlin and equally challenging. Rates range $360–$480 a day.

A popular and unique form of fishing in the L.A. area involves no hooks, bait, or poles. The great grunion runs, which take place March through August, are a spectacular natural phenomenon: Hundreds of thousands of small, silver fish wash up on Southern California beaches to spawn and lay their eggs in the sand. The **Cabrillo Museum** in San Pedro (tel. 213/548–7562) has entertaining and educational programs about grunion during most of the runs. There are certain seasons when touching the grunion is prohibited, so it's advisable to check with the **Fish and Game Department** (tel. 213/590–5132) before going to see them wash ashore.

Fitness and Health Clubs Many movies, TV shows, and songs have depicted the L.A. body as some kind of mythological creature possessing the secret of the three "T"s: tanning, toning, and tightening. There are dozens of health spa chains in the city that offer monthly and yearly memberships. **Nautilus Plus** and **Holiday Spa Health Clubs** are probably the most popular chains. The Holiday Club located south of Hollywood Boulevard (1607 Gower St., tel. 213/461–0227), is the flagship operation. This place has everything, including racquetball courts, indoor running tracks, pools, men's and women's weight and aerobics rooms, and a juice bar.

A few hotels in the city also have health spas, and some are open to the public. The Century Plaza Hotel in Beverly Hills (tel. 213/277–2000) also has weights, life cycles, aerobics, and saunas. The spa is open only to hotel guests at $15 per session. And if you're in town briefly on a layover, the Marriott Hotel at LAX (tel. 213/641–5700) has Universal weights, life cycles, a sauna, and an Olympic-size pool—all free to guests.

Golf The Department of Parks and Recreation maintains seven public 18-hole courses in Los Angeles. Reservations (tel. 213/485–5515) are required on weekends and holidays.

Rancho Park Golf Course (10460 W. Pico Blvd., tel. 213/838–7373) is one of the most heavily played links in the entire country. Rancho is a beautifully designed course with enough towering pines to make those who slice or hook want to forget they ever learned how to play golf. There's a 2-story driving range, a nine-hole pitch 'n' putt, a snack bar, and a pro shop where you can rent clubs.

Perhaps the most concentrated area of golf courses in the city can be found in Griffith Park. Here you'll find two splendid 18-hole courses along with a challenging nine-hole course. **Harding Golf Course** and **Wilson Golf Course** (both on Crystal Springs Dr., tel. 213/663–2555) are located about 1½ miles inside the Griffith Park entrance at Riverside and Los Feliz. Peaceful bridle paths surround the outer fairways, as the San Gabriel mountains make up the rest of the gallery in a scenic background. The nine-hole **Roosevelt Course** (tel. 213/665–2011) can be found by entering Griffith Park at the Hillhurst Street entrance.

Yet another course in the Griffith Park vicinity is the nine-hole **Los Feliz Pitch N' Putt** (3207 Los Feliz Blvd., tel. 213/663–7758). Other pitch 'n' putt courses include **Holmby Hills** (601 Club View Dr., West L.A., tel. 213/276–1604) and **Penmar** (1233 Rose Ave., Venice, tel. 213/396–6228).

Horseback Riding While horseback riding in Los Angeles is extremely popular, stables that rent horses are becoming an endangered species. Of the survivors, **Bar "S" Stables** (1850 Riverside Dr., Glendale, tel. 818/242–8443) will rent you a horse for $13 an hour. Riders who come here can take advantage of more than 50 miles of beautiful trails in the Griffith Park area. **Sunset River Trails** (on Rush St., at the end of Peck Rd., El Monte, tel. 818/444–2128) offers riders the nearby banks of the San Gabriel River to explore. **Sunset Stables** (at the end of Beachwood Dr., Hollywood, tel. 213/469–5450) offers a $25 "dinner cruise." At sunset, riders take a trail over the hill into Burbank, where they park their horses and have a feast at a Mexican restaurant.

Jogging Most true joggers don't care where they run (high schools and college tracks are good) or what the weather is like outside when they do it. But if you've got the time to drive to a more choice location to commence your leg-pumping exercises, here are a few suggestions:

A popular scenic course for students and downtown workers can be found at Exposition Park. Circling the Memorial Coliseum and Sports Arena is a jogging/workout trail with pull-up bars and other simple equipment spread out every several hundred yards. San Vicente Boulevard in Santa Monica has a wide grassy median that splits the street for several picturesque miles. Griffith Park offers several thousand acres of grassy hills for a course with more challenging terrain. Of course, the premium spot in Los Angeles for any kind of exercise can be found along one of the beaches.

Tennis And on the eighth day, God created the tennis court . . . at least it seems that way when you drive around most L.A. neighborhoods. If you want to play tennis, you'll have no problem finding a court in this town—although you might have to wait a while when you get there. Many public parks have courts that require an hourly fee. Lincoln Park, at Lincoln and Wilshire Boulevard in Santa Monica; Griffith Park, at Riverside and Los Feliz; and Barrington Park, on Barrington just south of Sunset in L.A., all have well-maintained courts with lights.

For a full rundown of all the public tennis courts in Los Angeles, contact the **L.A. Department of Recreation and Parks** (tel. 213/485–5515) or the **Southern California Tennis Association** (Los Angeles Tennis Center, UCLA Campus, Box 250015, L.A. 90024, tel. 213/208–3838).

If you're in town for just a few days and you don't have time to drive around looking for a court, you may very well be staying at a hotel that has facilities. For instance, the Century Plaza in Century City (tel. 213/277–2000) has eight rooftop courts overlooking the city; the Sheraton Towne House on Wilshire (tel. 213/382–7171) has four courts; and downtown the L.A. Bonaventure (tel. 213/624–1000) has eight courts for their guests.

Spectator Sports

If you enjoy watching professional sports, you'll never hunger for action in this town! Los Angeles is the home of some of the greatest franchises in pro basketball, football, and baseball.

Baseball   The **Dodgers** (tel. 213/224–1400) will try to muster up the old glory of "Dodger Blue" in another eventful season at the everpopular Dodger Stadium. Down the freeway a bit in Anaheim, the **California Angels** (tel. 213/625–1123) continue their race for the pennant in the American League West.

Basketball   While the great American pastime may be baseball, in the town where the four-time world champion **Los Angeles Lakers** (tel. 213/419–3182) continuously display what they call "showtime," basketball is king! The Lakers' home court is the Fabulous Forum in Inglewood. L.A.'s "other" team, the **Clippers** (tel. 213/748–6131), make their home at the L.A. Sports Arena in downtown next to the Coliseum.

Football   The **Los Angeles Raiders** (tel. 213/747–7111) still play at the L.A. Coliseum downtown, although there has been talk of a move east to Irwindale. In Anaheim, the **Los Angeles Rams** (tel. 213/625–1123) will continue their struggle to get back to the Super Bowl this year.

Golf   The hot ticket each February in this town is the Glen Campbell Los Angeles Open. The tournament attracts the best golfers in the world and is played in Pacific Palisades at the Riviera Country Club.

Hockey   The **L.A. Kings** (tel. 213/419–3182) put their show on ice at the Forum from November through April.

Polo   **Will Rogers State Park** (tel. 213/454–8212) offers lovely picnic grounds where you can feast while enjoying an afternoon chukker of polo. If it doesn't rain, games are played Saturdays at 2 and Sundays at 10.

Horse Racing   **Santa Anita** racetrack is still the dominant site for exciting Thoroughbred racing. With jockeys such as Pincay and Valenzuela in the saddle, you can always expect the best racing in the world at this beautiful facility. The track is located at Huntington Drive and Colorado Place in Arcadia (tel. 818/574–7223). **Hollywood Park** is another favorite racing venue. The new Cary Grant Pavilion was recently completed, bringing back a style that was lacking from this once great park for some time. The track is located next to the Forum in Inglewood, off Century Boulevard (tel. 213/419–1500). The racing season here goes from late April through mid-July. For harness racing, **Los Alamitos** (tel. 213/431–1361) has both day and night racing.

Dining

by Bruce David Colen

This past decade has seen Los Angeles emerge as one of the top gastronomic capitals of the world. It has been an amazing and delicious transformation. Where once the city was only known for its chopped Cobb salad, Green Goddess dressing, drive-in hamburger stands, and outdoor barbecues, today it has some of the best French and Italian restaurants in the United States, plus so many places featuring international cuisines that listing them all would sound like a roll call at the United Nations. Actually, there are so many new, *good* dining establishments opening every week that, currently, there are more chairs, banquettes, and booths than there are bodies to fill them. Net result? The fierce competition among upscale restauranteurs has made L.A. one of the least expensive big cities—both here and abroad—in which to eat well.

The natives tend to dine early, between 7:30 and 9 PM, a hold-over from when this was a "studio" town, and film making started at 6 AM. Advance reservations are essential at the "starred" restaurants, and at almost all restaurants on weekend evenings.

Highly recommended restaurants are indicated by a star ★.

Category	Cost*
Very Expensive	over $70
Expensive	$40–$70
Moderate	$20–$40
Inexpensive	under $20

*per person, without tax, service, or drinks

American
Beverly Hills

The Grill. This is the closest Los Angeles comes in looks and atmosphere to one of San Francisco's venerable bar-and-grills, with their dark wood paneling and brass trim. The food is basic American, cleanly and simply prepared, including fine steaks and chops, grilled fresh salmon, corned beef hash, braised beef ribs, and a great, creamy version of the Cobb salad. *9560 Dayton Way, tel. 213/276–0615. Evening valet parking. Dress: casual, but neat. AE, DC, MC, V. Closed Sun. Moderate.*
Ed Debevic's. This is a good place to take the kids and yourself, if you are yearning for the nostalgia of youth. Old Coca-Cola signs, a blaring juke box, gum-chewing waitresses in bobby sox, and meat loaf and mashed potatoes will take you back to the diners of the '50s. *134 N. La Cienega Blvd., tel. 213/659–1952. No weekend reservations; weekday reservations advised. Valet parking. Dress: casual. No credit cards. Inexpensive.*
RJ's the Rib Joint. There is a large barrel of free peanuts at the door, sawdust on the floor, and atmosphere to match. The outstanding salad bar has dozens of fresh choices and return privileges, and there are big portions of everything—from ribs, chili, and barbecued chicken, to mile-high layer cakes—at very reasonable prices. *252 N. Beverly Dr., tel. 213/274–RIBS. Valet parking at night. Dress: casual. AE, DC, MC, V. Inexpensive.*

Downtown Los Angeles Dining and Lodging

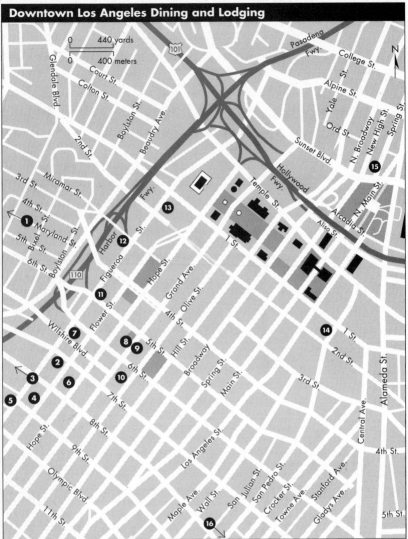

Dining

Checkers, **8**

Engine Co. #28, **7**

Horikawa, **14**

Mon Kee's Live Fish and Seafood Restaurant, **15**

Pacific Dining Car, **1**

Rex Il Ristorante, **10**

Seventh Street Bistro, **2**

Vickman's, **16**

Lodging

The Biltmore Hotel, **9**

Checkers Hotel, **8**

Figueroa Hotel, **5**

Holiday Inn L.A. Downtown, **3**

Hyatt Regency L.A., **6**

The New Otani and Garden, **13**

Orchid Hotel, **4**

Sheraton Grande Hotel, **12**

The Westin Bonaventure, **11**

Downtown **Checker's.** Located in a new, elegant small hotel, a southern relative of San Francisco's wonderful Campton Place, the restaurant features the California-American cuisine of Chef Jerry Comfort and a private club-like dining room that will make one give up thoughts of calling room service. The best bets are seafood sausage, smoked salmon with fennel toast, soft-shell-crab sandwich, roast pheasant, baked Virginia ham, rib-eye steak, and a Boston cream pie that would turn Beacon Hill bluebloods green with envy. *535 S. Grand Ave., tel. 213/624–0000. Valet parking. Jacket and tie required. AE, DC, MC, V. Moderate–Expensive.*

Pacific Dining Car. This is one of L.A.'s oldest restaurants, in a 1920s railroad car, with add-ons over the years. Best known for its well-aged steaks, rack of lamb, and an extensive California wine list at fair prices, it's a favorite haunt of politicians and lawyers around City Hall, and sports fans after the Dodger games. *1310 W. 6th St., tel. 213/483–6000. Valet parking. Open 24 hours. Reservations advised. Dress: casual. MC, V. Moderate–Expensive.*

Engine Co. #28. The ground floor of this National Historic Site was recently refurbished and refitted; now it's a very polished, bar and grill, crowded from day one. Reason? All-American food carefully prepared and served with obvious pride. Don't miss the corn chowder, "Firehouse" chili, grilled pork chop, smoked rare tenderloin, and grilled ahi tuna. And there's a great lemon meringue pie. *Corner of Figueroa St. and Wilshire Blvd. tel. 213/624–6996. Reservations required. Dress: jacket and tie required for lunch; casual for dinner. Valet parking. AE, MC, V. Closed weekend lunch. Moderate.*

Lawry's California Center. Out-of-towners envision this setting when they think of dining under the stars in the Big Orange: a terraced courtyard lush with flowers, ferns, and palm trees. There is a strolling mariachi band and, on weekends, a jazz group. The food is not that special, but the entrées—charbroiled New York steak, swordfish, grilled salmon, and hickory-smoked chicken—come with the works: a garden salad, freshly baked herb bread, corn on the cob, steamed vegetables, and a tortilla casserole. *570 West Ave. 26, tel. 213/225–2491. Parking lot. Reservations advised for dinner. Dress: casual. AE, MC, V. Garden dining May through mid-Nov. Closed Sun. lunch. Inexpensive–Moderate.*

Vickman's. Located next to the L.A. Produce Market, this bustling cafeteria opens at 3AM to accommodate fleets of truck drivers, restaurant and hotel buyers, stall owners, curious nightpeople, and customers at the nearby flower mart. The dishes are simple, hearty, and bountiful: ham and eggs, grits, stuffed pork chops, giant sandwiches, and a famous fresh strawberry pie. It's a fun place to go if you can't sleep. *1228 E. 8th St., tel. 213/622–3852. Dress: anything short of pajamas. No credit cards. Open 3 AM–3 PM daily. Inexpensive.*

Eastside **The Chronicle.** You will think you are in San Francisco's Sam's or the Tadish Grill, both very good places to be. The steaks, chops, prime rib, oysters, and other shellfish are excellent, and it has one of the best California wine lists south of the Napa Valley. *897 Granite Dr., tel. 818/792–1179. Valet parking. Reservations advised. Jacket and tie required. AE, MC, V. Moderate.*

Hollywood **L.A. Nicola.** Owner/chef Larry Nicola spent his early years in his family's produce market. His appreciation for fresh vegeta-

Beverly Hills and Hollywood Dining and Lodging

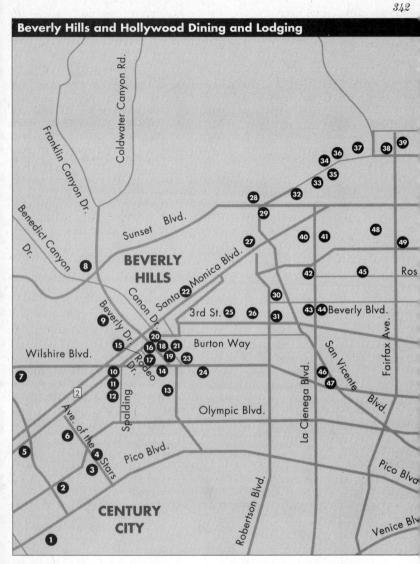

Dining

Antonio's Restaurant, **51**
The Bistro, **19**
The Bistro Garden, **23**
Border Grille, **49**
California Pizza Kitchen, **13**
Carnegie Deli, **20**
Cha Cha Cha, **61**

Champagne, **5**
Chan Dara, **55**
Chasen's, **30**
Chopstix, **52**
Citrus, **54**
Colette, **24**
Dan Tana's, **22**
The Dining Room, **14**
Ed Debevic's, **46**
El Cholo, **65**

Greenblatt's, **38**
The Grill, **17**
Hard Rock Cafe, **43**
Harry's Bar & American Grill, **4**
Jimmy's, **12**
Katsu, **59**
L.A. Nicola, **60**
L'Ermitage, **41**

L'Orangerie, **40**
La Toque, **37**
Le Chardonnay, **45**
Le Dome, **32**
Le St. Germain, **56**
Locanda Veneta, **31**
The Mandarin, **16**
Mandarin Wilshire, **47**
Nate 'n Al's, **18**
The Palm, **27**
Pastel, **15**

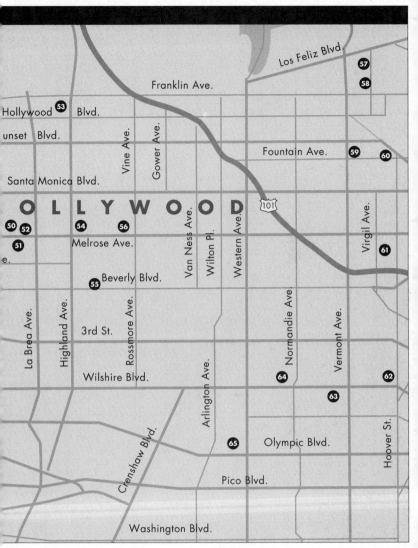

Pierre's Los
Feliz Inn, **57**
Prego, **9**
Primi, **1**
Restaurant Katzu, **58**
RJ's the Rib Joint, **21**
Spago, **28**
Tommy Tang's, **50**
Trader Vic's, **10**
Trumps, **42**
Tuttobene, **48**
The Windsor, **63**

Lodging
Beverly Hills
Comstock, **7**
Beverly Hills Hotel, **8**
The Beverly Hilton, **10**
Beverly House
Hotel, **11**
Century City Inn, **2**
Century Plaza Hotel, **6**
Château Marmont
Hotel, **36**

Four Seasons Los
Angeles, **26**
Hollywood Holiday
Inn, **53**
Hollywood
Roosevelt, **39**
Hyatt on Sunset, **34**
Hyatt Wilshire, **64**
J W Marriott Hotel at
Century City, **3**
L'Ermitage Hotel, **25**

Le Bel Age Hotel, **29**
Le Mondrian
Hotel, **33**
Ma Maison Sofitel
Hotel, **44**
Regent Beverly
Wilshire, **14**
Saint James's
Club, **35**
Sheraton Towne
House, **62**

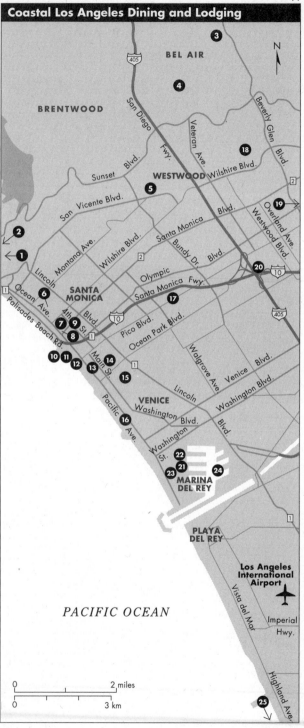

344

Coastal Los Angeles Dining and Lodging

Dining
Adriano's, **3**
Beaurivage, **1**
The Bel Air Hotel, **4**
The Chesterfield Hotel Deluxe, **19**
Chinois on Main, **14**
Daily Grill, **5**
Dynasty Room, **18**
Fennel, **8**
Gillilands, **13**
Gladstone's 4 Fish, **7**
La Scala-Malibu, **2**
Orleans, **15**
Valentino, **17**
West Beach Cafe, **16**

Lodging
Barnaby's Hotel, **24**
The Bel Air Hotel, **4**
Best Western Royal Palace Hotel, **20**
Carmel Hotel, **6**
Loews Santa Monica Beach Hotel, **10**
Marina Beach Hotel, **21**
Marina International Hotel, **22**
Miramar Sheraton, **9**
Pacific Shore, **11**
Palm Motel, **12**
The Ritz-Carlton, Marina del Rey, **23**
Sheraton at Redondo Beach, **25**
Westwood Marquis, **18**

bles, greens, and meats is evident in all his offerings, along with a penchant for off-beat American cooking, utilizing the bounty from California's farms and waters. Nicola raises the lowly hamburger to a place of eminence. And don't miss the grilled shark, veal chop with capers, or the appetizer of fried artichoke hearts. Perhaps the nicest thing about this California-style bistro, with its white walls and huge pails of fresh flowers, is its hideaway atmosphere, a place with style but no pretensions. *4326 Sunset Blvd., tel. 213/660–7217. Valet Parking. Reservations advised. Dress: casual. AE, DC, MC, V. Closed Sun. Moderate.*

West Hollywood **Chasen's.** It may no longer be Hollywood's "in" spot, but the clublike rooms are full of nostalgia, and have a quaintly formal charm. The dishes that Alfred Hitchcock, Gary Cooper, and Henry Fonda loved—and George Burns still does—are as good as ever: hobo steak, double-rib lamb chops, boiled beef with matzo dumplings, and the late Dave Chasen's famous chili. For enders, try the sensational banana shortcake or frozen eclair. This is a place for special celebrations. *9039 Beverly Blvd., tel. 213/271–2168. Valet parking. Weekend reservations suggested. Dress: a chance to look your very best. Jacket and tie required. No credit cards. Dinner only, Tues.–Sun. Expensive.*

The Palm. If you don't mind the roar of the jocks, or having the New York–style waiters rush you through your Bronx cheesecake, this is where you'll find the biggest and best steamed Maine lobsters, very good steaks and chops, great French fried onion rings, and paper-thin potato slices. If you have the roast beef hash for lunch, you'll have to skip dinner. A three-deep bar adds to the noise. *9001 Santa Monica Blvd., tel. 213/550–8811. Valet Parking. Reservations advised. Dress: casual. AE, DC, MC, V. Closed weekend lunch. Moderate–Expensive.*

The Hard Rock Cafe. Big burgers, rich milkshakes, banana splits, BLTs, and other pre-yuppie food delights, along with loud music, have made this '50s-era barn of a cafe the favorite of local teenagers. There is a large and busy bar for curious adults, many parents watching the kids. The place drew national attention—and spawned other Hard Rocks—for its fish-tail Cadillac jutting out of the roof, Fonzie's leather jacket on the wall, and Elvis's motorcycle. *8600 Beverly Blvd., tel. 213/276–7605. Valet parking. No reservations. Dress: you name it. AE, DC, MC, V. Inexpensive.*

Westside **West Beach Cafe.** It seems owner Bruce Madder can do no ★ wrong. Ten years ago, he opened this upscale restaurant within a Frisbee toss of all the voyeur action on the Venice beach strand. Next came **Rebecca's,** just across the street, where Mexican food is treated as semi-*haute cuisine* and idolized by the yuppie set. Then last year came the instant winner **DC-3,** a 21st-century architectural extravaganza at Santa Monica Airport. Best at the West Beach are Caesar salad, filet mignon taco, braised lamb shank, ravioli with pork and radicchio, fisherman's soup, and what many consider the best hamburger and fries in all of Los Angeles. There's also a fabulous selection of French wines and after-dinner liqueurs. *60 N. Venice Blvd., tel. 213/823–5396. Valet parking. Reservations advised. Dress: casual. AE, DC, MC, V. Moderate–Expensive.*

Gilliland's. While Gerri was teaching cooking in her native Ireland, she took a vacation in Southern California—and never went back. Instead, she created this charming little restaurant that offers the best of both culinary worlds, and showcases her fascination with Mediterranean dishes. The soda bread, Irish stew, and corned beef and cabbage are wonderful; and marvelous is the only word for her bitter lemon tart. Be sure to try the pasta dishes with California sauces or Provençal herbs. This is a warm and friendly place, just like its owner. *2424 Main St., Santa Monica, tel. 213/392–3901. Reservations advised. Dress: casual. AE, MC, V. Moderate.*

Gladstone's 4 Fish. Undoubtedly the most popular restaurant along the entire California coast, serving well over a million beachgoers a year. Perhaps not the greatest food in the world, but familiar seashore fare is prepared adequately, in large portions, and the prices are certainly right. Best bets: crab chowder, steamed clams, three-egg omelettes, hamburgers, barbecued ribs, and chili. And then there's the wonderful view, especially from the beach-side terrace—ideal for whale-, porpoise-, and people-watching. *17300 Pacific Coast Hwy, Pacific Palisades (corner of Sunset Blvd.), tel. 213/GL4–FISH. Valet parking. Reservations advised. Dress: casual. AE, DC, MC, V. Inexpensive–Moderate.*

Daily Grill. The Grill (*see* above) formula proved so popular that management decided to try a less pricey version in an area where rents are not as high as in Beverly Hills. The response has been spectacular, which means that at peak hours you'll probably have to wait for a table. But the chicken pot pie, alone, is worth the first come, first served ground rules. A Daily Grill sibling just opened on La Cienega Boulevard. *11677 San Vicente Blvd., tel. 213/442–0044. Validated parking. Dress: casual. AE, MC, V. Inexpensive.*

Cajun
Westside

Orleans. Jambalaya and gumbo dishes are hot—in more ways than one—at this spacious eatery where the cuisine was created with the help of New Orleans chef Paul Prudhomme. The blackened redfish is probably the best catch on the menu. *11705 National Blvd., West Los Angeles, tel. 213/479–4187. Reservations advised. Dress: informal. AE, DC, MC, V. Moderate.*

California
Beverly Hills
★

The Dining Room. In the totally remodeled Regent Beverly Wilshire, this elegant, European looking salon is the best thing that has happened to L.A. hotel dining in decades. Wonderful California cuisine, plus splendid service at surprisingly non-posh prices are featured. Adjoining is an equally attractive, sophisticated cocktail lounge, with romantic lighting and a show-tune pianist. *9500 Wilshire Blvd., tel. 213/275–5200. Valet parking. Reservations advised. Jacket and tie required. AE, DC, MC, V. Moderate–Expensive.*

California Pizza Kitchen. This is the place if you hanker for a good pizza at a fair price, but don't feel like the usual pizza-parlor surroundings. There's an immaculate, pleasingly modern dining room, plus counter service by the open kitchen and a wide, slightly esoteric choice of pizza toppings. The pasta offerings are equally interesting and carefully prepared. The few sidewalk tables are in great demand. *207 S. Beverly Dr., tel. 213/272–7878. Reservations advised. Dress: informal. No reservations. AE, MC, V. Inexpensive–Moderate.*

Century City

The Bistro Garden. A flower-banked outdoor dining terrace makes this the quintessential Southern California luncheon experience. It's chic and lively without being pretentious or "Hollywood." There's excellent smoked salmon, fresh cracked crab, steak tartare, calves' liver with bacon, and a very special apple pancake. *176 N. Canon Dr., 213/550–3900. Valet parking. Reservations required. Jacket required. AE, DC, MC, V. Closed Sun. Moderate–Expensive.*

West Hollywood
★ **Citrus.** Tired of being known only as one of this country's greatest pastry chefs, Michel Richard opened this contemporary restaurant to display the breadth of his talents. Some of the dishes are superb, in his blending of French and American cuisines. You can't miss with the delectable tuna burger, the thinnest angel hair, the deep-fried potatoes, the sautéed *foie gras*, the rare duck, and the sweetbread salads. Best get your doctor's permission before even looking at Richard's irresistible desserts. *6703 Melrose Ave., tel. 213/857–0034. Valet parking. Reservations required. Jacket required. AE, MC, V. Closed Sun. Moderate–Expensive.*

★ **Spago.** This is the restaurant that propelled owner/chef Wolfgang Puck into the national and international culinary spotlight. And he deserves every one of the accolades for raising California cuisine to an imaginative and joyous gastronomic level, using only the finest of West Coast produce. The proof is in the tasting: grilled baby Sonoma lamb, pizza with Santa Barbara shrimp, thumbnail-size Washington oysters topped with golden caviar, grilled free-range chickens, and from the North Pacific, baby salmon. As for Puck's incredible desserts, he's on Weight Watchers' Most Wanted List. This is the place to see *People* Magazine live, but you'll have to put up with the noise in exchange. Be safe, make reservations at least a week in advance. *1114 Horn Ave., tel. 213/652–4025. Valet parking. Reservations required. Dress: from black leather to Polo. Dinner only. AE, DC, MC, V. Moderate–Expensive.*

Trumps. At this smartly designed contemporary adobe building, with striking abstract art on the pure white walls, the best artist in the house is chef/co-owner Michael Roberts, a very imaginative young American who takes special pleasure in combining offbeat flavors that result in a delectable whole: Brie and apple bisque, salmon tartare with tomatillo, corn pancakes with mussels, duck breast and pickled pumpkin and gingersnap cheesecake. This is the perfect cure for jaded appetites, and a very popular rendezvous for L.A.'s tastemakers. It serves the best afternoon tea in town. *8764 Melrose Ave., tel. 213/855–1480. Reservations advised. Jacket required. AE, DC, MC, V. Closed weekend lunch. Moderate–Expensive.*

Westside
★ **The Bel Air Hotel.** Even if the food was terrible, one would not mind, since the romantic country garden setting is so totally satisfying. But the California-Continental cooking is first-rate, be it breakfast, lunch, or dinner. All in all, it's a not-to-be-missed experience. *701 Stone Canyon Rd., Bel Air, tel. 213/472–1211. Valet parking. Reservations advised. Jacket and tie required. AE, DC, MC, V. Expensive.*

Caribbean
Hollywood **Cha Cha Cha.** When the Cajun food craze cooled off among L.A. foodies, Caribbean cooking became the trend, and this small, all-white shack of a place became the hottest spot in town. Even with reservations, expect a wait. There's good cornmeal chicken, spicy swordfish, fried banana chips, and assorted flans. This is a hangout for celebrities gone slumming. *656 N. Virgil Ave., tel. 213/664–7723. Valet parking. Reservations required, but expect to wait. Dress: casual. AE, DC, MC, V. Moderate.*

Chinese
Beverly Hills
★

The Mandarin. Who said you find great Chinese food only in hole-in-the-wall places, with oilcloth on the tables? Here is a good-looking restaurant with the best crystal and linens, serving an equally splendid mixture of Szechuan and Chinese country cooking. Minced squab in lettuce-leaf tacos, Peking duck, a superb beggars chicken, scallion pancakes, and any of the noodle dishes are recommended. *430 N. Camden Dr., tel. 213/272-0267. Valet parking. Reservations required. Jacket required. AE, DC, MC, V. Closed weekend lunch. Moderate.*

Downtown

Mon Kee's Live Fish and Seafood Restaurant. The name says it all—except how good the cooking is or how morning-fresh the fish. The delicious garlic crab is addictive, the steamed catfish a masterpiece of gentle flavors. In fact, almost everything on the menu is excellent. This is a crowded, messy type of place, and be prepared to wait for a table. *679 N. Spring St., tel. 213/628-6717. Pay parking lot. No reservations. Dress: for scrounging. MC, V. Inexpensive–Moderate.*

Mid-Wilshire

Mandarin Wilshire. Roger Lee, former chef at the Beverly Hills Mandarin (*See* above), and his wife recently opened this unpretentious, cheerful little cafe, in a mini-shopping center. The menu lists nearly 150 different dishes, a repertoire that only a master such as Lee could handle in such a modest setting. There are large portions at friendly prices, with a helpful staff. *8300 Wilshire Blvd., tel. 213/658-6928. Free parking in front. Reservations required. Dress: casual. AE, DC, MC, V. Closed Sun. lunch. Inexpensive.*

West Hollywood

Chopstix. Never underestimate the ability of Californians to adopt, and adapt to, an ethnic food vogue. In this case it is dim sum, subtly doctored for non-Oriental tastes. The result is Chinese junk food served in a mod setting, at high-stool tables or at a diner-like counter. The dishes are appetizing, but don't expect a native Chinese to agree. *729 Melrose Ave., tel. 935-2944. No reservations. Take out. Dress: casual. AE, DC, MC, V. Inexpensive.*

Continental
Beverly Hills

The Bistro. The kitchen is not quite as good as Jimmy's, but nobody has ever questioned that this replica of a Parisian boîte is one of the most stylish dining rooms west of Europe. The original owner, director Billy Wilder, was responsible for the interior design: mirrored walls, etched glass partitions, giant bouquets of fresh flowers and soft lighting. The food is more American bistro than French. There is a delicious, juicy chopped veal steak, good veal medallions, Eastern lobster on tagliatelli, and, most likely, the greatest chocolate soufflé you've ever tasted. *246 North Canon Dr., tel. 213/273-5633. Valet parking. Reservations required. Jacket and tie required. AE, DC, MC, V. Closed Sun.; closed Sat. lunch. Moderate–Expensive.*

Century City

Jimmy's. When the Beverly Hills CEOs are not entertaining, they head here or to The Bistro (*See* above). Owner Jimmy Murphy provides the warmth in this decorator-elegant restaurant. The best dishes on the very broad menu include smoked Scottish salmon, prawns with herbs and garlic, saddle of lamb, Châteaubriand and pheasant breast with wild blueberry sauce. There's steak tartare at lunch. *201 Moreno Dr., tel. 213/879-2394. Valet parking. Reservations required. Jacket and tie required. AE, DC, MC, V. Expensive.*

Mid-Wilshire **The Windsor.** This is what L.A.'s upscale restaurants were like 40 years ago: a dark, quiet retreat with red leather booths and banquettes, where captains still prepare dishes table-side. Talk about the old days, the menu even has baked Alaska and crepes Suzette. Stick with the steak and chop entrées, and the Caesar salad. *3198 W. 7th St., tel. 213/382–1261. Valet parking. Reservations required. Jacket and tie required. AE, DC, MC, V. Moderate.*

Westwood **Dynasty Room.** This peaceful, elegant room in the Westwood Marquis Hotel has European flair, and tables set far enough apart for privacy. Besides well-handled Continental fare, there is a *cuisine minceur* menu for calorie counters. There's an especially lavish, excellent Sunday brunch. *930 Hilgard Ave., tel. 213/208–9765. Valet parking. Reservations required. Jacket and tie required. AE, DC, MC, V. Closed lunch. Moderate.*

Deli **Carnegie Deli.** Marvin Davis, the oil millionaire, got tired of
Beverly Hills jetting cheese-cake, pastrami, and lox back from the parent Carnegie in NYC, so he financed a Beverly Hills taste-alike to challenge Nate 'n Al's pre-eminence. His big guns are corned beef and pastrami sandwiches that are 4½ inches high, cheese blintzes under a snowcap of sour cream, and wonderfully creamy cole slaw. *300 N. Beverly Dr., tel. 213/275–3354. No reservations. Dress: casual. AE, DC, MC, V. Inexpensive.*
Nate 'n Al's. This famous gathering place for Hollywood comedians, gag writers, and their agents, serves first-rate matzo ball soup, lox and scrambled eggs, cheese blintzes, potato pancakes, and the best deli sandwiches west of Manhattan. *414 N. Beverly Dr., tel. 213/274–0101. Free parking. No reservations. Dress: casual. CB, DC. Inexpensive.*

West Hollywood **Greenblatt's.** Who ever heard of a deli famous for its extensive wine list? This one also serves wood-smoked ribs, rotisserie chicken, and 20 different salads, along with the usual sandwiches. *8017 Sunset Blvd., tel. 213/656–0606. Parking lot. No reservations. Dress: as you are. MC, V. Open 9AM–2AM. Inexpensive.*

French **Pastel.** The most successful business in the ultra-chic Rodeo
Beverly Hills Collection of high fashion boutiques is proof positive that the natives are hungry for dining bargains. Prix-fixe dinners, including a half bottle of wine, are just $28.50. For starters: duck pâté and a giant basket of crudités. Next, charbroiled prime rib, a perfect roasted chicken, or fresh grilled fish. And there are seven lovely desserts to agonize over. *421 N. Rodeo Dr., tel. 213/274–9775. Parking. Reservations advised. Jacket required. AE, DC, MC, V. Closed Sun. Moderate.*

Downtown **Seventh Street Bistro.** Set in a landmark art deco office build-
★ ing, this ground-floor restaurant is full of light and beautifully designed. It has all the sophistication and panache of a town house in Paris or Manhattan. The *nouvelle* Franco-Californian cuisine is splendid. The menu changes monthly, but not the enthusiasm of the bistro's loyal customers. *811 W. 7th St., tel. 213/627–1242. Valet parking at night. Reservations advised. Jacket and tie required. AE, DC, MC, V. Closed lunch Sat. and Sun. Moderate–Expensive.*

West Hollywood **L'Ermitage.** Despite a rather sedate, French country-house
★ setting, there's nothing mundane about chef Michel Blanchet's three-star classic French-California dishes. Specialties include escargot pancake, smoked salmon ravioli with leeks and caviar,

sea bass in a pastry crust, sweetbread stew, salmon tartare, and fabulous desserts. *730 N. La Cienega Blvd., tel. 213/652–5840. Reservations required. Valet parking. Jacket and tie required. AE, DC, MC, V. Closed lunch and Sun. Very Expensive.*

★ **L'Orangerie.** For sheer elegance and classic good taste, it would be hard to find a lovelier restaurant in the country. And the cuisine, albeit *nouvelle*-light, is as French as the l'orangerie at Versailles. Some of the specialties include coddled eggs served in the shell, topped with caviar, squab with foie gras, pot au feu, rack of lamb for two, and an unbeatable apple tart, served with a jug of double cream. *903 N. La Cienega Blvd., tel. 213/652–9770. Valet parking. Reservations required. Jacket and tie required. AE, DC, MC, V. Closed lunch. Very Expensive.*

La Toque. Amid the hurly-burly of Sunset Strip is this small, unassuming one-story building. Step through the door, and you'll imagine you've entered a French countryside inn. The charming hideaway is the province of Ken Frank, one of the nation's best young American, French-cooking chefs. Each day some new delight graces the menu: ravioli stuffed with foie gras and pheasant, fettuccine with egg and black truffle, venison seared with Armagnac, or grilled duck breast in a Calvados sauce. Be sure to order the roasted-shredded potato pancake with golden caviar and crème fraîche. *8171 Sunset Blvd., tel. 213/656–7515. Valet parking. Reservations required. Jacket required. AE, DC, MC, V. Closed Sun., closed Sat. lunch. Moderate–Expensive.*

Le Chardonnay. The interiors are Art Deco in this unabashed copy of a famous Left Bank bistro, circa 1920. It's a most romantic rendezvous, with comfortable, cozy booths, except for the high noise level. There are no complaints about the cooking, however: warm sweetbread salad, goat cheese ravioli, roast venison, grilled fish, Peking duck with a ginger and honey sauce, and lots of lush desserts. *8284 Melrose Ave., tel. 213/655–8880. Valet parking. Reservations required. Jacket required. AE, MC, V. Closed Sun.; closed Sat. lunch. Moderate.*

Le Dome. For some reason, local food critics have never given this brasserie the attention it deserves. Perhaps they are intimidated by the hordes of show and music biz celebrities that keep the place humming. By and large the food is wonderful, honest, down-to-earth French: cockles in white wine and shallot, veal ragout, marvelous veal sausage with red cabbage, and a genuine, stick-to-the-ribs cassoulet. *8720 Sunset Blvd., tel. 213/659–6919. Valet parking. Reservations required. Dress: any which way but formal. AE, DC, MC, V. Closed Sun. Moderate.*

★ **Chinois on Main.** The second of the Wolfgang Puck pack of restaurants, this one was designed in tongue-in-cheek kitsch by his wife, Barbara Lazaroff. Both the look of the place and Puck's merging of Chinese and French cuisines for contemporary tastes are great good fun. A few of the least resistible dishes on an irresistible menu include Mongolian lamb with eggplant, poached-and-curried oysters, whole catfish garnished with ginger and green onions, and rare duck with a wondrous plum sauce. The best desserts are the three different flavored crèmes brûlées. This is one of L.A.'s most crowded spots—and among the noisiest. Bring earplugs. *2709 Main St., Santa Monica, tel. 213/392–9025. Valet parking, evenings. Reservations required for dinner. Dress: informal. AE, DC, MC, V. No lunch Sat.–Tues. Expensive.*

Westside **Fennel.** Ocean Avenue has often been compared to a sea-bluff boulevard on the French Riviera; this is the closest you can come to the latest true Parisian cooking in California. It is very, very trendy with L.A.'s francophiles. Call in advance to find out which of three French chefs is in residence. *1535 Ocean Ave., tel. 213/394–2079. Valet parking. Reservations required. Jacket required. AE, DC, MC, V. Closed weekend lunch in winter. Expensive.*

Beaurivage. A charming, romantic restaurant designed in the fashion of an auberge on the Côte d'Azur, this is the best of the Malibu dining places with a view of the beach and ocean. The menu compliments the Provençal atmosphere: roast duckling Mirabelle, pasta with shellfish, a lovely mussel soup, filet Mignon with a three-mustard sauce, and in season, wild game specials. *26025 Pacific Coast Hwy, tel. 213/456–5733. Reservations required. Parking lot. Dress: no wetsuits or tank tops. AE, DC, MC, V. Closed lunch Tues.–Thurs. Moderate.*

★ **Champagne.** Patrick Healy, another young American who trained under some of the best chefs in France, has opened this attractive restaurant where cuisine, not people-watching, keeps patrons returning week after week. They have their choice of contemporary or traditional French dishes and spa cuisine selections. Two specialties include a three-layered eggplant and crayfish cake that's a real farmhouse cassoulet. The desserts are light and lovely. *10506 Santa Monica Blvd., tel. 213/470–8446. Valet parking. Reservations required. Jacket required. AE, DC, MC, V. Closed Mon., Dinner only. Moderate.*

Italian **Prego.** This is a super bargain in the highest of high-rent dis-
Beverly Hills tricts. The baby lamb chops, the large broiled veal chop, and the Florentine rib steak are among the best, dollar for dollar, in town. The baked in-house bread sticks are great. *362 N. Camden Dr., tel. 213/277–7347. Valet parking. Reservations advised. Dress: as you are. AE, DC, MC, V. Closed Sun. lunch. Inexpensive–Moderate.*

Primi. Valentino's younger, less expensive brother, with a menu that features a wide variety of appetizer-size portions of Northern Italian treats, including pasta and salad selections. This is a cheerful, contemporary setting, with a pleasant outside terrace. *10543 W. Pico Blvd., tel. 213/475–9235. Valet parking. No reservations. Jacket required. AE, DC, MC, V. Closed Sun. lunch. Inexpensive–Moderate.*

Century City **Harry's Bar & American Grill.** A more private, posh, uptown version of Prego, this restaurant is run by the same management. The decor and selection of dishes are acknowledged copies of Harry's Bar in Florence. But you'll find that for first-rate food—paper-thin carpaccio, excellent pastas, grilled fish and steaks, along with a fine hamburger, the check will be lower than in Italy. This is the best place to dine, before or after seeing a movie in the area. *2020 Ave. of the Stars, tel. 213/277–2333. Valet parking. Reservations advised. Jacket and tie required. AE, DC, MC, V. Closed Sun. lunch. Moderate.*

Downtown **Rex Il Ristorante.** Owner Mauro Vincenti probably knows more
★ about Italian cuisine than any restaurateur in the country. To create the ideal showcase for his talents, two ground floors of a historic art deco building were remodeled to resemble the main dining salon of the circa-1930 Italian luxury liner, *Rex*. The cuisine is equally special, the lightest of *cucina nuovo*. Be prepared for small and costly portions. *617 S. Olive St., tel. 213/*

627–2300. Valet parking. Reservations required. Jacket and tie required. AE, DC, MC, V. Closed Sun.; closed lunch Sat. and Mon. Very Expensive.

Adriano's. A five-minute drive north of Sunset Boulevard, through one of L.A.'s loveliest residential canyons, brings you to this countrified retreat near the top of the Santa Monica Mountains. There's nothing backwoods about the food, though. Specialties include lobster with linguini, a T-bone veal chop, wonderful polenta and risotto, roasted quail, and a delicious cheese soufflé. *2930 Beverly Glen Circle, tel. 213/475–9807. Free parking. Reservations required. Jacket required. AE, DC, MC, V. Closed Mon.; closed weekend lunch. Moderate–Expensive.*

West Hollywood **Locanda Veneta.** This relatively new trattoria is an Italian fa-
★ vorite. The food may be more finely wrought at one or two other spots, but the combination of a splendid Venetian chef, Antonio Tomassi and a *simpatico* co-owner, Jean Louis De Mori, have re-created the atmospheric equivalent of a genuine Italian trattoria, at reasonable prices. Specialties include fried whitebait, rissotto with porcini mushrooms, veal chop, ricotta and potato dumplings, linguini with clams, lobster ravioli with saffron sauce, and a super pear tart. *8638 W. 3rd St., tel. 213/ 274–1893. Valet parking. Reservations required. Dress: Casual. AE, DC, MC, V. Closed Sun.; closed Sat. lunch. Moderate.*

Tuttobene. If Silvio de Mori, Jean Louis's older brother, served nothing more than peanut butter sandwiches, his place would be doing SRO business. But this best-loved restaurateur, a genuinely gracious, caring host, happens to provide some of the most delectable trattoria dishes west of Tuscany. There are different, freshly baked breads every day, superb down-to-earth pastas and gnocci, luscious rissotto with wild mushrooms, picked-that-morning arugula salad—all at very fair prices. *945 N. Fairfax Ave., tel. 213/655–7051. Valet parking. Reservations required. Dress: casual. AE, MC, V. Moderate.*

Westside **Valentino.** Rated among the best Italian restaurants in the na-
★ tion, it's generally considered to have the best wine list outside Italy. Owner Piero Selvaggio is the man who introduced Los Angeles to the best and lightest of modern-day Italian cuisine, and the natives have loved him ever since. There's superb prosciutto, bresaola, fried calamari, lobster cannelloni, fresh broiled porcini mushrooms, and osso buco. *3115 Pico Blvd., Santa Monica, tel. 213/829–4313. Valet parking. Reservations required. Jacket required. AE, DC, MC, V. Closed Sun.; lunch, Fri. only. Expensive.*

La Scala Malibu. Malibu's most celebrity-crowded hangout has moved to brand new, cheerful quarters; in the process, the Northern Italian food has greatly improved, and the prices have come down a notch. You can't quite see the ocean, but, "There's Cher over there talking to Olivia Newton-John and Jack Lemmon, next to the table with Larry Hagman and Walter Matthau." *3874 Cross Creek Rd., tel. 213/456–1979. Reservations advised. Dress: casual. No lunch weekends. AE, MC, V. Moderate.*

Japanese **Horikawa.** A department store of Japanese cuisines including
Downtown sushi, teppan steak tables, tempura, sashimi, shabu-shabu, teriyaki, and a $50 per person *kaiseki* dinner. All are very good to excellent, but the sushi bar is the best. The decor is traditional Japanese, with private sit-on-the-floor dining rooms for

two to 24. *111 S. San Pedro St., tel. 213/680–9355. Valet parking. Reservations advised. Jacket and tie required. AE, DC, MC, V. Lunch Mon.–Fri. only. Moderate–Expensive.*

Los Feliz **Katsu.** This stark, simple, perfectly designed sushi bar with a
★ small table area serves the most exquisite and delicious Japanese delicacies in all of Southern California. This is a very special treat, for both eye and palate. *1972 N. Hillhurst Ave., tel. 213/665–1891. Valet parking. No lunch reservations; dinner reservations advised. Dress: informal. Beer, wine, and saki. AE, MC, V. Closed Sat. lunch. Moderate.*

Mexican **El Cholo.** This progenitor of the present-day, upscale South-
Hollywood land chain has been packing them in since the '20s. It serves good, bathtub-size margaritas, a zesty assortment of tacos, make-your-own tortillas, and, from June to September, green corn tamales. It's friendly and fun, with large portions at peso prices. *1121 S. Western Ave., tel. 213/734–2773. Parking lot. Reservations advised. Dress: casual. AE, MC, V. Inexpensive.*

West Hollywood **Border Grill.** Very trendy, very loud, this storefront place is owned by two female chefs with the most eclectic tastes in town. The menu ranges from crab tacos to vinegared and peppered grilled turkey to pickled pork sirloin. It's worth dropping by, if you don't mind not hearing anything that's said. *7407½ Melrose Ave., tel. 213/658–7495. Reservations advised. Dress: casual. AE, MC, V. Moderate.*

Antonio's Restaurant. Don't let the strolling mariachis keep you from listening to the daily specials, the true Mexico City dishes that put this unpretentious favorite several cuts above the ubiquitous taco-enchilada cantinas. The chayote (squash) stuffed with ground beef, ricotta, and a spicy tomato sauce; pork ribs in a sauce of pickled chipotle peppers; veal shank with garlic, cumin, and red pepper; and chicken stuffed with apples, bananas, and raisins are all definitely worth trying. Have the flan for dessert. *7472 Melrose Ave., tel. 213/655–0480. Valet parking. Dinner reservations advised. Dress: casual. AE, MC, V. Inexpensive–Moderate.*

Polynesian **Trader Vic's.** Sure it's corny, but this is the most restrained and
Beverly Hills elegant of the late Victor Bergeron's South Sea extravaganzas. Besides, who says "corn" can't be fun, and tasty, too. The crab Rangoon, grilled cheese wafers, skewered shrimp, grilled pork ribs, and the steaks, chops, and peanut butter-coated lamb cooked in huge clay ovens, are just fine. As for the array of exotic rum drinks, watch your sips. *9876 Wilshire Blvd., tel. 213/274–7777. Valet parking. Jacket and tie required. AE, DC, MC, V. Closed lunch. Moderate–Expensive.*

Thai **Chan Dara.** Here is excellent Thai food in a bright and shiny
Hollywood Swiss chalet, of all places. Try any of the noodle dishes, especially the ones with crab and shrimp. The place is noisy, but bearable. *310 N. Larchmont Blvd., tel. 213/467–1052. Reservations advised for parties of more than 4. Dress: for fun. AE, MC, V. Inexpensive.*

West Hollywood **Tommy Tang's.** A very "in" grazing ground for yuppies and celebs alike. So much people-watching goes on, nobody seems to notice the small portions on their plates. The kitchen features crisp duck marinated in ginger and plum sauce, blackened sea scallops, and a spinach salad tossed with marinated beef. There is also a sushi bar. *7473 Melrose Ave., tel. 213/651–1810. Valet* *parking. Reservations advised. Dress: informal. AE, DC, MC, V. Closed Sunday lunch. Moderate.*

Lodging

You can find almost any kind of accommodation in Los Angeles, from a simple motel room that allows you to park right in front of your room, to a posh hotel like the Beverly Hills, where an attendant will park your car and whisk you off to a spacious room or to your own bungalow.

Because L.A. is so spread out—it's actually a series of suburbs connected by freeways—it's a good idea to select a hotel room not only for its ambience, amenities, and price, but also for a location that is convenient to where you plan to spend most of your time. West Hollywood and Beverly Hills are trendy and central, while Hollywood itself has lost much of its legendary glamour. Westwood and Santa Monica are attractive but less accessible locations, and the more recently developed Century City offers new hotels and a large shopping mall.

It's best to plan ahead and reserve a room; many hotels offer special prices for weekend visits or may offer tickets to amusement parks or plays. A travel agent can help in making your arrangements.

Hotels are listed in categories, determined first by location: Downtown, Mid-Wilshire, Hollywood/West Hollywood, Beverly Hills/Bel Air, West Los Angeles, Santa Monica, Marina del Rey, and South Beach Cities. They are further divided, under location, into categories determined (roughly) by the price of a room for two people, on the European plan.

Highly recommended lodgings in each price category are indicated by a star ★ .

Category	Cost*
Very Expensive	over $155
Expensive	$110–$155
Moderate	$70–$110
Inexpensive	under $70

for a double room; not including tax

Downtown
Very Expensive

The Biltmore Hotel. Since its 1923 opening, the Biltmore has hosted such notables as Mary Pickford, J. Paul Getty, Eleanor Roosevelt, Princess Margaret, and several U.S. presidents. Now a historic landmark, it was renovated in 1986 for $35 million, with modern, updated guest rooms decorated in pastels. The lobby ceiling was painted by Italian artist Giovanni Smeraldi; imported Italian marble and plum-colored velvet grace the Grand Avenue Bar, which features excellent jazz nightly. Bernard's is an acclaimed Continental restaurant. The private, swank health club has a Roman bath motif. Banquet and meeting rooms serve up to 1,200; the special club floor boasts a library, wide-screen TV, and pocket billiards room. *506 S. Grand Ave., 90013, tel. 213/624–1011 or 800/245–8673. 704 rooms. Facilities: restaurant, lounge, entertainment, health club (fee). AE, DC, MC, V.*

Checkers Hotel. With its excellent pedigree and smaller scale, this is a brand-new sophisticated addition to the downtown hotel scene. Set in one of downtown's few remaining historic buildings—opened as the Mayflower Hotel in 1927—Checkers boasts the same management as the acclaimed Campton Place in San Francisco (one of the nation's top hotels). Rooms are furnished with oversize beds, upholstered easy chairs, writing tables, and minibars. A library is available for small meetings or tea. *535 S. Grand Ave., 90071, tel. 213/624–0000 or 800/628–4900. 190 rooms. Facilities: restaurant, rooftop spa and lap pool, exercise studio.*

Hyatt Regency Los Angeles. The Hyatt is located in the heart of the "new" downtown financial district, minutes away from the Convention Center, Dodger Stadium, and the Music Center. Each room has city views. The hotel is part of the Broadway Plaza, comprising 35 shops. Nearby tennis and health club facilities are available at an extra cost. *711 S. Hope St., 90017, tel. 213/683–1234 or 800/233–1234. 500 rooms. Facilities: restaurant, coffee shop, lounge, entertainment. AE, DC, MC, V.*

★ **Sheraton Grande Hotel.** Opened in 1983, this 14-story, 550-room mirrored hotel is near Dodger Stadium, the Music Center, and downtown's Bunker Hill District. Rooms have dark wood furniture, sofas, minibars; colors are aqua or copper; baths are marble. Butler service on each floor. Limousine service is available, and there are privileges at a local health club. *333 S. Figueroa St., 90071, tel. 213/617–1133 or 800/325–3535. 469 rooms. Facilities: 2 restaurants, nightclub, outdoor pool, 23 meeting rooms, 4 movie theaters. AE, DC, MC, V.*

The Westin Bonaventure. This is John Portman's striking masterpiece: a 35-story, circular-towered, mirrored-glass high rise in the center of downtown. Rooms have a wall of glass, clean lines, pale furnishings, and comfortable appointments. The outside elevators provide stunning views of the city; there are also 5 acres of ponds and waterfalls in the lobby, several restaurants, including Beaudry's Gourmet, and the Bona Vista revolving lounge at the top of the hotel. The grand ballroom seats 3,000. A popular Sunday brunch is served in the atrium lobby. Parking is expensive. *5th and Figueroa sts., 90071, tel. 213/624–1000 or 800/228–3000. 1,474 rooms. Facilities: restaurant, lounge, entertainment, pool, 5-level shopping arcade. AE, DC, MC, V.*

Expensive **The New Otani and Garden.** East meets West in L.A., and the
★ exotic epicenter downtown is at this 21-story ultramodern hotel surrounded by Japanese gardens and waterfalls. The decor combines a serene blend of Westernized luxury and Japanese simplicity. Each room has a refrigerator, alarm clock, color TV, phone in the bathroom; most provide a kimono. Concrete walls provide great noise control. A Thousand Cranes offers classic Japanese cuisine; Commodore Perry's, steak and lobster; and the Genji Bar features noted jazz artists. There is a large conference center. *120 S. Figueroa St., 90012, tel. 213/629–1200 or 800/421–8795 nationwide or 800/252–0197 in CA. 448 rooms. Facilities: restaurants, nightclub, sauna and massage (fee), parking (fee). AE, DC, MC, V.*

University Hilton Los Angeles. If you're doing business at USC, the Coliseum, or the Sports Arena, this is the best hotel in the area. All rooms have a view of the pool area, the lush gardens, or the nearby USC campus. It's well-equipped to handle banquets and conventions. *3530 S. Figueroa St., 90007, tel. 213/748–*

4141, 800/872-1104 outside CA, 800/445-8667 in CA. 241 rooms. Facilities: restaurant, coffee shop, lounge, pool, parking (fee). AE, DC, MC, V.

Moderate   **Figueroa Hotel.** This hotel has managed to keep its charming Spanish style intact as it enters its second half-century. There's a poolside bar. The hotel is on the Gray Line sightseeing tour route, and there is airport service every hour to LAX. *939 S. Figueroa St., 90015, tel. 213/627-8971; 800/421-9092 outside CA, 800/331-5151 in CA. 280 rooms. Facilities: restaurant, coffee shop, lounge, pool, free parking. AE, DC, MC, V.*

Holiday Inn L.A. Downtown. This offers Holiday Inn's usual professional staff, services, and standard room decor. It's close to the Museum of Contemporary Art and Dodger Stadium. Pets are allowed and there is plenty of free parking. *750 Garland Ave., 90017, tel. 213/628-5242 or 800/465-4329. 204 rooms. Facilities: restaurant, lounge, pool, parking. AE, DC, MC, V.*

Inexpensive   **Comfort Inn.** With its central location between downtown and Hollywood, near the Wilshire commercial district, it's very convenient for business types. The modern-style rooms offer color TVs and VCRs. *3400 W. 3rd St., 92020, tel. 213/385-0061. 130 rooms. Facilities: 24-hr. coffee shop, pool. AE, DC, MC, V.*

Orchid Hotel. One of the smaller downtown hotels, this is very reasonably priced. There are no frills, but the standard rooms are clean. There is no parking at the hotel, but public lots are close by. *819 S. Flower St., 90017, tel. 213/624-5855. 66 rooms. Facilities: color TV, coin-operated laundry. AE, DC, MC, V.*

Mid-Wilshire   **Hyatt Wilshire.** One of Wilshire Boulevard's largest hotels, this
Expensive–   12-story building's interior was renovated in 1987. There's a
Very Expensive   grand piano and concert pianist in the lobby. The Hyatt's corporate clients often use the large banquet and meeting rooms (for up to 400 people). Extras include the Hyatt Regency Club, a full-security floor, and an excellent Sunday champagne brunch. *3515 Wilshire Blvd., 90010, tel. 213/381-7411 or 800/233-1234. 397 rooms. Facilities: restaurant, cafeteria, lounge, disco, room service, laundry service, parking (fee). AE, DC, MC, V.*

Sheraton Towne House. Howard Hughes slept (and lived) here. A great example of L.A.'s best Art Deco architecture, this hotel—built in the 1920s—retains its original charm and elegance. Marble fireplaces and cedar-lined closets enhance the country-estate tone. It's convenient to Bullocks Wilshire shopping. *2961 Wilshire Blvd., 90010, tel. 213/382-7171 or 800/325-3535. 300 rooms. Facilities: restaurant, coffee shop, pool, tennis, parking (fee). AE, DC, MC, V.*

Hollywood/West   **Le Bel Age Hotel.** This is a wonderful location for an all-suite,
Hollywood   European-style hotel with a distinctive restaurant featuring
Very Expensive   fine Russian meals with an elegant French flair. There are
★   many extravagant touches, like three telephones with five lines in each suite, original art, private terraces with city views, and courtesy limousine service. *1020 N. San Vicente Blvd., West Hollywood 90069, tel. 213/854-1111 or 800/424-4443. 190 suites. Facilities: 2 restaurants, lounge, pool. AE, CB, DC, MC, V.*

Le Mondrian Hotel. This giant structure is a monument to the Dutch artist from whom the hotel takes its name. The outside of the 12-story hotel is actually a giant surrealistic mural; inside there's fine artwork. Accommodations are spacious, with pale wood furniture and curved sofas in the seating area. Private, chauffeured limo is at each guest's disposal. There's nouvelle cuisine at Cafe Piet. Convenient to major recording, film, and TV studios. *8440 Sunset Blvd., West Hollywood 90069, tel. 213/650–8999 or 800/424–4443. 243 suites. Facilities: restaurant, pool, health club, parking. AE, DC, MC, V.*

★ **The Saint James's Club/Los Angeles.** Also on the Sunset Strip, this is the latest in the prestigious chain of St. James's Clubs, and the first in the United States. The building has been around since the 1930s; today all the furnishings are exact replicas of Art Deco masterpieces, the originals of which are in New York's Metropolitan Museum of Art. A 30s-style supper club serves California cuisine along with piano entertainment. Club Bar and Lounge. *8358 Sunset Blvd., West Hollywood 90069, tel. 213/654–7100 or 800/225–2637. 63 rooms. Facilities: restaurant, health center, sauna, pool, secretarial services, small meeting facilities. AE, DC, MC, V.*

Expensive **Château Marmont Hotel.** Although planted on Sunset Strip amid giant billboards and much Hollywood glitz, this castle of Old World charm and French Normandy design still promises its guests a secluded hideaway close to Hollywood's hot spots. A haunt for many show-biz personalities (John Belushi spent his last night here) and discriminating world travelers since it opened in 1927, this is the ultimate in privacy. All kinds of accommodations are available, including fully equipped cottages, bungalows, and a penthouse. *8221 Sunset Blvd., West Hollywood 90046, tel. 213/656–1010 or 800/CHATEAU. 62 rooms. Facilities: dining room, gardens, pool, patios. AE, MC, V.*

Hollywood Roosevelt. This hotel across from Mann's Chinese Theater was once considered the state-of-the-art in Hollywood glamour and luxury before it gradually fell into disrepair. But in true Hollywood fashion, this site of the first Academy Awards ceremony made a comeback in 1985, thoroughly restored right down to the ornate lobby and elegant courtyard. The Olympic-size pool was decorated by artist David Hockney and the Tropicana Bar sits in the courtyard. *7000 Hollywood Blvd., Hollywood 90028, tel. 213/466–7000 or 800/950–7667. 320 rooms. Facilities: restaurant, lounge, 90 poolside cabanas, rental cars, airport transportation. AE, DC, MC, V.*

Hyatt on Sunset. In the heart of the Sunset Strip, this Hyatt is a favorite of music-biz execs and rock stars. There are penthouse suites, some rooms with private patios, and a rooftop pool. The rooms are decorated in peach colors and modern furniture. *8401 W. Sunset Blvd., 90069, tel. 213/656–4101 or 800/233–1234. 262 rooms. Facilities: restaurant, lounge, entertainment, pool, parking (fee). AE, DC, MC, V.*

Moderate **Hollywood Holiday Inn.** You can't miss this hotel, one of the tallest buildings in Hollywood. It's 23 stories, topped by Windows, a revolving restaurant-lounge. The rooms are decorated in light gray and rose. There is a safekeeping box in each room. The hotel is only minutes from the Hollywood Bowl, Universal Studios, and Mann's Chinese Theater, and it's a Gray Line Tour stop. *1755 N. Highland Ave., Hollywood 90028, tel. 213/462–7181 or 800/465–4329. 468 rooms. Facilities: restaurant, coffee shop, pool, coin laundry, parking. AE, CB, DC, MC, V.*

Inexpensive **Sunset Dunes Motel.** Across the street from two TV stations, this hotel with Spanish-style rooms is a popular stop for studio folk. Its Dunes restaurant is open until 10 PM; nearby is the family-oriented Spaghetti Factory. *5625 Sunset Blvd., Holly-*

wood 90028, tel. 213/467–5171. 56 rooms. Facilities: restaurant, lounge, free parking. AE, DC, MC, V.

Beverly Hills
Very Expensive
★

Beverly Hills Hotel. This is a California landmark: Beautiful grounds in a quiet location with tropical plants cover 12 acres. The lovely rooms are all different, decorated with traditional furniture and over-stuffed chairs and sofas. Movie stars often take the bungalows and congregate in the famous Polo Lounge. Breakfast and lunch are served in the Coterie Restaurant overlooking the heated pool. *9641 Sunset Blvd., Beverly Hills, 90210, tel. 213/276–2251 or 800/283–8885. 331 units. Facilities: 2 restaurants, pool, wading pool, exercise room, parking. AE, DC, MC, V.*

The Beverly Hilton. This large hotel complex has a wide selection of restaurants and shops. Most rooms have balconies. Trader Vic's and L'Escoffier are two of the city's better restaurants. There is a theater ticket desk, limo service, and free coffee lobby for hotel guests. *9876 Wilshire Blvd., Beverly Hills 90210, tel. 213/274–7777 or 800/445–8667. 592 rooms. Facilities: restaurants, pool, wading pool, exercise room, refrigerators, parking. AE, DC, MC, V.*

★ **L'Ermitage Hotel.** Old World charm with modern conveniences is a rewarding combination. Opened in 1976, it's won both the Mobil Five Star Award and the AAA Five Diamond Award; one of the only hotels on the West Coast to garner both, it's near Beverly Hills, elegant shopping, and 20th Century Fox. The suites have balconies and sunken living rooms with fireplaces. The fine Cafe Russe is reserved exclusively for hotel guests. Complimentary Continental breakfast; chauffeured limo within Beverly Hills. *9291 Burton Way, 90201, tel. 213/278–3344 or 800/424–4443. 114 rooms. Facilities: restaurant, pool, whirlpool, spa, private solarium, parking. AE, DC, MC, V.*

★ **Four Seasons Los Angeles.** This new hotel combines the best in East and West Coast luxury. Formal European decorative details are complemented by outpourings of flora from the porte cochère to the rooftop pool deck. There is an outstanding restaurant and a great shopping location within five minutes of Rodeo Drive and trendy Melrose Avenue. *300 S. Doheny Dr., 90048, tel. 213/273–2222 or 800/332–3442. 285 rooms. Facilities: restaurant, 1-hr. pressing service, pool, exercise equipment. AE, DC, MC, V.*

Ma Maison Sofitel Hotel. This two-year-old hotel offers first-class service and an intimacy usually reserved for small European-style hotels. The country French guest rooms are done in terra-cotta and blues, with small prints. The hotel is next to some of L.A.'s best shopping, restaurants, and boutiques. Unfortunately it also faces a large brick wall; insist on a northern view. *855 Beverly Blvd., 90048, on the fringe of Beverly Hills, tel. 213/278–5444 or 800/221–4542. 311 rooms. Facilities: 2 restaurants, 24-hour room service, pool, sauna, fitness center, parking. AE, DC, MC, V.*

Regent Beverly Wilshire. This famous hotel facing Rodeo Drive and the Hollywood Hills re-opened in 1989 after a major renovation, and is under new management. It remains stylish, with personal service and extras to match. There are great restaurants, limo service to the airport, and a multilingual staff. *9500 Wilshire Blvd., Beverly Hills 90212, tel. 213/275–4282 or 800/ 421–4354. 453 rooms. Facilities: restaurants, pool, health spas, parking (fee). AE, DC, MC, V.*

Expensive **Beverly Hills Comstock.** All accommodations at this hotel are smartly furnished suites featuring kitchen/living rooms, one bedroom, and bath. *10300 Wilshire Blvd., 90024, tel. 213/275–5575 or 800/343–2184. 150 rooms. Facilities: restaurant, pool, whirlpool, parking. AE, DC, MC, V.*

Moderate **Beverly House Hotel.** Small but elegantly furnished European-
★ style bed-and-breakfast hotel, it's near Century City and Beverly Hills shopping. *140 S. Lasky Dr., 90212, tel. 213/271–2145 or 800/432–5444. 50 rooms. Facilities: laundry, free parking. AE, DC, MC, V.*

West Los Angeles **Century Plaza Hotel.** This 20-story hotel (on 14 acres of tropical
Very Expensive plants and reflecting pools) features a new 30-story tower, lav-
★ ishly decorated with signature art and antiques; it's furnished like a mansion, with a mix of classic and contemporary. Each room has a refrigerator and balcony with ocean or city view. Complimentary "towncar service" is provided to Beverly Hills. There are four excellent restaurants: award-winning La Chaumiere for California/French cuisine, The Terrace for American/Continental, the Garden Pavilion for spa cuisine, and the Cafe Plaza, a French-style cafe. *2025 Ave. of the Stars, Century City 90067, tel. 213/277–2000 or 800/228–3000. 1,072 rooms. Facilities: 2 pools, whirlpools, parking. AE, CB, DC, MC, V.*

★ **J W Marriott Hotel at Century City.** This hotel, opened in 1988, is the West Coast flagship for the multi-faceted Marriott chain. Its elegant modern rooms are decorated in soft pastels and equipped with minibars, lavish marble baths, and facilities for the handicapped. The hotel offers complimentary limo service to Beverly Hills and boasts the 2,000-square-foot Presidential Suite and excellent service. *2151 Ave. of the Stars, Century City 90067, tel. 213/201–0440 or 800/228–9290. 375 rooms. Facilities: restaurant, indoor and outdoor pools, whirlpools, fitness center. AE, DC, MC, V.*

Moderate **Century City Inn.** This hotel is small but well-designed for comfort. Rooms have refrigerators, microwave oven, remote control TV and VCR, as well as a 10-cup coffee unit with fresh gourmet-blended coffee and tea. Baths have whirlpool tubs and a phone. Complimentary breakfast. *10330 W. Olympic Blvd., tel. 213/553–1000 or 800/553–1005. 46 rooms. Facilities: rental cars, parking. AE, DC, MC, V.*

Coastal Los **Bel Air Hotel.** A charming, secluded hotel (and celebrity mecca)
Angeles with lovely gardens and a creek complete with swans. The
Very Expensive rooms and suites are individually decorated in peaches and earth tones. *701 Stone Canyon Rd., Bel Air 90077, tel. 213/472–1211 or 800/648–4097 outside CA. 60 rooms, 32 suites. Facilities: pool, restaurant, lounge, parking. AE, DC, MC, V.*

Santa Monica **Loews Santa Monica Beach Hotel.** Set on the most precious of
Very Expensive L.A. real estate—beachfront—the Loews opened mid-1989 just south of the Santa Monica Pier. Most of the contemporary rooms have ocean views and private balconies; all guests have private access to the beach. Its restaurant, Riva, serves Northern Italian cuisine with an emphasis on seafood. *1700 Ocean Ave., 90401, tel. 213/458–6700 or 800/223–0888. 315 rooms, 35 suites. Facilities: restaurant, cafe, fitness center, indoor/outdoor pool, valet parking. AE, CB, DC, MC, V.*

Miramar Sheraton. This hotel, "where Wilshire meets the sea," is close to all area beaches, across the street from Pacific Palisades Park, and near deluxe shopping areas and many quaint eateries. The landscaping incorporates the area's second-largest rubber tree. Many rooms have balconies overlooking the ocean. The decor in some rooms is very contemporary, with bleached wood, marble, granite, glass, and bricks. A new wing has traditional furnishings. *101 Wilshire Blvd., 90403, tel. 213/394-3731 or 800/325-3535. 305 rooms. Facilities: 3 restaurants, lounge, entertainment, pool. AE, DC, MC, V.*

Expensive **Pacific Shore.** Formerly the Royal Inn of Santa Monica, this modern building is a 1/2-block from the beach and many restaurants. The attractive rooms are decorated with contemporary fabrics and modern furniture; some have ocean views. *1819 Ocean Ave., 90401, tel. 213/451-8711 or 800/622-8711. 169 rooms. Facilities: restaurant, lounge, pool, sauna, therapy pool, Jacuzzi, laundry facilities, Avis Rent-a-Car, gift shop, free parking. AE, CB, DC, MC, V.*

Inexpensive **Carmel Hotel.** This charming hotel from the 1920s is one block from the beach and the new Santa Monica Shopping Plaza, as well as from movie theaters and many fine restaurants. There's a Mexican-American restaurant on premises. *201 Broadway, 90401, tel. 213/451-2469. 110 rooms. Facilities: restaurant, parking, AE, DC, MC, V.*

Palm Motel. This quiet, unceremonious motel has old fashioned rooms. The decorative highlight is the color TVs, but they do offer complimentary coffee, tea, and cookies at breakfast. It's only a short drive away from several good restaurants. *2020 14th St., 90405, tel. 213/452-3822. 26 rooms. Facilities: self-service laundry, free parking. MC, V.*

Westwood Marquis. This hotel near UCLA is a favorite of corporate and entertainment types. Each individualized suite in its 15 stories has a view of Bel Air, the Pacific Ocean, and downtown L.A. Breakfast and lunch are served in the Garden Terrace, also famous for its Sunday brunch. The award-winning Dynasty Room features Continental cuisine plus special Minceur spa diet menu. European teas are served in the afternoon in the Westwood Lounge. *930 Hilgard Ave., 90024, tel. 213/208-8765 or 800/692-2140. 256 suites. Facilities: 2 pools, sauna, phones in bathrooms, banquet and meeting rooms, parking fee. AE, CB, DC, MC, V.*

Expensive **The Chesterfield Hotel Deluxe.** This new, more-than-comfortable hotel near the Century City business complex mixes California architecture with English fabrics and furnishings, epitomized in the red welcome carpet and the London phone booth at the entrance. *10320 W. Olympic Blvd., 90067, tel. 213/556-2777 or 800/243-7871. 126 rooms. Facilities: Exercise salon, sun deck, garden whirlpool, restaurant, London taxi courtesy service to surrounding areas. AE, DC, MC, V.*

Inexpensive–Moderate **Best Western Royal Palace Hotel.** This small hotel located just off I-405 has all suites, decorated with conservative, homey prints. Morning coffee and tea in room is complimentary, as is parking to hotel guests. Suites have kitchenettes. *2528 S Sepulveda Blvd., 90064, tel. 213/477-9066 or 800/528-1234. 32 rooms. Facilities: pool, Jacuzzi, exercise room, billiard room, laundry facilities. AE, DC, MC, V.*

Marina del Rey **Marina Beach Hotel.** Opened in 1986, this luxurious 9-story
Very Expensive high-rise hotel is high-tech in design, but softened by a pastel
★ decor accented in brass and marble. There are lovely touches like a gazebo on the patio. The restaurant Stones is known for

its fresh seafood. The hotel offers 24-hour free transportation to and from LAX. *4100 Admiralty Way, 90292, tel. 213/301–3000; 800/528–0444 nationwide, or 800/862–7462 in CA. 386 rooms. Facilities: restaurant, lounges, pool, parking (fee). AE, DC, MC, V.*

The Ritz-Carlton, Marina del Rey. Opened in 1990, this sumptuous property sits on some prime real estate at the northern end of a basin, offering a resplendent panoramic view of the Pacific. The extremely attractive rooms have marble baths, honor bars, and plenty of amenities—from maid service twice a day to plush terry robes. *4640 Admiralty Way, Marina del Rey 90292, tel. 213/823–3656. 306 rooms. Facilities: Pool, sun deck, fitness center, tennis courts, boutiques, complimentary transportation to LAX. AE, CB, DC, MC, V.*

Expensive **Marina International Hotel.** Directly across from an inland beach, this hotel is unique for its village-style luxury decor. Each of the very private rooms offers a balcony or patio. The Crystal Fountain restaurant has Continental cuisine. Boat charters are available for up to 200 people. *4200 Admiralty Way, 90292, tel. 213/301–2000; 800/528–0444 nationwide; 800/862–7462, in CA; 110 rooms, 25 bungalows. Facilities: restaurant, lounge, pool, airport transportation, free parking. AE, DC, MC, V.*

South Bay Beach Cities *Expensive– Very Expensive* **Sheraton at Redondo Beach.** Opened in 1987, this swank 5-story hotel overlooks the Pacific, across the street from the Redondo Beach Pier. There are plenty of amenities, including indoor and outdoor dining and a nightclub. The rooms are decorated in a seaside theme of light woods and bright colors. *300 N. Harbor Dr., Redondo Beach 90277, tel. 213/318–8888 or 800/325–3535. 339 rooms. Facilities: restaurant, lounge, entertainment, pool, exercise room, sauna, whirlpool, tennis, parking (fee). AE, DC, MC, V.*

Moderate **Barnaby's Hotel.** Modeled after a 19th-century English inn, ★ with four-poster beds, lace curtains, and antique decorations, Barnaby's also has an enclosed greenhouse pool. Rosie's Bar resembles a cozy pub, with live entertainment; Barnaby's Restaurant features Continental cuisine and curtained private booths. Afternoon tea is a highlight. An adjacent health club charges $10 per day. Weekend packages are available. *3501 Sepulveda Blvd., at Rosecrans, Manhattan Beach 90266, tel. 213/545–8466 or 800/552–5285. 128 rooms. Facilities: restaurant, lounge, pool. AE, DC, MC, V.*

Airport *Expensive* **Hyatt Hotel–LAX.** Earth tones and brass decorate this elegant 12-story building, the hotel closest to LAX, Hollywood Park, the Forum, and Marina del Rey. With business travelers in mind, it offers large meeting rooms with ample banquet space. Bilingual staff; concierge on duty 24 hours a day. *6225 W. Century Blvd., 90045, tel. 213/670–9000 or 800/233–1234. 596 rooms. Facilities: restaurant, coffee shop, lounge, entertainment, pool, sauna, exercise room, parking (fee). AE, DC, MC, V.*

The Los Angeles Airport Marriott. One of the first luxury hotels to be built in the airport area (it opened in 1973) is a fully equipped convention center convenient to the beach, Marina del Rey, Fisherman's Village, the Forum, and the Coliseum. Complimentary airport bus service gets you to LAX in just four minutes. Seven restaurants and lounges offer gourmet elegance, family-style dining, and lavish California-style buffets.

All guest rooms are designed for maximum space and comfort in relaxing earth tones, some with sitting areas and balcony. *5855 W. Century Blvd., 90045, tel. 213/641–5700 or 800/228–9290. 1,012 rooms. Facilities: restaurants, lounge, entertainment, pool, health club, laundry facilities, parking (fee). AE, DC, MC, V.*

★ **Stouffer Concourse Hotel.** A good place if you're looking for pampering but want to stay near the airport. Rooms and suites are done in soft pastels; many suites have private outdoor spas. The expansive, luxurious lobby is decorated in earth tones and brass. The Trattoria Grande restaurant features pasta and seafood specialties. *5400 W. Century Blvd., 90045, tel. 213/216–5858 or 800/468–3571. 750 rooms. Facilities: restaurants, lounge, entertainment, fitness center, pool, sauna, parking (fee). AE, DC, MC, V.*

Moderate **Pacifica Hotel.** Just 3 miles north of LAX and a few minutes from Marina del Rey, this deluxe Spanish-American-style hotel is convenient for business types. There is elegant as well as casual dining. The Culver's Club Lounge has lively entertainment and dancing. Extra special is the Shalamar Suite, with beautiful decorations and its own indoor pool. Package rates. *6161 Centinela Ave., Culver City 90230, tel. 213/649–1776 or 800/542–6082. 368 rooms. Facilities: restaurants, lounge, entertainment, pool, sauna, health club, free parking. AE, DC, MC, V.*

The Arts

For the most complete listing of weekly events, get the current issue of *Los Angeles* or *California* magazine. The Calendar section of the *Los Angeles Times* also offers a wide survey of Los Angeles arts events, as do the more irreverent free publications the *L.A. Weekly* and the *L.A. Reader.*

Most tickets can be purchased by phone (with a credit card) from **Teletron** (tel. 213/410–1062), **Ticketmaster** (tel. 213/480–3232), **Ticketron** (tel. 213/642–4242), **Good Time Tickets** (tel. 213/464–7383), or **Murray's Tickets** (tel. 213/234–0123).

Theater Even small productions might boast big names from "the business" (the Los Angeles entertainment empire). Many film and television actors love to work on the stage between "big" projects as a way to refresh their talents or regenerate their creativity in this demanding medium. Doing theater is also an excellent way to be seen by those who matter in the more glitzy end of show business. Hence there is a need for both large houses—which usually mount productions that are road-company imports of Broadway hits or, on occasion, the place where Broadway-bound material begins its tryout phase—and a host of small, intimate theaters for the talent that abounds in this city.

The following samples includes some of the major houses in the area:

Ahmanson Theater. With 2,071 seats making it the largest of the three-theater Music Center complex (with the Dorothy Chandler Pavilion and the Mark Taper Forum), its productions include both classics and new plays. The list of artists who have worked at this theater reads like a Who's Who of stage and screen. *135 N. Grand Ave., tel. 213/972-7654. Tickets: $32-$50. AE, DC, MC, V.*

James A. Doolittle. Located in the heart of Hollywood, this house offers an intimate feeling despite its 1,038-seat capacity. New plays, dramas, comedies, and musicals are presented here year round. *1615 N. Vine St., Hollywood, tel. 213/462-6666; charge line, 213/851-9750. Tickets: $26-$36. AE, DC, MC, V.*

John Anson Ford Theater. This 1,300-seat house in the Hollywood hills is best known for its Shakespeare and free summer jazz, dance, and cabaret concerts. *2580 Cahuenga Blvd., Hollywood, tel. 213/972-7211. Tickets: $10-$35. AE, MC, V.*

Mark Taper Forum. Also part of the Music Center, this house boasts 742 seats, excellent acoustics, and an intimate setting. The theater, under the direction of Gordon Davidson, is committed to new works and to the development of a community of artists. Many of its plays, including *Children of a Lesser God*, have gone on to Broadway. *135 N. Grand Ave., tel. 213/972-7353; charge line, 213/972-7654. Tickets: $17.50-$30. AE, DC, MC, V.*

Second City Theater. Built in 1911, this charming 282-seat theater (a former opera house) is decorated in an Old World style. The theater is now home to the infamous Second City comedy troupe. *214 Santa Monica Blvd., Santa Monica, tel. 213/451-0621. Tickets: $7-$15.*

Pantages. Once the home of the Oscar telecast and Hollywood premieres, this house is massive (2,300 seats) and (except for the acoustics) splendid. Musicals from Broadway are usually presented here. *6233 Hollywood Blvd., Hollywood, tel. 213/410-1062. Tickets: $15-$35. MC, V.*

Westwood Playhouse. An acoustically superior theater with great sightlines, the 498-seat playhouse showcases new plays, primarily musicals and comedies in the summer. Many productions come in from Broadway; two—*Perfectly Frank* and *Passionate Ladies*—went on to Broadway. Jason Robards and Nick Nolte got their starts here. *10886 Le Conte Ave., Westwood, tel. 213/208-6500 or 213/208-5454. Tickets: $17.50-$30. AE, DC, MC, V.*

Wilshire Theater. The interior of this newly renovated, 1,900-seat house is art deco-style; musicals from Broadway are the usual fare. *8440 Wilshire Blvd., Beverly Hills, tel. 213/642-4242. Tickets: $14.50-$30. MC, V.*

Concerts Los Angeles is not only the focus of America's pop/rock music recording scene; after years of being regarded as a cultural invalid, Los Angeles has finally come into its own as a center for classical music and opera.

The following is a list of Los Angeles' major concert halls:

The Ambassador Auditorium (300 W. Green St., Pasadena, tel. 818/304-6161). World-renowned soloists and ensembles perform in this elegant and acoustically impressive hall from September to May.

Dorothy Chandler Pavilion (135 N. Grand Ave., tel. 213/972-7211). Part of the Los Angeles Music Center and—with the Hollywood Bowl—the center of L.A.'s classical music scene, the 3,000-seat Pavilion is the home of the Los Angeles Philharmonic from November to April and the showcase for the Los Angeles Master Chorale Group, the Los Angeles Civic Light Opera, and, in the fall, the Joffrey Ballet.

The Greek Theater (2700 N. Vermont Ave., tel. 213/410-1062).

This open-air auditorium near Griffith Park offers some classical music in its mainly pop/rock/jazz schedule from June to October. Its Doric columns evoke the amphitheaters of ancient Greece.

The Hollywood Bowl (2301 Highland Ave., tel. 213/850–2000). Open since 1920, the Bowl is one of the world's largest outdoor amphitheaters, located in a park surrounded by mountains, trees, and gardens. The L.A. Philharmonic spends its summer season here. Concert-goers usually arrive early, bringing or buying picnic suppers. There are plenty of picnic tables, and box-seat subscribers can reserve a table right in their own box. Restaurant dining is available on the grounds (reservations recommended, tel. 213/851–3588). The seats are wooden, so you might bring or rent a cushion—and bring a sweater. A convenient way to enjoy the Hollywood Bowl experience without the hassle of parking is to take one of the Park-and-Ride buses, which leave from various locations around town; call the Bowl for information.

Royce Hall (405 N. Hilgard Ave. tel., 213/825–9261). Internationally acclaimed performers are featured in this 1,800-seat auditorium at UCLA. The university's **Schoenberg Hall,** smaller but with wonderful acoustics, also hosts a variety of concerts.

The Shrine Auditorium (665 W. Jefferson Blvd., tel. 213/749–5123). Built in 1926 by the Al Malaikah Temple, its decor could be termed basic Baghdad and beyond. Touring companies from all over the world, along with assorted gospel and choral groups, appear in this one-of-a-kind, 6,200-seat theater.

The Wilshire Ebell Theater (4401 W. 8th St., tel. 213/939–1128). The Los Angeles Opera Theatre comes to this Renaissance-style building (Spanish in architecture and design, built in 1924), as do a broad spectrum of other musical performers.

Wiltern Theater (Wilshire Blvd. and Western Ave., tel. 213/380–5005). Reopened in 1985 as a venue for the Los Angeles Opera Theater, the building was constructed in 1930, is listed in the National Register of Historic Places, and is a striking example of Art Deco in its green terra-cotta glory.

Dance In addition to Los Angeles' own Bella Lewitsky and the Los Angeles Chamber Ballet, yearly visiting dance companies include the Joffrey, American Ballet Theatre, Martha Graham, and Paul Taylor, to name a few. Most dance events in Los Angeles will be listed each Sunday in the *Los Angeles Times* Calendar section. The **Dance Resource Center of Greater Los Angeles** (tel. 213/281–1918) also offers current dance information.

UCLA Center for the Arts (405 N. Hilgard Ave., tel. 213/825–9261) attracts masters of modern dance, jazz, and ballet, including Martha Graham, Bella Lewitsky, Paul Taylor, Hubbard Street Dance Company, and Bejart, along with its own UCLA Dance Company. Rush tickets priced at $7 are available on the night of the performance for senior citizens and full-time students.

Film Spending two hours at a movie while visiting Los Angeles needn't be taking time out from sightseeing. Some of the country's most historic and beautiful theaters are found here, hosting first-run and revival films worth seeing, if only to visit the famed movie palaces.

Movie listings are advertised daily in the Calendar section of the papers. The most common price of admission to first-run movies, as of this writing, is $6.50–$7, but bargain prices as low as $3.50 are common for the first showing of the day.

Egyptian Theater (6712 Hollywood Blvd., tel. 213/467–6167). Built in 1922, this theater was also owned by Sid Grauman and was the site of many premieres. Now run by United Artists, it's been converted into a triple-screen facility for first-run movies, but the lobby retains the ornate Egyptian decor that made it famous.

Mann's Chinese Theater (6925 Hollywood Blvd., tel. 213/464–8111). Formerly owned by Sid Grauman, this Chinese pagoda structure is perhaps the world's best known movie theater. It still carries out one of the oldest of Hollywood traditions, its famous hand- and foot-printing ceremony.

Pacific Cinerama Dome (6360 Sunset Blvd., tel. 213/466–3401). This futuristic, geodesic structure was the first theater designed specifically for Cinerama in the United States. The gigantic screen and multitrack sound system create an unparalleled cinematic experience.

Nightlife

Nightlife in Los Angeles has come to mean anything from catching a stand-up routine at the Comedy Store to frenetic disco dancing at Chippendale's. This city offers a potpourri of specialized entertainment, not only in the hub of the city but also in the outlying suburbs.

Despite the high energy level of the nightlife crowd, Los Angeles nightclubs aren't known for keeping their doors open until the wee hours. This is an early-to-bed city, and it's safe to say that by 2 AM most jazz, rock, and disco clubs are closed for the night. Perhaps it's the temperate climate and the sports orientation of the city: most Angelenos want to be on the tennis court or out jogging by 9 AM, so a late night social life is out of the question.

Dress codes vary depending on the place you visit. Jackets are expected at more traditional nightspots like cabarets and hotels. Discos are generally casual, although some prohibit the wearing of jeans. The rule of thumb is to phone ahead and check the dress code, but on the whole, Los Angeles is oriented toward casual wear.

Consult *Los Angeles* and *California* magazines for current listings. The Sunday *Los Angeles Times* Calendar section and the free *L.A. Weekly* and *L.A. Reader* also provide listings.

Jazz **The Baked Potato.** At this tiny club, where they pack you in like sardines to hear jazz powerhouses, the featured item on the menu is, of course, baked potatoes. They're jumbo and stuffed with everything from steak to vegetables. *3787 Cahuenga Blvd. W, North Hollywood, tel. 818/980–1615. AE, MC, V.*

Catalina Bar and Grill. Big name acts and innovators like Latin-influenced saxophonist Paquito D' Rivera light up this top Hollywood jazz spot. Continental cuisine is served. *1640 N. Cahuenga Blvd., Hollywood, tel. 213/466–2210. AE, MC, V. Cover varies.*

Jax. This intimate club serves a wide variety of food, from sandwiches to steak and seafood, along with live music. *339 N.*

Brand Blvd., Glendale, tel. 818/500-1604. AE, MC, V. No cover.

The Lighthouse. One of Los Angeles' finest, the Lighthouse features a broad spectrum of music, from reggae to big-band. Jam sessions are frequent on weekends. Freddie Hubbard, Woody Herman, and Jimmy Witherspoon have all played here. The decor is wood, brass, and brick, with lots of plants. Dine on fettuccine, appetizers, or steaks while hearing the sounds. *30 Pier Ave., Hermosa Beach, tel. 213/372-6911 or 376-9833. MC, V with a $5 minimum. No cover.*

Marla's Memory Lane. Now owned by comedy star Marla Gibbs of "The Jeffersons" and "227" and newly remodeled, the room pops with blues, jazz, and easy listening. Kenny Burrell and Ernie Andrews play here from time to time. A new menu includes roast prime rib of beef and Alaskan king crab legs. *2323 W. Martin Luther King, Jr. Blvd., Central Los Angeles, tel. 213/294-8430. AE, DC, MC, V.*

Nucleus Nuance. This art deco restaurant features vintage jazz Friday and Saturday nights. *7267 Melrose Ave., West Hollywood, tel. 213/939-8666. AE, DC, MC, V.*

Vine Street Bar and Grill. This elegant club in the heart of Hollywood (across the street from the James Doolittle Theater) features two shows nightly. Past performers have included Eartha Kitt, Cab Calloway, and Carmen McRae. Italian food is served. *1610 N. Vine St., Hollywood, tel. 213/463-4375. AE, MC, V.*

Folk/Pop/Rock **At My Place.** This enterprise features a provocative blend of jazz/fusion, pop, and rhythm-and-blues music acts. Comedy performers open the weekend shows; some of the culinary specialties include quiche and potato skins. *1026 Wilshire Blvd., Santa Monica, tel. 213/451-8596. MC, V.*

The Central. Road crews, pop-act managers, and famous guitarists alike come to hear live music in the pop, soul, and jazz-fusion genres. Many celebrity musicians attend the Tuesday night jam sessions. *8852 Sunset Blvd., West Hollywood, tel. 213/855-9183. No credit cards.*

Gazzarri's. This Sunset Strip landmark is a venue for pure rock and roll with the younger crowd. Dress is casual. *9039 Sunset Blvd., West Hollywood, tel. 213/273-6606. No credit cards.*

McCabe's Guitar Shop. Folk, acoustic rock, bluegrass, and soul are offered in an intimate concert-hall setting. Coffee, herb tea, apple juice, and homemade sweets are served during intermission. *3101 Pico Blvd., Santa Monica, tel. 213/828-4497. Advanced tickets often necessary. AE, DC, MC, V. Closed Mon.-Thurs.*

The Palace. The in spot for the upwardly mobile, it's plush art deco—truly a palace—and boasts live entertainment, a fabulous sound system, full bar, and dining upstairs. Patrons dress to kill. *1735 N. Vine St., Hollywood, tel. 213/462-3000 or 213/462-6031. AE, MC, V.*

The Roxy. The premier Los Angeles rock club is classy and comfortable, offering performance art as well as theatrical productions. Many famous Los Angeles groups got their start here as opening acts. *9009 Sunset Blvd., West Hollywood, tel. 213/276-2222. No credit cards.*

The Strand. This major concert venue covers a lot of ground, hosting acts like Asleep at the Wheel, bluesman Albert King, rock vet Robin Trower, and Billy Vera in the same week. Who says you can't have it all? *1700 S. Pacific Coast Hwy., Redondo Beach, tel. 213/316–1700. AE, MC, V.*

The Troubador. In the early 1970s this was one of the hottest clubs in town for major talent. Business then became shaky for a few years as the music industry changed its focus, but now it's rolling again, this time with up-and-coming talent. The adjoining bar is a great place to see and be seen. *9081 Santa Monica Blvd., West Hollywood, tel. 213/276–6168. No credit cards.*

Cabaret **La Cage aux Folles.** This cabaret supper club features female impersonators who do impressions of such stars as Liza Minnelli and Barbra Streisand. The ambience, with a shocking-pink and stark-blue color scheme, resembles a European bistro of 40 years ago. It's unusual and fun. There's an extensive French/Continental menu. *643 N. La Cienega Blvd., West Hollywood, tel. 213/657–1091. AE, DC, MC, V. Closed Mon.*

Studio One Blackout. An elegant, classy night spot features excellent musical acts, singers, comedians and dancers. *652 N. La Peer, West Hollywood, tel. 213/659–0472. AE, MC, V.*

Disco/Dancing **China Club.** At this new West Coast branch of the hip New York dance club, a serious attitude and the latest in performance artwear will help you get in the door. *1600 N. Argyle, Hollywood, tel. 213/469–1600.*

Coconut Teaszer. Disco dancing, a great barbecue menu, and killer drinks make for lively fun. *8177 Sunset Blvd., tel. 213/654–4774.*

DC3. Hip and uptown, this club/restaurant in the Santa Monica Airport plays pop music until 2 AM. Look for an older, upscale crowd and sophisticated lighting effects. *2800 Donald Douglas Loop, Santa Monica, tel. 213/399–2323. AE, DC, MC, V.*

Samba E Saudade. The serious dance action in L.A. these days moves to a Latin beat. This Brazilian club dishes it up hot, with a sexy, infectious flair. *9300 W. Jefferson Blvd., Culver City, tel. 213/962–1953. Open Thurs. and Sun.*

The Stock Exchange. Along with Vertigo, this multilevel art deco palace is the hottest place to be downtown. It once was the Pacific Stock Exchange; now it's a star-filled dance spot. *618 S. Spring St., tel. 213/627–4400. AE, MC. Open Wed.–Sat.*

20/20. Once the Playboy Club, this night spot is where the beautiful people hang out, with plenty of mirrors for checking themselves out. Music runs from oldies to Top 40. *2020 Ave. of the Stars, Century City, tel. 213/933–2020. AE, MC, V.*

Vertigo. This New York-style club with a restrictive entrance policy, has a large dance floor, balcony bar, and restaurant. It's open Friday and Saturday until 4 AM, which is unusual for this city. *333 Boylston St., tel. 213/747–4849. MC, V.*

Country **The Palomino.** There's occasionally a wild crowd at this premier country showcase in Los Angeles. Good old boys and hip cowboys meet here, and everybody has a good time. *6907 Lankershim Blvd., North Hollywood, tel. 818/764–4010. AE, DC, MC, V.*

Comedy and Magic **Comedy and Magic Club.** This beachfront club features many magicians and comedians seen on TV and in Las Vegas. The Unknown Comic, Elayne Boosler, and Pat Paulsen have all played here. The menu features light American fare and many appetizers. *1018 Hermosa Ave., Hermosa Beach, tel. 213/372–2626. Reservations are suggested. AE, MC, V. Closed Mon.*

Comedy Store. L.A.'s premier comedy showcase for over a decade. Many famous comedians, including Robin Williams and

Steve Martin, make unannounced appearances here. The cover varies. *8433 Sunset Blvd., Hollywood, tel. 213/656–6225. AE, MC, V.*

The Improvisation. The Improv is a transplanted New York establishment; 18 years in the Big Apple, now seven in the Big Orange. Comedy is showcased, with some vocalists. The Improv was the proving ground for Liza Minnelli and Richard Pryor, among others. Reservations recommended. *8162 Melrose Ave., West Hollywood, tel. 213/651–2583 and 321 Santa Monica Blvd., Santa Monica, tel. 213/394–8664. MC, V for food and drinks only.*

Second City. The Chicago comedy institution behind SCTV and innumerable top performers has finally come to L.A. Improv is the specialty of the house, and it's almost always well done. *214 Santa Monica Blvd., Santa Monica, tel. 213/451–0621. $7–$15. AE, MC, V. Closed Mon.*

Excursions to Santa Catalina Island

When you approach Catalina Island through the typical early morning ocean fog, it's easy to wonder if perhaps there has been some mistake. What is a Mediterranean island doing 22 miles off the coast of California? Don't worry, you haven't left the Pacific—you've arrived at one of the Los Angeles area's most popular resorts.

Though lacking some of the sophistication of a European pleasure island, Catalina offers virtually unspoiled mountains and canyons, coves and beaches. It is Southern California without the freeways, a place to relax and play golf or tennis, go boating, hiking, diving, or fishing, or just lay on the beach. Avalon is the island's only "city," a charming old-fashioned beach community. Yachts are tied up in neat rows in the crescent-shaped bay, palm trees rim the main street, and there are plenty of restaurants and shops to attract the attention of day-trippers out strolling in the sunshine.

Of course, life was not always this leisurely on Catalina. Discovered by Juan Rodriguez Cabrillo in 1542, the island has sheltered many characters, from Russian fur trappers (seeking sea-otter skins), slave traders, pirates, and gold miners, to film makers and movie stars. Avalon was named in 1888 after the island of Avalon in Tennyson's *Idylls of the King*. In 1919, William Wrigley, Jr., chewing-gum magnate, purchased controlling interest in the company developing the island. Wrigley had the island's most famous landmark, the Casino, built in 1929, and he made Catalina the site of spring training for his Chicago Cubs baseball team. The Santa Catalina Island Conservancy, a nonprofit foundation, acquired about 86% of the island in 1974 to help preserve Catalina's natural resources.

A wide variety of tours offer samples of those resources, either by boat along the island's coast or by bus or van into Catalina's rugged interior country. Depending on which route you take, you can expect to see roving bands of buffalo, deer, goats, and boar, or unusual species of sea life, including such oddities as electric perch, saltwater goldfish, and flying fish. The buffalo originally came to the island in 1924 for the filming of *The Van ishing American;* apparently, they liked it well enough to stay

Although Catalina can certainly be done in a day, there are sev eral inviting, romantic hotels that promise to make it worth extending your stay for one or more nights. Between Memoria Day and Labor Day we strongly suggest you make reservation *before* heading out to the island. After Labor Day, rates drop dramatically and rooms are much easier to find.

Arriving and Departing

By Boat Boats to Catalina run from San Pedro and Long Beach. **Catali-na Express** (tel. 213/519–1212) makes the run in 90 minutes round-trip fare is $25 for adults. There is regularly scheduled service from San Pedro ($27.70 roundtrip) and Long Beach ($32 roundtrip). **Catalina Cruises** (tel. 800/888–5939) is a bit slower, taking two hours, and cheaper, charging about $20. Service is also available from Newport Beach through **Catalina Passenger Service** (tel. 714/673–5245), leaving from Balboa Pavilion. Ad vance reservations for all lines are recommended.

By Plane **Helitrans** (tel. 213/548–1314 or 800/262–1472) offers helicopter service from San Pedro's Catalina Island Terminal to Pebbly Beach, five minutes by van from Avalon. **Island Express** (tel. 213/491–5550) flies from San Pedro and Long Beach. The trip takes about 15 minutes and costs $53 one way. Commuter air service is available from Long Beach Airport and John Wayne Orange County Airport to Catalina's Airport in the Sky. Call **Allied Air Charter** (tel. 213/510–1163) for schedules and fares.

Guided Tours

The major tour operators on the island are the **Santa Catalina Island Co.** (tel. 213/510–2000 or 800/428–2566) and **Ultimate Destinations** (tel. 213/510–0575). Tours include: inland motor tour, Skyline Drive, coastal cruise to Seal Rocks (summer only), the Flying Fish boat trip (evenings, summer only), casi-no tour, Avalon scenic tour, and the glass-bottom boat tour. Advance reservations are highly recommended for the first four tours; the other three are offered several times daily. Costs vary from $4.50 for the casino tour (adults) to $17 for the four-hour inland motor tour; discounts are available for those under 12 and over 55. Catalina Adventure Tours also offers para-sailing, fishing, and diving.
The Catalina Conservancy (tel. 213/510–1421) offers walks led by docents.

Exploring

Catalina Island is one of the very few places in the L.A. envi-rons where walking is considered quite acceptable. In fact, you cannot bring a car onto the island nor can you rent one once you get there. If you are determined to have a set of wheels, rent a bicycle, or golf cart along Crescent Avenue as you walk in from the docks. To hike into the interior of the island you will need a permit, available for free from the L.A. County Department of Parks and Recreation (Island Plaza, Avalon, tel. 213/510–0688).

The **Visitors Center** and the **Chamber of Commerce Visitors Bureau** are good places to get your bearings, check into special events, and plan your itinerary. The Visitors Center (tel. 213/510–2000) is located on the corner of Crescent Avenue and Catalina Avenue, across from the Green Pier; the Chamber's Visitors Bureau is on the pier.

Housed on the northwest point of Crescent Bay is the **Casino.** The round structure is an odd mixture of Spanish, Moorish, and Art Deco modern style, with Art Deco murals on the porch as you enter. In the Casino are an art gallery, museum, movie theater (tel. 213/510–0179), and ballroom. Guided tours are available.

The Wrigley Memorial and Botanical Garden is 2 miles south of Avalon via Avalon Canyon Road. Wrigley's family commissioned this monument to Wrigley, replete with grand staircase and Spanish mausoleum with Art Deco touches. Despite the fact that the mausoleum was never used by the Wrigleys, who are buried in Los Angeles, the structure is worth a look, and the view from the mausoleum is worth even more. The garden is small but exceptionally well planted. Tram service between the Memorial and Avalon is available daily between 8 AM and 5 PM. There is a nominal entry fee.

If modern architecture interests you, be sure to stop by the **Wolfe House** (124 Chimes Rd.). Built in 1928 by noted architect Rudolph Schindler, its terraced frame is carefully set into a steep site, affording extraordinary views. The house is a private residence, rarely open for public tours, but you can get a good view of it from the path below it and from the street.

El Rancho Escondido is a working ranch in Catalina's interior, home to some of the country's finest Arabian horses. The ranch can be visited on the Inland Motor Tour.

Dining

The following credit-card abbreviations are used: AE, American Express; CB, Carte Blanche; DC, Diners Club; MC, MasterCard; V, Visa.

American
Inexpensive
(under $10)
The Sand Trap. Omelets are the specialty at this local favorite located on the way to Wrigley Botanical Garden. *Bird Park Rd., tel. 213/510–1349. No credit cards.*

Italian
Inexpensive
(under $10)
Antonio's Pizzeria. Spirited atmosphere, decent pizza, and appropriately messy Italian sandwiches. *2 locations: 230 Crescent Ave., tel. 213/510–0008 and 114 Sumner, tel. 213/510–0060. MC, V.*

Moderate
($10–$20)
Cafe Prego. This restaurant features an intimate setting on the waterfront, several good pasta dishes, and a hearty minestrone. *603 Crescent Ave., tel. 213/510–1218. AE, MC, V. Closed for lunch.*

Seafood
Moderate
($10–$20)
Pirrone's. A brand-new restaurant with bird's-eye view of the bay serving fresh seafood. *417 Crescent Ave., tel. 213/510–0333. MC, V. Open Mon.–Sat. for dinner, plus Sun. brunch, in winter.*

Lodging

Very Expensive   **Inn on Mt. Ada.** The former Wrigley Mansion is now the island's
($170–$440)   most exclusive hotel. There are only six rooms, the views spectacular, the grounds superbly planted. *Box 2560, Avalon
90704, tel. 213/510–2030. 6 rooms. AE, MC, V.*

Moderate–   **Glenmore Plaza Hotel.** This striking Victorian structure, dat-
Expensive   ing from 1891, has hosted Clark Gable, Teddy Roosevelt, and
($80–$180)   Amelia Earhart. Located near the beach, the hotel offers com-
plimentary breakfast and suites with whirlpool or Jacuzzi. *120
Sumner Ave., Avalon 90704, tel. 213/510–0017. 50 rooms. AE,
MC, V.*
Hotel Villa Portofino. This is a Mediterranean-style waterfront
hotel with a sun deck, art gallery, and Italian restaurant. *111
Crescent Ave., Avalon 90704, tel. 213/510–0555. 34 rooms. AE,
MC, V.*

Moderate   **Hotel Catalina.** A renovated Victorian building, 1/2-block from
($70–$100)   the beach, the Catalina offers a choice of rooms and cottages.
Extra touches include an attractive sun deck with Jacuzzi, and
free movies every afternoon. *129 Whittley Ave., Avalon 90704,
tel. 213/510–0027. 32 rooms, 4 cottages. AE, MC, V.*

Moderate   **Zane Grey Pueblo Hotel.** The former home of the famous Ameri-
($75–$125)   can novelist, this hotel offers a stunning harbor view from its
hilltop perch. Built in 1926 in Hopi Indian pueblo style, amenities include eccentric decor, a swimming pool, and a courtesy
bus. No phones or TVs in rooms; no children allowed. *199
Chimes Tower Rd., Avalon 90704, tel. 213/510–0966. 18 rooms.
AE, MC, V.*

Inexpensive   **Atwater Hotel.** This family-oriented hotel is 1/2-block from the
(under $70)   beach. *Box 737, Avalon 90704, tel. 213/510–1788. 84 rooms.
AE, CB, DC, MC, V.*

Excursion to Antelope Valley

The most memorable parts of a trip are often its surprises—the
places and people you stumble onto when you least expect to.
Antelope Valley, which makes up the western corner of the Mojave Desert, holds several unexpected pleasures. A sudden
turn along a desert road reveals a riot of flaming orange poppies on acres of rolling hills nestled between barren rises and
desolate flatlands. In the late summer and fall, after the flowers have faded, you can pick your own cherries, peaches, and
pears at nearby orchards incongruously set in the desert. Head
east and you can hike to the top of Saddleback Butte for a spectacular view of where the desert ends and the San Gabriel
Mountains begin, their snow-capped peaks a beautiful contrast
to the arid valley.

Another surprise is the valley's wildlife. No, don't look for the
hoary antlers of the antelope that lent their name to the area.
Once practically overrunning the region, the antelope went
into decline with the arrival of the railroad in 1876. They apparently refused to cross the tracks that blocked the route to their
traditional grazing grounds, and many starved to death. A se-
vere winter in the 1880s and the growth of ranching and farm-

ing in the early 1900s spelled the end for the few that had survived.

What you can see on an Antelope Valley safari is the eminently amusing and increasingly rare desert tortoise. Thanks to preservationists, a safe haven has been created for California's official state reptile. Visiting the tortoise in its natural habitat is a great opportunity for budding photographers; not noted for their speed, the tortoises make willing subjects. If birds are more your fancy, there is also a 40-acre wildlife sanctuary in the valley noted for its winged inhabitants.

Man, of course, has also made his mark in Antelope Valley. You'll find gold mines and historic railroad towns that still evoke the spirit of the Old West. About $40 million in gold and silver has been taken out of the hills between Rosamond and Mojave since a Mr. Hamilton hit pay dirt in the 1890s on what is now called Tropico Hill. The Burton Mining Company believes there is still some gold to be found in Tropico, and is today still excavating the same hill on which Hamilton made his fortune.

Arriving and Departing

By Car   Heading north from Los Angeles, I–5 will lead you to Highway 14, which runs north through Palmdale, Lancaster, Rosamond, and Mojave. It should take about 90 minutes to reach Palmdale and another hour between Palmdale and Mojave. To reach the **Antelope Valley California Poppy Reserve,** take the Avenue I exit in Lancaster off Highway 14 and head west about 10 miles. Rosemond and the **Tropico Mine** are just north of Lancaster on Highway 14. Take the Rosamond Boulevard exit and go west for three miles to Mojave-Tropico Road; turn north here and you will see the mine shortly. For the **Desert Tortoise Natural Area,** take Highway 14 about 4 miles past Mojave and then turn east on California City Boulevard through California City; turn left on Randsburg-Mojave Road and follow signs about 5 miles to the preserve. Take Avenue J (Rte. N5) east from Lancaster for about 19 miles to get to **Saddleback Butte State Park.** To reach the **Devil's Punchbowl Natural Area Park** and nearby **Hamilton Preserve,** take Highway 138 southwest from Palmdale; just past Pearblossom turn south on Route N6 (Longview Rd.) and go about 8 miles. On Highway 138, you can continue southeast along the San Gabriel Mountains, pick up I–15 south through the San Gabriel Mountains, pick up I-15 south through Cajon Pass, and return to Los Angeles via I–10 heading west.

Exploring

You can't miss the **Antelope Valley California Poppy Reserve;** its orange glow with dots of purple lupine and yellow goldfields and fiddleneck can be seen long before you reach the reserve itself. The best time to visit is between March and May, peak flower time. There are four short (1–2 mile) walking trails leading through the fields, some reaching wonderful viewpoints. While there is a perfectly serviceable picnic area by the parking lot, a snack on the bench atop Kitanemuk Vista (an easy five-minute stroll up a well-marked trail) offers much finer scenery. Do take a few minutes to walk through the visitor center. The uniquely designed building is burrowed into a hill to keep the building cooler during the summer and warmer dur-

ing the winter. You can pick up trail maps an*
formation. *Visitor Center open Mar.–May
Park day-use fee: $3 per car. For more informa
ules of guided tours, call the California Dept. of
Recreation, tel. 805/942–0662.*

You will find the area's orchards along State Highway 138 in
the communities of **Littlerock** and **Pearblossom,** and in **Leonia,**
just to the southwest of Lancaster. Harvesting season starts in
June. *Contact the Lancaster Chamber of Commerce and Visitors Center (44335 Lowtree, Lancaster 93534, tel. 805/948–4518) for more information.*

A short drive north of Lancaster to **Rosamond** will take you
back a long way in years. Gold was first discovered in Tropico
Hill in 1894, and Burton's Tropico Mine and Mill, hanging awkwardly against the hill, looks just as it did during the height of
the Gold Rush. Unfortunately, the high cost of liability insurance put an end to mine tours and led to the closing of an
informative museum, but you can still get a close look at the old
buildings and let your imagination fill in the sights and sounds
of a turn-of-the-century mining town.

The **Desert Tortoise Natural Area** is a good place to commune
with nature. Cars must be left behind as you stroll through the
preserve's peaceful and picturesque landscape. Be sure to do
two things: look around and consider the fact that there isn't a
sign of civilization to be seen; and breathe deeply, because you
won't often find air this fresh in and around Los Angeles or any
urban center. The best time of the year for viewing the tortoises is generally March through June, but avoid the midafternoon. The tortoises sensibly stay cool during the heat of
the day by retiring to their shallow burrows. Two warnings
about the natural area: The road into the area is wide and flat,
but not paved, so your car is bound to get a bit dusty; also, there
is no water available at the preserve. The preserve is open
land, there is no admission, and you may feel free to roam about
wherever you like. *For more information and to arrange
guided tours call the California City Recreation Department
(tel. 619/373–4278).*

East of Lancaster is **Saddleback Butte State Park,** a favorite
among hikers and campers. A 2½-mile trail leads to the 3,651-
foot summit of the butte for which the park is named, offering
some grand views. Throughout the park there is a great deal of
typical high-desert plant and animal life—stands of Joshua
trees, desert tortoises, golden eagles, and many other species
of reptiles, mammals, and birds. Near park headquarters is a
picnic area with tables, stoves, and rest rooms. The Los Angeles County Department of Parks and Recreation (tel. 805/259-
7721) offers a fact sheet on the various wildlife sanctuaries near
the park. *Information on camping at Saddleback Butte is
available from the State Dept. of Parks (tel. 805/942–0662).*

Further south is another popular spot for hikers—**Devils
Punchbowl Natural Area Park.** Once at the bottom of an ocean,
and currently nestled between the active San Andreas and San
Jacinto faults, the park offers a network of well-planned trails.
For a colorful fact sheet on the nearby **Hamilton Preserve**—40
acres of pinyon-juniper woodland sheltering numerous bird
species.

Antelope Valley is also home to **Edwards Air Force Base** and the **NASA Ames-Dryden Flight Research Facility** (off State Hwy. 14, northeast of Lancaster). Tours of the facility are available, with a film describing the history of flight test programs, a walk through a hangar, and a look at experimental aircraft. When the space shuttle is up, this is the place to see it land. *Free tours weekdays 10:15 AM and 1:15 PM. Call ahead (tel. 805/ 258-3446), as the base is occasionally closed for security reasons.*

Dining

Antelope Valley is not known for its fine dining. There are several fast-food and very average roadside restaurants in Lancaster, Palmdale, and Mojave. You might be better off to pack a gourmet picnic basket before you leave Los Angeles and dine alfresco at one of the many scenic spots you will come across throughout the valley.

13 Orange County

Sometime during the recessions of the 1970s, Middle Amer
packed up its bags and moved west, settling comfortably in (
ange County. Stretching between two major cities—L
Angeles and San Diego—Orange County is perhaps Americ
foremost suburb. Mickey Mouse rules, the average home co
$200,000, and finding the right wave or a volleyball game at t
beach are daily concerns among the younger set. The count
affluence continues to attract an ever-growing number of exc
sive shopping malls, new performing arts arenas, and luxurio
oceanfront resorts—along with traffic jams, slow-growth ini
atives, and an occasional metallic haze blotting the sky. It i
region some travelers love to hate, but when it comes to the
parks, shopping, and beach life, few places do it better than (
ange County.

Served by convenient airports and only an hour's drive fr
Los Angeles, Orange County is both a destination on its ov
and a very popular excursion from Los Angeles.

Getting Around

By Plane   Several airports are accessible to Orange County. **John Way
Orange County Airport (tel. 714/755–6500) is the county's ma
facility; it is 14 minutes from Anaheim and centrally locat
within the county. It is used by Alaska Airlines (tel. 800/42
0333), American West Airlines (tel. 800/AWA–WEST), Ame
can (tel. 800/433–7300), Delta (tel. 800/221–1212), TWA (t
800/221–2000), and United (800/241–6522).

Long Beach Airport (tel. 213/421–8295) is another good choi
for Orange County visits. It is about 20 minutes by coach fro
Anaheim. Airlines flying into Long Beach include Ameri
West, American Airlines, Delta, TWA, and United.

Anaheim is 35 miles from **Los Angeles International Airport,
miles from **Ontario Airport**.

Airport Coach (tel. 800/772–5299 in CA or 800/491–3500 outsi
CA) serves LAX to Anaheim, Long Beach, and Pasadena. T
fare to Anaheim is $12 one way, $22 round-trip, to Long Bea
$9 one way, $16 round-trip.

SuperShuttle (tel. 213/417–8427) provides 24-hour door-to-do
service from all the airports to all points in Orange Count
Fare to the Disneyland district is $10 a person from any airpor
Phone for other fares and reservations.

Prime Time Airport Shuttle (tel. 213/558–1606 or 818/901–990
offers service to LAX, Burbank Airport, and San Pedro Ha
bor. The company's motto is "We're on time, or you don't pay
The fare is $10 from Anaheim hotels to LAX. Children und
two ride free.

By Car   Two major freeways, I–405 and I–5, run north and sou
through Orange County. Past Laguna they merge into the I–
Try to stay away from these during rush hours (7–9 AM and 4-
PM) when they can slow for miles. Coming off I–405 is I–605, a
other major Orange County route. Highways 22, 55, and 91 g
west to the ocean and east to the mountains: Take Highway 91
Highway 22 to inland points (Buena Park, Anaheim) and tal
Highway 55 to Newport Beach.

Highway 1 (Pacific Coast Highway), allows easy access to beach communities, and it is the most scenic route. It follows the entire Orange County coast, from Huntington Beach to San Clemente.

By Train **Amtrak** (800/USA–RAIL) has several stops in Orange County: Santa Ana, San Juan Capistrano, San Clemente, Anaheim, and Fullerton. There are six departures daily. A special motor-coach also takes people to Disneyland from the Fullerton station.

By Bus In Southern California, relying on public transportation is usually a mistake, unless you have plenty of time and patience. The **Los Angeles RTD** has limited service to Orange County. At the downtown Los Angeles terminal, on Sixth Street, you can get the No. 460 to Anaheim; it goes to Knott's Berry Farm and Disneyland.

The **Orange County Transit Department** (tel. 714/636–7433) will take you virtually anywhere in the county, but, again, it will take time; OCTD buses go from Knott's Berry Farm and Disneyland to Huntington and Newport beaches. The No. 1 bus travels south along the coast.

Greyhound-Trailways (tel. 213/394–5433) has scheduled bus service to Orange County as well. For **Gray Line's** schedule and fare information, call 213/856–5900.

Pacific Coast (tel. 714/978–8855) offers transportation from Orange County hotels to the San Diego Zoo, Tijuana, the *Queen Mary/Spruce Goose*, and Knott's Berry Farm.

Scenic Drives Winding along the **Pacific Coast Highway** on the seaside edge of Orange County is an eye-opening experience. Here the contradictions of Southern California are revealed: the powerful, healing ocean vistas and the scars of commercial exploitation; the appealingly laid-back, simple beach life and the tacky bric-a-brac of the tourist trail. Oil rigs line the road from Long Beach south to Huntington Beach, suddenly giving way to pristine stretches of water and dramatic hillsides. Prototypical beach towns like Laguna Beach, Dana Point, and Corona del Mar serve as casual stopping points irregularly arrayed along the route. This is a classic coastline drive.

For a scenic mountain drive, try **Santiago Canyon Road,** which winds through the Cleveland National Forest in the Santa Ana Mountains. Tucked away in the mountains are Modjeska Canyon, Irvine Lake, and Silverado Canyon, of silver mining lore. The terrain is rugged and you feel as if you are nowhere near urban civilization.

Guided Tours

General-Interest Tours **Gray Line** (tel. 213/856–5900) has all-day tours to Disneyland and Knott's Berry Farm, as well as a combination tour of Knott's and Movieland Wax Museum.

For those who want specialized sightseeing services for small-group or personal tours, **The Orange County Experience** (tel. 714/680–3550), has been showing groups around the county for many years. Owner Louis Reichman is the author of *The Orange County Experience*. Stories behind Disneyland, Knott's Berry Farm, and some of Orange County's most interesting cities make up these insiders' tours. The Crystal Cathedral, Mission San Juan Capistrano, and many local beaches can be part of the tour. A special tour, "From Orange to Wine," visits the Callaway winery in scenic Rainbow Gap via the old Butterfield Stage Route.

Boat Tours At the **Cannery** in Newport Beach, you can hop a boat and go for a brunch cruise around the harbor on Sundays. Cruises last two hours and depart at 10 AM and 1:30 PM. Champagne brunches cost $25 per person. For more information call 714/675–5777.

Catalina Passenger Service (tel. 714/673–5245) at the Balboa Pavilion offers a full selection of sightseeing tours and fishing excursions to Catalina and around Newport Harbor. The 45-minute narrated tour of Newport Harbor, at $5, is the least expensive. Whale-watching cruises (Dec.–Mar.) are especially enjoyable. Narrated by a speaker from the American Cetacean Society, the tours follow the migration pattern of the giant gray whales.

Hornblower Yachts (tel. 714/548–8700) offers a number of special sightseeing brunch cruises. Whale-watching brunches (Jan.–Apr.) are scheduled each Saturday and Sunday; special cruises take place on such holidays as Valentine's Day, Easter, Halloween, Thanksgiving, and Christmas.

Walking Tours If you want to walk in Orange County, you have to drive somewhere first. For a respite from suburban sprawl and urban smog, the **Tucker Wildlife Preserve** in Modjeska Canyon (tel. 714/649–2760), 17 miles southeast of the city of Orange, is worth the effort. The preserve is a haven for more than 140 bird species, including seven varieties of hummingbird that are surprisingly amusing to watch.

Free walking tours of **Mission San Juan Capistrano** are offered every Sunday at 1 PM, whether the swallows are in town or not. The tours take in the ruins of the Great Stone Church, destroyed by an earthquake in 1812, the Serra Chapel, the mission's courtyards and fountains, and other historical sights.

Shopping Tours Several shopping shuttles help visitors make their own shopping tours. Six days a week, **South Coast Plaza's Shuttle Service** (tel. 714/241–1700) furnishes free round-trip transportation from many coastal area hotels to this ritzy shopping area. Santa Ana's **Main Place** (tel. 714/547–7800), a newly improved shopping center, offers several shuttles a day from Anaheim hotels. One-way fare is $2 adults, $1 children 12 and under. **The City Shopper** offers transportation to the Crystal Cathedral, the City Shopping Center in Orange, and local hotels for $1 one way. Information is available at hotels.

Important Addresses and Numbers

Tourist Information The main source of tourist information is the **Anaheim Area Convention and Visitors Bureau,** located at the Anaheim Convention Center (800 West Katella Ave., 92802, tel. 714/999–8999). The **Guest Information Hot Line,** (tel. 714/635–8900) offers information on entertainment, special events, and sightseeing tours in Orange County. This recording also describes amusement-park hours and major attractions.

Other area chambers of commerce and visitors bureaus are generally open Monday–Friday 9–5 and will help with information.

Buena Park Visitors Bureau (7711 Beach Blvd., 90261, tel. 714/994–1511).

Newport Harbor Chamber of Commerce (1470 Jamboree Rd., 92660, tel. 714/644–8211).

Huntington Beach Chamber of Commerce (Seacliff Village, 2213 Main St., 92648, tel. 714/536–8888).

Laguna Beach Chamber of Commerce (357 Glenneyre, 92651, tel. 714/494–1018).

Dana Point Chamber of Commerce (Box 12, 92629, tel. 714/496–1555).

San Juan Capistrano Visitors Center (inside the mission, 31882 Camino Capistrano, tel. 714/493–1424). **San Juan Capistrano Visitors Bureau** (31682 El Camino Real, 92675, tel. 714/493–4700).

San Clemente Tourism Bureau (31199 N. El Camino Real, 92672, tel. 714/492–1131).

Emergencies Dial 911 for **police** and **ambulance** in an emergency.

Orange County is so spread out and comprised of so many different communities that it is best to ask at your hotel for the closest emergency room. Here are a few: **Anaheim Memorial Hospital** (1111 W. La Palma, tel. 714/774–1450), **Western Medical Center** (1025 S. Anaheim Blvd., Anaheim, tel. 714/533–6220), **Hoag Memorial Hospital** (301 Newport Blvd., Newport Beach, tel. 714/645–8600), **South Coast Medical Center** (31872 Coast Hwy., South Laguna, tel. 714/499–1311).

Exploring Orange County

Residents have long battled the popular belief that Orange County's borders start and end at Disneyland. We take the more enlightened view that there are two sides to the county—the theme parks that dominate the inland area (of which Disneyland is certainly first and foremost), and the coastline. And so, we've divided our Exploring section into two parts.

As the county lacks a defined center, day trips will typically be destination oriented, rather than open explorations. If you're traveling with children, you can easily devote several full days to the theme parks: a day or two at Disneyland, a day at Knott's Berry Farm, and perhaps a day for driving between some of the area's lesser-known attractions. You'll have to head to the beach towns to rent a sailboard, or other water-sports paraphernalia. Cultural events take place at the Orange County Performing Arts Center. The coastline is the only place for meandering. Beach days can mix sunning, studying surf culture, and browsing through the small shops in the beach communities.

Inland Orange County

Numbers in the margin correspond with points of interest on the Orange County map.

Anaheim is indisputably the West's capital of family entertainment. With Disneyland, Knott's Berry Farm, and Movieland Wax Museum, there are as many rides and attractions and as much color and merriment as anyone could want. The Anaheim Convention Center attracts almost as many conventions as Disneyland attracts children. For many visitors to Anaheim, a family trip to Disneyland may be an added attraction of an Anaheim meeting.

❶ Perhaps more than any other attraction in the world, **Disneyland,** the lasting physical evidence of Walt Disney's dream, is a symbol of the enduring child in all of us, a place of wonder and enchantment—also an exceptionally clean, well-managed, and imaginatively developed wonder. Decades ago, when the Yippies staged a small demonstration there, the papers reported that a woman stepped from behind a stroller to remind them that there were children present. There always are—plus many jaded adults who find they can't help but enjoy themselves.

Disney built the park in 1955, and new attractions are added every year. The newest, open just a year, is Splash Mountain in the Bear County area of the park. The highlight here is an eight-passenger flume ride inspired by the Disney film *Song of the South*. The combination thrill-and-show ride features more than 100 of Disney's signature robotic characters, including Brer Fox, Brer Rabbit, and Brer Bear. At one point the flume drops 52 feet at 40 miles an hour, the longest, fastest flume ride anywhere, according to Disney.

Star Tours is based on the popular movie *Star Wars* and is guided by those charming robots C3PO and R2D2. The story goes like this: The robots are now working for an intergalactic travel agency and you go on a trip with them in a star speeder; as you head for space, you find yourself in the middle of a battle between the rebel and imperial forces. The very realistic ride uses flight simulator technology.

All of the old standbys in Disneyland are still going strong. Disney's ideal turn-of-the-century Main Street is what first greets visitors; through it are Tomorrowland, Frontierland, Fantasyland, and Adventureland. Tomorrowland is the site of Star Tours, and also of the popular *Captain EO*, the Michael Jackson 3D movie directed by Francis Ford Coppola. Space Mountain is a thrilling ride through space.

Fantasyland is the favorite domain of kids: The Pinocchio's Daring Journey ride takes you through this favorite puppet's escapade; a fly-through waterfall is only one element of the Peter Pan Flight; and logs turn into crocodiles in Snow White's Scary Adventure.

Frontierland takes visitors back to the Wild West. Big Thunder Mountain, one of the newer rides, is a runaway mine-car roller coaster. For a much more relaxing ride, the *Mark Twain* and *Columbia* river vessels take passengers on an exploration of the river, complete with Tom Sawyer's Island.

Time Out   **Blue Bayou,** featuring Creole food, is a great place to eat. It is located in the entrance to the Pirates of the Caribbean, so you can hear the antics in the background.

Adventureland's Jungle Cruise is another popular water-based ride, with jungle sounds and realistic snapping crocodiles. The Pirates of the Caribbean is a swashbuckling adventure with cannonballs flying overhead to the accompaniment of a catchy pirate tune. *1313 Harbor Blvd., Anaheim, tel. 714/999–4565. Admission: $25.50 adults, $20.50 children 3–12; this allows entrance to all the rides and attractions. In summer, open Sun.–Fri. 9 AM–midnight, Sat. 9 AM–1 AM; in fall, winter, and spring, open Mon.–Fri. 10–6, weekends 9–midnight.*

2 Knott's Berry Farm, another family tradition, is located in nearby Buena Park. Several decades ago, people used to come to a 10-acre fruit patch here for Mrs. Knott's home cooking and the re-created ghost town. Now Knott's is a 150-acre complex with more than 60 eating places, 60 shops, and 100 rides and attractions. The new Boomerang thrill ride gives the sensation that you are falling out as you take its six loops. Wild Water Wilderness, set in a California river wilderness park of the early 1900s, is a new attraction featuring a raging white-water river, cascading waterfall, and geysers, landscaped with indigenous California trees. Bigfoot Rapids, a white-water rafting ride, incorporates the legend of Bigfoot; the ride itself is more than ⅓-mile long. Floating rafts pass towering cliffs, race under waterfalls, and shoot the rapids. Bigfoot memorabilia—photos, footprints, etc.,—are on hand in the "ranger's station."

Time Out Don't forget what made Knott's famous: Mrs. Knott's fried chicken dinners and boysenberry pies at **Mrs. Knott's Chicken Dinner Restaurant,** just outside the park in Knott's Marketplace.

The other themed areas at Knott's include Camp Snoopy, a children's wonderland set in California's high Sierras; Ghost Town, an authentic 1880s Old West town; and Fiesta Village, a salute to California's Spanish heritage. Knott's is known for its daring thrill rides. "Montezooma's" Revenge accelerates from 0 to 55 mph in less than five seconds. The Corkscrew is the world's first upside-down roller coaster, featuring two 360-degree loops. And the Parachute Sky Jump falls 20 stories. *8039 Buena Park Blvd., Buena Park, tel. 714/220–5200. Admission: $21 adults, $16 children 3–12, $15 senior citizens over 60, expectant mothers, and handicapped visitors. Open in summer, Sun.–Fri. 10 AM–midnight, Sat. 10 AM–1 AM; in winter, Mon.–Fri. 10–6, Sat. 10–10, Sun. 10–7.*

3 Visitors will find 70 years of movie magic immortalized at **Movieland Wax Museum** in 240 wax sculptures of Hollywood's greatest stars. Realistic movie sets are the backdrop for such celebs as Bette Davis, Judy Garland, Marilyn Monroe, Redd Foxx, Sammy Davis, Jr., George Burns, Clint Eastwood, Mel Gibson, and Roger Moore. The Black Box is the newest attraction here; it takes visitors through scary scenes from *Alien, Halloween,* and *Altered States. 7711 Buena Park Blvd., 1 block north of Knott's, tel. 714/522–1155. Admission: $9.95 adults, $5.95 children. Open daily in summer 9–10; daily in winter 10–9.*

4 Garden Grove, a community adjacent to Anaheim and Buena Park, is the site of one of the most impressive churches in the country, the **Crystal Cathedral.** The domain of television evangelist Robert Schuller, the glass edifice resembles a four-pointed star. More than 10,000 panes of glass cover the weblike steel truss to form translucent walls. The feeling as you enter is nothing less than mystical. A *Newsweek* writer called the building, designed by the renowned architect Philip Johnson, "the most spectacular religious edifice in the world." In addition to tours of the cathedral, two pageants are offered yearly: "The Glory of Christmas" and "The Glory of Easter." These dramas, which include live animals in the cast, flying angels, and other special effects, are seen by more than 200,000 people each year.

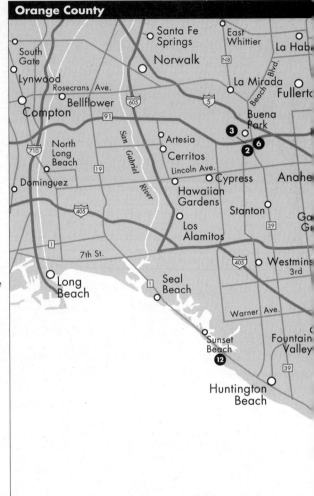

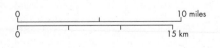

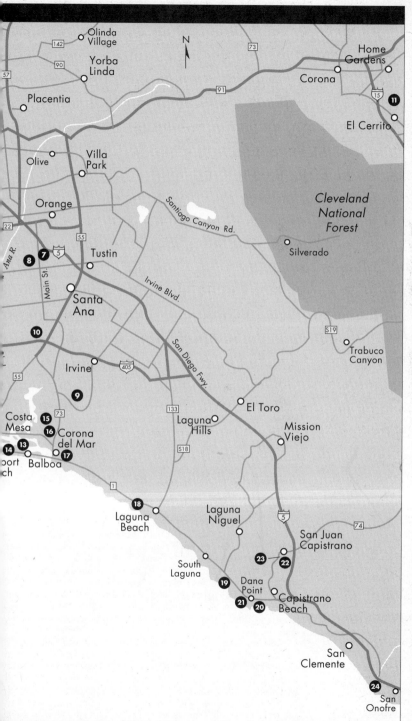

12141 Lewis St., Garden Grove, tel. 714/971–4013. Admission free. Usually open for self-guided tours Mon.–Sat. 9–3:30, Sun. 1:30–3:30. For reservations for the Easter and Christmas productions, call 714/54–GLORY.

⑤ Several unique museums fill the inland area. The **Anaheim Museum,** which recently moved to the Carnegie Library Building, constructed circa 1908, explores the prehistory and geology of the area as well as Anaheim's wine-producing story. *133 S. Anaheim Blvd., tel. 714/778–3301. Suggested admission: $1.50 adults, $1 senior citizens. Open Wed.–Fri. 10–4, Sat. noon–4, closed Sun.*

⑥ The **Museum of World Wars and Military History** will fascinate history buffs. Included in the $2-million collection are military field equipment, armor, uniforms, posters, and armored vehicles. *7884 E. La Palma Ave. (at Beach Blvd.), Buena Park, tel. 714/952–1776. Admission: $1 adults. Open daily from 11–6, Sun. noon–6.*

⑦ The **Bowers Museum** presents cultural arts of the Americas, the Pacific Rim, and Africa. Each year it does exhibitions of international, national, and regional scope. *2002 N. Main St., Santa Ana, tel. 714/972–1900. Admission free. Open Tues.– Sat. 10–5, Sun. noon–5.*

Santa Ana, the county seat, is undergoing a dramatic restoration in its downtown area. Gleaming new government buildings meld with turn-of-the-century structures to give a sense of **⑧** where the county came from and where it is going. The **Fiesta Marketplace** is a new downtown development that has been recognized as a grass-roots effort involving businesspeople and government. The Spanish-style, 4-block project brings life to one of the traditionally most successful Hispanic marketplaces in Southern California.

Known for its forward-looking concept of community planning, **⑨** Irvine is also a center for higher education. The **University of California at Irvine** was established on land donated by the Irvine Company in the mid-1950s. The Bren Events Center's Fine Art Gallery on campus sponsors exhibitions of 20th-century art (free, Tues.–Sat. 10–5). Tree lovers will be enthralled by the campus: it's an arboretum with more than 11,000 trees from all over the world. *Take the San Diego Freeway (I–405) to Jamboree Rd. Go west to Campus Dr. S.*

It is no small irony that the Costa Mesa/South Coast Metro area is known first for its posh shopping mall and then for its per-**⑩** forming arts center. **South Coast Plaza** (3333 South Bristol St. in Costa Mesa) attracts more than 20 million visitors a year, making it the busiest mall in Southern California. This is Adventureland for the credit card set, built around attractions named Polo/Ralph Lauren, Charles Jourdan, Godiva Chocolates and Courrèges. The adjacent **Orange County Performing Arts Center** (600 Town Center Dr., tel. 714/556–2787) is a world-class complex, hosting such notables as the Los Angeles Philharmonic, the Pacific Symphony, and the New York Opera. California Scenario, a 1.6-acre sculpture garden designed by artist Isamu Noguchi, connects the arts center and the mall, completing this unusual union of art and upscale consumerism. Noguchi uses sandstone, running water, concrete, and native plants to evoke different aspects of the California environment.

Time Out   For a quick, healthful meal during a South Coast Plaza visit, try **Forty Carats** on the lower level between Saks and Bullocks. This spin-off of a restaurant in Bloomingdale's department store has a selection of tasty natural muffins, carrot and pumpkin among them.

After you have sightseen yourself to exhaustion, you might want to try the ultimate in the California spa experience at **①** **Glen Ivy Hot Springs.** Thirty-five miles east of Anaheim, the spa is a day-use only resort. It features an Olympic-size mineral water pool, seven outdoor whirlpool baths, and a pool designed for tanning. The highlight is California's only European-style clay bath. Certified massage therapists are on duty. *Take Hwy. 91 east to I–15 south. Continue 8 mi to Temescal Canyon Rd. and exit. Make 2 immediate rights and take Glen Ivy Rd. to its end. Tel. 714/277–3529. Admission: $14.75 weekends and holidays; $12.50 weekdays. Open daily 10–6.*

The Coast

To explore Orange County's coast you need four things: a car, the Pacific Coast Highway, comfortable walking shoes, and a supply of sun block. The highway serves as the main thoroughfare for all the beach towns along the coast. Small in scale, these communities are eminently walkable, so park the car to have a look about. We'll start our tour in the north and head south.

Huntington Beach is a living museum of Southern California beach life. Each September, surfers from around the world converge on the city for its annual surfing competition. Unfortunately, Huntington pier, the best place to observe the sporting and social scene, is closed this year for a major renovation. The facelift will include a new theater, restaurant, and shopping complex scheduled to open this year across the street from the pier.

⑫ You won't find surfers at the **Bolsa Chica Ecological Reserve,** but you may well meet a great blue heron, light-footed clapper rail, or harlequin duck. Close to 200 different species of birds have been sighted at the 300-acre salt marsh located off the Pacific Coast Highway between Warner Avenue and Golden West Street. On the first Saturday of each month, from October through March, the Amigos de Bolsa Chica offer guided tours of the reserve (tel. 714/897–7003; call for a schedule).

Newport Beach is the county's bastion of high society. Yacht clubs and country clubs thrive and host one gala party after the next. The community got its start as a commercial shipping center, but now it has become one of the county's most popular recreation and shopping areas.

In this Beverly Hills-by-the-sea community, boats are as numerous as BMWs; nearly 10,000 of them bob gently on the swells in Newport Harbor. During the Christmas season the boats are decorated with more lights than most homes, making for lively, showy parades in and out of the harbor. In June, the annual Flight of the Snowbirds Regatta takes place; the first race was run in 1926.

The U-shaped harbor, with the mainland along one leg and Balboa Peninsula along the other, shelters eight small islands. **Balboa Island,** connected to the peninsula by a three-car ferry, is the most visited. You can drive directly to the island (via Jamboree, off the Pacific Coast Highway), but the ferry—one of the few remaining in the state—offers significantly more atmosphere. The Victorian Balboa Pavilion is the architectural jewel of the peninsula. Built in 1902 as a bath and boat house, the pavilion was a haven for the big band sound in the 1940s. Today it hosts boating facilities for harbor cruises, a sport fishing fleet, whale watching boats (December through February), and a restaurant. The **Newport Pier** dates back to 1888.

Near the pier is a section called the Fun Zone. It has a carnival feel with an old-fashioned Ferris wheel, arcades, and novelty concessions. And you can get a renowned Balboa Bar (chocolate covered frozen banana) here without going to Balboa Island. *To get to the Balboa Peninsula, take Hwy. 55 (Newport Freeway) southwest until it becomes Newport Blvd. At the end, bear left onto Balboa Blvd.*

The **Newport Harbor Art Museum** is internationally known for its impressive collection of works by California artists. The emphasis is on contemporary art, and there are many changing exhibits. Snacks are available in the Sculpture Garden Cafe. *850 San Clemente Dr., tel. 714/759–1122. A donation is requested. Open Tues.–Sun. 10–5.*

Fashion Island is another Newport Beach signature venue. Atrium Court, a Mediterranean-style plaza, is especially popular with upscale shoppers. Splash and Flash, with trendy swimwear; Amen Wardy, with the most haughty of women's fashions; and Posh, a unique men's store, are just some of the entries. In the first-floor court, you can relax to the sounds of a grand piano. A recent expansion and renovation has added several new stores. *On Newport Center Dr. between Jamboree and MacArthur blvds., just off Pacific Coast Hwy.*

Time Out   **Irvine Ranch Farmers' Market,** in Fashion Island shopping center, sells a vast array of fresh produce, deli fare, and any other exotic food that you can imagine. It is best to visit off-hours; the place is mobbed at lunchtime.

Just south of Newport Beach, **Corona del Mar** is a small jewel of a town with an exceptional beach. You can walk clear out onto the bay on a rough-and-tumble rock jetty. The town itself stretches only a few blocks along the Pacific Coast Highway, but some of the fanciest stores and ritziest restaurants in the county are located here. **Sherman Library and Gardens,** a lush botanical garden and library specializing in Southwest flora and fauna, offers a diversion from sun and sand. Colorful seasonal flowers adorn the grounds, and you can have pastries and coffee in the tea garden. *2647 E. Coast Hwy., Corona del Mar, tel. 714/673–2261. Admission: $2. Open daily 10:30–4.*

If Newport is a seaside Beverly Hills, **Laguna Beach** is the SoHo of the surf. About 60 art galleries peacefully coexist with the endless volleyball games and parades of people on Main Beach. Local shops offer crafts and current fashion in addition to canvases and sculptures. In the true spirit of the 60s, when Timothy Leary and his hippie cronies used to hang out in Laguna's fast-food joints along Pacific Coast Highway, the artistic style here can best be described as anything goes. Expect to see placid dune and ocean watercolors as well as shocking neon-colored works and out-of-the-ordinary assemblages of found objects.

⑱ The **Laguna Beach Museum of Art** has two locations. In Laguna Beach (307 Cliff Dr., tel. 714/494–6531), right near Heisler Park, the museum offers exhibits of historical and contemporary American art. The smaller gallery near the Carousel Court at South Coast Plaza (tel. 714/662–3366), offers smaller scale exhibits in the same vein.

In front of the Pottery Barn on the Coast Highway is a bit of local nostalgia—a life-size statue of Eiler Larson, the town greeter. For years, he stood at the edge of town saying hellos and goodbye to visitors.

Laguna's many festivals give it a worldwide reputation in the arts community. During July and August, the Sawdust Festival and Art-a-Fair, the Festival of the Arts, and the **Pageant of the Masters** take place. The Pageant of the Masters (tel. 714/494–1147) is Laguna's most impressive event, a blending of life and art. Live models and carefully orchestrated backgrounds are arranged in striking mimicry of famous paintings. Participants must hold a perfectly still pose for the length of their stay on stage. It is an impressive effort, requiring hours of training and rehearsal by the 400 or so residents who volunteer each year.

Going to Laguna without exploring its beaches would be a shame. To get away from the hubbub of Main Beach, go north to Woods Cove, off the Coast Highway at Diamond Street; it's especially quiet during the week. Big rock formations hide lurking crabs. As you climb the steps to leave, you'll see a stunning English-style mansion, once the home of Bette Davis. At the end of almost every street in Laguna, there is another little cove with its own beach.

⑲ The **Ritz Carlton** in Laguna Niguel is the classiest hotel for miles, and has become a watering hole for the movers and shakers of Orange County. Gleaming marble and stunning antiques fill this posh hotel, and traditional English tea is served each afternoon to the strains of live piano music. *33533 Ritz Carlton Dr., Laguna Niguel, tel. 714/240–2000.*

⑳ It's been a popular port town for some 150 years, but recently, **Dana Point** has really started to boom. New shops, restaurants, and hotels are opening at a fast pace. The town's harbor, set on a secluded cove surrounded by steep, jagged cliffs, is the main attraction. Boats can be rented at Dana Wharf Sportsfishing (tel. 714/496–5794) for fishing or other recreation. The beach is also a draw. In the summer, it's not unusual to see the adventurous parasailing above the sun worshipers; come winter, attention typically turns to whale-watching (for information, call 714/496–4794). Mariners Village is the harbor's shopping area, a nautically themed, not terribly original, affair.

㉑ The **Orange County Marine Institute** is a unique educational facility that helps adults and children explore the ocean environment. A 65-foot diesel sports-fishing boat is a floating laboratory; hands-on opportunities allow you to study marine life. Anchored near the institute is *The Pilgrim*, a full-size replica of the square-rigged vessel on which sailed Richard Henry

Dana, the author of *Two Years Before the Mast,* for whom the town is named. Tours of *The Pilgrim* are offered one Sunday each month. *Dana Point Harbor Dr. and Del Obispo, tel. 714/ 496–2274. Open daily 9–3.*

San Juan Capistrano is best known for its mission, and of course, for the swallows that migrate here each year from their winter haven in Argentina. The arrival of the birds on St. Joseph's Day, March 19, launches a week of celebration. After summering in the arches of the old stone church, the swallows head home on St. John's Day, October 23.

㉒ Founded in 1776 by Father Junipero Serra, **Mission San Juan Capistrano** was the major Roman Catholic outpost between Los Angeles and San Diego. Although the original Great Stone Church lies in ruins, due to an 1812 earthquake, many of the mission's adobe buildings have been restored and the grounds are well-kept. The impressive Serra Chapel is believed to be the oldest building still in use in California. The knowledgeable staff in the mission's visitors center can help you with a self-guided tour. *Camino Capistrano and Ortega Hwy., tel. 714/ 493–1111. Admission: $2 adults, $1 children under 11. Open daily 7:30–5.*

㉓ Near the mission is the post-modern **San Juan Capistrano Library,** built in 1983. Architect Michael Graves mixed classical design with the style of the mission for a striking effect. It has a courtyard with private places for reading as well as a running water fountain. *31495 El Camino Real. Open Mon.–Thurs. 10–9, Fri.–Sat. 10–5.*

Time Out The **Capistrano Depot** (26701 Verdugo St., tel. 714/496–8181) is not only a train station for Amtrak, but also a restaurant and jazz spot. White tablecloths, linen napkins, and flowers grace the restaurant, which specializes in rack of lamb, prime rib, and combinations of filet Mignon and scampi for dinner. It's a perfect way to see San Juan if you are based in Los Angeles—a train ride, a meal, and then a little sightseeing.

The southernmost city in Orange County, San Clemente, is probably best remembered as the site of the Western White House during the Nixon years. Casa Pacifica made the news often in those years. The house, on a massive 25.4-acre estate, is visible from the beach; just look up to the cliffs.

㉔ Perhaps even more controversial than Nixon's house is the **San Onofre Nuclear Power Plant,** lending an eerie feeling to the nearby beach, where surfers surf nonetheless. Off the Coast Highway, the San Onofre Nuclear Information Center is a must for those who want to know more about the mechanics of nuclear energy.

San Clemente also offers a wide selection of activities that make Southern California the playground that it is: swimming, surfing, sailing, fishing, and picnicking. San Clemente State Beach is one of the least crowded and most beautiful of the state beaches.

In the summer, San Clemente is a whirl for nine days during La Christianita Pageant. The three-act play commemorates the first baptism of a Native American in California. (This may or may not be an event you feel needs honoring. Christianized Native Americans throughout the state died in very large numbers.) The pageant is presented in La Christianita Bowl, 3 miles from a wilderness clearing where it was first presented. Soldiers, priests, Native American rites, and singing make up the colorful production.

For avid bicycle riders, the next 20 miles south of San Clemente is prime terrain. Camp Pendleton welcomes cyclists to use its roads. But don't be surprised if you see a troop helicopter taking off right beside you. This is the country's largest Marine Corps base. Training involves off-shore landings; overland treks are also conducted on the installation's three mountain ranges, five lakes, and 250 miles of roads.

What to See and Do with Children

Disneyland and Knott's Berry Farm are the prime attractions (*see* Exploring, above), but there are many other amusements designed for children and families.

Raging Waters is a water theme park sure to please the whole family. It's actually in southeast Los Angeles County, but not far from Anaheim. Clean beaches and river rapids (man-made), water slides, and safe water fun for the smallest of children are found here. *111 Via Verde, San Dimas, where I–10 and I–210 meet (take the Raging Waters Blvd. exit), tel. 714/592–6453. Admission: $14.95 adults, $8.50 children 42–48," children under 42" free, reduced prices for senior citizens and non-sliders. Open May–June, daily 10–6, the rest of the summer Mon.– Thurs. 10–9, weekends 9–10.*

Wild Rivers is Orange County's newest water theme park. It has more than 40 rides and attractions. Among them: a wave pool, several daring slides, a river inner-tube ride, and several places to eat and shop. *8800 Irvine Center Dr., Laguna Hills (just off I–405 at Irvine Center Dr.), tel. 714/768–WILD. Admission: $14.95 adults, $10.95 children 3–9; discounts after 4 PM. Open mid-May to mid-Sept. Call for hours.*

Hobby City Doll and Toy Museum houses antique dolls and toys from around the world in a replica of the White House. It is one of the world's largest hobby, craft, and collector centers. *1238 S. Beach Blvd., Anaheim, tel. 714/527–2323.*

La Habra Children's Museum features all kinds of diversions for children. The restored 1923 railroad depot has a beehive, railroad cars, and several touchable displays. *301 S. Euclid St., tel. 714/905–9793.*

Laguna Moulton Playhouse has a special children's theater with changing fare. *606 Laguna Canyon Rd. tel. 714/494–0743.*

Off the Beaten Track

If you find time to visit any of these spots during your trip to Orange County, you can term yourself local. These are some of the "in" spots that natives know well.

Lido Island. This beautiful island in Newport Harbor is the location of some of the most elegant homes in Orange County. It's an inviting spot for a walk and a great view of the boats. *Take Hwy. 55 to Pacific Coast Hwy. in Newport Beach. Turn left at the signal onto Via Lido and follow this street onto the island.*

Orange County Swapmeet. This is no ordinary flea market. With huge collection of items at big discounts, it's truly a Southern Californian way to spend the day, enjoying some beer and hot dogs in the sun. There are more than 1,000 vendors every Saturday and Sunday. Good bargains to look for include stereo equipment, plants, and artwork. *Orange County Fairgrounds, 88 Fair Dr., Costa Mesa (off Hwy. 55), tel. 714/751-3247.*

C'est Si Bon. This little cafe resembles quaint sidewalk cafes in Paris. It offers the best selection of coffee and croissants anywhere around; there is also a great selection of cheeses and pâtés. *Riverside Ave., off Pacific Coast Hwy. in Newport Beach, tel. 714/645-0447. Open Mon.–Fri. 6:30–6, Sat. 8–5, Sun. 8:30 AM–1:30 PM.*

Shopping

Shopping is Orange County's favorite indoor sport, and the region has the shops, malls, and arcades to prove it. Some of the most exclusive shopping areas in the world fill the Newport Beach area, and South Coast Plaza in Costa Mesa is the second-largest mall in the country. Following is just a small selection of the shopping available in the county.

South Coast Plaza's (Bristol and Sunflower sts.) 270 stores offer everything from tires to ball gowns. Saks Fifth Avenue, Nordstrom, Neiman Marcus, Bullocks, I. Magnin, May Company, Sears, the Broadway, and Robinson's are the department stores anchoring the mall. For literary buffs, there is a branch of the famous Rizzoli's International Bookstore.

Fashion Island on Newport Center Drive in Newport Beach sits on the top of a hill, so shoppers enjoy a distinct ocean breeze. It is an open-air, single level mall of more than 120 stores. Don't miss the Irvine Ranch Farmers Market, on the first level of the Atrium Court. This awesome market is a high quality, specialty gourmet store, surrounded by international eateries—a salsa bar, Italian bakery, and gourmet chocolate stand, to name a few.

The **City Shopping Center,** in Orange, is an enclosed mall enhanced with attractive landscaping. May Company and J.C. Penney are the department stores. **Buena Park Mall,** near Disneyland and Knott's, has more than 160 stores.

If you can look past the inflatable palm trees, unimaginative T-shirts and other tourist novelties, there is some good browsing to be done in Laguna Beach. This is Main Street USA kind of shopping, with antiques and crafts you won't find in a generic shopping mall. Dozens of art and custom jewelry shops dot the streets. There are more jewelers per capita in Laguna than in any other town in the country. Some of the more unusual Laguna stores include: **Chicken Little Emporium,** Coast Highway, with whimsical gifts and clothing; **From Laguna,** 241 Forest Avenue, for unique fashions; **Khyber Pass,** 384 Forest Avenue, with gifts from the Middle East and Afghanistan; and **Toni's Kids Closet,** Coast Highway, with designer children's clothing and handcrafted wooden toys.

Beaches

Huntington Beach State Beach runs for miles along Coast Highway (take Beach Blvd. if you are coming from inland). There are changing rooms, concessions, and lifeguard vigilance on the premises. **Bolsa Chica State Beach,** down the road and across from the Bolsa Chica Ecological Reserve, has facilities for barbecues and picnics.

Lower Newport Bay provides an enclave sheltered from the ocean. This area, off Coast Highway on Jamboree, is a 740-acre preserve for ducks and geese. **Newport Dunes Aquatic Park,** nearby, offers picnic facilities, changing rooms, and a place to launch boats.

Just south of Newport Beach, **Corona del Mar State Beach** has a tidepool and caves waiting to be explored. It also sports one of the best walks in the county—a beautiful rock pier jutting into the ocean.

The county's best place for scuba diving is in the **Marine Life Refuge,** which runs from Seal Rock to Diver's Cove in Laguna. Farther south, in South Laguna, **Aliso County Park** is a recreation area with a pier for fishing.

Doheny State Park, near the Dana Point Harbor, has food stands and shops nearby. Camping is permitted here; there are also picnic facilities and a pier for fishing. **San Clemente State Beach** is one of the least crowded. It has ample camping facilities and food stands. Boogie boards and small boats can be rented nearby as well.

Participant Sports

Orange County is a sportsperson's playground; from surfing to walking, from sailing to biking, there is something for everyone who wants to be active.

Bicycling Bicycles and roller skates are some of the most popular means of transportation along the beaches. Again, most beaches have rental stands. A bike path spans the whole distance from Marina del Rey all the way to San Diego, with some minor breaks. In Laguna, try the **Laguna Cyclery** (tel. 714/552–1798); in Huntington Beach, **Two Wheel Transit Authority** (tel. 714/951–4896).

Golf Golf is one of the most popular sports in Orange County, and owing to the climate, almost 365 days out of the year are perfect golf days. Here is a selection of golf courses:

Anaheim Hills Public Country Club (tel. 714/637–7311), **Costa Mesa Public Golf and Country Club** (tel. 714/540–7500), **Mile Square Golf Course,** Fountain Valley (tel. 714/545–3726), **Meadowlark Golf Course,** Huntington Beach (tel. 714/846–1364), **Rancho San Joaquin Golf Course,** Irvine (tel. 714/786–5522), **Costa del Sol Golf Course,** Mission Viejo (tel. 714/581–9040), **Newport Beach Golf Course** (tel. 714/852–8681), **San Clemente Municipal Golf Course** (tel. 714/361–8278), **San Juan Hills Country Club,** San Juan Capistrano (tel. 714/837–0361), **Aliso Creek Golf Course,** South Laguna (tel. 714/499–1919).

Snorkeling Corona del Mar is off-limits to boats; this fact—along with its two colorful reefs—make it a great place for snorkeling. Laguna Beach is also a good spot for snorkeling and diving; the whole beach area of this city is a marine preserve.

Surfing Orange County's signature sport may be too rough and tumble for some; you can get the same feel with a boogie board. Rental stands are found at all beaches. And body surfing is also a good way to start. Huntington Beach is popular for surfers and spectators. "The Wedge" at Newport Beach is one of the most famous surfing spots in the world. Don't miss the spectacle of surfers, who look tiny in the middle of the waves, flying through this treacherous place. San Clemente surfers are usually positioned right across from the San Onofre Nuclear Reactor.

Swimming All of the state, county, and city beaches in Orange County allow swimming. Make sure there is a manned lifeguard stand nearby and you are safe. Also keep on the lookout for posted signs about undertow, as it can be mighty nasty in certain places.

Tennis Most of the larger hotels have tennis courts. Here are some other choices; try the local Yellow Pages for further listings.

Huntington Beach **Edison Community Center** (21377 Magnolia St., tel. 714/960–8870) has four courts available on a first-come, first-served basis, or reservations can be made. The **Murdy Community Center** (70000 Norma Dr., tel. 714/960–8895) requires reservations.

Newport Beach Call the recreation department at 714/644–3151 for information about court use at **Corona del Mar High School,** 2102 East Bluff Street. There are eight courts for public use.

Laguna Beach Eight metered courts can be found at **Laguna Beach High School,** on Park Avenue. On Monday, Wednesday, and Friday, courts are also available at the **Irvine Bowl,** Laguna Canyon Road.

San Clemente There are four courts at **San Luis Rey Park,** on Avenue San Luis Rey. They are offered on a first-come, first-served basis. Call the recreation department at 714/361–8200 for further information.

Water Sports Rental stands for surfboards, windsurfers, small power boats, and sailboats, can almost always be found near most of the piers. Here are some of the more well-known rental places; **Hobie Sports** has three locations for surfboard and boogie board rentals—two in Dana Point (tel. 714/496–2366 or 714/496–1251) and one in Laguna (tel. 714/497–3304).

In the biggest boating town of all, Newport Beach, you can rent sailboats and small motorboats at **Balboa Boat Rentals** in the harbor (tel. 714/673–1320; open Fri.–Sun. 9 AM–sundown). Sailboats rent for $20 an hour, and motorboats for $26 an hour. You must have a driver's license, and some knowledge of boating is helpful; rented boats are not allowed out of the bay.

In Dana Point, power and sailboats can be rented at **Embarcadero Marina** (tel. 714/496–6177), near the launching ramp at Dana Point Harbor. Boat sizes vary—sailboats range $12–$50 for two hours, motorboats are $17 an hour.

Spectator Sports

Orange County has some of the best unplanned, casual spectator sports; besides the surfers, you are bound to catch a volleyball or basketball game at any beach on a weekend. Professional sports in Orange County include the following:

Baseball   The **California Angels** (tel. 714/634–2000) play at the Anaheim Stadium from April through October.

Football   The **Los Angeles Rams** (tel. 714/937–6767) have called Anaheim Stadium their home since 1980. The season runs from August through December.

Horse Racing   The **Los Alamitos Race Course** (tel. 714/995–1234) has quarter horse racing and harness racing on a ⅝-mile track. Thoroughbred racing is part of the fare here as well.

Horse Shows   Twice monthly at the **Orange County Fair Equestrian Center** (714/641–1328) show jumping is featured. Admission is free.

Dining

by Bruce David Colen   Orange County seems to prove that nothing improves the quality of restaurants quite so much as being in a high-rent district. Since the region became the nation's most costly place to buy a home, the dining scene is vastly improved. Interestingly, prices are not generally as high as in the upscale communities of Los Angeles and San Francisco. The growing number of luxury hotels, with dining rooms to match, has also broadened gastronomic choices. The French cuisine at Le Meridien, in Newport, is the best of any California hotel. Unless otherwise noted, a sport jacket or blazer are proper dining attire. It is always safest to call ahead for reservations.

Highly recommended restaurants are indicated by a star ★ .

Category	Cost*
Very Expensive	over $40
Expensive	$30–$40
Moderate	$15–$30
Inexpensive	under $15

*per person, without tax, service, or drinks

Anaheim
Expensive   **Bessie Wall's.** Citrus rancher John Wall built this house for his bride-to-be in 1927. It has been restored, and the rooms converted into dining areas decorated with Wall memorabilia. Bessie's favorite chicken and dumplings recipe is on the menu, which also features Southern California-Mexican dishes. The place is nostalgic fun. *1074 N. Tustin Blvd., tel. 714/630–2812. Reservations advised. AE, DC, MC, V. Closed Sat. lunch.*

JW'S. You would never guess you were in a hotel—the dining room looks like a French country inn, complete with a fireplace. The food is well-prepared classic French, featuring roasted saddle of lamb, venison, and wild boar. *Marriott Hotel, 700 W. Convention Way, tel. 714/750–8000. Reservations required. Jacket required. Valet parking. AE, MC, V, DC. Dinner only. Closed Sun.*

Overland Stage. A dining Disneyland of sorts. The theme is California in its Wild West days. There's a stagecoach over the entrance and all sorts of Western Americana bric-a-brac within. Some of the daily specials are equally intriguing: wild boar, buffalo, rattlesnake, bear, and elk. *1855 S. Harbor Blvd., tel. 714/750–1811. Reservations advised. AE, DC, MC, V. Closed for lunch weekends.*

Corona del Mar
Expensive

Trees. The contempory look, atmosphere, and menu of this upscale restaurant are among the most appealing in Orange County. The three dining rooms, with walls and table appointments done in shades of pink, surround a glassed-in atrium planted with towering ficus trees. Each room has its own fireplace, and satisfying cooking matches the setting: Maryland crab cakes, roast turkey dinners on Sunday; Chinese chicken salad, potstickers and spring rolls; veal sweetbreads in puff pastry. Don't pass up the apricot mousse dessert. There's also a piano bar. *440 Heliotrope Ave., tel. 714/673–0910. Reservations required. Jacket required. AE, DC, MC, V. Closed for lunch.*

Moderate
★

The Five Crowns. A surprisingly faithful replica of Ye Old Bell, England's oldest inn (ca. 1135). The barmaids and waitresses are costumed in Elizabethan dress; there's a wide array of British ales and, of course, Guinness stout. The roast beef with Yorkshire pudding and rack of lamb are very good, as are the fish dishes, all at reasonable prices. *3801 E. Pacific Coast Hwy., tel. 714/760–0331. Reservations required. AE, DC, MC, V. Dinner only, Mon.–Sat., and Sun. brunch.*

Costa Mesa
Expensive

Gemmel's. This sophisticated, charming restaurant is in a not very attractive, commercial neighborhood. But once you're through the front door, you'll think you're in New York or London. Chef Gemmel's cooking is cosmopolitan: He smokes his own salmon and makes a hearty duck pâté; there's smoked quail with dill and noodles, sautéed Maine lobster, and poached whitefish in a mustard sauce. All in all, worth dressing for. *3000 Bristol St., tel. 714/751–1074. Reservations required. AE, DC, MC, V. Closed Sat. lunch and Sun.*

Watercolors. The light, cheerful dining room has a cliff-top view of the harbor and an equally enjoyable Continental/California menu, along with low calorie choices. Try the baked breast of pheasant, roast rabbit, or grilled swordfish, and either the Caesar salad or poached spinach salad. *Dana Point Resort, tel. 714/661–5000. Dress: casual. Valet parking. Reservations advised. AE, DC, MC, V.*

Moderate–Expensive

Alfredo's. Northern Italian dishes served in a attractive, multilevel dining room, beneath a huge skylight. There's lots of cheerful greenery with service to match. Menu suggestions include mozzarella marinara, scampi sautéed with garlic and white wine, chicken and spinach cannelloni, and a fine seafood salad. Brunch is served on Sundays. *666 Anton Blvd., tel. 714/540–1550. Reservations recommended. Jacket required. AE, DC, MC, V. Closed Sat. lunch and Sun. dinner.*

Dana Point
Moderate

Chart House. This is one of the most popular of the small chain of steak and seafood houses in Southern California. Mud pie is the dessert everyone asks for. This particular location has a sensational view of the harbor from most of the tables and booths. *34442 Green Lantern, tel. 714/493–1183. Reservations advised. AE, DC, MC, V. Dinner only.*

Delaney's Restaurant. Seafood from nearby San Diego's fishing fleet is what this place is all about. Your choice is prepared as simply as possible. If you have to wait for a table, pass the time at the clam and oyster bar. *25001 Dana Dr., tel. 714/496–6196. Reservations advised. AE, DC, MC, V.*

Fullerton
Expensive

The Cellar. And it is just that, a subterranean dining room, with beamed ceiling and stone walls, wine casks and racks. The European and California wine list is among the best in the nation. The classic French cuisine is lightened up for the California palate. *305 N. Harbor Blvd., tel. 714/525–5682. Reservations required. AE, DC, MC, V. Dinner only; closed Sun. and Mon.*

Huntington Beach
Moderate

MacArthur Park. Modeled after the popular San Francisco restaurant, this casual eatery has a view of Huntington Harbor. Contemporary art hangs on brick walls. Standouts on the California menu are smoked filet Mignon appetizers and sweet potatoes with tequila-and-lime sauce. *16390 Pacific Coast Hwy., tel. 714/846–5553. Weekend reservations advised. AE, MC, V.*

Inexpensive

Texas Loosey's Chili Parlor & Saloon. This place features Tex-Mex cooking with hot fixings, plus steaks, ribs, and burgers. Country-western music is played at night. *14160 Beach Blvd., tel. 714/898–9797. Dress: casual. MC, V.*

Irvine
Moderate–Expensive

Chanteclair. This Franco-Italian country house is a lovely, tasteful retreat in an island of modern, high-rise office buildings. French Riviera-type cuisine is served; Châteaubriand for two and rack of lamb are recommended. *18912 MacArthur Blvd., tel. 714/752–8001. Reservations advised. Jacket required. AE, DC, MC, V. No lunch Sat., Sunday brunch.*

Moderate

Gulliver's. Jolly old England is the theme of this groaning board. Waitresses are addressed as "wenches" and busboys as "squires." Prime rib is the specialty. *18482 MacArthur Blvd., tel. 714/833–8411. Reservations advised. MC, V.*

Pavilion. Excellent Chinese food is offered in what resembles a formal eating hall in Chef Hu's native Taiwan. Specialties include steamed whole fish, ginger duck, and Hunan lamb. *14110 Culver Dr., tel. 714/551–1688. Reservations advised. AE, MC, V.*

Prego. A much larger version of the Beverly Hills Prego, this one is located in an attractive approximation of a Tuscan villa, with an outdoor patio. A favorite of Orange County's Yuppies, who rave about the watch-the-cooks-at-play open kitchen and the oak-burning pizza oven. Try the spit-roasted meats and chicken, or the charcoal-grilled fresh fish. Also try the California or Italian wines. *18420 Von Karman Ave., tel. 714/553–1333. Closed for lunch weekends. Dress: casual. Valet parking. AE, MC, V.*

Laguna Beach
Expensive
★

The Ritz-Carlton. The Dining Room in this oceanside resort hotel serves rather pretentious pseudo-*nouvelle* cuisine, but the lavish Sunday brunch served in The Cafe is considered the best in Southern California. Be sure to make reservations several days in advance and ask for a table on the terrace, overlooking the swimming pool. *33533 Ritz-Carlton Dr., Niguel, tel. 714/240–2000. Reservations required. AE, DC, MC, V. Dinner only in the Dining Room, lunch and dinner in The Cafe.*

Moderate **Las Brisas.** A longtime coastal favorite, this restaurant features a spectacular view of the rugged coastline from the clifftop terrace, wonderful margaritas, addictive guacamole, and *nouvelle* Mexican dishes. The first three compensate for the last. *361 Cliff Dr., tel. 714/497–5434. Reservations advised. AE, DC, MC, V.*

Partners Bistro. Beveled glass, antiques, and lace curtains adorn this neighborhood eatery. Fresh fish and tournedos of beef are featured on the somewhat Continental menu. *448 S. Coast Hwy., tel. 714/497–4441. Reservations recommended. MC, V.*

The White House. Bing Crosby and Cecil B. de Mille dined at this local hangout. The broad American menu has everything from bagels and lox to Mexican favorites. There's also a salad bar while you're making up your mind. *340 S. Coast Hwy., tel. 714/494–8088. No reservations. AE, DC, MC, V.*

Inexpensive **The Beach House.** A Laguna tradition, the Beach House has a white-water view from every table. Fresh fish, lobster, and steamed clams are the drawing cards. *619 Sleepy Hollow La., tel. 714/494–9707. Reservations advised. AE, MC, V.*

The Cottage. The menu is heavy on vegetarian dishes, and the price is right. Specialties include fresh fish, Victoria Beach scallops, and "chicken Alfredo." *308 N. Pacific Coast Hwy., tel. 714/494–3023. Weekend reservations advised. AE, MC, V.*

Tortilla Flats. This hacienda-styled restaurant specializes in first rate *chile rellenos, carne Tempiquena,* soft shell tacos, and beef or chicken *fajitas.* There's a wide selection of Mexican beers and tequilas. *1740 S. Coast Hwy., tel. 714/494–6588. Dinner reservations advised. AE, MC. V. Brunch only on Sun.*

Newport Beach **Antoine's.** This lovely, candlelit dining room is made for ro-
Expensive mance and quiet conversation. It serves the best French
★ cuisine of any hotel in Southern California; the fare is *nouvelle,* but neither skimpy nor tricky. *4500 MacArthur Blvd., tel. 714/476–2001. Reservations advised. Jacket and tie required. AE, DC, MC, V. Dinner only Mon.–Sat., Sun. brunch.*

★ **The Ritz.** One of the most pleasant and comfortable Southern California restaurants, the bar area has red leather booths, etched glass mirrors, and polished brass trim. Don't pass up the smorgasbord appetizer, the roast Bavarian duck, or the rack of lamb from the spit. This is one of those rare places that pleases everyone. *880 Newport Center Dr., tel. 714/720–1800. Reservations advised. Jacket required. AE, DC, MC, V. Closed Sat. lunch, closed Sun.*

Moderate **Le Biarritz.** Newport Beach natives have deep affection for this restaurant, with its country French decor, hanging greenery, and skylit garden room. There's food to match the mood: a veal and pheasant pâté, seafood crepes, boned duckling and wild rice, sautéed pheasant with raspberries, and warm apple tart for dessert. *414 N. Newport Blvd., tel. 714/645–6700. Reservations advised. AE, DC, MC, V. Closed weekend lunch.*

Bubbles Balboa Club. This whimsical take-off of a 1930s nightclub has cigarette "girls" and canned music from the Big Band era. While you're taking in the scene, order a steak or the grilled lamb chops. *111 Palm St., tel. 714/675–9093. Reservations advised. AE, DC, MC, V. Closed lunch.*

Cannery. The building was a cannery, and it has wonderful wharfside views. The seafood entrées are good, and the sandwiches at lunch are satisfying, but the location and lazy atmosphere are the real draw. *3010 Lafayette Ave., tel. 714/675-5777. Reservations advised. AE, DC, MC, V. Sunday brunch.*

Marrakesh. In a casbah setting, straight out of a Bob Hope "On the Road" movie, diners become part of the scene—you eat with your fingers while sitting on the floor or lolling on hassocks. Chicken *b'stilla*, rabbit *couscous*, and skewered pieces of marinated lamb are the best of the Moroccan dishes. It's what-the-heck-fun. *1100 W. Pacific Coast Hwy., tel. 714/645-8384. Reservations advised. AE, DC, MC, V. Closed lunch.*

Inexpensive

Crab Cooker. If you don't mind waiting in line, this shanty of a place serves fresh fish grilled over mesquite at low, low prices. The clam chowder and cole slaw are good, too. *2200 Newport Blvd., tel. 714/673-0100. No reservations. No credit cards.*

★ **El Torito Grill.** Southwestern cooking incorporating below-the-border specialties is the attraction here. The just-baked tortillas with a green pepper salsa, the turkey mole enchilada, and the blue corn duck tamalitos are good choices. The bar serves 20 different tequila brands and hand-shaken margaritas. *951 Newport Center Dr., tel. 714/640-2875. Reservations advised. AE, DC, MC, V.*

Orange
Very Expensive
★
Chez Cary. Orange County residents have been celebrating special events here for more than 25 years. It will be a costly evening, indeed. But you'll get excellent Continental cuisine with impeccable service, in an opulent, red plush dining room —and gold matchbooks imprinted with your name. *571 S. Main St., tel. 714/542-3595. Reservations required. Jacket and tie required. DC, MC, V. Closed lunch.*

Expensive

The Hobbit. This is the place to feast, if you can make reservations 2 to 3 months in advance. The 6-to 8-course French-Continental meal starts in the wine cellar at 7:30 and ends about three hours later. *2932 E. Chapman, tel. 714/997-1972. Reservations required far in advance. Jacket required. AE, DC, MC, V. One evening seating only.*

Moderate

La Brasserie. It doesn't look like a typical brasserie, but the varied French cuisine fits the name over the door. One dining room in the multi-floor house is done as an attractive, cozy library. There's also a most inviting bar-lounge. *202 S. Main, tel. 714/978-6161. Reservations advised. AE, DC, MC, V. Closed Sat. lunch and Sun.*

San Clemente
Moderate
Andreino's. Pasta is the key word at this Italian restaurant decorated with antiques, flowers, and lacy curtains. *1925 S. El Camino Real, tel. 714/492-9955. Reservations advised. AE, MC, V.*

Etienne's. Smack-dab in the center of town, this restaurant is housed in a white stucco historical landmark. There is outdoor seating on a terra-cotta patio with fountains. Indoors, the decor is Old French château. Only fresh fish is served; chateaubriand, frog legs, and other French favorites are on the menu, along with flaming desserts. *215 S. El Camino Real, tel. 714/492-7263. Reservations advised. AE, DC, MC, V. Closed for lunch Fri.; closed Sun.*

The Fish Tale. Twenty-five different kinds of beer are part of the fare at this seafood restaurant with turn-of-the-century decor. *111 W. Palizada, tel. 714/498-6072. Reservations recommended. AE, MC, V.*

Swallow's Cove. This elegant restaurant has peach linen cloths and high-backed upholstered chairs, with rosebuds on every table. The menu offers seafood, steak, and chicken; Chicken Judy—Mediterranean baked chicken—is a house special. *In the San Clemente Inn, 2600 Ave. del Presidente, tel. 714/492–6103. Weekend reservations advised. AE, DC, MC, V.*

San Juan Capistrano
Moderate

El Adobe. President Nixon memorabilia fills the walls in this early American-style eatery serving Mexican-American food. Mariachi bands play Wednesday–Sunday. *31891 Camino Capistrano, tel. 714/830–8620. AE, MC, V.*

L'Hirondelle. There are only 12 tables at this charming French inn. Duckling is the specialty, prepared three different ways. *31631 Camino Capistrano, tel. 714/661–0425. Reservations necessary. MC, V. Closed Mon.–Tues.*

Inexpensive

Swallow Inn. The food is Mexican, but the atmosphere is American West, complete with sawdust on the floor. Live entertainment Tuesday–Sunday. *31786 Camino Capistrano, tel. 714/493–3188. No credit cards.*

Santa Ana
Inexpensive

Saddleback Inn. The decor here takes Orange County back in time to hacienda days, blending Old Spain and Mission California. Slow-cooked barbecued roast beef is the house specialty; filet of sole amandine, barbecued baked chicken, and filet Mignon with bordelaise sauce are other possibilities. *1660 E. 1st St., tel. 714/835–3311. AE, V. Closed Sun.*

Lodging

Like cuisine, hotels have also come a long way in Orange County. Sophistication seems to grow with each new hotel opening. The beaches are the most expensive for lodging; family areas, like Anaheim, are full of more inexpensive, simpler motels, which are too numerous to list. Categories here are based on prices for summer; winter rates tend to be lower.

Highly recommended lodgings are indicated by a star ★ .

Category	Cost*
Very Expensive	over $110
Expensive	$80–$110
Moderate	$60–$80
Inexpensive	under $60

for a double room, not including tax

Anaheim
Very Expensive
★

Anaheim Hilton and Towers. This hotel is one of the largest on the West Coast. It is truly a city unto itself, complete with its own post office. The lobby is dominated by a bright, airy atrium, and rooms are decorated in pinks and greens with light wood furniture. *777 Convention Way, 92702, tel. 714/750–4321 or 800/445–8667. 1,600 rooms. Facilities: 4 restaurants, several lounges and shops, outdoor pool, new fitness center, hot tubs, sun deck, concierge. AE, DC, MC, V.*

Anaheim Marriott. With outstanding meeting facilities, this hotel caters to convention attendees. Its lobby is filled with windows and colorful Spanish tile. Rooms, decorated with pastels, have balconies. *700 W. Convention Way, 92802, tel. 714/750–8000. 1,042 rooms. Facilities: gift shops, beauty salon, 2 heated swimming pools, Jacuzzi, weight rooms, video games, 3 restaurants, lounge, and entertainment. AE, CB, DC, MC, V.*

Disneyland Hotel. Always bustling with activity, this hotel is connected to Disneyland by monorail. It encompasses a 60-acre resort that carries on the fun atmosphere of its neighbor. New towers and tropical village make for unique accommodations; rooms, decorated in contemporary colors, all have balconies with views of Disneyland or the hotel marina. *1150 W. Cerritos Ave., 92802, tel. 714/778–6600 or 800/MICKEY–1. 1,132 rooms. Facilities: waterfront bazaar with wares from all over the world, tennis courts, pool, marina with playland and pedal boats. AE, CB, DC, MC, V.*

Pan Pacific Anaheim. This hotel is geared toward the business traveler. Its distinctive atrium lobby has glass-enclosed elevators. Contemporary graphics fill the rooms. Nonsmoking rooms are available. *1717 S. West St., 92802, tel. 714/999–0990 or 800/821–8976. 507 rooms. Facilities: 3 restaurants, swimming pool, sun deck, and Jacuzzi. AE, DC, MC, V.*

Expensive **Anaheim Holiday Inn.** Large glass chandeliers greet the visitor to this establishment 1 block south of Disneyland. *1850 S. Harbor Blvd., 92802, tel. 714/750–2801. 312 rooms. Facilities: heated pool, sauna, suites, dining room, lounge, and coffee shop. AE, CB, DC, MC, V.*

Anaheim Plaza Resort. Soft pastels and plants fill the lobby of this hotel near Disneyland. Wheelchair units and suites are available. *1700 S. Harbor Blvd., 92602, tel. 714/772–5900 or 800/228–9000. 300 rooms. Facilities: heated pool, restaurant. AE, CB, DC, MC, V.*

Grand Hotel. Lobby and rooms are decorated in a pleasant plum-teal green combination. This property is adjacent to Disneyland and offers a free shuttle. Each room in the 9-story high rise has a balcony. *7 Freedman Way, 92802, tel. 714/772–7777. 242 rooms. Facilities: pool, gift shop, dining room, coffee shop, the Grand Dinner Theater. AE, CB, DC, MC, V.*

Inn at the Park. Mountains of all kinds can be seen from private balconies—the man-made Matterhorn at Disneyland and the Santa Ana Mountains. *1855 S. Harbor Blvd., 92802, tel. 714/750–1811. 500 rooms. Facilities: heated pool, exercise room, suites, restaurant, coffee shop, lounge with entertainment. AE, CB, DC, MC, V.*

Sheraton-Anaheim Motor Hotel. This Tudor-style hotel offers free shuttle to Disneyland. *1015 W. Ball Rd., 92802, tel. 714/778–1700 or 800/325–3535. 500 rooms. Facilities: dining room, coffee shop, deli, heated pool, suites, game room, bar. Wheelchair units. AE, CB, DC, MC, V.*

Moderate **Ramada Hotel Maingate.** A clean, reliable, two-year-old member of the worldwide chain, the hotel is across the street from Disneyland, with free shuttle service to the park. *1460 S. Harbor Blvd., 92802, tel. 714/772–6777. 467 rooms. Facilities: pool, restaurant. AE, MC, V.*

Quality Hotel and Conference Center. A large, open, red-tile lobby is filled with mirrors, plants, and flowers; rooms are decorated in greens and yellows. The hotel is close to Disneyland. *616 Convention Way, 92802, tel. 714/750–3131. 284 rooms. Facilities: suites, heated pool, gift shop, bar restaurant. AE, CB, DC, MC, V.*

Inexpensive **Hampton Inn.** Basic lodging at a basic price is offered here. *300 E. Katella Way, 92802, tel. 714/772–8713. 136 rooms. Facilities: pool, cable TV. AE, MC, V.*

Buena Park *Moderate*	**Buena Park Hotel and Convention Center.** A spiral staircase leading to the mezzanine centers a lobby of marble, brass, and glass. Sleeping rooms are done in blues, greens, and peaches. *7675 Crescent Ave., 90620, tel. 714/995-1111. 328 rooms. Facilities: heated pool, dining rooms, lounge, coffee shop. AE, CB, DC, MC, V.*
Costa Mesa *Very Expensive*	**Westin South Coast Plaza.** The lobby lounge dominates a sunken lobby here; rooms are all decorated in a different style. This is the perfect hotel for die-hard shoppers, who only have to cross the street to get to South Coast Plaza, one of the poshest shopping centers in the country. A special weekend package is available at 50% off regular price. *666 Anton Blvd., 92626, tel. 714/540-2500. 400 rooms. Facilities: volleyball, shuffleboard, tennis courts, 2 restaurants, 3 bars, live entertainment, gift shop. AE, CB, DC, MC, V.*
Dana Point *Very Expensive* ★	**Dana Point Resort.** This two-year-old resort brings Cape Cod to Southern California in pleasant shades of sea foam green and peach. The lobby is filled with large palm trees and original artwork. It is casual yet elegant; every room has an ocean view. A special parasailing package deal is offered. *25135 Park Lantern Ave., 92629, tel. 714/661-5000. 350 rooms. Facilities: 2 pools, 3 spas, health club, restaurant, and lounge. AE, CB, DC, MC, V.*
Moderate	**Marina Best Western.** Set right in the marina, this hotel is accessible to many restaurants and shops. All rooms have balconies and vary in size from a basic room to a family suite with kitchen and fireplace. *24800 Dana Point Dr., 92629, tel. 714/496-1203. 135 rooms. Facilities: pool. AE, CB, DC, MC, V.*
Huntington Beach *Expensive*	**Best Western Huntington Beach Inn.** This inn, decorated in light green and mauve, is right across from the ocean. *21112 Pacific Coast Hwy., 92648, tel. 714/536-1421. 94 rooms. Facilities: restaurant, pool, coffee shop, lounge, gift shop, par-3 golf course. AE, CB, DC, MC, V.*
Inexpensive	**Huntington Shore Motor Hotel.** Also across from the ocean, some rooms at this small hotel have ocean views. The cozy lobby is set off with a fireplace. The extra-large rooms are decorated in earth tones. Complimentary Continental breakfast is offered. *21002 Pacific Coast Hwy., 92648, tel. 714/536-8861. 50 rooms. Facilities: heated pool. AE, MC, V.*
Irvine *Very Expensive*	**Irvine Hilton and Towers.** This beautiful hotel has all the amenities of a first-class resort. It is elegantly decorated in pale earth tones; the marble lobby is flanked by glass-enclosed elevators. Weekend rates are a great deal. *17900 Jamboree Rd., 92714, tel. 714/863-3111. 550 rooms. Facilities: pool, Jacuzzi, tennis, workout room, entertainment, 2 restaurants, 2 cocktail lounges, concierge. AE, CB, DC, MC, V.* **Irvine Marriott.** Mauve and sea foam green fill this contemporary hotel, and flower arrangements beautify the lobby. *1800 Von Karman, 92715, tel. 714/553-0100. 502 rooms. Facilities: restaurant, indoor-outdoor pool, tennis courts, sports-oriented bar, massage room, concierge floors, American Airlines and Hertz Rent-a-Car desks. AE, CB, DC, MC, V.*
Moderate	**Airporter Inn Hotel.** To cater to business people, all rooms here have a work area and are decorated in earth tones. One deluxe suite even has its own private pool. *18700 MacArthur Blvd.,*

92715, tel. 714/833–2770. 213 rooms. Facilities: Heated pool, dining room, coffee shop, cocktails, suites. AE, DC, MC, V.

Laguna Beach
Very Expensive

Inn at Laguna. This Southwest-style inn has just been renovated and enlarged. It's got one of the best locations in town—close to Main Beach and one of Laguna's most popular watering holes, Las Brisas restaurant and bar, yet far away enough to be secluded. The inn is decorated in peacock blue and peach and overlooks the ocean from a high bluff. *211 N. Coast Hwy., 92651, tel. 714/497–9722. 70 rooms. Facilities: VCRs in the rooms, heated pool, Jacuzzi, complimentary continental breakfast. AE, CB, DC, MC, V.*

★ **Surf and Sand Hotel.** The largest hotel in Laguna, the Surf and Sand has a shopping area with antiques, clothing, and gift shops. Newly done rooms sport soft sand colors and wooden shutters; they feature private balconies and honor bars. *15555 S. Coast Hwy., 92651, tel. 714/497–4477. 157 rooms. Facilities: private beach, pool, lounge, concierge, 2 restaurants, art gallery, entertainment. AE, CB, DC, MC, V.*

Expensive–Very Expensive

The Carriage House. This New Orleans-style bed-and-breakfast is surrounded by a lush garden. Complimentary family-style breakfast is offered daily. Fresh fruit and wine gifts welcome guests. *1322 Catalina St., 92651, tel. 714/494–8945. 6 suites. No credit cards. 2-night minimum on weekends.*

Eiler's Inn. A light-filled atrium centers this newly remodeled B & B. All rooms are unique and decorated with antiques. Outdoor breakfast is served; in the afternoon there's wine and cheese, often to the accompaniment of live music. With only 12 rooms, you'll need to book well in advance. *741 S. Coast Hwy., 92651, tel. 714/494–3004. AE, MC, V.*

Moderate–Expensive

Hotel Laguna. This downtown landmark, the oldest hotel in Laguna, was totally redone three years ago. Lobby windows look out on manicured gardens, and a patio restaurant overlooks the ocean. *425 S. Coast Hwy., 92651, tel. 714/494–1151. 68 rooms. Facilities: 2 restaurants, private beach, lounge, entertainment. AE, CB, DC, MC, V.*

Laguna Niguel
Very Expensive
★

The Ritz-Carlton. The only Mobil five-star and AAA five-diamond resort in California, this hotel has become *the* place for the county's haute society. The Mediterranean architecture and extensive landscaping make it feel like an Italian country villa. *33533 Ritz Carlton Dr., 92677, tel. 714/240–2000. 393 rooms. Facilities: beach access, health club, 2 pools, 3 restaurants, 3 lounges and a club with entertainment, concierge. Adjacent to an ocean-view 18-hole golf course. AE, CB, DC, MC, V.*

Newport Beach
Very Expensive
★

Four Seasons Hotel. This four-year-old hotel lives up to the quality of its fellow chain members. Marble and antiques fill the airy lobby; all rooms—decorated with beiges, peaches, and other southwestern tones—have spectacular views. *690 Newport Dr., 92660, tel. 714/759–0808. 285 rooms. Facilities: pool, whirlpool, lighted tennis courts, health club, 2 restaurants, lounge, concierge. AE, CB, DC, MC, V.*

Hotel Meridien Newport Beach. An eye-catching cantilevered design is the trademark of this ultramodern hotel in Koll Center. Decor is Southern Californian with striking pastels. Weekend rates dip almost 50%. *4500 MacArthur Blvd., 92660, tel. 714/476–2001. 435 rooms. Facilities: restaurant, cafe,* *lounge, health club with Jacuzzi, pool, tennis courts, complimentary bicycles, concierge. AE, CB, DC, MC, V.*

The Newporter Resort. Terra-cotta reigns supreme at this recently redecorated and expanded resort. Upper Newport Bay is an added attraction for soothing walks or invigorating runs. Guests have access to the John Wayne Tennis Club right next door. *1107 Jamboree Rd., 92660, tel. 714/644–1700. 410 rooms. Other facilities: 9-hole par-3 golf course, jogging paths, exercise room, 3 pools, 2 restaurants, lounge, entertainment, concierge. AE, CB, DC, MC, V.*

Sheraton Newport Beach. Bamboos and palms decorate the lobby in this Southern California beach-style hotel. Vibrant teals, mauves, and peaches make up the color scheme. Complimentary morning paper, buffet breakfast, and cocktail parties are offered daily. *4545 MacArthur Blvd., 92660, tel. 714/833–0570. 338 rooms. Facilities: pool, Jacuzzi, tennis courts, restaurant, lounge, entertainment. AE, CB, DC, MC, V.*

Expensive **Marriott Hotel and Tennis Club.** A distinctive atrium surrounded by fountains greets guests. Location is directly across the street from Fashion Island shopping center. *900 Newport Center Dr., 92660, tel. 714/640–4000 or 800/228–9290. 600 rooms. Facilities: 2 pools, adjacent golf course, tennis courts, Jacuzzi, 2 restaurants, lounge, entertainment. AE, CB, DC, MC, V.*

Orange **Doubletree Inn.** This hotel has a dramatic lobby of marble and
Expensive granite with silent waterfalls cascading down the walls. The oversize guest rooms come equipped with a small conference table. Location is near the popular shopping center called The City. *100 The City Dr., 92668, tel. 714/634–4500. 450 rooms. Facilities: 2 concierge floors, 2 restaurants, bar, heated pool, 2 tennis courts, spa. AE, CB, DC, MC, V.*

Inexpensive **Best Western El Camino.** This motel is close to Knott's Berry Farm and Disneyland. The large lobby is comfortably decorated with overstuffed sofas. Complimentary Continental breakfast is offered. *3191 N. Tustin Ave., 92665, tel. 714/998–0360. 56 rooms. Facilities: heated pool. AE, CB, DC, MC, V.*

San Clemente **Ramada San Clemente.** This four-year-old mission-style hotel
Moderate is beautifully set on a lush hillside. The lobby has a dramatic vaulted ceiling. A private patio or balcony is part of each room. *35 Calle de Industrias, 92672, tel. 714/498–8800. 110 rooms. Facilities: pool, restaurant with American cuisine, lounge, cable TV, HBO in rooms. AE, CB, DC, MC, V.*

San Clemente Inn. Located in the secluded southern part of San Clemente, this inn is adjacent to the state beach. Refurbished each year in soft earth tones, all the condo units are equipped with bars and kitchens. *2600 Avenida del Presidente, 92672, tel. 714/492–6103. 96 units. Facilities: large pool, tennis exercise equipment, restaurant. MC, V.*

San Juan **Country Bay Inn.** Built in the 1930s, all the rooms here are dec-
Capistrano orated with antiques of brass, wood, and rattan. The rooms in
Moderate this cozy inn also all have a wood-burning fireplace. It is right
★ across from the beach, and some rooms have balconies or patios. Continental breakfast is complimentary; champagne is served on arrival. *34862 Pacific Coast Hwy., 92624, tel. 714/496–6656. 28 rooms. Facilities: Jacuzzi. AE, MC, V.*

The Arts

The biggest draw on the arts scene is the **Orange County Performing Arts Center** (600 Town Center Dr., tel. 714/556–ARTS) in Costa Mesa. Among the groups that perform here are the American Ballet Theatre, the New York City Ballet, the Opera Pacific, and symphony orchestras from around the country.

Concerts   The **Irvine Meadows Amphitheater** (8800 Irvine Center Dr., tel. 714/855–4515) is an open-air structure offering musical events from May through October.
Anaheim Stadium (2000 State College Blvd., tel. 714/937–6750) hosts a variety of musical events throughout the year.
The **Pacific Amphitheater** (Orange County Fairgrounds, Costa Mesa, tel. 714/634–1300) offers musical entertainment and stages plays from April through October.

Theater   **South Coast Repertory Theater** (655 Town Center Dr., tel. 714/957–4033), near the Orange County Performing Arts Center in Costa Mesa, has been a tradition in the county for the last 24 years. Twelve productions are offered each year on two different stages. A resident group of actors forms the nucleus for this facility's innovative productions.
La Mirada Theater for the Performing Arts (14900 La Mirada Blvd., tel. 714/994–6150) presents a wide selection of Broadway shows, concerts, and film series.
Muckenthaler Cultural Center (1201 W. Malvern Ave., tel. 714/738–6595) often presents cabaret theater. Located in a beautiful Spanish house, the center was a gift to the city of Fullerton by the Muckenthaler family.

Nightlife

Bars   The **Cannery** (3010 Layfayette Ave., tel. 714/675–5777) and the **Warehouse** (3450 Via Osporo, tel. 714/673–4700) are two crowded Newport Beach bars. The **Studio Cafe** (100 Main St., on the Balboa Peninsula, tel. 714/675–7760) presents jazz musicians every night.
In Laguna Beach, the **Sandpiper** (1183 Coast Hwy., tel. 714/494–4694) is a tiny dancing joint that attracts an eclectic crowd. And **Laguna's White House** (340 Coast Hwy., tel. 714/494–8088) has nightly entertainment that runs the gamut from rock to Motown, reggae to pop.

Comedy   The **Improvisation** (4255 Campus Dr., Irvine, tel. 714/854–5455) is probably the funniest place in the county. From well known to lesser known, comedians try out their acts nightly.

Country Western   **Bandstand** (1721 S. Manchester, Anaheim, tel. 714/956–1410) offers live country music Sunday, Tuesday, Thursday, and Friday. Other nights, there is Top-40 music. Six dance floors and four bars are part of the complex.

Dinner Theater   Several night spots in Orange County serve up entertainment with dinner. **Tibbie's Music Hall** (16360 Coast Hwy., Huntington Beach, tel. 714/840–5661) offers rowdy musical revues along with prime rib, fish, or chicken.
Medieval Times Dinner and Tournament (7662 Beach Blvd., tel. 714/521–4740) is a new Buena Park attraction that takes guests back to the days of knights and ladies. Knights on horseback compete in medieval games, sword fighting, and jousting. Din-

ner, all of which is eaten with your hands, includes vegetables, roast chicken, potatoes, pastry, and cocktails.

Other area dinner theaters include **The Grand Dinner Theater** (Grand Hotel, Anaheim, tel. 714/772–7777), **Curtain Call** (690 El Camino Real, Tustin, tel. 714/838–1540), and **Hampton's** (3503 S. Harbor Blvd., Santa Ana, tel. 714/979–7550).

Nightclubs   **Crackers** (710 Katella Ave., Anaheim, tel. 714/978–1828) is a zany restaurant and nightclub where waiters and waitresses double as on-stage performers. The live entertainment seven days a week varies, with music from the '40s to the '80s.

The Hop (18774 Brookhurst St., Fountain Valley, tel. 714/963–2366) is a 1950s–'60s-style dinner/nightclub owned by the Righteous Brothers. Nostalgia fills this fun place, which has a basketball court-dance floor and a '56 Chevy attached to the front of the DJ booth. Only music circa 1950–60 is played.

14 San Diego

Each year San Diego absorbs thousands of visitors who eventually become residents. They are drawn by the climate—sunny, dry, warm, and clear nearly all year round. They swim, surf, and sunbathe on long beaches facing the turquoise Pacific, where whales, seals, and dolphins frolic offshore. They tour oases of tropical palms, sheltered bays fringed by golden pampas grass, and far-ranging parklands blossoming with brilliantly hued and scented bougainvillea, jasmine, ice plant, and bird of paradise. They run, bike, and walk for hours down wide streets and paths planned for recreation, among the strong, tanned natives who thrive on San Diego's varied health, fitness, and sports scenes.

San Diego County is the nation's seventh largest—with a population of more than 2 million, it's larger than nearly a dozen U.S. states. It sprawls east from the Pacific Ocean through dense urban neighborhoods to outlying suburban communities that seem to sprout overnight on canyons and cliffs. The City of San Diego is the state's second largest, after Los Angeles. It serves as a base for the U.S. Navy's 11th Naval District and as a port for ships from many nations. Many of its long-time and recent residents were stationed here in the service and vowed to stay put. Others passed through on vacation or saw the city in movies and TV shows and became enamored with the city and its reputation as a prosperous Sunbelt playground. Since its beginnings, San Diego has attracted a steady stream of prospectors, drawn to the nation's farthest southwest frontier.

Tourism is San Diego's third largest industry, after manufacturing and the military. San Diego's politicians, business leaders, and developers have set the city's course toward a steadily increasing influx of visitors—which gives the residents some pleasant attractions and some not-so-enjoyable distractions: With growth comes congestion, even in San Diego's vast expanse.

Arriving and Departing

By Plane There are regularly scheduled nonstop flights into San Diego from many U.S. and Mexican cities. San Diego is served by Alaska Airlines (tel. 800/426–0333), America West (tel. 619/560–0727), American (tel. 619/232–4051), Braniff (tel. 619/231–0700), British Airways (tel. 800/247–9297), Continental (tel. 800/525–0280), Delta (tel. 619/235–4344), Northwest (tel. 619/239–0488), Pan American (tel. 800/221–1111), Piedmont (tel. 800/251–5720), Southwest (tel. 619/232–1221), Skywest (tel. 800/453–9417), Trans World (tel. 619/295–7009), United (tel. 619/234–7171), and USAir (tel. 800/428–4322).

From the Airport to Center City All flights arrive at Lindbergh Field, just 3 miles northwest of downtown. **San Diego Transit** Route 2 buses leave every 20–30 minutes, 5:30 AM–midnight, from the center traffic aisle at the East Terminal and the traffic island at the far west end of the West Terminal. The buses go to Fourth and Broadway, downtown. Fare is $1 per person. Taxi fare is $5–$6 plus tip to most center-city hotels. The **Super Shuttle Airport Limousine** (tel. 619/434–4567) is available to various neighborhoods. Also, many hotels offer free transportation. If you're driving to the downtown area, just follow signs to I-5 and go south for about 3 miles.

By Car I–5 stretches from Canada to the Mexican border and bisects San Diego. I–8 provides access from Yuma, Arizona and points east. Drivers coming from Nevada and the mountain regions beyond can reach San Diego on I-15. Avoid rush-hour periods when the traffic can be jammed for miles.

By Train **Amtrak** trains (tel. 800/USA-RAIL) from Los Angeles arrive at the Santa Fe Depot at Kettner Boulevard and Broadway, near the heart of downtown. There are additional stations in Del Mar and Oceanside, both located in north San Diego County. Eight trains operate daily in each direction.

By Bus **Greyhound-Trailways** (tel. 619/239-9171) offers frequent daily service between the downtown terminal at 120 West Broadway and Los Angeles, connecting with buses to all major U.S. cities. Many buses are express or nonstop, while others make stops at coastal towns en route.

Getting Around

Many attractions such as the Gaslamp Quarter, Balboa Park, and La Jolla, are best seen on foot. Various modes of public transportation can be used to reach any major tourist and shopping area, but it is best to have a car for exploring more remote coastal and inland regions. The International Information Center in Horton Plaza, at the corner of First Avenue and F Street, provides maps of the city.

By Bus Fares on **San Diego Transit** (tel. 619/233-3004) buses are $1, express buses are $1.25, and seniors pay 50¢ on any bus. A free transfer is included in the fare, but it must be requested upon boarding. Buses to most major attractions leave from Fourth and Broadway or Fifth and Broadway.

By Taxi Rates vary according to company. The average fare for one to five passengers is $2 for the first mile, $1.40 for each additional mile. Cab companies that serve most areas of the city are **Yellow Cab** (tel. 619/234-6161), **Orange Cab** (tel. 619/291-3333), **La Jolla Cab** (tel. 619/453-4222), **Co-op Silver Cabs** (tel. 619/280 -5555), **Coast Cab** (tel. 619/226-8294), and **Coronado Cab** (tel. 619/435-6211).

By Trolley The **San Diego Trolley** (tel. 619/233-3004) travels from the Sante Fe Depot to within 100 feet of the U. S.-Mexico border, stopping at 21 substations en route. The East County line connects midtown with Lemon Grove, La Mesa, and El Cajon. Passes, tokens, and schedules are available at The Transit Store (440 Broadway). Ticket vending machines, located at each station, require exact change; the basic fare is 50¢-$1.50 one way. Trolleys run daily 5AM-1AM.

By Ferry The San Diego-Coronado Ferry leaves from the Broadway Pier daily, every hour on the hour, 10 AM-10 PM. Fare is $1 each way.

By Limousine Limousine companies provide chauffeured service for business or pleasure. Some offer airport shuttles and customized tours. Rates vary and are based per hour, per mile, or both, with some minimums established. Companies offering a range of services include **A Touch of Class** (tel. 619/265-1995), **Olde English Livery Service** (tel. 619/232-6533), **La Jolla Limousines** (tel. 619/459-5891), and **Paul the Greek's** (tel. 619/287-6888).

Exploring San Diego *(Boxes Refer to Detail Maps)*

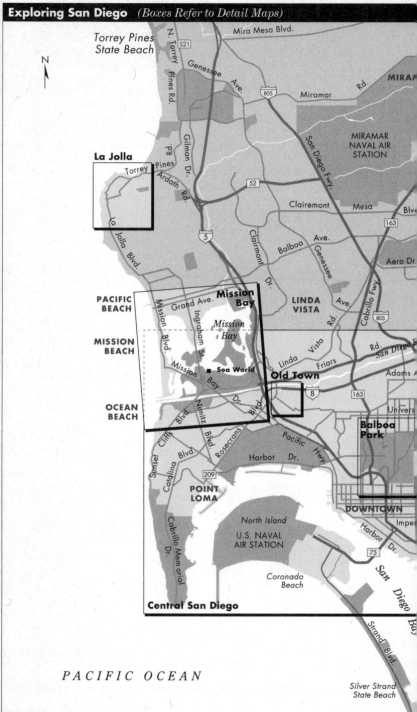

N

Torrey Pines State Beach

N. Torrey Pines Rd.

S21

Mira Mesa Blvd.

Genessee Ave.

805

Miramar Rd.

MIRAM

MIRAMAR NAVAL AIR STATION

La Jolla

Torrey Pines Rd.

Gilman Dr.

Ardath Rd.

52

San Diego Fwy.

Clairemont Mesa

Blvd

163

5

Clairemont Dr.

Balboa Ave.

Genessee Ave.

Aero Dr

Cabrillo Fwy.

805

PACIFIC BEACH

Grand Ave.

Mission Bay

Mission Bay

LINDA VISTA

MISSION BEACH

Mission Blvd.

Ingraham St.

Mission Bay

Sea World

Old Town

Linda Vista Rd.

Friars

Rd.

San Diego F

Adams A

la Jolla Blvd.

OCEAN BEACH

Mission Dr.

Blvd.

8

163

Univers

Nimitz Blvd.

Sunset Cliffs Blvd.

Catalina Blvd.

Rosecrans

Pacific Hwy

Balboa Park

Harbor Dr.

209

POINT LOMA

Cabrillo Memorial Dr.

North Island

U.S. NAVAL AIR STATION

DOWNTOWN

Imper

Harbor Dr.

75

San Diego Ba

Coronado Beach

Central San Diego

Strand Blvd.

PACIFIC OCEAN

Silver Strand State Beach

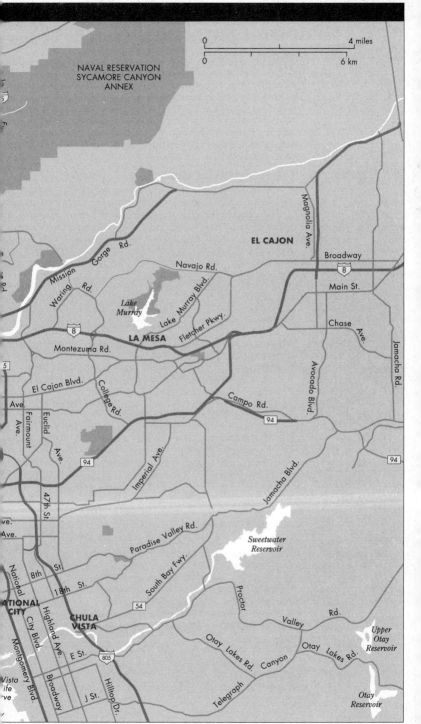

NAVAL RESERVATION
SYCAMORE CANYON
ANNEX

0   1   4 miles
0   6 km

EL CAJON

Magnolia Ave.

Broadway

8

Main St.

Mission Gorge Rd.

Navajo Rd.

Waring Rd.

Lake Murray

Lake Murray Blvd.

Fletcher Pkwy.

8

LA MESA

Chase Ave.

Montezuma Rd.

Jamacha Rd.

El Cajon Blvd.

College Rd.

Campo Rd.

Avocado Blvd.

94

Fairmount Ave.

Euclid Ave.

94

Imperial Ave.

47th St.

Jamacha Blvd.

94

Paradise Valley Rd.

Sweetwater Reservoir

ve.

Ave.

South Bay Fwy.

National City

8th St.

18th St.

54

Proctor Valley Rd.

Upper Otay Reservoir

City Blvd.

NATIONAL CITY

CHULA VISTA

Highland Ave.

E St.

805

Otay Lakes Rd. Canyon

Otay Lakes Rd.

Montgomery Blvd.

Vista ife ve.

Broadway

Hilltop Dr.

J St.

Telegraph

Otay Reservoir

Important Addresses and Numbers

Tourist   **The International Information Center** (tel. 619/236–1212) is in
Information   Horton Plaza, at the corner of First Avenue and F Street, in
the heart of downtown. Recorded visitor information is available (tel. 619/239–9696). *Open daily 8:30–5. Closed Thanksgiving and Christmas.*
Mission Bay Visitor Information Center is conveniently located
off I–5 at the Mission Bay side of the Clairemont Drive exit.
*2688 E. Mission Bay Dr., tel. 619/276–8200. Open daily 9–
dusk.*
Balboa Park Information Center. *1549 El Prado, in Balboa
Park, tel. 619/239–0512. Open daily 9:30–4.*

Emergencies   Dial 911 for **police** and **ambulance** in an emergency.

Doctor   Hospital emergency rooms with physicians on duty are open 24
hours. Major hospitals are: **UCSD Medical Center** (225 Dickin-
son, tel. 619/543–6400), **Mercy Hospital and Medical Center**
(4077 5th Ave., tel. 619/260–7000), **Scripps Memorial Hospital**
(9888 Genesee Ave., La Jolla, tel. 619/457–6150), and the **Veterans Administration Hospital** (3350 La Jolla Village Dr., La
Jolla, tel. 619/453–7500).

Weather/Beach   Tel. 619/289–1212 and 619/225–9492 for up-to-date informa-
Report   tion.

Guided Tours

Orientation Tours   Both **Gray Line Tours** (tel. 619/231–9922) and **San Diego Mini
Tours** (tel. 619/234–9044) offer daily four-hour sightseeing excursions. Gray Line uses 45-passenger buses; San Diego Mini
Tours uses 25-passenger buses. **Baubles, Bangles & Beans** (tel.
619/295–5015) features tours of San Diego and across the border. Each of the companies provides pickup at major hotels. We
recommend the **Molly Trolley Express** (tel. 619/233–9177),
which travels to almost every attraction and shopping area on
open-air trackless trolleys. Drivers double as tour guides. You
can take the full two-hour, narrated city tour, or get on and off
as you please. An all-day pass costs $6 per person. The trolley
carries 34 passengers and operates Tuesday–Sunday, 9–5.
Free one-hour bus tours of the downtown redevelopment area,
including the Gaslamp Quarter, are hosted by **Centre City Development Corporation** (tel. 619/696–3215). Groups of 43
passengers leave from 119 West F Street, downtown, every
Saturday at 10 AM. Reservations are necessary.

Special-Interest   **Pacific Horizon** (tel. 619/456–2719) specializes in hot-air bal-
Tours   loon rides over North County daily at sunrise and sunset,
including a one-hour ride and champagne toast.
Vintage Wine Tours (tel. 619/298–1666) will pick you up at your
hotel in a 1960s vintage Cadillac limousine and take you on a
six-hour tour through four wineries and the Deer Park Car Museum. A gourmet picnic lunch is included.
Old Town Tours (tel. 619/296–1004) offers dramatized tours of
California's first non-Native American community. Groups or
individuals are welcome; reservations are recommended.
San Diego Harbor Excursion (tel. 619/234–4111) and **Invader
Cruises** (tel. 619/234–8687) each sail with more than 100 passengers on narrated cruises of San Diego harbor. Both vessels
have snack bars. One-hour cruises depart several times daily

from the Broadway Pier. San Diego Harbor Excursion (which is highly recommended) offers a two-hour tour each day at 2 PM. Reservations are not necessary for any of the tours.

Mariposa Sailing Cruises (tel. 619/542–0646) offers morning and afternoon sailing tours of the harbor and San Diego Bay on the 35-foot cutter *Mariposa*.

Whale-watching Tours
California gray whales migrate south to Mexico from mid-December to mid-March. Up to 200 whales pass the San Diego coast each day, coming within yards of tour boats. Most tour companies will give a free second trip to any passenger who fails to sight a whale. *The Avanti* (tel. 619/222–0391), a 70-foot, luxury motor yacht, offers narrated tours twice a day on weekdays and three times a day on weekends. A "Sail with the Whales" trip is offered Wednesday-Saturday aboard a 1924 schooner from Bagheera Sailing Adventures (tel. 619/223–8808). A more intimate tour is conducted by **Sail San Diego** (tel. 619/548–4227) on a 38-foot Bristol sailing yacht. A full lunch and an informative lecture are provided for a maximum of six persons. Early booking is recommended due to space limitations.

Walking Tours
The Gaslamp Foundation (410 Island Ave., tel. 619/233–5227) leads 1½-hour guided walks of the restored downtown historical district, highlighting the Victorian architecture. Groups meet at the foundation office, near Horton Plaza (Sat. 10 AM and 1 PM). A donation is requested. Self-guided-tour brochures are available at the office Monday–Friday, 8:30–5.

Free walking tours that explore the gardens, architecture, and history of Balboa Park are given every Saturday at 10 AM by **Offshootours** (tel. 619/297–0289). Also offered are guided botanical tours of more than 7,000 species of exotic fauna and flora at the San Diego Zoo. The tour is free with zoo admission, and is offered on the last Sunday of each month.

Old Town Walking Tours (tel. 619/296–1004) leads strolls through 200 years of history in San Diego's original city center. Hourly tours leave daily 10–5 from 3977 Twiggs Street. There is a charge, and reservations are suggested.

Exploring San Diego

Exploring San Diego is an endless adventure, limited only by time and transportation constraints, which can be considerable if you don't have a car. San Diego is more of an endless chain of separate communities than it is a cohesive city. Many of the major attractions are 15 miles or so away from each other—which means a minimum ½-hour ride under the best of circumstances. The streets are fun for getting an up-close look at how San Diegans live, and if you've got a car, be sure to drive through Mission and Pacific beaches along Mission Boulevard for a good view of the vibrant, young, outrageous beach scene. But true Southern Californians use the freeways, which crisscross the county in a sensible fashion. Interstate 5 runs a direct north–south route through the county's coastal communities to the Mexico border. Interstates 805 and 15 do much the same inland, with Interstate 8 as the main east–west route. Highways 163 and 94 act as connectors.

If you are going to drive around San Diego, study your maps before you hit the road. The freeways are convenient and fast most of the time, but if you miss your turnoff or get caught in commuter traffic, you'll experience a none-too-pleasurable hallmark of Southern California living—freeway madness. Just go with the flow, use your indicators and don't push your luck. Southern California drivers rush around on a complex freeway system with the same fervor they demonstrate in scores of jogging marathons each year. They particularly enjoy speeding up at interchanges and entrance and exit ramps. Be sure you know where you're going before you join the freeway chase. Better yet, use public transportation or tour buses from your hotel, and save your energy for walking in the sun.

Downtown and the Embarcadero

Numbers in the margin correspond with points of interest on the Central San Diego map.

Long ignored by the local populace, downtown San Diego, just 3 miles south of the international airport, Lindbergh Field, is changing and growing rapidly, gaining status as a cultural and recreational center for the county's residents and visitors alike.

Downtown's natural attributes were obvious to its original booster, Alonzo Horton, who arrived in San Diego in 1867. Horton looked at the bay and the acres of flatland surrounded by hills and canyons and knew he had found San Diego's center. Though Old Town, under the Spanish fort at the Presidio, had been settled for years, Horton knew it was too far away from the water to take hold as the commercial center of San Diego. He bought 960 acres along the bay at 27.5¢ per acre and literally gave away the land for free to those who would develop the land or build houses. Within months, he had sold or given away 226 city blocks of land, and settlers were camping on their land in tents while building their houses and businesses. In 1868, Horton and other city fathers staked out 1,400 acres surrounding a mesa overlooking the harbor and created a permanent greenbelt overlooking downtown. That acreage officially became Balboa Park in 1911.

The transcontinental train arrived in 1885, and the great land boom was on. The population soared from 5,000 to 35,000 in less than a decade—a foreshadowing of San Diego's future. In 1887, the tile-domed Santa Fe Depot was constructed at the foot of Broadway, 2 blocks from the water. Freighters chugged in and out of the harbor, and by the early 1900s the navy had discovered this perfect West Coast command center. Today the navy has a strong presence in the harbor and on Point Loma and Coronado Island and is an integral part of the cityscape.

As downtown grew into San Diego's transportation and commerce hub, residential neighborhoods blossomed along the beaches and inland valleys. Downtown's business district gradually moved farther away from the original heart of downtown at Fifth and Market streets, past Broadway, and up toward the park. Downtown's waterfront fell into disrepute during World War I, when sailors, gamblers, prostitutes, and boozers were drawn like magnets to each other and the waterfront bars.

But Alonzo Horton's modern-day followers, city leaders intent on prospering while preserving San Diego's natural beauty, have reclaimed the waterfront. The San Diego Convention Center opened in November 1989 smack on the waterfront, its

sail-like roof soaring over the harbor. The $160-million center is
the result of two decades of impressive downtown development, and the dirt lots of the former warehouse district
surrounding the center now boast architecturally diverse hotels and restaurants.

❶ Your first view of downtown, no matter what your mode of
transportation, will likely include **The Embarcadero** along Harbor Drive. Though the entire waterfront has become a major
tourist attraction, as yet there is no tourist office on the Embarcadero. Your closest access to maps and brochures is at the
❷ recently restored **Santa Fe Depot,** just 2 blocks away at the corner of Broadway and Kettner Boulevard. There is a tourist
information booth inside the station, with bus schedules, maps,
and a Traveler's Aid booth. The cavernous waiting area inside
the depot was used for San Diego's premier society balls the
year restoration was completed, and the gleaming marble
floors and tile dome suited the elegant guests well. Now, although the station's regulars aren't part of the elite crowd, the
room has become a good home base for those exploring downtown. Tour buses for Mexico depart from here, and the
Greyhound-Trailways bus station is just a few blocks away, at
120 West Broadway. The bright red San Diego trolley departs
from across the street from the depot, at the corner of Kettner
Boulevard and C Street. A massive office and retail center is
under construction here; it will be the hub of several transportation services.

Begin your Embarcadero tour at the foot of Ash Street on Harbor Drive, where the harbor's collection of houseboats, ferries,
cruise ships, naval destroyers, tour boats, and a fair share of
❸ seals and seagulls begins. The *Star of India,* a beautiful wind-
jammer built in 1863, is docked at the foot of Grape Street on
Harbor Drive, across from the Spanish-style San Diego County
❹ Administration Center. The *Star of India* is part of the **Maritime Museum,** a collection of three ships that have been
restored and opened for tours. The Maritime Museum is located in the *Berkeley*, an 1898 paddlewheel boat by the B Street
Pier. *Tel. 619/234–9153. Ships open daily 9–8. Admission: $5
adults, $4 senior citizens and students, $10 families.*

A cement pathway runs from the *Star of India* along the water,
past restaurants and fish markets to the docks for harbor-tour
boats and whale-watching trips (which are scheduled from December to March during the grand migration of the gray
whales from the Pacific Northwest to southern Baja). This section of the Embarcadero, at Harbor Drive and the foot of
Broadway, has become a tourist gathering spot. A cluster of
streetfront windows sell tickets for tours; those waiting for
their boats grab a beer or ice cream at the '50s-style diner Bay
Cafe, and sit on the upstairs patio or on benches along the busy
pathway and watch the sailboats, paddlewheelers, and yachts
vie for space.

❺ The pink and blue **B Street Pier** is the terminal for San Diego's
burgeoning cruise business. Small ships travel from San Diego
to Catalina Island and Ensenada, Mexico, 80 miles south of San
Diego. Major cruise lines use San Diego as both a port of call
and a departure point for cruises to San Juan, Vancouver, and
the Panama Canal. The cavernous pier building has a cruise information center and a small, cool bar and gift shop. There is a
huge public parking lot ($3 a day) along the south side of the

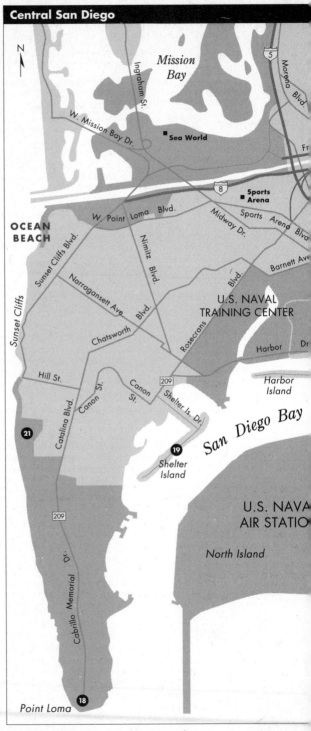

Central San Diego

Mission Bay

Sea World

Sports Arena

OCEAN BEACH

U.S. NAVAL TRAINING CENTER

Harbor Island

San Diego Bay

Shelter Island

U.S. NAVAL AIR STATION

North Island

Point Loma

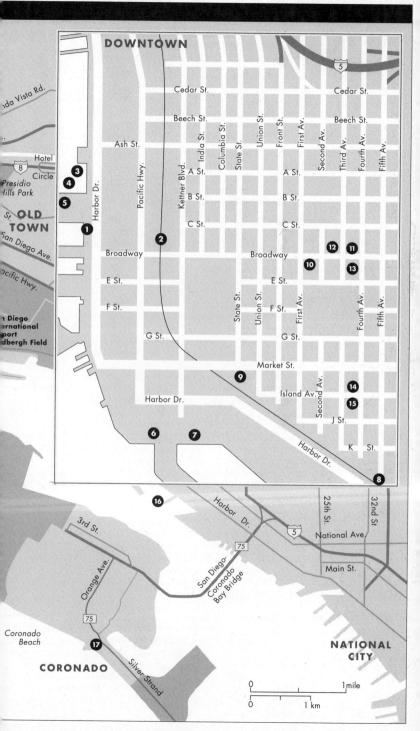

pier building. Since much of the parking along Harbor Drive is limited to two-hour meters, this lot is good if you're planning on taking your time touring the harbor. One of the newest, yet most traditional, boat trips is the **Bay Ferry** to Coronado Island, which runs hourly from 10 AM to 10 PM.

Back along the Embarcadero are traditional craft shops and gift shops, some awaiting restoration. The navy's 11th Naval District has control of the next few waterfront blocks, and a series of destroyers, submarines, and carriers cruise in and out, some staying for weeks at a time. The navy occasionally offers tours of these floating cities.

A steady stream of joggers, bicyclists, and serious walkers pick up speed as the Embarcadero pathway passes the Tuna Harbor, where the tuna fleet gathers. A new Fish Market restaurant has opened over the water at the end of the pier, offering spectacular views of the harbor and downtown.

6 **Seaport Village** (tel. 619/235–4013) is a privately developed and operated 14-acre shopping, dining, and recreational outdoor mall. Constructed with a designer's eye to ersatz history, the village's clapboard and adobe buildings house a seemingly unending series of specialty shops, snack bars, and restaurants—each with an independent theme. The Broadway Flying Horses Carousel, whose handcarved animals rose and fell at Coney Island during the turn of the century, is surrounded by inexpensive ethnic cafes and takeouts, and a video parlor for those who prefer their fun in the shade. Beside the wall is Seaport Village's official symbol, the 45-foot-high Mulkilteo Lighthouse, modeled after an 80-year-old light-house in Everett, Washington, and housing the San Diego Pier Cafe, a seafood restaurant. Seaport Village spreads from Harbor Drive to the waterfront. The Spanish-style, deserted San Diego Police Department Headquarters at the corner of Harbor Drive and Market Street is being incorporated into the village, and construction is underway on a nightlife/dining center and a multitiered parking garage. The parking lots along Harbor Drive fill up quickly, but there is additional parking up Market Street and Kettner Boulevard. Stay away from parking meters if you're planning to stay awhile, since they are patrolled frequently. Seaport Village's shops are open daily from 10 to 9, with restaurants closing closer to midnight.

Time Out Seaport Village is a great place for a meal, either at a sit-down restaurant or on the run. Picnic tables are scattered in the shade near the carousel, with take-out fare available from Greek, Italian, and Mexican cafes. Cookies, ice cream, candies, and popcorn are sold at stands throughout the village. The upstairs deck at the Harbor House restaurant is a good place to watch the sunset.

7 The mirrored towers of the **San Diego Marriott Hotel and Marina** mark the end of Seaport Village. The waterfront walkway continues past the hotel's marina, where hotel guests park their enormous, extravagant yachts. Farther on is a large park with a fishing pier and walking paths. Just past the Marriott is **8** the new, striking **San Diego Convention Center,** which has permanently transformed downtown. The 760,000-square-foot center, sitting right at the edge of the waterfront, posed incredible dilemmas for the builders. The center is well worth wandering through, and shows are frequently open to the public.

To reach the heart of downtown walk up Fifth Avenue from the Convention Center, up Market Street from Seaport Village, or up Broadway from the B Street Pier. The **Olde Cracker Factory,** at Market and State streets, houses antiques and collectibles shops.

Walking up Broadway, you'll pass the Santa Fe Depot and a collection of seedy bars and tattoo parlors. The condition of lower Broadway is a constant headache for downtown's promoters, but the businesses here are popular with sailors and fishermen released from long weeks aboard ship. A few blocks farther, at the corner of First Street and Broadway, is where downtown comes alive. Here you'll pass the **Spreckels Theater,** a grand old stage that now presents pop concerts and touring plays.

The grand **U.S. Grant Hotel,** built in 1910, is across the street. Far more elegant and formal than most San Diego hotels, the U.S. Grant has massive marble lobbies, with gleaming chandeliers and hospitable doormen. One block away is the **Westgate Hotel,** another deluxe accommodation for visiting celebrities and royalty. The Westgate is French Provincial in style, and has a nice piano bar on the main floor and an elegant French restaurant, Le Fountainbleu, at the top. The new 450-room Omni Hotel is connected to Horton Plaza and often hosts special events in conjunction with the plaza.

The theme of "shopping in adventureland" carries over from Seaport Village to downtown San Diego's centerpiece, **Horton Plaza.** Completed in August 1985, this shopping, dining, and entertainment mall fronts Broadway and G streets from First to Fourth avenues and covers more than 6 city blocks. Designed by Jon Jerde, Horton Plaza is far from what one imagines a shopping or city center to be. A collage of pastel colors with elaborate, colorful tilework marking benches and stairways, cloth banners waving in the air, and modern sculptures marking the entrances, rises in staggered levels six floors high, with great views of all of downtown, from the harbor to Balboa Park and beyond. There are four levels of parking, and the first three hours are free.

The International Visitor Information Center was opened in Horton Plaza by the San Diego Convention and Visitors Bureau in 1985, and it has become the traveler's best resource for information on all of San Diego (and Tijuana). Photos of San Diego's landmarks decorate the walls, and brochures and pamphlets in many languages are neatly arrayed by the counters. *11 Horton Plaza, street level at the corner of 1st and F sts., tel. 619/236–1212. Open daily 8:30–5:30.*

Long before Horton Plaza became the bright star on downtown's redevelopment horizon, the Gaslamp Quarter was gaining attention and respect. A 16-block National Historic District centered around Fourth and Fifth avenues from Broadway to Market Street, the quarter contains most of San Diego's Victorian-style commercial buildings from the late 1800s, when Market Street was the center of early downtown. At the turn of the century, downtown's business district moved farther west toward Broadway, and many of San Diego's first buildings fell into disrepair. The quarter became known as the Stingaree district, where hookers picked up sailors in lively taverns and dance halls. As the move for downtown redevelopment emerged, there was talk about destroying the buildings in the quarter, but in 1974, history buffs, developers, architects, and artists formed the Gaslamp Quarter Council, bent on preserving the district. Today, beaten-down flophouses have become choice office buildings. The brick sidewalks are lined with trees and benches, and the shops and restaurants tend toward individuality.

14 At the farthest end of the redeveloped quarter, the **Gaslamp Quarter Association** (410 Island Ave., tel. 619/233–5227) is headquartered in the William Heath Davis house, a restored 19th-century saltbox house. Walking tours of the historical district leave from here on Saturdays at 10 and 1. A $2 donation is suggested. If you can't make the tour, stop by the house and pick up a brochure and map.

Across the street from the Gaslamp Quarter Association's headquarters, at the corner of Island and Third, is the 100-
15 year-old **Horton Grand Hotel,** restored and operated in turn-of-the-century style. The hotel's central courtyard has become a popular wedding and party site. A small Chinese museum serves as a tribute to the surrounding Chinatown district, which is nothing more than a collection of modest homes that once housed Chinese laborers and their families.

Many of the quarter's landmark buildings are located on Fourth and Fifth streets, between Island and Broadway. Among the nicest are the Backesto Building, the Keating Building, the Louis Bank of Commerce, and the Mercantile Building, all on Fifth Street. The Golden Lion Tavern, at the corner of Fourth and F streets, is a magnificently restored turn-of-the-century tavern with a 12-foot mahogany bar and a spectacular stained-glass domed ceiling. The section of G Street between Sixth and Tenth avenues is becoming an art gallery district.

Coronado

Coronado Island is a charming, peaceful community, essentially left alone for decades to grow at its characteristic slow pace. It is a city unto itself, ruled by its own municipal government. Long-time residents live in grand Victorian homes handed down by their families for generations. The streets are wide, quiet, and friendly, with lots of neighborhood parks where young families mingle with the island's many senior citizens. The Coronado Municipal Golf Course, with its lovely setting under the bridge, is across the water from Seaport Village.

North Island Naval Air Station was established on the island across from Point Loma in 1911, and was the site of Charles Lindbergh's departure on his flight around the world. Today, high-tech air- and seacraft arrive and depart continuously from North Island, providing a real-life education in military armament. Coronado's long relationship with the navy has made it an enclave of sorts for retired military personnel.

Coronado is visible from both downtown and Point Loma, and accessible via the arching blue 2.2-mile-long San Diego–Coronado Bridge, a landmark just beyond downtown's skyline. The bridge handles more than 20,000 cars each day. There is a $1 toll for crossing the bridge into Coronado, but cars carrying two or more passengers can enter through the free car-pool lane. Rush hour tends to be slow, which is fine since the view of the harbor, downtown, and the island is breathtaking, day and night. Until the bridge was completed in 1969, visitors and residents relied on the Coronado Ferry, running across the harbor from downtown. When the bridge was opened, the ferry closed down, much to the chagrin of those fond of traveling at a leisurely pace. In 1987, the ferry returned, and with it came the island's most ambitious development in decades.

16 The Bay Ferry runs from the B Street Pier at downtown's Embarcadero to the **Old Ferry Landing,** which is actually a new development on an old site. Its buildings resemble the gingerbread domes of the Hotel del Coronado, the island's long-time main attraction. The Old Ferry Landing is similar to Seaport Village, with small shops and restaurants and lots of benches facing the water. Nearby, the elegant high-rise Le Meridien hotel accommodates many wedding receptions and gala banquets. The Bay Ferry is located at the B Street Pier, at Broadway and Harbor Drive. Boats depart hourly from 10 to 10. Fare is $1 each way.

A trackless trolley runs from the landing down Orange Avenue, the island's version of a downtown, to the Hotel del Coronado. Coronado's residents and commuting workers have quickly adapted to this traditional mode of transportation, and the ferry has become quite popular with bicyclists who shuttle their bikes across the harbor and ride the island's wide, flat boulevards for hours.

17 The **Hotel del Coronado** is the island's most prominent landmark. Selected as a National Historic Site in 1977, "the Del" (as natives say) celebrated its 100th anniversary in 1988. Celebrities, royalty, and politicians marked the anniversary with a weekend-long party that highlighted the hotel's colorful history. *1500 Orange Ave., tel. 619/435–6611. Free guided tours from the lobby Sat. 1 PM.*

The hotel is integral to the island's history. In 1884, two wealthy financiers, Elisha Spurr Babcock, Jr. and H. L. Story, stopped hunting grouse and rabbits on the undeveloped island long enough to appreciate the long stretches of virgin beaches and the view of San Diego's emerging harbor, and realized the island's potential. They decided to build a luxurious resort hotel, formed the Babcock-Story Coronado Beach Company, purchased the 4,100-acre land parcel for $110,000 in 1885, and in 1886 sold lots and shares in the new hotel.

It took only one year to build the 400-room main hotel, though it was a mighty effort that employed hundreds of Chinese laborers racing against the clock. All materials and laborers had to be ferried to the island and transported up Orange Avenue on the Babcock-Story Railroad, which was capable of transporting private railroad cars, thus popular with industrial tycoons. The hotel was completed in 1888, and Thomas Edison himself threw the switch as the Del became the world's first electrically lighted hotel. It has been a dazzling sight ever since.

The hotel's gingerbread architecture is recognizable all over the world, for it has served as a set for many movies, political meetings, and extravagant social happenings. The Duke of Windsor met Wallis Simpson here. Eight presidents have stayed here. The film *Some Like It Hot,* starring Marilyn Monroe, was filmed here. The hotel's underground corridors are lined with historical photos from the days when the hotel was first built. Of particular interest are the photos of the enormous tent city that was built during a major remodeling project in 1902. The tent city was so popular with guests that it was re-erected every summer until 1939.

Coronado's other main attraction is its 86 historical homes and sites. Many of the homes are turn-of-the-century mansions. The **Glorietta Bay Inn,** across the street from the Del, was the home of John Spreckels, original owner of North Island and the Hotel del Coronado. Nearby is the **Boat House,** a small replica of the hotel that once served as the launching point for deep-sea fishing craft, and which now houses a Chart House restaurant. The Boat House is a great spot for watching the sails in the harbor and watching the sun set over downtown. **Star Park,** on Loma Avenue, acts as a hub for five streets all designated as historical sites. Among the homes here is the Meade House, where L. Frank Baum wrote *The Wizard of Oz.*

Point Loma, Shelter Island, and Harbor Island

Point Loma curves around the San Diego Bay west of downtown and the airport, protecting the center city from the Pacific's tides and waves. Though its main streets are cluttered with hotels, fast-food shacks, and military installations, Point Loma is an old and wealthy enclave of stately family homes for military officers, successful Portuguese fishermen, and political and professional leaders. Its bayside shores front huge estates, with sailboats and yachts packed tightly in private marinas.

18 **Cabrillo National Monument,** named after the Portuguese explorer Juan Rodriguez Cabrillo, sits atop the very tip of Point Loma. Cabrillo was the first European to discover San Diego, which he called San Miguel, in 1542. In 1913, the monument grounds were set aside to commemorate his discovery. Begin your tour at the Visitor's Center, where films and lectures about the monument, the sea-level tide pools, and the gray whales migrating offshore are presented frequently. Signs along the walkways that edge the cliffs describe the views, with posters picturing the various navy, fishing, and pleasure craft that sail into and fly over the bay. A new statue of Cabrillo overlooks downtown from a windy promontory, where visitors gather to admire the stunning panorama over the bay from the snowcapped San Bernardino Mountains, some 200 miles northeast to the hills surrounding Tijuana. Rest rooms and water fountains are plentiful along the paths that climb to the monument's various view points, but there are no food facilities. Exploring the grounds consumes time and calories; bring a picnic lunch and rest on a bench overlooking the sailboats headed to sea.

The oil lamp of the Old Point Loma Lighthouse was first lit in 1855. The light, sitting in a brass and iron housing above a painstakingly refurbished white wooden house, shone through a state-of-the-art lens from France and was visible from the sea for 25 miles. Unfortunately, it was too high above the cliffs to guide navigators trapped in Southern California's thick offshore fog and low clouds. In 1891 a new lighthouse was built on the small shore under the slowly eroding 400-foot cliffs. The old lighthouse is open to visitors, and the Coast Guard still uses the newer lighthouse and a mighty foghorn to guide boaters through the narrow channel leading into the bay. *1800 Cabrillo Memorial Dr., tel. 619/557–5450. Admission: $1; $3 for parking. Open daily 9–5:15.*

19 **Shelter Island** sits in the narrow channel between Point Loma's eastern shore and the west coast of Coronado. In 1950 the port director thought there should be some use for the soil dredged to deepen the ship channel. Why not build an island?

His hunch paid off. Shelter Island's shores now support towering mature palms, a cluster of mid-range resorts and restaurants, and side-by-side marinas. It is the center of San Diego's yacht-building industry, and boats in every stage of construction are visible in the yacht yards. A long sidewalk runs from the landscaped lawns of the **San Diego Yacht Club** (tucked down Anchorage Street off Shelter Island Drive), past boat brokerages to the hotels and marinas, which line the inner shore facing Point Loma. On the bay side, fishermen launch their boats or simply stand on shore and cast off. Families relax at picnic tables on the grass, where there are fire rings and permanent barbecue grills, while strollers wander to the huge Friendship Bell, given to San Diegans by the people of Yokahama in 1960.

Scott Street, which runs along Point Loma's waterfront from Shelter Island to the Marine Corps recruiting center on Harbor Drive, is lined with deep-sea-fishing charters and whale-watching boats. This is a good spot to watch fishermen (and women) haul marlin, tuna, and puny mackerel off their boats.

20 **Harbor Island,** made from 3½ million tons of rock and soil from the San Diego Bay, forms a peninsula adjacent to the airport. Again, hotels and restaurants line the inner shores, but here the buildings are many stories high, and the views from the bayside rooms are spectacular. The bay shore has pathways and gardens and picnic spots for sightseeing or working off the calories from the island restaurants' fine meals. On the west point Tom Ham's Lighthouse restaurant has a Coast Guard-approved beacon shining from its tower.

21 **Sunset Cliffs Park** is at the western side of Point Loma near Ocean Beach. The cliffs are aptly named, since their main attraction is their vantage point as a fine sunset-watching spot. The dramatic coastline here seems to have been carved out of ancient rock. Certainly the waves make their impact, and each year more sections of the cliffs sport caution signs. Don't climb around on the cliffs when you see these signs. It's easy to lose your footing and slip in the crumbling sandstone, and the surf can get very rough. Small coves and beaches dot the coastline and are popular with surfers drawn to the pounding waves and locals from the neighborhood who name and claim their special spots. The homes along Sunset Cliffs Boulevard are lovely examples of Southern California luxury, with pink adobe mansions beside shingled Cape Cod-style cottages. To reach the cliffs from Cabrillo Monument take Catalina Boulevard to Hill Street. Turn left and drive straight to the cliffs. Sunset Cliffs Boulevard intersects Hill Street and runs through Ocean Beach to Interstate 8.

Balboa Park

*Numbers in the margin correspond with points of interest on
the Balboa Park map.*

If it were on the ocean, Balboa Park would encompass all that is
wonderful about San Diego. But you can see the ocean, or the
bay at least, from many points in the park's 1,400 acres of
cultural, recreational, and environmental delights. Balboa
Park's acreage had been set aside by the city founders in 1868.
Many of the park's ornate Moorish buildings were intended to
be temporary structures housing exhibits for the Panama-
California International Exposition of 1915 and the California
Pacific International Exposition of 1935–36. Most of San
Diego's museums are located in the park, making it San Diego's
cultural center. The museums offer free admission on a rotat-
ing basis on Tuesdays.

The Laurel Street Bridge, also known as Cabrillo Bridge, is the
park's official gateway that leads over a vast canyon, filled with
downtown commuter traffic on Highway 163, to El Prado, the
park's central pedestrian mall. At Christmas the bridge is lined
with colored lights. Bright pink blossoms on rows of peach
trees herald the coming of spring. At the final arch leading to
El Prado, the 100-bell carillon in the California Tower tolls the
hour. Figures of California's historical personages decorate
the base of the 200-foot spire, and a magnificent blue-tile dome
shines in the sun.

① **The Museum of Man** sits under the California Tower and houses
the extensive collection of archaeological and anthropological
exhibits first assembled for the 1915 exposition. One of that
fair's primary cultural highlights was the "Story of Man
Through the Ages" display, with artifacts called from expeditions throughout the world. Over the years the museum has
amplified that original theme and is now one of the finest anthropological museums in the country. Exhibits focus on
Southwestern, Mexican, and South American cultures, and the
museum sponsors ongoing expeditions and research in South
America. *Tel. 619/239–2001. Admission: $3 adults, $1 children
13–18. Open daily 10–4:30.*

② Next to the Museum of Man are the Simon Edison Center for
the Performing Arts, with three theaters, and the **Sculpture
Garden,** an outdoor exhibit of traditional and modernistic
sculptures. The Sculpture Garden Cafe, with tables set amid
the art, is open for lunch.

③ **The San Diego Museum of Art** faces the central parking lot,
where an empty parking space is rarer than any painting. Traffic is diverted from the rest of El Prado here, with the roadway
leading toward the park's southern circle of museums. Be sure
to check out the Museum of Art's special shows, which can be
quite adventurous—recent shows have included the paintings
of Dr. Seuss and Maurice Sendak, giving the kids something to
appreciate while the grownups admire the old masters. *Tel.
619/232–7931. Admission: $4. Open Tues.–Sun. 10–4:30.*

④ **The Timken Art Gallery,** next to the museum, is a private gallery housing works of European masters and a collection of
Russian icons. The Putnam Foundation operates the gallery,
which is the only privately owned building in the park. *Tel. 619/*

Balboa Park

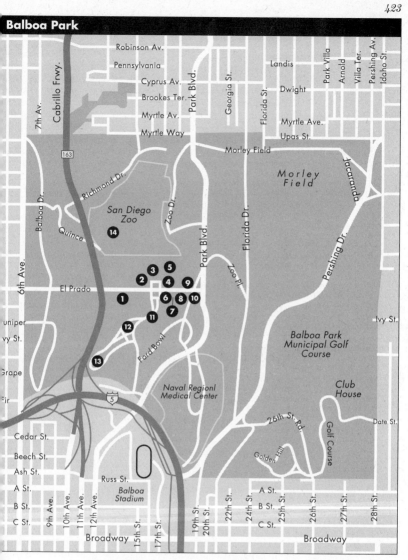

Robinson Av.
Pennsylvania
Cyprus Av.
Brookes Ter.
Myrtle Av.
Myrtle Way
7th Av.
Cabrillo Frwy.
Park Blvd.
Georgia St.
Florida St.
Landis
Dwight
Park Villa
Arnold
Villa Ter.
Pershing Av.
Idaho St.
Myrtle Ave.
Upas St.
163
Richmond Dr.
Balboa Dr.
Quince
San Diego Zoo
Zoo Dr.
Morley Field
Morley Field
Jacaranda
6th Ave.
El Prado
Park Blvd.
Florida Dr.
Zoo Pl.
Pershing Dr.
Ivy St.
Juniper
Ivy St.
Ford Bowl
Balboa Park Municipal Golf Course
Club House
Grape
Fir
5
Naval Regionl Medical Center
26th St. Rd.
Golden Hill
Golf Course
Date St.
Cedar St.
Beech St.
Ash St.
A St.
B St.
C St.
9th Ave.
10th Ave.
11th Ave.
12th Ave.
15th St.
17th St.
Russ St.
Balboa Stadium
19th St.
20th St.
22nd St.
24th St.
25th St.
A St.
B St.
C St.
26th St.
27th St.
28th St.
Broadway
Broadway

Botanical Building, **5**
Hall of Champions, **7**
House of Pacific Relations, **12**
Museum of Man, **1**
Museum of Photographic Arts, **8**

Natural History Museum, **9**
Organ Pavilion, **11**
Park Information Center, **6**
Reuben H. Fleet Space Theater and Science Center, **10**

San Diego Aerospace Museum, **13**
San Diego Museum of Art, **3**
San Diego Zoo, **14**
Sculpture Garden, **2**
Timken Art Gallery, **4**

239–5548. *Admission free. Open Tues.–Sat. 10–4:30, Sun*
1:30–4:30. *Closed Sept.*

The action gets lively in the next section of El Prado, where
mimes, jugglers, and musicians perform on long lawns beside
❺ the Lily Pond, in front of the graceful **Botanical Building.** Built
for the 1915 exposition, the latticework, open-air nursery
houses more than 500 types of tropical and subtropical plants.
The orchid collection is stunning, and there are benches beside
cool miniature waterfalls for resting away from the sun. The
Lily Pond is filled with giant koi fish and blooming water lilies
and is a popular spot for photographers. The Botanical Building is open daily from 10 to 4:30, and there is no admission fee.

❻ **The Park Information Center** (tel. 619/239–0512; open daily
9:30–4) is located in the House of Hospitality, across El Prado
from the pond. Many of the city's cultural groups also have offices in this building, which surrounds a peaceful patio and
Spanish fountain. Next door, The Cafe Del Rey Moro serves
drinks, lunch, and dinner. The flowering grotto hidden by eucalyptus trees behind the restaurant is a favored spot for
weddings.

❼ The **Hall of Champions,** a sports museum with a vast collection
of memorabilia honoring local athletes and sports history, is
next in line. The Hall of Champions has paintings and photographs of famous sports personalities. *Tel. 619/234–2544.*
Admission: $2 adults, 50¢ children 6–17. Open Mon.–Sat. 10–
4:30, Sun. 1:30–4:30.

❽ The **Museum of Photographic Arts,** one of the few museums in
the country dedicated solely to photography, celebrated its
sixth anniversary in 1989. MOPA exhibits the works of world-
renowned and relatively obscure photographers, highlighting
themes of human tragedy and celebration. *Tel. 619/239–5262.*
Admission: $2.50. Open daily 10–5, Thurs. 10–9.

Below MOPA in the basement of the Casa de Balboa is the **San
Diego Model Railroad Museum.** The room is filled with the
sounds of chugging engines, screeching brakes, and shrill whis-
tles when the six model train exhibits are in operation. *Tel. 619/
696–0199. Admission free. Open Fri. 11–4, weekends 11–5.*

The short flight of steps leading to the park's main fountain is
another gathering spot for street performers. On one side of
❾ the fountain is the **Natural History Museum,** with displays on
the plants and animals of Southern California and Mexico. Children seem particularly impressed by the dinosaur bones, while
amateur geologists, gemologists, and jewelers admire the collection of gems, including beautiful rose-colored tourmaline
crystals mined in San Diego County. *Tel. 619/232–3821. Admission: $4 adults, $1 children 3–11. Open daily 10–4:30.*

❿ The **Reuben H. Fleet Space Theater and Science Center** is on the
other side of the fountain. The Omnimax theater has a dome
overhead screen where fantastic films about nature, space, and
life seem to lift the viewer into the action. Films are shown regularly throughout the day and are informative and exhilarating. The Science Center is like a giant laboratory playground
where clever interactive exhibits teach children and adults
about basic and complex scientific principles. The center's gift
shop is akin to a museum, with toys and gadgets that inspire
the imagination. The Laserium has laser shows throughout

the day. *Tel. 619/238–1168. Theater admission: $5 adults, $3 children 5–15; laser shows: $5 adults, $3 children 6–17; Science Center admission: $1.50 adults, 75¢ children or included with price of theater ticket. Open daily 9:30–9:30.*

El Prado ends in a bridge that crosses over Park Boulevard to a perfectly tended rose garden and a seemingly wild cactus grove. From here you can see across the canyon to even more parkland, with picnic groves, sports facilities, and acres of ranging chaparral. Back along El Prado, roads and pathways lead to even more sights.

The main branch off El Prado goes south from the parking lot by the Museum of Art. A long island of flowers divides the road

⑪ curving around the **Organ Pavilion** and the 5,000-pipe Spreckels Organ, believed to be the largest outdoor organ in the world. Much of the time it is locked up on a stage before rows of benches where wanderers rest and regroup. Concerts are sometimes given on Sunday afternoons, and the organ is amazing to hear. On summer evenings local military bands, gospel groups, and barbershop quartets give concerts in the pavilion. At Christmas, the park's massive Christmas tree and life-size nativity display turn the Organ Pavilion into a seasonal wonderland.

⑫ The **House of Pacific Relations,** across from the pavilion, is really a cluster of stucco cottages representing various foreign countries. The buildings are open on Sundays, and individual cottages often present celebrations on their country's holidays. A large parking lot sits just behind the pavilion and is a good place to find a space, particularly if you're attending an evening cultural event.

⑬ This southern road ends at the Pan American Plaza and the **San Diego Aerospace Museum and International Aerospace Hall of Fame.** The building is unlike any other in the park. The Ford Motor Company commissioned the building for the 1935 exposition, when sleek, streamlined design was all the rage. A thin line of blue neon outlines the round building at night, giving it the appearance of a landlocked UFO. Exhibits about aviation and aerospace pioneers line the rotunda, and a collection of real and replicated aircraft fills the center. *Tel. 619/234–8291. Admission: $4 adults, $1 children 6–17. Open daily 10–4:30.*

The **San Diego Automotive Museum** (tel. 619/231–2886) is one of the newest museums in Balboa Park, situated in Pan American Plaza, between the Palisades Building and the International Aerospace Hall of Fame.

⑭ **The San Diego Zoo** is Balboa Park's most famous attraction. It ranges over 100 acres fronting Park Boulevard, and is surely one of the finest zoos and tropical gardens in the world. More than 3,200 animals of 777 species roam in expertly crafted habitats that spread down into, around, and up above the natural canyons. Equal attention has been paid to the flora; the zoo is an enormous botanical garden with one of the world's largest collections of subtropical plants. From the moment you walk through the entrance and face the swarm of bright pink flamingos and blue peacocks, you know you've entered a rare pocket of natural harmony. Exploring the zoo fully takes the stamina of a healthy hiker, but there are open-air trams running throughout the day on a 3-mile tour of 80% of the zoo's exhibits.

Tel. 619/234–3153. Admission: $8.50 adults, $2.50 children 3–15. Open daily 9–6:30; no entrance after 4 PM.

Old Town

Numbers in the margin correspond with points of interest on the Old Town San Diego map.

San Diego's Spanish and Mexican history and heritage are best evident in Old Town, just north of downtown at Juan Street, near the intersection of interstates 5 and 8. It wasn't until 1968 that Old Town became a state historic park. Fortunately, private efforts kept the area's history alive until then, and many of San Diego's oldest structures remain in good shape. Old Town also has many interesting shops and restaurants.

Though Old Town is often credited as being the first European settlement in Southern California, the true beginnings took
① place overlooking Old Town from atop **Presidio Park.** There, Father Junípero Serra established the first of California's missions, called San Diego Acala, in 1769. San Diego's Indians, called the San Diegueños by the Spaniards, were forced to abandon their seminomadic lifestyle and live at the mission. In 1774 the hilltop was declared a Royal Presidio, or fortress, and the mission was moved to its current location along the San Diego River, 6 miles east from the original site. The Indians lost more of their traditional grounds and ranches as the mission grew along the riverbed. In 1775 the Indians attacked and burned the mission, destroying religious objects and killing Franciscan Padre Luis Jayme. Their later attack on the presidio was less successful, and their revolt was short-lived. By 1800 around 1,500 Indians were living on the mission's grounds, receiving religious instruction and adapting to the Spanish way of life.

The pioneers living within the presidio's walls were mostly Spanish soldiers and poor Mexicans and mestizos, unaccustomed to farming San Diego's arid lands. They existed marginally until 1821, when Mexico gained independence from Spain, claimed its lands in California, and the Mexican flag flew over the presidio. The Mexican government, centered some 3,000 miles away in Monterey, stripped the Spanish missions of their land-holdings, and an aristocracy of landholders began to emerge. At the same time, settlers were beginning to move down from the presidio to what is now called Old Town.

In 1846, during the war between Mexico and the United States, a detachment of Marines raised the U.S. flag in Old Town; in 1850 San Diego became an incorporated city, with Old Town as its center.

Old Town's historic buildings are clustered around the main
② plaza along San Diego Avenue, called **California Plaza,** with a view of the presidio from behind the cannon by the flagpole. The plaza today serves much the same purpose as it did when it was first laid out. Art shows often fill the lawns around the plaza, and lounging and strolling are encouraged. San Diego Avenue is closed to traffic here, and the cars are diverted to Juan and Congress streets, both of which are also lined with shops and restaurants. There are plenty of free parking lots on the outskirts of Old Town, which is best seen by foot. Shopping

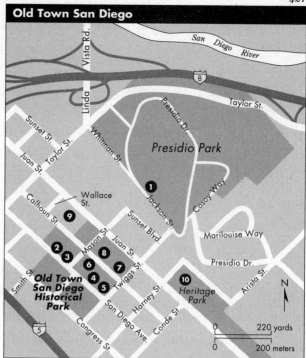

and eating are essential for a true Old Town tour, so bring your wallet and an appetite.

3 The Old Town State Historic Park office is located in **La Casa de Machado y Silvas,** on the south side of the plaza. Free guided tours of the park are available here daily at 2 PM, and there is a good booklet for sale that provides a brief history and self-guided-tour map for the 12-acre park. La Casa de Machado y Silvas was built in 1843 and housed families for more than a century; park rangers now show films and distribute information from the living room. The office is at the intersection of San Diego Avenue and Mason Street. *Tel. 619/237–6770. Open daily 10–5.*

The historic section of Old Town includes a collection of adobe **4** and log houses in a subdued Mexican colonial style. **La Casa de Pedrorena,** a hacienda-style home built in 1869, now houses a **5** Mexican restaurant and bakery. **La Casa de Altamirano** serves as the *San Diego Union* Newspaper Historical Building. A wood-frame structure prefabricated in Maine and shipped around Cape Horn in 1851, the building has been restored to replicate the newspaper's offices of 1868, when the first edition of the *San Diego Union* was printed.

6 **La Casa de Estudillo,** across Mason Street from the plaza, is an original Old Town adobe built in 1827. The house has been restored to its former grandeur as the home of the prestigious **7** Estudillo family, and it is now open for tours. **The Seeley Stable** became San Diego's stagecoach stop in 1867 and was the hub of Old Town until near the turn of the century, when the tracks of the Southern Pacific Railroad passing by the south side of the settlement became the favored route. The stables now house a collection of horse-drawn vehicles, Western memorabilia, and Indian artifacts. There is a $1 admission fee to tour the stables, where a slide show on San Diego history is presented three times a day.

❽ La Casa de Bandini, next to the stables, is one of the loveliest haciendas in San Diego. Built in 1829 by a Peruvian, Juan Bandini, the house served as Old Town's social center during Mexican rule. After Bandini lost his financial, political, and social standing through various political and business schemes, he lost the house in the 1850s. Albert Seeley, the stagecoach entrepreneur, purchased the home in 1869, added a second story, and turned it into the Cosmopolitan Hotel, a comfortable way station for travelers on the day-long trip south from Los Angeles. Surely it must have been a lovely hotel, with rooms overlooking the huge central gardens and patio. Casa Bandini's colorful gardens and main floor dining rooms now house a good Mexican restaurant run by the owners of other highly successful Old Town businesses.

❾ The unofficial center of Old Town is the **Bazaar del Mundo,** a shopping and dining enclave built to represent a colonial Mexican square. The central courtyard is always in blossom with magenta bougainvillea and scarlet hibiscus, with irises, poppies, and petunias in season. Ballet Folklorico and flamenco dancers perform in the outdoor gazebo on weekend afternoons, and the bazaar frequently holds arts and crafts exhibits and Mexican festivals in the courtyard. Colorful shops specializing in Latin American crafts and unusual gift items border the courtyard, which is shielded from shoppers by thick bushes and huge bird cages with cawing macaws and toucans.

❿ Heritage Park, up the Juan Street hill east of the Seeley Stables, is the headquarters for SOHO, the Save Our Heritage Organization. The climb up to the park is a bit steep, but the view of the harbor is great. SOHO has moved several grand Victorian homes and a temple from other parts of San Diego to the park, where they have been restored. The homes are now used for offices, shops, and restaurants.

Mission Bay

Numbers in the margin correspond with points of interest on the Mission Bay Area map.

Mission Bay is San Diego's monument to sports and fitness. Action and leisure are the main themes of this 4,600-acre aquatic park, 75% of which is public land. Admission to its 27 miles of bayfront beaches and 17 miles of ocean frontage is free. All you need for a perfect day is a bathing suit, shorts, and the right selection of playthings.

When explorer Juan Rodriguez Cabrillo first spotted the bay in 1542, he called it "Baja Falso." The ocean-facing inlet led to acres of swampland, inhospitable to boats and inhabitants. In the 1960s the city planners decided to dredge the swamp and build an artificial bay with acres of beaches and lawns for play. Only 25 percent of the land would be used for commercial property, and now just a handful of resort hotels break up the natural landscape. Drivers and train riders coming down to San

Diego from Los Angeles get a good view of the action and the park's most popular spots. Kite flying has become a fine art on the lawns facing Interstate 5, where the sky is flooded with the bright colors of huge, elaborate kites.

❶ The **Visitor Information Center** at the East Mission Bay Drive exit from Interstate–5 is an excellent tourist resource for the bay and all of San Diego. Leaflets and brochures for most of the area's attractions are provided free of charge, and information on transportation, reservations, and sightseeing is offered cheerfully. The center is a gathering spot for the runners, walkers, and exercisers taking part in group activities. From the low hill outside the building you can easily appreciate the bay's obvious charms. *2688 E. Mission Bay Dr., tel. 619/276–8200. Open daily 9–5:30.*

A 5-mile pathway runs through this section of the bay from the trailer park and miniature golf course south past the highrise Hilton Hotel to Sea World Drive. Playgrounds and picnic areas abound on the beach and low grassy hills of the park. Group gatherings, company picnics, and birthday parties are common along this stretch, where huge parking lots seem to expand to serve the swelling crowds on sunny days. On weekend evenings, the path is filled with a steady stream of exercisers jogging, speed walking, biking, and skating, releasing tension from their stressful day at the office. The water is filled with bathers (watch for signs indicating that the water is unsafe), water-skiers, fishermen, and boaters, some in one-person kayaks, others in crowded powerboats. The San Diego Crew Classic, which takes place in April, fills this section of the bay with crew teams from throughout the country.

❷ **Fiesta Island,** off Mission Bay and Sea World drives, is a smaller, artificial playground popular with jet- and water-skiers. In July, the annual Over-the-Line Tournament attracts thousands of players and oglers drawn by the baseball teams' raunchy names and outrageous behavior. Call 619/297–8480 for more information.

Ingraham Street is another main drag through the bay, from ❸ the shores of Pacific Beach to Sea World Drive. **San Diego Princess Resort** is the focal point of this part of the bay, with its lushly landscaped grounds, model yacht pond, and bayfront restaurants. Ducks and cottontail rabbits are as common as tourists, and the resort is a great family playground. Powerboats take off from Ski Beach, across Ingraham Street, which is also the site of the annual Miller Highlife Thunderboat Regatta, held in September. The noise from these boats is absolutely deafening, and the beach is packed from dawn until dark with thrill seekers.

West Mission Bay Drive runs from the ocean beyond Mission Boulevard to Sea World Drive. The pathways along the Mission Beach side of the bay are lined with vacation homes, many for rent by the month. Those fortunate to live here year round have the bay as their front yard, with wide sandy beaches, volleyball courts, and an endless stream of sightseers on the sidewalk. **Belmont Park,** an abandoned amusement park at the corner of Mission Boulevard and West Mission Bay Drive, has undergone restoration and now is a shopping and dining center between the bay and the Mission Beach boardwalk. Twinkling lights outline the old Belmont Park roller coaster, which has a dedi-

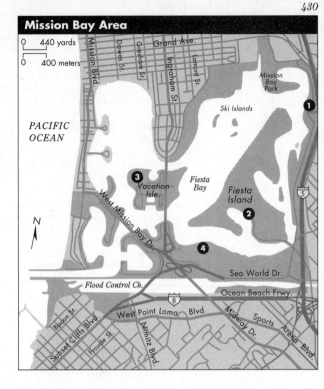

cated group of supporters who protect the coaster from destruction and continuously attempt to get it running again.

4 The world's largest marine life park, **Sea World,** is an ocean-oriented amusement park set amid tropical landscaping along the bay. The high Sky Tower has a glass elevator to the top, where the views of San Diego County from the ocean to the mountains are nicest in early morning and late evening. Recent additions include a bat ray pool and a new stadium for the ever-popular Shamu killer whale show. Summer nights feature concerts and fireworks displays. The Penguin Encounter has a moving sidewalk passing by a glass-enclosed artic environment, where hundreds of emperor penguins slide over glaciers into icy waters. The shark exhibit, with a variety of fierce-looking species, is especially popular with imaginative youngsters. *Sea World Dr., at west end of I–8, tel. 619/226–3901, Admission: $21 adults, $15.50 children 3–11. Open daily 9–5, later in summer.*

La Jolla

Numbers in the margin correspond with points of interest on the La Jolla map.

La Jollans have long considered their village to be the Monte Carlo of California, and with good cause. Its coastline curves into natural coves backed by verdant hillsides covered with lavish homes, now worth millions as housing values soar. Though La Jolla is considered part of San Diego, it has its own postal zone and a coveted sense of class. Movie stars and royalty frequent established hotels and private clubs, and the social scene is the stuff gossip columns are made of.

The Indians called it "La Hoya," meaning "the cave," referring to the caves dotting the shoreline. The Spaniards changed the name to La Jolla, meaning "the jewel," and its residents have cherished the name and its allusions ever since. Though development and construction have radically altered the town's once serene and private character, it remains a haven for the elite, a playground for those who can afford such luxuries.

To reach La Jolla from I–5 take the Ardath Road exit if you're traveling north, and drive slowly down this long hill so you can appreciate the breathtaking view. Traveling south, take the La Jolla Village Drive exit. If you enjoy meandering, the best way to reach La Jolla from the south is to drive through Mission and Pacific beaches on Mission Boulevard, past the crowds of roller skaters, bicyclists, and sunbathers headed to the beach. The clutter and congestion eases up as the street becomes La Jolla Boulevard, where quiet neighborhoods with winding streets lead down to some of the best surfing beaches in San Diego (*see* Beaches, below). The boulevard here is lined with expensive restaurants and cafes, and a few take-out spots.

Nautilus Street East leads up to **Mount Soledad,** the highest point in La Jolla. From the cross on top of the mountain you can see the coast from the county's northern border south far beyond downtown—barring smog and haze. It is an excellent spot for getting a true sense of San Diego's geography. Sunrise services are held here on Easter Sunday.

❶ La Jolla's primary coastal attraction is **Ellen Browning Scripps Park** at La Jolla Cove. In the park along the cliffs above the cove, towering palms line the sidewalk of Coast Boulevard, where strollers in evening dress are as common as Frisbee throwers. The Children's Pool, at the south end of the park, has a curving beach and shallow waters and is a wonderful place for small swimmers.

❷ The **La Jolla Caves** are at the farthest point north of the cove under the La Jolla Cave and Shell Shop (1325 Coast Blvd., tel. 619/454–6080). A trail leads down from the shop into the caves, with 133 steps down to the largest, Sunny Jim Cave. The waters at La Jolla Cove are an underwater preserve, and divers and snorkelers flock to these shores on sunny weekends.

Prospect Street, La Jolla's main boulevard, overlooks the cove from 1 block up. The street is lined with excellent restaurants, expensive boutiques, and a recent proliferation of office buildings and two-story shopping complexes. Many of the restaurants on the west side of the street have great views of the cove. At the corner of Prospect and Girard streets sits the charming **❸** pink **La Valencia Hotel.** Its grand lobby with floor-to-ceiling windows overlooking the cove is a popular wedding spot, and its Whaling Bar is the main hangout for La Jolla denizens. The hotel exudes a certain stuffiness, and as Prospect Street grows ever more crowded, lines of Mercedes and Jaguars crowd the valet stand at the hotel's entrance. Pretend you are visiting nobility and wander through the lobby and onto the outdoor balcony—the view is worth the deception.

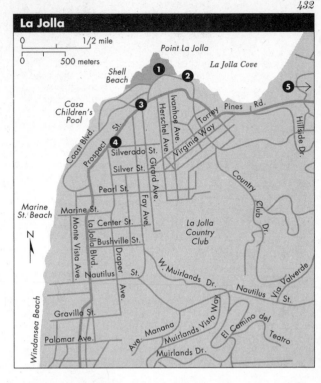

Like Prospect Street, Girard Street is lined with expensive
shops, where the wares are lovely to look at, even if highly
unaffordable. The shopping and dining district has spread to
Pearl Street and other side streets, with a steady parade of am-
blers and sightseers strolling about, chatting in many
languages. Wall Street, a quiet tree-lined boulevard, was once
the financial heart of La Jolla, but banks and investment houses
can now be seen throughout town. The nightlife scene is an active one here, with jazz clubs, piano bars, and watering holes
for the elite younger set coming and going with the trends.
Though the village has lost some of its charm and sense of being
a close-knit community, it has gained a cosmopolitan air that
makes it a popular vacation resort for the international set.

❹ The **La Jolla Museum of Contemporary Art** is the village's
cultural center, housed in a remodeled Irving Gill home. The
museum has a permanent collection of post-1950 art and often
exhibits shows of contemporary art, furnishings, and design.
Film series and lectures are held frequently in Sherwood Hall.
An excellent bookstore adjacent to the museum has a good collection of art books and magazines. *700 Prospect St., tel. 619/
454–3541. Admission: $3 adults, $1 students and seniors, 50¢
children under 12. Admission free Wed. after 5 P.M. Open Tues.
–Sun. 10–5, Wed. until 9.*

North of the cove on La Jolla Shores Drive is the La Jolla Beach
and Tennis Club, host of many tennis tournaments. La Jolla
Shores' beaches are some of the finest in San Diego, with long
❺ stretches allotted to surfers or swimmers. The **Scripps Institution of Oceanography,** up the hill from the shores, has a fine

aquarium with more than 20 huge tanks filled with colorful saltwater fish and helpful exhibits on how tides affect the shoreline. The fish are most active during feeding time, at 1:30 on Wednesday and Sunday. An outdoor tide-pool exhibit is filled with starfish, sea anemone, lobsters, crabs, and myriad sea creatures that inhabit the local shoreline. The bookstore has a nice selection of illustrated books and cards. There are paths leading down from the institute's buildings to the beaches at La Jolla Shores. The beach north of the Scripps Pier is a great tide-pooling spot, where you can find all sorts of sea creatures in the pools on shore. If you plan to stay at the beach be sure not to park at a meter. *8602 La Jolla Shores Dr., tel. 619/534–6933. Admission free, though contributions are appreciated. Open daily 9–5.*

San Diego for Free

San Diego's main attractions are its climate and natural beauty, which are accessible to all, free of charge. The 70 miles of beaches are free—no boardwalks with admission fees, no high-priced parking lots. All you need is a swimsuit and a towel. You can easily while away a week or two just visiting a different beach community each day, from the opulence of La Jolla to the laid-back hippie style of Ocean Beach (*see* Beaches, below). Nearly all of San Diego's major attractions in our Exploring section are situated amid huge parks, gardens, and waterfronts, with plenty of natural wonders to keep you amused.

Mission Bay is a massive playground for people of all ages, with beaches for sunning and swimming, playgrounds and picnic tables, and fire rings for nighttime bonfires. **Balboa Park** is similarly entrancing, with gorgeous gardens and recreational areas. The **Scripps Institution of Oceanography's Aquarium** requests donations but won't turn you away if you don't pay. Walking tours through Old Town are free, and the tour guides are great history teachers.

What to See and Do with Children

As if swimming, roller skating, biking, and hiking weren't enough, San Diego has plenty of additional activities to keep kids happy. The **San Diego Zoo** has children's petting zoos, where the animals are content to play nicely with curious kids. The animal nursery is a lot of fun for the little ones, who can spot baby chimps and antelopes playing with same bright-colored plastic toys that all kids enjoy.

Many of **Balboa Park's** museums have special exhibits for children. They seem particularly entranced by the Museum of Man's "Wonder of Life" exhibit, with see-through plastic models of babies in their mothers' wombs. The Natural History Museum's dinosaurs are always a hit. But best of all is the Science Center at the Rueben H. Fleet Space Theater, where the gadgets and hands-on experiments are clever and educational.

Mission Bay and many of the beaches have large playgrounds by the water. **The Children's Pool** at La Jolla Cove is a shallow cove protected from the waves, and safe for snorkeling.

In **Old Town,** Geppeto's toy store is a must-see for its inexpensive gadgets imported from Europe. There are plenty of incredibly expensive toys as well, but steer the kids toward the back shelves and they're sure to find some little treasure they'll enjoy. The carousels at Balboa Park and the zoo are good for burning up some energy.

Off the Beaten Track

Don't think you've finished seeing San Diego once you've hit all the main attractions. The real character of the place doesn't shine through until you've hit a few neighborhoods and mingled with the folks. Then you can say you've seen San Diego.

Mission Hills is an older neighborhood near downtown that has the charm and wealth of La Jolla and Point Loma, without the crowds. The prettiest streets are above Presidio Park and Old Town, where huge mansions with rolling lawns resemble Eastern estates. Drive along Fort Stockton Drive up from the Presidio, or Juan Street past Heritage Park in Old Town to Sunset Boulevard to see these homes. Washington Street runs up a steep hill from I–8 through the center of Mission Hills. Palmier's, at the corner of Washington Street and Goldfinch, is a French cafe and charcuterie with wonderful pâtés, pastries, and wines to eat there or to go. On Goldfinch, visit the Gathering, a neighborhood restaurant with great breakfasts and outdoor tables for reading the Sunday paper in the sun.

Hillcrest, farther up Washington Street beginning at First Avenue, is San Diego's Castro Street, the center for the homosexual community and artists of all bents. University Avenue and Fourth and Fifth streets are filled with cafes, boutiques, and excellent bookstores. The Guild Theater, on Fifth Street between University Avenue and Robinson, shows first-run foreign films and has nice balcony seating, unusual in this age of multiplexes. Words and Music, at Fourth Street and Robinson, is a great new and used bookstore with a baby grand piano in the center, where the proprietor often holds informal concerts. The Corvette Diner, on Fourth Street between University Avenue and Washington Street, is an outrageous '50s-diner sort of place, with burgers and shakes and campy waitpersons. Quel Fromage, a coffee house on University Avenue between Fourth and Fifth streets, has long been the place to go to discuss philosophical or romantic matters over espresso. Washington Street eventually becomes Adams Avenue, San Diego's Antique Row, with shops displaying an odd array of antiques and collectibles. Adams Avenue leads into Kensington and Talmadge, two lovely old neighborhoods overlooking Mission Valley.

Shopping

Most San Diego shops are open daily 10–6; department stores and shops within the larger malls stay open until 9 on weekdays. Almost every store will accept traveler's checks with proper identification (driver's license, passport). Aside from their own credit cards, major department stores usually accept American Express, MasterCard, and Visa.

Shopping Districts San Diego's shopping areas are a mélange of self-contained mega-malls, historic districts, quaint villages, funky neighborhoods, and chic suburbs.

Downtown. Horton Plaza, in the heart of center city, is a shopper's Disneyland—visually exciting multilevels of department stores, one-of-a-kind shops, fast-food counters, classy restaurants, a farmer's market, live theater, and cinemas. Free daily performances by jugglers, mimes, and musicians add to the festive atmosphere. Surrounding Horton Plaza is the 16-block Gaslamp Quarter, a redevelopment area featuring art galleries and antiques and specialty shops, housed in Victorian buildings.

Kensington/Hillcrest. These are two of San Diego's older, established neighborhoods, situated several miles north and east of downtown. Adams Avenue, in Kensington, is Antique Row. More than 20 dealers sell everything from postcards and kitchen utensils to cut glass and porcelain. Park Boulevard, in Hillcrest, is the city's center for nostalgia. Small shops, on either side of University Avenue, stock clothing, accessories, furnishings, and bric-a-brac from the 1920s–1960s.

Old Town. North of downtown, off I–5, this popular historic district is reminiscent of a colorful Mexican marketplace. Adobe architecture, flower-filled plazas, fountains, and courtyards highlight the shopping at Bazaar del Mundo. Smaller shopping complexes line the side streets and San Diego Avenue, where the finer galleries are scattered just blocks from Old Town's historic area.

Hotel Circle. The Hotel Circle area, northeast of downtown near I–8 and Freeway 163, has two major shopping centers. Fashion Valley and Mission Valley Center contain hundreds of shops, as well as restaurants, cinemas, and branches of almost every San Diego department store.

La Jolla/Golden Triangle. La Jolla, about 15 miles northwest of downtown, on the coast, is an ultrachic, ultraexclusive resort community. High-end and trendy boutiques line Girard Avenue and Prospect Street. Coast Walk, nestled along the cliff side of Prospect Street, offers several levels of sophisticated shops, galleries, and restaurants, as well as a spectacular ocean view. The Golden Triangle area, several miles east of coastal La Jolla, is served by two malls. La Jolla Village Square, just west of I–5, is an indoor shopping complex; University Towne Centre, farther inland, between I–5 and I–805, is an open-air village. Both centers feature the usual range of department stores, specialty shops, sportswear chains, restaurants, and cinemas.

Seaport Village. On the waterfront, a few minutes from downtown, Seaport Village offers quaint theme shops, restaurants, arts and crafts galleries, and commanding views of Coronado, the bridge, and passing ships.

Coronado. Across the bay, Coronado is accessible by car or ferry. Orange Avenue, in the center of town, has 6 blocks of ritzy boutiques and galleries. The elegant Hotel del Coronado, also on Orange Avenue, houses exclusive (and costly) specialty shops. Old Ferry Landing, where the new ferry lands, is a waterfront center similar to Seaport Village.

Beaches

Overnight camping is not allowed on any of the beaches, but there are campgrounds at some state beaches. Lifeguards are stationed at city beaches (from Sunset Cliffs to Black's Beach) in the summertime, but coverage in winter is erratic. Glass is prohibited on all beaches, and fires are allowed only in fire rings or barbecues. For a general beach and weather report, tel. 619/225-9494.

The beaches are listed from south to north. For information on Mission Bay, *see* Exploring.

Border Field State Beach. The southernmost San Diego beach is different from most California beaches. Located just north of the Mexican border, it is a marshy area with wide chaparrals and wildflowers, a favorite of horseback riders and hikers. Frequent sewage contamination from Tijuana makes the water unpleasant—if not downright dangerous—for swimming. Ample parking, rest rooms, fire rings. *Exit I-5 at Dairy Mart Rd. and head west along Monument Rd.*

South Beach. One of the few beaches where dogs are free to romp, this is a good beach for long, isolated walks. The often-contaminated water and rocky beach tend to keep crowds away. The downside: There are few facilities, such as rest rooms. *Located at the end of Seacoast Dr., take I-5 to Coronado Ave. and head west on Imperial Beach Ave. Turn left onto Seacoast Dr.*

Imperial Beach. A classic Southern California beach, where surfers and swimmers congregate to enjoy the water and waves. The Imperial Beach Municipal Pier, closed for several years due to storm damage, reopened in the summer of 1988. It provides a pleasant backdrop for the Frisbee games of the predominantly young crowd. Imperial Beach is also the site of the U.S. Open Sandcastle Competition every July. There are lifeguards on duty during the summer, parking lots, food vendors nearby, and rest room facilities. *Take Palm Ave. west from I-5 to where it ends at the water's edge.*

Silver Strand State Beach. Farther north on the isthmus of Coronado (commonly mislabeled an island), Silver Strand was set aside as a state beach in 1932. The name is derived from the tiny silver seashells found in abundance near the water. The water is relatively calm, making it ideal for families. Four parking lots provide room for more than 1,500 cars ($3 per car). There is also a campground and a wide array of facilities. *Take the Palm Ave. exit from I-5 west to State Hwy. 75; turn right and follow the signs.*

Coronado Beach. With the famous Hotel Del Coronado as a backdrop, this wide stretch of sandy beach is one of the largest in the county. It is surprisingly uncrowded on most days, as the locals go to the less touristy areas to the south or north. A perfect beach for sunbathing or games of Frisbee and smash ball (played with paddles and a large ball). Parking can be a little difficult on the busiest days, but there are plenty of rest rooms and service facilities, as well as fire rings. The view (even for a brief moment) as you drive over the Coronado Bridge makes it a worthwhile excursion. *From the bridge turn left on Orange Ave. and follow the signs.*

Sunset Cliffs. Back on the mainland, beneath the jagged cliffs on the west side of Point Loma peninsula, is one of the more secluded beaches in the area, popular primarily with surfers and locals. The tide goes out each day to reveal tide pools teeming with life at the south end of the peninsula, near Cabrillo Point. Farther north the waves attract surfers and the lonely coves attract sunbathers. Stairs are available at the foot of Bermuda and Santa Cruz avenues, but much of the access is limited to treacherous cliff trails. Another negative: There are no available facilities. *Take I–8 west to Sunset Cliffs Blvd. and head south.*

Ocean Beach. The northern end of this beach, past the second jetty, is known as Dog Beach, the only beach within San Diego city limits that allows dogs to romp around without a leash. The southern end of Ocean Beach, near the pier, is a hangout for surfers and transients. Much of the area, though, is a haven for local volleyball players, sunbathers, and swimmers. Limited parking, fire rings, and food vendors are available. *Reach Ocean Beach by taking I–8 west to Sunset Cliffs Blvd. and heading south. Turn right on Voltaire St., Saratoga Ave., or Newport Ave.*

Mission Beach. It's not Atlantic City, but the boardwalk stretching along Mission Beach is a popular spot for strollers, roller skaters, and bicyclists. The south end is a popular spot for surfers, swimmers, and volleyball players. Toward the north end, near the Belmont Park Roller Coaster, the newly refurbished Plunge (tel. 619/488–3110) offers freshwater swimming daily all year round, at a cost of $2 for adults and $1.75 for children and senior citizens. Parking can be a challenge, but there are plenty of rest rooms and restaurants in the area. *Exit I–5 at Garnet Ave. and head west to Mission Blvd. Turn south and look for parking.*

Pacific Beach. The boardwalk turns into a sidewalk, but there are still bike paths and picnic tables running along the beachfront. The beach is a favorite for local teens, and the blare of rock music can be annoying. Parking, too, can be a problem, although there is a small lot at the foot of Ventura Place. *Same directions as for Mission Beach, exept go north on Mission Blvd.*

Tourmaline Surfing Park and **Windansea Beach:** Immortalized in Tom Wolfe's 1965 novel, *The Pumphouse Gang,* these La Jolla beaches are two of the top surfing spots in the area. Tourmaline has a better parking area. *Take Mission Blvd. north (it turns into La Jolla Blvd.) and turn west on Tourmaline St. (for the surfing park) or Nautilus St. (for Windansea Beach).*

Marine Street Beach: This is a classic stretch of sand for sunbathing and Frisbee games. *Accessible from Marine St. off La Jolla Blvd.*

Children's Pool: For the tykes, a shallow lagoon with small waves and no riptide provides a safe, if crowded, haven. *It can be reached by following La Jolla Blvd. north. When it forks, take the left road, Coast Blvd.*

La Jolla Cove. Just north of the Children's Pool is La Jolla Cove, simply one of the prettiest spots in the world. A beautiful, palm-tree-lined park sits on top of cliffs formed by the incessant pounding of the waves. At low tide the tide pools and cliff caves provide a goal for explorers. Seals sun themselves on the rocks. Divers explore the underwater delights of the San Diego–La Jolla Underwater Park, an ecological reserve. The cove also is a favorite of rough-water swimmers. Buoys mark distances for them. The beach below the cove is almost nonexistent at high tide, but the cove is still a must-see. *Follow Coast Blvd. north to the signs; or take the La Jolla Village Dr. exit from I–5, head west to Torrey Pines Rd., turn left and drive down the hill to Girard Ave. Turn right and follow the signs.*

La Jolla Shores. One of the most popular and overcrowded beaches in the county. On holidays such as Memorial Day, all access routes are usually closed. The lures are a wide sandy beach, relatively calm surf, and a concrete boardwalk paralleling the beach. There are also a wide variety of facilities, from posh restaurants to snack shops, within easy walking distance. Go early to get a parking spot. *From I–5 take La Jolla Village Dr. west and turn left onto La Jolla Shores Dr. Head west to Camino del Oro or Vallecitos St. Turn right and look for parking.*

Black's Beach. Once the only legal nude beach in the country, before nudity was outlawed in the late 1970s. But that doesn't stop people from braving the treacherous cliff trails for a chance to take off their clothes. Above the beach, hang gliders and sail-plane enthusiasts launch from the Torrey Pines Glider Port. Due to the difficult access, the beach is always relatively uncrowded. The waves make it a favorite haunt for surfers. *Take Genesee Ave. west from I–5 and follow the signs to the glider port.*

Participant Sports

At least one stereotype of San Diego is true—it is an active, outdoors-oriented community. People recreate more than spectate. It is hard not to, with such a wide variety of choices available.

Bicycling On any given summer day Old Highway 101, from La Jolla to Oceanside, looks like a freeway for cyclists. Never straying more than a ¼-mile from the beach, it is easily the most popular and scenic ride around. Although the roads are narrow and winding, experienced cyclists like to follow Lomas Santa Fe Drive in Solana Beach east into beautiful Rancho Santa Fe, perhaps even continuing east on Del Dios Highway, past Lake Hodges, to Escondido. For more leisurely rides, Mission Bay, San Diego Harbor, and the Mission Beach boardwalk are all flat and scenic. San Diego even has a velodrome in Balboa Park, for those who like to race on a track. Tel. 619/239–0512 for more information.

Bikes can be rented at any number of bike stores, including **Alpine Rent A Bike** (tel. 619/273–0440) in Pacific Beach, **Hamel's Action Sports Center** (tel. 619/488–5050) in Mission Beach, and **California Bicycle** (tel. 619/454–0316) in La Jolla. A free comprehensive map of all county bike paths is available from the local office of the California Department of Transportation (tel. 619/237–6699).

Diving Enthusiasts from all over the world flock to La Jolla to skindive and scuba dive in the areas off the La Jolla Cove, so rich in ocean creatures and flora. The area marks the south end of the San Diego–La Jolla Underwater Park, an ecological preserve. Farther north, off the south end of Black's Beach, Scripps Canyon lies in about 60 feet of water. Accessible by boat, the canyon plummets to more than 175 feet in some sections. Another popular diving spot is off Sunset Cliffs in Point Loma, where lobster and a wide variety of sea life is relatively close to shore, although the strong rip currents make it an area best enjoyed by experienced divers.

Diving equipment and boat trips can be arranged through **San Diego Divers Supply** (tel. 619/224–3439), **Ocean Enterprises** (tel. 619/565–6054), or at the several **Diving Locker** locations throughout the area. It is illegal to take any wildlife from the ecological preserves in La Jolla or near Cabrillo Point. Spearfishing requires a license (available at most dive stores) and it is illegal to take out-of-season lobster and game fish out of the water. For general diving information contact the San Diego Marine Safety Service at tel. 619/225–9494.

Fishing Variety is the key. The Pacific Ocean is full of corbina, croaker, and halibut just itching to be your dinner. No license is required to fish from a public pier, such as the Ocean Beach pier. A fishing license from the State Department of Fish and Game, available at most bait and tackle stores, is required for fishing from the shoreline, although children under 15 won't need one.

Several companies offer half-day, daily, or multiday fishing expeditions in search of marlin, tuna, albacore, and other deepwater fish. **Fisherman's Landing** (tel. 619/222–0391), **H & M Landing** (tel. 619/222–1144), and **Seaforth Boat Rentals** (tel. 619/223–1681) are among the companies operating from San Diego. **Helgren's Sportfishing** (tel. 619/722–2133) offers trips from Oceanside Harbor.

Fitness Several hotels offer full health clubs, at least with weight machines, stationary bicycles, and spas, including, in the downtown area, the Omni San Diego (tel. 619/239–2200) and the U.S. Grant Hotel (tel. 619/232–3121). Hotels noted for health clubs in the outlying areas include the Hotel del Coronado (tel. 619/435–6611), Sheraton Grand (tel. 619/291–2900), Kona Kai Beach and Tennis Resort (tel. 619/222–1191), the San Diego Hilton Beach and Tennis Resort (tel. 619/276–4010), the La Costa Hotel and Spa (tel. 619/438–9111), and the Olympic Resort Hotel (tel. 619/438–8330). Guests of the Town and Country Hotel (tel. 619/291–7131) and the Hanalei Hotel (tel. 619/297–1101) have access to the tennis and racquetball courts, weight room, saunas, and other facilities of the nearby **Atlas Health Club** in Mission Valley (tel. 619/298–9321). The dozen **Family Fitness Centers** in the area—including centers in Mission Valley (tel. 619/281–5543), the Sports Arena area (tel. 619/224–2902), and La Jolla (tel. 619/457–3930)—and **Jack La Lanne Health Spas** (tel. 619/276–6070) allow nonmembers use of the facilities for a small fee. A company called **Sweat 'N Smile Inc.** (320 Upas St., San Diego, tel. 619/296–6776) offers fitness and recreation programs, including classes, volleyball, and baseball, geared to travelers.

Golf To list the more than 70 golf courses in San Diego County requires more space than we have here. Among the most popular public courses are the following:

Balboa Park Municipal Golf Course (Golf Course Dr., San Diego, tel. 619/232–2470). 18 holes, 5,900 yards, plus a neighboring nine-hole course, driving range, equipment rentals, clubhouse, restaurant.

Mission Bay Golf Course (2702 N. Mission Bay Dr., San Diego, tel. 619/273–1221). 18 holes, 3,175 yards, honors other memberships, reservations required, driving range, equipment rentals.

Rancho Bernardo Inn and Country Club (17550 Bernardo Oaks Dr., tel. 619/277–2146 or 800/542–6096). 18 holes, 6,329 yards, reservations required, driving range, equipment rentals, lodging.

Singing Hills Country Club (3007 Dehesa Rd., El Cajon, tel. 619/442–3425). 54 holes, honors other memberships, reservations required, driving range, equipment rentals, lodging.

Torrey Pines Municipal Golf Course (11480 N. Torrey Pines Rd., La Jolla, tel. 619/453–0380). 36 holes, reservations not required (but suggested), driving range, equipment rentals, lodging.

Whispering Palms Country Club (Via de la Valle, Rancho Santa Fe, tel. 619/756–2471). 27 holes, honors other memberships, reservations required, lodging.

Horseback Riding Expensive insurance has severely cut the number of stables offering horses for rent in San Diego County. The businesses that remain offer a wide variety of organized excursions. **Holidays on Horseback** (tel. 619/445–3997) in the East County town of Descanso leads rides ranging from a few hours to a few days in the Cuyamaca Mountains. They rent special, easy-to-ride steeds to make it a little easier for beginners. **Rancho San Diego Stables** (tel. 619/670–1861) is located near Spring Valley. South of Imperial Beach, near the Mexican border, **Hilltop Stables** (tel. 619/428–5441) and **Sandi's Rental Stables** (tel. 619/424–3124) lead rides through Border Field State Park.

Jogging There is no truth to the rumor that San Diego was created to be one big jogging track, but it often seems that way. From downtown, the most popular run is along the Embarcadero, which stretches around the bay. There are nice, uncongested sidewalks through most of the area. The alternative for downtown visitors is to head east to Balboa Park, where a labyrinth of trails snakes through the canyons.

Mission Bay may be the most popular jogging spot, renowned for its wide sidewalks and basically flat landscape. Trails head west around Fiesta Island from Mission Bay, providing distance as well as a scenic route.

The beaches, of course, are extremely popular with runners. But there is no reason to go where everyone else goes.

Running is one of the best ways to explore San Diego, especially along the coast. There are organized runs almost every weekend; check any local sporting goods store for more information. Some tips: Don't run in bike lanes and check the local newspaper's tide charts before heading to the beach.

Surfing A year-round sport (thanks to wetsuits in the winter) for people of all ages, surfing is not a hard sport to learn. Anyone can get on a board and paddle around. For the hard core, some of the most popular surfing spots are the Ocean Beach pier, Tourmaline Surfing Park in La Jolla, Windansea Beach in La Jolla, South Cardiff State Beach, and Swami's (Sea Cliff Roadside

Park) in Encinitas. Check the beach listings for directions. Be aware that most public beaches have separate areas for surfers.

Many local surf shops rent boards, including **Star Surfing Company** (tel. 619/273–7827) in Pacific Beach, **La Jolla Surf Systems** (tel. 619/456–2777), and **Hansen's Sporting Goods** (tel. 619/753–6595) in Encinitas.

Tennis   There are more than 1,300 courts spread around the county, most of them in private clubs. But there are a few public facilities. **Morley Field** (tel. 619/295–9278) in Balboa Park has 25 courts, 12 of which are lighted. However, nonmembers cannot make reservations, so it's first come, first served. There is a nominal fee for use of the courts. The **La Jolla Recreation Center** (tel. 619/454–2071) offers nine public courts near downtown La Jolla, five of them lighted. Use of the courts is free. There are 12 lighted courts at **Robb Field** (tel. 619/224–7581) in Ocean Beach, with a small day-use fee. In the eastern part of the city, the **Colina del Sol Recreation Center** (tel. 619/583–0303) charges a small fee for use of six lighted courts. Most high schools and community colleges also have courts open to the public on weekends.

The list of hotel complexes with tennis facilities includes the Bahia Resort Hotel (tel. 619/488–0551), the Hotel del Coronado (tel. 619/435–6611), the Kona Kai Beach and Tennis Resort (tel. 619/222–1191), La Costa Hotel and Spa (tel. 619/438–9111), and the Rancho Bernardo Inn and Country Club (tel. 619/487–1611). Intense tennis instruction is available at John Gardiner's Rancho Valencia Resort (tel. 619/756–1123 or 800/548–3664) in Rancho Santa Fe. Some of the larger private clubs: **Atlas Health Club** (tel. 619/298–9321), **San Diego Tennis and Racquet Club** (tel. 619/275–3270), and **Tennis La Jolla** (tel. 619/459–0869).

Waterskiing   Mission Bay is one of the most popular waterskiing areas in Southern California. It is best to get out early, when the water is smooth and the crowds small. The **Snug Harbor Marina** (tel. 619/434–3089) is small, but off the beaten path. Boats and equipment can be rented from **Seaforth Boat Rentals** (1641 Quivera Rd., near Mission Bay, tel. 619/223–1681). The private **San Diego and Mission Bay Boat and Ski Club** (2606 N. Mission Bay Dr., tel. 619/276–0830) operates a slalom course and ski jump in Mission Bay's Hidden Anchorage. Permission from the club or the Mission Bay Harbor Patrol (tel. 619/224–1862) must be obtained to use the course and jump.

Spectator Sports

San Diego doesn't have a professional basketball franchise, ever since the Clippers left for Los Angeles, but it has just about every other type of sporting team and event. For information on tickets to any event contact Teleseat (tel. 619/283–SEAT). San Diego Jack Murphy Stadium is located at the intersection of I–8 and I–805.

Baseball   From April through September the San Diego Padres (tel. 619/280–4636) slug it out for bragging rights in the National League at San Diego Jack Murphy Stadium. Tickets range from $3.50 to $8.50 and usually are readily available, unless the Padres are in the thick of the pennant race.

Football The Chargers (tel. 619/563–8281) have been one of the National Football League's most exciting teams since the merger with the American Football League. Originally a Los Angeles franchise, the Chargers fill San Diego Jack Murphy Stadium August through December.

Golf In January, La Costa Hotel and Spa (tel. 619/438–9111) hosts the prestigious **Tournament of Champions,** featuring the winners of the previous year's tournaments. The **San Diego Open** brings the pros to the Torrey Pines Municipal Golf Course (tel. 619/453–0380). The Stoneridge Country Club (tel. 619/487–2117) hosts the **Ladies Professional Golf Association** in the spring.

Horse Racing Begun 50 years ago by Bing Crosby, Pat O'Brien, and their Hollywood cronies, the annual summer meeting of the **Del Mar Thoroughbred Club** (tel. 619/755–1141) located on the Del Mar Fairgrounds "Where the Turf Meets the Surf" in Del Mar, attracts a horde of "Beautiful People," along with the best horses and jockeys in the country. The meeting begins in July and continues through early September, every day except Tuesday.

Dining

Local restaurateurs from time to time ask the question that so often interrupts their nightly slumbers: "Will San Diego ever be a *real* restaurant town?"

There are two answers to this question, neither quite satisfactory. San Diego certainly is a "restaurant town" in the sense that it offers one of the highest per capita ratios of eateries-to-population in the country; at last count there were 4,000 food service establishments in San Diego County. But it is not yet an eating capital in the style of Los Angeles and New York, where it is taken for granted that restaurant meals will be of high quality.

The city's gastronomic reputation rests primarily on its seafood, which is so popular that even modest restaurants make a point of offering several daily fish specials. It is hard to be more than a stone's throw from one or more seafood restaurants no matter where one stands in a shopping or tourist district, but bear in mind that the best seafood is found in the best restaurants, no matter what their culinary affiliation may be. And as is true elsewhere, restaurants with spectacular views—and there are many such in San Diego—often invest far more effort in washing the picture windows than in cooking.

The rules of dining out in San Diego are simple and pleasant. Most eateries serve lunch and dinner; breakfast is largely the province of hotels and coffee shops. Most restaurants accept reservations, but few require them, and waits are uncommon outside of the beach areas. Dress codes by and large do not exist beyond simple shirt-and-shoes requirements, except at a handful of top restaurants that require men to wear jackets. The city likes to dine around 7:30 PM, and it is at that hour that restaurants will be the most crowded. Few restaurants offer seating after 9:30 or 10 PM.

The principal restaurant locations are in the excitingly renovated downtown; in historic Old Town, site of the first non-native settlement and close to the downtown area; in the beach neighborhoods; and in exclusive La Jolla, a lovely neighborhood that slopes from the top of Mt. Soledad to the sea and attracts jet-setters and trendsetters from around the globe. Mission Valley, which remains a tourist center thanks to its concentration of hotels, sprouts restaurants like weeds but is a virtual desert when it comes to quality cuisine. A similar caveat must be offered about the large, tourist-oriented eateries on Shelter and Harbor islands, which in effect rent out their enjoyable views and lively atmospheres by charging hefty prices for mediocre food.

Restaurants are grouped first by location and then by type of cuisine. Highly recommended restaurants are indicated by a star ★.

Category	Cost*
Very Expensive	over $35
Expensive	$25–$35
Moderate	$15–$25
Inexpensive	under $15

per person, without tax, service, or drinks

Beaches
French
★

The Belgian Lion. A somewhat fusty, ugly duckling of a restaurant, The Belgian Lion serves one of the best roast ducklings to be found in the city, along with marvelously creamy soups, excellent braised sweetbreads, poached salmon in a delicious sorrel sauce, sauerkraut braised in champagne with smoked meats and sausages, and a rich cassoulet. The service and wine list are worthy of the menu, and although the decor lacks that certain *je ne sais quoi*, the place has a great deal of charm. *2265 Bacon St., tel. 619/223–2700. Dress: casual. Reservations suggested. AE, CB, DC, MC, V. Closed Sun. and Mon. Expensive.*

Mexican

Old Town Mexican Cafe. This old stand-by looks a touch seedy, but the burritos, enchiladas, and carne asada are satisfying enough so that lines are common even during the middle of the afternoon. Carnitas and shredded beef tacos are two of the dishes responsible for this restaurant's ongoing popularity with locals and visitors. This restaurant serves late, which makes it a good place at which to satisfy a midnight taco craving. *2489 San Diego Ave., tel. 619/297–4330. Dress: casual. Reservations accepted for groups. AE, MC, V. Inexpensive.*

Mixed Menu

Saska's. Walk through the doors and you're in the genuine heart of Old Mission Beach, whose lazy pulse still throbs here when the conversation in the bar turns to sports, especially San Diego's peculiar form of baseball called over-the-line. The food is simple but first-rate; choices include shellfish cocktails, a fine crab chowder, the fresh fish offerings of the day (simply but beautifully grilled), and some of the best steaks in town, especially the variously sized top sirloins. This is the only place that serves a full, quality menu until 3 AM nightly. *3768 Mission Blvd., tel. 619/488–7311. Dress: casual. Reservations accepted. AE, DC, MC, V. Moderate.*

Old Columbia Brewery & Grill. As the first microbrewery in San Diego, this eatery can be somewhat forgiven for paying more attention to its house brews than to its menu, a well-written but perfunctorily executed listing of snacks, burgers, salads, and entrées. The draw is the beer, tapped directly from

444

Avanti, **9**
The Belgian Lion, **17**
Cafe Pacifica, **16**
Dobson's, **24**
Fisherman's Grill, **5**
George's at the
Cove, **2**
Hard Rock Cafe, **7**
Issimo, **11**
Karinya, **12**
La Gran Tapa, **22**
La Valencia Hotel, **4**
L'Escargot, **10**
Manhattan, **8**
McCormick and
Schmick's, **13**
Old Columbia Brewery
& Grill, **19**
Old Town Mexican
Cafe, **15**
Pacifica Grill, **20**
Panda Inn, **25**
Rainwater's, **21**
Red Sails Inn, **18**
St. James Bar, **1**
Salvatore's, **23**
Saska's, **14**
Star of India, **6**
Top O' the Cove, **3**

San Diego Dining

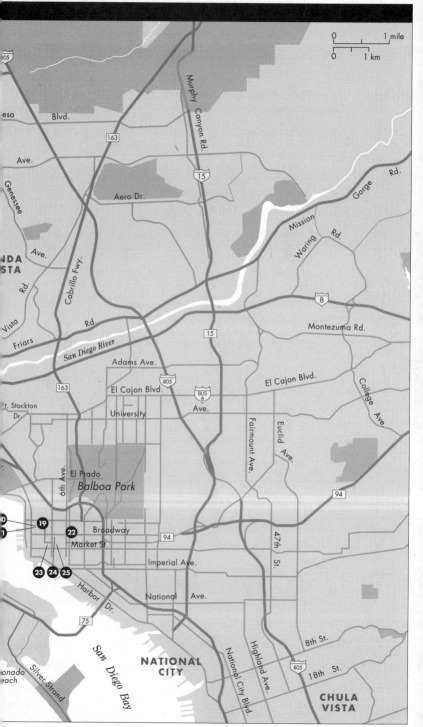

tanks in the adjacent brewing room. The best nibbles to go along with the Gaslamp Gold ale or the Downtown After Dark lager are beer-battered fish and chips, hefty onion rings, and oversized hamburgers. Downtown mingles here when the sun sets, and the action runs late. *1157 Columbia St., tel. 619/234–2739. Dress: casual. Reservations accepted. MC, V. Inexpensive.*

Red Sails Inn. This is not technically at the beach, since it is on the San Diego Bay side of Point Loma. It's an old favorite with old salts, though, and a natural for anyone in search of good, simple seafood at a waterfront location. The restaurant is surrounded by yacht basins and thus enjoys a large following among nautical types, who especially treasure its hearty, all-American breakfasts and late-night snacks. *2614 Shelter Island Dr., tel. 619/223–3030. Dress: casual. Reservations for large parties only. AE, DC, MC, V. Inexpensive.*

Seafood **Cafe Pacifica.** The menu changes daily to reflect the market availability of a globe-spanning selection of fish and shellfish. The approach is moderately nouvelle, which means that light, interesting sauces and imaginative garnishes are likely to be teamed with the simply cooked fillets of salmon, sea bass, swordfish, and so forth. Consider oysters and smoked fish as good opening courses, and don't miss the indulgent crème brûlée dessert. *2414 San Diego Ave., tel. 619/291–6666. Dress: informal. Reservations accepted. AE, DC, MC, V. No lunch weekends. Moderate.*

McCormick and Schmick's. Upon its opening in early 1988, this excellent seafood house offered a serious challenge to the city's older fish eateries. The menu changes frequently and may include as many as 100 options, all uniformly well prepared and ranging from a lovely selection of fresh oysters to Dungeness crabs, a fine crab-and-salmon Newburg, grilled baby salmon, and just about everything else that swims, crawls, or ruminates under the waves. The service is good, the upstairs courtyard pleasant, and a few choice tables have ocean views. An especially good choice for a lazy, self-indulgent lunch. *4190 Mission Blvd., tel. 619/581–3938. Dress: casual. Reservations suggested. AE, CB, DC, MC, V. Moderate.*

Thai **Karinya.** Designed and operated by a Thai architect, Karinya is rather soothingly pretty while still every bit as casual as the most beachy beachgoer could desire (and in San Diego, that's pretty casual). Start with the spicy salad called larb and the sweet noodles called mee krob, and then move along to the tart, savory tom yum gai soup. The entrée list gets hot and spicy with the curries (the beef penang nuah, and a fiery blend of shrimp and pineapple) and turns mild with myriad noodle dishes. Everything is quite good, including the service. *4475 Mission Blvd., tel. 619/270–5050. Dress: casual. Reservations accepted. AE, MC, V. Closed Mon., no lunch weekends. Inexpensive.*

Downtown **Panda Inn.** Clean, graceful lines and fine works of art replace
Chinese the paper lanterns and garish dragons that decorate most Chinese eateries, but, better yet, this is a place to which you can
★ take visiting Chinese friends with utter confidence. Thanks to superior kitchen and service staffs, this is not only the city's best Chinese restaurant, but one of its best restaurants, period. Its location in Horton Plaza, downtown San Diego's shopping and entertainment hub, makes it a natural place to

stop for "burnt" pork, sensational hot and pungent chicken and shrimp, succulent steamed dumplings, ridiculously delicious Szechuan-style green beans, and first-rate Peking duck. *506 Horton Plaza, tel. 619/233–7800. Dress: casual. Reservations accepted. AE, MC, V. Inexpensive.*

French-American ★ **Dobson's.** Consciously San Franciscan in style, Dobson's attracts the city's power structure during the day and well-heeled performing-arts patrons at night. The menu changes daily and is uniformly excellent, beginning with the always-available mussel bisque, and continuing with superb fish, veal, fowl, and beef entrées. The service and wine card also approach perfection. *956 Broadway Circle, tel. 619/231–6771. Reservations suggested. AE, MC, V. No lunch Sat. Closed Sun. Very Expensive.*

Italian **Salvatore's.** Situated in the lush, luxurious Meridian tower, Salvatore's makes the most of its surroundings and is a sophisticated milieu in which to lunch or dine. The Roman-born owners present a typically Roman menu, which is to say pan-Italian, with regional specialties from the tip of the Italian boot to the butter-loaded pastas of the far northern provinces. Presentations are spectacular, and for a dish of edible beauty, try the Caterina di Medici salad, or the excellent grilled swordfish, garnished to look like a pineapple. The pastas are uniformly superior. *750 Front St., tel. 619/544–1865. Reservations accepted. AE, MC, V. No lunch weekends. Closed Sun. Expensive.*

Mixed Menu **Rainwater's.** San Diego's answer to New York's Palm, this Eastern-style chophouse is the place to find oversize steaks, lobsters, veal and pork chops, prime ribs, and a rich, savory black bean soup accented with Madeira. Side dishes get as much attention as main events, so zero in on the wispy shoe-string potatoes, giant baked Idahos, steaming tangles of fried onion rings and the rich, satisfying creamed corn, all served in gargantuan portions. The wine list is also excellent. The mood is expansive, which makes it a favorite with movers, shakers, and dealmakers. *1202 Kettner Blvd. (2nd fl.), tel. 619/233–5757. Reservations accepted. AE, DC, MC, V. No lunch weekends. Very Expensive.*

Southwestern-Nouvelle **Pacifica Grill.** If you've never had canarditas (and you probably haven't), this is the place to visit for juicy chunks of slowly cooked duck, which one garnishes with any of a dozen spicy or savory condiments and rolls inside fresh, hot, blue corn tortillas. Since switching to the new Southwestern style of cooking, this ever-trendy restaurant has seen its popularity soar almost as high as the atrium that lights this beautifully remodeled warehouse. The place also serves superior seafood and wildly imaginative pastas. *1202 Kettner Blvd., tel. 619/696–9226. Reservations accepted. AE, CB, DC, MC, V. No lunch weekends. Moderate.*

Spanish **La Gran Tapa.** Carefully modeled to recall the fabled tapas bars that line the principal streets in Madrid, this noisy, busy in-spot daily prints up a lengthy menu of classic Spanish snacks and appetizers, with more substantial dishes and even an excellent hamburger thrown in for those who prefer traditional dining. The best bet is to order two or three tapas per person and let the whole table share. Choices include empanadas (spicy filled pies) made with pork and olives, spinach and cheese, or whatever the chef has dreamed up; tiny fried squid; miniature shrimp croquettes; shrimp in garlic sauce; fresh, hot potato chips, and much more. A good spot for late-night dining. *611 B St., tel. 619/234–8272. Dress: casual. Reservations accepted. AE, MC, V. No lunch Sat. Closed Sun. Moderate.*

La Jolla
California
★

George's at the Cove. A lovely, art-filled dining room, excellent service, a good view of La Jolla Cove, and an imaginative, well-prepared menu make this one of the city's best restaurants. Pay special attention to the seafood, but the pastas, beef and veal dishes, and poultry specialties are also uniformly excellent. Desserts are outsized, grandiose, and irresistible. *1250 Prospect St., tel. 619/454–4244. Reservations suggested. AE, CB, DC, MC, V. Very Expensive.*

Continental

Top O' The Cove. More or less synonymous with romance, Top O' The Cove has been the scene of thousands of marriage proposals in its 35-year history. Yet another place that boasts an extravagant view of La Jolla Cove, it also boasts a competent kitchen that turns out beautifully garnished, luxury fare dressed with creamy and well-seasoned sauces. The menu hits all the bases—beef, veal, fowl, and seafood—but pay special attention to the nightly specials. The decor is lush, and the wine list, at more than 800 entries, the recipient of countless awards. *1216 Prospect St., tel. 619/454–7779. Jacket and tie suggested. Reservations advised. AE, MC, V. Very Expensive.*

La Valencia Hotel. Depending on how you count them, there are from three to five dining rooms in La Jolla's famed and oh-so-fashionable "pink palace." Some locals just about live in the Whaling Bar dining room, which is why local shorthand designates the hotel "La V." Romantics will want to ascend the narrow tower to the Sky Room, however, which has the best (mostly French, and well-prepared) food in the hotel, as well as a view of the Pacific that stretches into infinity. The downstairs rooms feature better lunches than dinners, but in any case keep the seafood and poultry in mind. *1132 Prospect St., tel. 619/454–0771. Dress: casual. Reservations suggested. AE, CB, DC, MC, V. Moderate-Expensive.*

French

St. James Bar. A new offering from leading San Diego restaurateur Paul Dobson, the St. James Bar is a magnet for the area business folk at lunch, and the glitterati at night. All are drawn by the creamy mussel bisque, the sweetbreads in truffle juice sauce, the delicate poached Norwegian salmon in saffron sauce, and other beautifully realized offerings. One of the city's top five eateries, it offers expert cuisine in a luxurious setting that includes marble floors, art from a top gallery, and an incongruous but handsome 100-year-old bar rescued from a Montana saloon. *4370 La Jolla Village Dr., tel. 619/453–6650. AE, MC, V. No lunch Sat., closed Sun. Very Expensive.*

L'Escargot. Yes, you guessed it: this tiny hideaway in the Bird Rock district makes much of snails (escargot) and offers them in some 20 appetizer variations. To make something of a running joke, it also offers rich chocolate snails for dessert. In between these extremes lies some very solid, traditional French cooking, performed with flair by chef/proprietor Pierre Lustrat. Fresh fish, veal, beef, and duck dishes are equally rich and appealing. Skip the chocolate snails and instead order Lustrat's tarte tatin (upside-down apple tart) for dessert. He is so justly proud of it that his personalized license plates read "MA TATIN." *5662 La Jolla Blvd., tel. 619/459–6066. Jacket sug-*

gested. *Reservations advised. Dinner only. AE, MC, V. Expensive.*

Indian **Star of India.** As do so many chic, big-city neighborhoods, La Jolla hosts a good selection of upscale ethnic eateries. The Star of India is a case in point: Grander and more expensive than the city's other Indian houses, it also offers a better selection of dishes and a more talented kitchen staff. In addition to all the typical curries and kebabs, the menu offers several tandoori meats (baked in a special, super-heated oven), quite a number of vegetarian dishes, and a superb selection of freshly prepared Indian breads. *1025 Prospect St., tel. 619/459–3355. Dress: casual. Reservations accepted. DC, MC, V. Moderate.*

Italian **Issimo.** Beautifully composed plates are served in grand style ★ in a small jewel box of a dining room. Start with a pasta or the homemade pâté de foie gras (yes, this is an Italian place, but the foie gras is fabulous), and then move along to osso buco, baby lamb chops, veal sauté, or a steak in a delicate sauce. This restaurant also speaks seafood fluently, and the desserts rival those made by the finest European pastry chefs. *5634 La Jolla Blvd., tel. 619/454–7004. Jacket suggested. Reservations advised. MC, V. Closed Sun. Very Expensive.*

Avanti. For staid old La Jolla, this starkly modern restaurant with its mirrored ceiling and white, black, and chrome interior design, comes as a refreshing surprise. That's why it's such a popular meeting place for the trendy, successful natives looking for sophisticated fun with cuisine to match. There is an open-to-view kitchen where one can watch chef John Cooke prepare such appetite-arousing dishes as tiny pasta rings mixed with ricotta and pistachios; scampi sautéed in olive oil, minced garlic and white wine; beef filet topped with porcini mushroom sauce; chicken breasts grilled with radicchio. Counting calories? There's a spa menu, too. *875 Prospect Ave., 619/454–4288. Dinner only. Expensive. AE, MC, V.*

Manhattan. This little slice of the Big Apple became an overnight success when it brought a chic, cosmopolitan atmosphere and a rather good list of upscale Italian preparations to laidback but hungry La Jolla. The deep-fried calamari make an outstanding starter, and the selection of pastas includes both familiar favorites as well as some unusual, relatively exotic choices. The kitchen also does a good job with fish and shellfish, but its way with beef easily surpasses its talents in the veal department. Try the excellent ice cream specialties for dessert. Although Manhattan is located in the Empress Hotel, it is not a hotel dining room, since it is under separate management. *7766 Fay Ave., tel. 619/454–1182. Jacket suggested. Reservations accepted. No lunch weekends. AE, MC, V. Moderate.*

Mixed Menu **Hard Rock Cafe.** It seems that every other city has a Hard Rock Cafe, and now San Diego has one, too. The local college students and teens are rejoicing, and even their elders crack a smile when they stroll into this monument to ground chuck and Chuck Berry. Designed as a museum of rock 'n roll memorabilia, the place features Elton John's "Tutti Frutti" suit, guitars used by Def Leppard and Pink Floyd, and a pink Cadillac through the ceiling. Most diners ogle all this while munching on hefty burgers and fat onion rings, but if you take a close look at the menu, you'll also find excellent grilled fish, a fine, lime-marinated chicken, and homemade apple pie that almost matches Mom's. *909 Prospect St., tel. 619/456–5456. Dress: casual. No reservations. AE, MC, V. Inexpensive.*

Seafood **Fisherman's Grill.** The oyster bar serves up an exceptional selection of raw bivalves and generously sized shellfish cocktails, and the kitchen follows suit by offering creamy chowders, clever sandwiches, mesquite-broiled fish, and good, old-fashioned deep-fried shrimp coated with a zesty beer batter. *7825 Fay Ave., tel. 619/456–3733. Dress: casual. Reservations accepted. AE, MC, V. No lunch weekends. Inexpensive.*

Lodging

When choosing lodgings in San Diego, the first thing to consider is location. The city is made up of many regions, each one possessing its own unique characteristics. Consider the type of atmosphere you prefer. Do you want to be in the middle of a bustling metropolitan setting or would you rather have a serene beach bungalow? San Diego has all this and more. Also consider the hotel's proximity to attractions that you are most interested in seeing. And then of course, there's the price.

Highly recommended hotels are indicated by a star ★.

Category	Cost*
Very Expensive	over $150
Expensive	$90–$150
Moderate	$75–$90
Inexpensive	under $75

for a double room, not including tax

Coronado Coronado is a quiet, out-of-the-way place to stay, but if you plan to see many of San Diego's attractions, you'll probably spend a lot of time commuting across the bridge or riding the ferry.

Very Expensive **Hotel del Coronado.** Built in 1888, the Del has accommodated
★ such luminaries as the Duke and Duchess of Windsor, a number of U.S. presidents, countless movie stars including Marilyn Monroe, and other celebrities. A designated historical landmark, the white-frame Victorian structure has been maintained scrupulously to retain the flavor of its era. In the original structure, every room is different. For the guest who prefers a newer room, there is a high-rise wing adjacent to the original building. The Crown Room restaurant is well-known and there is nightly entertainment in one of the lounges. *1500 Orange Ave., 92118, tel. 619/435–6611. 700 rooms. Facilities: pool, tennis courts, beach. AE, DC, MC, V.*
Le Meridien. This elegant newcomer to the Coronado shoreline has taken its place as a gathering spot for the elite. The decor is French Country with touches of beachfront hideaway, antique armoires beside rattan chairs. The rooms looking over the water have breathtaking views of the downtown skyline. The restaurant, Marius, is among San Diego's best; Sunday brunch at the poolside brasserie is a Coronado happening. The hotel's spa offers a variety of luxurious beauty and fitness treatments. *2000 Second St., 92118, tel. 619/435–3000. 300 rooms. Facilities: pool, spa. AE, DC, MC, V.*

Expensive **Glorietta Bay Inn.** Built around the turn-of-the-century mansion of the Spreckels family, who once owned most of downtown San Diego, this is now a spotlessly maintained hotel. Located adjacent to the Coronado harbor, the Del, and Coronado village, it has many fine restaurants and quaint shops within walking distance. *1630 Glorietta Blvd., 92118, tel. 619/435–3101. 100 rooms. Facilities: tennis, golf, pool. AE, MC, V.*

Inexpensive **Coronado Motor Inn.** This motel is located away from the village toward the bay and the ferry stop. *266 Orange Ave., 92118, tel. 619/435–4121. 24 rooms. Facilities: pool. MC, V.*

Downtown Downtown San Diego is presently in the midst of a decade-long redevelopment effort. The revitalization has attracted many new hotels. There is much to be seen within walking distance of downtown accommodations—Seaport Village, the Embarcadero, the historic Gaslamp Quarter, a variety of theaters and night spots, the convention center, and the spectacular Horton Plaza shopping center. The zoo and Balboa Park are also nearby. For nonstop shopping, nightlife, and entertainment, the downtown area is an excellent location.

Very Expensive **Omni San Diego Hotel.** This high rise was completed in 1987 and is lavishly decorated with marble, brass, and glass. The rooms are luxurious and modern. The lobby lounge is packed every night with local financiers and weary shoppers from adjacent Horton Plaza. *910 Broadway Circle, 92101, tel. 619/239–2200 or 800/THE–OMNI. 450 rooms. Facilities: tennis courts, sauna, spa, pool, complete health club, lounge, disco, 2 restaurants. AE, MC, V.*

San Diego Marriott Hotel and Marina. This luxurious high rise consists of two 25-story towers offering panoramic views of the bay and/or city. The north-tower rooms all have balconies while only the suites in the south tower offer balconies. The rooms are stark but elegant, and the grounds have a lush, shaded waterfall by the pool. *333 W. Harbor Dr., 92101, tel. 619/234–1500 or 800/327–0200. 1,356 rooms. Facilities: 3 restaurants, 2 lounges with piano music, boutiques, full-service salon, jogging path, health spa, tennis courts, sauna, 2 outdoor pools, charter boat. AE, DC, MC, V.*

★ **U.S. Grant Hotel.** Originally built in 1910, this hotel, which faces the famed Horton Plaza, was renovated and reopened in 1985. The atmosphere is elegant and formal with crystal chandeliers and marble floors. All rooms feature mahogany furnishings. Butlers and concierges serve the guests splendidly. There are two restaurants, the Garden Room and the Grant Grill, a long-time favorite of high-powered business types. The use of an associated health club is included. *326 Broadway, 92101, tel. 619/232–3121. 280 rooms. AE, DC, MC, V.*

Westgate Hotel. This elegant high rise offers rooms uniquely furnished with genuine European antiques. Hand-cut Baccarat chandeliers adorn the lobby, which is modeled after the anteroom in the Palace of Versailles. The rooms feature Italian marble counters, oversize bathtubs, brass fixtures with 14-kt. gold overlay and breathtaking views of the harbor and the city (from the ninth floor up). Enjoy high tea and international coffees with piano accompaniment in the afternoon, and award-winning cuisine and white-gloved service in the Fountainebleu Room in the evening. The trolley can take you to Tijuana right from the hotel, and complimentary transportation is available

Bahia Resort Hotel, **8**
Balboa Park Inn, **22**
Britt House, **24**
Colonial Inn, **2**
Coronado Motor Inn, **31**
Dana Inn & Marina, **9**
Doubletree Hotel, **15**
Glorietta Bay Inn, **33**
Hanalei Hotel, **13**
Harbor Hill Guest House, **23**
Heritage Park Bed & Breakfast Inn, **12**
Horton Grand Hotel, **28**
Hotel del Coronado, **34**
Humphrey's Half Moon Inn, **20**
Hyatt Islandia, **10**
Kona Inn, **19**
Kona Kai Beach and Tennis Resort, **18**
Le Meridien, **32**
Mission Bay Motel, **4**
Ocean Manor Apartment Hotel, **17**
Omni San Diego Hotel, **29**
Padre Trail Inn, **11**
Prospect Park Inn, **3**
Radisson Harbor View, **30**
San Diego Marriott Hotel and Marina, **27**
San Diego Marriott Mission Valley, **16**
San Diego Princess Resort, **7**
Santa Clara Motel, **6**
Sheraton Harbor Island East, **21**
Surfer Motor Lodge, **5**
Torrey Pines Inn, **1**
Town and Country Hotel, **14**
U.S. Grant Hotel, **26**
Westgate Hotel, **25**

San Diego Lodging

0   1 mile
0   1 km

Murphy Canyon Rd.

Blvd.

Ave.

Genessee

Aero Dr.

Mission

Gorge Rd.

Waring Rd.

DA
TA

Ave.

Rd.

Cabrillo Fwy.

vista

Friars Rd.

16

San Diego River

Montezuma Rd.

13 **14** **15** Adams Ave.

El Cajon Blvd.

College Ave.

163

El Cajon Blvd.

Stockton Dr.

University

Ave.

Fairmount Ave.

Euclid Ave.

22

23

6th Ave.

El Prado
Balboa Park

24

94

30

Broadway

5

Market St.

94

6

47th St.

27

Imperial Ave.

28 **29**

Harbor Dr.

National Ave.

32

31

33

75

8th St.

34

Orange Ave.

**NATIONAL
CITY**

National City Blvd.

Highland Ave.

805

18th St.

nado
each

Silver Strand

San Diego Bay

**CHULA
VISTA**

within the downtown area. *1055 2nd Ave., 92101, tel. 619/238–1818. 223 rooms. AE, DC, MC, V.*

Expensive **Britt House.** This grand Victorian inn offers charming rooms, each uniquely furnished with antiques. Each room has a sitting area where fresh-baked goodies are served for breakfast. Lovely gardens surround the building and an elaborate high tea is served in the parlor every afternoon. In the Victorian tradition, there is a bathroom for every two rooms to share. Located within walking distance from Balboa Park and the zoo. Reservations are a must. *460 Maple St., 92101, tel. 619/234–2926. 10 rooms, 5 with bath. AE, MC, V.*

★ **Horton Grand Hotel.** This is San Diego's oldest Victorian hotel, built in 1886 and restored in 1986 in the fashion of an elegant, European-style tourist hotel. The charming rooms are furnished with period antiques and feature ceiling fans, gas-burning fireplaces, and diaries that provide guests with a sense of those who came before them and an opportunity to share with those who will come later. Each room is different from the next. The choicest rooms are those overlooking the garden courtyard that twinkles with miniature lights each evening. Afternoon high tea and evening jazz are offered. *311 Island Ave., 92101, tel. 619/544–1886. 110 rooms. Facilities: Chinatown museum, restaurant, lounge. AE, DC, MC, V.*

Moderate–Expensive **Balboa Park Inn.** Originally built in 1915, this charming European-style bed-and-breakfast inn was restored in 1982, with one- and two-bedroom suites with kitchenettes (for two–four people) housed in four 2-story buildings that are connected by courtyards. Each suite has a different flavor—Italian, French, Spanish, or early California. Some suites have fireplaces, wet bars, and whirlpool tubs. Continental breakfast and the morning paper are delivered to every suite. Balboa Park and the zoo are directly across the street. *3402 Park Blvd., 92103, tel. 619/298–0823. 25 suites with bath. Facilities: outdoor bar, room service. AE, DC, MC, V.*

Radisson Harbor View. Of the proliferation of new hotels opening downtown, the Radisson stands out for its location, practically on the off-ramp from Interstate 5, 6 blocks from the Embarcadero. The rooms are spotless and spacious, and they all have balconies looking out to the harbor. Business services and a health club are available. *1646 Front St., 92101, tel. 619/239–6800. 333 rooms. Facilities: pool, health club. AE, MC. V.*

Inexpensive **Harbor Hill Guest House.** Quaint, comfortable rooms in a 3-story home. Harbor view and kitchenettes are available. Continental breakfast included, families welcome. *2330 Albatross St., 92101, tel. 619/233–0638. 5 rooms. MC, V.*

Harbor Island/ Shelter Island Harbor Island and Shelter Island are two artificially made peninsulas located between downtown San Diego and the lovely community of Point Loma. Both peninsulas are bordered by grassy parks, tree-lined paths, lavish hotels, and wonderful restaurants. Harbor Island is closest to the downtown area and less than five minutes from the airport. Shelter Island is on the Point Loma side. Both islands command breathtaking views of the bay and the downtown skyline. Although some lodgings listed are not located directly on the islands, they are in the vicinity.

Very Expensive **Sheraton Harbor Island East.** Although less luxurious than the
★ neighboring Sheraton Grand, this hotel has more to offer

recreation-wise. There are 12 floors. If you want a view, request the eighth floor or above. The rooms all have sitting areas with tables and chairs, providing plenty of room to spread your belongings about. *1380 Harbor Island Dr., 92101, tel. 619/291–2900. 725 rooms. Facilities: tennis courts, sauna, spa, 2 pools, fitness facility. AE, DC, MC, V.*

Expensive **Humphrey's Half Moon Inn.** This sprawling South Sea-style re-
★ sort has many open areas with palm trees, beautiful green grass, and tiki torches. The recently restored rooms are standard but pleasant and some have views of the pool area or the bay. The restaurant, Humphrey's, is famous with the locals for its summer jazz concert series. *2303 Shelter Island Dr., 92106, tel. 619/224–3411 or 800/542–7400. 141 rooms. Facilities: putting green, pool, spa, bicycles. AE, DC, MC, V.*

Kona Kai Beach and Tennis Resort. This hotel also serves as a prestigious members-only club for locals, but all facilities are open to hotel guests. The rooms are simple and tasteful with Hawaiian decor. *1551 Shelter Island Dr., 92106, tel. 619/222–1191. 89 rooms. Facilities: health club, tennis courts, racquetball courts, pool, spa, private beach, 2 restaurants, lounge. AE, DC, MC, V.*

Moderate **Kona Inn.** Although not as luxurious as the rest of the hotels on
★ Shelter Island, this is a comfortable hotel in a beautiful location. For a small fee, Kona Inn guests have the privilege of using the tennis, pool, spa, racquetball, and health club facilities of the more lavish, neighboring sister hotel, the Kona Kai. *1901 Shelter Island Dr., 92106, tel. 619/222–0421. 82 rooms. AE, DC, MC, V.*

Hotel Circle Hotel Circle, as the name implies, is headquarters for a number of hotels and motels, most of them moderately priced and catering to the individual traveler. A car is an absolute necessity here, since the "circle" consists of hotels on both sides of I–8, the busiest stretch of freeway in San Diego. Although not particularly scenic or serene, Mission Valley is close to Balboa Park, the zoo, downtown, and the beaches. As a general rule, try to reserve a room that doesn't face the freeway.

Expensive **Doubletree Hotel.** One of the grandest hotels in the valley, this
★ brand-new high rise offers three floors reserved for nonsmokers. The decor is modern Southwestern. Children stay free and small pets are accepted. *901 Camino del Rio S, 92108, tel. 619/543–9000 or 800/528–0444. 350 rooms. Facilities: restaurant, lounge, spa, pool, fitness center. AE, DC, MC, V.*

San Diego Marriott Mission Valley. This high-rise hotel sits smack in the middle of the former San Diego River, now a dry riverbed being graded and transformed into a commercial zone with sleek office towers and elaborate shopping complexes. Though a bit out of the way, the Marriott has become a meeting place and second home for those doing business in the valley. The rooms are standard chain hotel fare, and comfortable. *8757 Rio San Diego Dr., 92108, tel. 619/692–3800 or 800/228–9290. 350 rooms. Facilities: pool, 2 tennis courts, health club. AE, DC, MC, V.*

Moderate–Expensive **Heritage Park Bed & Breakfast Inn.** This inn is located a few
★ minutes from Mission Valley in the Old Town area. The location is picturesque and quiet. Nine guest rooms are housed in a romantic Queen Anne–style mansion from 1889. Three of the rooms have private baths, the others share communal facilities.

The rooms are quaint and furnished with Victorian antiques. Breakfast and afternoon refreshments are included. *2470 Heritage Park Row, 92110, tel. 619/295-7088. 9 rooms. MC, V.*

Town and Country Hotel. Although the original part of this hotel was built in the '50s, it has been refurbished many times and two high-rise sections were added in the '70s. The rooms are decorated in quaint, colonial fashion. With the city's largest convention facilities until the new downtown Convention Center opened, it caters to convention and meeting groups, but the hotel is enough like a resort to attract tourists as well as conventioneers. *500 Hotel Circle N, 92108, tel. 619/291-7131. 1,000 rooms. Facilities: 6 restaurants, 5 lounges, 4 pools, golf, health club. AE, DC, MC, V.*

Moderate **Hanalei Hotel.** If I-8 were out of sight, you'd swear you were in
★ a tropical paradise. This hotel has a definite island feel with palm trees, waterfalls, Koi ponds, and tiki torches. There is a 2-story complex and a high rise. The 2-story complex rooms are poolside, and the high rise is built around a beautiful Hawaiian garden with ponds, palm trees, and plenty of spots to sit and take in the atmosphere. The rooms are clean and comfortable with Hawaiian decor. *2270 Hotel Circle S, 92108, tel. 619/297-1101. 425 rooms. Facilities: 2 restaurants, lounge, pool, spa. AE, MC, V.*

Inexpensive **Padre Trail Inn.** This standard, family-style motel is located
★ slightly southwest of Mission Valley. Historic Old Town, shopping, and dining are all within walking distance. *4200 Taylor St., 92110, tel. 619/297-3291. 100 rooms. Facilities: pool, restaurant, lounge. AE, DC, MC, V.*

La Jolla La Jolla is one of the world's most beautiful, prestigious beach communities. Million-dollar homes line the beaches and cascade down the hillsides. Expensive boutiques, galleries, and restaurants make up the village—the heart of La Jolla. La Jolla is also a popular vacation spot with many lodging possibilities even for those on a budget.

Expensive **Colonial Inn.** A tastefully restored Victorian-style building in the center of La Jolla, this hotel offers turn-of-the-century elegance with features such as fan windows and a mahogany-paneled elevator. You can get a view of the village or of the ocean, but the ocean view will cost considerably more. Boutiques, restaurants, and the cove are within walking distance. *910 Prospect St., 92307, tel. 619/454-2181 or 800/832-5525. 75 rooms. Facilities: restaurant, lounge, pool. AE, DC, MC, V.*

Moderate–Expensive **Prospect Park Inn.** This charming, European-style inn is newly redecorated. The rooms are quaint and some have balconies with sweeping ocean views. Located in the village, it is within walking distance from shops and restaurants and 1 block from the beach. The higher the floor, the more you pay. *1110 Prospect St., 92037, tel. 619/454-0133, 800/345-8577 (in CA), or 800/433-1609. 25 rooms. AE, MC, V.*

Moderate **Torrey Pines Inn.** Located on a bluff between La Jolla and Del Mar, this hotel commands a view of miles and miles of coastline. THe hotel stands adjacent to the Torrey Pines Golf Course, site of the annual San Diego Open PGA golf tournament every January. Nearby is scenic Torrey Pines State Beach. Downtown La Jolla is a 10-minute drive away. The inn is a nice, reasonable, out-of-the-way place to stay. *11480 Torrey Pines Rd., 92037, tel. 619/453-4420. 75 rooms. AE, DC, MC, V.*

Mission Bay and Beaches

Most people who come to San Diego would like to stay close to the water. San Diego has many beaches but there is a concentration of hotels on Mission and Pacific beaches. Both of these areas have a casual atmosphere and a busy coastal thoroughfare offering endless shopping, dining, and nightlife possibilities. Mission Bay Park, with its beaches, bike trails, boat-launching ramps, golf course, and grassy parks is also a hotel haven. You can't go wrong with any of these locations. There is always plenty of beautiful scenery and activities.

Very Expensive

Hyatt Islandia. Located in one of San Diego's most beautiful seashore areas, Mission Bay Park, the Islandia has lanai-style units and a high rise. The landscaping is lush and tropical in flavor and the room decor is tastefully modern with dramatic views of the bay area. This hotel is famous for its lavish Sunday buffet brunch. *1441 W. Mission Bay Dr., 92109, tel. 619/224–1234. 423 rooms. Facilities: pool, spa, 2 restaurants. AE, DC, MC, V.*

★ **San Diego Princess Resort.** This resort resembles a self-sufficient village with a wide range of amenities. Perhaps its greatest features are the marina and mile of beaches. The grounds are so beautifully landscaped that this resort has been the setting for many movies. Accommodations consist of individual cottages. Kitchens and bay views are available. With something for everyone, this hotel is favored by families, particularly during the summer. *1404 W. Vacation Rd., 92109, tel. 619/274–4630. 450 cottages. Facilities: 3 restaurants, 8 tennis courts, 5 pools, bicycle and boat rentals. AE, DC, MC, V.*

Moderate–Expensive

★ **Bahia Resort Hotel.** This huge complex is located on a 14-acre peninsula in Mission Bay Park. The ocean is also within walking distance. The rooms are studios and suites with kitchens, tastefully furnished. The price is good considering the location and amenities. *998 W. Mission Bay Dr., 92109, tel. 619/488–0551. 300 rooms. Facilities: tennis courts, water sport rentals, spa, pool, evening bay cruises. AE, DC, MC, V.*

Dana Inn & Marina. This hotel, which has an adjoining marina, offers a bargain in the Mission Bay Park area. The accommodations are not as grand as in the other hotels in the area but they're perfectly fine if you're not going to stay cooped up in your room. *1710 W. Mission Bay Blvd., 92109, tel. 619/222–6440. 125 rooms. Facilities: pool, spa. AE, DC, MC, V.*

Moderate

★ **Surfer Motor Lodge.** This hotel is located right on the beach and directly behind a new shopping center with many restaurants and boutiques. The rooms are plain, but the view from the upper floors of this high rise are very nice. *711 Pacific Beach Dr., 92109, tel. 619/483–7070. 52 rooms. Facilities: restaurant, cocktail lounge, swimming pool. AE, DC, MC, V.*

Inexpensive–Moderate

★ **Ocean Manor Apartment Hotel.** Units rent by the day, week, or month, and the owner says that some people have been coming every year for 20 years! This hotel is located in Ocean Beach, a community south of Mission Beach that doesn't have many lodging facilities. This is a charming place with a lovely view located right on Sunset Cliffs. The beach below has long since washed away, but there are beaches within walking distance. The rooms are studios or one- or two-bedroom suites with kitchens and living rooms. They are furnished plainly in 1950s style but are quaint and comfortable. There is no maid service, but fresh towels are always provided. This is a quiet place and the owners want to keep it that way. *1370 Sunset Cliffs Blvd.,*

92107, tel. 619/222–7901 or 619/224–1379. 20 rooms. Facilities: pool. MC, V.

Inexpensive **Mission Bay Motel.** Located ½-half block from the beach, this motel offers centrally located, modest units. Great restaurants and nightlife are within walking distance, but you might find the area a bit noisy. *4221 Mission Blvd., 92109, tel. 619/483–6440. 50 rooms. Facilities: pool. AE, MC, V.*

Santa Clara Motel. This is a small motel a block from the ocean and right in the middle of restaurant, nightlife, and shopping activity in Mission Beach. Location is the plus—kitchens are available, but there are no frills. Weekly rates are available. *839 Santa Clara Pl., 92109, tel. 619/488–1193. 25 rooms. AE, MC, V.*

The Arts

Top national touring companies perform regularly at the Civic Theatre, Golden Hall, Symphony Hall, and East County Performing Arts Center. San Diego State University, the University of California at San Diego, private universities, and community colleges present a wide variety of performing arts programs, from well-known artists to student performers. The daily *San Diego Union, Evening Tribune,* and the San Diego edition of the *Los Angeles Times* list current attractions and complete movie schedules. The *Reader,* a free weekly that comes out each Thursday, devotes an entire section to upcoming cultural events, as well as current theater and film reviews. *San Diego Magazine* publishes a monthly "What's Doing" column listing arts events throughout the county and reviews of current films, plays, and concerts.

It is best to book tickets well in advance, preferably at the same time you make hotel reservations, but half-price tickets to most theater, music, and dance events can be bought on the day of performance at **ARTS TIX Ticket Center** (121 Broadway, at 1st Ave., downtown, tel. 619/238–3810). Only cash is accepted. Advance full-price tickets can also be purchased through ARTS TIX.

Visa and MasterCard holders can buy tickets for many scheduled performances through **Teleseat** (tel. 619/283–7328), **Ticketmaster** (tel. 619/278–8497), and **Ticketron** (tel. 619/268–9686). Service charges vary according to event and most tickets are nonrefundable.

Theater **The Bowery Theatre** (1057 1st Ave., Kingston Playhouse, tel. 619/232–4088). While in search of a permanent home, the Bowery continues to be acclaimed by critics and local theatergoers for its premieres of high-quality works from current and upcoming super-star playwrights.

Coronado Playhouse (1755 Strand Way, Coronado, tel. 619/435–4856). This cabaret-type theater, near the Hotel del Coronado, stages regular dramatic and musical performances. Dinner packages are offered on Friday and Saturday.

Gaslamp Quarter Theatre (playhouse: 547 4th Ave., tel. 619/234–9583; showcase: 444 4th Ave., tel. 619/232–9608). The resident theater company performs comedies, dramas, mysteries, and musicals in the original 96-seat playhouse and in the new 250-seat showcase, both in the Gaslamp Quarter.

La Jolla Playhouse (Mandell Weiss Center for the Performing Arts, U. of California at San Diego, tel. 619/534–3960). Exciting and innovative presentations, early summer to fall, under the artist direction of Tony Award–winner Des McAnuff.

La Jolla Stage Company (750 Nautilus St., La Jolla, tel. 619/459 –7773). Lavish productions of Broadway favorites and popular comedies, staged year round in Parker Auditorium at La Jolla High School.

Lawrence Welk Village Theatre (8860 Lawrence Welk Dr., Escondido, tel. 619/749–3448). About a 45-minute drive from downtown, this famed dinner theater puts on polished Broadway-style productions with a professional cast.

Lyceum Theatre (Horton Plaza, tel. 619/235–8025). Home to the San Diego Repertory Theatre, San Diego's first resident acting company. Contemporary works are performed year round on the 550-seat Lyceum stage and in a flexible 225-seat space.

Marquis Public Theater (3717 India St., tel. 619/295–5654). Contemporary, experimental, and original plays are held on the main stage and in the smaller Gallery.

Mission Playhouse (1936 Quivira Way, Marina Village, tel. 619/ 226–0518). One of the oldest community theaters in San Diego performs a mixed bag of works, including up-to-the-minute versions of current plays.

Old Globe Theatre (Simon Edison Centre for the Performing Arts, Balboa Park, tel. 619/239–2255). The oldest professional theater in California performs classics, contemporary dramas, experimental works, and the famous summer Shakespeare Festival at the Old Globe and its sister theaters, the Cassius Carter Centre Stage and the Lowell Davies Festival Theatre.

San Diego Gilbert and Sullivan Company (Casa del Prado Theatre, Balboa Park, tel. 619/231–5714). Four different productions of Gilbert and Sullivan and related-style works are performed October–July.

Starlight Musicals (Starlight Bowl, Balboa Park, tel. 619/544–7827). A local summertime favorite is this series of popular musicals presented in an outdoor amphitheater mid-June–early September.

The Theatre in Old Town (4040 Twiggs St., tel. 619/298–0082). Mostly musical theater and Broadway hits are staged by the International Company of United States International University, October–June. All the seats are good in this cozy, barnlike structure.

Concerts **Open-Air Theater** (San Diego State U., tel. 619/594–5200). Top-name rock, reggae, and popular artists pack in the crowds for summer-long concerts under the stars.

Organ Pavilion (Balboa Park, tel. 619/239–0512). Robert Plimpton performs on the giant 1914 pipe organ at 2 PM on Sunday afternoons, except in January, and on most Monday evenings in summer. All concerts are free.

Sherwood Auditorium (700 Prospect St., La Jolla, tel. 619/459–0267). Many classical and jazz events are held in the 550-seat auditorium within La Jolla Museum of Contemporary Art. La Jolla Chamber Music Society presents nine concerts, August–May, of internationally acclaimed chamber ensembles, orchestras, and soloists. San Diego Chamber Orchestra, a 35-member ensemble, performs once a month, October–April.

Sports Arena (2500 Sports Arena Blvd., tel. 619/224–4176). Big-name rock stars play to more than 14,000 fans, using an end-stage configuration so that all seats face in one direction.

Symphony Hall (1245 7th Ave., tel. 619/699–4205). The San

Diego Symphony is the only California symphony with its own concert hall. The performance season runs November–May, with a series of outdoor pop concerts held in Mission Bay during the summer.

Opera **Civic Theatre** (202 C St., tel. 619/236–6510). The San Diego Opera draws international stars like Luciano Pavarotti, Joan Sutherland, and Kiri Te Kanawa. The season of four operas runs January–April in the 3,000-seat, state-of-the-art auditorium. English translations of works sung in their original languages are projected on a large screen above the stage.

Dance **3's Company** (tel. 619/296–9523). Interpretative dance presentations, incorporating live music, are staged at major theaters and concert halls around San Diego County.

California Ballet (tel. 619/560–5676). Four quality contemporary and traditional works, from story ballets to Ballanchine, are performed September–May. The *Nutcracker* is staged annually at the Civic Theatre, other ballets take place at Symphony Hall, East County Performing Arts Center, and Nautilus Bowl at Sea World.

Nightlife

The unbeatable variety of sun-and-surf recreational activities is considered the primary reason tourists love to visit San Diego, but most are unexpectedly delighted that the city gains new momentum after dark. The nightlife scene is one that's constantly growing and highly mercurial, since clubs aim to satisfy the crowd—one night, it's Top 40 or contemporary, the next, reggae, pop-jazz, or strictly rock'n'roll. Live pop and fusion jazz have become especially popular—some say it's the ideal music for what is perceived as the typical laid-back lifestyle. Discotheques and bars in Mission Valley and at the beaches tend to be the most crowded spots in the county on the weekends, but don't let that discourage you from visiting these quintessential San Diego hangouts. And should your tastes run to softer music, there are plenty of piano bars where frazzled nerves have a chance to wind down. Check the *Reader* for weekly band information or *San Diego* magazine's Restaurant & Nightlife Guide for the full range of nightlife possibilities.

California law prohibits the sale of alcoholic beverages after 2 AM. Bars and nightclubs usually stop serving at about 1:40 AM. You must be 21 to purchase and consume alcohol, and most places will insist on current identification. Be aware that California also has some of the most stringent drunk-driving laws, and roadblocks are not an uncommon sight.

Bars and Nightclubs **Anthony's Harborside.** An extra-spacious lounge looks out on the beautiful harbor and features jazz and contemporary Top-40 groups for dancing. *1355A N. Harbor Dr., downtown, tel. 619/232–6358. Open 11 AM–1:30 AM. Entertainment 8:30 PM–1:30 AM. AE, MC, V.*

The Hard Rock Cafe. This place has a great collection of rock and roll memorabilia. *909 Prospect St., La Jolla, tel. 619/456–5456.*

Mick's P.B. In this spectacular club rich with Honduran mahogany, chicly dressed singles from 25 to 45 dance to live contemporary rock and Top 40 by bands predominantly from out of town. *4190 Mission Blvd., Pacific Beach, tel. 619/581–*

3938. Open 8 PM–1:30 AM. Entertainment 9 PM–1:30 AM. AE, DC, MC, V.

Old Del Mar Cafe. Offering rock to reggae, fusion jazz to oldies, and virtually every other popular style of music, this combination woodsy cafe–lounge is considered one of the best intimate venues in the North County. *2730 Via de la Valle, Del Mar, tel. 619/455–0920. Entertainment 9 PM–1:30 AM. MC, V.*

Old Pacific Beach Cafe. Certainly one of Pacific Beach's most popular after-dark spots, showcasing the broadest range of musical styles—fusion and pop jazz, R&B, rambunctious rock'n'roll, and reggae. *4287 Mission Blvd., tel. 619/270–7522. Entertainment 9:30 PM–1:30 AM. MC, V.*

Jazz Clubs **B Street Cafe and Bar.** Downtown's hottest after-work happy hour leads to appearances by local jazz groups nightly. *425 W. B St., tel. 619/236–1707. Entertainment 8 PM–1 AM. AE, MC, V.*

Cargo Bar. The San Diego Hilton Hotel's nautical-theme bar with a can't-beat view of the bay and a don't-miss lineup of jazz and contemporary bands. *1775 E. Mission Bay Dr., tel. 619/276–4010. Open 5 PM–1:30 AM. Entertainment 8:30 PM–1 AM. AE, DC, MC, V.*

Elario's. A club on the top floor of the Summer House Inn with a sumptuous ocean view and an incomparable lineup of internationally acclaimed jazz musicians. *7955 La Jolla Shores Dr., La Jolla, tel. 619/459–0541. Entertainment 8 PM–1 AM. AE, DC, MC, V.*

Humphrey's. The premier promoter of the city's best jazz, folk, and light-rock summer concert series, held out on the grass. The rest of the year the music moves indoors for some first-rate jazz Sunday–Monday. *2241 Shelter Island Dr., tel. 619/224–3577. Entertainment 8 PM–midnight. AE, DC, MC, V.*

Rock Clubs **Bacchanal.** An all-concert venue that brings in a mixture of comedy, rock, nostalgia, jazz, R&B, and the like. *8022 Clairemont Mesa Blvd., Kearny Mesa, tel. 619/560–8022. Entertainment 8:30–11:30 PM. MC, V.*

Belly Up Tavern. Located in converted Quonset huts, this eclectic live-concert venue hosts critically acclaimed artists who play everything from reggae, rock, New Wave, Motown, and folk to—well, you name it. *143 S. Cedros Ave., Solana Beach, tel. 619/481–9022. Open 11 AM–1:30 AM. Entertainment 9:30 PM–1:30 AM. MC, V.*

Rio's. Some of the most intriguing and innovative local rock, blues, and reggae bands like to perform here. *4258 W. Point Loma Blvd., Loma Portal, tel. 619/225–9559. Open 7 PM–1:30 AM. Entertainment 9 PM–1:30 AM. AE, MC, V.*

Country/Western Clubs **Leo's Little Bit O'Country.** The largest country/western dance floor in the county—bar none. *680 W. San Marcos Blvd., San Marcos, tel. 619/744–4120. Open 4 PM–1 AM. Entertainment 8:30 PM–1 AM. Closed Mon. MC, V.*

Pomerado Club. The rustic dance hall, formerly a Pony Express station in the last century, now showcases the two-steppin' tunes of the house band, who are also the owners. *12237 Pomerado Rd., Poway, tel. 619/748–1135. Entertainment Fri.–Sat. 9 PM–1:30 AM. No credit cards.*

Comedy Clubs **Comedy Isle.** Located at the Bahia Resort Hotel, in the heart of Mission Beach, the Comedy Isle features comedians in its waterfront club and restaurant. *998 West Mission Bay Dr., tel.*

619/488–6872. Shows Tues., Wed., and Thurs. at 8:30 PM, Fri. and Sat. at 8:30 PM and 10:30 PM.

The Comedy Store. In the same tradition as the Comedy Store in West Hollywood, San Diego's version hosts some of the best national touring and local talent. *916 Pearl St., La Jolla, tel. 619/454–9176. Open Tues.–Thurs. 8–10:30 PM, Fri.–Sat. 8 PM–1 JAM. Days closed vary. AE, MC, V.*

The Improv. A superb art deco–style club with a distinct East Coast feel, where some of the big names in comedy present their routines. *832 Garnet Ave., Pacific Beach, tel. 619/483–4520. Open 6:30 PM–midnight. Entertainment 8 PM–midnight. AE, MC, V.*

Discos **Confetti.** A glitzy club popular with young professionals, students, and anyone with an inclination to party. It metamorphoses into the alternative-music club, **The Piranha Room,** on Sunday only. *5373 Mission Center Rd., Mission Valley, tel. 619/291–8635. Open weekdays 5 PM–2 AM, Sat. 7 PM–2 AM. AE, MC, V.*

Emerald City. Alternative dance music and an uninhibited clientele keep this beachtown spot unpredictable—which is just fine with everyone. *945 Garnet Ave., Pacific Beach, tel. 619/483–9920. Open 8:30 PM–2 AM. Closed Mon. No credit cards.*

Piano Bars **Top O' the Cove.** Show tunes and standards from the '40s to the '80s are the typical piano fare at this magnificent Continental restaurant in La Jolla. *1216 Prospect St., tel. 619/454–7779. Entertainment Wed.–Sun. 8 PM–midnight. AE, DC, MC, V.*

Westgate Hotel. One of the most elegant settings in San Diego offers piano music in the Plaza Bar. *1055 2nd Ave., downtown, tel. 619/238–1818. Open 11 AM–1 AM. Entertainment 8:30 PM–midnight. AE, DC, MC, V.*

Excursion to the San Diego North Coast

by Kevin Brass

A freelance writer, longtime North County resident Kevin Brass is a regular contributor to the San Diego edition of the Los Angeles Times, San Diego magazine, and other publications.

To say the north coast area of San Diego County is different from the city of San Diego is a vast understatement. From the northern tip of La Jolla to Oceanside, a half-dozen small communities developed separately from urban San Diego. In fact, they developed separately from each other, and each has its own flavorful history. Del Mar, for example, exists primarily because of the lure its wide beaches and Thoroughbred horse racing facility extended to the rich and famous. Just a couple of miles away, agriculture, not paparazzi, played a major role in the development of Solana Beach and Encinitas. Up the coast, Carlsbad still reveals elements of its heritage, roots directly tied to the old Mexican rancheros and the entrepreneurial instinct of John Frazier, who told people the area's water could cure common ailments. In the late 19th century, not far from the current site of the posh La Costa Hotel and Spa, he attempted to turn the area into a massive replica of a German mineral springs resort.

Today, the North Coast is a booming population center. An explosion of development in the early 1980s turned the area into a northern extension of San Diego. The freeways started to take on the typically cluttered characteristics of most Southern California freeways.

Excursion to the San Diego North Coast

Beyond the freeways, though, the co[...]
tained their charm. Some of the finest [...]
and attractions in San Diego County can [...]
true slice of So Cal heritage. From the pl[...]
hills of Rancho Santa Fe and the beachfro[...]
diff, to Mission San Luis Rey, a well-p[...]
California's first white settlers in Oceanside, the North Coast
is a distinctly different place.

Arriving and Departing

By Car I–5, the main freeway artery connecting San Diego to Los Angeles, follows the coastline. To the west, running parallel to
I–5, is Old Highway 101, which never strays more than ¼-mile
from the ocean. Beginning north of La Jolla, where it is known
as Torrey Pines Road, Old Highway is a designated scenic
route, providing access to the beauty of the coastline.

By Train **Amtrak** (tel. 619/239–9021 or 800/872–7245) operates trains
daily between Los Angeles, Orange County, and San Diego.
The last train leaves San Diego at approximately 9 PM each
night; the last arrival is at 11:30 PM. There are stops in Oceanside
and Del Mar.

By Bus **The San Diego Transit District** (tel. 619/433–8202) covers the
city of San Diego up to Del Mar, where the **North County Transit District** takes over, blanketing the area with efficient, on-
time bus routes.

Greyhound-Trailways (tel. 619/239–9171) has regular routes
connecting San Diego to points north, with stops in Del Mar,
Solana Beach, Encinitas, and Oceanside.

By Taxi Several companies are based in the North County, including
Amigo Cab (tel. 619/436–TAXI) and **Bill's Cab Co.** (tel. 619/755
–6737).

By Plane **Palomar Airport** (tel. 619/758–6233), located in Carlsbad 2
miles east of I–5 on Palomar Airport Road, is a general aviation
airport run by the County of San Diego and open to the public.
There are no commercial airlines flying out of Palomar Airport.

Guided Tours

Flight Trails Helicopters (2192 Palomar Airport Rd., tel. 619/
438–8424) offers whirlybird tours of the area from the air.

Exploring

*Numbers in the margin correspond with points of interest on
the San Diego North Coast map.*

Any journey around the North Coast area naturally begins at
the beach, and this one begins at **Torrey Pines State Beach,** just
south of Del Mar. At the south end of the wide beach, perched
on top of the cliffs, is the **Torrey Pines State Reserve,** one of only
two places (the other place is Santa Rosa Island off the coast of
northern California) where the Torrey pine tree grows naturally. The park has a museum and an excellent set of hiking trails
that snake through the 1,100-acre park, which is filled with exotic California shrubbery and features picturesque views from
the cliffs. *Tel. 619/755–2063. There is a small admission
charge. Open daily 9 AM–sunset.*

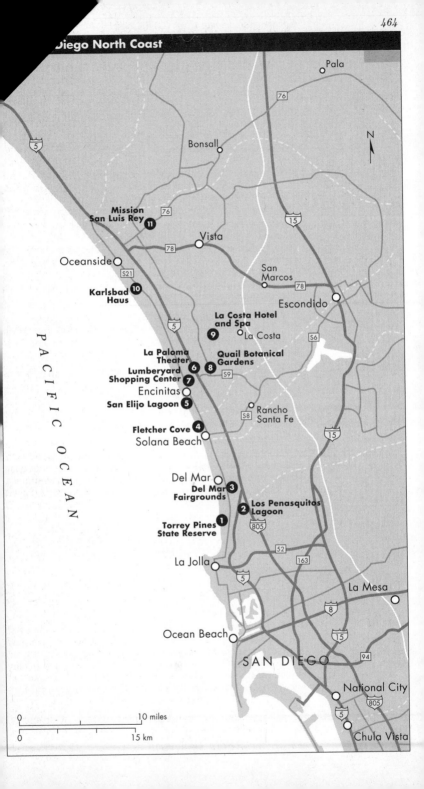

2 To the east of the state beach is **Los Penasquitos Lagoon,** one of the many natural estuaries that flow inland between Del Mar and Oceanside. Following Old Highway 101, the road leads into the small village of **Del Mar,** best known for its volatile political scene, celebrity visitors, and wide beaches. Years of battles and compromises between developers and residents have resulted in Del Mar Plaza, a cleverly hidden shopping/dining complex at the intersection of Highway 101 and 15th Street. The plaza's three restaurants are outstanding, and the shops and galleries carry exquisite, exclusive items. The top level has a large deck with plenty of benches and chairs looking out over the coastline. A left turn at 15th Street leads to Seagrove Park, a small, extremely pleasant stretch of grass overlooking the ocean. Turning right on Coast Boulevard provides access to Del Mar's beautiful beaches, particularly popular with Frisbee and volleyball players.

3 Less than ½-mile north, Coast Boulevard merges with Old Highway 101. Across the road is the **Del Mar Fairgrounds,** home to more than 100 different events a year, ranging from a cat show to an auto race. *Via de la Valle Rd. exit west from I–5, tel. 619/755–1161.*

The fairgrounds also host the annual summer meeting of the **Del Mar Thoroughbred Club** (aka "Where the Turf Meets the Surf"). The track brings the top horses and jockeys to Del Mar, along with a cross section of the rich and famous eager to bet on the ponies. Crooner Bing Crosby and his Hollywood buddies, Pat O'Brien, Gary Cooper, and Oliver Hardy, among others, organized the track in the 1930s, primarily because Crosby thought it would be fun to have a track near his Rancho Santa Fe home. Del Mar soon developed into a regular stop for the stars of stage and screen.

During the off-season, horse players can still gamble at the fairgrounds, thanks to a satellite wagering facility. Races from other California tracks are televised, and people can bet as if the races were being run right there. Times vary, depending on which tracks in the state are operating. *Tel. 619/755–1141. Racing season: July–Sept., daily except Tuesdays. Post time is 2 PM.*

Following Via de la Valle Road east from I–5 leads to the exclusive community of **Rancho Santa Fe,** one of the richest areas in the country. Groves of huge, drooping eucalyptus trees, first imported to the area by a railroad company looking to grow trees for railroad ties, cover the hills and valleys, hiding the posh estates. The little village of Rancho has some elegant and quaint—and overpriced—shops and restaurants. But it is no accident that there is little else to see or do in Rancho; the residents guard their privacy religiously. Even the challenging Rancho Santa Fe Golf Course, the original site of the Bing Crosby Pro-Am and considered one of the best courses in Southern California, is still open only to members of the Rancho Santa Fe community.

4 Back along the coast, along Old Highway 101 north of Del Mar, is the city of **Solana Beach,** a quiet little beach city. A highlight of Solana Beach is **Fletcher Cove,** located at the west end of Lomas Santa Fe Drive, called Pill Box by the locals because of a bunkerlike lifeguard station on the cliffs above the beach. Early Solana settlers used dynamite to blast the cove out of the cliffs. It is an easy-access beach, with a large parking lot replete with a small basketball court, a favorite of local pick-up game players.

North of Solana Beach, separating Solana Beach from Cardiff, **5** is the **San Elijo Lagoon,** home to many migrating birds. Trails wind around the entire area.

Continuing along Old Highway 101, past the cluster of hillside homes that comprises Cardiff, past the campgrounds of the San Elijo State Beach, the palm trees of Sea Cliff Roadside Park (Swami's to the locals) and the golden domes of the Self Realization Fellowship mark the entrance to downtown **Encinitas.** The Self Realization Fellowship was built at the turn of the century and serves as a retreat and place of worship for the followers of a Native American religious sect.

Another landmark of old Encinitas (which incorporated as a city in 1986, including the communities of Cardiff, Leucadia, **6** and Olivenhain) is the **La Paloma Theater** on the north end of town on Old Highway 101 (at the corner of Encinita Blvd., tel. 619/436–5808). The theater was built in the Roaring '20s as a stop for traveling vaudeville troupes. It has served as a concert hall, movie theater, and meeting place for the area ever since. Plays are still being rehearsed and performed here.

7 A newer landmark of Encinitas is the **Lumberyard Shopping Center,** a collection of small stores and restaurants that anchors the downtown shopping area. There is a huge selection of shopping centers inland at the intersection of Encinitas Boulevard and El Camino Real.

But Encinitas is known as the "Flower Capital of the World," not the "Shopping Center Capital of the World." Although the flower industry is not as prevalent as it once was, the city is still the home of Paul Ecke Poinsettias, the largest producer of the popular Christmas flower. A sampling of the area's dedication **8** to horticulture can be found at the **Quail Botanical Gardens,** home to thousands of different varieties of plants. *Encinitas Blvd. east from I–5 and turn left on Quail Gardens Dr., tel. 619/436–3036.*

Old Highway 101 continues north through Leucadia, a small community best known for its small art galleries and stores. At the north end of Leucadia (which means sheltered paradise in Greek), La Costa Avenue meets Highway 101. Following La Costa Avenue east, past the Batiquitos Lagoon, leads to the fa- **9** mous **La Costa Hotel and Spa** (tel. 619/438–9111), fat farm to the stars. It is also noted for its excellent golf and tennis facilities and restaurants.

La Costa is technically part of the city of Carlsbad, which is centered farther north, west of the Tamarack Avenue and Elm Avenue exits of I–5. In Carlsbad, Old Highway 101 is called Carlsbad Boulevard. Large rancheros owned by wealthy Mexicans were the first settlements inland, while the coastal area was developed by an entrepreneur, John Frazier, who lured people to the area with talk of the healing powers of mineral water bubbling from a coastal well. The water was found to have the same properties as water from the German mineral wells of Karlsbad, hence the name of the new community. Remnants **10** from the era, including the original well, are found at the **Alt Karlsbad Haus,** a small museum and gift shop. *2802A Carlsbad*

Blvd., tel. 619/729–6912. Admission free. Open 10–5 PM, Mon.–Sat., Sun. 1–4:30 PM.

North of Carlsbad is **Oceanside,** home of Camp Pendleton, the country's largest marine base, as well as a beautiful natural harbor teeming with activity. Oceanside Harbor is the North Coast center for fishing, sailing and all ocean water sports. Oceanside Pier is a favorite hangout for fishing enthusiasts. You can call for general harbor information (tel. 619/722–1418).

⓫ Oceanside is also home to **Mission San Luis Rey,** the largest and one of the best-preserved missions in the area. Built by Franciscan friars in 1798 to help educate and convert local Indians, San Luis Rey was the 18th and largest of the California missions. A picnic area, gift shop, and museum are on the grounds. Self-guided tours are available through the grounds, where retreats are held. *Tel. 619/757–3651. Take Mission Ave. east from I–5. Open Mon.–Sat. 10–4, Sun. 1–4.*

Dining

North County can be regarded as two distinct regions, the burgeoning and depressingly suburban inland area along Interstate 15, and the handsome coastal stretch built along Interstate 5. Inland offers little of interest to the serious eater, but the coastal strip, laced with affluent and somewhat avantgarde communities, is growing increasingly sophisticated. With some exceptions, the food in the waterside restaurants is unrewarding, but there can be no quibbling about the views or the unique ambience that can be found there. The local dress code appreciates sharp sportswear, but jeans, the area's standard uniform, are acceptable everywhere. Be warned that restaurants in Del Mar can be jammed during the late-July to early-September racing season, but it is exactly at this time of year that these restaurants are the most exciting.

Cardiff
Moderate
($15–$25)

The Triton. The beach and the sunset over the Pacific are the chief attractions of this outdoor dining spot. The seafood is average, when the surf is up the waiters tend to disappear, but it's fun, especially at lunch. *2530 South Highway 101, tel. 619/ 436–8877. Dress: casual. AE, DC, MC, V.*

Inexpensive
(under $15)

Los Olas. Funky and inexpensive Los Olas, across the street from the beach in Cardiff, serves good food, especially the chimichangas, tasty fried burritos with heaps of guacamole and sour cream. The beachside atmosphere is better suited for lunch than dinner, though. *2655 S. Hwy. 101, tel. 619/942– 1860. Dress: casual. MC, V.*

Del Mar
Very Expensive
(over $35)

Remington's. A luxurious and friendly atmosphere make Remington's worth the high prices. The menu is exceptional and offers lobster, beef, lamb, and veal dishes. *2010 Jimmy Durante Blvd., tel. 619/755–5104. Jackets suggested. Reservations accepted. MC, V.*

Moderate
($15–$25)

The Brigantine. One of the stronger links in a chain of local fish restaurants, this one has a popular Oyster Bar. Unlucky gamblers from the nearby Del Mar Racetrack find the fair prices particularly attractive. *3263 Camino del Mar, tel. 619/481– 1166. Dress: casual. AE, MC, V.*

Cilantros. For a taste of gourmet Mexican food—creative dishes full of subtle spices—Cilantros in Del Mar offers a wide variety of unusual creations, including shark *fajitas* and chicken with a mild chile sauce. The inexpensive tapas menu, with such delicacies as crab tostadas and three-cheese quesadillas, is a little easier on the wallet. *3702 Via de la Valle, Del Mar, tel. 619/259–8777. Dress: casual. Reservations recommended. AE, MC, V.*

Jake's. A favorite of the racetrack crowd, Jake's is nestled on the shoreline, with the sort of view that turns one's thoughts to romance, not the Daily Double. There is a fresh fish special each day, as well as a different pizza offering. If you're really pressed for time you can order a quick snack from the bar menu. *1660 Coast Blvd., tel. 619/755–2002. Dress: casual. Reservations suggested. AE, MC, V. Closed for lunch Sat.*

Portofino's. This classy little restaurant attempts to re-create the atmosphere of the posh Riviera resort from which it gets its name. Homemade pasta and the seafood dishes are popular. *1108 1st St., tel. 619/942–8442. Dress: casual. Reservations accepted. AE, DC, MC, V.*

Encinitas
Moderate
($15–$25)

Piret M. This charming, sun-dappled French bistro looks as much like a sophisticated gourmet boutique (with delicacies for sale) as it does a countryside restaurant. The menu features hearty soups and quiches, crisp fresh salads, a savory lamb ragout, large but elegant sandwiches, French omelets, and the sort of rich desserts that threaten the firmest of resolves. *897 1st St., tel. 619/942–5152. Dress: casual. Reservations suggested. AE, MC, V.*

Inexpensive
(under $15)

Santa Fe Grill. Despite its Mexican-sounding name, the Santa Fe Grill offers a straightforward selection of hamburgers, prime rib, and seafood dishes. *162 S. Rancho Santa Fe Rd., tel. 619/944–7455. Dress: casual. Reservations accepted. AE, MC, V.*

La Costa
Very Expensive
(over $35)

Pices. Located near the La Costa Country Club, Pices represents the upper class of North Coast seafood restaurants. Traditional seafood, such as scallops and shrimp, is served in innovative and tasty dishes. *7640 El Camino Real, tel. 619/436–9362. Jackets required. Reservations accepted. AE, CB, DC, MC, V.*

Rancho Santa Fe
Very Expensive
(over $35)

Mille Fleurs. This gem of a French auberge brightens a tiny village surrounded by country estates, just a few miles from the county's famous vegetable farms, where the chef shops daily. The tempting cuisine enriches the romantic atmosphere. *6009 Paseo Delicias, tel. 619/756–3085. Jacket and tie requested. Reservations advised. AE, DC, MC, V.*

Solana Beach
Expensive
($25–$35)

Frederick's. This husband-and-wife-owned, friendly, relaxed bistro serves traditional French dishes with California-fresh overtones. Leave room for the freshly baked bread and one of the lush desserts. The menu changes weekly. *128 S. Acacia St., tel. 619/755–2432. Dress: casual. DC, MC, V. Closed Sun. and Mon. Closed for lunch.*

Inexpensive
(under $15)

Chung King Loh. One of the better Chinese restaurants along the coast, Chung King Loh offers an excellent variety of Mandarin and Szechuan dishes. *552 Stevens Ave., tel. 619/481–0184. Dress: casual. AE, MC, V. No lunch Sun.*

Fidel's. Rich in North County tradition, both Fidel's restaurants serve a wide variety of well-prepared dishes in a low-key, pleasant atmosphere. The original restaurant in Solana Beach, a 2-story building with an outdoor patio area, is particularly nice. *607 Valley Ave., Solana Beach, tel. 619/755–5292; 3003 Carlsbad Blvd., Carlsbad, tel. 619/729–0903. Dress: casual. AE, MC, V.*

Lodging

The prices below reflect the cost of a room for two people not including tax (7%). Many hotels offer discount rates from October to May.

Carlsbad
Very Expensive (over $95)
La Costa Hotel and Spa. This famous resort has recently gone through a $100-million renovation, and the style is now mildly Southwestern. Some contemporary rooms are decorated in rose and turquoise. You'll find all amenities, including supervised children's activities and a movie theater. *Costa del Mar Rd., 92009, tel. 619/438–9111 or 800/853–6564. 478 rooms. Facilities: 5 restaurants, pool, exercise room, golf, tennis, theater. AE, DC, MC, V.*

Expensive ($75–$95)
Carlsbad Inn Beach and Tennis Resort. This hotel is near the beach and features modern amenities—Jacuzzis, health club, two restaurants, pool, and video room—and an old-world feel in the rooms. *3075 Carlsbad Blvd., 92008, tel. 619/434–7020. 200 rooms. AE, MC, V.*

Moderate ($55–$75)
Best Western Beach View Lodge. These clean and airy units across the street from the beach are within walking distance of all Carlsbad amenities. Jacuzzi swim, a therapy pool, and a sauna are all available. *3180 Carlsbad Blvd., 92008, tel. 619/729–1151. 41 rooms. Facilities: Jacuzzi, sauna, swimming pool. AE, CB, DC, MC, V.*

Inexpensive (under $55)
Carlsbad Lodge. The lodge is more than an easy walk from the beach, but there is a nice park nearby. The rooms are clean and pleasant. *3570 Pio Pico Dr., 92008, tel. 619/729–2383. 66 rooms. Facilities: Jacuzzi, sauna, swimming pool. AE, CB, DC, MC, V.*

Del Mar
Moderate ($55–$75)
Stratford Inn. Just outside of town and 3 blocks from the ocean, this inn offers a pleasant atmosphere. Rooms are clean and well-maintained; some have ocean views. Suites are available. Note: Not all rooms are air-conditioned, so be sure to ask before you reserve. *710 Camino del Mar, 92014, tel. 619/755–1501. 110 rooms. Facilities: 2 pools, Jacuzzi. AE, CB, DC, MC, V.*

Encinitas
Expensive ($75–$95)
Sanderling Place Inn. The Sanderling is perched on a hill with a stupendous view of the ocean, and the location is the main attraction of this hotel, along with the convenience of a Boathouse restaurant next door. *85 Encinitas Blvd., 92024, tel. 619/942–7455. 92 rooms. Facilities: Jacuzzi, pool, restaurant. AE, DC, MC, V.*

Inexpensive (under $55)
Budget Motels of America. This motel is adjacent to the freeway and within a block of the beach. Some rooms have VCRs and in-room movies—a good deal. *133 Encinitas Blvd., 92024, tel. 619/944–0260. 124 rooms. AE, DC, MC, V.*
Moonlight Beach Hotel. This folksy, laid-back motel is a favorite with those who want to stay put for a few days in a casual setting. All rooms have kitchens, and the beach is just a few blocks away. *233 2nd St., 92024, tel. 619/753–0623. 24 rooms. AE, MC, V.*

Leucadia	**Pacific Surf Motel.** It will never be compared with The Ritz, but
Inexpensive	it is clean, comfortable, and near all the shops and restaurants
(under $55)	of Encinitas. *1076 N. Hwy. 101, 92024, tel. 619/436–8763. 30 rooms. AE, MC, V.*
Oceanside	**Oceanside TraveLodge.** Near the beach and centrally located.
Inexpensive	*1401 N. Hill St., 92054, tel. 619/722–1244. 30 rooms. AE, CB,*
(under $55)	*DC, MC, V.*
Rancho Santa Fe	**John Gardiner's Rancho Valencia Resort.** This small, exclusive
Very Expensive	tennis resort is immensely popular with those who crave soli-
(over $95)	tude. The 20 Spanish-style casitas with red-tile roofs have two
	suites each; each suite has a fireplace. Tennis is the operative
	word here—with 18 courts and a resident pro—and guests
	usually include a tennis clinic in their stay. *5921 Valencia Cir-*
	cle, Rancho Santa Fe, tel. 619/756–1123 or 800/548–3664. 43
	rooms. Facilities: 18 tennis courts, 2 pools, croquet court, ele-
	gant restaurant. AE, DC, MC, V.

Excursion to Anza-Borrego Desert State Park

Every spring the stark desert landscape east of the Cuyamaca Mountains explodes with color. It's the annual blooming of the wildflowers in the Anza-Borrego Desert State Park, less than a two-hour drive from central San Diego. The beauty of this annual spectacle, as well as the natural quiet and blazing climate, lures tourists and natives to the area.

The area features a desert and not much more, but it is one of the favorite parks of those Californians who travel widely in their state. People seeking bright lights and glitter should look elsewhere. The excitement in this area stems from watching a coyote scamper across a barren ridge or a brightly colored bird resting on a nearby cactus, or from a waitress delivering another cocktail to a poolside chaise lounge. For hundreds of years, the only humans to linger in the area were from the San Dieguito, Kamia, and Cahuilla tribes, but the extreme temperature eventually forced them to leave, too. It wasn't until 1774, when Mexican explorer Captain Juan Bautista de Anza first blazed a trail through the area as a shortcut from Sonora to San Francisco, that modern civilization had its first glimpse of the oddly beautiful wasteland.

Today, more than 500,000 acres of desert are included in the Anza-Borrego Desert State Park, making it the largest state park in the United States. It is also one of the few parks in the country where people can camp anywhere. No campsite is necessary; just follow the trails and pitch a tent anywhere in the park.

Following the trails is an important point, since vehicles are prohibited to drive off the road in most areas of the park. However, there are 14,000 acres set aside in the east part of the desert near Ocotillo Wells for off-road enthusiasts. General George S. Patton conducted field training in the Ocotillo area to prepare for the World War II invasion of North Africa, and the area hasn't been the same since.

The little town of Borrego Springs acts
ral playground. Not exactly like Palm
wild crowds and preponderance of
Borrego is basically a small retiremen
average age of residents about 50. Fo¡
communing with the desert without a s¡
Borrego provides several pleasant hotel

We recommend visiting this desert between October and May
because of the extreme summer temperatures. Winter temperatures are comfortable, but nights (and sometimes days) are
cold, so bring a warm jacket.

Arriving and Departing

By Car Take I–8 east to Highway 79 north. Turn east on Highway 78.

By Bus The **Northeast Rural Bus System** (NERBS, tel. 619/765–0145)
connects Julian, Borrego Springs, Oak Grove, Ocotillo Wells,
Agua Caliente, Ramona, and many other small communities
with El Cajon, east of downtown San Diego.

By Plane Borrego Springs Airport (tel. 619/767–5388) has the nearest
runway.

Important Addresses and Numbers

For general information about the Borrego and desert areas,
contact the **Borrego Chamber of Commerce** (tel. 619/767–5555).
For information on the state park, contact the Visitor Center,
Anza-Borrego Desert State Park (Box 299, Borrego Springs
92004, tel. 619/767–5311). You can call the Visitor Center for
information on when the wildflowers are blooming, or you can
send a self-addressed postcard and they'll send it back when
the flowers bloom. For campsite information, call **MISTIX** (tel.
800/444–7275).

Exploring

The **Anza-Borrego Desert State Park** is too vast to even consider
exploring all its areas. Most people stay in the hills
surrounding Borrego Springs. An excellent underground **Visitor Information Center** (tel. 619/767–5311) and museum is
reachable by taking the Palm Canyon Drive spur west from the
traffic circle in the center of town. The rangers are helpful and
always willing to suggest areas to camp or hike. There is also a
brief slide show about the desert shown throughout the day. A
short, very easy trail from the Visitor Center to the campground will take you past many of the cacti illustrated in
Visitor Center displays.

One of the most popular camping and hiking areas is **Palm Canyon,** just a few minutes west of the visitor information center. A
1½-mile trail leads to a small oasis with a waterfall and palm
trees. If you find palms trees lining city streets in San Diego
and Los Angeles amusing, seeing this grove of native palms
around a pool in a narrow desert valley may give you a new vi-
sion of the dignity of this tree. The Borrego Palm Canyon
campground (on the desert floor a mile or so below the palm oasis) is one of only two developed campgrounds with flush toilets
and showers in the park. (The other is Tamarisk Grove Camp-

ground at the intersection of Highway 78 and Yaqui Pass Road.)

Other points of interest include **Split Mountain** (take Split Mountain Rd. south from Hwy. 78 at Ocotillo Wells), a narrow gorge with 600-foot perpendicular walls. You can drive the mile from the end of the paved road to the gorge in a passenger car if you are careful (don't get stuck in the sand). Don't attempt the drive in bad weather, when the gorge can quickly fill with a torrent of water.

On the way to Split Mountain (while you are still on the paved road), you'll pass a grove of the park's unusual **elephant trees** (10 feet tall, with swollen branches and small leaves). There is a self-guided nature trail; pick up a brochure at the parking lot.

You can get a good view of the Borrego Badlands from **Font's Point,** off Borrego-Salton Seaway (S22). The badlands are a maze of steep ravines that are almost devoid of vegetation. Park rangers sometimes give guided tours of the region above the badlands. You drive your own car in a caravan behind the ranger, stopping for closer looks and detailed information.

There is little to do in **Borrego Springs** itself except lie in the sun, lie in the shade, or take advantage of the hot days and recreate in the sun. The challenging 18-hole Rams Hill Country Club course is open to the public (tel. 619/767-5000), as is the Borrego Roadrunner Club (tel. 619/767-5652), but you'll have to know a member to play the private 18 holes of the De Anza Country Club located in the north end of the valley (tel. 619/767-5105).

For tennis fans, the Borrego Tennis Club (tel. 619/767-9725) has four lighted courts open to the public. One of the best and most appreciated deals in town is the Borrego Springs High School pool, located at the intersection of Saddle and Cahuilla roads, which is open to the public during the summer.

Most people prefer to explore the desert in a motorized vehicle. While it is illegal to ride two- or four-wheel vehicles off the trails in the state park, the **Ocotillo Wells State Vehicular Recreation Area** (tel. 619/767-5391), reached by following Highway 78 east from Borrego, is a popular haven for off-road enthusiasts. The sand dunes and rock formations are challenging as well as fun. Camping is permitted throughout the area, but water is not available. The only facilities are in the small town (or, perhaps, it should be called no more than a corner) of Ocotillo Wells.

To the east of Anza-Borrego is the Salton Sink, a basin that (although not as low as Death Valley) comprises more dry land below sea level than anywhere else in the hemisphere. The Salton Sea is the most recent of a series of lakes here, divided from the Gulf of California by the delta of the Colorado River. The current lake was created in 1905-7 when the Colorado flooded north through canals meant to irrigate the Imperial Valley. The water is extremely salty, even saltier than the Pacific Ocean, and it is primarily a draw for fishermen seeking corvina, croaker, and tilopia. Some boaters and swimmers also use the lake. The state runs a pleasant park with sites for day camping, RVs, and primitive camping. *Take Hwy. 78 east to Hwy. 111 north, tel. 619/393-3052.*

Bird-watchers particularly will love the **Salton Sea National Wildlife Refuge.** A hiking trail and observation tower make it easy to spot the dozens of varieties of migratory birds stopping at Salton Sea. *At the south end of Salton Sea, off Hwy. 111, tel. 619/348-5278.*

For hunters, the **Wister Wildlife Area** (tel. 619/348-0577), off Highway 111 on the east side of Salton Sea, controls the hunting of water fowl in the area. There are campsites available.

Lodging

If camping is not your thing, there are two very nice resorts near Borrego Springs that offer fine amenities without the overdevelopment of Palm Springs. Prices are based on the cost of a room for two, not including tax (7%).

Expensive (over $70) **Ram's Hill Country Club.** A relatively new hacienda-style country club in the middle of the desert. Patio units are on the golf course. *Box 664, Borrego Springs 92004, tel. 619/767-5028. 20 units. Facilities: tennis courts, Jacuzzi. AE, MC, V.*

Moderate ($50-$70) **La Casa del Zorro.** A small low-key resort complex in the heart of the desert where you need only walk a few hundred yards to be alone out under the sky, and you may well see roadrunners crossing the highway. The accommodations are in comfortable 1-3 bedroom ranch-style houses complete with living rooms and kitchens. *3845 Yaqui Pass Rd., 92004, tel. 619/767-5323 or 800/325-8274. 77 suites, 94 rooms, 19 casitas. Facilities: tennis courts, golf course, horseback riding, bicycles. AE, CB, DC, MC, V.*

Overland Junction. One of the largest facilities in the area. *221 Palm Canyon Dr., 92004, tel. 619/767-5342. 44 rooms. Facilities: 144 RV spaces, pools, Jacuzzi, laundromat. AE, CB, DC, MC, V.*

15 Palm Springs

*by Aaron
Sugarman*

What do you get when you start with dramatic scenery, add endless sunshine, mix in deluxe resorts, and spice things up with a liberal dash of celebrities? Palm Springs, a mecca for socialites, sun worshippers, and star gazers.

This fashionable desert resort community, nestled beneath 10,831-foot Mt. San Jacinto, sports more than 70 golf courses in a 20-mile radius, more than 300 tennis courts, 35 miles of bicycle trails, horseback riding, 7,000 or so swimming pools, and even cross-country skiing. Those inclined to less strenuous activities are attracted by such names as Gucci, I. Magnin, and Saks Fifth Avenue. It's often said that socializing is the top industry in Palm Springs; after a few days here, you're sure to agree.

Year-round, Palm Springs is both a vacation retreat and a residence for celebrities and famous politicians. Bob Hope is the city's honorary mayor, and Gene Autry, Frank Sinatra, Gerald Ford, and other luminaries can be spotted at charity events and restaurants and on the golf course. Carrie Fisher and Bette Midler have done stints at the Palms spa, while Donna Mills, Goldie Hawn, and Kurt Russell have been poolside stars at the Ingleside Inn. Palm Springs resorts are not new territory to celebrity visitors: Esther Williams once practiced her strokes at the El Mirador pool, Spencer Tracy played chess at the Racquet Club, and Joan Bennett pedaled her bicycle down Palm Canyon Drive.

Palm Springs became a haven for the stars in 1930, after the arrival of noted silent-film pros Charlie Farrell and Ralph Bellamy. For $30 an acre, the two actors bought 200 acres. This was the beginning of the Palm Springs Racquet Club, which soon listed Ginger Rogers, Humphrey Bogart, and Clark Gable among its members. Today you can take a tour that points out the homes of the celebrities of yesterday and today. Some of the most impressive include the Frank Sinatra, Elvis Presley, and Liberace estates.

The desert's stunning natural beauty is a major contributor to its magnetism. Nature dominates the area: City buildings are restricted to a height of 30 feet; flashing, moving, and neon signs are prohibited, preserving an intimate village feeling; and 50% of the land consists of open spaces with palm trees and desert vegetation.

This beauty is particularly evident in the canyon's surrounding Palm Springs. Lush Tahquitz Canyon, one of the five canyons that line the San Jacinto Mountains, was the setting for Shangri La in the original version of *Lost Horizon*. The original inhabitants of these rock canyons were the Cahuilla Indians. Their descendents came to be known as Agua Caliente—"hot water"—Indians, named after the hot mineral springs that flowed through their reservation. The Agua Caliente still own about 30,000 acres of Palm Springs desert, making them one of the richest tribes in the country.

Despite the building restrictions, Palm Springs provides an array of sophisticated spots, from the outstanding Desert Museum and Annenberg Theatre to the chic shops and galleries along the palm-tree-lined Palm Canyon Drive. The trendy El Paseo Drive, 10 miles south of Palm Springs in neighboring Palm Desert, is often compared to Rodeo Drive in Beverly Hills.

One brief comment on the weather: While daytime temperatures average a pleasantly warm 88° Fahrenheit, you are still in the desert. And that means during the middle of the day in the summer it is going to be very hot—sometimes uncomfortably hot. You're bound to be told that "it is a dry heat." It is. But it is still desert hot: Plan activities in the morning and late afternoon, and wear a hat and plenty of sunscreen if you're out for a midday stroll.

Arriving and Departing

By Plane Major airlines serving Palm Springs Municipal Airport include Alaska Airlines, America West, American Airlines, American Eagle, Continental Airlines, Skywest/Delta Connection, Trans World Airlines, United Airlines, and United Express. The airport is about 2 miles east of the city's main downtown intersection; most hotels provide service to and from the airport.

By Train **Amtrak** passenger trains service the Indio area, 20 miles east of Palm Springs. For information and reservations call 800/USA–RAIL. From Indio, **Greyhound-Trailways** bus service is available to Palm Springs.

By Bus **Greyhound-Trailways** Bus Lines (311 N. Indian Ave., tel. 619/325–2053).

By Car Palm Springs is about a two-hour drive east of Los Angeles and a three-hour drive northeast of San Diego. Highway 111 brings you right onto Palm Canyon Drive, the main thoroughfare in Palm Springs. From Los Angeles take the San Bernardino Freeway (I-10E) to Highway 111. From San Diego, I-15N connects with the Pomona Freeway (I-60E), leading to the San Bernardino Freeway (I-10E). If you're coming from the Riverside area, you might want to try the scenic Palms-to-Pines Highway (Hwy. 74). This 130-mile route begins in Hemet and connects directly with Highway 111; the trek from snowcapped peaks to open desert valley is breathtaking.

Getting Around

Downtown Palm Springs is distinctly walkable. Beyond that, you will find that having a car is the easiest way to get around and take in nearby attractions like the Aerial Tramway and El Paseo Drive.

By Bus **SunBus** serves the entire Coachella Valley from Desert Hot Springs to Coachella with regular routes. Call 619/323–4010 or 619/323–4058 for route and schedule information. The company also operates the **Sun Trolley,** which runs up and down Palm Canyon Drive from December through mid-May; the trolley runs from 9 AM to 7:30 PM. The fare is 50¢.

By Taxi **Desert Cab** (tel. 619/325–2868) and **Caravan Yellow Cab** (tel. 619/346–2981).

By Car The easiest way to get around Palm Springs is by automobile. If you're not driving to Palm Springs, you might do well to check with one of the many rental agencies, all of which offer fairly competitive rates. Agencies include Avis (tel. 619/325–1331), Aztec (tel. 619/325–2294), Budget (tel. 619/327–1404), Dollar (tel. 619/325–7334), Enterprise (tel. 619/328–9393), Hertz (tel. 619/778–5120), and National (tel. 619/327–4100).

Important Addresses and Numbers

Tourist Information **The City of Palm Springs Tourism Division** (100 S. Palm Canyon, tel. 800/34–SPRINGS) provides tourist information and maintains an information desk in the airport's main terminal.

Greater Palm Springs Convention and Visitors Bureau (tel. 619/327–8411) is located 300 yards north of the airport at Airport Park Plaza (255 N. Cielo, Suite 315).

Emergencies Dial 911 for **police** and **ambulance** in an emergency.

Doctor **Desert Hospital** (tel. 619/323–6511).

Dentist Dental emergency service is available from R. Turnage D.D.S. (tel. 619/327–8448) 24 hours a day.

Guided Tours

Orientation Tours **Gray Line Tours** (tel. 619/325–0974) offers several good general bus tours, from the hour-long Palm Springs Special highlight tour to the Palm Springs and Living Desert tour through Palm Springs, Cathedral City, Rancho Mirage, and Palm Desert, with stops at a date shop and the Living Desert. Prices are $14.25 for adults, $8.25 for children. Most departures are in the morning; call for reservations. Pick-up and drop-off service is available to most hotels. For a different perspective on the desert, try floating over the valley in a balloon. Trip lengths and prices vary; call **Fantasy Balloon Flights** (tel. 619/568–0997), **Sunrise Balloons** (tel. 619/346–7591), and the **American Balloon Society** (tel. 619/568–6700) for information.

Special-Interest Tours In Palm Springs, special-interest tours usually view celebrity homes. **Gray Line** and **Palm Springs Celebrity Tours** (tel. 619/325–2682) both cover this turf well. Prices range from $10 to $14 for adults. **Desert Off-Road Adventures** (tel. 619/773–3187) takes to the wilds with jeep tours of canyons, unexpected waterfalls, and other off-the-beaten-track attractions. Customized helicopter tours are available from **Sunrise Balloons:** 40-minute trips start at $270 for two people.

Exploring

Numbers in the margin correspond with points of interest on the Palm Springs map.

Palm Springs proper is pretty easy to understand. Palm Canyon Drive runs north-south through the heart of downtown; the intersection with Tahquitz-McCallum is pretty much the center of the main drag. Heading south, Palm Canyon Drive splits: South Palm Canyon Drive leads you to the Indian Canyons and East Palm Canyon takes you through the growing satellite resort areas of Cathedral City, Rancho Mirage, and Palm Desert. The Aerial Tramway is at the northern limits of Palm Springs. Joshua Tree National Monument is about an hour's drive north.

Most Palm Springs attractions can be seen in anywhere from an hour or two to an entire day. Do you want to take the tram up Mount San Jacinto, see the view and come right back down, or spend the day hiking? Would you rather linger for a picnic lunch in one of the Indian Canyons, or double back for a snack and people-watching at Hyatt's sidewalk cafe? Your best bet is to look at the list of sights and activities as if it were an à la carte menu and pick and choose according to your appetite. To help you organize your outings, we will start in the north and work our way south and southeast. A separate tour of Joshua Tree follows.

Palm Springs and Environs

1 The **Palm Springs Aerial Tramway** is the place for a real over- view of the desert. The 2½-mile ascent brings you to an elevation of 8,516 feet in under 20 minutes. On clear days, which are common, the view stretches 75 miles from the peak of Mt. San Gorgonio in the north to the Salton Sea in the south- east. Mt. San Jacinto State Park offers 54 miles of hiking trails and camping and picnic areas; the Nordic Ski Center is open for cross-country skiing November 15 to April 15, snow permit- ting. *Tram cars depart at least every 30 min. from 10 AM week- days and 8 AM weekends. Last car up is at 8 PM, last car down 9:45 PM; May–Labor Day, last car up is at 9 PM, last car down at 10:45 PM. Cost: $13.95 adults, $8.95 children 3–12. Closed for 2–4 wks after Labor Day for maintenance. Call 619/325–1391 for information; 619/325–4227 for ski and weather conditions.*

Strolling down **Palm Canyon Drive,** Palm Springs's version of Main Street, should satisfy even the most avid shopper. With a good pair of comfortable walking shoes you should be able to walk from one end of the drive to the other in a couple of hours. Some exceptional art galleries, such as the **Elaine Horwitch collection** of studios, have taken root along the route and are well worth the browsing time. *Elaine Horwitch Galleries, 1090 N. Palm Canyon Dr., tel. 619/325–3490. Open Mon.–Sat. 9:30–5:30, Sun. noon–5.*

Downtown, horse-drawn carriages promenade the city streets to the narrative of their driver/guides. **Carriage Trade Ltd.** (tel. 619/327–3214) charges $20 for one to four people. Rides start at the Hyatt Regency (285 N. Palm Canyon Drive).

2 Downtown Palm Springs is not without its historical treasures. The **Village Green Heritage Center** comprises two 19th-century pioneer homes. The adobe house built by "Judge" John McCallum in 1885 is now a museum housing the major por- tion of the collection of the Palm Springs Historical Society. McCallum, a San Francisco attorney, brought his family to the area hoping to restore the health of his son, who had been taken ill during a typhoid epidemic. Next door is the Cornelia White House, built in 1894 from railroad ties. Inside are such histori- cal tidbits as the first telephone in Palm Springs. *221 and 223 S. Palm Canyon Dr. Nominal admission. Both open Wed.–Sun. noon–3, Thurs.–Sat. 10–4. Closed June–mid-Oct.*

3 If further evidence is needed to prove that the desert is no bar- ren wasteland, there is the **Desert Museum.** Art exhibits here tend to favor a Western flavor, from California Contemporary to shows like the "Art and Treasures of the Old West" from the Buffalo Bill Historical Center. But it is not unusual to catch a Matisse exhibition or works from the impressive Armand Ham- mer Collection that toured the region in 1988. Natural-history and science exhibits illuminate aspects of the surrounding de- sert. The museum's Annenberg Theatre has featured Liza Minnelli and Frank Sinatra in concert. *Museum Dr., just north of Tahquitz Way (on the south side of the Desert Fashion Pla- za), tel. 619/325–7186. Admission: $4 adults, $2 children un-*

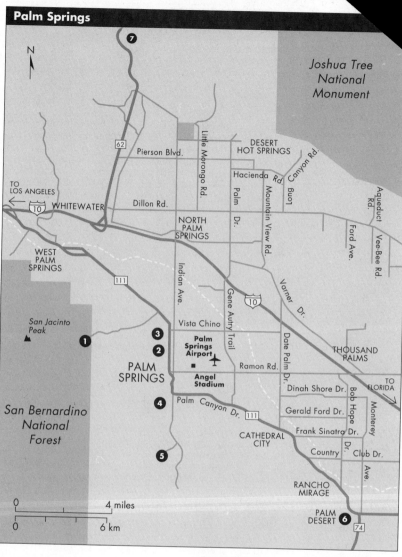

Palm Springs

N

Joshua Tree National Monument

TO LOS ANGELES

10 WHITEWATER

62

Pierson Blvd.

DESERT HOT SPRINGS

Hacienda Rd.

Long Canyon Rd.

Dillon Rd.

Little Morongo Rd.

Palm Dr.

Mountain View Rd.

Ford Ave.

Aqueduct Rd.

Vee-Bee Rd.

NORTH PALM SPRINGS

WEST PALM SPRINGS

111

Indian Ave.

Gene Autry Trail

Vista Chino

Varner Dr.

10

San Jacinto Peak

1

3

2

Palm Springs Airport

THOUSAND PALMS

PALM SPRINGS

Ramon Rd.

Date Palm Dr.

TO FLORIDA

Angel Stadium

Dinah Shore Dr.

Bob Hope Dr.

Monterey

4

Palm Canyon Dr.

111

Gerald Ford Dr.

San Bernardino National Forest

CATHEDRAL CITY

Frank Sinatra Dr.

Country Dr.

Club Dr.

Ave.

5

RANCHO MIRAGE

PALM DESERT **6**

74

0   4 miles

0   6 km

Desert Museum, **3**

Indian Canyons, **5**

Joshua Tree National Monument, **7**

Living Desert Reserve, **6**

Moorten Botanical Garden, **4**

Palm Springs Aerial Tramway, **1**

Village Green Heritage Center, **2**

7

der 17. *Open Tues.–Fri. 10–4, weekends until 5. Closed Mon. and June 5–Sept. 22.*

4 A short drive or distinctly long walk farther south on Palm Canyon is the **Moorten Botanical Garden.** More than 2,000 plant varieties cover the 4-acre site in settings that stimulate the plants' original environments. Indian artifacts and rock, crystal, and wood forms are exhibited. *1701 S. Palm Canyon Dr., tel. 619/327–6555. Nominal admission fee. Open daily 9–4:30.*

5 The **Indian Canyons** begin 5 miles south of downtown Palm Springs. Inside this Indian-owned sanctuary, visitors can gaze at pictographs, bedrock mortar holes for grinding grain, and stone houses and shelters built atop high cliff walls, all relics of ancient American history. Streams of icy mountain water wind through the dense growth of willows, sycamores, mesquite, and groves of stately Washingtonia palms. Bands of wild ponies roam through Murray Canyon, and Andreas Canyon has towering rock faces and mysterious crevices and caves. Desert wildlife scampers around the more than 3,000 palm trees in Palm Canyon. Experiencing the canyons leaves visitors with the sensation of slipping through a time warp into a prehistoric era. *End of S. Palm Canyon Dr., tel. 619/327–2714. Admission: $3 adults, 75¢ children. Open Sept.–June daily 8–5.*

6 Bighorn sheep, coyotes, eagles, and other desert wildlife roam in naturalistic settings at the **Living Desert Reserve,** in Palm Desert. There is a 6-mile nature walk, a walk through an aviary, a coyote grotto, a desert reptile exhibit, and regularly scheduled animal shows. This is a particularly enjoyable learning experience for children. *47-900 Portola Ave., less than 2 mi south of Hwy. 111. Admission: $5 adults, $2 children 6–15. Open daily 9–5, closed mid-June–Aug.*

Time Out Tired from all your hiking around? Then sample the healing waters that have made Palm Springs famous for centuries. The Cahuilla Indians have leased 8 acres of land to form the site of the **Palm Springs Spa Hotel.** Visit the inhalation room with its soothing menthol vapors, and of course, the mineral baths. Facials and massage are also available. *100 N. Indian Ave., tel. 619/325–1461. Prices begin at $25. Open daily, 10–5.*

Joshua Tree National Monument
7 **Joshua Tree National Monument** is about a one-hour drive from Palm Springs, whether you take I-10 north to Highway 62 to the Oasis Visitor Center or I-10 south to the Cottonwood Visitor Center. The northern part of the park is in the Mojave (or high) Desert and has the Joshua trees. The southern part is Colorado (or low) Desert; you'll see fine displays of wildflowers here in the spring. It is possible to drive through the monument and come back to Palm Springs from the other direction. This would be a good long day's exploring, but you would travel through the two major California deserts.

On the northern route to the national monument, you may want to consider stopping at the **Big Morongo Wildlife Reserve.** Once an Indian village, then a cattle ranch, and now a regional park, the reserve is a serene natural oasis supporting a wide variety of plants, birds, and animals. There is a shaded meadow for picnics and choice hiking trails. *From I-10 or Indian Ave., take Hwy. 62 east to East Dr. Admission free. Open 8–sunset.*

The monument itself is immense, complex, and ruggedly beautiful. It marks the meeting place of the Mojave and Colorado deserts with mountains of twisted rock and exposed granite monoliths, lush oases shaded by tall, elegant fan palms, and natural cactus gardens. Extensive stands of Joshua trees, which look like something Muppet-maker Jim Henson designed to amuse kids, give the monument its name. The trees were originally named by early white settlers who felt their unusual forms resembled Joshua raising his arms toward heaven. With so much to see—the monument covers more than ½-million acres—the **Oasis Visitor Center** is probably the best place to start. The center has an excellent selection of free and low-cost brochurs, books, posters, and maps as well as several educational exhibits. Knowledgeable and helpful rangers are on hand to answer questions and offer advice. *Hwy. 62 to the town of 29 Palms, follow the signs a short distance south to the Visitor Center. There is a $5 per-vehicle entry fee to the monument.*

Right at the Visitor Center is the **Oasis of Mara.** Inhabited first by Indians and later by prospectors and homesteaders, the oasis now provides a good home for birds, small mammals, and other wildlife. Once inside the monument, you will find nine campgrounds with tables, fireplaces, and rest rooms and several picnic areas for day use. Beyond those basics, sights range from the Hidden Valley, a legendary cattle rustlers' hideout reached by a trail winding through massive boulders; and the Lost Horse Mine, a remnant of the gold-mining days; to Keys View, an outstanding scenic point commanding a superb sweep of valley, mountain, and desert. Sunrise and sunset are magic times to be at the monument, when the light throws rocks and trees into high relief before (or after) bathing the hills in brilliant shades of red, orange, and gold. The National Parks Service map available at the Visitor Center tells you where to find these and other impressive sights within the monument.

Palm Springs for Free

The North Palm Canyon Gallery Association (tel. 619/322–0966) regularly offers a free "art stroll" touring the area galleries.

There are two dozen or so municipal and school **tennis courts** scattered throughout Palm Springs that are absolutely free. Check the "Courts and Courses" listing in *Desert Guide*, available at most hotels, at the Convention and Visitors Bureau, and at the Palm Springs Tourism Division.

What to See and Do with Children

The Dinosaur Gardens are a must-see. Claude Bell designed and built the 150-foot-long brontosaurus and matching Tyrannosaurus rex right off the main highway. The dinosaurs starred in the movie *Pee Wee's Big Adventure. 5800 Seminole Dr., Cabazon, just off I-10, just before Hwy. 111, 18 mi northwest of Palm Springs, no phone. Open Wed.–Mon. 9–5.*

At the **Palm Springs Swim Center,** an Olympic-size swimming pool has a separate swimming section for children only. Swimming instruction is available for all ages, *411 S. Pavilion, adjacent to Sunrise Way and Ramon Rd., tel. 619/323–8278. Hours and admission vary by season.*

Kids can also make a splash at the **Oasis Water Resort.** Tubing, water slides, "Squirt City," and other watery delights will entertain a wide range of age groups. *1500 Gene Autry Trail, between Hwy. 111 and Ramon Rd., tel. 619/325-7873. Hours and admission prices vary by season.*

California Angels spring training baseball games, with a requisite autograph hunt, make for a fun afternoon (*see* Spectator Sports below for more information).

Aerial Tramway (*see* Exploring, above).

The Living Desert (*see* Exploring, above).

Indian Canyons Hiking and picnic areas, Indian cultural remains (*see* Exploring, above).

Off the Beaten Track

Dog sled races in Palm Springs? Why not? The **Moosehead Championship Sled Dog Races** are held in January, atop Mt. San Jacinto. Take the Aerial Tramway up. Call 619/325-1391 for more information.

The Eldorado Polo Club (50-950 Madison Blvd., Indio, tel. 619/342-2223) is known as the "Winter Polo Capital of the West." Pack a picnic hamper and hobnob with the elite from November to April. Admission is free, except for a $5 charge on Sundays.

Shopping

The Palm Springs area is full of custom boutiques and lively art galleries. The resort community also has several large air-conditioned indoor malls with major department stores and chic boutiques. El Paseo in nearby Palm Desert is the desert's other shopping mecca, with its own collection of upscale and elegant galleries and shops. Most stores are open 10-5 or 6, Monday-Saturday. A fair number are open on Sunday, typically noon-5. The sales tax in Palm Springs is 6½%.

Shopping Districts **Palm Canyon Drive** is Palm Springs' main shopping destination. It began as a dusty two-way dirt road and is now a one-way, three-lane thoroughfare with parking on both sides. Its shopping core extends from Alejo Road on the north to Ramon Road on the south. Furs, jewelry, sportswear, home furnishings, books, shoes, and crafts will tempt you on this busy street. Anchoring the center of the drive is the Desert Fashion Plaza, sporting big names like Saks Fifth Avenue, I. Magnin, Gucci, and many smaller surprises.

The Courtyard at the Bank of Palm Springs Center brings Paris to Palm Springs. Expect to be dazzled by the high fashion of Rodier and Yves St. Laurent. There's also a six-screen movie theater.

El Paseo Village is touted as a true shopping experience rather than a shopping center. Unique stores, architecturally designed with a Spanish motif, are clustered among flower-lined paths and fountained courtyards. Don't miss Polo/Ralph Lauren (73-111 El Paseo, tel. 619/340-1414), featuring Lauren's classic fashions and accessories for men and women, and Cabale Cachet (73-111 El Paseo, tel. 619/346-5805), for a fine collection of European haute couture.

The Palm Desert Town Center is the desert's latest major addition to convenient and stylish shopping. Five major department stores anchor the center including Bullocks and The May Co. There are also seven movie theaters and a skating rink.

Rancho las Palmas at Highway 111 and Bob Hope Drive, Rancho Mirage, offers gourmet kitchenware, antiques, imported chocolate and confections, and fine restaurants.

Department Stores The exclusive **I. Magnin** (151 S. Palm Canyon Dr., tel. 619/325–1571) is a department store with class, so do expect the latest fashions, but don't expect flea market prices. Another **I. Magnin** (tel. 619/325–1531) is located at Desert Fashion Plaza. Other major department stores can be found in the various malls listed above.

Specialty Shops **Jacqueline's** (Desert Fashion Plaza, tel. 619/322–4114) features
Jewelry beautiful original designs; rings are a specialty.
Robanns (125 S. Palm Canyon Dr., tel. 619/325–9603) offers an elegant collection.

Discount Although Palm Springs is known for glamor and high prices, the city does offer bargains if you know where to look. Several outlets can be found in the **Loemann's Shopping Center** (2500 N. Palm Canyon Dr.), including **Fieldcrest-Cannon** (tel. 619/322–3229), **Dansk** (tel. 619/320–3304), and **Loemann's** (tel. 619/322–0388).

Participant Sports

The *Desert Guide* from Palm Springs Life, available at most hotels, the Convention and Visitors Bureau, and the Palm Springs Tourism Division, lists "Courts and Courses," with a map showing all of the city's golf courses and tennis courts and information on whether the facilities are public or private.

Bicycling There are more than 35 miles of bike trails, with six mapped-out city tours. Trail maps are available at the **Palm Springs Recreation Department** (401 S. Pavilion, tel. 619/323–8276) and bike-rental shops. You can rent a bike at **Mac's Bike Rental** (70–155 Highway 111, tel. 619/327–5721) and **Burnett's Bicycle Barn** (429 S. Sunrise Way, tel. 619/325–7844).

Golf Palm Springs is known as the "Winter Golf Capital of the World." The area has more than 70 golf courses within its limits, a number of which are open to the public. Among these are the **Palm Springs Municipal Golf Course** (1885 Golf Club Dr., tel. 619/328–1005) and **Fairchilds Bel Aire Greens** (1001 El Cielo Rd., tel. 619/327–0332). Don't be surprised to spy well-known politicians and Hollywood stars on the greens.

Hiking Nature trails abound in the Indian Canyons, Mt. San Jacinto State Park and Wilderness, and Living Desert Reserve (*see* Exploring, above).

Physical Fitness The **Clark Hatch Physical Fitness Center** (Hyatt Regency Suites Hotel, 285 N. Palm Canyon Dr., tel. 619/322–2778) is the latest in a worldwide chain of Hatch health clubs. The facilities are high-quality and low-key. Fees are $10 daily, $60 monthly.

Tennis Of the 350 or so tennis courts in the area, you'll find these open to the public: the **Palm Springs Tennis Center** (1300 Baristo Rd., tel. 619/320–0020), nine lighted courts; **Ruth Hardy Park** (Tamarisk and Caballeros, no phone), eight lighted courts, with no court fee; and **Demuth Park** (4375 Mesquite Ave., tel. 619/323–8279), four lighted courts.

Polo A new draw to desert life is the chance to learn to play polo. Just behind Eldorado in Indio, **Empire polo field** (tel. 619/342–9631) offers polo lessons as well as an inside show stadium and a balloon-launching field.

Spectator Sports

Baseball The **California Angels** hold their annual spring training and play a number of exhibition games in Palm Springs during March and early April. Games typically begin at 1 PM at Palm Springs Angels Stadium, east of Sunrise Way near Ramon Road. Reserved and general admission seats are available. Call 619/323–8272 for more information.

Golf More than 100 golf tournaments are presented in Palm Springs; the two most popular are the **Bob Hope Desert Classic** (Jan.) and the **Dinah Shore Championship** (Mar. or Apr.). Call the Convention and Visitors Bureau or Palm Springs Tourism for exact dates and places.

Tennis The **Newsweek Champions Cup** tournament (Feb. or Mar.), held at Hyatt Grand Champions Resort in Indian Wells, has attracted the likes of Boris Becker and Yannick Noah.

Dining

So many L.A. natives have second homes or condos "down in the Springs" that local restaurateurs are outdoing themselves to match the Big City's standards—and more and more are succeeding. Most of the restaurants listed below can be found on or near Highway 111, running from Palm Springs to Palm Desert.

Category	Cost*
Expensive	over $35
Moderate	$15–$30
Inexpensive	under $15

per person, without tax, service, or drinks

Palm Springs
Expensive
Melvyn's Restaurant. "Lifestyles of the Rich and Famous" calls this Old World-style spot "one of the 10 best." Snugly nestled into the gardens of the Ingleside Inn, weekend brunch here is a Palm Springs tradition. Nightly piano bar. *200 W. Ramon Rd., tel. 619/325–2323. Dress: jacket required. Reservations recommended. AE, MC, V.*

Le Vallauris. Formerly a private club, this stylish, rather romantic setting is now open to the public. The cuisine ranges from classic French to *nouvelle* desert. *385 W. Tahquitz-McCallum Way, tel. 619/325–5059. Valet parking. Jacket and tie required. Reservations recommended. AE, DC, MC, V.*

Moderate–Expensive
Lyon's English Grille. When was the last time you had real honest-to-goodness roast beef and Yorkshire pudding the way only the Brits can make it? Lyon's has it and other old-country favorites. Good value and good food make this a popular stop for the locals. *233 E. Palm Canyon Dr., tel. 619/327–1551.*

Dress: casual. Reservations suggested. AE, CB, DC, MC, V. Closed for lunch. Closed summer.

Moderate **Banducci's Bit of Italy.** Homemade dishes are served in a friendly, family atmosphere; try the cannelloni or lasagna. There's a piano bar, too. *1260 S. Palm Canyon Dr., tel. 619/ 325–2537. Dress: casual. Reservations suggested. AE, MC, V. Closed for lunch.*

Bono. Palm Springs' mayor, Sonny Bono, of Sonny and Cher fame, serves the Southern Italian dishes his mother used to make. It's a favorite feeding station for show biz folk and the curious, and a good place for pasta, chicken, veal, and scampi dishes. *1700 N. Indian Ave., tel. 619/322–6200. Valet parking. Reservations advised. Dress: casual. AE, MC, V. Dinner only.*

Brussels Cafe. The best spot in town for people-watching is this sidewalk cafe in the heart of Palm Canyon Drive. Try the Belgian waffles or homemade pâté. Beers from around the world are featured, and there's nightly entertainment. *109 S. Palm Canyon Dr., tel. 619/320-4177. Dress: casual. Reservations not usually necessary. AE, CB, DC, MC, V.*

Cafe St. James. Dine on a plant-filled balcony and watch the passing parade below. The lunch menu features excellent salads and thick, imaginative samdwiches. *254 N. Palm Canyon Dr., tel. 619/320–8041. Dress: casual. Reservations recommended. AE, CB, DC, MC, V. Closed Mon.*

Las Casuelas Original. A long-time favorite among natives and visitors alike, it's got great—in size and taste—margaritas and average Mexican dishes: crab enchilada, carne asada, lobster Ensenada. It gets very, very crowded during winter months. *368 N. Palm Canyon Dr., tel. 619/325–3213. Dress: casual. Reservations recommended. AE, DC, MC, V.*

Flower Drum. Related to New York's highly popular Flower Drum, this health-conscious Chinese restaurant features Hunan, Peking, Shanghai, Canton, and Szechuan cuisines in a Chinese village setting. *424 S. Indian Ave., tel. 619/323–3020. Dress: casual to dressy. Reservations recommended. AE, MC, V.*

Rennick's. This local landmark recently celebrated its silver [76] cholesterol counts. Fresh fish and grilled items are recommended. *100 N. Indian Ave., tel. 619/325–1461. Reservations suggested. AE, DC, MC, V.*

Riccio's. Tony Riccio, formerly of the Marquis and Martoni's, in Hollywood, knows the old-fashioned Italian food that comforts his steady patrons: fettucine Alfredo, veal piccata, chicken Vesuvio, and a luscious Italian cheesecake. *2155 N. Palm Canyon Dr., tel. 619/325–2369. Valet parking. Jacket required. Reservations recommended. AE, DC, MC, V. Closed lunch.*

Inexpensive **Di Amico's Steak House.** Hearty eaters will enjoy this early-California-style restaurant. Prime Eastern corn-fed beef, liver steak vaquero, and son-of-a-gun stew are featured. *1180 S. Palm Canyon Dr., tel. 619/325–9191. Dress: casual. Reservations recommended. MC, V. Closed Sunday lunch.*

Elmer's Pancake and Steak House. Forget about Aunt Jemima. Elmer's offers 25 varieties of pancakes and waffles. There are steaks, chicken, and seafood on the dinner menu. A children's menu is available, too. *1030 E. Palm Canyon Dr., tel. 619/327– 8419. No reservations. Dress: casual. MC, V.*

Louise's Pantry. Another local landmark, in the center of downtown Palm Springs for almost 40 years, its down-home cooking 1940s-style features chicken and dumplings and short ribs of beef. You can get soup, salad, entrée, beverage, and dessert for under $15. There's usually a line to get in. *124 S. Palm Canyon Dr., tel. 619/325–5124. Dress: casual. No credit cards.*

Cathedral City, Rancho Mirage, Palm Desert
Expensive

Dominick's. An old favorite of Frank Sinatra's and what's left of his "rat pack." Steaks, pasta, and veal dishes are the order of the day. *70–030 Hwy. 111, tel. 619/324–1711. Dress: casual. Reservations advised. AE, DC, MC, V. Closed lunch.*

Mama Gina's. Generally considered the best Italian food in the Palm Springs area, this attractive, simply furnished trattoria was opened by the son of the original Mama Gina in Florence, Italy. There is an open kitchen where you can watch the chef from Tuscany prepare specialties including deep fried artichokes, fettuccine with porcini mushrooms, and prawns with artichoke and zucchini. The soups are excellently robust. *73–705 El Paseo, tel. 619/568–9898. Dress: informal. Reservations required. AE, DC, MC, V. Closed lunch.*

Wally's Desert Turtle. If price is no object and you like plush, gilded decor, then this is where you'll be surrounded by the golden names of Palm Springs and Hollywood society. Old-fashioned French cooking is served: rack of lamb, imported Dover sole, braised sea bass, veal Oscar, chicken Normande, and dessert soufflés. *71–775 Hwy. 111, tel. 619/568–9321. Valet parking. Jacket required. Reservations required. MC, V. Dinner daily, lunch Fri.*

Moderate

The Rusty Pelican. Fresh seafood is flown in from both coasts and served in a nautical atmosphere. The Oyster Bar shucks to order. There's live entertainment and dancing. *72–191 Hwy. 111, Palm Desert, tel. 619/346–8065. Dress: casual. Reservations suggested. AE, CB, DC, MC, V.*

The Wilde Goose. The award-winning restaurant is popular with celebrities for its beef and lamb Wellington and five varieties of duck. A specialty of the house is duck with apricot and Triple Sec sauce. Dependable food and service. *67–938 Hwy. 111, Cathedral City, tel. 619/328–5775. Reservations recommended. AE, MC, V. Closed for lunch.*

Inexpensive

Stuft Pizza. What would any listing be without at least one pizza parlor? This one is popular for its thick, Chicago-style crusts and generous heaps of fresh toppings. *67–555 Hwy. 111, Cathedral City, tel. 619/321–2583. No credit cards.*

La Quinta
Expensive
★

Cunard's. Robert Cunard converted his French-style villa to a restaurant three years ago, and hired chef Jay Trubee to devise a Franco/Italian menu. Today, the warm atmosphere and inventive cuisine have made it the area's biggest hit. *73–045 Calle Cadiz, tel. 619/564–4443. Dinner only. Jacket and tie requested. Reservations advised. MC, V. Closed July and August.*

Lodging

One of the reasons Palm Springs attracts so many celebrities, entertainment-industry honchos, and other notables is its stock of luxurious hotels. There is a full array of resorts, inns, clubs, spas, lodges, and condos, from small and private to big and bustling. Room rates cover an enormous range—from $20 to $1,600 a night—and also vary widely from summer to winter season. It is not unusual for a hotel to drop its rates from 50 to

60% during the summer (June through early Sept.). For a growing number of off-season travelers, the chance to stay in a $180 room for $60 is an offer they just can't refuse.

Don't even think of visiting here during winter and spring holiday seasons without advance reservations. The Palm Springs Chamber of Commerce (tel. 619/325–1577), the Convention and Visitors Bureau (tel. 619/327–8411), and Palm Springs Tourism (tel. 800/34–SPRINGS) can help you with hotel reservations and information. For a more complete hotel guide complete with prices, pick up a copy of the *Convention and Visitors Bureau's Accommodations Guide* or the *Palm Springs Tourism Accommodations Guide*.

Highly recommended hotels are indicated by a star ★.

Category	Cost*
Very Expensive	over $150
Expensive	$100–$150
Moderate	$70–$100
Inexpensive	under $70

for a double room, not including tax

Rentals. Condos, apartments, and even individual houses may be rented by the day, week, month, or longer period. Rates start at about $400 a week for a one-bedroom condo, $500–$600 a week for two bedrooms, and $3,200 for a three-bedroom house for a month. Contact **The Rental Connection** (170 E. Palm Canyon Dr., Palm Springs 92264, tel. 619/320–7336; 800/468–3776; in CA, 800/232–3776). For small, exclusive hotels, contact **Palm Springs' Best-Kept Secrets** (tel. 800/344–5646).

Palm Springs
Very Expensive

Doubletree Resort at Desert Princess. This three-year-old luxury resort hotel has a full slate of amenities: 18-hole championship golf course, tennis and raquetball courts, pools, spas, and health club. *Vista Chino at Desert Princess Dr., tel. 619/322–7000. 300 rooms and suites. Facilities: 3 restaurants. AE, CB, DC, MC, V.*

Hyatt Regency Suites. Located stage center in the heart of downtown shopping at the Desert Fashion Plaza, the hotel has a striking 6-story asymmetrical lobby and three restaurants, including fine Continental cuisine at Le Jardin and a popular sidewalk cafe. *285 N. Palm Canyon Dr., tel. 619/322–9000. 194 suites. Facilities: health club, pool. AE, CB, DC, MC, V.*

★ **La Mancha Private Pool Villas and Court Club.** Only 4 blocks from downtown Palm Springs, this Hollywood-esque retreat blocks out the rest of the world. Villas are oversized and opulent; one is even equipped with a screening room and private pool. *444 N. Avenida Cabilleros, tel. 619/323–1773. Facilities: tennis courts, paddle tennis courts, pool, 2 croquet lawns. AE, CB, DC, MC, V.*

Palm Springs Hilton Resort and Racquet Club. The cool, white marble elegance of this plant-filled resort hotel just off Palm Canyon Drive and its two superb restaurants make it a top choice for the city. *400 E. Tahquitz Way, tel. 619/320–6868. 257 units. Facilities: tennis courts, pool, body spa, Jacuzzi. AE, CB, DC, MC, V.*

The Palm Springs Marquis. Posh, desert-modern style marks this centrally located hotel, featuring a gourmet restaurant and cafe, plus extensive meeting and convention facilities. *150 S. Indian Ave., tel. 619/322–2121. 262 units. Facilities: 2 pools, Jacuzzi, health spa, tennis courts. AE, CB, DC, MC, V.*

Sundance Villas. Beautifully decorated, spacious villas include fireplace, wet bar, kitchen, and private patio for dining or sunning. Each villa has a private pool or Jacuzzi. The hotel also has tennis courts. Not for the weak of pocketbook. *303 Cabrillo Rd., tel. 619/325–3888. 19 villas. AE, MC, V.*

Expensive **Gene Autry Hotel.** Well decked-out for activities, this hotel has six tennis courts, three swimming pools, two therapy spas, horseback riding, hiking, and desert tours. Dining and entertainment are offered nightly. *4200 E. Palm Canyon Dr., tel. 619/328–1171. 187 units. AE, CB, DC, MC, V.*

★ **Ingleside Inn.** A hacienda-style inn furnished with antiques, each room here is equipped with a steam shower and whirlpool. *200 W. Ramon Rd., tel. 619/325–0046. 29 units. Facilities: pool, Jacuzzi, sauna. AE, MC, V.*

Racquet Club of Palm Springs. Built by Charlie Farrell and Ralph Bellamy in 1933, the Racquet Club marked the beginning of Palm Springs glamour era. It is said Marilyn Monroe was "discovered" on the tennis courts. *2743 N. Indian Ave., tel. 619/325–1281. 120 units. Facilities: 4 pools, therapy pool, sauna, tennis courts, cocktail lounge. AE, CB, DC, MC, V.*

Moderate **Courtyard by Marriott.** This new property represents the Marriott chain's effort to expand into comfortable, smaller hotels offering a good value. The concept works nicely. *1300 Tahquitz Way, tel. 619/322–6100. 149 rooms. Facilities: restaurant, pool, weight room. AE, MC, V.*

Tuscany Manor Apartment-Hotel. These lovely apartments have a pool and therapeutic pool. Esther Williams shot her first movie here. *350 Chino Canyon Rd., tel. 619/325–2349. 24 units. MC, V.*

Villa Royale. A charming bed-and-breakfast, each unit is individually decorated in an international theme. Some rooms have private Jacuzzis and fireplaces. *1620 Indian Trail, tel. 619/327–2314. 34 units. AE, MC, V.*

Inexpensive **Mira Loma Hotel.** Small, with a friendly family atmosphere, this hotel has rooms and suites decorated in 1940s Hollywood Art Deco style. Marilyn Monroe slept here. *1420 N. Indian Ave., tel. 619/320–1178. 12 units. Facilities: pool. AE, MC, V.*

Monte Vista Hotel. Located in a prime Palm Canyon Drive location, this hotel is replete with swimming pool and comfortable accommodations. *414 N. Palm Canyon Dr., tel. 619/325–5641. 32 units. AE, MC, V.*

Mt. View Inn. A friendly atmosphere and convenient location make this small inn a great favorite. The inn has a swimming pool. *200 S. Cahuilla Rd., tel. 619/325–5281. 11 units. No credit cards.*

Westward Ho Seven Seas Hotel. A swimming pool, therapy pool, and cocktail lounge grace this modest property. *701 E. Palm Canyon Dr., tel. 619/320–2700. 209 units. AE, MC, V.*

Outside Palm Springs
Very Expensive **Hyatt Grand Champions Resort.** This elegant resort takes its fun seriously with two 18-hole golf courses, tennis courts featuring three court surfaces, the largest tennis stadium in the West, and a health club with a full complement of workout equipment and pampering treatments. Jasmine's *nouvelle* American menu is getting raves; the more casual Trattoria

mixes Italian and Californian cuisine with delightful results. *44 -600 Indian Wells La., Indian Wells, tel. 619/341-1000. 334 units. AE, CB, DC, MC, V.*

Marriott's Desert Springs Resort and Spa. The most luxurious spa facilities in the desert, two 18-hole golf courses, and a complex of waterways with boat transport around the resort let you know this is no run-of-the-mill resort. *74855 Country Club Dr., Palm Desert, tel. 619/341-2211. 891 rooms. Facilities: 16 tennis courts, 5 restaurants, European spa. AE, CB, DC, MC, V.*

★ **The Ritz Carlton Rancho Mirage.** The newest, poshest gem in the desert collection is located on a 650-foot-high plateau in the foothills of the Santa Rosas, adjacent to a reserve for bighorn sheep. Needless to say, it has all the amenities you would expect from one of the world's classiest hotel chains. *68-900 Frank Sinatra Dr., Rancho Mirage, tel. 619/321-8282. 221 rooms, 19 suites. AE, CB, DC, MC, V.*

Expensive **Two Bunch Palms.** Reputedly built by Al Capone to escape the pressures of gangsterdom in 1920s Chicago, this collection of white-walled villas and mineral pools is still something of a secret hideaway. Antiques capture the flavor of the pre-World War II years. *67-425 Two Bunch Palms Trail, Desert Hot Springs 92240, tel. 619/329-8791 or 800/472-4334. 44 villas. Facilities: thermal pools, tennis courts, restaurant. AE, MC, V.*

The Arts

For complete listings of upcoming events, pick up a copy of *Palm Springs Life* magazine or Palm Springs Life's *Desert Guide*, a free monthly publication found in any hotel.

The McCallum Theatre (73-000 Fred Waring Dr., Palm Desert, tel. 619/325-0698) in the Bob Hope Cultural Center is probably the desert's premier venue for the performing arts. Since opening in January 1988 with a tribute to Bob Hope, the theater has hosted such varied artists as Rudolph Nureyev and the Paris Ballet, the Los Angeles Philharmonic, pantomimist Marcel Marceau, and a rock-and-roll revival starring Fabian.

The Annenberg Theatre (Museum Dr., just north of Tahquitz Way, on the south side of the Desert Fashion Plaza, tel. 619/325-7186) of the Palm Springs Desert Museum is the area's other major arts center. Featured performers have ranged from the Second City improv troupe to Liza Minnelli, Frank Sinatra, and a slew of international musicians in its Sunday Afternoon Concerts series.

Concerts **The College of the Desert** (43-500 Monterey Ave., Palm Desert, tel. 619/346-8041). This is home to the annual Joanna Hodges Piano Conference and Competition.

Theater **VPG Theatre** (225 S. El Cielo Rd., tel. 619/320-9898). Home of the Valley Players Guild, the VPG offers a lively mix of theater fare.

Nightlife

Two good sources for finding current nightlife attractions are the *Desert Sun* (the local newspaper) and *Guide* magazine, a monthly publication distributed free at most downtown merchants' counters.

Live entertainment, ranging from soft dinner music to song-and-dance numbers, is frequently found in the city's hotels and restaurants. The piano bars at **Rennick's** and **Melvyn's Ingleside Inn** are popular. **Moody's Supper Club** (1480 S. Palm Canyon Dr., tel. 619/323–1806) has an inviting party atmosphere, and you can hear everything from Puccini to pop.

Jazz **The Great American Bar & Grill** (777 E. Tahquitz Way, tel. 619/322–1311) is a cool place for jazz on Monday and Tuesday nights. **Brussels Cafe** (tel. 619/320–4177) features jazz and blues Sunday nights.

Discos Between the flashing lights of its Top-40 disco and the retro memorabilia in its new '50s–'60s room, **Cecil's** (1775 E. Palm Canyon Dr., tel. 619/320–4202) is bound to keep you dancing. **Mary's** (1700 N. Indian Ave., tel. 619/322–6200), below Bono's restaurant, is one of Palm Spring's newest clubs, catering to an older, Hollywood crowd. Contemporary music is played here. **Zelda's** (169 N. Indian Ave., tel. 619/325–2375) is another nightclub that regularly attracts a full house and a young crowd.

Country There's live country music at the **Cactus Corral** (67–501 E. Palm Canyon Dr., Cathedral City, tel. 619/321–8558).

Comedy Clubs **The Comedy Haven.** Stand-up comics and improv groups dished up with American/Italian fare. *Desert Fashion Plaza (enter parking lot from Tahquitz Way), tel. 619/320–7855. Shows start at 9 PM.* **The Laff Stop.** Stand-up comedy shows are the nightly attraction, interspersed with live and recorded music of the '50s, '60s, and '70s. *Corner of Tahquitz and Caballeros, across from the Convention Center, tel. 619/327–8889.*

16 The Mojave Desert and Death Valley

by Aaron
Sugarman
When most people put together their "must-see" list of California attractions, the desert is not usually jockeying for position with the top contenders. What with the heat and the vast, seemingly empty tracts of land, the desert is certainly no Disneyland. But then, that's precisely why it deserves a closer look. The desert is truly one of our last frontiers. It offers an overwhelming richness of natural beauty: rolling waves of sand dunes, black cinder cones thrusting up hundreds of feet into the air from a blistered desert floor, riotous sheets of wildflowers, the bizarre shape of the Joshua tree basking in an orange glow at sunset, unspoiled valleys surrounded by rings of mountains, and a silence both dramatic and startling in its abundance.

Unlike cities, which regularly tear down and build over their history, the progress of man is preserved with striking clarity in the desert. An archaeological site in Calico was determined to be approximately 200,000 years old; stone tools and other artifacts uncovered there are believed to be the oldest evidence of man's activity in the Americas. Petroglyphs—prehistoric rock art—are scattered throughout the California deserts. There is a bewildering array of images, deer and mountain sheep, human figures, spears and shields, and seemingly abstract geometric patterns, carved from 2,000 to 10,000 years ago. The more recent, and romanticized, past is on display, too. Ghost towns, gold mills, old rail stations, and other pieces of the Old West dot the countryside. At times it is easy to feel you would do anything to trade your car in for a horse.

What is probably most surprising about the desert is its accessibility. The days of the 20-mule team and the railroad, which brought prosperity to the towns it reached in the late 1800s and early 1900s, are long gone. A surprisingly large amount of the desert can be seen from the comfort of your air-conditioned car. And don't despair if you are without air-conditioning—just avoid the middle of the day and the middle of the summer, good advice for all desert travel. Believe everything you've ever heard about desert heat; it can be brutal. A temperature of 134° was once recorded at Furnace Creek in Death Valley, the hottest place on the planet. But during mornings and evenings, particularly in the spring and fall, the temperature ranges from cool and crisp to pleasantly warm and dry: perfect for hiking and driving. And while the air at Death Valley can certainly be quite still, much of the desert is breezy, if not downright windy.

The Mojave desert begins just north of the San Bernardino Mountains along the northern edge of Los Angeles and extends north 150 miles into the Eureka Valley and east 200 miles to the Colorado River. Death Valley lies north and east of the Mojave, bordering Nevada. Mojave, with elevations ranging from 3,000 to 5,000 feet above sea level, is known as the High Desert; Death Valley, with points at almost 300 feet below sea level, is the lowest spot in the United States.

Due to the vast size of California's deserts, an area about as big as Ohio, and the weather, careful planning is essential for an enjoyable desert adventure. Conveniences, facilities, trails, gas stations, and supermarkets do not lurk just around the corner from many desert sights. Different pieces of the desert can be easily handled in day trips, more extensive exploring will require overnight stays; it's a good idea to know in advance which approach you will be taking. Reliable maps are a must—

signage is limited, and occasionally comple
The Automobile Club of America (AAA) is pr
source for maps. Other important accessories in
pass, extra food and water, sunglasses, extra clothe
or cool nights), a hat (if you're going to do any walking a
the sun), and plenty of sunscreen. Other than that, a pair o
oculars can come in handy, and don't forget your came
You're likely to see things you've never seen before.

Getting Around

By Car The vast Mojave Desert is shaped like a giant *L*, with one leg
north and the other east. To travel north through the Mojave,
take I–10 east out of Los Angeles to I–15 north. Just through
the Cajon Pass, pick up U.S. 395, which runs north through
Victor Valley, Boron, the Rand Mining District, and China
Lake. To travel east, continue on I–15 to Barstow. From
Barstow there are two routes: I–40, which passes through the
mountainous areas of San Bernardino County, whisks by the
Providence Mountains and enters Arizona at Needles (noted
for being the home town of Snoopy's brother Spike in the "Peanuts" cartoons); or the more northerly I–15, which passes
south of Calico, near Devil's Playground and the Kelso Sand
Dunes, and then veers northeast toward Las Vegas.

Death Valley National Monument can be entered from the
southeast or the west. Exit U.S. 395 at either State Highway
190 or 178 to enter from the west. From the southeast: Take
Hwy. 127 north from I–15 and then link up with either Highway 178, which travels west into the valley and then cuts north
past Funeral Peak, Badwater, Dante's View, and Zabriskie
Point before meeting up with Highway 190 at Furnace Creek,
or continue on Highway 127 north for 28 miles and then take
Highway 190 west straight into the middle of Death Valley.

Guided Tours

The following organizations regularly sponsor hikes, tours,
and outings in the California deserts. Call or write them for
more information.
The Audubon Society (Western Division, 555 Audubon Pl., Sacramento, CA 95825, tel. 916/481–5332).
The California Native Plant Society (909 12th St., Suite 116,
Sacramento, CA 95814, tel. 916/447–CNPS).
The Nature Conservancy (785 Market St., San Francisco, CA
94103, tel. 415/777–0487).
The Sierra Club (730 Polk St., San Francisco, CA 94109, tel.
415/776–2211).

Important Addresses and Numbers

Tourist Information **Bureau of Land Management** (BLM) (California Desert District Office, 1695 Spruce St., Riverside, CA 92507, tel. 714/276–
6394) can also provide information on BLM campgrounds.

Emergencies **BLM Rangers** (tel. 714/276–6419). **Police:** *San Bernardino
County Sheriff* (tel. 619/256–1796). **Hospital:** *Community Hospital* (Barstow, tel. 619/256–1761).

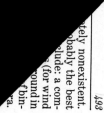

...oring

...bers in the margin correspond with points of interest on ...ojave Desert map.

...gh the Mojave desert is a vast, sprawling space, many of ...sitable attractions are conveniently laid out on a north– ...axis along U.S. 395 and Highway 178, and an east–west ...that runs between I–15 and I–40. We'll describe tours stretching roughly 120 miles along each axis, and a third tour that winds its way through Death Valley, which lies between the two routes. Keep in mind that there are a very limited number of hotels in the desert, so if you plan to spend the night somewhere, make sure your tour leaves you time to get to places like Furnace Creek in Death Valley, or Barstow, where there are some rooms to be found.

The Western Mojave

❶ On I–15, just before you reach U.S. 395 on the northbound tour, you cross Cajon Pass, riding over the infamous **San Andreas Fault**— an apocalyptic way to start a desert trip.

❷ About 70 miles later you enter the **Rand Mining District,** consisting of the towns of Randsburg, Red Mountain, and Johannesburg. Randsburg is one of the very few authentic goldmining communities that hasn't become a ghost town. The town first boomed with the discovery of gold in the Rand Mountains in 1895, and along with the neighboring towns, grew to support the successful Yellow Aster Mine. Rich tungsten ore was discovered during World War I and silver in 1919. All told, the total money brought in by these precious metals is estimated at more than $35 million. Thankfully, Randsburg still sports its authentic Old West heritage. The picturesque town has some original gold-rush buildings, plus a few antiques shops, a general store, and the **Randsburg Desert Museum,** which is crammed with mining and frontier life memorabilia. *U.S. 395 to Johannesburg, then follow the signs 1 mi southwest to Randsburg. The museum, tel. 619/374–2111, is open weekends, 10–5.*

❸ Just to the northwest of the Rand Mining District is **Red Rock Canyon State Park.** Red Rock Canyon is a feast for the eyes with its layers of pink, white, red, rust, and brown rocks. Entering the park from the south, you pass through a narrow, steepwalled gorge and enter a wide bowl tinted pink by what was once hot volcanic ash. The human history of this area goes back some 20,000 years to the ancient canyon dwellers known only as the Old People. Mojave Indians roamed the land for several hundred years until Gold-Rush fever hit the region in the midto late 1800s; remains of mining operations dot the countryside. The canyon was later invaded by filmmakers, and it has starred in numerous Westerns. The state park can be found on either side of Highway 14 about 10 miles south of where it meets U.S. 395. You can reach the informative ranger station by heading northwest on Abbott Drive from Highway 14.

❹ The nearby **Petroglyph Canyons** provide one of the desert's most amazing spectacles. The two canyons, commonly called Big and Little Petroglyph, contain what is probably the greatest concentration of rock art in the country. Scratched or pecked into the shiny desert varnish (oxidized minerals) that coats the canyon's dark basaltic rocks are thousands of images.

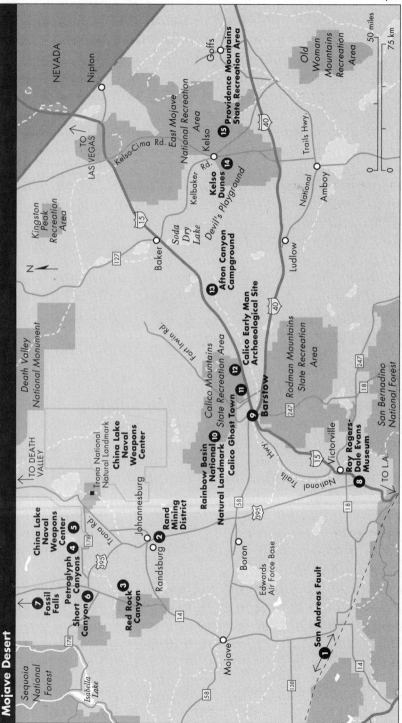

Some are figures of animals and people, some seemingly abstract—maybe just the doodles of ancient man! All are exceptionally preserved and protected. The feeling of living
⑤ history is incredible. The canyons are in the **U.S. Naval Weapons Center at China Lake,** and access is limited. Weekend tours must be arranged in advance through the **Maturango Museum** (China Lake Blvd. and Las Flores Ave., Ridgecrest, tel. 619/375–6900), which will also provide you with background on what you will see.

⑥ Heading northwest, you will find **Short Canyon** about ½-mile from the intersection of Highway 14 and U.S. 395. Sierra snows and natural springs feed the stream that flows down the rocky canyon, spills over a falls, and then sinks into the sand. In good years, there are large beds of wildflowers; in very dry years there are still some splashes of color. In the spring, a ½-mile hike along the stream brings you to a 20-foot waterfall. Head west on the canyon road you'll find just south of Brady's Cafe on U.S. 395, but only after checking on current road conditions with the BLM (tel. 714/276–6394) or Red Rock Canyon State Park (tel. 805/942–0662).

⑦ **Fossil Falls** is another 20 miles up 395. On the way you'll pass Little Lake, a good place to see migrating waterfowl in the spring and fall, including several varieties of ducks and geese and probably pelicans as well. The area just north of the lake is often covered with wildflowers. As you pass the lake, **Red Hill** comes into view ahead of you. The hill is a small volcano that was active in the neighborhood of 20,000 years ago. Approaching the falls you cross a large volcanic field; the falls themselves drop an impressive distance along the channel cut by the Owens River through the hardened lava flows. Mammoth bones and human tools dating back 10,000 to 20,000 years ago have been found in the area. *The falls are about 20 mi north of the intersection of Hwy 14 and U.S. 395, then a ½-mile east on Cinder Cone Rd. A dirt road leads south to a parking area. There are usually BLM signs directing the way.*

The Eastern Mojave We'll start the eastward tour in **Victorville,** less than 20 miles from Cajon Pass. First off, notice the bit of river you see flowing along the eastern side of the freeway, near Mojave Narrows Regional Park—this is one of the few places where the Mojave River runs above ground. For the most part, the 150-mile-long river flows from the San Bernardino Mountains north and east under the desert floor. The park itself offers boat rentals, an
⑧ equestrian center, fishing, and camping. Then there is the **Roy Rogers-Dale Evans Museum,** exhibiting the personal and professional memorabilia of the famous Western stars. Yes, Roy's faithful horse Trigger is there, too. *Mojave Narrows Park, 18000 Yates Rd., tel. 619/245–2226, is open daily 7:30 AM–dusk; there is a $3 per vehicle entry fee. The Roy Rogers-Dale Evans Museum, 15650 Seneca Rd., tel. 619/243–4547, is open daily 9–5; admission: $3 adults, $2 ages 13–16 and senior citizens, $1 ages 6–12.*

⑨ Continue along I–15 to **Barstow.** Barstow was established in 1886 when a subsidiary of the Atchison, Topeka and Santa Fe Railroad began construction of a depot and hotel at this junction of its tracks and the 35th-parallel transcontinental lines. The **Desert Information Center** (831 Barstow Rd., tel. 619/256–8617) contains exhibits about desert ecology, wildflowers, wildlife, and other features of the desert environment; a help-

ful and knowledgeable staff is on hand to answer any questions
you may have.

There is a natural impulse to describe many areas of the desert
as seemingly belonging to another planet. **Rainbow Basin,** 8
miles north of Barstow, looks just as you would expect Mars to
look like (maybe it's because some of those old Martian movies
were actually filmed there). There is a tremendous sense of upheaval; huge slabs of red, orange, white, and green stone tilt at
crazy angles like ships about to capsize. At points along the
spectacularly scenic 6-mile drive it is easy to imagine you are
alone in the world, hidden among the colorful badlands that
give the basin its name. Hike the many washes and you are likely to see the fossilized remains of creatures that roamed the basin 12 to 16 million years ago: mastodons, large and small
camels, rhinos, dog-bears, birds, and insects. Do leave any
fossils you find where they are—they are protected by Federal
law. *Take Fort Irwin Rd. about 5 mi north to Fossil Bed Rd., a
graded dirt road, and head west 3 mi. Call the Desert Information Center in Barstow (tel. 619/256–8617) for more information.*

After a 10-mile drive northeast from Barstow, you can slip into
the more recent past at **Calico Ghost Town.** Calico became a
wild—and rich—mining town after a rich deposit of silver was
found around 1881. In 1886, after more than $85 million worth
of silver, gold, and other precious metals were harvested from
the multicolored "calico" hills, the price of silver fell and the
town slipped into decline. "Borax" Smith helped revive the
town in 1889 when he started mining the unglamorous but prof-
itable mineral borax there, but that boom busted by the turn of
the century. The effort to restore the ghost town was started
by Walter Knott of Knott's Berry Farm fame in 1960. Knott
handed the land over to San Bernardino County in 1966 and it
became a regional park. Today, the 1880s come back to life as
you stroll the wooden sidewalks of Main Street, browse through
several Western shops, roam the tunnels of Maggie's Mine, and
take a ride on the Calico-Odessa Railroad. Special festivals in
March, May, October, and November add to Calico's Old West
flavor. *Ghost Town Rd., 3 mi north of I–15, tel. 619/254–2122.
There is a $4 per vehicle entry fee. The town is open 9–5 daily.*

If you're at all curious about life 200,000 years ago, the **Calico
Early Man Archeological Site** is a must-see. Nearly 12,000 tools
—scrapers, cutting tools, choppers, hand picks, stone saws,
and the like—have been excavated from the site since 1964.
Prior to finding the site, many archaeologists believed the first
humans came to North America "only" 10,000 to 20,000 years
ago. Dr. Louis Leakey, the noted archaeologist, was so impressed with the findings that he became the Calico Project director from 1963 to his death in 1972; his old camp is now a
visitor's center and museum. The Calico excavations provide a
rare opportunity to see artifacts, buried in the walls and floors
of the excavated pits, fashioned by the earliest known Americans. *15 mi northeast of Barstow via I–15; take Minneola Rd.
north for 3 mi. The site is open Wed.–Sun. 8–4:30, closed Mon.
and Tues. Guided tours of the dig are offered Wed. at 1:30 and
3:30, Thurs.–Sun. at 9:30, 11:30, 1:30 and 3:30. Trail maps are
available for self-guided tours.*

Thanks to its colorful, steep walls, **Afton Canyon** is often called
the Grand Canyon of the Mojave. The canyon was carved out

over many thousands of years by the rushing waters of the Mojave River, which makes another of its rare above-ground appearances here. And where you find water in the desert, you'll find trees, grasses, and wildlife. The canyon has been a popular spot for a long time; Indians and later white settlers following the Mojave Trail from the Colorado River to the Pacific coast, often set up camp here, near the welcomed presence of water. *About 38 mi from Barstow on I–15; take the Afton turnoff and follow a good dirt road about 3 mi southwest.*

⑭ Although there is a broad range of terrain that qualifies as desert, nothing says "desert" quite like graceful, wind-blown sand dunes. And the white sand **Kelso Dunes,** located about 40 miles southeast of Baker, are perfect, pristine desert dunes. The dunes cover 70 square miles, often at heights of 500–600 feet, and they can be reached in an easy ½-mile walk from where you have to leave your car. When you reach the top of one of the dunes, kick a little bit of sand down the lee side and find out why they say the sand "sings." In Kelso, there is a Mission Revival depot dating from 1925, one of the very few of its kind still standing. *I–15 to Baker, then take Kelbaker Rd. south for 35 mi to the town of Kelso. The dunes are another 7 mi ahead.*

⑮ Our last stops in the Eastern Mojave are the **Providence Mountains State Recreation Area** and the **Mitchell Caverns Natural Preserve.** The recreation area's visitor center, at an elevation of 4,300 feet, offers spectacular views of mountain peaks, dunes, buttes, rocky crags, and desert valleys. The caves, known as El Pakiva and Tecopa, offer a rare opportunity to see all three types of cave formations—dripstone, flowstone, and erratics —in one place. The year-round 65° temperature is also a nice break from the heat. *Take I–40 east from Barstow 100 mi to Essex Rd., then head northwest for 16 mi to the state recreation area. If you have a 4-wheel-drive vehicle, you can continue south from Kelso on Kelbaker Rd. about 3 mi to the poleline road; bear left and drive about 12 mi over Foshay Pass to Essex Rd. Guided tours of the caves are offered Sept.–June, weekdays at 1:30 PM, weekends and holidays at 1:30 and 3; weekends only during the summer. Tours gather at the visitor center.*

Death Valley *Numbers in the margin correspond with points of interest on the Death Valley map.*

The topography of Death Valley National Monument is like a mini-lesson in geology. Two hundred million years ago seas covered the area, depositing layers of sediment and fossils. Between 5 million and 35 million years ago, faults in the earth's crust and volcanic activity pushed and folded the ground, causing mountain ranges to rise and the valley floor to drop. Later the valley was filled periodically by lakes, which eroded the surrounding rocks into fantastic formations and deposited the salts that now cover the floor of the basin. Today, the area sports an astounding variety of physical features: 14 square miles of sand dunes, 200 square miles of crusty salt flats, 11,000-foot mountains, hills and canyons of many colors. There are more than 1,000 species of plants and trees—21 of which are unique to the valley, like the yellow Panamint Daisy, and the blue-flowered Death Valley sage.

❶ Starting from the northernmost tip of the monument, **Scotty's Castle** is an odd apparition rising out of a desert canyon. This $2.5-million Moorish mansion, begun in 1924 and never com-

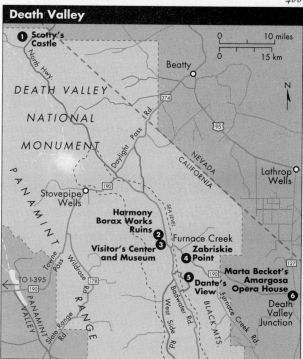

Death Valley

❶ Scotty's Castle

Beatty

DEATH VALLEY

NATIONAL

MONUMENT

North Hwy.

374

Daylight Pass Rd.

95

NEVADA
CALIFORNIA

Lathrop Wells

PANAMINT

Stovepipe Wells

190

Harmony Borax Works Ruins ❷

SEA LEVEL

❸

Visitor's Center and Museum

Furnace Creek

Zabriskie
❹ Point

TO I-395

190

Towne Pass

Wildrose Rd.

178

RANGE

Slate Range Rd.

West Side Rd.

Badwater Rd.

❺ Dante's View

BLACK MTS.

Marta Becket's Amargosa Opera House

127

190

Furnace Creek Rd.

❻

Death Valley Junction

PANAMINT
VALLEY

0   10 miles

0   15 km

N

pleted, takes its name from Walter Scott, better known as Death Valley Scotty. An ex-cowboy, prospector, and performer in Buffalo Bill's Wild West Show, Scotty always told people the castle was his, financed by gold from a secret mine. That secret mine was, in fact, a Chicago millionaire named Albert Johnson, who was advised by doctors to spend time in a warm, dry climate. The house sports works of art, imported carpets, handmade European furniture, and a tremendous pipe organ. While it would probably all look perfectly normal in Beverly Hills, in Death Valley it is the wildest of mirages. *Located on the North Hwy 190N. Admission: $4 adults, $2 children 6–11. Grounds open 7 AM to 6 PM daily; tours 8–5.*

❷ Following Highway 190 south, you'll come to the remains of the famed **Harmony Borax Works,** from which the renowned 20-mule teams hauled borax to the railroad town of Mojave. Those teams were a sight to behold: 20 mules hitched up to a single massive wagon, carrying a load of 10 tons of borax to a town 165 miles away through burning desert. The teams plied the route between 1884 and 1907, when the railroad finally arrived in Zabriskie. You can visit the ruins of the Harmony Borax Works. The Borax Museum, 2 miles farther south, houses original mining machinery and historical displays in a building that used to serve as a boarding house for miners; the adjacent structure is the original mule-team barn. *Look for the Harmony Borax Works Rd. on Hwy 190, about 50 mi south of Scotty's Castle; take the road west a short distance to the ruins.*

❸ Between the ruins and the museum you will see a sign for the **Visitor's Center** at Furnace Creek. The center provides guided

walks, exhibits, helpful publications, and more helpful rangers. *Open 8–8. Call the National Park Service in Death Valley
(tel. 619/786–2331) for more information on visitor's center
services.*

❹ **Zabriskie Point,** about 4 miles south of the visitor's center, is
one of the monument's most scenic spots. Not particularly high
—only about 710 feet—it overlooks a striking badlands panorama with wrinkled, cinammon-color hills. You might rec-
ognize it from the film *Zabriskie Point* by the Italian director
Antonioni. When Highway 178 splits off from Highway 190, fol-
❺ low it south about 13 miles to **Dante's View.** This viewpoint is
more than 5,000 feet up in the Black Mountains. In the dry desert air, you can see most of the 110 miles the valley is stretched
across. The oasis of Furnace Creek is a green spot to the north.
The view up and down is equally astounding: The tiny blackish
patch far below you is Badwater, the lowest point in the country
at 280 feet below sea level; on the western horizon is Mt. Whitney, the highest spot in the continental United States at 14,495
feet. Those of you in great shape may want to try the 14-mile
hike up to Telescope Peak. The view, not surprisingly, is
breathtaking; so is the 3,000-foot elevation gain of the hike.
The best time to visit any of these viewpoints is early morning
or late afternoon when the light highlights the colors and
shapes of the surrounding desert.

Just outside the monument, at Death Valley Junction, is an un-
❻ expected pleasure to rival Scotty's Castle—**Marta Becket's
Amargosa Opera House.** Marta Becket is an artist and dancer
from New York who first saw the town of Amargosa when she
was on tour in 1964. Three years later she came back and had a
flat tire in the same place, and on impulse she decided to buy a
boarded-up theater amid a complex of run-down Spanish colonial buildings. Today, the population of the town is still two people and a dozen cats, but three nights a week, cars, motor
homes, and buses roll in to catch the show she has been presenting for more than 20 years. To compensate for the sparse
crowds her show attracted in the early days, Becket painted
herself an audience, making the theater a masterpiece of
trompe l'oeil painting. Now she often performs her blend of
classical ballet, mime, and 19th-century melodrama to sell-out
crowds. After the show, you can meet her in the adjacent art
gallery, where she sells her paintings and autographs her posters and books. *Amargosa Opera House, Box 8, Death Valley
Junction, CA 92328, tel. 619/852–4316. Call ahead for reservations. Performances Nov.–Apr., Fri., Sat., and Mon. at 8:15
PM; May and Oct., shows Sat. only. The opera house is closed
during the summer. Admission is by donation: $5 adults, $3
children.*

What to See and Do with Children

Many of the desert's attractions should delight children. The
following are of particular interest; for more information, *see*
the Exploring section, above.

The Rand Mining District
The Roy Rogers-Dale Evans Museum, Victorville
Calico Ghost Town
Mitchell Caverns
Marta Becket's Amargosa Opera House

Off the Beaten Track

The desert is not a particularly well-beaten track to begin with, but some spots are a bit farther out of the way, or more difficult to reach. **Trona Pinnacles National Natural Landmark,** just west of the China Lake Naval Weapons Center, is not easy to get to. There are several dirt roads leading to the "tufa" area—where towering spires of calcium carbonate reach heights of up to 140 feet. Unfortunately, the best road to the area changes depending on the weather; you either have to be lucky enough to follow someone who knows the best way, or keep trying until you get there. And forget about it if the roads are wet. Still, the pinnacles are considered the best examples of tufa towers in the country, and the area is probably a great place to film a science-fiction flick. *Take Hwy 178 north from U.S. 395 for 29 mi. There you will find a dirt intersection; turn southeast and go ½-mile to a fork. Continue south via the right fork, cross some railroad tracks, and continue about 5 mi to the pinnacles.*

Lodging

Death Valley   **Furnace Creek Inn.** The rambling stone structure tumbling down the side of a hill is something of a desert oasis. There are pleasantly cool dining rooms, a heated pool, tennis courts, golf, riding, and a cocktail lounge with entertainment. *Box 1, Death Valley 92328, tel. 619/786–2345. 67 rooms and suites. AE, CB, DC, MC, V. Closed mid-May–mid-Oct. Double rooms start at $250, with breakfast and dinner.*

Furnace Creek Ranch. An annex of the inn, about 1 mile away on the valley floor. Originally crew headquarters for a borax company, the newer section has very good rooms. The ranch also features a coffee shop, steak house, cocktail lounge, and a general store. *Box 1, Death Valley 92328, tel. 619/786–2345. 225 rooms. AE, CB, DC, MC, V. Double rooms start at $67.75 for rooms with TV and telephone.*

Stove Pipe Wells Village. A landing strip for light aircraft is an unusual touch for a motel, as is a heated mineral pool, but the rest is pretty basic. The property includes a dining room, grocery store, pool, and cocktail lounge. *Hwy 190, tel. 619/786–2387. 82 rooms. MC, V. $50 and up.*

Barstow   **Best Western Desert Villa.** A slightly above-average AAA-approved motel with a pool and whirlpool. *1984 E. Main St., tel. 619/256–1781. 79 units. AE, CB, DC, MC, V. $52 and up.*

Camping

The Mojave Desert and Death Valley have about two dozen campgrounds in a variety of desert settings. Listed below is a sampling of what is available. For further information the following booklets are useful: *High Desert Recreation Resource Guide,* from the Mojave Chamber of Commerce (15836 Sierra Hwy., Mojave, CA 93591); *San Bernardino County Regional Parks,* from the Regional Parks Department (825 E. 3rd St., San Bernardino, CA 92415); and *California Desert Camping,* from the Bureau of Land Management (California Desert District Office, 1695 Spruce St., Riverside, CA 92507).

Death Valley **Mahogany Flat** (east of Hwy. 178). Ten well-shaded tent spaces in a forest of juniper and piñon pine. Tables, pit toilets; no water. Open Apr.–Nov.

Mesquite Springs (Hwy. 190 near Scotty's Castle). Sixty tent or RV spaces, some shaded, with stoves or fireplaces, tables, flush toilets, water.

Wildrose (west of Hwy. 178). Thirty-nine tent or RV sites, some shaded, in a canyon. Stoves or fireplaces, tables, water, pit toilets.

Mojave Desert **Mid-Hills Campground** (123 mi east of Barstow via I–40). Hiking, horseback riding, in a wooded setting. Thirty campsites, pit toilets, water.

Mojave Narrows (I–15). Eighty-seven camping units, hot showers. Secluded picnic areas and two lakes surrounded by cottonwoods and cattails. Fishing, rowboat rentals, bait shop, specially designed trail for the handicapped.

Owl Canyon Campground (12 mi. north of Barstow and 1 mi. east of Rainbow Basin). Thirty-one camping units, cooking grills, vault toilets, water.

Index

Personal Itinerary

Departure *Date*

Time

Transportation

Arrival *Date*   *Time*

Departure *Date*   *Time*

Transportation

Accommodations

Arrival *Date*   *Time*

Departure *Date*   *Time*

Transportation

Accommodations

Arrival *Date*   *Time*

Departure *Date*   *Time*

Transportation

Accommodations

Personal Itinerary

Arrival *Date*   *Time*

Departure *Date*   *Time*

Transportation

Accommodations

Arrival *Date*   *Time*

Departure *Date*   *Time*

Transportation

Accommodations

Arrival *Date*   *Time*

Departure *Date*   *Time*

Transportation

Accommodations

Arrival *Date*   *Time*

Departure *Date*   *Time*

Transportation

Accommodations

Personal Itinerary

Arrival *Date*   *Time*

Departure *Date*   *Time*

Transportation

Accommodations

Arrival *Date*   *Time*

Departure *Date*   *Time*

Transportation

Accommodations

Arrival *Date*   *Time*

Departure *Date*   *Time*

Transportation

Accommodations

Arrival *Date*   *Time*

Departure *Date*   *Time*

Transportation

Accommodations

Addresses

Name	Name
Address	Address
Telephone	Telephone
Name	Name
Address	Address
Telephone	Telephone
Name	Name
Address	Address
Telephone	Telephone
Name	Name
Address	Address
Telephone	Telephone
Name	Name
Address	Address
Telephone	Telephone
Name	Name
Address	Address
Telephone	Telephone
Name	Name
Address	Address
Telephone	Telephone
Name	Name
Address	Address
Telephone	Telephone

Fodor's Travel Guides

U.S. Guides

Alaska
Arizona
Boston
California
Cape Cod
The Carolinas & the
 Georgia Coast
The Chesapeake
 Region
Chicago
Colorado
Disney World & the
 Orlando Area

Florida
Hawaii
The Jersey Shore
Las Vegas
Los Angeles
Maui
Miami & the Keys
New England
New Mexico
New Orleans
New York City
New York City
 (Pocket Guide)

New York State
Pacific North Coast
Philadelphia
The Rockies
San Diego
San Francisco
San Francisco
 (Pocket Guide)
The South
Texas
USA
The Upper Great
 Lakes Region

Virgin Islands
Virginia & Maryland
Waikiki
Washington, D.C.

Foreign Guides

Acapulco
Amsterdam
Australia
Austria
The Bahamas
The Bahamas
 (Pocket Guide)
Baja & the Pacific
 Coast Resorts
Barbados
Belgium &
 Luxembourg
Bermuda
Brazil
Budget Europe
Canada
Canada's Atlantic
 Provinces
Cancun, Cozumel,
 Yucatan Peninsula
Caribbean
Central America
China

Eastern Europe
Egypt
Europe
Europe's Great
 Cities
France
Germany
Great Britain
Greece
The Himalayan
 Countries
Holland
Hong Kong
India
Ireland
Israel
Italy
Italy's Great Cities
Jamaica
Japan
Kenya, Tanzania,
 Seychelles
Korea

Lisbon
London
London Companion
London
 (Pocket Guide)
Madrid & Barcelona
Mexico
Mexico City
Montreal &
 Quebec City
Morocco
Munich
New Zealand
Paris
Paris (Pocket Guide)
Portugal
Puerto Rico
 (Pocket Guide)
Rio de Janeiro
Rome
Saint Martin/
 Sint Maarten
Scandinavia

Scandinavian Cities
Scotland
Singapore
South America
South Pacific
Southeast Asia
Soviet Union
Spain
Sweden
Switzerland
Sydney
Thailand
Tokyo
Toronto
Turkey
Vienna
Yugoslavia

Special-Interest Guides

Bed & Breakfast
 Guide to the Mid-
 Atlantic States

Bed & Breakfast
 Guide to New
 England
Cruises & Ports
 of Call

A Shopper's Guide
 to London
Health & Fitness
 Vacations
Shopping in Europe

Skiing in North
 America
Sunday in New York
Touring Europe